Mrs. Langtry as Pauline, in the "Lady of Lyons."

THE DRAMATIC WORKS

OF

Edward Bulwer Lytton

(LORD LYTTON)

THE DUCHESS DE LA VALLIERE.
THE LADY OF LYONS; OR, LOVE AND PRIDE.
RICHELIEU; OR, THE CONSPIRACY.
NOT SO BAD AS WE SEEM; OR, MANY SIDES TO A CHARACTER.
MONEY
THE RIGHTFUL HEIR.
WALPOLE.
DARNLEY.

VOLUME IX.

WILDSIDE PRESS

PREFATORY NOTE TO THE KNEBWORTH EDITION.

THE first four Dramatic Works in this volume were produced by Lord Lytton within an interval of fifteen years. Two of these have, ever since their first performance, held their ground among the stock pieces on the English stage. The earliest of all his plays—Mr. Bulwer's maiden play of "The Duchess de la Vallière"—was the only one which failed at once to secure popular approbation as an acting drama. Brought out at Covent Garden Theatre upon Wednesday, the 4th January, 1837, with a rather indifferent cast (save only that Macready was the Marquess de Bragelone), it was withdrawn after nine representations. Published immediately afterwards by the Messrs. Saunders and Otley, it has since then retained its repute simply as a work of art in the closet.

"The Lady of Lyons," which was dashed off a twelve-month afterwards, literally upon the spur of the moment, achieved, upon the other hand, a brilliant success. Macready having, a year prior to this, undertaken the management of Covent Garden Theatre, while talking over the responsibilities of the enterprise, had one day exclaimed to the Author, "Oh! that I could get a play like the 'Honeymoon!'" Within a fortnight from the utterance of that ejaculation, the manuscript of the "Lady of Lyons" was placed as a gift in the hands of the Manager. Brought out anonymously, on Thursday, the 15th February, 1838, its reception was triumphant, and at the close of another fortnight the authorship was acknowledged upon the play bills.

A similar welcome, on Thursday, the 7th March, 1839, was accorded to the historical drama of "Richelieu," Macready making his mark as the Cardinal as unmistakably as he had previously done in the *rôle* of Claude Melnotte. During that same year, Lord Lytton, upon Thursday, the 31st October, placed upon the boards of the Haymarket his play of "The Sea Captain," which, in spite of its having a brilliant run during that season, was subsequently, in obedience to the author's desire, withdrawn, not merely from the stage, but from publication. The root idea of that drama was several years afterwards re-adapted by Lord Lytton, under the title of "The Rightful Heir."

The last drama of the four, "Not so Bad as we Seem," was distinctly a *pièce de circonstance*. It was written—like "The Lady of Lyons,"—in obedience to a sudden impulse and with singular rapidity. It originated one winter's evening in the banqueting hall at Knebworth, after some amateur theatricals, the actors in which were a cluster of artists and men of letters, pre-eminent among whom was Charles Dickens. Lord Lytton and his guests upon that occasion projected together the establishment of a benevolent institution for the help of their less fortunate brothers of the pen and pencil, to be called "The Guild of Art and Literature." In furtherance of this project the host had said, "Undertake to act a play yourselves and I engage to write it." Hence the production of this five-act drama, the original cast of which, as having now a peculiar interest of its own, is here prefixed to it as a literary curiosity. The play, which rapidly poured three thousand pounds into the coffers of the newly created Guild, was first performed on Friday, the 16th May, 1851, in the presence of Her Majesty and the Prince Consort, in a temporary theatre erected in the late Duke of Devonshire's town house in Piccadilly.

CONTENTS.

THE DUCHESS DE LA VALLIERE..	9
THE LADY OF LYONS; OR, LOVE AND PRIDE..	71
RICHELIEU; OR, THE CONSPIRACY...	107
NOT SO BAD AS WE SEEM; OR, MANY SIDES TO A CHARACTER......................	179
MONEY...	221
THE RIGHTFUL HEIR...	271
WALPOLE; OR, EVERY MAN HAS HIS PRICE..	321
DARNLEY...	355

THE DUCHESS DE LA VALLIERE.

DRAMATIS PERSONÆ.

LOUIS THE FOURTEENTH	. . . . .	MR. VANDENHOFF.
THE DUKE DE LAUZUN	⎫	MR. W. FARREN.
COUNT DE GAMMONT	⎬ *Courtiers*	MR. PRITCHARD.
MARQUIS DE MONTESPAN	⎭	MR. WEBSTER.
THE MARQUIS DE BRAGELONE, *Betrothed to Mademoiselle de la Vallière*		MR. MACREADY.
BERTRAND, *the Armorer*	. . . .	MR. TILBURY.

Courtiers, Gentlemen of the Chamber, Priests, &c.

MADAME DE LA VALLIERE	. . .	MRS. W. WEST.
MADEMOISELLE (afterwards Duchess) DE LA VALLIERE		MISS HELEN FAUCIT.
MADAME DE MONTESPAN	. . .	MISS PELHAM.
ABBESS	. . . . . .	MRS GARRICK.

Nuns, Ladies, Maids of Honor, &c.

First performed on Wednesday, the 4th of January, 1837, at Covent Garden Theatre.

PROLOGUE.

Spoken by Mr. H. Wallack.

To paint the Past, yet in the Past portray
Such shapes as seem dim prophets of To-day;—
To trace, through all the garish streams of art,
Nature's deep fountain—woman's silent art;—
On the stirr'd surface of the soften'd mind
To leave the print of holier truths behind;—
And, while through joy or grief—through calm or **strife,**
Bound the wild Passions on the course of Life,
To share the race—yet point the proper goal,
And make the Affections preachers to the Soul;—
Such is the aim with which a gaudier age
Now woos the brief revival of the stage;—
Such is the moral, though unseen it flows,
In Lauzun's wiles and soft La Vallière's woes;
Such the design our Author boldly drew,
And, losing boldness, now submits to you.

Not new to climes where dreamy FABLE dwells—
That magic Prospero of the Isle of Spells—
Now first the wanderer treads, with anxious fear,
The fairy land whose flowers allured him here.
Dread is the court our alien pleads before;
Your verdict makes his exile from the shore.
Yet, e'en if banish'd, let him think, in pride,
He trod the path with no unhallow'd guide;
Chasing the light, whose face, though veil'd and dim,
Perchance a meteor, seem'd a star to him,
Hoping the ray might rest where TRUTH appears
Beneath her native well—your smiles and tears.

When a wide waste, to Law itself unknown,
Lay that fair world the DRAMA calls its own;
When all might riot on the mines of Thought,
And Genius starved amidst the wealth it wrought;
He who now ventures on the haunted soil
For nobler laborers won the rights of toil,
And his the boast—that Fame now rests in ease
Beneath the shade of her own laurel-trees.
Yes, if with all the critic on their brow,
His clients once have grown his judges now,

And watch, like spirits on the Elysian side,
Their brother ferried o'er the Stygian tide,
To where, on souls untried, austerely sit
(The triple Minos)—Gallery—Boxes—Pit—
'Twill soothe to think, howe'er the verdict end,
In every rival he hath served a friend.

But well we know, and, knowing, we rejoice,
The mightiest Critic is the PUBLIC VOICE.
Awed, yet resign'd, our novice trusts in you,
Hard to the practised, gentle to the new.
Whate'er the anxious strife of hope and fear,
He asks no favor—let the stage be clear.
If from the life his shapes the poet draws,
In man's deep breast lie all the critic's laws:
If not, in vain the nicely-poised design,
Vain the cold music of the labor'd line,
Before our eyes, behold the living rules;—
The soul has instincts wiser than the schools!
Yours is the Great Tribunal of the Heart,
And touch'd Emotion makes the test of Art.
Judges august!—the same in every age,
While Passions weave the sorcery of the Stage,—
While Nature's sympathies are Art's best laws,—
To you a stranger has referr'd his cause:—
If the soft tale he woos the soul to hear
Bequeaths the moral, while it claims the tear,
Each gentler thought to faults in others shown
He calls in court—a pleader for his own!

THE DUCHESS DE LA VALLIERE.

ACT I.—SCENE I.

Time, sunset. On the foreground an old Château; beyond, Vineyards and Woods, which present, through their openings, Views of a River, reflecting the sunset. At a distance, the turrets of the Convent of the Carmelites.

MADAME *and* MADEMOISELLE DE LA VALLIERE.

Mdlle. de la Vall. 'Tis our last eve, my mother!
Mme. de la Vall.   Thou regrett'st it,
My own Louise! albeit the court invites thee—
A court beside whose glories, dull and dim
The pomp of Eastern kings, by poets told;
A court——
Mdlle. de la Vall. In which I shall not see my mother!
Nor these old walls, in which, from every stone,
Childhood speaks eloquent of happy years;
Nor vines and woods, which bade me love the earth,
Nor yonder spires, which raised that love to God!— [*The Vesper bell tolls.*
The vesper bell!—my mother, when, once more,
I hear from those gray towers that holy chime,
May thy child's heart be still as full of Heaven,
And callous to all thoughts of earth, save those
Which mirror Eden in the face of Home!
Mme. de la Vall. Do I not know thy soul?—through every snare
My gentle dove shall 'scape with spotless plumes.
Alone in courts, I have no fear for *thee:*—
Some natures take from Innocence the lore
Experience teaches; and their delicate leaves,
Like the soft plant, shut out all wrong, and shrink
From vice by instinct, as the wise by knowledge:
And such is thine! *My* voice thou wilt not hear,
But Thought shall whisper where my voice would warn,
And Conscience be thy mother and thy guide!
Mdlle. de la Vall. Oh, may I merit all thy care, and most
Thy present trust!—Thou'lt write to me, my mother,
And tell me of thyself: amidst the court
My childhood's images shall rise. Be kind
To the poor cotters in the wood;—alas!
They'll miss me in the winter!—and my birds?—
Thy hand will feed them?——
Mme. de la Vall.   And that noble heart
That loves thee as my daughter should be loved—

The gallant Bragelone?*—should I hear
Some tidings Fame forgets—if in the din
Of camps I learn thy image makes his solace,
Shall I not write of *him?*—
    Mdlle. de la Vall. [*with indifference*]. His name will breathe
Of home and friendship;—yes!—
    Mme. de la Vall.   Of nought beside?
    Mdlle. de la Vall. Nay, why so pressing?—let me change the theme.
The king?—you have seen him;—is he, as they say,
So fair—so stately?
    Mme. de la Vall. Ay, in truth, my daughter,
A king that wins the awe he might command.
Splendid in peace, and terrible in war;
Wise in the council—gentle in the bower.
    Mdlle. de la Vall. Strange, that so often through mine early dreams
A royal vision flitted;—a proud form,
Upon whose brow nature had written "empire;"
While, on the lip,—love, smiling, wrapp'd in sunshine
The charmèd world that was its worshipper—
A form like that which clothed the gods of old,
Lured from Olympus by some mortal maid,—
Youthful it seemed—but with ambrosial youth;
And beautiful—but half as beauty were
A garb too earthly for a thing divine:—
Was it not strange, my mother?
    Mme. de la Vall.   A child's fancy,
Breathed into life by thy brave father's soul.
He taught thee, in thy cradle yet, to lisp
Thy sovereign's name in prayer—and still together,
In thy first infant creed, were link'd the lessons
"TO HONOR GOD AND LOVE THE KING;" it was
A part of that old knightly faith of France
Which made it half religion to be loyal.
    Mdlle. de la Vall. It might be so. I have preserved the lesson,
Ev'n with too weak a reverence.—Yet, 'tis strange!
A dream so oft renew'd!—
    Mme. de la Vall.   Here comes thy lover!
Thou wilt not blame him if his lips repeat
The question mine have ask'd? Alphonso, welcome!

SCENE II.

BRAGELONE, MADAME *and* MADEMOISELLE DE LA VALLIERE.

    Brage. My own Louise!—ah! dare I call thee so?
War never seem'd so welcome! since we part,
Since the soft sunshine of thy smiles must fade

---

* The author has, throughout this play, availed himself of the poetical license to give to the name of Bragelone the Italian pronunciation, and to accent the final *e*.

From these dear scenes, it soothes, at least to think
I shall not linger on the haunted spot,
And feel, forlorn amidst the gloom of absence,
How dark is all once lighted by thine eyes.
      [MME. DE LA VALLIERE *retires into the chateau.*
 Mdlle. de la Vall. Can friendship flatter thus?—or wouldst thou train
My ear betimes to learn the courtier's speech?
 Brage. Louise! Louise! this is our parting hour:
Me war demands—and thee the court allures.
In such an hour, the old romance allow'd
The maid to soften from her coy reserve,
And her true knight, from some kind words, to take
Hope's talisman to battle!—Dear Louise!
Say, canst thou love me?—
 Mdlle. de la Vall.   Sir!—I!—love!—methinks
It is a word that——
 Brage.   Sounds upon thy lips
Like "land" upon the mariner's, and speaks
Of home and rest after a stormy sea.
Sweet girl, my youth has pass'd in camps; and war
Hath somewhat scathed my manhood ere my time.
Our years are scarce well-mated: the soft spring
Is thine, and o'er my summer's waning noon
Grave autumn creeps. Thou say'st "I flatter!"—well
Love taught me first the golden words in which
The honest heart still coins its massive ore.
But fairer words, from falser lips, will soon
Make *my* plain courtship rude. Louise! thy sire
Betroth'd us in thy childhood: I have watch'd thee
Bud into virgin May, and in thy youth
Have seem'd to hoard my own!—I think of *thee*,
And I am youthful still! The passionate prayer—
The wild idolatry—the purple light
Bathing the cold earth from a Hebe's urn;—
Yea, all the soul's divine excess which youth
Claims as its own, came back when first I loved thee!
And yet so well I love, that if thy heart
Recoil from mine,—if but one single wish,
A shade more timid than the fear which ever
Blends trembling twilight with the starry hope
Of maiden dreams, would start thee from our union,—
Speak, and my suit is tongueless!
 Mdlle. de la Vall.   Oh, my lord!
If to believe all France's chivalry
Boasts not a nobler champion,—if to feel
Proud in your friendship, honor'd in your trust,—
If this be love, and I have known no other,
Why then——
 Brage. Why then, thou lov'st me!
 Mdlle. de la Vall. [*aside*].   Shall I say it?
I feel 'twere to deceive him! Is it love?
Love, no, it is *not* love!—[*Aloud.*] My noble lord,
As yet I know not all mine own weak heart;

I would not pain thee, yet would not betray.
Legend and song have often painted love,
And my heart whispers not the love which should be
The answer to thine own:—thou hadst best forget me!
   Brage. Forget!
   Mdlle. de la Valle. I am not worthy of thee!
   Brage.   Hold!—
My soul is less heroic than I deem'd it.
Perchance my passion asks too much from thine
And would forestall the fruit ere yet the blossom
Blushes from out the coy and maiden leaves.
No! let *me* love; and say, perchance the time
May come when *thou* wilt bid me *not* forget thee.
Absence may plead my cause; it hath some magic;
I fear not contrast with the courtier-herd;
And thou art not Louise if thou art won
By a smooth outside and a honey'd tongue,
No! when thou seest these hunters after power,
These shadows, minion'd to the royal sun,—
Proud to the humble, servile to the great,—
Perchance thou'lt learn how much one honest heart,
That never wrong'd a friend or shunn'd a foe,—
How much the old hereditary knighthood,
Faithful to God, to glory, and to love,
Outweighs a universe of cringing courtiers!
Louise, I ask no more!—I bide my time!

          Re-enter MME. DE LA VALLIERE *from the château.*

   Mme. de la Vall. The twilight darkens. Art thou, now Alphonso,
Convinced her heart is such as thou wouldst have it?
   Brage. It is a heavenly tablet—but my name
Good angels have not writ there!
   Mme. de la Vall.   Nay, as yet,
Love wears the mask of friendship: she must love thee.
   Brage. [*half incredulously*]. Think'st thou so?
   Mme. de la Vall.   Ay, be sure!
   Brage.   I'll think so too.
                        [*Turns to* MDLLE. DE LA VALLIERE.
Bright lady of my heart!—[*Aside.*] By Heaven! 'tis true!
The rose grows richer on her cheek, like hues
That in the silence of the virgin dawn,
Predict, in blushes, light that glads the earth.
Her mother spoke aright;—ah, yes, she loves me!
Bright lady of my heart, farewell! and yet
Again—farewell!
   Mdlle. de la Vall. Honor and health be with you!
   Mme. de la Vall. Nay, my Louise, when warriors wend to battle,
The maid they serve grows half a warrior too;
And does not blush to bind on mailed bosoms
The banner of her colors.
   Brage.   Dare I ask it?

Mdlle. de la Vall. A soldier's child could never blush, my lord,
To belt so brave a breast;—and yet,—well, wear it.
   [*Placing her scarf round* BRAGELONE'S *hauberk.*
   Brage. Ah! add for thy sake.
   Mdlle. de la Vall.   For the sake of one
Who honors worth, and ne'er since Bayard fell,
Have banners flaunted o'er a knight more true
To France and Fame;—
   Bage.   And love?
   Mdlle. de la Vall.   Nay, hush, my lord;
I said not that.
   Brage.   But France and Fame shall say it!
Yes, if thou hear'st men speak of Bragelone,
If proudest chiefs confess he bore him bravely,
Come life, come death, his glory shall be thine,
And all the light it borrow'd from thine eyes,
Shall gild thy name. Ah! scorn not *then* to say,
" He loved me well!" How well! God shield and bless thee!
   [*Exit* BRAGELONE.
   Mdlle. de la Vall. [*aside*]. Most worthy love! *why* can I love him not?
   Mme. de la Vall. Peace to his gallant heart! when next we meet,
May I have gain'd a son—and thou—
   Mdlle. de la Vall. [*quickly*].   My mother,
This night let every thought be given to *thee!*
Beautiful scene, farewell!—farewell, my home!
And thou, gray convent, whose inspiring chime
Measures the hours with prayer, that morn and eve
Life may ascend the ladder of the angels,
And climb to heaven! serene retreats, farewell!
And now, my mother!—no! some hours must yet
Pass ere our parting.
   Mme. de la Vall.   Cheer thee, my Louise!
And let us now within; the dews are falling—
   Mdlle. de la Vall. And I forgot how ill thy frame may bear them.
Pardon!—within, within!—
   [*Stopping short and gazing fondly on* MME. DE LA VALLIERE.
      Your hand, dear mother?   [*Exeunt.*

SCENE III.

An old Armory, of the heavy French Architecture preceding the time of Francis the First, in the Castle of BRAGELONE. BERTRAND, *the armorer, employed in polishing a sword.*

   Bert. There now? I think this blade will scarcely shame
My gallant master's hand; it was the weapon,
So legends say, with which the old Lord Rodolph
Slew, by the postern gate, his lady's leman!
Oh, we're a haughty race—we old French lords;
Our honor is unrusted as our steel,
And, when provoked, as ruthless!

Enter BRAGELONE.

Brage.   Ah, old Bertrand!
Why, your brave spirit, 'mid these coats of mail,
Grows young again. So! this, then, is the sword
You'd have me wear. God wot! a trenchant blade,
Not of the modern fashion.

Bert.   My good lord,
Yourself are scarcely of the modern fashion.
They tell me, that to serve one's king for nothing,
To deem one's country worthier than one's self,
To hold one's honor not a phrase to swear by,—
They tell me, now, all *this* is out of fashion.
Come, take the sword, my lord!—you have your father's
Stout arm and lordly heart: they're out of fashion,
And yet you keep the one—come, take the other.

Brage. Why you turn satirist!

Ber.   Satirist! what is that?

Brage. Satirists, my friend, are men who speak the truth
That courts may say—they do not know the fashion!
Satire on Vice is Wit's revenge on fools
That slander Virtue. How now! look ye, Bertrand!
Methinks there is a notch here.

Ber.   Ay, my lord;
I would not grind it out;—'twas here the blade
Clove through the helmet, ev'n unto the chin,
Of that irreverent and most scoundrel Dutchman
Who stabb'd you, through your hauberk-joints—what time
You placed your breast before the king.

Brage.   Hence, ever
Be it believed, that, in his hour of need,
A king's sole safeguard are his subjects' hearts!
Ha, ha! good sword! that was a famous stroke!
Thou didst brave deeds that day, thou quaint old servant,
Though now—thou'rt not the fashion.

Ber.   Bless that look,
And that glad laugh! they bring me back the day
When first old Bertrand arm'd you for the wars,—
A fair-faced stripling; yet, beshrew my heart,
You spurr'd that field before the bearded chins,
And saved the gallant Lord La Vallière's standard,
And yet you were a stripling then.

Brage.   La Vallière!
The very name goes dancing through my veins.
Bertrand, look round the armory. Is there nought
I wore that first campaign? Nay, nay! no matter,
I wear the *name within* me. Hark ye, Bertrand!
We're not so young as then we were: when next
We meet, old friend, we both will end our labors,
And find some nook, amidst yon antique trophies,
Wherein to hang this idle mail.

Ber.   Huzza!
The village dames speak truth—my Lord will marry!
And I shall nurse, in these old wither'd arms,

Another boy—for France another hero.
Ha, ha! I am so happy.
   Brage.   Good old man!
Why this is like my father's hall—since thus
My father's servants love me.
   Ber.   All must love you!
   Brage. All!—let me think so.   [*Bugle sounds.*
                Hark, the impatient bugle!
I hear the neigh of my exultant charger,
Breathing from far the glorious air of war.
Give me the sword!

           Enter Servant, *with a letter.*

              Her mother's hand!—" Louise,
Arrived at court, writes sadly, and amidst
The splendor pines for home,"—I knew she would!
My own Louise!—" Speaks much of the king's goodness;"—
Goodness to her!—that thought shall give the king
A tenfold better soldier!—" From thy friend,
Who trusts ere long to hail thee as her son."
Her son!—a blessed name. These lines shall be
My heart's true shield and ward away each weapon.
He who shall wed Louise has conquer'd Fate,
And smiles at earthly foes!—Again the bugle!
Give me your hand, old man. My fiery youth
Went not to battle with so blithe a soul
As now burns in me. So! she pines for home—
I knew she would—I knew it! Farewell, Bertrand!   [*Exit* BRAGELONE.
   Ber. Oh! there'll be merry doings in the hall
When my dear lord returns! A merry wedding,
And then—and then—oh, such a merry christening!
How well I fancy his grave manly face
Brightening upon his first-born.   [*As he is going.*

           Re-enter BRAGELONE.

   Brage.   Ho, there! Bertrand!
One charge I had forgot:—Be sure they train
The woodbine richly round the western wing—
My mother's old apartment. Well, man! well!
Do you not hear me?
   Ber.   *You,* my lord! the woodbine?
   Brage. Yes; see it duly done. I know she loves it;
It clambers round her lattice. I would not
Have one thing absent she could miss.
                             Remember!   [*Exit* BRAGELONE
   Ber. And this is he whom warriors call "the Stern!"
The dove's heart beats beneath that lion breast.
Pray Heaven his lady may deserve him! Oh,
What news for my good dame!—i' faith, I'm glad
I was the first to learn the secret. So,
This year a wife—next year a boy! I'll teach
The young rogue how his father clove the Dutchman

Down to the chin! Ha, ha! old Bertrand now
Will be of use again on winter nights,—
I know he'll be the picture of his father.   [*Exit* BERTRAND.

SCENE IV.

An Antechamber in the Palace of Fontainebleau.

Enter LAUZUN *and* GRAMMONT *at opposite doors.*

Lau. Ah, Count, good day! Were you at court last night?
Gram. Yes; and the court has grown the richer by
A young new beauty.
Lau.   So!—her name?
Gram.   La Vallière.
Lau. Ay, I have heard;—a maid of honor?
Gram.   Yes.
The women say she's plain.
Lau.   The women! oh,
The case it is that's plain—*she* must be lovely.
Gram. The dear, kind gossips of the court declare
The pretty novice hath conceived a fancy—
A wild, romantic, innocent, strange fancy—
For our young king; a girlish love, like that
Told of in fairy tales: she saw his picture,
Sigh'd to the canvas, murmur'd to the colors,
And—fell in love with carmine and gambouge.
Lau. The simple dreamer! Well, she saw the king?
Gram. And while she saw him, like a rose, when May
Breathes o'er its bending bloom, she seem'd to shrink
Into her modest self, and a low sigh
Shook blushes (sweetest rose-leaves!) from her beauty.
Lau. You paint it well.
Gram.   And ever since that hour
She bears the smiling malice of her comrades
With an unconscious and an easy sweetness;
As if alike *her* virtue and *his* greatness
Made love impossible: so, down the stream
Of purest thought, her heart glides on to danger.
Lau. Did Louis note her?—Has he heard the gossip?
Gram. Neither, methinks: his Majesty is cold.
The art of pomp, and not the art of love,
Tutors his skill—Augustus more than Ovid.
Lau. The time will come. The king as yet is young,
Flush'd with the novelty of sway, and fired
With the great dream of cutting Dutchmen's throats:
A tiresome dream—the poets call it "Glory."
Gram. So much the better,—'tis one rival less;
The handsome king would prove a dangerous suitor.
Lau. Oh, hang the danger! He must have a mistress;

'Tis an essential to a court: how many
Favors, one scarcely likes to ask a king,
One flatters from a king's inamorata !
We courtiers fatten on the royal vices;
And, while the king lives chaste, he cheats, he robs me
Of ninety-nine per cent. !

 Gram.   Ha, ha ! Well, duke,
We meet again to-night. You join the revels ?
Till then, adieu.

 Lau.   Adieu, dear count.   [*Exit* GRAMMONT.
            The king
Must have a mistress: I must lead that mistress.
The times are changed !—'twas by the sword and spear
Our fathers bought ambition—vulgar butchers !
But now our wit's our spear—intrigue our armor;
The antechamber is our field of battle;
And the best hero is—the cleverest rogue ?   [*Exit* LAUZUN.

SCENE V.

Night—the Gardens of the Fontainebleau, brilliantly illuminated with colored lamps—Fountains, vases, and statues in perspective*—A pavilion in the background—to the right the Palace of the Fontainebleau, illuminated. Enter Courtiers, Ladies, etc.

A Dance.

Enter LOUIS *followed by* Courtiers, *etc.*

 Louis. Fair eve and pleasant revels to you all !
Ah, Duke !—a word with you.   [Courtiers *give way.*
      Thou hast seen, my Lauzun,
The new and fairest floweret of our court,
This youngest of the graces—sweet La Vallière,
Blushing beneath the world's admiring eyes ?

 Lau. [*Aside*]. (So, so !—he's caught !) Your Majesty speaks warmly;
Your praise is just—and grateful—

 Louis.   Grateful ?

 Lau.   Ay.
Know you not, Sire, it is the jest, among
The pretty prattlers of the royal chamber,
That this young Dian of the woods has found
Endymion in a king—a summer dream,
Bright, but with vestal fancies !—scarcely love,
But that wild interval of hopes and fears
Through which the child glides, trembling, to the woman ?

 Louis. Blest thought ! Oh, what a picture of delight
Your words have painted !—

 Lau.   While we speak, behold,
Through yonder alleys, with her sister planets,
Your moonlight beauty gleams.

 * The effect of the scene should be principally made by jets-d'eau, waterfalls, etc.

Louis.   'Tis she !—this shade
Shall hide us !—quick—   [*Enters one of the bosquets.*
  Lau. [*following him*].   I trust my creditors
Will grow the merrier from this night's adventure.

        Enter MDLLE. DE LA VALLIERE *and* Maids of Honor.

  First Maid. How handsome looks the Duke de Guiche to-night !
  Second Maid. Well, to my taste, the graceful Grammont bears
The bell from all !—
  Third Maid.   But, then, that charming Lauzun
Has so much wit.
  First Maid.   And which, of all these gallants,
May please the fair La Vallière most ?
  Mdlle. de la Vall.   In truth,
I scarcely mark'd them; when the king is by,
Who can have eye, or ear, or thought for others ?
  First Maid. You raise your fancies high !
  Second Maid.   And raise them vainly !
The king disdains all love !
  Mdlle. de la Vall.   Who spoke of love ?
The sunflower, gazing on the Lord of heaven,
Asks but its sun to shine !—Who spoke of love ?
And who would wish the bright and lofty Louis
To stoop from glory ? Love should not confound
So great a spirit with the herd of men.
Who spoke of love ?——
  First Maid.   My country friend, you talk
Extremely well; but some young lord will teach you
To think of Louis less, and more of love.
  Mdlle. de la Vall. Nay, ev'n the very presence of his greatness
Exalts the heart from each more low temptation.
He seems to walk the earth as if to raise
And purify our wandering thoughts, by fixing
Thought on himself;—and she who thinks on Louis
Shuts out the world, and scorns the name of love !
  First Maid. Wait till you're tried—   [*Music.*
                But, hark ! the music chides us
For wasting this most heavenly night so idly.
Come ! let us join the dancers.   [*Exeunt* Maids.
  [*As* LA VALLIERE *follows, the* King *steals from the bosquet, and takes her
      hand, while* LAUZUN *retires in the opposite direction.*
  Louis.   Sweet La Vallière !
  Mdlle. de la Vall. Ah !—
  Louis. Nay, fair lady, fly not, ere we welcome
Her who gives night its beauty !
  Mdlle. de la Vall.   Sire, permit me !
My comrades wait me.
  Louis.   What ! my loveliest subject
So soon a rebel ? Silent !—Well, *be* mute,
And teach the world the eloquence of blushes.
  Mdlle. de la Vall. I may not listen—
  Louis.   What if *I* had set
Thyself the example ? What if *I* had listen'd,

Veil'd by yon friendly boughs, and dared to dream
That one blest word which spoke of Louis absent
Might charm his presence, and make Nature music?
 Mdlle. de la Vall. You did not, Sire! you could not!
 Louis.   Could not hear thee,
Nor pine for these divine, unwitness'd moments,
To pray thee, dearest lady, to divorce
No more the thought of love from him who loves thee.
And—faithful still to glory—swears thy heart
Unfolds the fairest world a king can conquer!
Hear me, Louise!
 Mdlle. de la Vall. No, Sire; forget those words!
I am not what their foolish meaning spoke me,
But a poor simple girl, who loves her king,
And honor *more*. Forget, and do not scorn me!
         [*Exit* MDLLE. DE LA VALLIERE.
 Louis. Her modest coyness fires me more than all
Her half-unconscious and most virgin love.

   Enter Courtiers, Ladies, Guests, &c.; LAUZUN, GRAMMON, *and*
       MONTESPAN.

Well, would the dancers pause awhile?
 Lau.   Ev'n pleasure
Wearies at last.
 Louis.   We've but to change its aspect,
And it resumes its freshness. Ere the banquet
Calls us, my friends, we have prepared a game
To shame the lottery of this life, wherein
Each prize is neighbor'd by a thousand blanks.
Methinks it is the duty of a monarch
To set the balance right, and bid the wheel
Shower nought but prizes on the hearts he loves.
What ho, there! with a merry music, raise
Fortune, to show how Merit conquers Honors!   [*Music.*
  [*The Pavilion at the back of the stage opens, and discovers the Temple of
   Fortune superbly illuminated. Fortune; at her feet, a wheel of light;
   at either hand, a golden vase, over each of which presides a figure—the
   one representing* Merit, *the other* Honor.
 Louis. Approach, fair dames and gallants! Aye, as now,
May fortune smile upon the friends of Louis!
  [*The* Courtiers *and* Ladies *group around the vases. From the one over
   which* Merit *presides they draw lots, and receive in return from*
   Honor *various gifts of jewels, etc.*

   Enter MDLLE. DE LA VALLIERE *at the back of the stage.*

 Louis [*to Malle. de la Vall.*]. Nay, if you smile not on me, then the scene
Hath lost its charm.
 Mdlle. de la Vall. Oh, Sire, all eyes are on us!
 Louis. All eyes *should* learn where homage should be render'd.
 Mdlle. de la Vall. I pray you, Sire——
 Lau.   Will't please your Majesty
To try your fortune?

Louis. Fortune! Sweet La Vallière,
I only seek my fortune in thine eyes.

  Music. Louis *draws, and receives a diamond bracelet.* Ladies
   crowd round.

First Lady. How beautiful!

Second Lady. Each gem were worth a duchy!

Third Lady. Oh, happy she upon whose arm the king
Will bind the priceless band!

Louis [*approaching Mdlle. de la Vall.*]. Permit me, lady. [*Clasps the bracelet.*

Lau. Well done—well play'd! In that droll game call'd Woman,
Diamonds are always trumps for hearts.

First Lady.   Her hair's
Too light!

Second Lady. Her walk is so provincial!

Third Lady. D'ye think she paints?

Lau.   Ha, ha! What envious eyes,
What fawning smiles, await the king's new mistress!

ACT II.—SCENE I.

The Gardens of the Fontainebleau.

Enter Bragelone.

Brage. Why did we suffer her to seek the court?
It is a soil in which the reptile Slander
Still coils in slime around the fairest flower.
Can it be true?—Strange rumors pierced my tent
Coupling her name with—pah!—how foul the thought is!—
The maid the king loves!—Fie! I'll not believe it!
I left the camp—sped hither: if she's lost,
Why then!—down—down, base heart! wouldst *thou* suspect her?
Thou—who shouldst be her shelter from suspicion?
But I may warn, advise, protect, and save her—
Save—'tis a fearful word!

Enter Lauzun.

Lau.   Lord Bragelone!
Methought your warrior spirit never breathed
The air of palaces! No evil tidings,
I trust, from Dunkirk?

Brage.   No. The *fleur-de-lis*
Rears her white crest unstain'd. Mine own affairs
Call me to court.

Lau.   Affairs! I hate the word;
It sounds like debts.

Brage. [*Aside*]. This courtier may instruct me.
[*Aloud.*] Our king—he bears him well?

Lau.   Oh, bravely. Marquis;
Engaged with this new palace of Versailles
It costs some forty millions!

Brage.   Ay, the People
Groan at the burthen.
    Lau.   People!—what's the *People?*
I never heard that word at court! The *People!*
    Brage. I doubt not, duke. The People, like the **Air**,
Is rarely heard, save when it speaks in thunder.
I pray you grace for that old-fashion'd phrase.
What is the latest news?
    Lau.   His Majesty
Dines half an hour before his usual time.
That's the last news at court!—it makes sensation!
    Brage. Is there no weightier news? I heard at Dunkirk
How the king loved a——loved a certain maiden—
The brave La Vallière's daughter.
    Lau.   How, my lord,
How can you vegetate in such a place?
I fancy the next tidings heard at Dunkirk
Will be that—Adam's dead!
    Brage.   The news is old, then?
    Lau. News! *news,* indeed! Why, by this time, our lackeys
Have worn the gossip threadbare. News!—
    Brage.   The lady
(She is a soldier's child) hath not yet barter'd
Her birthright for ambition? She rejects him?
Speak!—She rejects him?
    Lau.   Humph!
    Brage.   Oh, duke, I know
This courtier air—this most significant silence—
With which your delicate race are wont to lie
Away all virtue! Shame upon your manhood!
Speak out, and say Louise La Vallière lives
To prove to courts—that woman *can* be honest!
    Lau. Marquis, you're warm.
    Brage.   You dare not speak;—I knew it!
    Lau. Dare not?
    Brage.   Oh, yes, you dare, with hints and smiles,
To darken fame—to ruin the defenceless—
Blight with a gesture—wither with a sneer!
Did I say "dare not?"—No man dares it better!
    Lau. My lord, these words must pass not!
    Brage.   Duke, forgive me!
I am a rough, stern soldier—taught from youth
To brave offence, and by the sword alone
Maintain the license of my speech. Oh, say—
Say but one word!—say this poor maid is sinless,
And, for her father's sake—(*her father* loved me!)
I'll kneel to thee for pardon!
    Lau.   Good, my lord,
I know not your interest in this matter:
'Tis said that Louis loves the fair La Vallière;
But what of that?—good taste is not a crime!
'Tis said La Vallière does not hate the king;
But what of that?—it does but prove her—loyal!

I know no more. I trust you're satisfied;
If not——
 Brage. Thou liest!
 Lau.   Nay, then, draw!
    [*They fight—after a few passes,* LAUZUN *is disarmed.*
 Brage.   There, take
Thy sword. Alas! each slanderer wears a weapon
No honest arm can baffle—*this* is edgeless. [*Exit* BRAGELONE.
 Lau. Pleasant! This comes, now, of one's condescending
To talk with men who cannot understand
The tone of good society. Poor fellow! [*Exit* LAUZUN.

SCENE II.

Enter MADEMOISELLE DE LA VALLIERE.

 Mdlle. de la Vall. He loves me, then! He loves me! Love! wild word!
Did I say love? Dishonor, shame, and crime
Dwell on the thought! And yet—and yet—*he loves me!*

  [*Re-enter* BRAGELONE, *at the back of the stage.—She takes out the King's picture.*

Mine early dreams were prophets!—Steps! The king?
 Brage. No, lady; pardon me;—a joint mistake;
You sought the king—and *I* Louise la Vallière!
 Mdlle. de la Vall. You here, my lord!—you here!
 Brage.   There was a maiden
Fairer than many fair; but sweet and humble,
And good and spotless, through the vale of life
She walk'd, her modest path with blessings strew'd
(For all men bless'd her); from her crystal name,
Like the breath i' the mirror, even envy pass'd:
I sought that maiden at the court; none know her.
May I ask you—where now Louise la Vallière?
 Mdlle. de la Vall. Cruel!—unjust! You were my father's friend,
Dare you speak thus to me?
 Brage.   Dare! dare!—'Tis well.
You have learnt your state betimes!——
 Mdlle. de la Vall.   My state, my lord!
I know not by what right you thus assume
The privilege of insult!
 Brage.   Ay, reproach!
The harlot's trick—for shame! Oh, no, your pardon!
You are too high for shame: and so—farewell!
 Mdlle. de la Vall. My lord!—my lord, in pity—No!—*in justice,*
Leave me not thus!
 Brage.   Louise!
 Mdlle. de la Vall.   Have they belied me?
Speak, my good lord!—What crime have I committed?
 Brage. No crime—at courts! 'Tis only Heaven and Honor

That deem it aught but—most admired good fortune!
Many, who swept in careless pride before
The shrinking, spotless, timorous La Vallière,
Will now fawn round thee, and with bended knees
Implore sweet favor of the king's kind mistress.
Ha, ha!—this is not crime! Who calls it crime?
Do prudes say "Crime?" Go, bribe them, and they'll swear
Its name is greatness. Crime, indeed!—ha, ha!

 Mdlle. de la Vall. My heart finds words at length!—'Tis false!
 Brage.   'Tis false!
Why, speak again!—say once more it is false—
'Tis *false!*—again, *'tis false!*

 Mdlle. de la Vall. Alas, I'm wretched!
 Brage. No, lady, no! not wretched, if not guilty!
  [MADEMOISELLE DE LA VALLIERE, *after walking to and fro in great agitation, seats herself on one of the benches of the garden, and covers her face with her hands.*

 Brage. [*aside*]. Are these the tokens of remorse? No, matter!
I loved her well! And love is pride, not love,
If it forsake ev'n guilt amidst its sorrows!
[*Aloud.*] Louise!—Louise!—Speak to thy friend, Louise!
Thy father's friend!—thine own!

 Mdlle. de la Vall.   This hated court!
Why came I hither? Wherefore have I closed
My heart against its own most pleading dictates?
Why clung to virtue, if the brand of vice
Sear my good name?

 Brage.   That, when thou pray'st to Heaven,
Thy soul may ask for *comfort*—not *forgiveness!*

 Mdlle. de la Vall. [*rising eagerly*]. A blessed thought! I thank thee!

 Brage.   Thou art innocent!
Thou hast denied the king?

 Mdlle. de la Vall.   I *have* denied him.

 Brage. Curst be the lies that wrong'd thee!—doubly curst
The hard, the icy selfishness of soul,
That, but to pander to an hour's caprice,
Blasted that flower of life—fair fame! Accurst
The king who casts his purple o'er his vices!

 Mdlle. de la Vall. Hold!—thou malign'st thy king!

 Brage.   He spared not **thee**.

 Mdlle. de la Vall. The king!—Heaven bless him!

 Brage.   Would'st thou madden me?
Thou!—No—thou lov'st him not?—thou hid'st thy face!
Woman, thou tremblest! Lord of Hosts, for this
Hast thou preserved me from the foeman's sword,
And through the incarnadined and raging seas
Of war upheld me?—made both life and soul
The sleepless priests to that fair idol—Honor?
Was it for this? I loved thee not, Louise,
As gallants love! Thou wert this life's IDEAL,
Breathing through earth the Lovely and the Holy,
And clothing Poetry in human beauty!
When in this gloomy world they spoke of sin,

I thought of thee, and smiled—for thou wert sinless!
And when they told of some diviner act
That made our nature noble, my heart whisper'd—
"So would have done Louise!"—'Twas thus I loved thee!
To lose thee, I can bear it; but to lose,
With thee, all hope, all confidence, of virtue—
This—*this* is hard!—Oh! I am sick of earth!

 Mdlle. de la Vall. Nay, speak not thus;—be gentle with me. Come,
I am not what thou deem'st me, Bragelone;
Woman I am, and weak. Support, advise me!
Forget the lover, but be still the friend.
Do not desert me—*thou!*

 Brage.   Thou lov'st the king!

 Mdlle. de la Vall. But I can fly from love.

 Brage.   Poor child! And whither?

 Mdlle. de la Vall. Take me to the old castle, to my mother.

 Brage. The king can reach thee there!

 Mdlle. de la Vall.   He'll not attempt it.
Alas! in courts, how quickly men forget!

 Brage. Not till their victim hath surrender'd all!
Hadst thou but yielded, why thou might'st have lived
Beside his very threshold, safe, unheeded;
But thus, with all thy bloom of heart unrifled,—
The fortress storm'd, not conquer'd,—why man's pride,
If not man's lust, would shut thee from escape!
Art thou in earnest,—wouldst thou truly fly
From gorgeous infamy to tranquil honor,
God's house alone may shelter thee!

 Mdlle. de la Vall.   The convent!
Alas! alas! to meet those eyes no more!
Never to hear that voice!

 Brage. [*departing*]. Enough.

 Mdlle. de la Vall.   Yet, stay!
I'll see him once! one last farewell—and then—
Yes, to the convent!

 Brage.   I have done!—and yet,
Ere I depart, take back the scarf thou gav'st me.
Then didst "thou honor worth!" now, gift and giver
Alike are worthless.

 Mdlle. de la Vall. Worthless! Didst thou hear me?
Have I not said that——

 Brage.   Thou wouldst see the king!
Vice first, and virtue after! O'er the marge
Of the abyss thou tremblest. One step more,
And from all heaven the Angels shall cry "*Lost!*"
Thou ask'st that single step! Wouldst thou be saved?
Lose not a moment.—Come!

 Mdlle. de la Vall. [*in great agony*]. Beside that tree,
When stars shone soft, he vow'd for aye to love me!

 Brage. Think of thy mother! At this very hour
She blesses Heaven that thou wert born—the last
Fair scion of a proud and stainless race.
To-morrow, and thy shame may cast a shade

Over a hundred 'scutcheons, and thy mother
Feel thou wert born that *she* might long to die !
Come !
   Mdlle. de la Vall.   I am ready—take my hand.
                                  [*Her eye falls on the bracelet.*
                              Away !

This is his gift ! And shall I leave him thus ?
Not one kind word to break the shock of parting—
   Brage. And break a mother's heart !
   Mdlle. de la Vall.   Be still ! Thou'rt man !
Thou canst not feel as woman feels !—her weakness
Thou canst not sound. O Louis, Heaven protect thee !
May fate look on thee with La Vallière's eyes !
Now I am ready, sir. Thou'st seen how weak
Woman is ever where she loves. *Now*, learn,
Proportion'd to that weakness is the strength
With which she conquers love ! O Louis, Louis !
Quick ! take me hence !—
   Brage.   The heart she wrongs hath saved her !
And is that all !—The shelter for mine age—
The Hope that was the garner for Affection—
The fair and lovely tree, beneath whose shade
The wearied soldier thought to rest at last,
And watch life's sun go calm and cloudless down,
Smiling the day to sleep—all, all lie shatter'd !
No matter. I have saved thy soul from sorrow,
Whose hideous depth thy vision cannot fathom.
Joy !—I have saved thee !
   Mdlle. de la Vall.   Ah ! when last we parted
I told thee, of thy love I was not worthy.
Another shall replace me !
   Brage. [*smiling sadly*]. Hush ! Another !
No !—See, I wear thy colors still ! Though Hope
Wanes from the plate, the dial still remains,
And takes no light from stars ! I—*I* am nothing !
But thou—Nay, weep not ! Yet these tears are honest:
Thou hast not lived to make the Past one blot,
Which life in vain would weep away ! Poor maiden !
I could not cheer thee *then*. *Now*, joy !—I've saved thee !
                        [*Exeunt* MDLLE. DE LA VALLIERE *and* BRAGELONE.

SCENE III.

The King's Cabinet at Fontainebleau; the King seated at a table, covered with papers, etc., writing.*

Enter LAUZUN.

Louis. Lauzun, I sent for you. Your zeal has served me,
And I am grateful. There, this order gives you
The lands and lordship of De Visci.
  Lau.   Sire,
How shall I thank your goodness?
  Louis.   Hush!—by silence!
  Lau. [*aside*]. A king's forbidden fruit has pretty windfalls!
  Louis. This beautiful Louise! I never loved
Till now.
  Lau. She yields not yet?
  Louis.   But gives refusal
A voice that puts ev'n passion to the blush
To own one wish so soft a heart denies it!
  Lau. A woman's No! is but a crooked path
Unto a woman's Yes! Your Majesty
Saw her to-day?
  Louis.   No!—Grammont undertakes
To bear, in secret, to her hand, some lines
That pray a meeting.—I await his news.   [*Continues writing.*
  Lau. [*aside*]. I'll not relate my tilt with Bragelone.
First, I came off the worst.—No man of sense
Ever confesses that! And, secondly,
This most officious, curious, hot-brain'd Quixote
Might make him jealous; jealous kings are peevish;
And, if he fall to questioning the lady,
She'll learn who told the tale, and spite the teller.
Oh! the great use of logic!
  Louis.   'Tis in vain
I strive by business to beguile impatience!
How my heart beats!—Well, count!

Enter GRAMMONT.

  Gram.   Alas, my liege!
  Louis. Alas!—Speak out!
  Gram.   The court has lost La Vallière!
  Louis. Ha!—lost!
  Gram.   She has fled, and none guess whither.
  Louis.   Fled!
I'll not believe it!—Fled!
  Lau.   What matters, sire?
No spot is sacred from the king!
  Louis.   By Heaven
I *am* a king!—Not all the arms of Europe

---

* To some it may be interesting to remember that this cabinet, in which the most powerful of the Bourbon kings is represented as rewarding the minister of his pleasures, is the same as that in which is yet shown the table upon which Napoleon Bonaparte (son of a gentleman of Corsica) signed the abdication of the titles and dominions of Charlemagne!

Could wrest one jewel from my crown. And she—
What is my crown to her! I am a king!
Who stands between the king and her he loves
Becomes a traitor—and may find a tyrant!
Follow me! [*Exit* LOUIS.
    Gram. Who e'er heard of maids of honor
Flying from kings?
    Lau. Ah, had *you* been a maid,
How kind you would have been, you rogue!—Come on!
[*Exeunt* LAUZUN *and* GRAMMONT.

SCENE IV.

The Cloisters of a Convent—Night—Thunder and Lightning, the latter made visible through the long oriel windows.

    Mdlle. de la Vall. [*rising*]. Darkly the night sweeps on.
        No thought of sleep
Steals to my heart. What sleep is to the world
Prayer is to me—life's balm, and grief's oblivion!
Yes, ev'n before the altar of my God,
Unhallow'd fire is raging through my veins—
Heav'n on my lips, but earth within my heart—
And while I pray *his* memory prompts the prayer,
And all I ask of Heaven is—" Guard my Louis!"
Forget him—*that* I dare not pray! I would not,
Ev'n if I could, be happy, and forget him! [*Thunder.*
Roll on, roll on, dark chariot of the storm,
Whose wheels are thunder!—the rack'd elements
Can furnish forth no tempest like the war
Of passions in one weak and erring heart! [*The bell tolls one.*
Hark to night's funeral knell! How through the roar
Of winds and thunder thrills that single sound,
Solemnly audible!—the tongue of time,
In time's most desolate hour!—it bids us muse
On worlds which love can reach not! Life runs fast
To its last sands! To bed, to bed!—to tears
And wishes for the grave!—to bed, to bed! [*A trumpet is heard without.*

    Two or three Nuns *hurry across the stage.*

    First Nun. Most strange!
    Second Nun. In such a night, too! The great gates,
That ne'er unclose save to a royal guest,
Unbarr'd!
    Mdlle. de la Vall. What fear, what hope, by turns distracts me!
[*The trumpet sounds again.*
    First Nun. Hark! in the court, the ring of hoofs!—the door
Creaks on the sullen hinge!
    Lau. [*without*]. Make way!—the king!

Enter LOUIS *and* LAUZUN.

Mdlle. de la Vall. [*rushing forward*]. Oh, Louis!—oh, beloved! [*Then pausing abruptly.*] No, touch me not!
Leave me! in pity leave me! Heavenly Father,
I fly to thee! Protect me from his arms—
Protect me from myself!
    Louis.   Oh bliss!—Louise!

Enter Abbess *and other* Nuns.

Abbess. Peace, peace! What clamor desecrates the shrine
And solitudes of God?
    Lau.   Madam, your knee—
The king!
    Abbess. The king!—you mock me, sir!
    Louis [*quitting* MDLLE. DE LA VALLIERE]. Behold
Your sovereign, reverend mother! We have come
To thank you for your shelter of this lady,
And to reclaim our charge.
    Abbess.   My liege, these walls
Are sacred even from the purple robe
And sceptred hand.
    Louis.   She hath not ta'en the vow!
She's free!—we claim her!—she is of our court!
Woman,—go to!
    Abbess.   The maiden, sire, is free
Your royal lips have said it!—She is free!
And if this shrine her choice, whoe'er compels her
Forth from the refuge, doth incur the curse
The Roman Church awards to even kings!
Speak, lady!—dost thou claim against the court
The asylum of the cloister?
    Louis.   Darest thou brave us?
    Lau. [*aside to Louis*]. Pardon, my liege!—reflect! Let not the world
Say that the king—
    Louis.   Can break his bonds!—Away!
I was a man before I was a king!
                [*Approaching* MDLLE. DE LA VALLIERE.
Lady, we do command your presence! [*Lowering his voice.*] Sweet!
Adored Louise!—if ever to your ear
My whispers spoke in music—if my life
Be worth the saving, do not now desert me!
    Mdlle. de la Vall. Let me not hear him, Heaven!—Strike all my senses!
Make—make me dumb, deaf, blind,—but keep me honest!
    Abbess. Sire, you have heard her answer!
    Louis [*advancing passionately, pauses, and then with great dignity*].
                      Abbess, no!
This lady was intrusted to our charge—
A fatherless child!—the king is now her father!
Madam, we would not wrong you; but we know
That sometimes most unhallow'd motives wake
Your zeal for converts!—This young maid is wealthy,
And nobly born!—Such proselytes may make
A convent's pride, but oft a convent's victims!

No more!—we claim the right the law awards us,
Free and alone to commune with this maiden.
If then her choice go with you—be it so;
We are no tyrant! Peace!—retire!
  Abbess.   My liege!
Forgive—
  Louis. We do! Retire!   [LAUZUN, *the* Abbess, etc., *withdraw*.
  Louis.   We are alone!
  Mdlle. de la Vall. Alone!—No, God is present, and the conscience!
  Louis. Ah! fear'st thou, then, that heart that would resign
Ev'n love itself to guard one pang from thee?
  Mdlle. de la Vall. I *must* speak!—Sire, if every drop of blood
Were in itself a life, I'd shed them all
For one hour's joy to thee!—But fame and virtue—
My father's grave—my mother's lonely age—
These, these—   [*Thunder*.
              I hear their voice!—the fires of Heaven
Seem to me like the eyes of angels, and
Warn me against myself!—Farewell!
  Louis.   Louise,
I will not hear thee! What! farewell! that word
Sounds like a knell to all that's worth the living!
Farewell! why, then, farewell all peace to Louis,
And the poor king is once more but a thing
Of state and forms. The impulse and the passion—
The blessed air of happy human life—
The all that made him envy not his subjects,
Dies in that word! Ah, canst thou—dar'st thou say it?
  Mdlle. de la Vall. Oh, speak not thus!—Speak harshly! threat, command!—
Be all the king!
  Louis.   The king! he kneels to thee!
  Mdlle. de la Vall. I'm weak—be generous! My own soul betrays me;
But *thou* betray me not!
  Louis.   Nay, hear me, sweet one!
Desert me not this once, and I will swear
To know no guiltier wish—to curb my heart—
To banish hope from love—and nurse no dream
Thy spotless soul itself shall blush to cherish!
Hear me, Louise—thou lov'st me?
  Mdlle. de la Vall.   Love thee, Louis!
  Louis. Thou lov'st me,—then confide! Who loves, *trusts* ever!
  Mdlle. de la Vall. Trust thee!—ah! *dare* I?
  Louis [*clasping her in his arms*]. Ay, till death! What ho!
Lauzun! I say!

                    Enter LAUZUN.

  Mdlle. de la Vall. No, no!
  Louis.   *Not trust me*, dearest?
          [*She falls on his shoulder—the* Abbess *and* Nuns *advance*.
  Abbess. Still firm!
  Lau.   No, madam!—Way there for the king!

ACT III.—SCENE I.

An Antechamber in the Palace of MADAME LA DUCHESSE DE LA VALLIERE *at Versailles.*

Enter LAUZUN *and* MADAME DE MONTESPAN *at opposite doors.*

Lau. Ha! my fair friend, well met!—how fares Athenè?

Mme. de Mon. Weary with too much gaiety! Now, tell me,
Do *you* ne'er tire of splendor? Does this round
Of gaudy pomps—this glare of glitt'ring nothings—
Does it ne'er pall upon you? To my eyes
'Tis as the earth would be if turf'd with scarlet,
Without one spot of green.

Lau.   We all feel thus
Until we are used to it. Art has grown *my* nature.
And if I see green fields, or ill-dressed people,
I cry "How artificial!" With me, "*Nature*"
Is "Paris and Versailles." The word, "a man,"
Means something noble, that one sees at court.
Woman's the thing Heaven made for wearing trinkets
And talking scandal. That's my state of nature!
You'll like it soon; you have that temper which
Makes courts its element.

Mme. de Mon.   And how?—define, sir.

Lau. First, then—but shall I not offend?

Mme. de Mon.   Be candid.
I'd know my faults, to make them look like virtues.

Lau. First, then, Athenè, you've an outward frankness.
Deceit in you looks honester than truth.
Thoughts, at court, like faces on the stage,
Require some rouge. You rouge your thoughts so well,
That one would deem their only fault, that nature
Gave them too bright a bloom!

Mme. de Mon.   Proceed!

Lau.   Your wit
Is of the true court breed—it plays with nothings;
Just bright enough to warm, but never burn—
Excites the dull, but ne'er offends the vain.
You have much energy; it looks like feeling!
Your cold ambition seems an easy impulse;
Your head most ably counterfeits the heart,
But never, like the heart, betrays itself!
Oh! you'll succeed at court!—you see I know you!
Not so this new-made duchess—young La Vallière.

Mme. de Mon. The weak, fond fool!

Lau.   Yes, weak—*she* has a heart;
Yet *you*, too, love the king!

Mme. de Mon.   And she does *not!*
She loves but *Louis*—I but love the *king*:
Pomp, riches, state, and power—these, who would love not?

Lau. Bravo! well said!—Oh, you'll succeed at court!
I knew it well! it was for this I chose you—
Induced your sapient lord to waste no more

Your beauty in the shade—for this prepared
The duchess to receive you to her bosom,
Her dearest friend; for this have duly fed
The king's ear with your praise, and clear'd your way
To rule a sovereign and to share a throne.
   Mme. de Mon. I know thou hast been my architect of power;
And, when the pile is built—
   Lau. [*with a smile*].   Could still o'erthrow it,
If thou couldst play the ingrate!
   Mme. de Mon.   I!—nay!
   Lau.   Hear me.
Each must have need of each. Long live the king!
Still let his temples ache beneath the crown.
But all that kings can give—wealth, rank, and power—
Must be for *us*—the king's friend and his favorite.
   Mme. de Mon. But is it easy to supplant the duchess?
All love La Vallière! Her meek nature shrinks
Ev'n from our homage; and she wears her state
As if she pray'd the world to pardon greatness.
   Lau. And thus destroys herself! At court, Athenè,
Vice, to win followers, takes the front of virtue,
And looks the dull plebeian things called *moral*
To scorn, until they blush to be unlike her.
Why is De Lauzun not her friend? Why plotting
For a new rival? Why?—Because De Lauzun
Wins not the power he look'd for from her friendship!
She keeps not old friends!—and she makes no new ones!
For who would be a friend to one who deems it
A crime to ask his Majesty a favor?
"*Friends*" is a phrase at court that means *Promotion!*
   Mme. de Mon. Her folly, I confess, would not be mine.
But, grant her faults—the king still loves the duchess!
   Lau. Since none are by, I'll venture on a treason,
And say, the king's a man!—and men will change!
I have his ear, and you shall win his eye.
'Gainst a new face, and an experienced courtier,
What chance hath this poor, loving, simple woman?
Besides, she has too much conscience for a king!
He likes not to look up, and feel how low,
Ev'n on the throne that overlooks the world,
His royal greatness dwarfs beside that heart
That never stoop'd to sin, save when it loved him!
   Mme. de Mon. You're eloquent, my lord!
   Lau.   Ah! of such natures
You and I know but little!—[*Aside.*] This must cease,
Or I shall all disclose my real aims!
[*Aloud.*] The king is with the duchess?
   Mme. de Mon.   Yes.
   Lau.   As yet
She doth suspect you not?
   Mme. de Mon.   Suspect!—the puppet!
No; but full oft, her head upon my bosom,
Calls me her truest friend!—invites me ever

To amuse the king with my enlivening sallies,—
And still breaks off, in sighing o'er the past,
To wish her spirit were as blithe as mine,
And fears her Louis wearies of her sadness.

 Lau. So, the plot ripens!—ere the king came hither,
I had prepared his royal pride to chafe
At that sad face, whose honest sorrow wears
Reproach unconsciously! You'll learn the issue!
Now, then, farewell!—We understand each other! [*Exit* LAUZUN.

 Mme. de Mon. And once I loved this man!—and still might love him,
But that I love ambition! Yes, my steps
Now need a guide; but once upon the height,
And I will have no partner! Thou, lord duke,
With all thine insolent air of proud protection,
Thou shalt wait trembling on my nod, and bind
Thy fortune to my wheels! O man!—vain man!
Well sung the poet,—when this power of beauty
Heaven gave our sex, it gave the only sceptre
Which makes the world a slave! And I will wield it!
           [*Exit* MME. DE MONTESPAN.

SCENE II.

The scene opens and discovers the KING, *and the* DUCHESS DE LA VALLIERE *at chess.*

 Louis. But one move more!
 Duch. de la Vall.   Not so! I check the king.
 Louis. A vain attempt!—the king is too well guarded!
There,—check again! Your game is lost!
 Duch. de la Vall.   As usual,
Ev'n from this mimic stage of war you rise
Ever the victor.   [*They leave the table and advance.*
 Louis.   'Twere a fairer fortune,
My own Louise, to reconcile the vanquish'd!
 Duch. de la Vall. [*sadly*]. My best-loved Louis!
 Louis.   Why so sad a tone?
Nay, smile, Louise!—Love thinks himself aggrieved
If Care casts shadows o'er the heart it seeks
To fill with cloudless sunshine! Smile, Louise!
Ev'n unkind words were kinder than sad looks.
There—*now* thou gladd'st me!
 Duch. de la Vall.   Yet ev'n thou, methought,
Didst wear, this morn, a brow on which the light
Shone less serenely than its wont!
 Louis.   This morn!
Ay, it is true!—This morn I heard that France
Hath lost a subject monarchs well might mourn!
Oh! little know the world how much a king,
Whose life is past in *purchasing* devotion,
Loses in one who merited all favor

And scorned to ask the least! A king, Louise,
Sees but the lackeys of mankind. The true
Lords of our race—the high chivalric hearts—
Nature's nobility—alas, are proud,
And stand aloof, lest slaves should say they flatter!
Of such a mould was he whom France deplores.

Duch. de la Vall. Tell me his name, that I, with thee, may mourn him.

Louis. A noble name, but a more noble bearer;
Not to be made by, but to make, a lineage.
Once, too, at Dunkirk, 'twixt me and the foe,
He thrust his gallant breast, already seamed
With warrior-wounds, and *his* blood flow'd for mine.
Dead!—his just merits all unrecompensed!—
Obscured, like sun-light, by the suppliant clouds!
He should have died a marshal! Death did wrong
To strike so soon! Alas, brave Bragelone!

Duch. de la Vall. Ha!—did I hear aright, my liege—my Louis?
That name—that name!—thou saidst not "Bragelone"?

Louis. Such was his name, not often heard at court.
Thou didst not know him? What! thou art pale! thou weepest!—
Thou art ill! Louise, look up! [*He leads her to a seat.*

Duch. de la Vall. Be still, O conscience!
I did not slay him!—Died *too soon!* Alas!
He should have died with all his hopes unblighted,
Ere I was—what I am!

Louis. What mean these words?

Duch. de la Vall. How did death strike him?—what disease?

Louis. I know not.
He had retired from service; and in peace
Breathed out his soul to some remoter sky!
France only guards his fame! What was he to thee
That thou shouldst weep for him?

Duch. de la Vall. Hast thou ne'er heard
We were betrothed in youth?

Louis [*agitated and aside*]. Lauzun speaks truth!
I'd not her virgin heart—she loved another!
[*Aloud.*] Betrothed! You mourn him deeply!

Duch. de la Vall. Sire, I do.
That broken heart!—I was its dream—its idol!
And with regret is mingled—what repentance?

Louis [*coldly*]. Repentance, madam! Well, the word is gracious!

Duch. de la Vall. Pardon! oh, pardon! But the blow was sudden;
How can the heart play courtier with remorse?

Louis. Remorse!—again. Why be at once all honest,
And say you love me not!

Duch. de la Vall. Not love you, Louis?

Louis. Not if you feel repentance to have loved!

Duch. de la Vall. What! think'st thou, Louis, I should love thee more
Did I love virtue less, or less regret it?

Louis. I pray you truce with these heroic speeches;
They please us in romance—in life they weary.

Duch. de la Vall. Louis, do I deserve this?

Louis. Rather, lady.

Do *I* deserve the mute reproach of sorrow?
Still less these constant, never-soothed complaints—
This waiting-woman jargon of "*lost virtue.*"

  Duch. de la Vall. Sire, this from you!

  Louis.   Why, oft, could others hear thee,
Well might they deem thee some poor village Phœbe,
Whom her false Lubin had deceived, and left,
Robb'd of her only dower! and not the great
Duchess la Vallière, in our realm of France
Second to none but our anointed race,
The envy of the beauty and the birth
Of Europe's court—our city of the world:
Is it so great disgrace, Louise la Vallière,
To wear, unrivall'd, in thy breast, the heart
Of Bourbon's latest, nor her least, of kings?

  Duch. de la Vall. Sire, when your deigned to love me, I had hoped
You knew the sunshine of your royal favor
Had fallen on a lowly flower. Let others
Deem that the splendor consecrates the sin!
I'd loved thee with as pure and proud a love,
If thou hadst been the poorest cavalier
That ever served a king—thou know'st it, Louis!

  Louis. I would not have it so! my fame, my glory,
The purple and the orb, are part of me;
And thou shouldst love them for my sake, and feel
I were not Louis were I less the king.
Still weeping! Fie! I tell thee tears freeze back
The very love I still would bear to thee!

  Duch. de la Vall. "Would *still!*"—didst thou say "*still?*"

  Louis.   Come, lady
Woman, to keep her empire o'er the heart,
Must learn its nature—mould unto its bias—
And rule by never differing from our humors.

  Duch. de la Vall. I'll school my features, teach my lips to smile,
Be all thou wilt; but say not "*still,*" dear Louis!

  Louis. Well, well! no further words; let peace be with us.
[*Aside.*] By Heaven, she weeps with yet intenser passion!
It must be that she loved this Bragelone,
And mourns the loftier fate that made her mine!
[*Aloud.*] This gallant soldier, madame, your betrothed,
Hath some share in your tears?

  Duch. de la Vall.   Oh, name him not;
My tears are all unworthy dews to fall
Upon a tomb so honor'd!

  Louis.   Grant me patience!
These scenes are very tedious, fair La Vallière.
In truth, we kings have, in the council-chamber,
Enough to make us tearful;—in the bower
We would have livelier subjects to divert us.

  Duch. de la Vall. Again forgive me! I am sick at heart;
I pray you pardon;—these sad news have marr'd
The music of your presence, and have made me
Fit but for solitude. I pray you, sire,

Let me retire; and when again I greet you,
I'll wear the mien you'd have me!
    Louis.   Be it so!
Let me no more disturb you from your thoughts;
They must be sad. So brave—and your betroth'd!
Your grief becomes you.
    Duch. de la Vall. You forgive me, Louis?
We do not part unkindly?
    Louis.   Fair one, no!   [*Exit* LA VALLIERE.
    Louis. She was my first love, and my fondest.—*Was!*
Alas, the word must come!—I love her yet,
But love wanes glimmering to that twilight—friendship!
Grant that she never loved this Bragelone;
Still, tears and sighs make up dull interludes
In passion's short-lived drama! She is good,
Gentle, and meek,—and I do think she loves me,
(A truth no king is sure of!)—But, in fine,
I have begun to feel the hours are long
Pass'd in her presence! what I hotly sought,
Coldly I weary of. I'll seek De Lauzun:
I like his wit—I almost like his knavery;
It never makes us yawn, like high-flown virtues.
Thirst, hunger, rest—these are the wants of peasants:
A courtier's wants are titles, place, and gold;
But a poor king, who has these wants so sated,
Has only one want left—to be amused!   [*Exit* LOUIS.

SCENE III.

Re-enter the DUCHESS DE LA VALLIERE.

    Duch. de la Vall. Louis! dear Louis!—Gone! alas! and left me
Half in displeasure!—I was wrong, methinks,
To—no!—I was not wrong to *feel* remorse,
But wrong to give it utterance!

               Enter MADAME DE MONTESPAN.
    Mme. de Mon.   What! alone,
Fair friend? I thought the king——
    Duch. de la Vall.   Has gone, in anger;
Cold, and in anger.
    Mme. de Mon.   What, with *thee*, dear lady?
On the smooth surface of that angel meekness
I should have thought no angry breath could linger.
But men and kings are——
    Duch. de la Vall.   Hush! I was to blame.
The king's all goodness. Shall I write to him?
Letters have not our looks—and, oh, one look!
How many hardest hearts one look hath won,

A life consumed in words had woo'd in vain!
 Mme. de Mon. To-night there is high revel at the court;
There you may meet your truant king.
 Duch. de la Vall.   To-night
An age!—How many hours to-night?
 Mme. de Mon.   You know
My office makes my home the royal palace;
I serve the queen, and thus shall see your Louis
Ere the sun set.
 Duch. de la Vall. You!—happy *you!*
 Mme. de Mon.   Perchance
(The king is ever gracious to your friends,
And knows me of the nearest), I might whisper,
Though with less sweet a tone, your message to him,
And be your dove, and bear you back the olive?
 Duch. de la Vall. My kind Athenè!
 Mme. de Mon.   Nay, 'tis yours the kindness,
To wear my love so near your heart. But, tell me,
Since you accept my heraldry, the cause
Of strife between you in this court of love.
 Duch. de la Vall. Alas! I know not, save that I offended!
The wherefore boots the heart that loves to know?
 Mme. de Mon. Not much, I own, the poor defendant—woman,
But much the advocate; I need the brief.
 Duch. de la Vall. Methinks his kingly nature chafes to see
It cannot rule the conscience as the heart;
But, tell him, ever henceforth I will keep
Sad thoughts for lonely hours.—Athenè, tell him,
That if he smile once more upon Louise,
The smile shall never pass from that it shines on;
Say—but I'll write myself. [*Sits down to the table and writes.*
 Mme. de Mon. [*aside*]. What need of schemes—
Lauzun's keen wit—Athenè's plotting spirit?
She weaves herself the web that shall ensnare her!
 Duch. de la Vall. There; back these feeble words with all thy beauty,
Thy conquering eyes, and thy betwiching smile,
Sure never suit can fail with such a pleader!
And now a little while to holier sadness,
And thine accursing memory, Bragelone!
 Mme. de Mon. Whom speak you of?—the hero of the Fronde?
Who seem'd the last of the old Norman race,
And half preserved to this degenerate age
The lordly shape the ancient Bayards wore!
 Duch. de la Vall. You praise him well! He was my father's friend,
And should have been his son. We were affianced,
And—but no more! Ah! cruel, cruel Louis!
You mourn'd for him—how much more cause have *I!*
 Mme. de Mon. [*quickly*]. What! he is dead? your grief the king resented?
Knew he your troth had thus been plighted?
 Duch. de la Vall.   Yes:
And still he seem'd to deem it sin to mourn him!
 Mme. de Mon. [*aside.*] A clue—another clue—that I will follow,
Until it lead me to the throne!—[*Aloud.*] Well, cheer thee;

Trust your true friend; rely on my persuasion.
Methinks I never task'd its powers till now.
Farewell, and fear not! Oh! I'll plead your cause,
As if myself the client!—[*Aside.*] Thou art sentenced!
[*Exit* MADAME DE MONTESPAN.

Duch. de la Vall. 'Tis a sweet solace still to have a friend—
A friend in *woman!* Oh, to what a reed
We bind our destinies, when man we love!
Peace, honor, conscience lost—if I lose him,
What have I left? How sinks my heart within me!
I'll to my chamber; there the day of tears
Lends night its smile! *And I'm the thing they envy!*
[*Exit* DUCHESS DE LA VALLIERE.

SCENE IV.

The Gardens of Versailles—LAUZUN, GRAMMONT, *and* Courtiers.

Lau. 'Tis now the hour in which our royal master
Honors the ground of his rejoicing gardens
By his illustrious footsteps!—there, my lords,
That is the true style-courtier!

Gram. Out upon you!
Your phrase would suit some little German prince,
Of fifteen hundred quarterings and five acres,
And not the world's great Louis! 'Tis the hour
When Phœbus shrinks abash'd, and all the stars
Envy the day that it beholds the king!

Enter LOUIS.

Louis. My lords,
Pray you be cover'd. Hark ye, dear De Lauzun.
[*Exeunt the* Courtiers, *as the* King *takes* LAUZUN *aside.*
The fair De Montespan?

Lau. Is worth the loving;
And, by mine honor, while we speak she comes!
A happy fortune. Sire, may I withdraw? [*Exit.*

Enter MADAME DE MONTESPAN. [*Salutes the* King *and passes on.*]

Louis. Fair madam, we had hoped you with you brought
Some bright excuse to grace our cheerless presence
With a less short-lived light! You dawn upon us
Only to make us more regret your setting.

Mme. de Mon. Sire, if I dared, I would most gladly hail
A few short moments to arrest your presence,
And rid me of a soft, yet painful duty.

Louis. 'Tis the first time, be sure, so sweet a voice
E'er craved a sanction for delighting silence.
Speak on, we pray thee!

Mme. de Mon. Gracious sire, the duchess,

Whom you have lately left, she fears, in anger,
Besought me to present this letter to you.
    Louis [*takes the letter, and aside*]. She blushes while she speaks!—'Tis passing strange,
I ne'er remark'd those darkly-dreaming eyes,
That melt in their own light!
    [*Reads and carelessly puts up the letter.*
                      It scarcely suits
Her dignity, and ours, to choose a witness
To what hath chanced between us. She is good;
But her youth, spent in some old country castle,
Knows not the delicate spirit of a court.
    Mme. de Mon. She bade me back her suit. Alas! my liege,
Who can succeed, if fair La Vallière fail?
    Louis. She bade thee?—she was prudent! Were *I* woman,
And loved, I'd not have chosen such a herald.
    Mme. de Mon. Love varies in its colors with all tempers;
The duchess is too proud to fear a rival,
Too beautiful to find one. May I take
Some word of comfort back to cheer her sadness,
Made doubly deep by thoughts of your displeasure,
And grief for a dear friend?
    Louis.   Ay, *that's* the sadness!
    Mme. de Mon. He was a gallant lord, this Bragelone,
And her betrothed. Perchance in youth she loved him,
Ere the great sun had quench'd the morning star!
    Louis. She loved him!—think'st thou so?
    Mme. de Mon.   Indeed I know not;
But I have heard her eloquent in praise,
And seen her lost in woe. You will forgive her!
    Louis. Forgive her?—there's no cause!
    Mme de Mon.   Now, bless you, sire,
For that one word. My task is done.
    Louis.   Already?
    Mme. de Mon. What can I more? Oh, let me hasten back!
What rapture must be hers who can but fill
An atom of the heart of godlike Louis!
How much more the whole soul!—To lose thy love
Must be, not grief, but some sublime despair,
Like that the Roman felt who lost a world!
    Louis [*aside*]. By Heaven, she fires me!—a brave, royal spirit,
Worthy to love a king!
    Mme. de Mon.   To know thee hers,
What pride!—what glory! Though all earth cried "Shame!"
Earth could not still the trumpet at her heart,
That, with its swelling and exultant voice,
Told her the earth was but the slave of Louis,
And *she* the partner! And, O hour of dread!
When (for the hour must come) some fairer form
Shall win thee from her—still, methinks, 'twould be
A boast to far posterity to point
To all the trophies piled about thy throne,
And say—" He loved me once!"—O sire, your pardon;
I am too bold.

Louis. Why, this were love, indeed,
Could we but hope to win it. And such love
Would weave the laurel in its wreaths of myrtle.
Beautiful lady! while thou speak'st, I dream
What love should be,—and feel where love is not!
Thou com'st the suitor, to remain the judge;
And I could kneel to thee for hope and mercy.
   Mme. de Mon. Ah, no!—ah, no!—she is my friend. And if
She love not as I love—I mean, I *might* love—
Still she *believes* she loves thee. Tempt me not.
Who could resist thee! Sire, farewell! [*Exit* MADAME DE MONTESPAN.
   Louis. Her voice
Is hush'd; but still its queen-like music lingers
In my rapt ears. I dreamt Louise had loved me;
She who felt love disgrace! Before the true,
How the tame counterfeit grows pale and lifeless,
By the sad brow of yon devout La Vallière
I feel a man, and fear myself a culprit!
But this high spirit wakes in mine the sense
Of what it is—I *am* that Louis whom
The world has called "The Great!"—and in her pride
Mirror mine own. This jaded life assumes
The zest, the youth, the glory of *excitement!*
To-night we meet again;—speed fast, dull hours! [*Exit* LOUIS.

SCENE V.

*Grand Saloon in the Palace of Versailles—in the background the suite of apartments is seen in perspective—*Courtiers, Ladies, etc.

   First Cour. [*approaching the Duch. de la Vall.*]. Madam, your goodness is
        to France a proverb!
If I might dare request, this slight memorial
You would convey to our most gracious master?
The rank of colonel in the royal guard
Is just now vacant. True, I have not served;
But I do trust my valor is well-known:
I've kill'd three noted swordsmen in a duel!—
And, for the rest, a word from you were more
Than all the laurels Holland gave to others.
   Duch de la Vall. My lord, forgive me! I might ill deserve
The friendship of a monarch, if, forgetting
That honors are the attributes of merit;—
And they who sell the service of the public
For the false coin, soft smiles and honey'd words
Forged in the antechambers of a palace,
Defraud a people to degrade a king!
If you have merits, let *them* plead for you;
Nor ask in whispers what you claim from justice.

Mme. de Mon. [*to first Courtier, as the Duch. de la Vall. turns away*].
    Give me the paper.   Hush! the king shall see it!   [*Music.*

Enter the KING, GRAMMONT, *and other* Courtiers.   *He pauses by the* QUEEN, *and accosts her respectfully in dumb show.*

    Gram. [*aside.*] With what a stately and sublime decorum
His majesty throws grandeur o'er his foibles!
He not disguises vice; but makes vice kingly—
Most gorgeous of all sensualists!
    Lau.   How different
His royal rival in the chase of pleasure,
The spendthrift, sauntering Second Charles of England!
    Gram. Ay, Jove to Comus!
    Lau.   Silence! Jove approaches!

    [*The crowd breaks up into groups; the* King *passes slowly from each till he joins the* DUCHESS DE LA VALLIERE; *the* Courtiers *retire.*

    Louis. Why, this is well. I thank you.
    Duch. de la Vall.   And forgive me?
    Louis. Forgive you! You mistake me: wounded feeling
Is not displeasure.   Let this pass, Louise.
Your lovely friend has a most heavenly smile!
    Duch. de la Vall. And a warm heart. In truth, my liege, I'm glad
You see her with my eyes.
    Louis.   You have no friend
Whose face it glads me more to look upon. [*Aside, and gazing on* MONTESPAN.
(What thrilling eyes!)—[*Aloud.*]   My thanks are due to her,
For, with the oil of her mellifluous voice,
Smoothing the waves the passing breeze had ruffled.

    [*Joins* MADAME DE MONTESPAN, *and leads her through the crowd to the back of the stage.*

    Lau. Your grace resolves no more to be content
Eclipsing others.   You eclipse yourself.
    Duch. de la Vall. I thought you were a friend, and **not a flatterer.**
    Lau. Friendship would lose its dearest privilege
If Friendship were forbidden to admire!
Why, ev'n the king admires your grace's friend,—
Told me to-day she was the lovliest lady
The court could boast.   Nay, see how, while they speak,
He gazes on her.   How his breathing fans
The locks that shade the roses of her cheek!
    Duch. de la Vall. Ha! Nay, be still, my heart.
    Lau.   It is but friendship;
But it looks wondrous warm!
    Duch. de la Vall.   He cannot mean it!
And yet—and yet—he lingers on her hand—
He whispers!
    Lau.   How the gossips gaze and smile!
There'll be much scandal.
    Duch. de la Vall. Lauzun!—what!—thou think'st not—
No, no, thou canst not think——
    Lau.   That courts know treachery.

That women are ambitious, or men false;
I will not think it.   Pshaw!

Duch. de la Vall.   My brain swims round!
Louis, of late, hath been so changed.   How fair
She looks to-night!—and, oh, *she* has not fallen!
He comes—he nears us—he has left her.   Fie!
My foolish fancies wronged him!

Lau.   The spell works.

Mme. de Mon. [*as the king quits her, to First Courtier, giving him back the paper*]. My lord, your suit is granted.

First Cour.   Blessings, madam!
          [*The other* Courtiers *come round him.*

Second Cour. Her influence must be great.   I know three dukes
Most pressing for the post.

Third Cour.   A rising sun,
Worthier of worship than that cold La Vallière.
The king as well, methinks, might have no mistress,
As one by whom no courtier grew the richer.
          [*The* Courtiers *group round* MADAME DE MONTESPAN.

Louis. My lords, you do remember the bright lists
Which, in the place termed thenceforth " *The Carrousel,*" *
We sometime held?—a knightly tournament,
That brought us back the age of the first Francis!

Lau. Of all your glorious festivals, the greatest!
Who but remembers?

Duch. de la Vall. [*Aside*]. Then he wore my colors.
How kind to bring back to my yearning heart
That golden spring-time of our early loves!

Louis. Next week we will revive the heroic pageant,
Proud plumes shall wave, and levell'd spears be shiver'd;
Ourself will take the lists, and do defy
The chivalry of our renownèd France,
In honor of that lady of our court
For whom we wear the colors, and the motto
Which suits her best—" *Most bright where all are brilliant!*"

Gram. Oh, a most kingly motion!

Louis.   Ere we part,
Let each knight choose his colors and his lady.
Ourself have set the example.
          [*The* Courtiers *mingle with the* Ladies, *etc., many* Ladies *give their colors.*

Duch. de la Vall. [*timidly*]. Oh, my Louis!
I read thy heart; thou hast chosen this device
To learn thy poor Vallière to be proud.
Nay, turn not from my blessings.   Once before
You wore my colors, though I gave them not.
To-night I give them!—Louis loves me still!
          [*Takes one of the knots from her breast, and presents it.*

Louis. Lady, the noblest hearts in France would beat
More high beneath your badge.   Alas! *my* service

---

* The *Place du Carrousel* was so named from a splendid festival given by Louis. On the second day, devoted to knightly games, the king, who appeared in the character of *Roger*, carried off four prizes. All the crown jewels were prodigalized on his arms and the trappings of his horse

Is vow'd already *here*.
>   [*Turning to* Madame de Montespan, *and placing a knot of her colors over his order of the Saint Esprit.*]
>   These are my colors!

Duch. de la Vall. How! How!
>   [*The* King *converses apart with* Madame de Montespan.]

Lau. [*to the Duch. de la Vall.*] Be calm, your grace; a thousand eyes
Are on you. Give the envious crowd no triumph.
Ah! had *my* fortune won so soft a heart
I would have——

Duch. de la Vall. Peace!—Away! Betray'd!—Undone!

ACT IV.—SCENE I.

The Gardens at Versailles.

Enter Lauzun.

Lau. So far, so prosperous! From the breast of Louis,
The blooming love it bore so long a summer
Falls like a fruit o'er-ripe; and, in the court,
And o'er the king, this glittering Montespan
Queens it without a rival,—awes all foes,
And therefore makes all friends. State, office, honors,
Reflect her smile, or fade before her frown.
So far, so well! Enough for Montespan.
For Lauzun now!—I love this fair La Vallière,
As well, at least, as woman's worth the loving;
And if the jewel has one trifling flaw,
The gold 'tis set in will redeem the blemish.
The king's no niggard lover; and her wealth
Is vast. I have the total in my tablets—
(Besides estates in Picardy and Provence.)
I'm very poor—my debtors very pressing.
I've robb'd the duchess of a faithless lover,
To give myself a wife, and her a husband.
Wedlock's a holy thing,—and wealth a good one!

Enter Louis.

Louis. The day is long—I have not seen Athenè.
Pleasure is never stagnant in her presence;
But every breeze of woman's changeful skies
Ripples the stream, and freshens e'en the sunshine.

Lau. 'Tis said, your Majesty, "that contrast's sweet,"
And she you speak of well contrasts another.
Whom once——

Louis.   I loved; and still devoutly honor.
This poor La Vallière!—could we will affection,
I would have never changed. And even now

I feel Athenè has but charm'd my senses,
And my void heart still murmurs for Louise !
I would we could be friends, since now not lovers,
Nor dare be happy while I know her wretched.
   Lau. Wearies she still your Majesty with prayers,
Tender laments, and passionate reproaches ?
   Louis. Her love outlives its hopes.
   Lau.   An irksome task
To witness tears we cannot kiss away,
And with cold friendship freeze the ears of love !
   Louis. Most irksome and most bootless !
   Lau.   Haply, sire,
In one so pure, the charm of wedded life
Might lull keen griefs to rest, and curb the love
Thou fliest from to the friendship that thou seekest ?
   Louis. I've thought of this. This Duke De Longueville loves her,
And hath besought before her feet to lay
His princely fortunes.
   Lau. [*quickly*].   Ha !—and she—
   Louis.   Rejects him.
   Lau. Sire, if love's sun, once set, bequeaths a twilight,
'Twould only hover o'er some form whom chance
Had link'd with Louis—some one (though unworthy)
Whose presence took a charm from brighter thoughts
That knit it with the past.
   Louis.   Why, how now, duke !—
Thou speak'st not of thyself !
   Lau.   I dare not, sire !
   Louis. Ha, ha !—poor Lauzun !—what ! the soft La Vallière
Transfer her sorrowing heart to thee ? Ha, ha !
   Lau. My name is not less noble than De Longueville's;
My glory greater, since the world has said
Louis esteems me more.
   Louis.   *Esteems !* No;—*favors !*
And thou dost think that she, who shrunk from love,
Lest love were vice, would wed the wildest lord
That ever laugh'd at virtue ?
   Lau.   Sire you wrong me,
Or else you (pardon me) condemn yourself.
Is it too much for one the king calls friend
To aspire to one the king has call'd——
   Louis.   Sir, hold !
I never so malign'd that hapless lady
As to give *her* the title only due
To such as Montespan, who glories in it—
The *last* my *mistress;* but the first my *victim:*
A nice distinction, taught not in your logic,
Which, but just now, confused esteem and favor.
Go to ! we kings are not the dupes you deem us.
   Lau. [*aside*]. So high ! I'll win La Vallière to avenge me,
And humble this imperial vanity.
[*Aloud.*] Sire, I offend ! Permit me to retire,
And mourn your anger; nor presume to guess

Whence came the cause.   And, since it seems your *favor*
Made me aspire too high, in that I loved
Where you, sire, made love noble, and half-dream'd
Might be—nay, *am* not—wholly there disdain'd—
  Louis. How, duke?
  Lau.   I do renounce at once
The haughty vision.   Sire, permit my absence.
  Louis. Lauzun, thou hintest that, were suit allow'd thee,
La Vallière might not scorn it;—is it so?
  Lau. I crave your pardon, sire.
  Louis.   Must I ask twice?
  Lau. I do believe, then, sire, with time and patience,
The duchess might be won to—*not reject me!*
  Louis. Go, then, and prove thy fortune.   We permit thee.
And, if thou prosperest, why then love's a riddle,
And woman is—no matter!   Go, my lord!
We did not mean to wound thee.   So, forget it!
Woo when thou wilt—and wear what thou can'st win.
  Lau. My gracious liege, Lauzun commends him to thee;
And if one word, he merit not, may wound him,
He'll think of favors words can never cancel.
Memory shall med'cine to his present pain.
God save you, sire!—[*Aside*] to *be* the dupe I deem you!   [*Exit* LAUZUN.
  Louis. I love her not; and yet, methinks, am jealous!
Lauzun is wise and witty—knows the sex;
What if she do?—No! I will not believe it.
And what is she to me?—a friend—a friend!
And I would have her wed.   'Twere best for both—
A balm for conscience—an excuse for change!
'Twere best:—I marvel much if she'll accept him!   [*Exit* LOUIS.

SCENE II.

A private apartment in the Palace of the DUCHESS DE LA VALLIERE.

Enter the DUCHESS DE LA VALLIERE.

  Duch. de la Vall. He loves me, then, no longer!   All the words
Earth knows shape but one thought—"He loves no longer!"
Where shall I turn?   My mother—my poor mother!
Sleeps the long sleep! 'Tis better so!   Her life
Ran to its lees.   I will not mourn for her.
But it is hard to be alone on earth!
This love, for which I gave so much, is dead,
Save in my heart; and love, surviving love,
Changes its nature, and becomes despair!
Ah, me!—ah, me! how hateful is this world!

Enter Gentleman of the Chamber.

  Gent. The Duke de Lauzun!
  Duch. de la Vall.   News, sweet news, of Louis!

Enter LAUZUN.

Lau. Dare I disturb your thoughts?

Duch. de la Vall.   My lord, you're welcome!
Came you from court to-day?

Lau.   I left the king
But just now, in the gardens.

Duch. de la Vall. [*eagerly*]. Well!

Lau.   He bore him
With his accustom'd health!

Duch. de la Vall.   Proceed.

Lau.   Dear lady,
I have no more to tell.

Duch. de la Vall. [*aside*]. Alas! *No message!*

Lau. We did converse, 'tis true, upon a subject
Most dear to one of us. Your grace divines it?

Duch. de la Vall. [*joyfully*]. Was it of *me* he spoke?

Lau.   Of you
I spoke, and *he* replied. I praised your beauty—

Duch. de la Vall. You praised!

Lau.   Your form, your face—that wealth of mind
Which, play'd you not the miser, and conceal'd it,
Would buy up all the coins that pass for wit.
The king, assenting, wish'd he might behold you
As happy—as your virtues should have made you.

Duch. de la Vall. 'Twas said in mockery!

Lau.   Lady, no!—in kindness.
Nay, more (he added), would you yet your will
Mould to his wish—

Duch. de la Vall. His wish!—the lightest!

Lau.   Ah!
You know not how my heart throbs while you speak!
Be not so rash to promise; or, at least,
Be faithful to perform!

Duch. de la Vall.   You speak in riddles.

Lau. Of your lone state and beautiful affections,
Form'd to make Home an Eden, our good king,
Tenderly mindful, fain would see you link
Your lot to one whose love might be your shelter.
He spake, and all my long-conceal'd emotions
Gush'd into words, and I confess'd—O lady,
Hear me confess once more—how well I love thee!

Duch. de la Vall. You dared?—and *he*—the king—

Lau.   Upon me smiled,
And bade me prosper.

Duch. de la Vall.   Ah!
               [*Sinks down and covers her face with her hands.*

Lau.   Nay, nay, look up!
The heart that could forsake a love like thine
Doth not deserve regret. Look up, dear Lady!

Duch. de la Vall. He bade thee prosper!

Lau.   Pardon! My wild hope
Outran discretion.

Duch. de la Vall. Louis bade thee prosper!

Lau. Ah, if this thankless—this remorseless love
Thou could'st forget! Oh, give me but thy friendship,
And take respect, faith, worship, all, in Lauzun!

Duch. de la Vall. Consign me to another! Well, 'tis well!
Earth's latest tie is broke!—earth's hopes are over!

Lau. Speak to me, sweet Louise!

Duch. de la Vall. So, thou art he
To whom this shatter'd heart should be surrender'd?—
And thou, the high-born, glittering, scornful Lauzun,
Would take the cast-off leman of a king,
Nor think thyself disgraced! Fie!—fie! thou'rt shameless!

Lau. You were betray'd by love, and not by sin,
Nor low ambition. Your disgrace is honor
By the false side of dames the world calls spotless.

Duch. de la Vall. Go, sir, nor make me scorn you. If I've err'd,
I know, at least, the majesty of virtue,
And feel—what you forget.

Lau. Yet hear me, madam!

Duch. de la Vall. Go, go! You are the king's friend—you were mine;
I would not have you thus debased—refused
By one at once the fallen and forsaken!
His friend shall not be shamed so!
[*Exit the* DUCH. DE LA VALLIERE.

Lau. [*passing his hand over his eyes*]. I do swear
These eyes are moist! And he who own'd this gem
Casts it away, and cries "divine" to tinsel!
So falls my hope. My fortunes call me back
To surer schemes. Before that ray of goodness
How many plots shrunk, blinded, into shadow!
Lauzun forgot himself, and dreamt of virtue!
[*Exit* LAUZUN.

SCENE III.

Gentleman of the Chamber, *and* BRAGELONE, *as a Franciscan friar.*

Gent. The duchess gone! I fear me that, to-day,
You are too late for audience, reverend father.

Brage. Audience!—a royal phrase!—it suits the duchess.
Go, son; announce me.

Gent. By what name, my father?

Brage. I've done with names. Announce a nameless monk,
Whose prayers have risen o'er some graves she honors.

Gent. [*aside*]. My lady is too lavish of her bounty
To these proud shavelings: yet, methinks, this friar
Hath less of priest than warrior in his bearing.
He awes me with his stern and thrilling voice,
His stately gesture, and imperious eye.
And yet, I swear, he comes for alms!—the varlet!
Why should I heed him?

Brage.   Didst thou hear? Begone! [*Exit* Gentleman.
Yes, she will know me not. My lealest soldier,
One who had march'd, bare-breasted, on the steel,
If I had bid him cast away the treasure
Of the o'er-valued life; the nurse that rear'd me,
Or mine own mother, in these shroudlike robes,
And in the immature and rapid age
Which, from my numb'd and withering heart, hath crept
Unto my features, now might gaze upon me,
And pass the stranger by. Why should she know me,
If they who loved me know not? Hark! I hear her:
That silver footfall!—still it hath to me
Its own peculiar and most spiritual music,
Trembling along the pulses of the air,
And dying on the heart that makes its echo!
'Tis she! How lovely yet!

Enter the Duchess de la Valliere.

Duch. de la Vall.   Your blessing, father.
Brage. Let courts and courtiers bless the favor'd duchess:
Courts bless the proud; Heaven's ministers, the humble.
Duch. de la Vall. He taunts me, this poor friar! Well my father,
I have obey'd your summons. Do you seek
Masses for souls departed?—or the debt
The wealthy owe the poor?—say on!
Brage. [*aside*].   Her heart
Is not yet harden'd! Daughter, such a mission
Were sweeter than the task which urged me hither:
You had a lover once—a plain, bold soldier;
He loved you well!
Duch. de la Vall. Ah, Heaven!
Brage.   And you forsook him.
Your choice was natural—some might call it noble!
And this blunt soldier pardon'd the *desertion*,
But sunk at what his folly term'd *dishonor*.
Duch. de la Vall. O father, spare me!—if dishonor were,
It rested but with me.
Brage.   So deem'd the world,
But not that foolish soldier!—he had learn'd
To blend his thoughts, his fame, *himself*, with thee;
Thou wert a purer, a diviner self;
He loved thee as a warrior worships glory;
He loved thee as a Roman honor'd virtue;
He loved thee as thy sex adore ambition;
And when Pollution breathed upon his idol
It blasted glory, virtue, and ambition,
Fill'd up each crevice in the world of thought,
And poison'd earth with thy contagious shame!
Duch. de la Vall. Spare me! in mercy, spare me!
Brage.   This poor fool,
This shadow, living only on thy light,
When thou wert darken'd, could but choose to die.
He left the wars; no fame, since *thine* was dim:

He left his land;—what home without Louise?
It broke—that stubborn, stern, unbending heart—
It broke! and, breaking, its last sigh—forgave thee!

Duch. de la Vall. And I live on!

Brage. One eve, methinks, he told me,
Thy hand around his hauberk wound a scarf;
And thy voice bade him "Wear it for the sake
Of one who honor'd worth!" Were those the words?

Duch. de la Vall. They were. Alas! alas!

Brage. He wore it, lady,
Till memory ceased. It was to him the token
Of a sweet dream; and, from his quiet grave,
He sends it now to thee.—Its hues are faded.

Duch. de la Vall. Give it me!—let me bathe it with my tears!
Memorial of my guilt—

Brage. [*in a soft and tender accent*]. And *his* forgiveness!

Duch. de la Vall. That tone! ha! while thou speakest, in thy voice,
And in thy presence, there is something kindred
To him we jointly mourn: thou art—

Brage. His brother:
Of whom, perchance, in ancient years he told thee;
Who, early wearied of this garish world,
Fled to the convent-shade, and found repose.

Duch. de la Vall. [*approaching*]. Ay, is it so?—thou'rt Bragelone's brother?
Why, then, thou art what *he* would be, if living—
A friend to one most friendless!

Brage. Friendless—Ay,
Thou hast learnt, betimes, the truth, that man's wild passion
Makes but its sport of virtue, peace, affection;
And breaks the plaything when the game is done!
Friendless!—I pity thee!

Duch. de la Vall. Oh! holy father,
Stay with me!—succour me!—reprove, but guide me:
Teach me to wean my thoughts from earth to heaven,
And be what God ordain'd his chosen priests—
Foes to our sin, but friends to our despair.

Brage. Daughter, a heavenly and a welcome duty,
But one most rigid and austere: there is
No composition with our debts of sin.
God claims thy soul; and, lo! his creature there!
Thy choice must be between them—God or man,
Virtue or guilt; a Louis or—

Duch. de la Vall. A Louis!
Not mine the poor atonement of the choice;
I am, myself, the Abandon'd One!

Brage. I know it;
Therefore my mission and my ministry.
When he who loved thee died, he bade me wait
The season when the sicklied blight of shame
Creeps o'er the bloom of Passion, when the way
Is half prepared by Sorrow to Repentance,
And seek you then,—*he* trusted not in vain:
Perchance an idle hope, but it consoled him.

Duch. de la Vall. No, no!—not idle!—in my happiest hours,
When the world smiled, a void was in this heart
The world could never fill: thy brother knew me!
Brage. I do believe thee, daughter. Hear me yet;
My mission is not ended. When thy mother
Lay on the bed of death (she went before
The sterner heart the same blow broke more slowly),—
As thus she lay, around the swimming walls
Her dim eyes wander'd, searching through the shadows,
As if the spirit, half-redeem'd from clay,
Could force its will to shape, and, from the darkness,
Body a daughter's image—(nay, be still!)
Thou wert not there;—alas! thy shame had murder'd
Even the blessed sadness of that duty!
But o'er that pillow watch'd a sleepless eye,
And by that couch moved one untiring step,
And o'er that suffering rose a ceaseless prayer;
And still thy mother's voice, whene'er it call'd
Upon a daughter—found a son!
Duch. de la Vall. O Heaven!
Have mercy on me!
Brage. Coldly through the lattice
Gleam'd the slow dawn, and, from their latest sleep,
Woke the sad eyes it was not *thine* to close!
And, as they fell upon the haggard brow,
And the thin hairs—grown gray, but not by Time—
Of that lone watcher—while upon her heart
Gush'd all the memories of the mighty wrecks
Thy guilt had made of what were once the shrines
For Honor, Peace, and God!—that aged woman
(She was a hero's wife) upraised her voice
To curse her child!
Duch. de la Vall. Go on!—be kind, and kill me!
Brage. Then he, whom thoughts of what he *was* to *thee*
Had made her son, arrested on her lips
The awful doom, and, from the earlier past,
Invoked a tenderer spell—a holier image!
Painted thy gentle, soft, obedient childhood—
Thy guileless youth, lone state, and strong temptation;
Thy very sin the overflow of thoughts
From wells whose source was innocence; and thus
Sought, with the sunshine of thy maiden spring,
To melt the ice that lay upon her heart,
Till all the mother flow'd again!
Duch. de la Vall. And she!
Brage. Spoke only once again! She died—and *bless'd* thee!
Duch. de la Vall. [*rushing out*]. No more!—I *can* no more!—my heart is breaking!
Brage. The angel hath not left her!—if the plumes
Have lost the whiteness of their younger glory,
The wings have still the instinct of the skies,
And yet shall bear her up!
Louis [*without*]. We need you not, sir;
Ourself will seek the duchess.

Brage. The King's voice!
How my flesh creeps!—my foe, and her destroyer!
The ruthless, heartless—
 [*His hand seeks rapidly and mechanically for his sword hilt*
 Why, why!—where's my sword?
O Lord! I do forget myself to dotage:
The soldier, now, is a poor helpless monk,
That hath not even curses. Satan, hence!
Get thee behind me, Tempter!—There, I'm calm.

SCENE IV.

Louis *and* Bragelone.

Louis. I can no more hold parley with impatience,
But long to learn how Lauzun's courtship prospers.
She is not here. At prayers, perhaps. The duchess
Hath grown devout. A friar!—Save you, father!
 Brage. I thank thee, son.
 Louis. He knows me not. Well, monk
Are you her grace's almoner?
 Brage. Sire, no!
Louis. So short, yet know us?
 Brage. Sire, I do. You are
The man—
 Louis. How, priest!—the *man!*
 Brage. The word offends you?
The king, who raised a maiden to a duchess.
That maiden's father was a gallant subject:
Kingly reward!—you made his daughter duchess.
That maiden's mother was a stainless matron:
Her heart you broke, though mother to a duchess!
That maiden was affianced from her youth
To one who served you well—nay, saved your life:
His life you robb'd of all that gave life value:
And yet—you made his fair betroth'd a duchess!
You are that king. The world proclaims you "Great;"
A million warriors bled to buy your laurels;
A million peasants starved to build Versailles:
Your people famish; but your court is splendid!
Priests from the pulpit bless your glorious reign;
Poets have sung you greater than Augustus;
And painters placed you on immortal canvas,
Limn'd as the Jove whose thunders awe the world:
But to the humble minister of Heaven,
You are the king who has betray'd his trust—
Beggar'd a nation but to bloat a court,
Seen in men's lives the pastime to ambition,
Look'd but on virtue as the toy for vice;
And, for the first time, from a subject's lips,
Now learns the name he leaves to Time and God!

Louis. Add to the bead-roll of that king's offences,
That when a foul-mouth'd monk assumed the rebel,
The monster-king forgave him. Hast thou done?

Brage. Your changing hues belie your royal mien;
Ill the high monarch veils the trembling man!

Louis. Well, you are privileged! It ne'er was said
The Fourteenth Louis, in his proudest hour,
Bow'd not his sceptre to the Church's crozier.

Brage. Alas! *the Church!* 'Tis true, this garb of serge
Dares speech that daunts the ermine, and walks free
Where stout hearts tremble in the triple mail.
But wherefore?—Lies the virtue in the robe,
Which the moth eats? or in these senseless beads?
Or in the name of Priest? The Pharisees
Had priests that gave their Saviour to the cross!
No! we have high immunity and sanction,
That Truth may teach humanity to Power,
Glide through the dungeon, pierce the armed throng,
Awaken Luxury on her Sybarite couch,
And, startling souls that slumber on a throne,
Bow kings before that priest of priests—THE CONSCIENCE!

Louis [*aside*]. An awful man! unlike the reverend crew
Who praise my royal virtues in the pulpit,
And—ask for bishoprics when church is over!

Brage. This makes us sacred. The profane are they
Honoring the herald while they scorn the mission.
The king who serves the Church, yet clings to Mammon;
Who fears the pastor, but forgets the flock;
Who bows before the monitor, and yet
Will ne'er forego the sin, may sink, when age
Palsies the lust and deadens the temptation,
To the priest-ridden, not repentant, dotard,
For pious hopes hail superstitious terrors,
And seek some sleek Iscariot of the *Church*,
To sell salvation for the thirty pieces!

Louis [*aside*]. He speaks as one inspired!

Brage. Awake!—awake!
Great though thou art, awake thee from the dream
That earth was made for kings—mankind for slaughter—
Woman for lust—the people for the palace!
Dark warnings have gone forth; along the air
Lingers the crash of the first Charles's throne!
Behold the young, the fair, the haughty king!
The kneeling courtiers, and the flattering priests;
Lo! where the palace rose, behold the scaffold—
The crowd—the axe—the headsman—and the victim!
Lord of the silver lilies, canst thou tell
If the same fate await not thy descendant!
If some meek son of thine imperial line
May make no brother to yon headless spectre!
And when the sage who saddens o'er the end
Tracks back the causes, tremble, lest he find
The seeds, thy wars, thy pomp, and thy profusion

Sow'd in a heartless court and breadless people,
Grew to the tree from which men shaped the scaffold,—
And the long glare of thy funereal glories
Light unborn monarchs to a ghastily grave!
Beware, proud King! the Present cries aloud,
A prophet to the future! Wake!—beware!
[*Exit* BRAGELONE.

Louis. Gone! Most ill-omen'd voice and fearful shape!
Scarce seem'd it of the earth; a thing that breathed
But to fulfil some dark and dire behest;
To appal us, and to vanish.—The quick blood
Halts in my veins. Oh! never till this hour
Heard I the voice that awed the soul of Louis,
Or met one brow that did not quail before
My kingly gaze! And this unmitred monk!
I'm glad that none were by.—It was a dream;
So let its memory like a dream depart.
I am no tyrant—nay, I love my people.
My wars were made but for the fame of France!
My pomp! why, tush!—what king can play the hermit?
My conscience smites me not; and but last eve
I did confess, and was absolved!—A bigot;
And half, methinks, a heretic! I wish
The Jesuits had the probing of his doctrines.
Well, well, 'tis o'er!—What ho, there!

Enter Gentleman of the Chamber.

Louis.   Wine! Apprise
Once more the duchess of our presence.—Stay!
Yon monk, what doth he here?
Gent.   I know not, sire,
Nor saw him till this day.
Louis.   Strange!—Wine!
[*Exit* Gentleman.

SCENE V.

DUCHESS DE LA VALLIERE *and* LOUIS.

Louis.   Well, madam,
We've tarried long your coming, and meanwhile
Have found your proxy in a madman monk,
Whom, for the future, we would pray you spare us.

Re-enter Gentleman *with wine.*

So, so! the draught restores us. Fair La Valliere,
Make not yon holy man your confessor;
You'll find small comfort in his lectures.
Duch. de la Vall.   Sire,
His meaning is more kindly than his manner.
I pray you, pardon him.

Louis.   Ay, ay ! No more;
Let's think of him no more. You had, this morn,
A courtlier visitant, methinks—De Lauzun ?
    Duch. de la Vall.   Yes, sire.
    Louis.   A smooth and gallant gentleman.
You're silent. Silence is assent; 'tis well !
    Duch. de la Vall. [*aside*]. Down, my full heart ! The duke declares your wish
Is that—that I should bind this broken heart
And—no ! I cannot speak—
               [*With great and sudden energy*]
                 You wish me wed sire?
    Louis. 'Twere best that you should wed; and yet, De Lauzun
Is scarce the happiest choice.—But as thou wilt.
    Duch. de la Vall. " 'Twere best that I should wed ! "—thou saidst it, Louis;
Say it once more !
    Louis. In honesty, I think so.
    Duch. de la Vall. My choice is made, then—I obey the fiat,
And will become a bride !
    Louis.   The duke has sped !
I trust he loves thyself, and not thy dower.
    Duch. de la Vall. The duke ! what, hast thou read so ill this soul
That thou couldst deem thus meanly of that book
Whose every page was bared to thee ? A bitter
Lot has been mine—and this sums up the measure.
Go, Louis ! go !—All glorious as thou art—
Earth's Agamemnon—the great king of men—
Thou wert not worthy of this woman's heart !
    Louis. Her passion moves me !—Then your choice has fallen
Upon a nobler bridegroom ?
    Duch. de la Vall.   Sire, it hath !
    Louis. May I demand that choice.
    Duch. de la Vall.   Too soon thou'lt learn it.
Not yet ! Ah me !
    Louis.   Nay, sigh not, my sweet duchess
Speak not so sadly. What though love hath past,
Friendship remains; and still my fondest hope
Is to behold thee happy. Come !—thy hand;
Let us be friends ! We are so !
    Duch. de la Vall.   *Friends !*—no more !
So, it hath come to this ! I am contented !
Yes—we are friends !
    Louis.   And when your choice is made,
You will permit your friend to hail your bridals ?
    Duch. de la Vall. Ay, when my choice is made
    Louis.   This poor De Lauzun
Hath then no chance ? I'm glad of it, and thus
Seal our new bond of friendship on your hand.
Adieu !—and Heaven protect you !
                                       [*Exit* LOUIS.
    Duch. de la Vall. [*gazing after him*]. Heaven hath *heard* thee;
And in this last most cruel, but most gracious,
Proof of thy coldness, breaks the lingering chain
That bound my soul to earth.

Enter Bragelone.

                         O holy father!
Brother to him whose grave my guilt prepared,
Witness my firm resolve, support my struggles,
And guide me back to Virtue through Repentance!
   Brage. Pause, ere thou dost decide.
   Duch. de la Vall.   I've paused too long.
And now, impatient of this weary load,
Sigh for repose.
   Brage.   O Heaven, receive her back!
Through the wide earth, the sorrowing dove hath flown
And found no haven; weary though her wing
And sullied with the dust of lengthen'd travail,
Now let her flee away and be at rest!
The peace that man has broken—THOU restore,
Whose holiest name is FATHER!
   Duch. de la Vall.   Hear us, Heaven.

ACT V.—SCENE I.

Enter Madame de Montespan, Grammont, *and* Courtiers.

   Mme. de Mon. So she has fled from court—the saintly duchess;
A convent's grate must shield this timorous virtue.
Methinks they're not so many to assail it!
Well, trust me, one short moon of fast and penance
Will bring us back the recreant novice——
   Gram.   And
End the eventful comedy by marriage.
Lauzun against the world were even odds;
But Lauzun *with* the world—what saint can stand it?
   Mme. de Mon. [*aside*]. Lauzun!—the traitor! What! to give my rival
The triumph to reject the lawful love
Of him whose lawless passion first betray'd me!
   Gram. Talk of the devil! Humph—you know the proverb.

Enter Lauzun.

   Lau. Good day, my friends. Your pardon, madam; I
Thought 'twas the sun that blinded me.—[*Aside*]. Athenè!
Pray you a word.
   Mme. de Mon. [*aloud, and turning away disdainfully*]. We are not at leisure, duke.
   Lau. Ha! [*aside*]. Nay, Athenè, spare your friend these graces.
Forget your state one moment; have you ask'd
The king the office that you undertook
To make my own? My creditors are urgent.
   Mme. de Mon. [*aloud*]. No, my lord duke, I have not ask'd the king!
I grieve to hear your fortunes are so broken,
And that your honor'd and august device,
To mend them by your marriage, fail'd.
   Gram.   She hits him
Hard on the hip. Ha, ha!—the poor De Lauzun!

Lau. Sir !—Nay, I'm calm !

Mme. de Mon. Pray, may we dare to ask
How long you've loved the duchess ?

Lau. Ever since
You were her friend and confidante.

Mme. de Mon. You're bitter.
Perchance you deem your love a thing to boast of.

Lau. To boast of !—Yes ! 'Tis something ev'n to love
The only woman Louis ever *honor'd !*

Mme. de Mon. [*laying her hand on* LAUZUN's *arm*]. Insolent ! You shall rue this !
　　If I speak
Your name to Louis, coupled with a favor,
The suit shall be your banishment !

　　　　　　　[*Exit* MADAME DE MONTESPAN.

First Courtier Let's follow.
Ha ! ha !—Dear duke, your game, I fear, is lost !
You've play'd the knave, and thrown away the king.

Courtiers. Ha ! ha !—Adieu ! [*Exeunt.*

Lau. Ha ! ha !—The devil take you !
So, she would ruin me ! Fore-arm'd—fore-warn'd !
I have the king's ear yet, and know some secrets
That could destroy her ! Since La Valliere's flight,
Louis grows sad and thoughtful, and looks cold
On her vain rival, who too coarsely shows
The world the stuff court ladies' hearts are **made of.**
She will undo herself—and I will help her.
Weave on thy web, false Montespan, weave on;
The bigger spider shall devour the smaller.
The war's declared—'tis clear that one must fall:—
I'l be polite—the *lady* to the wall !

　　　　　　　[*Exit* LAUZUN.

SCENE II.

Sunset—the old Château of La Vallière—the Convent of the Carmelites at a distance—the same scene as that with which the play opens.

Enter the DUCHESS DE LA VALLIERE *and* BRAGELONE *from the Château.*

Duch. de la Vall. Once more, ere yet I take farewell of earth,
I see mine old, familiar, maiden home !
All how unchanged !—the same the hour, the scene,
The very season of the year !—the stillness
Of the smooth wave—the stillness of the trees,
Where the winds sleep like dreams !—and, oh ! the calm
Of the blue heavens around yon holy spires,
Pointing, like gospel truths, through calm and storm,
To man's great home !

Brage. [*aside*]. Oh ! how the years recede !
Upon this spot I spoke to her of love,
And dreamt of bliss for earth ! [*The vesper-bell tolls.*

Duch. de la Vall. Hark ! the deep sound,

That seems a voice from some invisible spirit,
Claiming the world for God.—When last I heard it
Hallow this air, here stood my mother, living;
And I—was then a mother's *pride!*—and yonder
Came thy brave brother in his glittering mail;
And—ah! these thoughts are bitter!—were he living,
How would he scorn them!

 Brage. [*who has been greatly agitated*]. No!—ah, no!—thou wrong'st him!

 Duch. de la Vall. Yet, were he living, could I but receive
From his own lips my pardon, and his blessing,
My soul would deem one dark memorial razed
Out of the page most blister'd with its tears!

 Brage. Then have thy wish! and in these wrecks of man
Worn to decay, and rent by many a storm,
Survey the worm the world call'd Bragelone.

 Duch. de la Vall. Avaunt!—avaunt!—I dream!—the dead return'd
To earth to mock me!—No! this hand is warm!
I have one murther less upon my soul.
I thank thee, Heaven!—[*swoons*].

 Brage. [*supporting her*]. The blow strikes home; and yet
What is my life to her? Louise!—She moves not;
She does not breathe; how still she sleeps! I saw her
Sleep in her mother's arms, and then, in sleep
She smiled. *There's no smile now!*—poor child! One kiss!
It is a brother's kiss—it has no guilt;
Kind Heaven, it has no guilt.—I have survived
All earthlier thoughts: her crime, my vows, effaced them.
A brother's kiss!—Away! I'm human still;
I thought I had been stronger; God forgive me!
Awake, Louise!—awake! She breathes once more.
The spell is broke; the marble warms to life!
And I—freeze back to stone!

 Duch. de la Vall.   I heard a voice
That cried "Louise!"—Speak, speak!—my sense is dim,
And struggles darkly with a blessed ray
That shot from heaven.—My shame hath not destroy'd thee!

 Brage. No!—life might yet serve *thee!*—and I lived on,
Dead to all else. I took the vows, and then,
Ere yet I laid me down, and bade the Past
Fade like a ghost before the dawn of heaven,
One sacred task was left.—If love was dust,
Love, like ourselves, hath an immortal soul,
That doth survive whate'er it takes from clay;
And that—the holier part of love—became
A thing to watch thy steps—a guardian spirit
To hover round, disguised, unknown, undream'd of,
To soothe the sorrow, to redeem the sin,
And lead thy soul to peace!

 Duch. de la Vall. O bright revenge!
Love strong as death, and nobler far than woman's!

 Brage. To *peace*—ah, let me deem so!—the mute cloister.
The spoken ritual, and the solemn veil,
Are nought themselves;—the Huguenot abjures

The monkish cell, but breathes, perchance, the prayer
That speeds as quick to the Eternal Throne !
In our own souls must be the solitude;
In our own thoughts the sanctity !—'Tis *then*
The feeling that our vows have built the wall
Passion can storm not, nor temptation sap,
Gives calm its charter, roots out wild regret,
And makes the heart the world-disdaining cloister.
This—this is peace ! but pause, if in thy breast
Linger the wish of earth. Alas ! all oaths
Are vain, if nature shudders to record them—
The subtle spirit 'scapes the sealèd vessel !
The false devotion is the true despair !

   Duch. de la Vall. Fear not !—I feel 'tis not the walls of stone.
Told beads, nor murmur'd hymns, that bind the heart,
Or exorcise the world; the spell's the thought
That where most weak we've banish'd the temptation,
And reconciled, what earth would still divide,
The human memories and the immortal conscience.

   Brage. Doubt fades before the accents. On the day
That gives thee to the veil we'll meet once more.
Let mine be man's last blessing in this world.
Oh ! tell me then, thou'rt happier than thou hast been;
And when we part, I'll seek some hermit cell
Beside the walls that compass thee, and prayer,
Morning and night, shall join our souls in heaven.

   Duch. de la Vall. Yes, generous spirit ! think not that my future
Shall be repining as the past. Thou livest,
And conscience smiles again. The shatter'd bark
Glides to its haven. Joy ! the land is near.
   [*Exit* Duchess de la Valliere *into the Château.*

   Brage. So, it is past !—the secret is disclosed !
The hand she did reject on earth has led her
To holier ties. I have not lived in vain !
Yet who had dream'd, when through the ranks of war
Went the loud shout of " France and Bragelone ! "
That the monk's cowl would close on all my laurels ?
A never-heard philosopher is life !—
Our happiest hours are sleep's;—and sleep proclaims
Did we but listen to its warning voice,
That REST is earth's elixir. Why, then, pine
That, ere our years grow feverish with their toil,
Too weary-worn to find the rest they sigh for,
We learn betimes THE MORAL OF REPOSE ?
I will lie down, and sleep away this world.
The pause of care, the slumber of tired passion,
Why, why defer till night is well-nigh spent ?
When the brief sun that gilt the landscape sets,
When o'er the music on the leaves of life
Chill silence falls, and every fluttering hope
That voiced the world with song has gone to rest,
Then let thy soul, from the poor laborer, learn
" Sleep's sweetest taken soonest ! "

[*As he moves away, his eye falls upon a glove dropped by the* DUCHESS DE LA VALLIERE—*he takes it up.*

And this hath touch'd her hand!—it were a comfort
To hoard a single relic!
　　　[*Kisses the glove, and then suddenly dropping it.*
　　　　No!—'Tis sinful!
　　　　　　　　　　　　[*Exit* BRAGELONE.

SCENE III.

The exterior of the Gothic Convent of the Carmelites—The windows illumined—Music heard from within—A crowd without—Enter Courtiers, Ladies, Priests, etc., *and pass through the door of the chapel, in the centre of the building.*

Enter LAUZUN *from a door in the side wing of the Convent—to him,* GRAMMONT.

Lau. Where hast thou left the king?
Gram. 　　　　　　　Not one league hence.
Lau. Ere the clock strikes, La Vallière takes the veil.
Gram. Great Heaven! so soon!—and Louis sent me on,
To learn how thou hadst prosper'd with the duchess.
He is so sanguine—this imperious king,
Who never heard a "No" from living lips!
How did she take his letter?
Lau. 　　　　　In sad silence;
Then mused a little while, and some few tears
Stole down her cheeks, as, with a trembling hand,
She gave me back the scroll.
Gram. 　　　　　You mean her answer.
Lau. No; the king's letter. "Tell him that I thank him;"
(Such were her words;) "but that my choice is made;
And ev'n this last assurance of his love
I dare not keep: 'tis only when I pray,
That I may think of him. This is my answer."
Gram. No more?—no written word?
Lau. 　　　　　　　None, Grammont. Then
She rose and left me; and I heard the bell
Calling the world to see a woman scorn it.
Gram. The king will never brook it. He will grasp her
Back from this yawning tomb of living souls.
The news came on him with such sudden shock;
The long noviciate thus abridged! and she—
Ever so waxen to his wayward will!—
She cannot yet be marble.
Lau. 　　　　　Wrong'd affection
Makes many a Niobe from tears. Haste, Grammont,
Back to the king, and bid him fly to save,
Or nerve his heart to lose, her. I will follow,—
My *second* charge fulfill'd.
Gram. 　　　　　And what is that?
Lau. Revenge and justice!—Go! 　　　[*Exit* GRAMMONT.

Lau. [*looking down the stage*]. I hear her laugh—
I catch the glitter of her festive robe !
Athenè comes to triumph—and to tremble !

SCENE IV.

MADAME DE MONTESPAN, Courtiers, *and* LAUZUN.

Mme. de Mon. [*aside*]. Now for the crowning cup of sparkling fortune !
A rarer pearl than Egypt's queen dissolved
I have immersed in that delicious draught,
A woman's triumph o'er a fairer rival !
   [*As she turns to enter the convent, she perceives* LAUZUN.
What ! you here, duke !
   Lau.   Ay, madam; I've not yet
To thank you for—my banishment !
   Mme. de Mon.   The Ides
Of March are come—not over !
   Lau.   Are they not ?
For some they may be ! You are here to witness—
   Mme. de Mon. My triumph !
   Lau.   And to take a *friend's* condolence.
I bear this letter from the king !
   Mme. de Mon.   The king ?
            [*Reads the letter.*
" We do not blame you; blame belongs to love,
And love had nought with you." What ! what ! I tremble !
" The duke de Lauzun, of these lines the bearer,
Confirms their purport: from our royal court
We do excuse your presence." Banish'd, duke ?
Is that the word ?—What, banish'd !
   Lau.   Hush !—you mar
The holy silence of the place. 'Tis true;
You read aright. Our gracious king permits you
To quit Versailles. Versailles is not the world.
   Mme. de Mon. Perdition !—banish'd !
   Lau.   You can take the veil.
Meanwhile, enjoy *your triumph !*
   Mme. de Mon.   Triumph !—Ah !
She triumphs o'er me to the last. My soul
Finds hell on earth—and hers make earth a heaven !
   Lau. Hist !—will you walk within ?
   Mme. de Mon.   O, hateful world !
What ?—hath it come to this ?
   Lau.   You spoil your triumph !
   Mme. de Mon. Lauzun, I thank thee—thank thee—thank—and curse thee.
            [*Exit* MADAME DE MONTESPAN
   Lau. [*looking after her with a subdued laugh*]. Ha, ha !—the *broken* heart
      can know no pang

Like that which racks the *bad* heart when its sting
Poisons itself.   Now, then, away to Louis.
The bell still tolls: there's time.   This soft La Vallière!
The only thing that ever baffled Lauzun,
And felt not his revenge!—revenge, poor soul!
Revenge upon a dove!—she shall be saved
From the pale mummies of yon Memphian vault,
Or the great Louis will be less than man,—
Or that fond sinner will be more than woman. [*Exit* LAUZUN.

SCENE V.

The interior of the Chapel of the Carmelite Convent—On the foreground, Courtiers, Ladies, *etc.—At the back of the stage, the altar, only partially seen through the surrounding throng—The officials pass to and fro, swinging the censers—The stage darkened—Lights suspended along the aisle, and tapers by the altar.*

As the scene opens, solemn music, to which is chaunted the following

HYMN.

Come from the world, O weary soul,
For run the race and near the goal!
Flee from the net, O lonely dove,
Thy nest is built the clouds above!
Turn, wild and warm with panting fear,
And slake thy thirst, thou wounded deer,
    In Jordan's holy springs!

Arise! O fearful soul, arise!
For broke the chain and calm the skies!
As moths fly upward to the star,
The light allures thee from afar.
Though earth is lost, and space is wide,
The smile of God shall be thy guide,
    And Faith and Hope thy wings!

[*As the Hymn ends,* BRAGELONE *enters, and stands apart in the background.*
First Cour. Three minutes more, and earth has lost La Vallière!
Second Cour. So young!—so fair!
Third Cour.   'Twas whisper'd, that the king
Would save her yet!
First Cour.   What! snatch her from the altar?
He durst not, man!

    Enter LOUIS, GRAMMONT, *and* LAUZUN.

Louis.   Hold! we forbid the rites!
    [*As the* King *advances hastily up the aisle,* BRAGELONE *places himself before him.*
Back monk! revere the presence of the king;
Brage. And thou the palace of the King of the kings;

Louis. Dotard! we claim our subject.
Brage. She hath past
The limit of your realm. Ye priests of Heaven,
Complete your solemn task!—The church's curse
Hangs on the air. Descendant of Saint Louis,
Move—and the avalanche falls!
[*The* DUCHESS DE LA VALLIERE, *still dressed in the bridal and gorgeous attire assumed before the taking of the veil, descends from the altar.*
Duch. de la Vall. No, holy friend!
I need it not; my soul is my protector.
Nay, thou mayst trust me.
Brage. [*after a pause*]. Thou art right.—I trust thee.
Louis [*leading the Duch. de la Valliere to the front of the stage*]. Thou hast not ta'en the veil?—Ev'n Time had mercy.
Thou art saved!—thou art saved!—to love—to life!
Duch. de la Vall. Ah, sire!
Louis. Call me not sire!—forget that dreary time
When thou wert duchess, and myself the king.
Fly back, fly back, to those delicious hours
When *I* was but thy lover and thy Louis!
And thou my dream—my bird—my fairy flower—
My violet, shrinking in the modest shade
Until transplanted to this breast—to haunt
The common air with odors! Oh, Louise!
Hear me!—the fickle lust of change allured me,
The pride thy virtues wounded arm'd against thee,
Until I dream'd I loved thyself no longer;
But now this dread resolve, this awe of parting,
Re-binds me to thee—bares my soul before me—
Dispels the lying mists that veil'd thine image,
And tells me that I never loved but thee!
Duch. de la Vall. I am not then despised!—thou lov'st me still!
And when I pray for thee, my heart may feel
That it hath nothing to forgive!
Louis. Louise!
Thou dost renounce this gloomy purpose?
Duch. de la Vall. Never!
It is not gloomy!—think'st thou it is gloom
To feel that, as my soul becomes more pure,
Heaven will more kindly listen to the prayers
That rise for *thee?*—is that thought *gloom,* my Louis?
Louis. Oh! slay me not with tenderness! Return!
And if thy conscience startle at my love,
Be still my friend—my angel!
Duch. de la Vall. I am weak,
But, in the knowledge of my weakness, strong!
I could not breathe the air that's sweet with thee,
Nor cease to love!—in flight my only safety;
And were that flight not made by solemn vows
Eternal, it were bootless; for the wings
Of my wild soul know but two bournes to speed to—
Louis and Heaven! And, oh, in Heaven at last
My soul, unsinning, may unite with Louis!

Louis. I do implore thee!—

Duch. de la Vall.   No! thou canst not tempt me!
My *heart* already is the nun.

Louis.   Thou know'st not
I have dismiss'd thy rival from the Court.
Return!—though mine no more, at least thy Louis
Shall know no second love.

Duch. de la Vall.   What! wilt thou, Louis,
Renounce for me eternally my rival,
And live alone for——

Louis.   Thee! Louise, I swear it!

Duch. de la Vall. [*raising her arms to Heaven*]. Father, at length, I dare to hope for pardon,
For now remorse may prove itself sincere!
Bear witness, Heaven! I never loved this man
So well as now! and never seem'd *his* love
Built on so sure a rock! Upon thine altar
I lay the offering. I revoke the past;
For Louis, Heaven was left—and now I leave
Louis, when tenfold more beloved, for Heaven!
Ah! pray with me! Be this our latest token—
This memory of sweet moments—sweet, though sinless!
Ah! pray with me! that I may hive till death
The thought—" we pray'd together for forgiveness!"

Louis. Oh! wherefore never knew I till this hour
The treasure I shall lose! I dare not call thee
Back from the Heaven where thou art half already!
Thy soul demands celestial destinies,
And stoops no more to earth. Be thine the peace,
And mine the penance! Yet these awful walls,
The rigid laws of this severest order,
Yon spectral shapes, this human sepulchre,—
And thou, the soft, the delicate, the highborn,
The adored delight of Europe's mightiest king,—
Thou canst not bear it!

Duch. de la Vall.   I have borne much worse—
Thy change and thy desertion!—Let it pass!
There is no terror in the things without;
Our souls alone the palace or the prison;
And the one thought that I have fled from sin
Will fill the cell with images more glorious,
And haunt its silence with a mightier music,
Than ever throng'd illumined halls, or broke
From harps by mortal strung!

Louis.   I will not hear thee!
I cannot brave these thoughts. Thy angel voice
But tells me what a sun of heavenly beauty
Glides from the earth, and leaves my soul to darkness.
This is *my* work!—'twas I for whom that soul
Forsook its native element; for me,
Sorrow consumed thy youth, and conscience gnaw'd
That patient, tender, unreproachful heart.
And now this crowns the whole! the priest—the altar—

The sacrifice—the victim ! Touch me not !
Speak not ! I am unmann'd enough already.
I—I—I choke ! These tears—let them speak for me.
Now ! now thy hand—farewell ! farewell, for ever !

[*Exit* Louis.

Duch. de la Vall. Be firm, my heart, be firm !
[*After a pause, turning to* Bragelone, *with a slight smile.*
'Tis past ! we've conquered !
[*The* Duchess de la Valliere *re-ascends to the altar—the crowd close around.*
[*Music.*

CHORUS.

Hark ! to the nuptial train are open'd wide
The Eternal Gates. Hosanna to the bride !

Gram. She has ta'en the veil—the last dread rite is done.
Abbess [*from the altar*]. Sister Louise ! before the eternal grate
Becomes thy barrier from the living world,
It is allow'd thee once more to behold
The face of men, and bid farewell to friendship.
Brage. [*aside*]. Why do I shudder ? why shrinks back my being
From our last gaze, like Nature from the Grave ?
One moment, and one look, and o'er her image
Thick darkness falls, till Death, that morning star,
Heralds immortal day. I hear her steps
Treading the mournful silence; o'er my soul
Pauses the freezing time. O Lord, support me !
One effort more—one effort !—Wake, my soul !
'Tis thy last trial; wilt thou play the craven ?
[*The crowd give way, the* Duchess de la Valliere *in the habit of the Carmelite nuns, passes down the steps of the altar, led by the* Abbess—*As she pauses to address those whom she recognizes in the crowd, the chorus chaunts :—*

Sister, look and speak thy last,
From the world thou'rt dying fast;
While farewell to life thou'rt giving,
Dead already to the living.

Duch. de la Vall. [*coming to the front of the stage, sees* Lauzun]. Lauzun: thou serv'st a king, whate'er his faults,
Who merits all thy homage: honor—love him.
His glory needs no friendship; but in sickness
Or sorrow, *kings* need love. Be faithful, Lauzun !
And, far from thy loud world, one lowly voice
Shall not forget thee.
Brage. [*aside*]. All the strife is hush'd !
My heart's wild sea lies mute !
Duch. de la Vall. [*approaching* Bragelone, *and kneeling to him*]. Now ! friend and father,
Bless the poor Nun !
Brage. As Duchess of La Vallière

Thou wert not happy; as the Carmelite Sister,
Say—*art* thou happy?
   Duch. de la Vall.   Yes!
   Brage. [*laying his hand on her head*]. O Father, bless her!

CHORUS.

Hark! in Heaven is mirth!
                Jubilate!
Grief leaves guilt on earth!
                Jubilate!
Joy for sin forgiven!
                Jubilate!
Come, O Bride of Heaven!
                Jubilate!

                        [*Curtain falls slowly.*

THE LADY OF LYONS;

OR,

LOVE AND PRIDE.

TO

THE AUTHOR OF "ION,"

WHOSE GENIUS AND EXAMPLE HAVE ALIKE CONTRIBUTED
TOWARDS THE REGENERATION OF

The National Drama,

THIS PLAY IS INSCRIBED.

PREFACE.

An indistinct recollection of the very pretty little tale, called "The Bellows-Mender," suggested the plot of this Drama. The incidents are, however, greatly altered from those in the tale, and the characters entirely re-cast.

Having long had a wish to illustrate certain periods of the French history, so, in the selection of the date in which the scenes of this play are laid, I saw that the era of the Republic was that in which the incidents were rendered most probable, in which the probationary career of the hero could well be made sufficiently rapid for dramatic effect, and in which the character of the time itself was depicted by the agencies necessary to the conduct of the narrative. For during the early years of the first and most brilliant successes of the French Republic, in the general ferment of society, and the brief equalization of ranks, Claude's high-placed love, his ardent feelings, his unsettled principles (the struggle between which makes the passion of this drama), his ambition, and his career, were phenomena that characterized the age, and in which the spirit of the nation went along with the extravagance of the individual.

The play itself was composed with a twofold object. In the first place, sympathizing with the enterprise of Mr. Macready, as Manager of Covent Garden, and believing that many of the higher interests of the Drama were involved in the success or failure of an enterprise equally hazardous and disinterested, I felt, if I may so presume to express myself, something of the Brotherhood of Art; and it was only for Mr. Macready to think it possible that I might serve him in order to induce me to make the attempt.

Secondly, in that attempt I was mainly anxious to see whether or not, after the comparative failure on the stage of "The Duchess de la Vallière," certain critics had truly declared that it was not in my power to attain the art of dramatic construction and theatrical effect. I felt, indeed, that it was in this that a writer, accustomed to the narrative class of composition, would have the most both to learn and *un*learn. Accordingly, it was to the development of the plot and the arrangement of the incidents that I directed my chief attention;—and I sought to throw whatever belongs to poetry less into the diction and the "felicity of words" than into the construction of the story, the creation of the characters, and the spirit of the pervading sentiment.

The authorship of the play was neither avowed nor suspected until the play had established itself in public favor. The announcement of my name was the signal for attacks, chiefly political, to which it is now needless to refer. When a work has outlived for some time the earlier hostilities of criticism, there comes a new race of critics to which a writer may, for the most part, calmly trust for a fair consideration, whether of the faults or the merits of his performance.

DRAMATIS PERSONÆ.

BEAUSEANT, *a rich gentleman of Lyons, in love with, and refused by, Pauline Deschappelles* . . . MR. ELTON.

GLAVIS, *his friend, also a rejected suitor to Pauline* MR. MEADOWS.

COLONEL (afterwards General) DAMAS, *cousin to Mme. Deschappelles, and an officer in the French army* . . . . MR. BARTLEY.

MONSIEUR DESCHAPPELLES, *a Lyonnese merchant, father to Pauline* . . . . . MR. STRICKLAND.

GASPAR . . . . MR. DIDDEAR.
CLAUDE MELNOTTE . . . . . MR. MACREADY.
FIRST OFFICER . . . . . . MR. HOWE.
SECOND OFFICER . . . . . . MR. PRITCHARD.
THIRD OFFICER . . . . . . MR. ROBERTS.

Servants, Notary, etc.

MADAME DESCHAPPELLES . . . . MRS. W. CLIFFORD.
PAULINE, *her daughter* . . . . . MISS HELEN FAUCIT.
THE WIDOW MELNOTTE, *mother to Claude* . . MRS. GRIFFITH.
JANET, *the innkeeper's daughter* . . . MRS. EAST.
MARIAN, *maid to Pauline* . . . . MISS GARRICK.

Scene—Lyons and the neighborhood.

Time—1795–1798.

First performed on Thursday, the 15th of February, 1838, at Covent Garden Theatre.

THE LADY OF LYONS;

OR,

LOVE AND PRIDE.

ACT I.—SCENE I.

A room in the house of M. Deschappelles, *at Lyons.* Pauline *reclining on a sofa;* Marian, *her maid, fanning her—Flowers and notes on a table beside the sofa*—Madame Deschappelles *seated—The gardens are seen from the open window.*

Mme. Deschap. Marian, put that rose a little more to the left.—[Marian *alters the position of a rose in* Pauline's *hair.*]—Ah, so!—that improves the hair,—the *tournure*, the *je ne sais quoi!*—You are certainly very handsome, child!—quite my style;—I don't wonder that you make such a sensation!—Old, young, rich, and poor, do homage to the Beauty of Lyons!—Ah, we live again in our children,—especially when they have our eyes and complexion!

Pauline [*languidly*]. Dear mother, you spoil your Pauline!—[*Aside.*] I wish I knew who sent me these flowers!

Mme. Deschap. No, child!—If I praise you, it is only to inspire you with a proper ambition.—You are born to make a great marriage.—Beauty is valuable or worthless according as you invest the property to the best advantage.—Marian, go and order the carriage!

[*Exit* Marian.

Pauline. Who *can* it be that sends me, every day, these beautiful flowers?—how sweet they are!

Enter Servant.

Servant. Monsieur Beauseant, Madam.

Mme. Deschap. Let him enter. Pauline, this is another offer!—I know it is!—Your father should engage an additional clerk to keep the account-book of your conquests.

Enter Beauseant.

Beau. Ah, ladies how fortunate I am to find you at home!—[*Aside.*] How lovely she looks!—It is a great sacrifice I make in marrying into a family in trade!—they will be eternally grateful!—[*Aloud.*] Madam, you will permit me a word with your charming daughter.—[*Approaches* Pauline, *who rises disdainfully.*]—Mademoiselle, I have ventured to wait upon you, in a hope that you must long since have divined. Last night, when you outshone all the beauty of Lyons, you completed your conquest over me! You know that my fortune is not exceeded by any estate in the province,—you know that, but for the Revolution, which has defrauded me of my titles, I should be noble. May I, then, trust that you will not reject my alliance? I offer you my hand and heart.

Pauline [*aside*]. He has the air of a man who confers a favor!—[*Aloud.*] Sir, you are very condescending—I thank you humbly; but, being duly sensible of my own demerits, you must allow me to decline the honor you propose. [*Curtsies, and turns away.*

Beau. Decline! impossible!—you are not serious!—Madam, suffer me to appeal to *you.* I am a suitor for your daughter's hand—the settlements shall be worthy her beauty and my station. May I wait on M. Deschappelles?

Mme. Deschap. M. Deschappelles never interferes in the domestic arrangements,—you are very obliging. If you were still a marquis, or if my daughter were intended to marry a commoner,—why, perhaps, we might give you the preference.

Beau. A commoner!—we are all commoners in France now.

Mme. Deschap. In France, yes; but there is a nobility still left in the other countries in Europe. We are quite aware of your good qualities, and don't doubt that you will find some lady more suitable to your pretensions. We shall be always happy to see you as an acquantance, M. Beauseant!—My dear child, the carriage will be here presently.

Beau. Say no more, madam!—say no more!—[*Aside*]. Refused! and by a merchant's daughter!—refused! It will be all over Lyons before sunset!—I will go and bury myself in my château, study philosophy, and turn woman-hater. Refused! they ought to be sent to a madhouse!—Ladies, I have the honor to wish you a very good morning.   [*Exit.*

Mme. Deschap. How forward these men are!—I think, child, we kept up our dignity. Any girl, however inexperienced, knows how to accept an offer, but it requires a vast deal of address to refuse one with proper condescension and disdain. I used to practise it at school with the dancing-master.

Enter DAMAS.

Damas. Good morning, cousin Deschappelles.—Well, Pauline, are you recovered from last night's ball?—So many triumphs must be very fatiguing. Even M. Glavis sighed most piteously when you departed; but that might be the effect of the supper.

Pauline. M. Glavis, indeed!

Mme. Deschap. M. Glavis?—as if my daughter would think of M. Glavis!

Damas. Hey-day!—why not?—His father left him a very pretty fortune, and his birth is higher than yours, cousin Deschappelles. But perhaps you are looking to M. Beauseant,—his father was a marquis before the Revolution.

Pauline. M. Beauseant!—Cousin, you delight in tormenting me!

Mme. Deschap. Don't mind him, Pauline!—Cousin Damas, you have no susceptibility of feeling,—there is a certain indelicacy in all your ideas.—M. Beauseant knows already that he is no match for my daughter!

Damas. Pooh! pooh! one would think you intended your daughter to marry a prince!

Mme. Deschap. Well, and if I did?—what then?—Many a foreign prince—

Damas [*interrupting her*]. Foreign prince!—foreign fiddlestick!—you ought to be ashamed of such nonsense at your time of life.

Mme. Deschap. My time of life!—That is an expression never applied to any lady till she is sixty-nine and three-quarters;—and only then by the clergyman of the parish.

Enter Servant.

Servant. Madame, the carriage is at the door.   [*Exit.*

Mme. Deschap. Come, child, put on your bonnet—you really have a very thorough-bred air—not at all like your poor father.—[*Fondly*]. Ah, you little coquette! when a young lady is always making mischief, it is a sure sign that she takes after her mother!

Pauline. Good day, cousin Damas—and a better humor to you.—[*Going back to the table and taking the flowers*]. Who *could* have sent me these flowers?

[*Exeunt* PAULINE *and* MADAME DESCHAPPELLES.

Damas. That would be an excellent girl if her head had not been turned. I fear she is now become incorrigible! Zounds, what a lucky fellow I am to be still a bachelor! They may talk of the devotion of the sex—but the most faithful attachment in life is that of a woman in love—with herself.   [*Exit.*

SCENE II.

The exterior of a small Village Inn—sign, the Golden Lion—A few leagues from Lyons, which is seen at a distance.

Beau. [*behind the scenes*]. Yes, you may bait the horses; we shall rest here an hour.

Enter BEAUSEANT *and* GLAVIS.

Gla. Really, my dear Beauseant, consider that I have promised to spend a day or two with you at your château,—that I am quite at your mercy for my entertainment,—and yet you are as silent and as gloomy as a mute at a funeral, or an Englishman at a party of pleasure.

Beau. Bear with me!—the fact is that I am miserable.

Gla. You—the richest and gayest bachelor in Lyons?

Beau. It is because I am a bachelor that I am miserable.—Thou knowest Pauline—the only daughter of the rich merchant, Mons. Deschappelles?

Gla. Know her?—who does not?—as pretty as Venus, and as proud as Juno.

Beau. Her taste is worse than her pride.—[*Drawing himself up.*] Know, Glavis, she has actually refused *me!*

Gla. [*aside*]. So she has me!—very consoling! In all cases of heart-ache, the application of another man's disappointment draws out the pain and allays the irritation.—[*Aloud.*] Refused you! and wherefore?

Beau. I know not, unless it be because the Revolution swept away my father's title of Marquis,—and she will not marry a commoner. Now, as we have no noblemen left in France,—as we are all citizens and equals, she can only hope that, in spite of the war, some English Milord or German Count will risk his life, by coming to Lyons, that this *fille du Roturier* may condescend to accept him. Refused me, and with scorn!—By Heaven, I'll not submit to it tamely:—I'm in a perfect fever of mortification and rage.—Refuse *me*, indeed!

Gla. Be comforted, my dear fellow,—I will tell you a secret. For the same reason she refused ME!

Beau. You!—that's a very different matter! But give me your hand, Glavis,—we'll think of some plan to humble her. *Mille diables!* I should like to see her married to a strolling player!

Enter Landlord *and his* Daughter *from the Inn.*

Land. Your servant, citizen Beauseant,—servant, sir. Perhaps you will take dinner before you proceed to your château; our larder is most plentifully supplied.

Beau. I have no appetite.

Gla. Nor I. Still it is bad travelling on an empty stomach. What have you got? [*Takes and looks over the bill of fare.*]

[*Shout without.*] "Long live the Prince!—Long live the Prince!"

Beau. The Prince!—what Prince is that? I thought we had no princes left in France.

Land. Ha, ha! the lads always call him Prince. He has just won the prize in the shooting-match, and they are taking him home in triumph.

Beau. Him! and who's Mr. Him?

Land. Who should he be but the pride of the village, Claude Melnotte?—Of course you have heard of Claude Melnotte?

Gla. [*giving back the bill of fare*]. Never had that honor. Soup—ragout of hare—roast chicken, and, in short, all you have!

Beau. The son of old Melnotte, the gardener?

Land. Exactly so—a wonderful young man.

Beau. How, wonderful?—Are his cabbages better than other people's?

Land. Nay, he don't garden any more; his father left him well off. He's only a genus.

Gla. A what?

Land. A genius!—a man who can do everything in life except anything that's useful;—that's a genus.

Beau. You raise my curiosity;—proceed.

Land. Well, then, about four years ago, old Melnotte died, and left his son well to do in the world. We then all observed that a great change came over young Claude: he took to reading and Latin, and hired a professor from Lyons, who had so much in his head that he was forced to wear a great full-bottom wig to cover it. Then he took a fencing-master, and a dancing-master, and a music-master; and then he learned to paint; and at last it was said that young Claude was to go to Paris, and set up for a painter. The lads laughed at him at first; but he is a stout fellow, is Claude, and as brave as a lion, and soon taught them to laugh the wrong side of their mouths; and now all the boys swear by him, and all the girls pray for him.

Beau. A promising youth, certainly! And why do they call him Prince?

Land. Partly because he is at the head of them all, and partly because he has such a proud way with him, and wears such fine clothes—and, in short, looks like a prince.

Beau. And what could have turned the foolish fellow's brain? The Revolution, I suppose?

Land. Yes—the revolution that turns us all topsy-turvy—the revolution of Love.

Beau. Romantic young Corydon! And with whom is he in love?

Land. Why—but it is a secret, gentlemen.

Beau. Oh! certainly.

Land. Why, then, I hear from his mother, good soul! that it is no less a person than the Beauty of Lyons, Pauline Deschappelles.

Beau. and Glavis. Ha, ha!—Capital!

Land. You may laugh, but it is as true as I stand here.

Beau. And what does the Beauty of Lyons say to his suit?

Land. Lord, sir, she never even condescended to look at him, though when he was a boy he worked in her father's garden.

Beau. Are you sure of that?

Land. His mother says that Mademoiselle does not know him by sight.

Beau. [*taking Glavis aside*]. I have hit it,—I have it;—here is our revenge! Here is a prince for our haughty damsel. Do you take me?

Gla. Deuce take me if I do!

Beau. Blockhead!—it's as clear as a map. What if we could make this elegant clown pass himself off as a foreign prince?—lend him money, clothes, equipage for the purpose?—make him propose to Pauline?—marry Pauline? Would it not be delicious?

Gla. Ha, ha!—Excellent! But how shall we support the necessary expenses of his highness?

Beau. Pshaw! Revenge is worth a much larger sacrifice than a few hundred louis;—as for details, my valet is the trustiest fellow, in the world, and shall have the appointment of his highness's establishment. Let's go to him at once, and see if he be really this Admirable Crichton.

Gla. With all my heart;—but the dinner?

Beau. Always thinking of dinner! Hark ye, landlord; how far is it to young Melnotte's cottage? I should like to see such a prodigy.

Land. Turn down the lane,—then strike across the common,—and you will see his mother's cottage.

Beau. True, he lives with his mother.—[*Aside*]. We will not trust to an old woman's discretion; better send for him hither. I'll just step in and write a note. Come, Glavis.

Gla. Yes,—Beauseant, Glavis, and Co., manufacturers of princes, wholesale and retail,—an uncommonly genteel line of business. But why so grave?

Beau. You think only of the sport,—I of the revenge. [*Exeunt within the Inn.*

SCENE III.

The interior of MELNOTTE'S *cottage; flowers placed here and there; a guitar on an oaken table, with a portfolio, etc.; a picture on an easel, covered by a curtain; fenciug-foils crossed over the mantelpiece; an attempt at refinement in spite of the homeliness of the furniture, etc.; a staircase to the right conducts to the upper story.*

[*Shout without*]. "Long live Claude Melnotte!" "Long live the Prince!"

The Widow Mel. Hark!—there's my dear son;—carried off the prize, I'm sure; and now he'll want to treat them all.

Claude Mel. [*opening the door*]. What! you will not come in, my friends! Well, well,—there's a trifle to make merry elsewhere. Good day to you all,—good day!

[*Shout*]. "Hurrah! Long live Prince Claude!"

Enter CLAUDE MELNOTTE, *with a rifle in his hand.*

Mel. Give me joy, dear mother!—I've won the prize!—never missed one shot! Is it not handsome, this gun?

Widow. Humph!—Well, what is it worth, Claude?

Mel. Worth! What is a riband worth to a soldier? Worth! everything! Glory is priceless!

Widow. Leave glory to great folks. Ah! Claude, Claude, castles in the air cost a vast deal to keep up! How is all this to end? What good does it do thee to learn Latin, and sing songs, and play on the guitar, and fence, and dance, and paint pictures? All very fine; but what does it bring in?

Mel. Wealth! wealth, my mother! Wealth to the mind—wealth to the heart—high thoughts—bright dreams—the hope of fame—the ambition to be worthier to love Pauline.

Widow. My poor son!—The young lady will never think of thee.

Mel. Do the stars think of us? Yet if the prisoner see them shine into his dungeon, wouldst thou bid him turn away from *their* lustre? Even so from this low cell, poverty, I lift my eyes to Pauline and forget my chains.—[*Goes to the picture and draws aside the curtain.*] See, this is her image—painted from memory. Oh, how the canvas wrongs her!—[*Takes up the brush and throws it aside.*] I shall never be a painter! I can paint no likeness but one, and that is above all art. I would turn soldier—France needs soldiers! But to leave the air that Pauline breathes! What is the hour?—so late? I will tell thee a secret, mother. Thou knowest that for the last six weeks I have sent every day the rarest flowers to Pauline?—she wears them. I have seen them on her breast. Ah, and then the whole universe seemed filled with odors! I have now grown more bold—I have poured my worship into poetry—I have sent the verses to Pauline—I have signed them with my own name. My messenger ought to be back by this time. I bade him wait for the answer.

Widow. And what answer do you expect, Claude?

Mel. That which the Queen of Navarre sent to the poor troubadour:—"Let me see the Oracle that can tell nations I am beautiful!" She will admit me. I shall hear her speak—I shall meet her eyes—I shall read upon her cheek the sweet thoughts that translate themselves into blushes. Then—then, oh, then—she may forget that I am the peasant's son!

Widow. Nay, if she will but hear thee talk, Claude?

Mel. I foresee it all. She will tell me that desert is the true rank. She will give me a badge—a flower—a glove! Oh rapture! I shall join the armies of the republic—I shall rise—I shall win a name that beauty will not blush to hear. I shall return with the right to say to her—"See, how love does not level the proud, but raise the humble!" Oh, how my heart swells within me!—Oh, what glorious prophets of the future are youth and hope!

[*Knock at the door*

Widow. Come in.

Enter GASPAR.

Mel. Welcome, Gaspar, welcome. Where is the letter? Why do you turn away, man? where is the letter? [GASPAR *gives him one.*] This! This is mine, the one I intrusted to thee. Didst thou not leave it?

Gaspar. Yes, I left it.

Mel. My own verses returned to me. Nothing else!

Gaspar. Thou wilt be proud to hear how thy messenger was honored. For thy sake, Melnotte, I have borne that which no Frenchman can bear without disgrace.

Mel. Disgrace, Gaspar! Disgrace?

Gaspar. I gave thy letter to the porter, who passed it from lackey to lackey till it reached the lady it was meant for.

Mel. It reached her, then;—you are sure of that! It reached her,—well, well!

Gaspar. It reached her, and was returned to me with blows. Dost hear, Melnotte? with blows! Death! are we slaves still, that we are to be thus dealt with, we peasants?

Mel. With blows? No, Gaspar, no; not blows!

Gaspar. I could show thee the marks if it were not so deep a shame to bear them. The lackey who tossed thy letter into the mire swore that his lady and her mother never were so insulted. What could thy letter contain, Claude?

Mel. [*looking over the letter*]. Not a line that a serf might not have written to an empress. No, not one.

Gaspar. They promise thee the same greeting they gave me, if thou wilt pass that way. Shall we endure this, Claude?

Mel. [*wringing* GASPAR's *hand*]. Forgive me, the fault was mine, I have brought this on thee; I will not forget it; thou shalt be avenged! The heartless insolence!

Gaspar. Thou art moved, Melnotte; think not of me; I would go through fire and water to serve thee; but,—a blow! It is not the *bruise* that galls,—it is the *blush*, Melnotte.

Mel. Say, what message?—How insulted!—Wherefore?—What the offence?

Gaspar. Did you not write to Pauline Deschappelles, the daughter of the rich merchant?

Mel. Well?—

Gaspar. And are you not a peasant—a gardener's son?—that was the offence. Sleep on it, Melnotte. Blows to a French citizen, blows! [*Exit.*

Widow. Now you are cured, Claude!

Mel. [*tearing the letter*]. So do I scatter her image to the winds—I will stop her in the open streets—I will insult her—I will beat her menial ruffians—I will—— [*Turns suddenly to* Widow.] Mother, am I humpbacked—deformed—hideous?

Widow. You!

Mel. A coward—a thief—a liar?

Widow. You!

Mel. Or a dull fool—a vain, drivelling, brainless idiot?

Widow. No, no.

Mel. What am I then—worse than all these? Why, I am a peasant! What has a peasant to do with love? Vain revolutions, why lavish your cruelty on the great? Oh that we—we, the hewers of wood and drawers of water—had been swept away, so that the proud might learn what the world would be without us! [*Knock at the door.*

Enter Servant *from the Inn.*

Servant. A letter for Citizen Melnotte.

Mel. A letter! from her perhaps—who sent thee?

Servant. Why, Monsieur—I mean Citizen—Beauseant, who stops to dine at the Golden Lion, on his way to his château.

Mel. Beauseant!—[*Reads*].

"Young man, I know thy secret—thou lovest above thy station: if thou hast wit, courage, and discretion, I can secure to thee the realization of thy most sanguine hopes; and the sole condition I ask in return is, that thou shalt be steadfast to thine own ends. I shall demand from thee a solemn oath to marry her whom thou lovest; to bear her to thine home on thy wedding night. I am serious—if thou wouldst learn more, lose not a moment, but follow the bearer of this letter to thy friend and patron,—CHARLES BEAUSEANT."

Mel. Can I believe my eyes? Are our own passions the sorcerers that raise up for us spirits of good or evil? I will go instantly.

Widow. What is this, Claude?

Mel. "Marry her whom thou lovest"—"bear her to thine own home."—Oh, revenge and love; which of you is the stronger?—[*Gazing on the picture.*] Sweet face, thou smilest on me from the convas: weak fool that I am, do I then love her still? No, it is the vision of my own romance that I have worshipped: it is the reality to which I bring scorn for scorn. Adieu, mother: I will return anon. My brain reels—the earth swims before me.—[*Looks again at the letter.*] No, it is *not* a mockery; I do *not* dream! [*Exit.*

ACT II.—SCENE I.

The Gardens of M. DESCHAPPELLES' *house at Lyons—the house seen at the back of the stage.*

Enter BEAUSEANT *and* GLAVIS.

Beau. Well, what think you of my plot? Has it not succeeded to a miracle? The instant that I introduced his Highness the Prince of Como to the pompous mother and the scornful daughter, it was all over with them: he came—he saw—he conquered: and, though it is not many days since he arrived, they have already promised him the hand of Pauline.

Gla. It is lucky, though, that you told them his highness travelled incognito, for fear the Directory (who are not very fond of princes) should lay him by the heels; for he has a wonderful wish to keep up his rank, and scatters our gold about with as much coolness as if he were watering his own flower-pots.

Beau. True, he is damnably extravagant; I think the sly dog does it out of malice. However, it must be owned that he reflects credit on his loyal subjects, and makes a very pretty figure in his fine clothes, with my diamond snuff-box.

Gla. And my diamond ring! But do you think he will be firm to the last? I fancy I see symptoms of relenting: he will never keep up his rank, if he once let out his conscience.

Beau. His oath binds him! he cannot retract without being foresworn, and those low fellows are always superstitious! But, as it is, I tremble lest he be discovered: that bluff Colonel Damas (Madame Deschappelles' cousin) evidently suspects him: we must make haste and conclude the farce: I have thought of a plan to end it this very day.

Gla. This very day! Poor Pauline: her dream will be soon over.

Beau. Yes, this day they shall be married; this evening, according to his oath, he shall carry his bride to the Golden Lion, and then pomp, equipage, retinue, and title, all shall vanish at once; and her Highness the Princess shall find that she has refused the son of a Marquis, to marry the son of a gardener.—Oh, Pauline! once loved, now hated, yet still not relinquished, thou shalt drain the cup to the dregs,—thou shalt know what it is to be humbled!

Enter from the house, MELNOTTE, *as the Prince of Como, leading in* PAULINE; MADAME DESCHAPPELLES, *fanning herself; and* COLONEL DAMAS.

[BEAUSEANT *and* GLAVIS *bow respectfully.* PAULINE *and* MELNOTTE *walk apart.*

Mme. Deschap. Good morning, gentlemen; really I am so fatigued with laughter; the dear Prince is so entertaining. What wit he has! Any one may see that he has spent his whole life in courts.

Damas. And what the deuce do you know about courts, cousin Deschappelles? You women regard men just as you buy books—you never care about what is in them, but how they are bound and lettered. 'Sdeath, I don't think you would even look at your Bible if it had not a title to it.

Mme. Deschap. How coarse you are, cousin Damas!—quite the manners of a barrack—you don't deserve to be one of our family; really we must drop your acquaintance when Pauline marries. I cannot patronize any relations that would discredit my future son-in-law, the Prince of Como.

Mel. [*advancing*]. These are beautiful gardens, madame, (BEAUSEANT *and* GLAVIS *retire*) —who planned them?

Mme. Deschap. A gardener named Melnotte, your highness—an honest man who knew his station. I can't say as much for his son—a presuming fellow, who,—ha! ha! actually wrote verses—such doggerel!—to my daughter.

Pauline. Yes, how you would have laughed at them, Prince!—*you,* who write such beautiful verses!

Mel. This Melnotte must be a monstrous impudent person!

Damas. Is he good-looking?

Mme. Deschap. I never notice such *canaille*—an ugly, mean-looking clown, if I remember right.

Damas. Yet I heard your porter say he was wonderfully like his highness.

Mel. [*taking snuff*]. You are complimentary.

Mme. Deschap. For shame, cousin Damas!—like the Prince, indeed!

Pauline. Like you! Ah, mother, like our beautiful prince! I'll never speak to you again, cousin Damas.

Mel. [*aside*]. Humph!—rank is a great beautifier! I never passed for an Apollo while I was a peasant; if I am so handsome as a prince, what should I be as an emperor! [*Aloud.*] Monsieur Beauseant, will you honor me? [*Offers snuff.*

Beau. No, your highness; I have no small vices.

Mel. Nay, if it were a vice, you'd be sure to have it, Monsieur Beauseant.

Mme. Deschap. Ha! ha!—how very severe!—what wit!

Beau. [*in a rage and aside*]. Curse his impertinence!

Mme. Deschap. What a superb snuff-box!

Pauline. And what a beautiful ring!

Mel. You like the box—a trifle—interesting perhaps from associations—a present from Louis XIV. to my great-great-grandmother. Honor me by accepting it.

Beau. [*plucking him by the sleeve*]. How!—what the devil! My box—are you mad? It is worth five hundred louis.

Mel. [*unheeding him, and turning to* PAULINE]. And you like this ring? Ah, it has, indeed a lustre since your eyes have shone on it [*placing it on her finger*]. Henceforth hold me, sweet enchantress, the Slave of the Ring.

Gla. [*pulling him*]. Stay, stay—what are you about? My maiden aunt's legacy—a diamond of the first water. You shall be hanged for swindling, sir.

Mel. [*pretending not to hear*]. It is curious, this ring; it is the one with which my grandfather, the Doge of Venice, married the Adriatic!

[Madame *and* PAULINE *examine the ring.*

Mel. [*to* BEAUSEANT *and* GLAVIS]. Fie, gentlemen! princes must be generous?—[*Turns to* DAMAS, *who watches them closely.*] These kind friends have my interest so much at heart, that they are as careful of my property as if it were their own!

Beau and Gla. [*confusedly*]. Ha! ha!—very good joke that!

[*Appear to remonstrate with* MELNOTTE *in dumb show.*

Damas. What's all that whispering? I am sure there is some juggle here: hang me, if I think he is an Italian after all. Gad, I'll try him. Servitore umillissimo, Eccellenza.*

---

* Your Excellency's most humble servant.

Mel. Hum—what does he mean, I wonder?

Damas. Godo di vedervi in buona salute.*

Mel. Hem—hem!

Damas. Fa bel tempo—che si dice di nuovo?†

Mel. Well, sir, what's all that gibberish?

Damas. Oh, oh!—only Italian, your highness!—The Prince of Como does not understand his own language!

Mel. Not as you pronounce it; who the deuce could?

Mme. Deschap. Ha! ha! cousin Damas, never pretend to what you don't know.

Pauline. Ha! ha! cousin Damas; *you* speak Italian, indeed!

[*Makes a mocking gesture at him.*

Beau. [*to* GLAVIS]. Clever dog!—how ready!

Gla. Ready, yes; with my diamond ring!—Damn his readiness!

Damas. Laugh at me!—laugh at a Colonel in the French army!—the fellow's an impostor; I know he is. I'll see if he understands fighting as well as he does Italian.—[*Goes up to him, and aside.*] Sir, you are a jackanapes.—Can you construe that?

Mel. No, sir; I never construe affronts in the presence of ladies; by-and-by I shall be happy to take a lesson—or give one.

Damas. I'll find the occasion, never fear!

Mme. Deschap. Where are you going, cousin?

Damas. To correct my Italian. [*Exit.*

Beau. [*to* GLAVIS]. Let us after, and pacify him; he evidently suspects something.

Gla. Yes!—but my diamond ring!

Beau. And my box!—We are over-taxed fellow-subjects!—we must stop the supplies, and dethrone the prince.

Gla. Prince!—he ought to be heir-apparent to King Stork.

[*Exeunt* BEAUSEANT *and* GLAVIS.

Mme. Deschap. Dare I ask your highness to forgive my cousin's insufferable vulgarity?

Pauline. Oh yes!—you will forgive his manner for the sake of his heart.

Mel. And the sake of his cousin.—Ah, madam, there is one comfort in rank,—we are so sure of our position that we are not easily affronted. Besides, M. Damas has bought the right of indulgence from his friends, by never showing it to his enemies.

Pauline. Ah! he is, indeed, as brave in action as he is rude in speech. He rose from the ranks to his present grade, and in two years!

Mel. In two years!—two years, did you say?

Mme. Deschap. [*aside*]. I don't like leaving girls alone with their lovers; but, with a prince, it would be so ill-bred to be prudish. [*Exit.*

Mel. You can be proud of your connection with one who owes his position to merit—not birth.

Pauline. Why, yes; but still—

Mel. Still what, Pauline!

Pauline. There is something glorious in the heritage of command. A man who has ancestors is like a representative of the past.

Mel. True; but, like other representatives, nine times out of ten he is a silent member. Ah, Pauline! not to the past, but to the future, looks true nobility, and finds its blazon in posterity.

Pauline. You say this to please me, who have no ancestors; but you, prince, must be proud of so illustrious a race!

Mel. No, no! I would not, were I fifty times a prince, be a pensioner on the dead! I honor birth and ancestry when they are regarded as the incentives to exertion, not the title-

---

* I am glad to see you in good health.
† Fine weather. What news is there?

deeds to sloth! I honor the laurels that overshadow the graves of our fathers;—it is our fathers I emulate, when I desire that beneath the evergreen I myself have planted, my own ashes may repose! Dearest! couldst thou but see with my eyes!

Pauline. I cannot forego pride when I look on thee, and think that thou lovest me. Sweet Prince, tell me again of thy palace by the Lake of Como; it is so pleasant to hear of thy splendors since thou didst swear to me that they would be desolate without Pauline; and when thou describest them, it is with a mocking lip and a noble scorn, as if custom had made thee disdain greatness.

Mel. Nay, dearest, nay, if thou wouldst have me paint
The home to which, could love fiulfil its prayers,
This hand would lead thee, listen!*—A deep vale
Shut out by Alphine hills from the rude world;
Near a clear lake, margin'd by fruits of gold
And whispering myrtles; glassing softest skies,
As cloudless, save with rare and roseate shadows,
As I would have thy fate!

 Pauline.   My own dear love!

 Mel. A palace lifting to eternal summer
Its marble walls, from out a glossy bower
Of coolest foliage musical with birds,
Whose songs should syllable thy name! At noon
We'd sit beneath the arching vines, and wonder
Why Earth could be unhappy, while the Heavens
Still left us youth and love! We'd have no friends
That were not lovers; no ambition, save
To excel them all in love; we'd read no books
That were not tales of love—that we might smile
To think how poorly eloquence of words
Translates the poetry of hearts like ours!
And when night came, amidst the breathless Heavens
We'd guess what star should be our home when love
Becomes immortal; while the perfumed light
Stole through the mists of alabaster lamps,
And every air was heavy with the sighs
Of orange-groves and music from sweet lutes,
And murmurs of low fountains that gush forth
I' the midst of roses!—Dost thou like the picture?

 Pauline. Oh, as the bee upon the flower, I hang
Upon the honey of thy eloquent tongue!
Am I not blest? And if I love too wildly,
Who would not love thee like Pauline?

 Mel. [*bitterly.*]   Oh, false one!
It is the *prince* thou lovest, not the *man:*
If in the stead of luxury, pomp, and power,
I had painted poverty, and toil, and care,
Thou hadst found no honey on my tongue;—Pauline,
That is not love!

---

* The reader will observe that Melnotte evades the request of Pauline. He proceeds to describe a home, which he does not say he possesses, but to which he would lead her, "*could Love fulfil its prayers.*" This caution is intended as a reply to a sagacious critic who censures the description, because it is not an exact and prosaic inventory of the characteristics of the Lake of Como!—When Melnotte, for instance, talks of birds " that syllable the name of Pauline" (by the way, a literal translation from an Italian poet), he is not thinking of ornithology, but probably of the Arabian Nights. He is venting the extravagant, but natural, enthusiasm of the poet and the lover.

Pauline. Thou wrong'st me, cruel Prince!
At first, in truth, I might not have been won,
Save through the weakness of a flatter'd pride;
But *now*,—oh! trust me,—couldst thou fall from power
And sink——
    Mel. As low as that poor gardener's son
Who dared to lift his eyes to thee?—
    Pauline. Even then,
Methinks thou wouldst be only made more dear
By the sweet thought that I could prove how deep
Is woman's love! We are like the insects, caught
By the poor glittering of a garish flame;
But, oh, the wings once scorch'd, the brightest star
Lures us no more; and by the fatal light
We cling till death!
    Mel. Angel!
    [*Aside.*] O conscience! conscience!
It must not be;—her love hath grown a torture
Worse than her hate. I will at once to Beauseant,
And—ha! he comes. Sweet love, one moment leave me.
I have business with these gentlemen— I—I
Will forwith join you.
    Pauline. Do not tarry long! [*Exit.*

Enter BEAUSEANT *and* GLAVIS.

    Mel. Release me from my oath,—I will not marry her!
    Beau Then thou art perjured.
    Mel. No, I was not in my senses when I swore to thee to marry her! I was blind to all but her scorn!—deaf to all but my passion and my rage! Give me back my poverty and my honor!
    Beau. It is too late,—you must marry her! and this day. I have a story already coined, and sure to pass current. This Damas suspects thee,—he will set the police to work!—thou wilt be detected—Pauline will despise and execrate thee. Thou wilt be sent to the common gaol as a swindler.
    Mel. Fiend!
    Beau. And in the heat of the girl's resentment (you know of what resentment is capable) and the parents' shame, she will be induced to marry the first that offers—even perhaps your humble servant.
    Mel. You! No; that were worse—for thou hast no mercy! I will marry her—I will keep my oath. Quick, then, with the damnable invention thou art hatching;—quick, if thou wouldst not have me strangle thee or myself.
    Gla. What a tiger! Too fierce for a prince;—he ought to have been the Grand Turk.
    Beau. Enough—I will dispatch; be prepared.
[*Exeunt* BEAUSEANT *and* GLAVIS.

Enter DAMAS *with two swords.*

    Damas. Now, then, sir, the ladies are no longer your excuse. I have brought you a couple of dictionaries; let us see if your highness can find out the Latin for *bilbo*.
    Mel. Away, sir! I am in no humor for jesting.
    Damas. I see you understand something of the grammar; you decline the non-substantive "small-swords" with great ease; but that won't do—you must take a lesson in *parsing*.
    Mel. Fool!

Damas. Sir, as sons take after their mother, so the man who calls me a fool insults the lady who bore me; there's no escape for you—fight you shall, or——

Mel. Oh, enough! enough!—take your ground.

[*They fight;* DAMAS *is disarmed.* MELNOTTE *takes up the sword and returns it to* DAMAS *respectfully.*

A just punishment to the brave soldier who robs the state of its best property—the sole right to his valor and his life.

Damas. Sir, you fence exceedingly well; you must be a man of honor—I don't care a jot whether you are a prince; but a man who has carte and tierce at his fingers' ends must be a gentleman.

Mel. [*aside.*] Gentleman! Ay, I was a gentleman before I turned conspirator; for honest men are the gentlemen of Nature! Colonel, they tell me you rose from the ranks.

Damas. I did.

Mel. And in two years!

Damas. It is true; that's no wonder in our army at present. Why the oldest general in the service is scarcely thirty, and we have some of two-and-twenty.

Mel. Two-and-twenty!

Damas. Yes; in the French army, now a days, promotion is not a matter of purchase. We are all heroes, because we may be all generals. We have no fear of the cypress, because we may all hope for the laurel.

Mel. A general at two-and-twenty! [*turning away*]—Sir, I may ask you a favor one of these days.

Damas. Sir, I shall be proud to grant it. It is astonishing how much I like a man after I've fought with him. [*Hides the swords.*

Enter MADAME DESCHAPPELLES *and* BEAUSEANT.

Mme. Deschap. Oh, prince,—prince!—What do I hear? You must fly—you must quit us!

Mel. I!—

Beau. Yes, prince: read this letter, just received from my friend at Paris, one of the Directory; they suspect you of designs against the Republic: they are very suspicious of princes, and your family take part with the Austrians. Knowing that I introduced your highness at Lyons, my friend writes to me to say that you must quit the town immediately, or you will be arrested,—thrown into prison, perhaps guillotined! Fly!—I will order horses to your carriage instantly. Fly to Marsailles; there you can take ship to Leghorn.

Mme. Deschap. And what's to become of Pauline? Am I not to be mother to a princess, after all?

Enter PAULINE *and* MONSIEUR DESCHAPPELLES.

Pauline [*throwing herself into* MELNOTTE'S *arms.*] You must leave us!—Leave Pauline!

Beau. Not a moment is to be wasted.

M. Deschap. I will go to the magistrates and inquire—

Beau. Then he is lost; the magistrates, hearing he is suspected, will order his arrest.

Mme. Deschap. And I shall not be a princess-dowager!

Beau. Why not? There is only one thing to be done:—send for the priest—let the marriage take place at once, and the prince carry home a bride?

Mel. Impossible!—[*Aside.*] Villain.

Mme. Deschap. What, lose my child?

Beau. And gain a princess!

Mme Deschap. Oh, Monsieur Beauseant, you are so very kind, it must be so,—we ought not to be selfish, my daughter's happiness at stake. She will go away, too, in a carriage and six!

Pauline. Thou art here still,—I cannot part from thee,—my heart will break.

SCENE I.]   THE LADY OF LYONS.   87

Mel. But thou wilt not consent to this hasty union?—thou wilt not wed an outcast—a fugitive?

Pauline. Ah! if thou art in danger, who should share it but Pauline?

Mel. [*aside*]. Distraction!—If the earth could swallow me!

M. Deschap. Gently! gently! The settlements—the contracts—my daughter's dowry!

Mel. The dowry!—I am not base enough for that; no, not one farthing!

Beau. [*to* MADAM]. Noble fellow!—Really your good husband is too mercantile in these matters. Monsieur Deschappelles, your hear his highness: we can arrange the settlements by proxy; 'tis the way with people of quality.

M. Deschap. But——

Mme. Deschap. Hold your tongue!—Don't expose yourself!

Beau. I will bring the priest in a trice. Go in all of you and prepare; the carriage shall be at the door before the ceremony is over.

Mme. Deschap. Be sure there are six horses, Beauseant! You are very good to have forgiven us for refusing you; but you see—a prince!

Beau. And such a prince! Madam, I cannot blush at the success of so illustrious a rival.—[*Aside.*] Now will I follow them to the village, enjoy my triumph, and to-morrow, in the hour of thy shame and grief, I think, proud girl, thou wilt prefer even these arms to those of the gardener's son.   [*Exit.*

Mme. Deschap. Come, Monsieur Deschappelles, give your arm to her highness that is to be.

M. Deschap. I don't like doing business in such a hurry; 'tis not the way with the house of Deschappelles & Co.

Mme. Deschap. There, now, you fancy you are in the counting-house, don't you?

[*Pushes him to* PAULINE.

Mel. Stay, stay, Pauline—one word. Have you no scruple, no fear? Speak—it is not yet too late.

Pauline. When I loved thee, thy fate became mine. Triumph or danger—joy or sorrow—I am by thy side.

Damas. Well, well, prince, thou art a lucky man to be so loved. She is a good little girl in spite of her foibles—make her as happy as if she were not to be a princess [*slapping him on the shoulder*]. Come, sir, I wish you joy—young—tender—lovely;—zounds, I envy you!

Mel. [*who has stood apart in gloomy abstraction*]. Do you?*

ACT III.—SCENE I.

The exterior of the Golden Lion—time, twilight. The moon rises during the scene.

Enter Landlord *and his* Daughter *from the Inn.*

Land. Ha—ha—ha! Well, I never shall get over it. Our Claude is a prince with a vengeance now. His carriage breaks down at my inn—ha—ha!

---

* On the stage the following lines are added:—

"Do you? Wise judges are we of each other.
'Woo, wed, and bear her home!' So runs the bond
To which I sold myself,—and then—what then?
Away?—I will not look beyond the hour.
Like children in the dark, I dare not face
The shades that gather round me in the distance.
You envy me—I thank you—you may read
My joy upon my brow—I thank you, sir!
If hearts had audible language, you would hear
What mine would answer when you talk of *envy!*"

Janet. And what airs the young lady gives herself! "Is this the best room you have, young woman?" with such a toss of the head.

Land. Well, get in, Janet: get in and see to the supper: the servants must sup before they go back. [*Exeunt.*

Enter BEAUSEANT *and* GLAVIS.

Beau. You see our princess is lodged at last—one stage more, and she'll be at her journey's end—the beautiful palace at the foot of the Alps!—ha—ha!

Gla. Faith, I pity the poor Pauline—especially if she's going to sup at the Golden Lion [*makes a wry face*]. I shall never forget that cursed ragout.

Enter MELNOTTE *from the Inn.*

Beau. Your servant, my prince; you reigned most worthily, I condole with you on your abdication. I am afraid that your highness's retinue are not very faithful servants. I think they will quit you in the moment of your fall—'tis the fate of greatness. But you are welcome to your fine clothes—also the diamond snuff-box, which Louis XIV. gave to your great-great-grandmother.

Gla. And the ring, with which your grandfather the Dodge of Venice married the Adriatic.

Mel. I have kept my oath, gentlemen—say, have I kept my oath?

Beau. Most religiously.

Mel. Then you have done with me and mine—away with you!

Beau. How, knave?

Mel. Look you, our bond is over. Proud conquerors that we are, we have won the victory over a simple girl—compromised her honor—embittered her life—blasted, in their very blossoms, all the flowers of her youth. This is your triumph,—it is my shame! [*Turns to* BEAUSEANT.] Enjoy thy triumph, but not in my sight. I *was* her betrayer—I *am* her protector! Cross but her path—one word of scorn, one look of insult—nay, but one quiver of that mocking lip, and I will teach thee that bitter word thou hast graven eternally in this heart—*Repentance!*

Beau. His highness is most grandiloquent.

Mel. Highness me no more! Beware! Remorse has made me a new being. Away with you! There is danger in me. Away!

Gla. [*aside.*] He's an awkward fellow to deal with: come away, Beauseant.

Beau. I know the respect due to rank. Adieu, my prince. Any commands at Lyons? Yet hold—I promised you 200 louis on your wedding-day; here they are.

Mel. [*dashing the purse to the ground*]. I gave you revenge, I did not sell it. Take up your silver, Judas; take it.—Ay, it is fit you should learn to stoop.

Beau. You will beg my pardon for this some day. [*Aside to* GLAVIS.] Come to my château—I shall return hither to-morrow, to learn how Pauline likes her new dignity.

Mel. Are you not gone yet?

Beau. Your highness's most obedient, most faithful—

Gla. And most humble servants. Ha! ha! [*Exeunt* BEAUSEANT *and* GLAVIS.

Mel. Thank heaven I had no weapon, or I should have slain them. Wretch! what can I say? Where turn? On all sides mockery—the very boors within—[*Laughter from the Inn*].—'Sdeath, if even in this short absence the exposure should have chanced. I will call her. We will go hence. I have already sent one I can trust to my mother's house. There, at least, none can insult her agony—gloat upon her shame! There alone must she learn what a villain she has sworn to love. [*As he turns to the door enter* PAULINE *from the Inn.*

Pauline. Ah! my lord, what a place! I never saw such rude people. They stare and wink so. I think the very sight of a prince, though he travels *incognito*, turns their honest heads. What a pity the carriage should break down in such a spot! You are not well—the drops stand on your brow—your hand is feverish.

Mel. Nay, it is but a passing spasm;—the air——

Pauline. Is not the soft air of your native south—
How pale he is!—indeed thou art not well.
Where are our people? I will call them.
 Mel.   Hold!
I—I am well.
 Pauline.   Thou art!—Ah! now I know it.
Thou fanciest, my kind lord—I know thou dost—
Thou fanciest these rude walls, these rustic gossips,
Brick'd floors, sour wine, coarse viands, vex Pauline;
And so they might, but thou art by my side,
And I forget all else.

   Enter Landlord, *the* Servants *peeping and laughing over his shoulder.*

 Land.   My lord—your highness—
Will your most noble excellency choose—
 Mel. Begone, sir!   [*Exit* Landlord *laughing.*
 Pauline.   How could they have learn'd thy rank?
One's servants are so vain!—nay, let it not
Chafe thee, sweet prince!—a few short days and we
Shall see thy palace by its lake of silver,
And—nay, nay, spendthrift, is thy wealth of smiles
Already drain'd, or dost thou play the miser?
 Mel. Thine eyes would call up smiles in deserts, fair one.
Let us escape these rustics: close at hand
There is a cot, where I have bid prepare
Our evening lodgment—a rude, homely roof,
But honest, where our welcome will not be
Made torture by the vulgar eyes and tongues
That are as death to Love! A heavenly night!
The wooing air and the soft moon invite us.
Wilt walk? I pray thee, now,—I know the path,
Ay, every inch of it!
 Pauline.   What, *thou!* methought
Thou wert a stranger in these parts? Ah, truant,
Some village beauty lured thee;—thou art now
Grown constant?
 Mel.   Trust me.
 Pauline.   Princes are so changeful!
 Mel. Come, dearest, come.
 Pauline.   Shall I not call our people
To light us?
 Mel. Heaven will lend its stars for torches!
It is not far.
 Pauline. The night breeze chills me.
 Mel.   Nay,
Let me thus mantle thee;—it is not cold.
 Pauline. Never beneath thy smile!
 Mel. [*aside.*]   O Heaven! forgive me!   [*Exeunt.*

SCENE II.

MELNOTTE'S *cottage—*Widow *bustling about—a table spread for supper.*

Widow. So, I think that looks very neat. He sent me a line, so blotted that I can scarcely read it, to say he would be here almost immediately. She must have loved him well indeed to have forgotten his birth; for though he was introduced to her in disguise, he is too honorable not to have revealed to her the artifice, which her love only could forgive. Well, I do not wonder at it; for though my son is not a prince, he ought to be one, and that's almost as good. [*Knock at the door.*] Ah! here they are.

Enter MELNOTTE *and* PAULINE.

Widow. Oh, my boy—the pride of my heart!—welcome, welcome! I beg pardon, ma'am, but I do love him so!

Pauline. Good woman, I really—why prince, what is this?—does the old lady know you? Oh, I guess, you have done her some service. Another proof of your kind heart? is it not?

Mel. Of my kind heart, ay!

Pauline. So you know the prince?

Widow. Know him, madam?—Ah, I begin to fear it is you who know him not!

Pauline. Do you think she is mad? Can we stay here, my lord? I think there's something very wild about her.

Mel. Madam, I—no, I cannot tell her; my knees knock together: what a coward is a man who has lost his honor! Speak to her—speak to her [*to his mother*]—tell her that—O Heaven, that I were dead!

Pauline. How confused he looks!—this strange place?—this woman—what can it mean?—I half suspect—Who are you, madam!—who are you! can't you speak? are you struck dumb?

Widow. Claude, you have not deceived her?—Ah, shame upon you! I thought that, before you went to the altar, she was to have known all.

Pauline. All! what!—My blood freezes in my veins!

Widow. Poor lady!—dare I tell her, Claude? [MELNOTTE *makes a sign of assent.*] Know you not then, madam, that this young man is of poor though honest parents? Know you not that you are wedded to my son, Claude Melnotte?

Pauline. Your son! hold—hold! do not speak to me.—[*Approaches* MELNOTTE, *and lays her hand on his arm.*]—Is this a jest? is it? I know it is, only speak—one word—one look—one smile. I cannot believe—I who loved thee so—I cannot believe that thou art such a—No, I will not wrong thee by a harsh word—Speak!

Mel. Leave us—have pity on her, on me: leave us.

Widow. Oh, Claude, that I should live to see thee bowed by shame! thee of whom I was so proud! [*Exit by the staircase.*

Pauline. Her son—her son!

Mel. Now, lady, hear me.

Pauline. Hear thee!
Ay, speak—her son! have fiends a parent? speak,
That thou mayst silence curses—speak!

Mel. No, curse me:
Thy curse would blast me less than thy forgiveness.

Pauline [*laughing wildly*]. "This is thy palace, where the perfumed light
Steals through the mist of alabaster lamps,
And every air is heavy with the sighs
Of orange-groves, and music from the sweet lutes,
And murmurs of low fountains, that gush forth

I' the midst of roses!" Dost thou like the picture?
This is my bridal home, and *thou* my bridegroom.
O fool—O dupe—O wretch!—I see it all—
Thy by-word and the jeer of every tongue
In Lyons. Hast thou in thy heart one touch
Of human kindness? if thou hast, why, kill me,
And save thy wife from madness. No, it cannot—
It cannot be: this is some horrid dream:
I shall wake soon.—[*Touching him.*] Art flesh art man? or but
The shadows seen in sleep? It is too real.
What have I done to thee? how sinn'd against thee,
That thou shouldst crush me thus?

  Mel.   Pauline, by pride
Angels have fallen ere thy time: by pride—
That sole alloy of thy most lovely mould—
The evil spirit of a bitter love,
And a revengeful heart, had power upon thee.
From my first years my soul was fill'd with thee:
I saw thee midst the flow'rs the lowly boy
Tended, unmark'd by thee—a spirit of bloom,
And joy, and freshness, as if Spring itself
Were made a living thing, and wore thy shape!
I saw thee, and the passionate heart of man
Enter'd the breast of the wild-dreaming boy.
And from that hour I grew—what to the last
I shall be—thine adorer! Well, this love
Vain, frantic, guilty, if thou wilt, became
A fountain of ambition and bright hope;
I thought of tales that by the winter hearth
Old gossips tell—how maidens sprung from kings
Have stoop'd from their high sphere; how love, like death
Levels all ranks, and lays the shepherd's crook
Beside the sceptre. Thus I made my home
In the soft palace of a fairy Future!
My father died; and I, the peasant-born,
Was my own lord. Then did I seek to rise
Out of the prison of my mean estate;
And, with such jewels as the exploring mind
Brings from the caves of knowledge, buy my ransom
From those twin gaolers of the daring heart—
Low birth and iron fortune. Thy bright image
Glass'd in my soul, took all the hues of glory,
And lured me on to those inspiring toils
By which man masters men! For thee I grew
A midnight student o'er the dreams of sages.
For thee I sought to borrow from each grace,
And every muse, such attributes as lend
Ideal charms to love. I thought of thee,
And passion taught me poesy—of thee,
And on the painter's canvas grew the life
Of beauty! Art became the shadow
Of the dear starlight of thy haunting eyes!
Men call'd me vain—some mad—I heeded not;

But still toil'd on—hoped on—for it was sweet,
If not to win, to feel more worthy thee?

Pauline. Has he a magic to exorcise hate!

Mel. At last, in one mad hour, I dared to pour
The thoughts that burst their channels into song,
And sent them to thee—such a tribute, lady,
As beauty rarely scorns, even from the meanest.
The name—appended by the burning heart
That long'd to show its idol what bright things
It had created—yea, the enthusiast's name,
That should have been thy triumph, was thy scorn!
That very hour—when passion, turn'd to wrath,
Resembled hatred most—when thy disdain
Made my whole soul a chaos—in that hour
The tempters found me a revengeful tool
For their revenge! Thou hadst trampled on the worm—
It turn'd and stung thee!

Pauline. Love, sir, hath no sting.
What was the slight of a poor powerless girl
To the deep wrong of this most vile revenge?
Oh, how I loved this man!—a serf!—a slave!

Mel. Hold, lady! No, not slave! Despair is free!
I will not tell thee of the throes—the struggles—
The anguish—the remorse: No, let it pass!
And let me come to such most poor atonement
Yet in my power. Pauline!——

[*Approaching her with great emotion, and about to take her hand.*

Pauline. No, touch me not!
I know my fate. You are, by law, my tyrant;
And I—O Heaven!—a peasant's wife! I'll work—
Toil—drudge—do what thou wilt—but touch me not;
Let my wrongs make me sacred!

Mel. Do not fear me.
Thou dost not know me, madam: at the altar
My vengeance ceased—my guilty oath expired!
Henceforth, no image of some marble saint,
Niched in cathedral aisles, is hallow'd more
From the rude hand of sacrilegious wrong.
I am thy husband—nay, thou need'st not shudder;—
Here, at thy feet, I lay a husband's rights.
A marriage thus unholy—unfulfill'd—
A bond of fraud—is, by the laws of France,
Made void and null. To-night sleep—sleep in peace.
To-morrow, pure and virgin as this morn
I bore thee, bathed in blushes, from the shrine,
Thy father's arms shall take thee to thy home.
The law shall do thee justice, and restore
Thy right to bless another with thy love.
And when thou art happy, and hast half forgot
Him who so loved—so wrong'd thee, think at least
Heaven left some remnant of the angel still
In that poor peasant's nature!

Ho! my mother!

Enter Widow.

Conduct this lady—(she is not my wife;
She is our guest,—our honor'd guest, my mother)—
To the poor chamber, where the sleep of virtue,
Never, beneath my father's honest roof,
Ev'n villains dared to mar! Now, lady, now,
I think thou wilt believe me. Go, my mother!

Widow. She is not thy wife!

Mel. Hush, hush! for mercy's sake! Speak not, but go.

[Widow *ascends the stairs;* PAULINE *follows weeping—turns to look back.*

Mel. [*sinking down*]. All angels bless and guard her!

ACT IV.—SCENE I.

*The cottage as before—*MELNOTTE *seated before a table—writing implements, etc.—(Day breaking.)*

Mel. Hush, hush!—she sleeps at last!—thank Heaven, for a while she forgets even that I live! Her sobs, which have gone to my heart the whole, long, desolate night, have ceased!—all calm—all still! I will go now; I will send this letter to Pauline's father: when he arrives, I will place in his hands my own consent to the divorce, and then, O France! my country! accept among thy protectors, thy defenders—the peasant's Son! Our country is less proud than custom, and does not refuse the blood, the heart, the right hand of the poor man.

Enter Widow.

Widow. My son, thou hast acted ill; but sin brings its own punishment. In the hour of thy remorse, it is not for a mother to reproach thee.

Mel. What is past is past. There is a future left to all men, who have the virtue to repent, and the energy to atone. Thou shalt be proud of thy son yet. Meanwhile, remember this poor lady has been grievously injured. For the sake of thy son's conscience, respect, honor, bear with her. If she weep, console—if she chide, be silent. 'Tis but a little while more—I shall send an express fast as horse can speed to her father. Farewell! I shall return shortly.

Widow. It is the only course left to thee—thou wert led astray, but thou art not hardened. Thy heart is right still, as ever it was when, in thy most ambitious hopes thou wert never ashamed of thy poor mother.

Mel. Ashamed of thee; No, if I yet endure, yet live, yet hope,—it is only because I would not die till I have redeemed the noble heritage I have lost—the heritage I took unstained from thee and my dead father—a proud conscience and an honest name. I shall win them back yet—heaven bless you! [*Exit.*

Widow. My dear Claude! How my heart bleeds for him.

[PAULINE *looks down from above, and after a pause descends.*

Pauline. Not here!—he spares me that pain at least: so far he is considerate—yet the place seems still more desolate without him. Oh, that I could hate him—the gardener's son!—and yet how nobly he—no—no—no I will not be so mean a thing as to forgive him!

Widow. Good morning, madam; I would have waited on you if I had known you were stirring.

Pauline. It is no matter, ma'am—your son's wife ought to wait on herself.

Widow. My son's wife—let not that thought vex you, madam—he tells me that you will have your divorce. And I hope I shall live to see him smile again. There are maidens in this village, young and fair, madam, who may yet console him.

Pauline. I dare say—they are very welcome—and when the divorce is got—he will marry again. I am sure I hope so. [*Weeps.*

Widow. He could have married the richest girl in the province, if he had pleased it; but his head was turned, poor child! he could think of nothing but you. [*Weeps.*

Pauline. Don't weep, *mother.*

Widow. Ah, he has behaved very ill, I know, but love is so headstrong in the young. Don't weep, madam.

Pauline. So, as you were saying—go on.

Widow. Oh, I cannot excuse him, ma'am—he was not in his right senses.

Pauline. But he always—always [*sobbing*] loved—loved me then?

Widow. He thought of nothing else. See here—he learnt to paint that he might take your likeness [*uncovers the picture*]. But that's all over now—I trust you have cured him of his folly;—but, dear heart, you have had no breakfast!

Pauline. I can't take anything—don't trouble yourself.

Widow. Nay, madam, be persuaded; a little coffee will refresh you. Our milk and eggs are excellent. I will get out Claude's coffee-cup—It is of real Sèvres; he saved up all his money to buy it three years ago, because the name of *Pauline* was inscribed on it.

Pauline. Three years ago! Poor Claude!—Thank you; I think I will have some coffee. Oh! if he were but a poor gentleman, even a merchant: but a gardener's son—and what a home! —Oh no,—it is too dreadful!

[*They seat themselves at the table,* BEAUSEANT *opens the lattice and looks in.*

Beau. So—so—the coast is clear! I saw Claude in the lane—I shall have an excellent opportunity. [*Shuts the lattice and knocks at the door.*

Pauline [*starting*]. Can it be my father?—he has not sent for him yet? No, he cannot be in such a hurry to get rid of me.

Widow. It is not time for your father to arrive yet; it must be some neighbor.

Pauline. Don't admit any one.

[Widow *opens the door,* BEAUSEANT *pushes her aside and enters.*
Ha! Heavens! that hateful Beauseant! This is indeed bitter!

Beau. Good morning, madam! O widow, your son begs you will have the goodness to go to him in the village—he wants to speak to you on particular business; you'll find him at the inn, or the grocer's shop, or the baker's, or at some other friend's of your family—make haste.

Pauline. Don't leave me, mother!—don't leave me.

Beau. [*with great respect*]. Be not alarmed, madam. Believe me your friend—your servant.

Pauline. Sir, I have no fear of you, even in this house! Go, madam, if your son wishes it; I will not contradict his commands whilst, at least he has still the right to be obeyed.

Widow. I don't understand this; however, I sha'n't be long gone. [*Exit.*

Pauline. Sir, I divine the object of your visit—you wish to exult in the humiliation of one who humbled you. Be it so; I am prepared to endure all—even your presence!

Beau. You mistake me, madam—Pauline, you mistake me! I come to lay my fortune at your feet. You must already be disenchanted with this impostor; these walls are not worthy to be hallowed by **your beauty**! Shall that form be clasped in the arms of a base-born peasant? Beloved, beautiful Pauline! fly with me—my carriage waits without—I will bear you to a home more meet for your reception. Wealth, luxury, station—all shall yet be yours. I forget your past disdain—I remember only your beauty and my unconquerable love!

Pauline. Sir! leave this house—it is humble: but a husband's roof, however lowly, is, in the eyes of God and man, the temple of a wife's honor! Know that I would rather starve— yes—with him who has betrayed me, than accept your lawful hand, even were you the prince whose name he bore!—Go.

Beau. What! is not your pride humbled yet?

Pauline. Sir, what was pride in prosperity in affliction becomes virtue.

Beau. Look round: these rugged floors—these homely walls—this wretched struggle of poverty for comfort—think of this! and contrast with such a picture the refinement, the luxury, the pomp, that the wealthiest gentleman of Lyons offers to the loveliest lady. Ah, hear me!

Pauline. Oh! my father!—why did I leave you?—why am I thus friendless? Sir, you see before you a betrayed, injured, miserable woman!—respect her anguish!

[MELNOTTE *opens the door silently, and pauses at the threshold.*

Beau. No! let me rather thus console it; let me snatch from those lips one breath of that fragrance which never should be wasted on the low churl thy husband.

Pauline. Help! Claude!—Claude!—Have I no protector?

Beau. Be silent! [*showing a pistol.*] See, I do not come unprepared even for violence. I will brave all things—thy husband and all his race—for thy sake. Thus, then, I clasp thee!

Mel. [*dashing him to the other end of the stage*]. Pauline—look up, Pauline! thou art safe.

Beau. [*levelling his pistol*]. Dare you thus insult a man of my birth, ruffian?

Pauline. Oh, spare him—spare my husband!—Beauseant—Claude—no—no [*faints*].

Mel. Miserable trickster! shame upon you! brave devices to terrify a woman! Coward!—you tremble—you have outraged the laws—you know that your weapon is harmless—you have the courage of the mountebank, not the bravo!—Pauline, there is no danger.

Beau. I wish thou wert a gentleman—as it is, thou art beneath me.—Good day, and a happy honeymoon.—[*Aside*]. I will not die till I am avenged. [*Exit.*

Mel. I hold her in these arms—the last embrace!
Never, ah never more, shall this dear head
Be pillow'd on the heart that should have shelter'd
And has betray'd!—Soft—soft! one kiss—poor wretch!
No scorn on that pale lip forbids me now!
One kiss—so ends all record of my crime!
It is the seal upon the tomb of hope,
By which, like some lost, sorrowing angel, sits
Sad memory evermore;—she breathes—she moves—
She wakes to scorn, to hate, but not to shudder
Beneath the touch of my abhorrèd love. [*Places her on a seat.*
There—we are strangers now!

Pauline. All gone—all calm—
Is *every* thing a dream? thou art safe, unhurt—
I do not love thee;—but—but I am woman,
And—and—no blood is spilt?

Mel. No, lady, no;
My guilt hath not deserved so rich a blessing
As even danger in thy cause.

Enter WIDOW.

Widow. My son, I have been everywhere in search of you; why did you send for me?

Mel. I did not send for you.

Widow. No! but I must tell you your express has returned.

Mel. So soon! impossible!

Widow. Yes, he met the lady's father and mother on the road; they were going into the country on a visit. Your messenger says that Monsieur Deschappelles turned almost white with anger when he read your letter. They will be here almost immediately. Oh, Claude, Claude! what will they do to you? How I tremble! Ah, madam! do not let them injure him—if you knew how he doated on you.

Pauline. Injure him! no, ma'am, be not afraid;—my father! how shall I meet him? how go back to Lyons? the scoff of the whole city! Cruel, cruel, Claude [*in great agitation*]. Sir, you have acted most treacherously.

Mel. I know it, madam.

Pauline [*aside*]. If he would but ask me to forgive him!—I never can forgive you, sir.

Mel. I never dared to hope it.

Pauline. But you are my husband now, and I have sworn to—to love you, sir.

Mel. That was under a false belief, madam; Heaven and the laws will release you from your vow.

Pauline. He will drive me mad! if he were but less proud—if he would but ask me to remain—hark, hark—I hear the wheels of the carriage—Sir—Claude, they are coming; have you no word to say ere it is too late? Quick—speak.

Mel. I can only congratulate you on your release. Behold your parents!

Enter MONSIEUR *and* MADAME DESCHAPPELLES *and* COLONEL DAMAS.

M. Deschap. My child! my child!

Mme. Deschap. Oh, my poor Pauline!—what a villanous hovel this is! Old woman, get me a chair—I shall faint—I certainly shall. What will the world say? Child, you have been a fool. A mother's heart is easily broken.

Damas. Ha, ha! most noble Prince—I am sorry to see a man of your quality in such a condition; I am afraid your highness will go to the House of Correction.

Mel. Taunt on, sir; I spared *you* when you were unarmed—I am unarmed now. A man who has no excuse for crime is indeed defenceless!

Damas. There's something fine in the rascal, after all!

M. Deschap. Where is the impostor?—Are you thus shameless, traitor? Can you brave the presence of that girl's father?

Mel. Strike me, if it please you—you *are* her father.

Pauline. Sir—sir, for my sake;—whatever his guilt, he has acted nobly in atonement.

Mme. Deschap. Nobly! Are you mad, girl? I have no patience with you—to disgrace all your family thus!—Nobly! Oh you abominable, hardened, pitiful, mean, ugly villain!

Damas. Ugly! Why he was beautiful yesterday!

Pauline. Madame, this is his roof, and he is my husband. Respect your daughter, or let blame fall alone on her.

Mme. Deschap. You—you—Oh, I'm choking.

M. Deschap. Sir, it were idle to waste reproach upon a conscience like yours—you renounce all pretensions to the person of this lady?

Mel. I do. [*Gives a paper.*] Here is my consent to a divorce—my full confession of the fraud which annuls the marriage. Your daughter has been foully wronged—I grant it, sir; but her own lips will tell you that, from the hour in which she crossed this threshold, I returned to my own station, and respected hers. Pure and inviolate, as when yestermorn you laid your hand upon her head, and blessed her, I yield her back to you. For myself—I deliver you for ever from my presence. An outcast and a criminal, I seek some distant land, where I may mourn my sin, and pray for your daughter's peace. Farewell—farewell to you all, for ever!

Widow. Claude, Claude, you will not leave your poor old mother? *She* does not disown you in your sorrow—no, not even in your guilt. No divorce can separate a mother from her son.

Pauline. This poor widow teaches me my duty. No, mother,—no, for you are now *my* mother also!—nor should any law, human or divine, separate the wife from her husband's sorrows. Claude—Claude—all is forgotten—forgiven—I am thine for ever!

Mme. Deschap. What do I hear?—Come away, or never see my face again.

M. Deschap. Pauline, *we* never betrayed you!—do you forsake us for him?

Pauline [*going back to her father*]. Oh no—but you will forgive him too; we will live together—he shall be your son.

M. Deschap. Never! Cling to him and forsake your parents! His home shall be yours—his fortune yours—his fate yours: the wealth I have acquired by honest industry shall never enrich the dishonest man.

Pauline. And you would have a wife enjoy luxury while a husband toils! Claude, take me; thou canst not give me wealth, titles, station—but thou canst give me a true heart. I will work for thee, tend thee, bear with thee, and never, never shall these lips reproach thee for the past.

Damas. I'll be hanged if I am not going to blubber!

Mel. This is the heaviest blow of all!—What a heart I have wronged!—Do not fear me, sir; I am not all hardened—I will not rob her of a holier love than mine. Pauline!—angel of love and mercy!—your memory shall lead me back to virtue!—The husband of a being so beautiful in her noble and sublime tenderness may be poor,—may be low-born;—(there is no guilt in the decrees of providence!)—but he should be one who can look thee in the face without a blush,—to whom thy love does not bring remorse,—who can fold thee to his heart, and say,—"*Here* there is no deceit!"——I am not that man!

Damas [*aside to* MELNOTTE]. Thou art a noble fellow, notwithstanding; and wouldst make an excellent soldier. Serve in my regiment. I have had a letter from the Directory—our young general takes the command of the army in Italy,—I am to join him at Marseilles,—I will depart this day, if thou wilt go with me.

Mel. It is the favor I would have asked thee, if I dared. Place me wherever a foe is most dreaded,—wherever France most needs a life!

Damas. There shall not be a forlorn hope without thee!

Mel. There is my hand!—mother, your blessing. I shall see you again,—a better man than a prince,—a man who has bought the right to high thoughts by brave deeds. And thou!—thou! so wildly worshipped, so guiltily betrayed,—all is not yet lost!—for thy memory, at least, must be mine till death! If I live, the name of him thou hast once loved shall not rest dishonored;—if I fall, amidst the carnage and the roar of battle, my soul will fly back to thee, and love shall share with death my last sigh!—More—more would I speak to thee!—to pray!—to bless! But no;—When I am less unworthy I will utter it to Heaven!—I cannot trust myself to——[*turning to* DESCHAPPELLES] Your pardon, sir; they are my last words—Farewell! [*Exit.*

Damas. I will go after him.—France will thank me for this.

Pauline [*starting from her father's arms*]. Claude!—Claude!—my husband!

M. Deschap. You have a father still!

ACT V.

Two years and a half from the date of Act IV.

SCENE I.

The Streets of Lyons.

Enter First, Second, *and* Third Officers.

First Officer. Well, here we are at Lyons, with gallant old Damas: it is his native place.

Second Officer. Yes; he has gained a step in the army since he was here last. The Lyonnese ought to be very proud of stout General Damas.

Third Officer. Promotion is quick in the French army. This mysterious Morier,—the hero of Lodi, and the favorite of the commander-in-chief,—has risen to a colonel's rank in two years and a half.

Enter DAMAS, *as a General.*

Damas. Good morrow, gentlemen; I hope you will amuse yourselves during our short stay at Lyons. It is a fine city: improved since I left it. Ah! it is a pleasure to grow old,—when the years that bring decay to ourselves do but ripen the prosperity of our country. You have not met with Morier?

First Officer. No: we were just speaking of him.

Second Officer. Pray, general, can you tell us who this Morier really is?

Damas. Is!—why a colonel in the French army.

Third Officer. True. But what was he at first?

Damas. At first? Why a baby in long clothes, I suppose.

First Officer. Ha, ha! Ever facetious, general.

Second Officer. [*to* Third]. The general is sore upon this point; you will only chafe him. —Any commands, general?

Damas. None. Good day to you.   [*Exeunt* Second *and* Third Officers.

Damas. Our comrades are very inquisitive. Poor Morier is the subject of a vast deal of curiosity.

First Officer. Say interest, rather, general. His constant melancholy, the loneliness of his habits,—his daring valor, his brilliant rise in the profession,—your friendship, and the favors of the commander-in-chief,—all tend to make him as much the matter of gossip as of admiration. But where is he, general? I have missed him all the morning.

Damas. Why, captain, I'll let you into a secret. My young friend has come with me to Lyons in hopes of finding a miracle.

First Officer. A miracle!

Damas. Yes, a miracle! in other words,—a constant woman.

First Officer. Oh! an affair of love!

Damas. Exactly so. No sooner did he enter Lyons than he waved his hand to me, threw himself from his horse, and is now, I warrant, asking every one who can know anything about the matter, whether a certain lady is still true to a certain gentleman!

First Officer. Success to him! and of that success there can be no doubt. The gallant Colonel Morier, the hero of Lodi, might make his choice out of the proudest families in France.

Damas. Oh, if pride be a recommendation, the lady and her mother are most handsomely endowed. By the way, captain, if you should chance to meet with Morier, tell him he will find me at the hotel.

First Officer. I will, general.   [*Exit.*

Damas. Now will I go to the Deschappelles, and make a report to my young Colonel. Ha! by Mars, Bacchus, Apollo, Virorum,—here comes Monsieur Beauseant!

Enter BEAUSEANT.

Good morrow, Monsieur Beauseant! How fares it with you?

Beau. [*aside*]. Damas! that is unfortunate;—if the Italian campaign should have filled his pockets, he may seek to baffle me in the moment of my victory. [*Aloud.*] Your servant, general,—for such, I think, is your new distinction! Just arrived in Lyons?

Damas. Not an hour ago. Well, how go on the Deschappelles? Have they forgiven you in that affair of young Melnotte? You had some hand in that notable device,—eh?

Beau. Why, less than you think for! The fellow imposed upon me. I have set it all right now. What has become of him? He could not have joined the army, after all. There is no such name in the books.

Damas. I know nothing about Melnotte. As you say, I never heard the name in the Grand Army.

Beau. Hem!—You are not married, general?

Damas. Do I look like a married man, sir?—No, thank Heaven! My profession is to make widows, not wives.

Beau. You must have gained much booty in Italy! Pauline will be your heiress—eh?

Damas. Booty! Not I! Heiress to what? Two trunks and a portmanteau,—four horses,—three swords,—two suits of regimentals, and six pair of white leather inexpressibles! A pretty fortune for a young lady!

Beau. [*aside*]. Then all is safe! [*Aloud*]. Ha! ha! Is that really all your capital, General Damas? Why, I thought Italy had been a second Mexico to you soldiers.

Damas. All a toss-up, sir. I was not one of the lucky ones! My friend Morier, indeed, saved something handsome. But our commander-in-chief took care of him, and Morier is a thrifty, economical dog,—not like the rest of us soldiers, who spend our money as carelessly as if it were our blood.

Beau. Well, it is no matter! I do not want fortune with Pauline. And you must know, General Damas, that your fair cousin has at length consented to reward my long and ardent attachment.

Damas. You!—the devil! Why, she is already married! There is no divorce!

Beau. True; but this very day she is formally to authorize the necessary proceedings,—this very day she is to sign the contract that is to make her mine within one week from the day on which her present illegal marriage is annulled.

Damas. You tell me wonders!—Wonders! No; I believe anything of women!

Beau. I must wish you good morning. [*As he is going, enter* DESCHAPPELLES.

M. Deschap. Oh, Beauseant! well met. Let us come to the notary at once.

Damas [*to Deschap.*]. Why, cousin!

M. Deschap. Damas, welcome to Lyons. Pray call on us; my wife will be delighted to see you.

Damas. Your wife be—blessed for her condescension! But [*taking him aside*] what do I hear? Is it possible that your daughter has consented to a divorce?—that she will marry Monsieur Beauseant?

M. Deschap. Certainly. What have you to say against it? A gentleman of birth, fortune, character. We are not so proud as we were; even my wife has had enough of nobility and princes!

Damas. But Pauline loved that young man so tenderly!

M. Deschap. [*taking snuff*]. That was two years and a half ago!

Damas. Very true. Poor Melnotte!

M. Deschap. But do not talk of that impostor; I hope he is dead or has left the country. Nay, even were he in Lyons at this moment, he ought to rejoice that, in an honorable and suitable alliance, my daughter may forget her sufferings and his crime.

Damas. Nay, if it be all settled, I have no more to say. Monsieur Beauseant informs me that the contract is to be signed this very day.

M. Deschap. It is; at one o'clock precisely. Will you be one of the witnesses?

Damas. I?—No; that is to say—yes, certainly!—at one o'clock I will wait on you.

M. Deschap. Till then, adieu—come Beauseant.

[*Exeunt* BEAUSEANT *and* DESCHAPELLES.

Damas. The man who sets his heart upon a woman
Is a chameleon, and doth feed on air;
From air he takes his colors—holds his life,—
Changes with every wind,—grows lean or fat,
Rosy with hope, or green with jealousy,
Or pallid with despair—just as the gale
Varies from North to South—from heat to cold!
Oh, woman! woman! thou shouldst have few sins
Of thine own to answer for! Thou art the author
Of such a book of follies in a man,
That it would need the tears of all the angels
To blot the record out!

Enter MELNOTTE, *pale and agitated.*

I need not tell thee ! Thou hast heard—
    Mel.   The worst !
I have !
    Damas. Be cheer'd; others are fair as she is !
    Mel. Others ! The world is crumbled at my feet !
She *was* my world; fill'd up the whole of being—
Smiled in the sunshine—walk'd the glorious earth—
Sate in my heart—was the sweet life of life.
The Past was hers; I dreamt not of a Future
That did not wear her shape ! Mem'ry and Hope
Alike are gone. Pauline is faithless ! Henceforth
The universal space is desolate !
    Damas.   Hope yet.
    Mel.   Hope, yes !—one hope is left me still—
A soldier's grave ! Glory has died with love.
I look into my heart, and, where I saw
Pauline, see Death !
[*After a pause*].—But am I not deceived ?
I went but by the rumor of the town;
Rumor is false,—I was too hasty ! Damas,
Whom hast thou seen ?
    Damas.   Thy rival and her father.
Arm thyself for the truth.—He heeds not—
    Mel.   She
Will never know how deeply she was loved !
The charitable night, that wont to bring
Comfort to-day, in bright and eloquent dreams,
Is henceforth leagued with misery ! Sleep, farewell,
Or else become eternal ! Oh, the waking
From false oblivion, and to see the sun,
And know she is another's !——
    Damas.   Be a man !
    Mel. I am a man !—it is the sting of woe
Like mine that tells us we are men !
    Damas.   The false one
Did not deserve thee.
    Mel.   Hush !—No word against her !
Why should she keep, through years and silent absence,
The holy tablets of her virgin faith
True to a traitor's name ! Oh, blame her not;
It were a sharper grief to think her worthless
Than to be what I am ! To-day,—to-day !
They said "To-day !" This day, so wildly welcomed—
This day, my soul had singled out of time
And mark'd for bliss ! This day ! oh, could I see her,
See her once more unknown; but hear her voice.
So that one echo of its music might
Make ruin less appalling in its silence.
    Damas. Easily done ! Come with me to her house;
Your dress—your cloak—moustache—the bronzed hues
Of time and toil—the name you bear—belief
In your absence, all will ward away suspicion.

Keep in the shade. Ay, I would have you come.
There may be hope? Pauline is yet so young,
They may have forced her to these second bridals
Out of mistaken love.
    Mel.   No, bid me hope not!
Bid me not hope! I could not bear again
To fall from such a heaven! One gleam of sunshine,
And the ice breaks and I am lost! Oh, Damas,
There's no such thing as courage in a man;
The veriest slave that ever crawl'd from danger
Might spurn me now. When first I lost her, Damas,
I bore it, did I not? I still had hope,
And now I—I——   [*Bursts into an agony of grief.*
    Damas.   What, comrade! all the women
That ever smiled destruction on brave hearts
Were not worth tears like these!
    Mel.   'Tis past—forget it.
I am prepared; life has no further ills!
The cloud has broken in that stormy rain,
And on the waste I stand, alone with Heaven.
    Damas. His very face is changed; a breaking heart
Does its work soon!—Come, Melnotte, rouse thyself:
One effort more. Again thou'lt see her.
    Mel.   See her!
There is a passion in that simple sentence
That shivers all the pride and power of reason
Into a chaos!
    Damas.   Time wanes;—come, ere yet
It be too late.
    Mel.   Terrible words—"*Too late!*"
Lead on. One last look more, and then——
    Damas.   Forget her!
    Mel. Forget her! yes—For death remembers not.   [*Exeunt.*

SCENE II.

A room in the house of Monsieur Deschappelles; Pauline *seated in great dejection.*

    Pauline. It is so, then. I must be false to Love,
Or sacrifice a father! Oh, my Claude,
My lover, and my husband! Have I lived
To pray that thou mayest find some fairer boon
Than the deep faith of this devoted heart,—
Nourish'd till now—now broken?

                     Enter Monsieur Deschappelles.

    M. Deschap.   My dear child,
How shall I thank—how bless thee? Thou hast saved,

I will not say my fortune—I could bear
Reverse, and shrink not—but that prouder wealth
Which merchants value most—my name, my credit—
The hard-won honors of a toilsome life:—
These thou hast saved, my child!

Pauline.   Is there no hope?
No hope but this?

M. Deschap. None. If, without the sum
Which Beauseant offers for thy hand, this day
Sinks to the west—to-morrow brings our ruin!
And hundreds, mingled in that ruin, curse
The bankrupt merchant! and the insolvent herd
We feasted and made merry cry in scorn,
"How pride has fallen!—Lo, the bankrupt merchant!"
My daughter, thou hast saved us!

Pauline.   And am lost!

M. Deschap. Come, let me hope that Beauseant's love—
Pauline.   His love!
Talk not of love. Love has no thought of self!
Love buys not with the ruthless usurer's gold
The loathsome prostitution of a hand
Without a heart? Love sacrifices all things
To bless the thing it loves! *He* knows not love.
Father, his love is hate—his hope revenge!
My tears, my anguish, my remorse for falsehood—
These are the joys that he wrings from our despair!

M. Deschap. If thou deem'st thus, reject him! Shame and ruin
Were better than thy misery;—think no more on't.
My sand is wellnigh run—what boots it when
The glass is broken? We'll annul the contract:
And if to-morrow in the prisoner's cell
These aged limbs are laid, why still, my child,
I'll think thou art spared; and wait the Liberal Hour
That lays the beggar by the side of kings!

Pauline. No—no—forgive me! You, my honor'd father,—
You, who so loved, so cherish'd me, whose lips
Never knew one harsh werd! I'm not ungrateful;
I am but human!—hush! *Now,* call the bridegroom—
You see I am prepared—no tears—all calm;
But, father, *talk no more of love!*

M. Deschap.   My child,
'Tis but one struggle; he is young, rich, noble;
Thy state will rank first 'mid the dames of Lyons;
And when this heart can shelter thee no more,
Thy youth will not be guardianless.

Pauline.   I have set
My foot upon the ploughshare—I will pass
The fiery ordeal. [*Aside.*] Merciful Heaven, support me!
And on the absent wanderer shed the light
Of happier stars—lost evermore to me!

Enter MADAME DESCHAPPELLES, BEAUSEANT, GLAVIS, *and* NOTARY.

Mme. Deschap. Why, Pauline, you are quite in *déshabille*—you ought to be more alive to the importance of this joyful occasion. We had once looked higher, it is true; but you see, after all, Monsieur Beauseant's father *was* a Marquis, and that's a great comfort. Pedigree and jointure!—you have them both in Monsieur Beauseant. A young lady decorously brought up should only have two considerations in her choice of a husband; first, is his birth honorable? secondly, will his death be advantageous? All other trifling details should be left to parental anxiety.

Beau. [*approaching and waving aside Madame*]. Ah, Pauline! let me hope that you are reconciled to an event which confers such rapture upon me.

Pauline. I am reconciled to my doom.

Beau. Doom is a harsh word, sweet lady.

Pauline [*aside*]. This man must have some mercy—his heart cannot be marble. [*Aloud.*] Oh, sir, be just—be generous! Seize a noble triumph—a great revenge! Save the father, and spare the child.

Beau. [*aside*]. Joy—joy alike to my hatred and my passion! The haughty Pauline is at last my suppliant. [*Aloud.*] You ask from me what I have not the sublime virtue to grant—a virtue reserved only for the gardener's son! I cannot forego my hopes in the moment of their fulfilment! I adhere to the contract—your father's ruin or your hand.

Pauline. Then all is over. Sir, I have decided.

[*The clock strikes one.*

Enter DAMAS *and* MELNOTTE.

Damas. Your servant, cousin Deschappelles. Let me introduce Colonel Morier.

Mme. Deschap. [*curtsying very low*]. What, the celebrated hero? This is, indeed, an honor! [MELNOTTE *bows, and remains in the background.*

Damas [*to Pauline*]. My little cousin, I congratulate you. What, no smile—no blush? You are going to be divorced from poor Melnotte, and marry this rich gentleman. You ought to be excessively happy!

Pauline. Happy!

Damas. Why, how pale you are, child!—Poor Pauline! Hist—confide in me! Do they force you to this?

Pauline. No!

Damas. You act with your own free consent?

Pauline. My own consent—yes.

Damas. Then you are the most—I will not say what you are.

Pauline. You think ill of me—be it so—yet if you knew all——

Damas. There is some mystery—speak out, Pauline.

Pauline [*suddenly*]. Oh, perhaps you can save me! you are our relation—our friend. My father is on the verge of bankruptcy—this day he requires a large sum to meet demands that cannot be denied; that sum Beauseant will advance—this hand the condition of the barter. Save me if you have the means—save me! You will be repaid above!

Damas. [*aside*]. I recant—Women are not so bad after all! [*Aloud.*] Humph, child! I cannot help you—I am too poor.

Pauline. The last plank to which I clung is shivered.

Damas. Hold—you see my friend Morier: Melnotte is his most intimate friend—fought in the same fields—slept in the same tent. Have you any message to send to Melnotte? any word to soften this blow?

Pauline. He knows Melnotte—he will see him—he will bear to him my last farewell— [*approaches* MELNOTTE]—He has a stern air—he turns away from me—he despises me!—Sir one word I beseech you.

Mel. Her voice again! How the old time comes o'er me!

Damas [to Madame.] Don't interrupt them. He is going to tell her what a rascal young Melnotte is; he knows him well, I promise you.

Mme. Deschap. So considerate in you, cousin Damas!

[DAMAS *approaches* DESCHAPPELLES; *converses apart with him in dumb show—*DESCHAPPELLES *shows him a paper, which he inspects and takes.*

Pauline. Thrice have I sought to speak; my courage fails me.—
Sir, is it true that you have known—nay, are
The friend of—Melnotte?

Mel.   Lady, yes!—Myself
And misery know the man!

Pauline.   And you will see him,
And you will bear to him—ay—word for word,
All that this heart, which breaks in parting from him,
Would send, ere still for ever?

Mel.   He hath told me
You have the right to choose from out the world
A worthier bridegroom;—he forgoes all claim,
Even to murmur at his doom. Speak on!

Pauline. Tell him, for years I never nursed a thought
That was not his;—that on his wandering way,
Daily and nightly, pour'd a mourner's prayers.
Tell him ev'n now that I would rather share
His lowliest lot,—walk by his side, an outcast,—
Work for him, beg with him,—live upon the light
Of one kind smile from him,—than wear the crown
The Bourbon lost!

Mel. [aside].   Am I already mad?
And does delirium utter such sweet words
Into a dreamer's ear? *[Aloud].* You love him thus,
And yet desert him?

Pauline.   Say, that, if his eye
Could read this heart,—its struggles, its temptations,—
His love itself would pardon that desertion!
Look on that poor old man,—he is my father;
He stands upon the verge of an abyss!—
He calls his child to save him! Shall I shrink
From him who gave me birth?—withhold my hand,
And see a parent perish? Tell him this,
And say—that we shall meet again in Heaven!

Mel. Lady—I—I—what is this riddle?—what
The nature of this sacrifice?

Pauline [*pointing to* DAMAS]. Go, ask him!

Beau. [*from the table*]. The papers are prepared—we only need
Your hand and seal.

Mel.   Stay, lady—one word more.
Were but your duty with your faith united,
Would you still share the low-born peasant's lot?

Pauline. Would I? Ah, better death with him I love
Than all the pomp—which is but as the flowers
That crown the victim!—*[Turning away.]* I am ready.

[MELNOTTE *rushes to* DAMAS.

Damas.   There—
This is the schedule—this the total.

Mel. Peace, old man!
I have a prior claim. Before the face
Of man and Heaven I urge it; I outbid
Yon sordid huckster for your priceless jewel, etc.
—*Lady of Lyons, Act V., Sc. 2.*

SCENE II.] *THE LADY OF LYONS.* 105

  Beau. [*to* DESCHAPPELLES, *showing notes*]. These
Are yours the instant she has sign'd; you are
Still the great House of Lyons!
   [*The* Notary *is about to hand the contract to* PAULINE, *when* MELNOTTE *seizes
    it and tears it.*
  Beau.   Are you mad?
  M. Deschap. How, sir! What means this insult?
  Mel.   Peace, old man!
I have a prior claim. Before the face
Of man and Heaven I urge it; I outbid
Yon sordid huckster for your priceless jewel. [*Giving a pocket-book.*
There is the sum twice told! Blush not to take it:
There's not a coin that is not bought and hallow'd
In the cause of nations with a soldier's blood!
  Beau. Torments and death!
  Pauline.   That voice! Thou art—
  Mel.   Thy husband!
          [PAULINE *rushes into his arms.*
Look up! Look up, Pauline!—for I can bear
Thine eyes! The stain is blotted from my name.
I have redeem'd mine honor. I can call
On France to sanction thy divine forgiveness!
Oh, joy!—Oh, rapture! By the midnight watchfires
Thus have I seen thee! thus foretold this hour!
And 'midst the roar of battle, thus have heard
The beating of thy heart against my own!
  Beau. Fool'd, duped, and triumph'd over in the hour
Of mine own victory! Curses on ye both!
May thorns be planted in the marriage-bed!
And love grow sour'd and blacken'd into hate
Such as the hate that gnaws me!
  Damas.   Curse away
And let me tell thee, Beauseant, a wise proverb
The Arabs have,—" Curses are like young chickens,
[*Solemnly.*] And still come home to roost!"
  Beau.   Their happiness
Maddens my soul! I am powerless and revengeless! [*To* MADAME.
I wish you joy! Ha! ha! the gardener's son!   [*Exit.*
  Damas [*to* GLAVIS]. Your friend intends to hang himself! Methinks
You ought to be his travelling companion!
  Gla. Sir, you are exceedingly obliging!   [*Exit.*
  Pauline.   Oh
My father, you are saved,—and by my husband!
Ah, blessed hour!
  Mel.   Yet you weep still, Pauline.
  Pauline. But on thy breast!—*these* tears are sweet and holy!
  M. Deschap. You have won love and honor nobly, sir!
Take her;—be happy both!
  Mme. Deschap.   I'm all astonish'd!
Who, then, is Colonel Morier?
  Damas.   You behold him!
  Mel. Morier no more after this happy day!
I would not bear again my father's name

Till I could deem it spotless ! The hour's come !
Heaven smiled on conscience ! As the soldier rose
From rank to rank, how sacred was the fame
That cancell'd crime, and raised him nearer thee !

  Mme. Deschap. A Colonel and a hero ! Well, that's something !
He's wondrously improved ! I wish you joy, sir !

  Mel. Ah ! the same love that tempts us into sin,
If it be true love, works out its redemption;
And he who seeks repentance for the Past
Should woo the Angel Virtue in the Future.

RICHELIEU;

OR,

THE CONSPIRACY.

"Le Comte de Soissons, et le Duc de Bouillon, avaient une bonne armée, et ils savaient la conduire; et pour plus grande sûreté, tandis que cette armée devait s'avancer, on devait, assassiner le Cardinal et faire soulever Paris. . . Les Conjurés faisaient un traité avec l'Espagne pour introduire des troupes en France, et pour y mettre tout en confusion dans une Régence qu'on croyait prochaine, et dont chacun espérait profiter. . . Richelieu avait perdu toute sa faveur, et ne conservait que l'avantage d'être nécessaire. Le bonheur du Cardinal voulut encore que le complot fut découvert, et qu'une copie du traité lui tombât entre les mains."—*Voltaire, Hist. Gen*

PREFACE.

The administration of Cardinal Richelieu, whom (despite all his darker qualities) Voltaire and history justly consider the true architect of the French monarchy, and the great parent of French civilization, is characterized by features alike tragic and comic. A weak king—an ambitious favorite; a despicable conspiracy against the minister, nearly always associated with a dangerous treason against the State—these, with little variety of names and dates, constitute the eventful cycle through which, with a dazzling ease, and an arrogant confidence, the great luminary fulfilled its destinies. Blent together, in startling contrast, we see the grandest achievements and the pettiest agents;—the spy—the mistress—the capuchin;—the destruction of feudalism;—the humiliation of Austria;—the dismemberment of Spain.

Richelieu himself is still what he was in his own day—a man of two characters. If, on the one hand, he is justly represented as inflexible and vindictive, crafty and unscrupulous; so, on the other, it cannot be denied that he was placed in times in which the long impunity of every licence required stern examples—that he was beset by perils and intrigues, which gave a certain excuse to the subtlest inventions of self-defence—that his ambition was inseparably connected with a passionate love for the glory of his country—and that, if he was her dictator, he was not less her benefactor. It has been fairly remarked, by the most impartial historians, that he was no less generous to merit than severe to crime—that, in the various departments of the State, the Army, and the Church, he selected and distinguished the ablest aspirants—that the wars which he conducted were, for the most part, essential to the preservation of France, and Europe itself, from the formidable enroachments of the Austrian House—that, in spite of those wars, the people were not oppressed with exorbitant imposts—and that he left the kingdom he had governed in a more flourishing and vigorous state than at any former period of the French history, or at the decease of Louis XIV.

The cabals formed against this great statesman were not carried on by the patriotism of public virtue, or the emulation of equal talent: they were but court struggles, in which the most worthless agents had recourse to the most desperate means. In each, as I have before observed, we see combined the twofold attempt to murder the minister, and to betray the country. Such, then, are the agents, and such the designs with which truth, in the drama as in history, requires us to contrast the celebrated Cardinal;—not disguising his foibles or his vices, but not unjust to the grander qualities (especially the love of country), by which they were often dignified, and, at times, redeemed.

The historical drama is the concentration of historical events. In the attempt to place upon the stage the picture of an era, that licence with dates and details, which Poetry permits, and which the highest authorities in the Drama of France herself have sanctioned, has been, though not unsparingly, indulged. The conspiracy of the Duc de Bouillon is, for instance, amalgamated with the *dénouement* of *The Day of Dupes;* * and circumstances connected with the treason of Cinq Mars (whose brilliant youth and gloomy catastrophe tend to subvert poetic and historic justice, by seducing us to forget his base ingratitude and his perfidious apostasy)

---

* " Le Cardinalse croit perdu, et prépare sa retraite. Ses amis lui conseillent de tenter enfin auprès du Roi un nouvel effort. Le Cardinal va trouver le Roi à Versailles. Le Roi, qui avait sacrifié son ministre par faiblesse, se remit par faiblesse entre ses mains, et il lui abandonne ceux qui l'avaient perdu. Ce jour qui est encore à present appellé La Journée des Dupes, fut celui du pouvoir absolu du Cardinal."—*Voltaire, Hist. Gen.*

are identified with the fate of the earlier favorite Baradas,* whose sudden rise and as sudden fall passed into a proverb. I ought to add, that the noble romance of "Cinq Mars" suggested one of the scenes in the fifth act; and that for the conception of some portion of the intrigue connected with De Mauprat and Julie, I am, with great alterations of incident, and considerable if not entire reconstruction of character, indebted to an early and admirable novel by the author of "Picciola."†

LONDON, *March*, 1839.

NOTE.

THE length of the play necessarily requires curtailments on the stage—the principal of which are enclosed within brackets. Many of the passages thus omitted, however immaterial to the audience, must obviously be such as the *reader* would be least inclined to dispense with—viz., those which, without being absolutely essential to the business of the stage, contain either the subtler strokes of character, or the more poetical embellishments of description. An important consequence of these suppressions is, that Richelieu himself is left, too often and too unrelievedly, to positions which place him in an *amiable* light, without that shadowing forth of his more sinister motives and his fiercer qualities, which is attempted in the written play. Thus, the *character* takes a degree of credit due only to the *situation*. To judge the author's conception of Richelieu fairly, and to estimate how far it is consistent with historical portraiture, the play must be *read*.

* " En six mois il (le Roi) fit (Baradas) premier Ecuyer, premier Gentil-homme de la Chambre, Capitaine de St. Germain, et Lieutenant de Roi, en Champagne. En moins de temps encore, on lui ôta tout, et des débris de sa grandeur, à peine lui resta-t-il de quoi payer ses dettes: de sorte que pour signifier une grande fortune dissipée aussi qu'acquise on disait en commun proverbe, Fortune de Baradas."—*Anquetil*.

† It may be as well, however, to caution the English reader against some of the impressions which the eloquence of both the writers I refer to are calculated to leave. They have exaggerated the more evil, and have kept out of sight the nobler qualities of the Cardinal.

TO

THE MARQUIS OF LANSDOWNE, K.G.,
ETC., ETC.,

THIS DRAMA

IS INSCRIBED

IN TRIBUTE TO THE TALENTS WHICH COMMAND, AND THE
QUALITIES WHICH ENDEAR, RESPECT.

DRAMATIS PERSONÆ.

LOUIS THE THIRTEENTH	MR. ELTON.
GASTON, DUKE OF ORLEANS, *brother to Louis XIII.*	MR. DIDDEAR.
BARADAS, *favorite of the King, First Gentleman of the Chamber, Premier Ecuyer, etc.*	MR. WARDE.
CARDINAL RICHELIEU	MR. MACREADY.
THE CHEVALIER DE MAUPRAT	MR. ANDERSON.
THE SIEUR DE BERINGHEN, *in attendance on the King,* one of the Conspirators	MR. VINING.
JOSEPH, *a Capuchin, Richelieu's confidant*	MR. PHELPS.
HUGUET, *an officer of Richelieu's household guard — a Spy*	MR. G. BENNETT.
FRANÇOIS, *First Page to Richelieu*	MR. HOWE.
FIRST COURTIER	MR. C. J. SMITH.
CAPTAIN OF THE ARCHERS	MR. T. MATHEWS.
FIRST SECRETARY OF STATE	MR. TILBURY.
SECOND SECRETARY OF STATE	MR. YARNOLD.
THIRD SECRETARY OF STATE	MR. W. H. PAYNE.
GOVERNOR OF THE BASTILE	MR. WALDRON.

Courtiers, Pages, Conspirators, Officers, Soldiers, etc.

JULIE DE MORTEMAR, *an Orphan, ward to Richelieu*	MISS HELEN FAUCIT.
MARIAN DE LORME, *Mistress to Orleans, but in Richelieu's pay*	MISS CHARLES.
PAGE TO BARADAS	MISS E. PHILLIPS.

* Properly speaking, the King's First Valet de Chambre—a post of great importance at that time.

First performed on Thursday, the 7th of March, 1839, at Covent Garden Theatre.

THE GREAT LORD CARDINAL.

RICHELIEU;

OR,

THE CONSPIRACY.

ACT I.

FIRST DAY.

SCENE I.—*A room in the house of* MARION DE LORME; *a table towards the front of the stage (with wine, fruits, etc.) at which are seated* BARADAS, *Four Courtiers, splendidly drest in the costume of* 1641-2;—*the* DUKE OF ORLEANS *reclining on a large fauteuil;*—MARION DE LORME *standing at the back of his chair, offers him a goblet, and then retires. At another table,* DE BERINGHEN, DE MAUPRAT, *playing at dice; other* Courtiers, *of inferior rank to those at the table of the* Duke, *looking on.*

Orle. [*drinking*]. Here's to our enterprise!
Bar. [*glancing at* MARION]. Hush, sir!
Orle. [*aside*]. Nay, Count,
You may trust her; she doats on me; no house
So safe as Marion's. *[At our statelier homes
The very walls do play the eaves-dropper.
There's not a sunbeam creeping o'er our floors
But seems a glance from that malignant eye
Which reigns o'er France; our fatal greatness lives
In the sharp glare of one relentless day.
But Richelieu's self forgets to fear the sword
The myrtle hides; and Marion's silken robe
Casts its kind charity o'er fiercer sins
Than those which haunt the rosy path between
The lip and eye of beauty.—Oh, no house
So safe as Marion's.]
Bar. Still, we have a secret,
And oil and water—woman and a secret—
Are hostile properties.
Orle. Well—Marion, see
How the play prospers yonder.
[MARION *goes to the next table, looks on for a few moments, then exit.*
Bar. [*producing a parchment*]. I have now
All the conditions drawn; it only needs
Our signatures: upon receipt of this,
(Whereto is join'd the schedule of our treaty
With the Count-Duke,† the Richelieu of the Escurial,)
Bouillon will join his army with the Spaniard,
March on to Paris,—there, dethrone the King:

---

* The passages enclosed in brackets are omitted in representation.   † Olivares, Minister of Spain.

You will be Regent; I, and ye, my Lords,
Form the new Council. So much for the core
Of our great scheme.
  Orle.   But Richelieu is an Argus;
One of his hundred eyes will light upon us,
And then—good-bye to life.
  Bar.   To gain the prize
We must destroy the Argus:—ay, my Lords,
The scroll the core, but blood must fill the veins,
Of our design;—while this despatch'd to Bouillon,
Richelieu despatch'd to heaven!—The last *my* charge,
Meet here to-morrow night. *You*, sir, as first
In honor and in hope, meanwhile select
Some trusty knave to bear the scroll to Bouillon;
Midst Richelieu's foes *I'll* find some desperate hand
To strike for vengeance, while we stride to power.
  Orle. So be it;—to-morrow, midnight. Come, my Lords.
    [*Exeunt* ORLEANS, *and the* Courtiers *in his train. Those at the other table rise, salute* ORLEANS, *and reseat themselves.*
  De Ber. Double the stakes.
  De Mau.   . Done.
  De Ber.   Bravo; faith, it shames me
To bleed a purse already *in extremis*.
  De Mau. Nay, as you've had the patient to yourself
So long, no other doctor should despatch it. [DE MAUPRAT *throws and loses.*
  Omnes. Lost! Ha, ha!—poor De Mauprat!
  De Ber.   One throw more?
  De Mau. No; I am bankrupt [*pushing gold*]. There goes all—except
My honor and my sword.   [*They rise.*
  De Ber.   Long cloaks and honor
Went out of vogue together, when we found
We got on much more rapidly without them;
The sword, indeed, is never out of fashion,—
The devil has care of *that*.
  First Gamester. Ay, take the sword
To Cardinal Richelieu:—he gives gold for steel,
When worn by brave men.
  De Mau. Richelieu!
  De Ber. [*to* BARADAS]. At that name
He changes color, bites his nether lip.
Ev'n in his brightest moments whisper "Richelieu,"
And you cloud all his sunshine.
  Bar.   I have mark'd it,
And I will learn the wherefore.
  De Mau. The Egyptian
Dissolved her richest jewel in a draught:
Would I could so melt time and all its treasures,
And drain it thus.   [*Drinking.*
  De Ber. Come, gentlemen, what say ye,
A walk on the parade?
  Omnes. Ay; come, De Mauprat.
  De Mau. Pardon me; we shall meet again ere nightfall.
  Bar. I'll stay and comfort Mauprat.

De Ber.   Comfort!—when
We gallant fellows have run out a friend,
There's nothing left—except to run him through!
There's the last act of friendship.
    De Mau.   Let me keep
That favor in reserve; in all beside
Your most obedient servant.
        [*Exeunt* DE BERINGHEN, *etc. Mannet* DE MAUPRAT *and* BARADAS.
    Bar.   You have lost—
You are not sad.
    De Mau.   Sad!—Life and gold have wings,
And must fly one day; open, then, their cages
And wish them merry.
    Bar.   You're a strange enigma:—
Fiery in war—and yet to glory lukewarm;
All mirth in action—in repose all gloom—
These are extremes in which the unconscious heart
Betrays the fever of deep-fix'd disease.
Confide in me! our young days roll'd together
In the same river, glassing the same stars
That smile i' the heaven of hope;—alike we made
Bright-wingèd steeds of our unform'd chimeras,
Spurring the fancies upward to the air,
Wherein we shaped fair castles from the cloud.
Fortune of late has sever'd us—and led
Me to the rank of Courtier, Count and Favorite,—
You to the titles of the wildest gallant
And bravest knight in France;—are you content?
No;—trust in me—some gloomy secret——
    De Mau.   Ay:—
A secret that doth haunt me, as, of old,
Men were possess'd of fiends!—where'er I turn,
The grave yawns dark before me!—I *will* trust you;—
Hating the Cardinal, and beguiled by Orleans,
You know I join'd the Languedoc revolt—
Was captured—sent to the Bastile——
    Bar.   But shared
The general pardon, which the Duke of Orleans
Won for himself and all in the revolt,
Who but obey'd his orders.
    De Mau.   Note the phrase;—
"*Obey'd his orders.*" Well, when on my way
To join the duke in Languedoc, I (then
The down upon my lip—less man than boy)
Leading young valors—reckless as myself,
Seized on the town of Faviaux, and displaced
The royal banners for the rebel. Orleans
(Never too daring), when I reach'd the camp,
Blamed me for acting—mark—*without his orders;*
Upon this quibble Richelieu razed my name
Out of the general pardon.
    Bar.   Yet released you
From the Bastile——

De Mau. To call me to his presence,
And thus address me:—" You have seized a town
Of France, without the orders of your leader,
And for this treason, but one sentence—DEATH."
    Bar. Death !
    De Mau. " I have pity on your youth and birth,
Nor wish to glut the headsman;—join your troop,
Now on the march against the Spaniards;—change
The traitor's scaffold for the soldier's grave;
Your memory stainless—they who shared your crime
Exiled or dead—your king shall never learn it."
    Bar. O tender pity !—O most charming prospect !
Blown into atoms by a bomb, or drill'd
Into a cullender by gunshot !—Well ?—
    De Mau. You have heard if I fought bravely.—Death became
Desired as Daphne by the eager Daygod.
Like him I chased the nymph—to grasp the laurel !
I could not die !
    Bar. Poor fellow !
    De Mau. When the Cardinal
Review'd the troops—his eye met mine;—he frown'd,
Summon'd me forth—" How's this !" quoth he; " you have shunn'd
The sword—beware the axe !—'twill fall one day !"
He left me thus—we were recall'd to Paris,
And—you know all !
    Bar. And, knowing this, why halt you,
Spell'd by the rattle-snake,—while in the breasts
Of your firm friends beat hearts, that vow the death
Of your grim tyrant ?—Wake !—Be one of us;
The time invites—the king detests the Cardinal,
Dares not disgrace—but groans to be deliver'd
Of that too great a subject—join your friends,
Free France, and save yourself.
    De Mau. Hush ! Richelieu bears
A charmèd life;—to all, who have braved his power,
One common end—the block.
    Bar. Nay, if he live,
The block your doom;—
    De Mau. Better the victim, Count,
Than the assassin.—France requires a Richelieu,
But does not need a Mauprat. Truce to this;—
All time one midnight, where my thoughts are spectres.
What to my fame ?—What love ?—
    Bar. Yet dost thou love *not ?*
    De Mau. Love ?—I am young——
    Bar. And Julie fair ! [*Aside.*] it is so,
Upon the margin of the grave—his hand
Would pluck the rose that I would win and wear !
[*Aloud.*] [Thou lov'st—
    De Mau. Who, lonely in the midnight tent,
Gazed on the watch-fires in the sleepless air,
Nor chose one star amidst the clustering hosts
To bless it in the name of some fair face

Set in his spirit, as that star in Heaven ?
For our divine affections, like the spheres,
Move over, ever musical.
  Bar.   You speak
As one who fed on poetry.
  De Mau.   Why, man,
The thoughts of lovers stir with poetry
As leaves with summer-wind.—The heart that loves
Dwells in an Eden, hearing angel-lutes,
As Eve in the First Garden. Hast thou seen
My Julie, and not felt it henceforth dull
To live in the common world—and talk in words
That clothe the feelings of the frigid herd ?
Upon the perfumed pillow of her lips—
As on his native bed of roses flushed
With Paphian skies—Love smiling sleeps:—Her voice
The blest interpreter of thoughts as pure
As virgin wells where Dian takes delight,
Or fairies dip their changelings !—In the maze
Of her harmonious beauties—Modesty
(Like some severer grace that leads the choir
Of her sweet sisters) every airy motion
Attunes to such chaste charm, that Passion holds
His burning breath, and will not with a sigh
Dissolve the spell that binds him !—Oh those eyes
That woo the earth—shadowing more soul than lurks
Under the lids of Psyche !—Go !—thy lip
Curls at the purfled phrases of a lover—
Love thou, and if thy love be deep as mine,
Thou wilt not laugh at poets.
  Bar. [*aside*].   With each word
Thou wak'st a jealous demon in my heart,
And my hand clutches at my hilt.—
  De Mau. [*gaily*].   No more !—
I love !—Your breast holds both my secrets !—Never
Unbury either !—Come, while yet we may,
We'll bask us in the noon of rosy life:—
Lounge through the gardens,—flaunt it in the taverns,—
Laugh,—game,—drink,—feast:—If so confined my days,
Faith, I'll enclose the knights.—Pshaw ! not so grave;
I'm a true Frenchman !—*Vive la bagetelle !*
      [*As they are going out, enter* HUGUET *ana four* Arquebusiers.
  Hug. Messire De Mauprat,—I arrest you !—Follow
To the Lord Cardinal.
  De Mau.   You see, my friend,
I'm out of my suspense !—the tiger's play'd
Long enough with his prey.—Farewell !—Hereafter
Say, when men name me, " Adrien de Mauprat
Lived without hope, and perish'd without fear !"
         [*Exeunt* DE MAUPRAT, HUGUET, *etc.*
  Bar. Farewell !—I trust forever ! I design'd thee
For Richelieu's murderer——but, as well his martyr !
In childhood you the stronger—and I cursed you;

In youth the fairer—and I cursed you still;
And now my rival!—While the name of Julie
Hung on thy lips—I smiled—for then I saw,
In my my mind's eye, the cold and grinning Death
Hang o'er thy head the pall!—Ambition, Love,
Ye twin-born stars of daring destinies,
Sit in my house of Life!—By the king's aid
I will be Julie's husband—in despite
Of My Lord Cardinal!—by the king's aid
I will be minister of France—in spite
Of my Lord Cardinal!—And then—what then?
The king loves Julie—feeble prince—false master—
[*Producing and gazing on the parchment.*
Then, by the aid of Bouillon, and the Spaniard,
I will dethrone the king; and all—ha!—ha!—
All, in despite of my Lord Cardinal! [*Exit.*

SCENE II.

A room in the Palais Cardinal, the walls hung with arras. A large screen in one corner. A table covered with books, papers, etc. A rude clock in a recess. Busts, statues, book-cases, weapons of different periods and banners suspended over RICHELIEU'S *chair.*

RICHELIEU *and* JOSEPH.

Rich. And so you think this new conspiracy
The craftiest trap yet laid for the old fox?——
Fox!—Well, I like the nickname! What did Plutarch
Say of the Greek Lysander?
 Joseph.   I forget.
 Rich. That where the lion's skin fell short, he eked it
Out with the fox's! A great statesman, Joseph,
That same Lysander!
 Joseph.   Orleans heads the traitors.
 Rich. A very wooden head, then! Well?
 Joseph.   The favorite,
Count Baradas—
 Rich. A weed of hasty growth;
First gentleman of the chamber—titles, lands,
And the king's ear!—It cost me six long winters
To mount as high, as in six little moons
This painted lizard——But I hold the ladder
And when I shake—he falls! What more?
 Joseph.   A scheme
To make your orphan-ward an instrument
To aid your foes. You placed her with the queen,
One of the royal chamber,—as a watch
I' th' enemy's quarters—
 Rich.   And the silly child
Visits me daily,—calls me "Father,"—prays
Kind Heaven to bless me—And for all the rest

As well have placed a doll about the queen !
She does not heed who frowns—who smiles; with whom
The king confers in whispers; notes not when
Men who last week were foes, are found in corners
Mysteriously affectionate; words spoken
Within closed doors she never hears;—by chance
Taking the air at keyholes—Senseless puppet !
No ears—nor eyes !—and yet she says, " She loves me ! "
Go on——

    Joseph. Your ward has charm'd the king——
    Rich.   Out on you !
Have I not, one by one, from such fair shoots
Pluck'd the insidious ivy of his love?
And shall it creep around my blossoming tree
Where innocent thoughts, like happy birds, make music
That spirits in Heaven might hear ? They're sinful, too,
Those passionate surfeits of the rampant flesh,
The church condemns them; and to us, my Joseph,
The props and pillars of the church, most hurtful.
The king is weak—whoever the king loves
Must rule the king; the lady loves another,
The other rules the lady—thus we're balk'd
Of our own proper sway—The king must have
No goddess but the State:—the State—that's Richelieu !

    Joseph. This not the worst;—Louis, in all decorous,
And deeming you her least compliant guardian,
Would veil his suit by marriage with his minion,
Your prosperous foe, Count Baradas !

    Rich.   Ha ! ha !
I have another bride for Baradas.

    Joseph. You, my lord ?
    Rich.   Ay—more faithful than the love
Of fickle woman:—when the head lies lowliest,
Clasping him fondest;—Sorrow never knew
So sure a soother,—and her bed is stainless !

    Joseph [*aside*]. If of the grave he speaks, **I do not wonder**
That priests are bachelors !

Enter FRANÇOIS.

    Fran.   Mademoiselle de Mortemar.
    Rich. Most opportune—admit her.   [*Exit* FRANÇOIS.
                                     In my closet
You'll find a rosary, Joseph; ere you tell
Three hundred beads, I'll summon you. Stay, Joseph;—
I did omit an Ave in my matins,—
A grievous fault;—atone it for me, Joseph;
There is a scourge within; I am weak, you strong.
It were but charity to take my sin
On such broad shoulders. Exercise is healthful.

    Joseph. I ! guilty of such criminal presumption
As to mistake myself for you—No, never !
Think it not ! [*Aside.*] Troth, a pleasant invitation !   [*Exit* JOSEPH.

Enter JULIE DE MORTEMAR.

Rich. That's my sweet Julie!—why, upon this face
Blushes such daybreak, one might swear the morning
Were come to visit Tithon.
 Julie [*placing herself at his feet*]. Are you gracious?—
May I say "Father?"
 Rich.   Now and ever!
 Julie.   Father!
A sweet word to an orphan.
 Rich.   No; not orphan
While Richelieu lives; thy father loved me well;
My friend, ere I had flatterers (now, I'm great,
In other phrase, I'm friendless)—he died young
In years, not service, and bequeath'd thee to me;
And thou shalt have a dowry, girl, to buy
Thy mate amidst the mightiest. Drooping?—sighs?
Art thou not happy at the court?
 Julie.   Not often.
 Rich. [*aside*]. Can she love Baradas? Ah! at thy heart
There's what can smile and sigh, blush and grow pale,
All in a breath? Thou art admired—art young;
Does not his majesty commend thy beauty—
Ask thee to sing to him?—and swear such sounds
Had smooth'd the brows of Saul?
 Julie.   He's very tiresome,
Our worthy king.
 Rich. Fie! kings are never tiresome,
Save to their ministers. What courtly gallants
Charm ladies most?—De Sourdiac, Longueville, or
The favorite Baradas?
 Julie.   A smileless man—
I fear and shun him.
 Rich.   Yet he courts thee?
 Julie.   Then
He is more tiresome than his Majesty.
 Rich. Right, girl, shun Baradas. Yet of these flowers
Of France, not one, in whose more honied breath
Thy heart hears summer whisper?

Enter HUGUET.

 Hug.   The Chevalier
De Mauprat waits below.
 Julie [*starting up*]. De Mauprat!
 Rich.   Hem!
He has been tiresome too!—Anon.   [*Exit* HUGUET.
 Julie.   What doth he?—
I mean—I—Does your Eminence—that is—
Know you Messire de Mauprat?
 Rich.   Well!—and you—
Has he address'd you often?
 Julie.   Often!—No—
Nine times; nay, ten; the last time, by the lattice
Of the great staircase. [*In a melancholy tone.*] The Court sees him rarely.

Rich. Not quite so quick, friend Huguet; Messire de Mauprat is a patient man, etc.—*Richelieu, Act I., Sc. 2.*

SCENE II.] RICHELIEU. 121

    Rich. A bold and forward royster!
    Julie.   *He?* nay, modest,
Gentle, and sad, methinks.
    Rich.   Wears gold and azure?
    Julie. No; sable.
    Rich.   So you note his colors, Julie?
Shame on you, child; look loftier. By the mass,
I have business with this modest gentleman.
    Julie. You're angry with poor Julie. There's no cause.
    Rich. No cause—you hate my foes?
    Julie.   I do!
    Rich.   Hate Mauprat?
    Julie. Not Mauprat. No, not Adrien, father.
    Rich.   Adrien!
Familiar!—Go, child; no, not *that* way; wait
In the tapestry chamber; I will join you,—go.
    Julie. His brows are knit; I dare not call him father!
But I *must* speak—Your Eminence——
    Rich. [*sternly.*]   Well, girl!
    Julie.   Nay,
Smile on me—one smile more, there, now I'm happy.
Do not rank Mauprat with your foes; he is not,
I know he *is* not; he loves France too well.
    Rich. Not rank De Mauprat with my foes? So be it.
I'll blot him from that list.
    Julie   That's my own father.   [*Exit* JULIE.
    Rich. [*ringing a small bell on the table*].   Huguet!

Enter HUGUET.

De Mauprat struggled not, nor murmured?
    Hug. No; proud and passive.
    Rich.   Bid him enter.—Hold!
Look that he hide no weapon. Humph, despair
Makes victims sometimes victors. When he has enter'd
Glide round unseen;—place thyself yonder [*pointing to the screen*]; watch him;
If he show violence—(let me see thy carbine;
So, a good weapon;)—if he play the lion,
Why—the dog's death.
    Hug.   I never miss my mark.
    [*Exit* HUGUET; RICHELIEU *seats himself at the table, and slowly arranges the papers before him. Enter* DE MAUPRAT, *preceded by* HUGUET, *who then retires behind the screen.*
    Rich. Approach, sir.—Can you call to mind the hour,
Now three years since, when in this room, methinks,
Your presence honor'd me?
    De Mau.   It is, my Lord,
One of my most——
    Rich. [*drily*]. Delightful recollections.*

---

* There are many anecdotes of the irony, often so terrible, in which Richelieu indulged. But he had a love for humor in its more hearty and genial shape. He would send for Boisrobert "to make him laugh,"—and grave ministers and magnates waited in the ante-room, while the great cardinal listened and responded to the sallies of the lively wit.

 De Mau. [*aside*]. St. Denis! doth he make a jest of axe
And headsman?
 Rich. [*sternly*]. I did then accord you
A mercy ill requited—you still live?
 De Mau. To meet death face to face at last.
 [*Rich.*   Your words
Are bold.
 De Mau. My deeds have not belied them.
 Rich.   Deeds!
O miserable delusion of man's pride.
Deeds! cities sack'd, fields ravaged, hearths profaned,
Men butcher'd! In your hour of doom behold
The *deeds* you boast of! From rank showers of blood,
And the red light of blazing roofs, you build
The rainbow glory, and to shuddering conscience
Cry,—Lo, the bridge to Heaven!
 De Mau.   If war be sinful,
Your hand the gauntlet cast.
 Rich.   It was so, sir.
Note the distinction:—I weigh'd well the cause
Which made the standard holy; raised the war
But to secure the peace. France bled—I groan'd;
But look'd beyond; and, in the vista, saw
France saved, and I exulted. You—but you
Were but the tool of slaughter—knowing nought,
Foreseeing nought, nought hoping, nought lamenting,
And for nought fit—save cutting throats for hire.
Deeds, marry, deeds!
 De Mau.   If you would deign to speak
Thus to your armies ere they march to battle,
Perchance your Eminence might have the pain
Of the throat-cutting to yourself.
 Rich. [*aside*].   He has wit,
This Mauprat—[*Aloud*]. Let it pass; there is against you
What you can less excuse.] Messire de Mauprat,
Doom'd to sure death, how hast thou since consumed
The time allotted thee for serious thought
And solemn penitence?
 De Mau. [*embarrassed*]. The time, my lord?
 Rich Is not the question plain? I'll answer for thee.
Thou hast sought nor priest nor shrine; no sackcloth chafed
Thy delicate flesh. The rosary and the death's-head
Have not, with pious meditation, purged
Earth from the carnal gaze. What thou hast *not* done
Brief told; what done, a volume! Wild debauch,
Turbulent riot;—for the morn the dice-box—
Noon claim'd the duel—and the night the wassail;
These, your most holy, pure preparatives,
For death and judgment. Do I wrong you, sir?
 De Mau. I was not always thus:—if changed my nature,
Blame that which changed my fate.—Alas, my lord,
[There is a brotherhood which calm-eyed reason
Can wot not of betwixt despair and mirth.

My birth-place mid the vines of sunny Provence,
Perchance the stream that sparkles in my veins
Came from that wine of passionate life which, erst,
Glow'd in the wild heart of the troubadour:
And danger, which makes steadier courage wary,
But fevers me with an insane delight;
As one of old who on the mountain crags
Caught madness from a Mænad's haunting eyes.
Were you, my lord,—whose path imperial power,
And the grave cares of reverent wisdom, guard
From all that tempts to folly meaner men,—]
Were you accursed with that which you inflicted—
By bed and board, dogg'd by one ghastly spectre—
The while within you youth beat high, and life
Grew lovelier from the neighboring frown of death—
The heart no bud, nor fruit—save in those seeds
Most worthless, which spring up, bloom, bear, and wither
In the same hour—Were this your fate, perchance,
You would have err'd like me!

  Rich.   I might, like you,
Have been a brawler and a reveller;—not,
Like you, a trickster, and a thief.—

  De Mau. [*advancing threateningly*]. Lord Cardinal!
Unsay those words!—   [HUGUET *deliberately raises the carbine.*

  Rich. [*waving his hand*]. Not quite so quick, friend Huguet;
Messire de Mauprat is a patient man,
And he can wait!—

       You have outrun your fortune;—
I blame you not, that you would be a beggar—
Each to his taste!—But I do charge you, sir,
That, being beggar'd, you would coin false moneys
Out of that crucible, called DEBT.—To live
On means not yours—be brave in silks and laces,
Gallant in steeds—splendid in banquets;—all
Not *yours*—ungiven—uninherited—unpaid for;—
This is to be a trickster; and to filch
Men's art and labor, which to them is wealth,
Life, daily bread,—quitting all scores with—" Friend,
You're troublesome!"—Why this, forgive me,
Is what—when done with a less dainty grace—
Plain folks call " *Theft!*" You owe eight thousand pistoles,
Minus one crown, two liards!——

  De Mau. [*aside*].   The old conjuror!
'Sdeath, he'll inform me next how many cups
I drank at dinner!

  Rich.   This is scandalous,
Shaming your birth and blood. I tell you, sir,
That you must pay your debts.

  De Mau.   With all my heart,
My lord. Where shall I borrow, then, the money?

  Rich. [*aside and laughing*]. A humorous dare-devil!—The very man
To suit my purpose—ready, frank, and bold! [*Rising and earnestly*
Adrien de Mauprat, men have called me cruel;—

I am not;—I am *just!*—I found France rent asunder,—
The rich men despots, and the poor banditti;—
Sloth in the mart, and schism within the temple;
Brawls festering to rebellion; and weak laws
Rotting away with rust in antique sheaths.
I have re-created France; and, from the ashes
Of the old feudal and decrepit carcase,
Civilization on her luminous wings
Soars, phœnix-like, to Jove! What was my art?
Genius, some say,—some, fortune,—witchcraft, some.
Not so;—my art was JUSTICE!—Force and fraud
Misname it cruelty—you shall confute them!
My champion YOU? You met me as your foe,
Depart my friend—You shall not die.—France needs you.
You shall wipe off all stains,—be rich, be honor'd,
Be great.——
        [DE MAUPRAT *falls on his knee*—RICHELIEU *raises him.*
       I ask, sir, in return, this hand,
To gift it with a bride, whose dower shall match,
Yet not exceed, her beauty.
  De Mau.   I, my lord,—[*hesitating*]
I have no wish to marry.
  Rich.   Surely, sir,
To die were worse.
  De Mau.   Scarcely; the poorest coward
Must die,—but knowingly to march to marriage—
My lord, it asks the courage of a lion!
  Rich. Traitor, thou triflest with me! I know *all!*
Thou hast dared to love my ward—my charge.
  De Mau.   As rivers
May love the sunlight—basking in the beams,
And hurrying on!—
  Rich.   Thou hast told her of thy love?
  De Mau. My lord, if I had dared to love a maid,
Lowliest in France, I would not so have wronged her,
As bid her link rich life and virgin hope
With one, the deathman's gripe might, from her side,
Pluck at the nuptial altar.
  Rich.   I believe thee;
Yet since she knows not of thy love, renounce her;
Take life and fortune with another!—Silent?
  De Mau. Your fate has been one triumph—you know **not**
How bless'd a thing it was in my dark hour
To nurse the one sweet thought you bid me banish.
Love hath no need of words;—nor less within
That holiest temple—the Heaven-builded soul—
Breathes the recorded vow. Base knight,—false lover
Were he, who barter'd all, that brighten'd grief,
Or sanctified despair, for life and gold.
Revoke your mercy;—I prefer the fate
I look'd for!
  Rich.   Huguet! to the tapestry chamber
Conduct your prisoner, [*To* MAUPRAT.]

                        You will there behold
The executioner:—your doom be private—
And Heaven have mercy on you !
    De Mau.   When I am dead,
Tell her, I loved her.
    Rich.   Keep such follies, sir,
For fitter ears;—go- -
    De Mau.   Does he mock me?
                                      [*Exeunt* DE MAUPRAT, HUGUET.
    Rich.   Joseph,
Come forth,

                      Enter JOSEPH.
            Methinks your cheek hath lost its rubies;
I fear you have been too lavish of the flesh;
The scourge is heavy.
    Joseph.   Pray you, change the subject.
    Rich. You good men are so modest !—Well, to business !
Go instantly—deeds—notaries !—bid my stewards
Arrange my house by the Luxembourg—*my* house
No more !—a bridal present to my ward,
Who weds to-morrow.
    Joseph.   Weds, with whom?
    Rich.   De Mauprat.
    Joseph. Penniless husband !
    Rich.   Bah ! the mate for beauty
Should be a man, and not a money-chest !
When her brave sire lay on his bed of death,
I vow'd to be a father to his Julie:—
And so he died—the smile upon his lips !
And when I spared the life of her young lover,
Methought I saw that smile again !—Who else,
Look you, in all the court —who else so well,
Brave, or supplant the favorite;—balk the king—
Baffle their schemes?—I have tried him:—He has honor
And courage;—qualities that eagle-plume
Men's souls,—and fit them for the fiercest sun,
Which ever melted the weak waxen minds
That flutter in the beams of gaudy Power !
Besides, he has taste, this Mauprat:—When my play
Was acted to dull tiers of lifeless gapers,*
Who had no soul for poetry, I saw him
Applaud in the proper places:—trust me, Joseph,
He is a man of an uncommon promise !
    Joseph. And yet your foe.

---

* The Abbé Arnaud tells us that the queen was a little avenged on the cardinal by the ill success of the tragi-comedy of " Mirame "—more than suspected to be his own—though presented to the world under the foster-name of Desmarets. Its representation (says Pelisson) cost him 300,000 crowns. He was so transported out of himself by the performance, that at one time he thrust his person half out of his box to show himself to the assembly; at another time he imposed silence on the audience, that they might not lose " *des endroits encore plus beaux !*" He said afterwards to Desmarets:—" Eh bien, les Français n'auront donc jamais de goût. Ils n'ont pas été charmés de Mirame !" Arnaud says pithily,—" On ne pouvoit alors avoir d'autre satisfaction des offenses d'un homme qui étoit maitre de tout, et redoutable à toute le monde." Nevertheless, his style in prose, though not devoid of the pedantic affectations of the time, often rises into very noble eloquence.

Rich.   Have I not foes enow?
Great men gain doubly when they make foes friends.
Remember my grand maxims:—First employ
All methods to conciliate.*
    Joseph.   Failing these?
    Rich. [*fiercely.*] All means to crush: as with the opening, and
The clenching of this little hand, I will
Crush the small venom of these stinging courtiers.
So, so, we've baffled Baradas.
    Joseph.   And when
Check the conspiracy!
    Rich.   Check, check? Full way to it.
Let it bud, ripen, flaunt i' the day, and burst
To fruit,—the Dead Sea's fruit of ashes; ashes
Which I will scatter to the winds.
                         Go, Joseph;
When you return, I have a feast for you;
The last great act of my great play: the verses,
Methinks, are fine,—ah, very fine.—*You* write
Verses! †—[*aside*] *such* verses!—You have wit, discernment.
    Joseph [*aside.*] Worse than the scourge! Strange that so great a statesman
Should be so bad a poet.
    Rich.   What dost thou say?
    Joseph. That it is strange so great a statesman should
Be so sublime a poet.
    Rich.   Ah, you rogue;
Laws die, Books never. Of my ministry
I am not vain! but of my muse, I own it.
Come, you shall hear the verses now.   [*Takes up a MS.*
    Joseph.   My lord,
The deeds, the notaries!
    Rich.   True, I pity you;
But business first, then pleasure.   [*Exit* JOSEPH.
    Rich. [*seats himself and reading*]. Ah, sublime!

                   Enter DE MAUPRAT *and* JULIE.

    De Mau. Oh, speak, my lord—I dare not think you mock me.
And yet—
    Rich.   Hush—hush—This line must be consider'd!
    Julie. Are we not both your children?
    Rich.   What a couplet!——
How now! Oh, sir—you live!

---

* " Vialart remarque une chose qui peut expliquer la conduite de Richelieu en d-autres circonstances :—c'est que les seigneurs à qui leur naissance ou leur mérite pouvoit permettre des prétensions, il avoit pour système, de leur accorder au-delà même de leurs droit et de leurs espérances, mais, aussi, une fois comblés—si, au lieu de reconnoitre ses services ils se levoient contre lui, et ils traitoit sans miséricorde."—*Anquetil.* See also the Political Testament, and the Mémoires de Cardinal Richelieu, in Petitot's collection.

† " Tantôt fanatique—tantôt fourbe—fonder les religieuses de Calvaire—*faire des vers.*" Thus speaks Voltaire of Father Joseph. His talents and influence with Richlieu, grossly exaggerated in his own day, are now rightly estimated.

    " C'étoit en effet un homme infatigable—portant dans les entreprises, l'activité, la souplèsse, l'opiniâtreté propre à les faire réussir."—*Anquetil.* He wrote a Latin poem, called " La Turciade," in which he sought to excite the kingdoms of Christendom against the Turks. But the inspiration of Tyrtæus was denied to Father Joseph.

De Mau.   Why, no, methinks,
Elysium is not life!
    Julie.   He smiles!—you smile,
My father! From my heart for ever, now,
I'll blot the name of orphan!
    Rich.   Rise, my children,
For ye are mine—mine both;—and in your sweet
And young delight—your love (life's first-born glory)—
My own lost youth breathes musical!
    De Mau.   I'll seek
Temple and priest henceforward, were it but
To learn Heaven's choicest blessings.
    Rich.   Thou shalt seek
Temple and priest right soon; the morrow's sun
Shall see across these barren thresholds pass
The fairest bride in Paris.—Go, my children,
Even *I* loved once!—Be lovers while ye may!
How is it with you, sir! You bear it bravely:
You know, it asks the courage of a lion.   [*Exeunt* JULIE *aud* DE MAUPRAT.
    Rich. O godlike Power! Woe, Rapture, Penury, Wealth,—
Marriage and Death, for one infirm old man
Through a great empire to dispense—withhold—
As the will whispers! And shall things—like motes
That live in my daylight—lackeys of court wages,
Dwarf'd starvelings—manikins, upon whose shoulders
The burthen of a province were a load
More heavy than the globe on Atlas,—cast,
Lots for my robes and sceptre? France! I love thee!
All Earth shall never pluck thee from my heart!
My mistress France—my wedded wife,—sweet France,
Who shall proclaim divorce for thee and me!   [*Exit* RICHELIEU.

ACT II.

SECOND DAY.

SCENE I.—*A splendid apartment in* MAUPRAT'S *new house. Casements opening to the Gardens, beyond which the domes of the Luxembourg Palace.*

Enter BARADAS.

Bar. Mauprat's new home:—too splendid for a soldier!
But o'er his floors—the while I stalk—methinks
My shadow spreads gigantic to the gloom
The old rude towers of the Bastile cast far
Along the smoothness of the jocund day.—
Well, thou hast 'scaped the fierce caprice of Richelieu;
But art thou farther from the headsman, fool?
Thy secret I have whisper'd to the king;
Thy marriage makes the king thy foe.—Thou stand'st
On the abyss—and in the pool below
I see a ghastly, headless phantom mirror'd;—
Thy likeness ere the marriage moon hath waned.
Meanwhile—meanwhile—ha—ha, if thou art wedded,
Thou art not wived.

Enter MAUPRAT [*splendidly dressed*].

De Mau. Was ever fate like mine?
So blest and yet so wretched!
 Bar. Joy, De Mauprat!—
Why, what a brow, man, for your wedding-day!
 De Mau. Jest not!—Distraction!
 Bar. What, your wife a shrew
Already? Courage, man—the common lot!
 De Mau. Oh! that she were less lovely, or less loved!
 Bar. Riddles again!
 De Mau. You know what chanced between
The cardinal and myself.
 Bar. This morning brought
Your letter:—faith a strange account! I laugh'd
And wept at once for gladness.
 De Mau. We were wed
At noon;—the rite perform'd, came hither!—scarce
Arrived, when——
 Bar. Well?—
 De Mau. Wide flew the doors, and lo,
Messire de Beringhen, and this epistle!
 Bar. 'Tis the king's hand!—the royal seal!
 De Mau. Read—read—
 Bar. [*reading*]. "Whereas Adrien de Mauprat, Colonel and Chevalier in our armies, being already guilty of High Treason, by the seizure of our town of Faviaux, has presumed, without our knowledge, consent, or sanction, to connect himself by marriage with Julie de

Mortemar, a wealthy orphan, attached to the person of Her Majesty, without our knowledge or consent—We do hereby proclaim and declare the said marriage contrary to law. On penalty of death, Adrien de Mauprat will not communicate with the said Julie de Mortemar by word or letter, save in the presence of our faithful servant, the Sieur de Beringhen, and then with such respect and decorum as are due to a demoiselle attached to the Court of France, until such time as it may suit our royal pleasure to confer with the Holy Church on the formal annulment of the marriage, and with our Council on the punishment to be awarded to Messire de Mauprat, who is cautioned, for his own sake, to preserve silence as to our injunction, more especially to Mademoiselle de Mortemar

"Given under our hand and seal at the Louvre.

"LOUIS."

    Bar. [*returning the letter*].   Amazement!—Did not
Richelieu say, the king
Knew not your crime?
    De Mau.   He said so.
    Bar.   Poor De Mauprat!—
See you the snare, the vengeance worse than death,
Of which you are the victim?
    De Mau.   Ha!
    Bar. [*aside*].   It works!
    [JULIE *and* DE BERINGHEN *in the Gardens.*
You have not sought the cardinal yet to——
    De Mau.   No!
Scarce yet my sense awaken'd from the shock;
Now I will seek him.
    Bar.   Hold, beware!—Stir not
Till we confer again.
    De Mau.   Speak—out, man!
    Bar.   Hush!
Your wife!—De Beringhen—Be on your guard—
Obey the royal orders to the letter.
I'll look around your palace. By my troth
A princely mansion!
    De Mau.   Stay—
    Bar.   So new a bridegroom
Can want no visitors;—Your servant, madam!
Oh! happy pair—Oh, charming picture!

    [*Exit through a side door*

    Julie.   Adrien,
You left us suddenly—Are you not well?
    De Mau. Oh, very well—that is—extremely ill!
    Julie. Ill, Adrien?   [*Taking his hand.*
    De Mau.   Not when I see thee.
    [*He is about to lift her hand to his lips when* DE BERINGHEN *coughs and pulls his mantle.* MAUPRAT *drops the hand and walks away.*
    Julie.   Alas!
Should he not love me?
    De Ber. [*aside*]. Have a care; I must
Report each word—each gesture to his majesty.
    De Mau. Sir, if you were not in his Majesty's service,
You'd be most officious, impudent,
Damn'd busy-body ever interfering
In a man's family affairs.

De Ber.   But as
I do belong, sir, to his Majesty—
    De Mau. You're lucky!—Still, were we a story higher,
'Twere prudent not to go too near the window.
    Julie. Adrien, what have I done? Say, am I changed
Since yesterday?—or was it but for wealth,
Ambition, life—that—that—you swore you loved me?
    De Mau. I shall go mad!—I do, indeed I do—
    De Ber. [*aside*]. Not love her! that were highly disrespectful.
    Julie. You do—what, Adrien?
    De Mau.   Oh! I do, indeed——
I do think, that this weather is delightful!
A charming day! the sky is so serene!
And what a prospect!—[*to* DE BERINGHEN]. Oh! you popinjay!
    Julie. He jests at me!—he mocks me!—yet I love him,
And every look becomes the lips we love!
Perhaps I am too grave?—You laugh at Julie;
If laughter please you, welcome be the music!
Only say, Adrien, that you love me.
    De Mau. [*kissing her hand*].   Ay;
With my whole heart I love you!——
                                Now, sir, go,
And tell that to his Majesty!—Who ever
Heard of its being a state offence to kiss
The hand of one's own wife?
    Julie.   He says he loves me,
And starts away, as if to say "I love you"
Meant something *very* dreadful.—Come, sit by me,—
I place your chair!—fie on your gallantry!
    [*They sit down; as he pushes his chair back, she draw hers nearer.*
Why must this strange Messire De Beringhen
Be always here? He never takes a hint.
Do you not wish him gone?
    De Mau.   Upon my soul
I do, my Julie!—Send him for your *bouquet,*
Your glove, your—anything.
    Julie.   Messire de Beringhen,
I dropp'd my glove in the gardens by the fountain,
Or the alcove, or—stay, no, by the statue
Of Cupid; may I ask you to——
    De Ber.   To send for it?
Certainly [*ringing a bell on the table*]. André, Pierre, (your rascals, how
Do ye call them?)

                     Enter Servants.

                Ah—*Madame* has dropp'd her glove
In the gardens, by the fountain,—or the alcove;
Or—stay—no, by the statue—eh?—of Cupid.
Bring it.
    De Mau. Did ever now one pair of shoulders
Carry such waggon-loads of impudence
Into a gentleman's drawing-room?
                        Dear Julie.

I'm busy—letters—visitors—the devil!
I do beseech you leave me—I say—leave me.
    Julie [*weeping*]. You are unkind.   [*Exit.*
    [*As she goes out,* MAUPRAT *drops on one knee and kisses the hem of her mantle, unseen by her.*
    De Ber.   Ten millions of apologies——
    De Mau. I'll not take one of them. I have, as yet,
Withstood all things—my heart—my love—my rights.
But Julie's tears!——When is this farce to end?
    De Ber. Oh! when you please. His Majesty requests me,
As soon as you infringe his gracious·orders,
To introduce you to the Governor
Of the Bastile. I should have had that honor
Before, but, gad, my foible is good-nature;
One can't be hard upon a friend's infirmities.
    De Mau. I know the king can send me to the scaffold—
Dark prospect!—but I'm used to it; and if
The Church and Council, by this hour to-morrow,
One way or other settle not the matter,
I will——
    De Ber. What, my dear Sir?
    De Mau.   Show you the door,
My dear, dear sir; talk as I please, with whom
I please, in my own house, dear sir, until
His Majesty shall condescend to find
A stouter gentleman than you, dear sir,
To take me out; and now you understand me,
My dear, most dear—oh damnably dear sir!
    De Ber. What, almost in a passion! you will cool
Upon reflection. Well, since *Madame's* absent,
I'll take a small refreshment. Now, don't stir;
Be careful;—how's your Burgundy?—I'll taste it—
Finish it all before I leave you. Nay,
No form;—you see I make myself at home.
                            [*Exit* DE BERINGHEN.
    De Mau. [*going to the door through which* BARADAS *had passed*]. Baradas! Count!

Enter BARADAS.

          You spoke of snares—of vengeance
Sharper than death—be plainer.
    Bar.   What so clear?
Richelieu has but two passions—
    De Mau.   Richelieu!
    Bar.   Yes!
Ambition and revenge—in you both blended.
First for ambition—Julie is his ward,
Innocent—docile—pliant to his will—
He placed her at the court—foresaw the rest—
The king loves Julie!
    De Mau.   Merciful Heaven! The king!
    Bar. Such Cupids lend new plumes to Richelieu's wings:
But the court etiquette must give such Cupids

The veil of Hymen—(Hymen but in name).
He look'd abroad—found you his foe:—*thus* served
Ambition—by the grandeur of his ward,
And vengeance—by dishonor to his foe!
    De Mau. Prove this.
    Bar.   You have the proof—the royal Letter:—
Your strange exemption from the general pardon,
Known but to me and Richelieu; can you doubt
Your friend to acquit your foe? The truth is glaring—
Richelieu alone could tell the princely lover
The tale which sells your life,—or buys your honor!
    De Mau. I see it all? Mock pardon—hurried nuptials—
False bounty!—all!—the serpent of that smile!
Oh! it stings home!
    Bar.   You yet shall crush his malice;
Our plans are sure:—Orleans is at our head;
We meet to-night; join us, and with us triumph.
    De Mau. To-night?—Oh, Heaven!—my marriage night!—Revenge!
    Bar. What class of men, whose white lips do not curse
The grim, insatiate, universal tyrant?
We, noble-born—where are our antique rights—
Our feudal seigniories—our castled strength,
That did divide us from the base Plebeians,
And make our swords our law—where are they? Trod
To dust—and o'er the graves of our dead power
Scaffolds are monuments—the kingly house
Shorn of its beams—the Royal Sun of France
'Clipsed by this blood-red comet. Where we turn,
Nothing but Richelieu!—armies—church—state—laws,
But mirrors that do multiply his beams.
He sees all—acts all—Argus and Briaræus—
Spy at our boards—and deathsman at our hearths;
Under the venom of one laidley nightshade,
Wither the lilies of all France.
    De Mau. [*impatiently*]. But Julie—
    Bar. [*unheeding him*]. As yet the Fiend that serves hath saved his power
From every snare; and in the epitaphs
Of many victims dwells a warning moral
That preaches caution. Were I not assured
That what before was hope is ripen'd now
Into most certain safety, trust me, Mauprat,
I still could hush my hate and mark thy wrongs,
And say "Be patient!" *Now*, the King himself
Smiles kindly when I tell him that his peers
Will rid him of his priest. You knit your brows,
Noble impatience!—Pass we to our scheme!
'Tis Richelieu's wont, each morn, within his chapel
(Hypocrite worship ended), to dispense
Alms to the Mendicant-friars,—in that guise
A band (yourself the leader) shall surround
And seize the despot.
    De Mau.   But the king?—but Julie?
    Bar. The king, infirm in health, in mind more feeble,

Is but the plaything of a minister's will.
Were Richelieu dead—his power were mine; and Louis
Soon should forget his passion and your crime.
But whither now?

De Mau.   I know not; I scarce hear thee;
A little while for thought: anon I'll join thee;
But now, all air seems tainted, and I loathe
The face of man!   [*Exit* DE MAUPRAT *through the Gardens.*

Bar.   Start from the chase, my prey,
But as thou speed'st the hell-hounds of revenge
Pant in thy track and dog thee down.
         [*Enter* DE BERINGHEN, *his mouth full, a napkin in his hand.*

De Ber.   Chevalier,
Your cook's a miracle,—what, my host gone?
Faith, count, my office is a post of danger—
A fiery fellow, Mauprat! touch and go,—
Match and saltpetre,—pr—r—r—r—!

Bar.   You
Will be released ere long. The king resolves
To call the bride to court this day.

De Ber.   Poor Mauprat!
Yet, since *you* love the lady, why so careless
Of the king's suit?

Bar.   Because the lady's virtuous,
And the king timid. Ere he win the suit,
He'll lose the crown,—the bride will be a widow,—
And I—the Richelieu of the Regent Orleans.

De Ber. Is Louis still so chafed against the Fox
For snatching yon fair dainty from the Lion?

Bar. So chafed, that Richelieu totters. Yes, the king
Is half conspirator against the cardinal.
Enough of this. I've found the man we wanted,—
The man to head the hands that murder Richelieu,—
The man, whose name the synonym for daring.

De Ber. He must mean me! No, count; I am, I own,
A valiant dog—but still——

Bar.   Whom can I mean
But Mauprat?—Mark, to-night we meet at Marion's.
There shall we sign; thence send this scroll [*showing it*] to Bouillon.
You're in that secret [*affectionately*]—one of our new Council.

De Ber. But to admit the Spaniard—France's foe—
Into the heart of France—dethrone the king—
It looks like treason, and I smell the headsman.

Bar. Oh, sir, too late to falter: when we meet
We must arrange the separate, coarser scheme,
For Richelieu's death. Of this despatch De Mauprat
Must nothing learn. He only bites at vengeance,
And he would start from treason.—We must post him
Without the door at Marion's—as a sentry.
[*Aside*]—So, when his head is on the block—his tongue
Cannot betray our more august designs!

De Ber. I'll meet you if the king can spare me.—[*Aside.*] No!
I am too old a goose to play with foxes,

I'll roost at home. Meanwhile, in the next room
There's a delicious pâté,—let's discuss it.
　　Bar. Pshaw! a man fill'd with a sublime ambition
Has no time to discuss your pâtés.
　　De Ber.　　　　　　　Pshaw!
And a man fill'd with as sublime a pâté
Has no time to discuss ambition.—Gad,
I have the best of it!

　　　　　Enter JULIE *hastily with first* Courtier.

　　Julie [*to* Courtier]. A summons, sir,
To attend the Louvre?—On *this* day, too?
　　Cour.　　　　　　　Madame,
The royal carriage waits below.—Messire [*to* DE BERINGHEN]
You will return with us.
　　Julie　　　What can this mean?—
Where is my husband?
　　Bar.　　　　He has left the house,
Perhaps till nightfall—so he bade me tell you.
Alas, were I the lord of such fair treasure—
　　Julie [*impatiently*]. Till nightfall?—Strange—my heart misgives me!
　　Cour.　　　　　　　Madame,
My orders will not brook delay.
　　Julie [*to* BARADAS].　　You'll see him—
And you will tell him!
　　Bar.　　　　From the flowers of Hybla
Never more gladly did the bee bear honey,
Than I take sweetness from those rosiest lips,
Though to the hive of others!
　　Cour. [*to* DE BERINGHEN]. Come, Messire.
　　De Ber. [*hesitating*]. One moment, just to—
　　Cour.　　　　　　　Come, sir.
　　De Ber.　　　　　　　I shall not
Discuss the pâté after all. 'Ecod,
I'm puzzled now. I don't know who's the best of it!
　　　　　　　[*Exeunt* JULIE, DE BERINGHEN, *and* Courtier.
　　Bar. Now will this fire his fever into madness!
All is made clear: Mauprat *must* murder Richelieu—
Die for that crime;—I shall console his Julie—
This will reach Bouillon!—from the wrecks of France
I shall carve out—who knows—perchance a throne!
All in despite of my Lord Cardinal.—

　　　　　Enter DE MAUPRAT *from the Gardens.*

　　De Mau. Speak! can it be?—Methought, that from the terrace
I saw the carriage of the king—and Julie!
No!—no!—my frenzy peoples the void air
With its own phantoms!
　　Bar.　　　Nay, too true.—Alas!
Was ever lightning swifter, or more blasting,
Than Richelieu's forkèd guile?
　　De Mau.　　　　I'll to the Louvre——

Bar. And lose all hope !—The Louvre !—the sure gate
To the Bastile !
  De Mau.   The king——
  Bar.   Is but the wax,
Which Richelieu stamps ! Break the malignant *seal*,
And I will raze the print. Come, man, take heart !
Her virtue well could brave a sterner trial
Than a few hours of cold imperious courtship.
Were Richelieu *dust*—no danger !
  De Mau.   Ghastly Vengeance !
To thee, and thine august and solemn sister,
The unrelenting Death, I dedicate
The blood of Armand Richelieu ! When Dishonor
Reaches our hearths Law dies and Murther takes
The angel shape of Justice !
  Bar.   Bravely said !
At midnight,—Marion's !—Nay, I cannot leave thee
To thoughts that——
  De Mau.   Speak not to me !—I am yours !—
But speak not ! There's a voice within my soul,
Whose cry could drown the thunder.—Oh ! if men
Will play dark sorcery with the heart of man,
Let them, who raise the spell, beware the Fiend !   [*Exeunt.*

SCENE II.

A room in the Palais Cardinal (as in the First Act).

RICHELIEU *and* JOSEPH.

FRANÇOIS *writing at a table.*

  Joseph. Yes;—Huguet taking his accustom'd round,—
Disguised as some plain burgher,—heard these rufflers
Quoting your name:—he listen'd,—" Pshaw," said one,
" We are to seize the Cardinal in his palace
To-morrow ! "—" How ? " the other ask'd :—" You'll hear
The whole design to-night: the Duke of Orleans
And Baradas have got the map of action
At their fingers' end."—" So be it," quoth the other,
" I will be there,—Marion de Lorme's—at midnight ! "
  Rich. I have them, man,—I have them !
  Joseph.   So they **say**
Of you, my lord ;—believe me, that their plans
Are mightier than you deem. You must employ
Means no less vast to meet them !
  Rich.   Bah ! in policy
We foil gigantic danger, not by giants,
But dwarfs.—The statues of our stately fortune

Are sculptured by the chisel—not the axe!*
Ah! were I younger—by the knightly heart
That beats beneath these priestly robes, † I would
Have pastime with these cut-throats!—Yea,—as when
Lured to the ambush of the expecting foe,—
I clove my pathway through the plumed sea!
Reach me yon falchion, François,—not that bauble
For carpet-warriors,—yonder—such a blade
As old Charles Martel might have wielded when
He drove the Saracen from France.

[FRANÇOIS *brings him one of the long two-handed swords worn in the middle ages.*

With this
I, at Rochelle, did hand to hand engage
The stalwart Englisher,—no mongrels, boy,
Those island mastiffs,—mark the notch—a deep one
His casque made here,—I shore him to the waist!
A toy—a feather—then! [*Tries to wield, and lets it fall.*
You see, a child could
Slay Richelieu now.

Fran. [*his hand on his hilt*]. But *now*, at your command
Are other weapons, my good lord.

Rich. [*who has seated himself as to write, lifts the pen*].

True,—THIS!
Beneath the rule of men entirely great
The pen is mightier than the sword. Behold
The arch-enchanter's wand!—itself a nothing!—
But taking sorcery from the master-hand
To paralyze the Cæsars—and to strike
The loud earth breathless!—Take away the sword—
States can be saved without it!   [*Looking on the clock.*
                    'Tis the hour,—
Retire, sir.   [*Exit* FRANÇOIS.

[*A knock is heard. A door concealed in the arras opens cautiously. Enter* MARION DE LORME.

Joseph. [*amazed*]. Marion de Lorme!
Rich.   Hist! Joseph!
Keep guard.
                                [JOSEPH *retires to the principal entrance*
        My faithful Marion!
Marion.   Good, my Lord,
They meet to-night in my poor house. The Duke
Of Orleans heads them.

---

* Richelieu not only employed the lowest, but would often consult men commonly esteemed the dullest. "Il disait que dans des choses de très grande importance, il avait expérimenté, que les moins sages donnaient souvent les meilleurs expédiens."—*Le Clerc.*

† Both Richelieu and Joseph were originally intended for the profession of arms. Joseph had served before he obeyed the spiritual inspiration to become a Capuchin. The death of his brother opened to Richelieu the bishopric of Luçon; but his military propensities were as strong as his priestly ambition. I need scarcely add that the cardinal, during his brilliant campaign in Italy, marched at the head of his troops in complete armor. It was under his administration that occurs the last example of proclaiming war by the chivalric defiance of herald and cartel. Richelieu valued himself much on his personal activity,—for his vanity was as universal as his ambition. A nobleman of the house of Grammont one day found him employed in *jumping*, and with all the *savoir vivre* of a Frenchman and a courtier, offered to jump against him. He suffered the cardinal to jump higher, and soon after found himself rewarded by an appointment. Yet, strangely enough, this vanity did not lead to a patronage injurious to the state; for never before in France was ability made so essential a requisite in promotion. He was lucky in finding the cleverest fellow among his adroitest flatterers.

"WITH THIS, I AT ROCHELLE DID HAND TO HAND ENGAGE THE STALWART ENGLISHER!"
—*Richelieu*, Act II., Sc. 2.

Rich.   Yes, go on.
Marion.   His Highness
Much question'd if I knew some brave, discreet,
And vigilant man, whose tongue could keep a secret,
And who had those twin qualities for service,
The love of gold, the hate of Richelieu.—
Rich.   You?—
Marion. Made answer, "Yes—my brother;—bold and trusty;
Whose faith, my faith could pledge;"—the Duke then bade me
Have him equipp'd and arm'd—well mounted—ready
This night to part for Italy.
Rich.   Aha!—
Has Bouillon too turn'd traitor?—So, methought!—
What part of Italy?
Marion.   The Piedmont frontier,
Where Bouillon lies encamp'd.
Rich.   Now there is danger!
Great danger!—If he tamper with the Spaniard,
And Louis list not to my counsel, as,
Without sure proof, he will not,—France is lost.
What more?
Marion. Dark hints of some design to seize
Your person in your palace. Nothing clear—
His Highness trembled while he spoke—the words
Did choke each other.
Rich.   So!—Who is the brother
You recommended to the Duke?
Marion.   Whoever
Your Eminence may father!—
Rich.   Darling Marion!*
       [*Goes to the table, and returns with a large bag of gold.*
There—pshaw—a trifle!—What an eye you have!
And what a smile—child!—[*kisses her.*]—Ah! you fair perdition—
'Tis well I'm old!
Marion [*aside and seriously*]. What a great man he is!
Rich. You are sure they meet?—the hour?
Marion.   At midnight.
Rich.   And
You will engage to give the Duke's Despatch
To whom I send?
Marion.   Ay, marry!
Rich. [*aside*].   Huguet? No;
He will be wanted elsewhere.—Joseph?—zealous,
But too well known—too much the *elder* brother!
Mauprat?—alas! it is his wedding-day!—

---

* Voltaire openly charges Richelieu with being the lover of Marion de Lorme; and the great poet of France, Victor Hugo, has sacrificed History to adorn her with qualities which were certainly not added to her personal charms. She was not less perfidious than beautiful. Le Clerc, properly, refutes the accusation of Voltaire against the discretion of Richelieu, and says, very justly, that if the great minister had the frailties of human nature, he learnt how to veil them,—at least when he obtained the scarlet. In earlier life he had been prone to gallantries which a little prepossessed the king (who was formal and decorous, and threw a singular coldness into the few attachments he permitted to himself), against the aspiring intriguer. But these gayer occupations died away in the engagement of higher pursuits or of darker passions.

François!—the Man of Men!—unnoted—young—
Ambitious—[*Goes to the door.*]—François!

Enter FRANÇOIS

Rich. Follow this fair lady;
(Find him the suiting garments Marion,) take
My fleetest steed:—arm thyself to the teeth;
A packet will be given you—with orders,
No matter what!—The instant that your hand
Closes upon it—clutch *it*, like your honor,
Which Death alone can steal, or ravish—set
Spurs to your steed—be breathless, till you stand
Again before me.—Stay, sir!—You will find me
Two short leagues hence—at Ruelle, in my castle.
Young man, be blithe!—for—note me—from the hour
I grasp that packet—think your guardian Star
Rains fortune on you!—

   Fran. If I fail—
   Rich. Fail—fail!
In the lexicon of youth, which Fate reserves
For a bright manhood, there is no such word
As—*fail!*—(You will instruct him further, Marion)
Follow her—but at distance;—speak not to her,
Till you are housed.—Farewell, boy! Never say
"*Fail*" again.

   Fran. I will not!
   Rich. [*patting his locks*]. There's my young hero!—
[*Exeunt* FRANÇOIS, MARION.

   Rich. So, they would seize my person in this palace?—
I cannot guess their scheme;—but my retinue
Is here too large!—a single traitor could
Strike impotent the faith of thousands;—Joseph,
Art sure of Huguet?—Think—we hang'd his Father!

   Joseph. But you have bought the Son;—heap'd favors on him!
   Rich. Trash!—favors past—that's nothing.—In his hours
Of confidence with you, has he named the favors
To *come*—he counts on?

   Joseph. Yes:—a Colonel's rank,
And letters of Nobility.

   Rich. What Huguet!—
[*Here* HUGUET *Enters, as to address the* CARDINAL, *who does not perceive him.*
   Hug. My own name, soft—[*glides behind the screen*].
   Rich. Colonel and Nobleman!
My bashful Huguet—that can never be!—
We have him not the less—we'll *promise it!*
And see the King withholds!—Ah, kings are oft
A great convenience to a minister!
No wrong to Huguet either;—Moralists
Say, hope is sweeter than Possession!—Yes!—
We'll count on Huguet! Favors *past* do gorge
Our dogs! leave service drowsy—dull the scent,
Slacken the speed;—favors *to come*, my Joseph,
Produce a lusty, hungry gratitude,

A ravenous zeal, that of the commonest cur
Would make a Cerberus.—You are right, this treason
Assumes a fearful aspect:—but once crush'd,
Its very ashes shall manure the soil
Of power; and ripen such full sheaves of greatness,
That all the summer of my fate shall seem
Fruitless beside the autumn !

[HUGUET *holds up his hand menacingly, and creeps out.*

Joseph. The saints grant it !
Rich. [*solemnly*]. Yes—for sweet France, Heaven grant
    it !—O my country,
For thee—thee only—though men deem it not—
Are toil and terror my familiars !—I
Have made thee great and fair—upon thy brows
Wreath'd the old Roman laurel:—at thy feet
Bow'd nations down.—No pulse in my ambition
Whose beatings were not measured from thy heart !
[In the old times before us, patriots lived
And died for liberty.—

Joseph. As you would live
And die for despotry—

Rich. False monk, not so,
But for the purple and the power wherein
State clothes herself.—I love my native land
Not as Venetian, Englisher, or Swiss,
But as a Noble and a Priest of France;
" All things for France "—lo, my eternal **maxim** !
The vital axle of the restless wheels
That bear me on ! With her I have entwined
My passions and my fate—my crimes—my virtues—*

---

* Richelieu did in fact so thoroughly associate himself with the State, that in cases where the extreme penalty of the law had been incurred, Le Clerc justly observes that he was more inexorable to those he had favored—even to his own connections—than to other and more indifferent offenders. It must be remembered, as some excuse for his unrelenting sternness, that before his time the great had been accustomed to commit any disorder with impunity, even the crime of treason;—" auparavant on ne faisoit poser les armes aux rebelles qu'en leur accordant quelque récompense." On entering into the administration, he therefore laid it down as a maxim necessary to the existence of the State, that " no crime should be committed with impunity."

To carry out this maxim, the long-established license to crime made even justice seem cruel. But the victims most commiserated, from their birth or accomplishments, as Montmorenci, or Cinq Mars, were traitors in actual conspiracy against their country, and would have forfeited life in any land where the punishment of death existed, and the lawgiver was strong enough to vindicate the law. Richelieu was, in fact, a patriot unsoftened by philantrophy. As in Venice (where the favorite aphorism was—" Venice first, Christianity next,"[1]) so, with Richelieu the primary consideration was, " What will be best for the country ?" He had no abstract principle whether as a politician or a priest, when applied to the world that lay beyond the boundaries of France. Thus he, whose object was to found in France a splendid and imperious despotism, assisted the Parliamentary party in England, and signed a treaty of alliance and subsides with the Catalan rebels, for the establishment of a republic in Barcelona: to convulse other monarchies was to consolidate the growing monarchy of France. So he, who completely crushed the Protestant party at home, braved all the wrath of the Vatican, and even the resentment of the King, in giving the most essential aid to the Protestants abroad.

There was, indeed, a largeness of view in his hostility to the French Huguenots, which must be carefully distinguished from the intolerance of the mere priest. He opposed them, not as a Catholic, but as a statesman. The Huguenots were strong republicans, and had formed plans for dividing France into provincial commonwealths; and the existence of Rochelle was absolutely incompatible with the integrity of the French monarchy. It was a second capital, held by the Huguenots, claiming independent authority and the right to treat with foreign powers. Richelieu's final conquest was marked by a humanity that had nothing of the bigot. The Huguenots obtained a complete amnesty, and had only to regret the loss of privileges and fortifications which could not have existed with any security to the rest of France.

[1] " Pria Veneziana, poi Christiane."

Hated and loved and schemed, and shed men's blood,
As the calm crafts of Tuscan Sages teach
Those who would make their country great. Beyond
The map of France—my heart can travel not,
But fills that limit to its farthest verge;
And while I live—Richelieu and France are one.]
We priests, to whom the Church forbids in youth
The plighted one—to manhood's toil denies
The soother helpmate—from our wither'd age
Shuts the sweet blossoms of the second spring
That smiles in the name of Father—we are yet
Not holier than Humanity, and must
Fulfil Humanity's condition—Love !
Debarred the Actual, we but breathe a life
To the chill Marble of the Ideal—Thus,
In thy unseen and abstract Majesty,
My France, my Country, I have bodied forth
A thing to love. What are these robes of state,
This pomp, this palace ? perishable baubles !
In this world two things only are immortal—
Fame and a People !

Enter HUGUET.

Hug.   My Lord Cardinal,
Your Eminence bade me seek you at this hour.
    Rich. Did I ?—True, Huguet.—So—you overheard
Strange talk amongst these gallants ? Snares and traps
For Richelieu ?—Well—we'll balk them ; let me think—
The men-at-arms you head—how many ?*
    Hug.   Twenty,
My Lord.
    Rich. All trusty ?
    Hug.   Yes, for ordinary
Occasions—if for great ones, I would change
Three-fourths at least.
    Rich.   Ay, what are great occasions ?
    Hug. Great bribes !
    Rich. [*to* JOSEPH]. Good lack, he knows some paragons
Superior to great bribes !
    Hug.   True Gentlemen
Who have transgress'd the laws—and value life
And lack not gold ;—your Eminence alone
Can grant them pardon. *Ergo*, you can trust them !
    Rich. Logic !—So be it—let these *honest* twenty
Be arm'd and mounted.—[*Aside.*] So they meet at midnight,
The attempt on me to-morrow—Ho ! we'll strike
'Twixt wind and water.—[*Aloud.*] Does it need much time
To find these ornaments to Human Nature ?
    Hug. My Lord—the trustiest of them are not birds

---

* The guard attached to Richelieu's person was, in the first instance, fifty arquebusiers, afterwards increased to two companies of cavalry and two hundred musqueteers. Huguet is therefore to be considered merely as the lieutenant of a small detachment of this little army. In point of fact, the subdivisions of the guard took it in turns to serve.

That love the daylight.—I do know a haunt
Where they meet nightly—
   Rich.   Ere the dawn be gray,
All could be arm'd, assembled, and at Ruelle
In my old hall?
   Hug.   By one hour after midnight.
   Rich.   The castle's strong. You know its outlets, Huguet?
Would twenty men, well posted, keep such guard
That not one step—(and Murder's step is stealthy)—
Could glide within—unseen?
   Hug.   A triple wall—
A drawbridge and portcullis—twenty men
Under my lead, a month might hold that castle
Against a host.
   Rich.   They do not strike till morning,
Yet I will shift the quarter—Bid the grooms
Prepare the litter—I will hence to Ruelle
While daylight last—and one hour after midnight
You and your twenty saints shall seek me thither!
You're made to rise!—You are, sir;—eyes of lynx,
Ears of the stag, a footfall like the snow;
You are a valiant fellow;—yea, a trusty,
Religious, exemplary, incorrupt,
And precious jewel of a fellow, Huguet!
If I live long enough,—ay, mark my words—
If I live long enough, you'll be a Colonel—
Noble, perhaps!—One hour, sir, after midnight.
   Hug. You leave me dumb with gratitude, My Lord;
I'll pick the trustiest—[*aside.*] Marion's house can furnish!
                                                      [*Exit* HUGUET.
   Rich. How like a spider shall I sit in my hole,
And watch the meshes tremble.
   Joseph.   But, my Lord,
Were it not wiser still to man the palace,
And seize the traitors in the act?
   Rich.   No; Louis,
Long chafed against me—Julie stolen from him,
Will rouse him more. He'll say I hatch'd the treason,
Or scout my charge:—He half desires my death;
But the despatch to Bouillon, some dark scheme
Against *his* crown—*there* is our weapon, Joseph;
With that, all safe—without it, all his peril!
Meanwhile to my old castle; *you* to court,
Diving with careless eyes into men's hearts,
As ghostly churchmen should do! See the King,
Bid him peruse that sage and holy treatise,
Wherein 'tis set forth how a Premier should
Be chosen from the Priesthood—how the King
Should never listen to a single charge
Against his servant, nor conceal one whisper
That the rank envies of a court distil
Into his ear—to fester the fair name
Of my—I mean his Minister!—Oh! Joseph,

A most convincing treatise.*
         Good—all favors,
If François be but bold, and Huguet honest.
Huguet—I half suspect—he bow'd too low—
'Tis not his way.
 Joseph. This is the curse, my Lord,
Of your high state;—suspicion of all men.
 Rich. [*sadly*]. True;—true;—my leeches bribed to poisoners;—pages
To strangle me in sleep.—My very King
(This brain the unresting loom, from which was woven
The purple of his greatness) leagued against me.
Old—childless—friendless—broken—all forsake—
All—all—but—
 Joseph. What?
 Rich.   The indomitable heart
Of Armand Richelieu!
 Joseph.   Nought beside?
 Rich.   Why, Julie,
My own dear foster-child, forgive me;—yes;
This morning, shining through their happy tears,
Thy soft eyes bless'd me!—and thy Lord,—in danger,
He would forsake me not.
 Joseph.   And Joseph——
 Rich. [*after a pause.*]   You—
Yes, I believe you—yes—for all men fear you
And the world loves you not. And I, friend Joseph,
I am the only man who could, my Joseph,
Make you a Bishop.† Come, we'll go to dinner,
And talk the while of methods to advance
Our Mother Church.‡ Ah, Joseph,—*Bishop Joseph!*

---

* This tract, on the "Unity of the Minister," contains all the doctrines, and many more to the same effect, referred to in the text, and had a prodigious influence on the conscience of the poor King. At the onset of his career, Richelieu, as deputy of the clergy of Poitou, complained in his harangue to the King that ecclesiastics were too rarely summoned to the royal councils, and invoked the example of the Druids.

† Joseph's ambition was not, however, so moderate; he refused a bishopric, and desired the cardinal's hat, for which favor Richelieu openly supplicated the Holy See, but contrived somehow or other never to effect it, although two ambassadors applied for it at Rome.

‡ The peculiar religion of Père Joseph may be illustrated by the following anecdote:—An officer, whom he had dismissed upon an expedition into Germany, moved by conscience at the orders he had received, returned for further explanations, and found the Capuchin *disant sa messe.* He approached and whispered, "But, my father, if these people defend themselves—" "Kill all" (*Qu' on tue tout*), answered the good father, continuing his devotions.

ACT III.

SECOND DAY (MIDNIGHT).

SCENE I.—RICHELIEU'S *Castle at Ruelle. A Gothic Chamber. Moonlight at the window, occasionally obscured.*

  Rich. [*reading*].* " In silence, and at night, the Conscience feels
That life should soar to nobler ends than Power."
So sayest thou, sage and sober moralist !
But wert thou tried ? Sublime Philosophy,
Thou art the Patriarch's ladder, reaching heaven,
And bright with beck'ning angels—but, alas !
We see thee, like the Patriarch, but in dreams,
By the first step—dull-slumbering on the earth.
I am not happy !—with the Titan's lust
I woo'd a goddess, and I clasp a cloud.
When I am dust, my name shall, like a star,
Shine through wan space, a glory—and a prophet
Whereby pale seers shall from their aëry towers
Con all the ominous signs, benign or evil,
That make the potent astrologue of kings.
But shall the Future judge me by the ends
That I have wrought—or by the dubious means
Through which the stream of my renown hath run
Into the many-voiced unfathom'd Time ?
Foul in its bed lie weeds—and heaps of slime,
And with its waves—when sparkling in the sun,
Ofttimes the secret rivulets that swell
Its might of waters—blend the hues of blood.
Yet are my sins not those of CIRCUMSTANCE,
That all-pervading atmosphere, wherein
Our spirits, like the unsteady lizard, take
The tints that color, and the food that nurtures ?
† O ! ye, whose hour-glass shifts its tranquil sands
In the unvex'd silence of a student's cell;
Ye, whose untempted hearts have never toss'd
Upon the dark and stormy tides were life
Gives battle to the elements,—and man
Wrestles with man for some slight plank, whose weight
Will bear but one—while round the desperate wretch
The hungry billows roar—and the fierce Fate,
Like some huge monster, dim-seen through the surf,

---

* I need not say that the great length of this soliloquy adapts it only for the closet, and that but few of the lines are retained on the stage. To the reader, however, the passages omitted in representation will not, perhaps, be the most uninteresting in the play, and may be deemed necessary to the completion of the Cardinal's portrait,—action on the stage supplying so subtly the place of words in the closet. The self-assured sophistries which, in the text, mingle with Richlieu's better-founded arguments, in apology for the darker traits of his character, are to be found scattered throughout the writings acribed to him. The reader will observe that in this self-confession lies the latent poetical justice, which separates happiness from success.

† Retained in representation.

Waits him who drops;—ye safe and formal men,
Who write the deeds, and with unfeverish hand
Weigh in nice scales the motives of the Great,
Ye cannot know what ye have never tried!
History preserves only the fleshless bones
Of what we are—and by the mocking skull
The would-be wise pretend to guess the features!
Without the roundness and the glow of life
How hideous is the skeleton! Without
The colorings and humanities that clothe
Our errors, the anatomists of schools
Can make our memory hideous!
                          I have wrought
Great uses out of evil tools—and they
In the time to come may bask beneath the light
Which I have stolen from the angry gods,
And warn their sons against the glorious theft,
Forgetful of the darkness which it broke.
I have shed blood—but I have had no foes
Save those the State had *—if my wrath was deadly,
'Tis that I felt my country in my veins,
And smote her sons as Brutus smote his own. †
And yet I am not happy—blanch'd and sear'd
Before my time—breathing an air of hate,
And seeing daggers in the eyes of men,
And wasting powers that shake the thrones of earth
In contest with the insects—bearding kings
And braved by lackies ‡—murder at my bed;
And lone amidst the multitudinous web,
With the dread Three—that are the Fates who hold
The woof and shears—the Monk, the Spy, the Headsman.
And this is power? Alas! I am not happy.   [*After a pause.*
And yet the Nile is fretted by the weeds
Its rising roots not up: but never yet
Did one least barrier by a ripple vex
My onward tide, unswept in sport away.
Am I so ruthless then that I do hate
Them who hate me? Tush, tush! I do not hate;
Nay, I forgive. The Statesman writes the doom,
But the Priest sends the blessing. I forgive them,
But I destroy; forgiveness is mine own,

---

* It is well known that when, on his death-bed, Richelieu was asked if he forgave his enemies; he replied, "I never had any, but those of the State." And this was true enough, for Richelieu and the State were one.

† Richelieu's vindication of himself from cruelty will be found in various parts of Petitot's Collection, vols. xxi. xxx. (*bis*).

‡ Voltaire has a striking passage on the singular fate of Richelieu, recalled every hour from his gigantic schemes to frustrate some miserable cabal of the ante-room. Richelieu would often exclaim, that "Six pieds de terre," as he called the king's cabinet, "lui donnaient plus de peine que tout le reste de l'Europe." The death of Wallenstein, sacrificed by the Emperor Ferdinand, produced a most lively impression upon Richelieu. He found many traits of comparison between Ferdinand and Louis—Wallenstein and himself. In the Memoirs —now regarded by the best authorities as written by his sanction, and in great part by himself—the great Frenchman bursts (when alluding to Wallenstein's murder) into a touching and pathetic anathema on the *miseee de cette vie* of dependence on jealous and timid royalty, which he himself, while he wrote, sustained. It is worthy of remark, that it was precisely at the period of Wallenstein's death that Richelieu obtained from the king an augmentation of his guard.

Destruction is the State's! For private life,
Scripture the guide—for public, Machiavel.
Would fortune serve me if the Heaven were wroth!
For chance makes half my greatness. I was born
Beneath the aspect of a bright-eyed star,
And my triumphant adamant of soul
Is but the fixed persuasion of success.
Ah!—here!—that spasm!—again!—How Life and Death
Do wrestle for me momently? And yet
The King looks pale. I shall outlive the King!
And then, thou insolent Austrian—who didst gibe
At the ungainly, gaunt, and daring lover,*
Sleeking thy looks to silken Buckingham,—
Thou shalt—no matter!—I have outlived love.
O! beautiful—all golden—gentle youth!
Making thy palace in the careless front
And hopeful eye of man—ere yet the soul
Hath lost the memories which (so Plato dream'd)
Breathed glory from the earlier star it dwelt in—
Oh! for one gale from thine exulting morning,
Stirring amidst the roses, where of old
Love shook the dew-drops from his glancing hair!
Could I recall the past—or had not set
The prodigal treasures of the bankrupt soul
In one slight bark upon the shoreless sea;
The yoked steer, after his day of toil,
Forgets the goad, and rests—to me alike
Or day or night—Ambition has no rest!
Shall I resign?—who can resign himself?
For custom is ourself; as drink and food
Become our bone and flesh—the aliments
Nurturing our nobler part, the mind—thoughts, dreams,
Passions, and aims, in the revolving cycle
Of the great alchemy—at length are made
Our mind itself; and yet the sweets of leisure—
An honor'd home—far from these base intrigues—
An eyrie on the heaven-kiss'd heights of wisdom—
[*Taking up the book.*
Speak to me, moralists!—I'll heed thy counsel.
Were it not best——

Enter FRANÇOIS *hastily, and in part disguised.*

    Rich. [*flinging away the book*]. Philosophy, thou liest!—Quick—the despatch
Power—Empire! Boy—the packet!
    Fran. Kill me, my Lord.
    Rich.   They knew thee—they suspected—
They gave it not——
    Fran.   He gave it—*he*—the Count
De Baradas—with his own hand he gave it!

---

* Richelieu was commonly supposed, though I cannot say I find much evidence for it, to have been too presuming in an interview with Anne of Austria (the Queen), and to have bitterly resented the contempt she expressed for him. The Duke of Buckingham's frantic and Quixotic passion for the Queen is well known.

Rich. Baradas! Joy! out with it!

Fran. Listen,
And then dismiss me to the headsman.

Rich. Ha!
Go on.

Fran. They led me to a chamber—There
Orleans and Baradas, and some half-score,
Whom I know not—were met——

Rich. Not more!

Fran. But from
The adjoining chamber broke the din of voices,
The clattering tread of arm'd men; at times
A shriller cry, that yell'd out, "Death to Richelieu!"

Rich. Speak not of *me:* thy *country* is in danger!
The adjoining room—So, so—a *separate* treason!
The one thy ruin, France!—the meaner crime,
Left to their tools, my murder!

Fran. Baradas
Question'd me close—demurr'd—until, at last,
O'erruled by Orleans,—gave the packet—told me
That life and death were in the scroll—this gold——

Rich. Gold is no proof——

Fran. And Orleans promised thousands.
When Bouillon's trumpets in the streets of Paris
Rang out shrill answer. Hastening from the house,
My footstep in the stirrup, Marion stole
Across the threshold, whispering, "Lose no moment
Ere Richelieu have the packet: tell him too—
Murder is in the winds of Night, and Orleans
Swears, ere the dawn the Cardinal shall be clay."
She said, and trembling fled within; when, lo!
A hand of iron griped me; through the dark
Gleam'd the dim shadow of an arm'd man:
Ere I could draw—the prize was wrested from me,
And a hoarse voice gasp'd—"Spy, I spare thee, for
This steel is virgin to thy Lord!" with that
He vanish'd.—Scared and trembling for thy safety
I mounted, fled, and kneeling at thy feet,
Implore thee to acquit my faith—but not,
Like him, to spare my life.

Rich. Who spake of *life?*
I bade thee grasp that treasure as thine *honor*—
A jewel worth whole hecatombs of lives!
Begone!—redeem thine honor—back to Marion—
Or Baradas—or Orleans—track the robber—
Regain the packet—or crawl on to Age—
Age and gray hairs like mine—and know, thou hast lost
That which had made thee great and saved thy country.—
See me not till thou'st bought the right to seek me.—
Away!—Nay, cheer thee, thou hast not fail'd yet.—
There's no such word as "fail!"

Fran. Bless you, my Lord,

For that one smile!—I'll wear it on my heart
To light me back to triumph.* [*Exit*.

    Rich.   The poor youth!
An elder had ask'd life!—I love the young!
For as great men live not in their own time,
But the next race,—so in the young, my soul
Makes many Richelieus. He will win it yet.
François!—He's gone. My murder! Marion's warning!
This bravo's threat! Oh for the morrow's dawn!
I'll set my spies to work—I'll make all space
(As does the Sun) a Universal Eye—
Huguet shall track—Joseph confess—ha! ha!
Strange, while I laugh'd I shudder'd—and ev'n now
Through the chill air the beating of my heart
Sounds like a death-watch by a sick man's pillow;
If Huguet *could* deceive me—hoofs without—
The gates unclose—steps near and nearer!

                Enter JULIE.

    Julie.   Cardinal!
My father! [*Falls at his feet*.
    Rich.   Julie at this hour!—and tears!
What ails thee?
    Julie.   I am safe; I am with thee!—
    Rich. Safe! why in all the storms of this wide world
What wind would mar the violet?
    Julie.   That man—
Why did I love him?—clinging to a breast
That knows no shelter?
                    Listen—late at noon—
The marriage-day—ev'n then no more a lover—
He left me coldly,—well,—I sought my chamber
To weep and wonder—but to hope and dream.
Sudden a mandate from the King—to attend
Forthwith his pleasure at the Louvre.
    Rich.   Ha!
You did obey the summons; and the King
Reproach'd your hasty nuptials.
    Julie.   Were that all!
He frown'd and chid; proclaim'd the bond unlawful:
Bade me not quit my chamber in the palace,
And there at night—alone—this night—all still—
He sought my presence—dared—thou read'st the heart,
Read mine!—I cannot speak it!
    Rich.   He a king,—
You—woman; well— you yielded!
    Julie.   Cardinal—
Dare you say "yielded?"—Humbled and abash'd,

---

* The fear and the hatred which Richelieu generally inspired were not shared by his dependents and those about his person, who are said "to have adored him."—"Ses domestiques le regardaient comme le meilleur des maitres."—*Le Clerc.* In fact, although "*Il eioit orgueilleux et colere,*"—he was "*en meme temps, affable et plein de douceur dans l'abord;*" and he was no less generous to those who served than severe to those who opposed him.

He from the chamber crept—this Mighty Louis;
Crept like a baffled felon !—yielded—Ah !
More royalty in woman's honest heart
Than dwells within the crown'd majesty
And sceptred anger of a hundred kings !
Yielded !—Heavens !—yielded !

  Rich.   To my breast,—close—close !
The world would never need a Richelieu, if
Men—bearded, mail'd men—the Lords of Earth—
Resisted flattery, falsehood, avarice, pride,
As this poor child with the dove's innocent scorn
Her sex's tempters, Vanity and Power !—
He left you—well !

  Julie.   Then came a sharper trial !
At the King's suit the Count de Baradas
Sought me to soothe, to fawn, to flatter, while
On his smoothe lip insult appear'd more hateful
For the false mask of pity: letting fall
Dark hints of treachery, with a world of sighs
That Heaven had granted to so base a Lord
The heart whose coldest friendship were to him
What Mexico to Misers ! Stung at last
By my disdain, the dim and glimmering sense
Of his cloak'd words broke into bolder light,
And THEN—ah ! then, my haughty spirit fail'd me !
Then I was weak—wept—oh ! such bitter tears !
For (turn thy the face aside and let me whisper
The horror to thine ear) then did I learn
That he—that Adrien—that my husband—knew
The King's polluting suit, and deemed it *honor!*
Then all the terrible and loathsome truth
Glared on me ;—coldness—waywardness, reserve
Mystery of looks—words—all unravell'd—and
I saw the impostor, where I had loved the god !

  Rich. I think thou wrong'st thy husband—but proceed.

  Julie. Did you say, "wrong'd" him ?—Cardinal, my father,
Did you say "wrong'd ?" Prove it, and life shall grow
One prayer for thy reward and his forgiveness.

  Rich. Let me know all.

  Julie.   To the despair he caused
The courtier left me; but amid the chaos
Darted one guiding ray—to 'scape—to fly—
Reach Adrien, learn the worst—'twas then near midnight:
Trembling I left my chamber—sought the Queen—
Fell at her feet—reveal'd the unholy peril—
Implored her aid to flee our joint disgrace.
Moved, she embraced and soothed me; nay, preserved;
Her words sufficed to unlock the palace-gates:
I hasten'd home—but home was desolate,—
No Adrien there ! Fearing the worst I fled
To thee, directed hither. As my wheels
Paused at thy gates—the clang of arms behind—
The ring of hoofs—

SCENE II.] *RICHELIEU.*

Rich.   'Twas but my guards, fair trembler.
(So Huguet keeps his word, my omens wrong'd him.)
   Julie. Oh, in one hour what years of anguish crowd!
   Rich. Nay there's no danger now, Thou needest rest.
Come, thou shalt lodge beside me. Tush! he cheer'd,
My rosiest Amazon—thou wrong'st thy Theseus.
All will be well—yes, yet all well.
                    [*Exeunt through a side door.*

SCENE II.

Enter HUGUET—DE MAUPRAT, *in complete armor, his visor down. The moonlight obscured at the casement.*

   Hug.   Not here!
   De Mau. Oh, I will find him, fear not. Hence and guard
The galleries where the menials sleep—plant sentries
At every outlet—Chance should throw no shadow
Between the vengeance and the victim! Go!
Ere yon brief vapor that obscures the moon,
As doth our deed pale conscience, pass away,
The mighty shall be ashes.
   Hug.   Will you not
A second arm?
   De Mau.   To slay one weak old man?—
Away! No lesser wrongs than mine can make
This murder lawful. Hence!
   Hug.   A short farewell!
                                [*Exit* HUGUET.

   Re-enter RICHELIEU [*not perceiving* DE MAUPRAT].
   Rich. How heavy is the air!—the vestal lamp
Of the sad Moon, weary with vigil, dies
In the still temple of the solemn heaven!
The very darkness lends itself to fear—
To treason——
   De Mau. And to death!
   Rich.   My omens lied not!
What art thou wretch?
   De Mau.   Thy doomsman!
   Rich.   Ho, my guards!
Huguet! Montbrassil! Vermont!
   De Mau.   Ay, thy spirits
Forsake thee, wizard; thy bold men of mail
Are *my confederates*. Stir not! but one step,
And know the next—thy grave!
   Rich.   Thou liest, knave!
I am old, infirm—most feeble—but thou liest!
Armand de Richelieu dies not by the hand
Of man—the stars have said it *—and the voice

---

* In common with his contemporaries, Richelieu was credulous in astrology and less lawful arts. He was too fortunate a man not to be superstitious.

Of my own prophet and oracular soul
Confirms the shining sibyls! Call them all
Thy brother butchers! Earth has no such fiend—
No! as one parricide of his father-land,
Who dares in Richelieu murder France!

  De Mau.   Thy stars
Deceive thee, Cardinal; thy soul of wiles
May against kings and armaments avail,
And mock the embattled world; but powerless now
Against the sword of one resolved man,
Upon whose forehead thou hast written shame!

  Rich. I breathe; he is not a hireling. Have I wronged thee?
Beware surmise—suspicion—lies! I am
Too great for men to speak the truth of me!

  De Mau. Thy *acts* are thy accusers, Cardinal!
In his hot youth, a soldier, urged to crime
Against the State, placed in your hands his life;—
You did not strike the blow—but o'er his head,
Upon the gossamer thread of your caprice,
Hover'd the axe. His the brave spirit's hell,
The twilight terror of suspense;—your death
Had set him free; he purposed not, nor pray'd it.
One day you summon'd—mock'd him with smooth pardon—
Shower'd wealth upon him—bade an angel's face
Turn Earth to Paradise——

  Rich.   Well!
  De Mau.   Was this mercy?
A Cæsar's generous vengeance?—Cardinal, no!
Judas, not Cæsar, was the model! You
Saved him from death for shame; reserved to grow
The scorn of living men—to his dead sires
Leprous reproach—scoff of the age to come—
A kind convenience—a Sir Pandarus
To his own bride, and the august adulterer!
Then did the first great law of human hearts,
Which with the patriot's, not the rebel's, name
Crown'd the first Brutus, when the Tarquin fell,
Make Misery royal—raise this desperate wretch
Into thy destiny! Expect no mercy!
Behold De Mauprat!   *[Lifts his vizor.*

  Rich.   To thy knees, and crawl
For pardon; or, I tell thee, thou shalt live
For such remorse, that, did I hate thee, I
Would bid thee strike, that I might be avenged!
It was to save my Julie from the King,
That in thy valor I forgave thy crime;—
It was, when thou—the rash and ready tool—
Yea, of that shame thou loath'st—didst leave thy hearth
To the polluter—in these arms thy bride
Found the protecting shelter thine withheld. *[Goes to the side door.*
Julie de Mauprat—Julie!

Enter JULIE.

Lo! my witness!

De Mau. What marvel's this?—I dream! my Julie—*thou!*
This, thy beloved hand?

Julie. Henceforth all bond
Between us twain is broken. Were it not
For this old man, I might, in truth, have lost
The right—now mine—to scorn thee!

Rich. So, you hear her?

De Mau. Thou with some slander hast her sense infected!

Julie. No, sir; he did excuse thee in despite
Of all that wears the face of truth. Thy *friend*—
Thy *confidant*—familiar—*Baradas*—
Himself reveal'd thy baseness.

De Mau. Baseness!

Rich. Ay;
That *thou* didst *court* dishonor.

De Mau. Baradas!
Where is thy thunder, Heaven?—Duped!—snared!—undone?
Thou—thou couldst not believe him! Thou dost love me!
Love cannot feed upon falsehoods!

Julie [*aside*]. Love him!—Ah!
Be still, my heart! [*Aloud.*] Love you I did:—how fondly,
Woman—if women were my listeners now—
Alone could tell!—For ever fled my dream:
Farewell—all's over!

Rich. Nay, my daughter, these
Are but the blinding mists of day-break love
Sprung from its very light, and heralding
A noon of happy summer.—Take her hand
And speak the truth, with which your heart runs over—
That this Count Judas—this Incarnate Falsehood—
Never lied more, than when he told thy Julie
That Adrien loved her not—except, indeed,
When he told Adrien, Julie could betray him.

Julie [*embracing* DE MAUPRAT]. You love me, then!—you love me!—and they wrong'd you!

De Mau. Ah! couldst thou doubt it?

Rich. Why, the very mole
Less blind than thou! Baradas loves thy wife;—
Had hoped her hand—aspired to be that cloak
To the King's will, which to thy bluntness seems
The Centaur's poisonous robe—hopes even now
To make thy corpse his footstool to thy bed!
Where was thy wit, man?—Ho! these schemes are glass!
The very sun shines through them.

De Mau. O, my Lord.
Can you forgive me?

Rich. Ay, and save you!

De Mau. Save!—
Terrible word!—O, save *thyself;*—these halls
Swarm with thy foes: already for thy blood
Pants thirsty Murder!

Julie. Murder!

Rich. Hush! put by
The woman. Hush! a shriek—a cry—a breath
Too loud, would startle from its horrent pause
The swooping Death! Go to the door, and listen!—
Now for escape!

De Mau. None—none! Their blades shall pass
This heart to thine.

Rich. [*drily*]. An honorable outwork
But much too near the citadel. I think
That I can trust you now [*slowly, and gazing on him*]:—yes; I can trust you.
How many of my troop league with you?

De Mau. All!—
We *are* your troop!

Rich. And Huguet?

De Mau. Is our captain.

Rich. A retributive Power!—This comes of spies!
All? then the lion's skin's too short to-night,—
Now for the fox's!——

Julie. A hoarse, gathering murmur!
Hurrying and heavy footsteps!

Rich. Ha!—the posterns?

De Mau. No egress where no sentry!

Rich. Follow me—
I have it!—to my chamber—quick! Come, Julie!
Hush! Mauprat, come!
[*Murmur at a distance.*]—Death to the Cardinal!

Rich. Bloodhounds, I laugh at ye!—ha! ha!—we will
Baffle them yet.—Ha!—ha! [*Exeunt* JULIE, MAUPRAT, RICHELIEU

Hug. [*without*]. This way—this way!

SCENE III.

Enter HUGUET *and the* Conspirators.

Hug. De Mauprat's hand is never slow in battle;
Strange, if it falter now! Ha! gone!

First Con. Perchance
The fox had crept to rest; and to his lair
Death, the dark hunter, tracks him.

[*Enter* MAUPRAT, *throwing open the doors of the recess in which a bed, whereon* RICHELIEU *lies extended.*

De Mau. Live the King!
Richelieu is dead!

Hug. [*advancing towards the recess;* MAUPRAT *following, his hand on his dagger*].
Are his eyes open?

De Mau. Ay,
As if in life!

Hug. [*turning back*]. I will not look on him.
You have been long.

De Mau.   I watch'd him till he slept.
Heed me.—No trace of blood reveals the deed;—
Strangled in sleep. His health had long been broken—
Found breathless in his bed. So runs our tale,
Remember! Back to Paris—Orleans gives
Ten thousand crowns, and Baradas a lordship,
To him who first gluts vengeance with the news
That Richelieu is in heaven! Quick, that all France
May share your joy!
    Hug.   And you?
    De Mau.   Will stay, to crush
Eager suspicion—to forbid sharp eyes
To dwell too closely on the clay; prepare
The rites, and place him on his bier—this *my* task.
I leave to you, sirs, the more grateful lot
Of wealth and honors. Hence!
    Hug.   I shall be noble!
    De Mau. Away!
    First Con.   Five thousand crowns!
    Omnes. To horse!—to horse!   [*Exeunt* Conspirators.

SCENE IV.

Still night—A room in the house of Count De Baradas, *lighted, &c.*

Orleans *and* De Beringhen.

De Ber. I understand. Mauprat kept guard without:
Knows nought of the despatch—but heads the troop
Whom the poor Cardinal fancies his protectors.
Save us from such protection!
    Orle.   Yet, if Huguet,
By whose advice and proffers we renounced
Our earlier scheme, should still be Richelieu's minion,
And play us false—
    De Ber.   The fox must then devour
The geese he gripes (I'm out of it, thank Heaven!)
And you must swear you smelt the trick, but seem'd
To approve the deed—to render up the doers.

Enter Baradas.

Bar. Julie is fled:—the King, whom now I left
To a most thorny pillow, vows revenge
On her—on Mauprat—and on Richelieu! Well;
We loyal men anticipate his wish
Upon the last—and as for Mauprat,—   [*Showing a writ.*
    De Ber.   Hum!
They say the devil invented printing! Faith,
He has some hand in writing parchment—eh, Count?
What mischief now?

Bar.   The King, at Julie's flight
Enraged, will brook no rival in a subject—
So on this old offence—the affair of Faviaux—
Ere Mauprat can tell tales of *us*, we build
His bridge between the dungeon and the grave.
     Orle. Well; if our courier can but reach the army,
The cards are ours!—and yet, I own, I tremble.
Our names are in the scroll—discovery, death!
     Bar. Success, a crown!
     De Ber. [*apart to* BARADAS]. Our future Regent is
No hero.
     Bar. [*to* DE BERINGHEN]. But his rank makes others valiant;
And on his cowardice I mount to power.
Were Orleans Regent—what were Baradas?
Oh! by the way—I had forgot, your Highness,
Friend Huguet whisper'd me, "Beware of Marion:
I've seen her lurking near the Cardinal's palace."
Upon that hint, I've found her lodging elsewhere.
     Orle. You wrong her, Count. Poor Marion!—she adores me.
     Bar. [*apologetically*]. Forgive me, but—

Enter Page.

     Page.   My Lord, a rude, strange soldier,
Breathless with haste, demands an audience.
     Bar.   So!—
The Archers?
     Page. In the ante-room, my Lord,
As you desired.
     Bar.   'Tis well—admit the soldier.
Huguet!—I bade him seek me here.

Enter HUGUET.

     Hug.   My Lords,
The deed is done. Now, Count, fulfil your word,
And makes me noble.
     Bar.   Richelieu dead?—art sure?
How died he?
     Hug.   Strangled in his sleep:—no blood,
No tell-tale violence.
     Bar.   Strangled?—monstrous villain!
Reward for murder! Ho, there!   [*Stamping.*

Enter Captain *with five* Archers.

     Hug.   No, thou durst not!
     Bar. Seize on the ruffian—bind him—gag him! Off
To the Bastile!
     Hug.   Your word—your plighted faith!
     Bar. Insolent liar! ho, away!
     Hug.   Nay, Count;
I have that about me, which——
     Bar.   Away with him! [*Exeunt* HUGUET *and* Archers.
Now, then, all's safe; Huguet must die in prison,
So Mauprat:—coax or force the meaner crew

To fly the country. Ha, ha! thus, your highness,
Great men make use of little men.
 De Ber.   My Lords,
Since our suspense is ended—you'll excuse me;
'Tis late—and, *entre nous*, I have not supp'd yet!
I'm one of the new Council now, remember;
I feel the public stirring here already;
A very craving monster. *Au revoir!*   [*Exit* DE BERINGHEN.
 Orle. No fear, now Richelieu's dead.
 Bar.   And could he come
To life again, he could not keep life's life—
His power,—nor save De Mauprat from the scaffold,—
Nor Julie from these arms—nor Paris from
The Spaniard—nor your highness from the throne!
All ours! all ours! in spite of my Lord Cardinal!

     [*Enter* Page.

 Page. A gentleman, my Lord, of better mien
Than he who last——
 Bar. Well, he may enter. [*Exit* Page.
 Orle.   Who
Can this be?
 Bar. One of the conspirators:
Mauprat himself, perhaps.

     Enter FRANÇOIS.

 Fran.   My Lord——
 Bar.   Ha, traitor!
In Paris still!
 Fran. The packet—the dispatch—
Some knave play'd spy without, and reft it from me,
Ere I could draw my sword.
 Bar.   Play'd spy *without!*
Did he wear armor?
 Fran. Ay, from head to heel.
 Orle. One of our band. Oh, heavens!
 Bar.   Could it be Mauprat?
Kept guard at the *door*—knew *nought of the dispatch*—
How HE!—and yet, who other?
 Fran.   Ha, De Mauprat!
The night was dark—his vizor closed.
 Bar.   'Twas he!
How could he guess?—'sdeath if he should betray us.
His hate to Richelieu dies with Richelieu—and
He was not great enough for treason. Hence!
Find Mauprat—beg, steal, filch, or force it back,
Or, as I live, the halter——
 Fran. By the morrow
I will regain it [*aside*], and redeem my honor! [*Exit* FRANÇOIS.
 Orle. Oh, we are lost—
 Bar. Not so! But cause on cause
For Mauprat's seizure—silence—death! Take courage.

Orle. Should it once reach the King, the Cardinal's arm
Could smite us from the grave.
  Bar.   Sir, think it not!
I hold De Mauprat in my grasp. To-morrow,
And France is ours! Thou dark and fallen Angel,
Whose name on earth's AMBITION—thou that mak'st
Thy throne on treasons, stratagems, and murder,—
And with thy fierce and blood-red smile canst quench
The guiding stars of solemn empire—hear us
(For we are thine)—and light us to the goal!

ACT IV.

THIRD DAY.

SCENE I.—*The Gardens of the Louvre.*—ORLEANS, BARADAS, DE BERINGHEN, Courtiers, &c.

 Orle. How does my brother bear the Cardinal's death?
 Bar. With grief, when thinking of the toils of State;
With joy, when thinking on the eyes of Julie:—
At times he sighs, "Who now shall govern France?"
Anon exclaims—"Who now shall baffle Louis?"

   Enter LOUIS *and other* Courtiers. [*They uncover.*]

 Orle. Now, my liege, now, I can embrace a brother.
 Louis. Dear Gaston, yes.—I do believe you *love* me;—
Richelieu denied it—sever'd us too long.
A great man, Gaston! Who shall govern France?
 Bar. Yourself, my liege. That swart and potent star
Eclipsed your royal orb. He served the country,
But did he *serve*, or seek to *sway* the *King?*
 [*Louis.* You're right—he was an able politician—
That's all:—between ourselves, Count, I suspect
The largeness of his learning—specially
In falcons *—a poor huntsman, too!
 Bar.   Ha—ha!
Your Majesty remembers——
 Louis.   Ay, the blunder
Between the *greffier* and the *souillard* when—   [*Checks and crosses himself.*
Alas! poor sinners that we are! we laugh
While this great man—a priest, a cardinal,
A faithful servant—out upon us!—

---

* Louis XIII. is said to have possessed some natural talents, and in earlier youth to have exhibited the germs of noble qualities; but a blight seems to have passed over his maturer life. Personally brave, but morally timid,—always governed, whether by his mother or his minister, and always repining at the yoke. The only affection amounting to a passion that he betrayed, was for the sports of the field; yet it was his craving weakness (and this throws a kind of false interest over his character) to wish to be loved. He himself loved no one. He suffered the only woman who seems to have been attached to him to wither in a convent;—he gave up favorite after favorite to exile or the block. When Richelieu died, he said coldly, " Voilà un grand politique mort!" and when the ill-fated but unprincipled Cinq Mars, whom he called " *le cher ami*," was beheaded, he drew out his watch at the fatal hour, and said with a smile, " I think at this moment that *le cher ami fait une vilaine mine*." Nevertheless, his conscience at times (for he was devout and superstitious) made him gentle, and his pride and honor would often, when least expected, rouse him into haughty but brief resistence to the despotism under which he lived.

Bar.   Sire,
If my brow wear no cloud, 'tis that the Cardinal
No longer shades the King.
   Louis [*looking up at the skies*]. Oh, Baradas!
Am I not to be pitied?—what a day
For—
   Bar. Sorrow?—No, Sire!
   Louis.   Bah! for *hunting*, man,
And Richlieu's dead; 'twould be an indecorum
Till he is buried—[*yawns*]—life is very tedious.
I made a madrigal on life last week:
You do not sing,* Count?—Pity; you should learn.
Poor Richelieu had no ear—yet a great man.
Ah! what a weary weight devolves upon me!
These endless wars—these thankless Parliaments—
The snares in which he tangled States and Kings,
Like the old fisher of the fable, Proteus,
Netting great Neptune's wariest tribes, and changing
Into all shapes when Craft pursued himself:
Oh, a great man!
   Bar.   Your royal mother said so,
And died in exile.
   Louis [*sadly*]. True: I loved my mother.†
   Bar. The Cardinal dies.—Yet day revives the earth;
The rivers run not back. In truth, my liege,
Did your high orb on others shine as him,
Why, things as dull in their own selves as I am
Would glow as brightly with the borrow'd beam. ‡
   Louis. Ahem!—He was too stern.
   Orle.   A very Nero.
   Bar. His power was like the Capitol of old—
Built on a human skull.
   Louis.   And, had he lived,
I know another head, my Baradas,
That would have propp'd the pile: I've seen him eye thee
With a most hungry fancy.
   Bar. [*anxiously*].   Sire, I knew
You would protect me.
   Louis.   Did you so? of course!
And yet he had a way with him—a something
That always——But no matter—he is dead.

* Louis had some musical taste and accomplishment, wherewith he often communicated to his favorites some of that wearisome *ennui* under which he himself almost unceasingly languished.

† One of Louis's most bitter complaints against Richelieu was the continued banishment of the Queen Mother. It is impossible, however, not to be convinced that the return of that most worthless intriguante was wholly incompatible with the tranquillity of the kingdom. Yet, on the other hand, the poverty and privation which she endured in exile are discreditable to the generosity and the gratitude of Richelieu; she was his first patron, though afterwards his most powerful persecutor.

‡ In his Memoirs, Richelieu gives an amusing account of the insolence and arts of Baradas, and observes, with indignant astonishment, that the favorite was never weary of repeating to the King that he (Baradas) would have made just as great a minister as Richelieu. It is on the attachment of Baradas to La Cressias, a maid of honor to the Queen Mother, of whom, according to Baradas, the King was enamoured also, that his love for the Julie de Mortemar of the play has been founded. The secret of Baradas's sudden and extraordinary influence with the King seems to rest in the personal adoration which he professed for Louis, with whom he affected all the jealousy of a lover, but whom he flattered with the ardent chivalry of a knight. Even after his disgrace he placed upon his banner, "Fiat voluntas tua."

And, after all, men call his King "The Just," *
And so I am. Dear Count, this silliest Julie,
I know not why, she takes my fancy. Many
As fair, and certainly more kind; but yet
It is so. Count I am no lustful Tarquin,
And do abhor the bold and frontless vices
Which the Church justly censures; yet, 'tis sad
On rainy days to drag out weary hours †—
Deaf to the music of a woman's voice—
Blind to the sunshine of a woman's eyes.
It is no sin in Kings to seek amusement;
And that is all I seek. I miss her much—
She has a silver laugh—a rare perfection.

 Bar. Richelieu was most disloyal in that marriage.]

 Louis [*querulously*]. He knew that Julie pleased me:—a clear proof
He never loved me!

 Bar   Oh, most clear!—But now
No bar between the lady and your will!
This writ makes all secure; a week or two
In the Bastile will sober Mauprat's love,
And leave him eager to dissolve a hymen
That brings him such a home.

 Louis.   See to it, Count.   [*Exit* BARADAS.
I'll summon Julie back. A word with you.
 [*Takes aside* First Courtier, *and* DE BERINGHEN, *and passes, conversing with
them, through the Gardens.*

      Enter FRANÇOIS.

 Fran. All search, as yet, in vain for Mauprat!—Not
At home since yesternoon—a soldier told me
He saw him pass this way with hasty strides;
Should he meet Baradas—they'd rend it from him—
And then—benignant Fortune smiles upon me—
I am thy son!—if thou desert'st me now,
Come, Death, and snatch me from disgrace. But, no,
There's a great Spirit ever in the air
That from prolific and far-spreading wings
Scatters the seeds of honor—yea, the walls
And moats of castled forts—the barren seas—
The cell wherein the pale-eyed student holds
Talk with melodious science—all are sown
With everlasting honors, if our souls
Will toil for fame as boors for bread—

      Enter MAUPRAT.

 De Mau.   Oh, let me—
Let me but meet him foot to foot—I'll dig

---

* Louis was called The Just, but for no other reason than that he was born under the Libra.

† Louis XIII. did not resemble either his father or his son in the ardor of his attachments; if not wholly Platonic, they were wholly unimpassioned: yet no man was more jealous, or more unscrupulously tyrannical when the jealousy was aroused.

The Judas from his heart;—albeit the King
Should o'er him cast the purple !
Fran.   Mauprat ! hold:—
Where is the——
De Mau. Well ! What wouldst thou ?
Fran.   The despatch !
The packet.—Look on me—I serve the Cardinal—
You know me.—Did you not keep guard last night
By Marion's house ?
De Mau.   I did;—no matter now !
They told me, *he* was *here !*—
Fran.   O joy ! quick—quick—
The packet thou didst wrest from me ?
De Mau.   The packet ?
What, art thou he I deem'd the Cardinal's spy
(Dupe that I was)—and overhearing Marion—
Fran. The same—restore it ! haste !
De Mau.   I have it not:
Methought it but reveal'd our scheme to Richelieu,
And, as we mounted, gave it to——

Enter BARADAS.

                       Stand back !
Now, villain ! now—I have thee !
         [*To* FRANÇOIS.] Hence, sir !—*Draw !*
Fran. Art mad ?—the King's at hand ! leave *him* to Richelieu !
Speak—the despatch—to whom—
   De Mau. [*dashing him aside, and rushing to* BARADAS]. Thou triple slanderer !
I'll set my heel upon thy crest !   [*A few passes.*
   Fran.   Fly—fly !—
The King !

Enter at one side LOUIS, ORLEANS, DE BERINGHEN, Courtiers, *&c. ; at the other, the* Guards *hastily.*

   Louis.   Swords drawn—before our very palace !
Have our laws died with Richelieu ?
   Bar.   Pardon, Sire,—
My crime but self-defence.* [*Aside to* King.] It is De Mauprat !
   Louis. Dare he thus brave us ?
               [BARADAS *goes to the* Guard, *and gives the writ.*
   De Mau.   Sire, in the Cardinal's name—
   Bar. Seize him—disarm—to the Bastile !
      [DE MAUPRAT *seized, struggles with the* Guard—FRANÇOIS *restlessly endeavoring to pacify and speak to him—when the gates open. Enter* RICHELIEU—JOSEPH—*followed by* Arquebusiers.
   Bar.   The Dead
Return'd to life !

---

* One of Richelieu's severest and least politic laws was that which made duelling a capital crime. Never was the punishment against the offence more relentlessly enforced; and never were duels so desperate and so numerous. The punishment of death must be evidently ineffectual so long as to refuse a duel is to be dishonored, and so long as men hold the doctrine, however wrong, that it is better to part with the life that Heaven gave than the honor man makes. In fact, the greater the danger he incurred, the greater was the punctilio of the cavalier of that time in braving it.

Louis. What a *mock* death! this tops
The Infinite of Insult.

De Mau. [*breaking from the* Guards]. Priest and Hero!—
For you are both—protect the truth!

Rich. [*taking the writ from the* Guard]. What's this?

De Ber. Fact in Philosophy. Foxes have got
Nine lives, as well as cats!

Bar. Be firm, my liege.

Louis. I have assumed the sceptre—I will wield it!

Joseph. The tide runs counter—there'll be shipwreck somewhere.

[Baradas *and* Orleans *keep close to the* King, *whispering and prompting him when* Richelieu *speaks.*

Rich. High treason—Faviaux! still that stale pretence!
My liege, bad men (ay, Count, most *knavish* men!)
Abuse your royal goodness. For this soldier,
France hath none braver—and his youth's hot folly,
Misled—(by whom *your Highness* may conjecture!)—
Is long since cancell'd by a loyal manhood.—
I, Sire, have pardon'd him.

Louis. And we do give
Your pardon to the winds. Sir, do your duty!

Rich. What, Sire?—you do not know—Oh, pardon me—
You know not yet, that this brave, honest heart,
Stood between mine and murder!—Sire! for my sake—
For your old servant's sake—undo this wrong.
See, let me rend the sentence.

Louis. At your peril!
This is too much:—Again, sir, do your duty!

Rich. Speak not, but go:—I would not see young Valor
So humbled as grey Service.

De Mau. Fare you well!
Save Julie, and console her.

Fran. [*aside to* Mauprat]. The despatch!
Your fate, foes, life, hang on a word!—to whom?

De Mau. To Huguet.

Fran. Hush—keep counsel!—silence—hope!

[*Exeunt* Mauprat *and* Guard.

Bar. [*aside to* François]. Has he the packet?

Fran. He will not reveal—
[*Aside.*] Work, brain!—beat, heart!—"*There's no such word as fail!*"

[*Exit* François.

Rich. [*fiercely*]. Room, my Lords, room!—the Minister of France
Can need no intercession with the King. [*They fall back*

Louis. What means this false report of death, Lord Cardinal?

Rich. Are you then anger'd, Sire, that I live still?

Louis. No; but such artifice—

Rich. Not mine:—look elsewhere!
Louis—my castle swarm'd with the assassins.

Bar. [*advancing*]. We have punished them already. Huguet now
In the Bastile.—Oh! my Lord, *we* were prompt
To avenge you—*we* were—

Rich. We?—Ha, ha! you hear,
My liege! What page, man, in the last court grammar

Made you a plural? Count, you have seized the *hirelings*:—
Sire, shall I name the *master?*

  Louis.   Tush, my Lord,
The old contrivance:—ever does your wit
Invent assassins, that ambition may
Slay rivals——
  Rich.   Rivals, Sire, in what?
Service to France? *I have none!* Lives the man
Whom Europe, paled before your glory, deems
Rival to Armand Richelieu?
  Louis.   What, so haughty!
Remember, he who made, can unmake.
  Rich.   Never!
Never! Your anger can recall your trust,
Annul my office, spoil me of my lands,
Rifle my coffers,—but my name—my deeds,
Are royal in a land beyond your sceptre!
Pass sentence on me, if you will; from Kings,
Lo! I appeal to time! [Be just, my liege—
I found your kingdom rent with heresies
And bristling with rebellion; lawless nobles
And breadless serfs; England fomenting discord;
Austria—her clutch on your dominion; Spain
Forging the prodigal gold of either Ind
To arm'd thunderbolts. The Arts lay dead,
Trade rotted in your marts, your Armies mutinous,
Your Treasury bankrupt. Would you now revoke
Your trust, so be it! and I leave you, sole
Supremest Monarch of the mightiest realm,
From Ganges to the Icebergs:—Look without;
No foe not humbled!—Look within; the Arts
Quit for your schools—their old Hesperides
The golden Italy! while through the veins
Of your vast empire flows in strengthening tides
TRADE, the calm health of nations!
              Sire, I know
Your smoother courtiers please you best—nor measure
Myself with them,—yet sometimes I would doubt
If Statesmen rock'd and dandled into power
Could leave such legacies to kings!   [LOUIS *appears irresolute*
  Bar. [*passing him whispers*].   But Julie,
Shall I not summon her to court?]
  Louis. [*motions to* BARADAS, *and turns haughtily to the* Cardinal].   Enough!
Your Eminence must excuse a longer audience.
To your own palace:—For our conference, this
Nor place—nor season.
  Rich.   Good my liege, for *Justice*
All place a temple, and all season, summer!—
Do you deny me justice?—Saints of Heaven!
He turns from me!—*Do you deny me Justice?*
For fifteen years, while in these hands dwelt Empire,
The humblest craftsman—the obscurest vassal—
The very leper shrinking from the sun,

Though loathed by Charity, might ask for justice!—
Not with the fawning tone and crawling mien
Of some I see around you—Counts and Princes—
Kneeling for *favors;*—but, erect and loud,
As men who ask man's rights!—my liege, my Louis,
Do you refuse me justice—audience even—
In the pale presence of the baffled Murther?*

    Louis. Lord Cardinal—one by one you have sever'd from me
The bonds of human love. All near and dear
Mark'd out for vengeance—exile or the scaffold.
You find me now amidst my trustiest friends,
My closest kindred;—you would tear them from me;
They murder *you* forsooth, since *me* they love!
Eno' of plots and treasons for one reign!
Home!—Home! and sleep away these phantoms!
    Rich.   Sire!
I——patience, Heaven!—sweet Heaven! Sire, from the foot
Of that Great Throne, these hands have raised aloft
On an Olympus, looking down on mortals
And worshipp'd by their awe—before the foot
Of that high throne,—spurn you the grey-hair'd man,
Who gave you empire—and now sues for safety?
    Louis. No:—when we see your Eminence in truth
At the *foot* of the throne—we'll listen to you.   [*Exit* LOUIS.
    Orle.   Saved!
    Bar. For this, deep thanks to Julie and to Mauprat!
    Rich. My lord de Baradas—I pray your pardon—
You are to be my successor!—your hand, sir!
    Bar. [*aside*]. What can this mean?
    Rich.   It trembles, see! it trembles!
The hand that holds the destinies of nations
Ought to shake less!—poor Baradas—poor France!
    Bar. Insolent——   [*Exeunt* BARADAS *and* ORLEANS.

SCENE II.

    Rich. Joseph—Did you hear the King?
    Joseph. I did—there's danger! Had you been less haughty †——
    Rich. And suffer'd slaves to chuckle—" See the Cardinal—
How meek his Eminence is to-day "—I tell thee
This is a strife in which the loftiest look
  Is the most subtle armor——
    Joseph.   But——

---

* For the haughty and rebuking tone which Richelieu assumed in his expostulations with the King, see his Memoirs (*passim*) in Petitot's collection, vols. 22-30 (*bis*). Montesquieu, in one of his brilliant antitheses, says well of Richelieu, " Ill avila le roi, mais il illustra le règne."

† However, "*orgueilleux*" and "*colere*" in his disputes with Louis, the Cardinal did not always disdain recourse to the arts of the courtier; once, after an angry discussion with the King, in which, as usual, Richelieu got the better, Louis, as they quitted the palace together, said, rudely, " Sortez le premier; vous êtes bien le roi de France." " Si je passe le premier," replied the minister, after a moment's hesitation, and with great adroitness, " ce ne peut être que comme le plus humble de vos serviteurs;" and he took a flambeau from one of the pages to light the King as he walked before him—" en reculant et sans tourner le dos."

IRVING AS RICHELIEU.

Rich.   No time
For ifs and buts. I will accuse these traitors!
François shall witness that De Baradas
Gave him the secret missive for De Bouillon,
And told him life and death were in the scroll.
I will—I will—

   Joseph.   Tush! François is your creature;
So they will say, and laugh at you!—*your witness*
Must be that same Despatch.

   Rich.   Away to Marion!

   Joseph. I have been there—she is seized—removed—imprisoned—
By the Count's orders.

   Rich.   Goddess of bright dreams,
My country—shalt thou lose me now, when most
Thou need'st thy worshipper? My native land!
Let me but ward this dagger from thy heart,
And die—but on thy bosom!

                     Enter JULIE.

   Julie.   Heaven! I thank thee!
It cannot be, or this all-powerful man
Would not stand idly thus.

   Rich.   What dost *thou* here?
Home!

   Julie. Home!—is *Adrien there?*—you're dumb—yet strive
For words; I see them trembling on your lip,
But choked by pity. It *was* truth—all truth!
Seized—the Bastile—and in your presence, too!
Cardinal, where is Adrien?—Think—he saved
Your life:—your name is infamy, if wrong
Should come to his!

   Rich.   Be soothed, child.

   Julie.   Child no more;
I love, and I am woman! Hope and suffer—
Love, suffering, hope,—what else doth make the strength
And majesty of woman?—Where is Adrien?

   Rich. [*to* JOSEPH]. Your youth was never young—you never loved:—
Speak to her—

   Joseph.   Nay, take heed—the King's command,
'Tis true—I mean—the—

   Julie [*to* RICHELIEU]. Let thine eyes meet mine:
Answer me but one word—I am a wife—
I ask thee for my *home*—my FATE—my ALL!
Where is my *husband?*

   Rich.   You are Richelieu's ward,
A soldier's bride: they who insist on truth
Must out-face fear;—you ask me for your husband?
There—where the clouds of Heaven look darkest, o'er
The domes of the Bastile!

   Julie.   I thank you, father;
You see I do not shudder. Heaven forgive you
The sin of this desertion!

   Rich. [*detaining her*]. Whither wouldst thou?

Julie. Stay me not. Fie! I should be there already.
I am thy ward, and haply he may think
Thou'st taught *me* also to forsake the wretched!

Rich. I've fill'd those cells—with many—traitors all.
Had *they* wives too?—Thy memories, Power, are solemn!
Poor sufferer!—think'st thou that yon gates of woe
Unbar to love? Alas! if love once enter,
'Tis for the last farewell; between those walls
And the mute grave *—the blessed household sounds
Only heard once—while hungering at the door,
The headsman whets the axe.

    Julie.   O, mercy! mercy!
Save him, restore him, father! Art thou not
The Cardinal-King?—the Lord of life and death—
Beneath whose light, as deep beneath the moon,
The solemn tides of Empire ebb and flow?
Art thou not Richelieu?

    Rich.   Yesterday I was!—
To-day a very weak old man!—to-morrow,
I know not what!

    Julie.   Do you conceive his meaning?
Alas! I cannot. But, methinks, my senses
Are duller than they were!

    Joseph.   The King is chafed
Against his servant. Lady, while we speak,
The lackey of the ante-room is not
More powerless than the Minister of France.

[*Rich.* And yet the air is still; Heaven wears no cloud;
From Nature's silent orbit starts no portent
To warn the unconscious world; albeit this night
May with a morrow teem which, in my fall,
Would carry earthquake to remotest lands,
And change the Christian globe. What wouldst thou, woman?
Thy fate and his, with mine, for good or ill,
Are woven threads. In my vast sum of life
Millions such units merge.]

                Enter First Courtier.

    First Cour.   Madame de Mauprat!
Pardon, your Eminence—Even now I seek
This lady's home—commanded by the King
To pray her presence.

    Julie. [*clinging to* RICHELIEU]. Think of my dead father!—
Think, how, an infant, clinging to your knees,
And looking to your eyes, the wrinkled care
Fled from your brow before the smile of childhood,
Fresh from the dews of Heaven! Think of this,
And take me to your breast.

    Rich.   To those who send you!—
And say you found the virtue they would slay
Here—couch'd upon this heart, as at an altar,

---

* "Selon l'usage de Louis XIII., faire arrêter quelqu'un pour crime d'état, et le faire mourir, l'était à peu près la même chose."—*Le Clerc.*

Rich. "Mark, where she stands!—around her form I draw the awful circle of our solemn church," etc.—*Richelieu, Act IV., Sc. 2.*

And shelter'd by the wings of sacred Rome!
Begone!

 First Cour. My Lord, I am your friend and servant—
Misjudge me not: but never yet was Louis
So roused against you:—shall I take this answer?—
It were to be your foe.

 Rich.   All time my foe,
If I, a Priest, could cast this holy sorrow
Forth from her last asylum!

 First Cour.   He is lost!   [*Exit* First Courtier

 Rich. God help thee, child! She hears not! Look upon her!
The storm, that rends the oak, uproots the flower.
Her father loved me so! and in that age
When friends are brothers! She has been to me
Soother, nurse, plaything, daughter. Are these tears?*
Oh! shame, shame!—dotage!

 Joseph.   Tears are not for eyes
That rather need the lightning, which can pierce
Through barrèd gates and triple walls, to smite
Crime, where it cowers in secret!—The Despatch!
Set every spy to work;—the morrow's sun
Must see that written treason in your hands,
Or rise upon your ruin.

 Rich.   Ay—and close
Upon my corpse!—I am not made to live—
Friends, glory, France, all reft from me;—my star
Like some vain holiday mimicry of fire,
Piercing imperial Heaven, and falling down
Rayless and blacken'd, to the dust—a thing
For all men's feet to trample! Yea!—to-morrow
Triumph or death! Look up, child!—Lead us, Joseph.
     [*As they are going out, enter* BARADAS *and* DE BERINGHEN

 Bar. My Lord, the King cannot believe your Eminence
So far forgets your duty, and his greatness,
As to resist his mandate! Pray you, Madam,
Obey the King—no cause for fear!

 Julie.   My father!

 Rich. She shall not stir!

 Bar.   You are not of her kindred—
An orphan—

 Rich. And her country is her mother!

 Bar. The country is the King!

 Rich.   Ay, is it so?—
Then wakes the power which in the age of iron
Burst forth to curb the great, and raise the low.
Mark, where she stands!—around her form I draw
The awful circle of our solemn church!

---

* Like Cromwell and Rienzi, Richelieu appears to have been easily moved to tears. The Queen-Mother who put the hardest interpretation on that humane weakness, which is natural with very excitable temperaments, said that "il pleurait quand il voulait." I may add, to those who may be inclined to imagine that Richelieu appears in parts of this scene too dejected for consistency with so imperious a character, that it is recorded of him that "quand ses affaires ne réuississoient pas, il se trouvoit abbattu et epouvanté, et quand il obtenoit ce qu'il souhaitoit, il étoit fier et insultant."

Set but a foot within that holy ground,
And on thy head—yea, though it wore a crown—
I launch the curse of Rome!

Bar. I dare not brave you!
I do but speak the orders of my King,
The church, your rank, power, very word, my Lord,
Suffice you for resistance:—blame yourself,
If it should cost you power!

Rich. That *my* stake.—Ah!
Dark gamester! *what is thine?* Look to it well!—
Lose not a trick.—By this same hour to-morrow
Thou shalt have France, or I thy head!

Bar. [*aside to* DE BERINGHEN]. He cannot
Have the Despatch?

De Ber. No: were it so, your stake
Were lost already.

Joseph [*aside*]. Patience is your game:
Reflect, you have not the Despatch!

Rich. O! monk!
Leave patience to the saints—for *I* am human!
Did not thy father die for France, poor orphan?
And now they say thou hast *no* father!—Fie!
Art thou not pure and good?—if so, thou art
A part of that—the Beautiful, the Sacred—
Which, in all climes, men that have hearts adore,
By the great title of their mother country!

Bar. [*aside*]. He wanders!

Rich. So cling close unto my breast,
Here where thou droop'st lies France. I am very feeble—
Of little use it seems to either now.
Well, well—we will go home.

Bar. In sooth, my Lord,
You do need rest—the burthens of the State
O'ertask your health!

Rich. [*to* JOSEPH]. I'm patient, see!

Bar. [*aside*]. His mind
And life are breaking fast!

Rich. [*overhearing him.*] Irreverent ribald!
If so, beware the falling ruins! Hark!
I tell thee, scorner of these whitening hairs,
When this snow melteth there shall come a flood!
Avaunt! my name is Richelieu—I defy thee!
Walk blindfold on ; behind thee stalks the headsman.
Ha! ha!—how pale he is! Heaven save my country! [*Falls back in Joseph's arms.*
[BARADAS *exit, followed by* DE BERINGHEN, *betraying his exultation by his gestures.*

ACT V.

FOURTH DAY.

SCENE I.—*The Bastile—a Corridor; in the back-ground the door of one of the condemned cells.*

Enter JOSEPH *and* Gaoler.

 Gaoler. Stay, father; I will call the Governor.   [*Exit* Gaoler.
 Joseph. He has it, then—this Huguet;—so we learn
From François;—Humph! Now if I can but gain
One moment's access, all is ours! The Cardinal
Trembles 'tween life and death. His life is power;
Smite one—slay both! No Æsculapian drugs,
By learnèd quacks baptized with Latin jargon,
E'er bore the healing which that scrap of parchment
Will medicine to Ambition's flagging heart.
France shall be saved—and Joseph be a bishop.

Enter Governor *and* GAOLER.

 Gov. Father, you wish to see the prisoners Huguet
And the young knight De Mauprat?
 Joseph.   So my office,
And the Lord Cardinal's order, warrant, son!
 Gov. Father, it cannot be: Count Baradas
Has summon'd to Louvre Sieur de Mauprat.
 Joseph. Well, well! But Huguet——
 Gov.   Dies at noon.
 Joseph.   At noon!
No moment to delay the pious rites
Which fit the soul for death. Quick—quick—admit me!
 Gov. You cannot enter, monk! Such are my orders!
 Joseph. Orders, vain man!—the Cardinal still is minister.
His orders crush all others!
 Gov. [*lifting his hat*].   Save his king's!
See, monk, the royal sign and seal affix'd
To the Count's mandate. None may have access
To either prisoner, Huguet or De Mauprat,
Not even a priest, without the special passport
Of Count de Baradas. I'll hear no more!
 Joseph. Just Heaven! and are we baffled thus? Despair!
Think on the Cardinal's power—beware his anger.
 Gov. I'll not be menaced, Priest! Besides, the Cardinal
Is dying and disgraced—all Paris knows it.
You hear the prisoner's knell!   [*Bell tolls*
 Joseph.   I do beseech you—
The Cardinal is *not* dying. But one moment,
And—hist!—five thousand pistoles!—
 Gov.   How! a bribe!—

And to a soldier, grey with years of honor!
Begone!

    Joseph. Ten thousand—twenty!—

    Gov.   Gaoler; put
This monk without our walls.

    Joseph.   By those grey hairs—
Yea, by this badge [*touching the cross of St. Louis worn by the* Governor]—The
    guerdon of your valor—
By all your toils—hard days and sleepless nights—
Borne in your country's service, noble son—
Let me but see the prisoner!—

    Gov.   No!

    Joseph.   He hath
Secrets of state—papers in which——

    Gov. [*interrupting*].   I know—
Such was his message to Count Baradas:
Doubtless the Count will see to it!

    Joseph.   The Count!
Then not a hope!—You shall——

    Gov.   Betray my trust!
Never—not one word more. You heard me, gaoler!

    Joseph. What can be done!—Distraction! Richelieu yet
Must—what?—I know not! Thought, nerve, strength, forsake me.
Dare you refuse the Church her holiest rights?

    Gov. I refuse nothing—I obey my orders.

    Joseph. And sell your country to her parricides!
Oh, tremble yet!—Richelieu——

    Gov.   Begone!

    Joseph.   Undone!   [*Exit* JOSEPH.

    Gov. A most audacious shaveling—interdicted
Above all others by the Count.

    Gaoler.   I hope, sir,
I shall not lose my perquisites. The Sieur
De Mauprat will not be reprieved?

    Gov.   Oh, fear not:—
The Count's commands by him who came from Mauprat
Are to prepare headsman and axe by noon;
The Count will give you perquisites enough—
Two deaths in one day!

    Gaoler.   Sir, may Heaven reward him!
Oh, by the way, that troublesome young fellow,
Who calls himself the prisoner Huguet's son
Is here again—implores, weeps, raves to see him.

    Gov. Poor youth, I pity him!

                Enter DE BERINGHEN, *followed by* FRANÇOIS.

    De Ber. [*to* FRANÇOIS]. Now, pirthee, friend,
Let go my cloak; you really discompose me.

    Fran. No, they will drive me hence: my father! Oh!
Let me but see him once—but once—one moment!

    De Ber. [*to* Governor]. Your servant, Messire; this poor rascal, Huguet,
Has sent to see the Count de Baradas
Upon state secrets, that afflict his conscience.

The Count can't leave his Majesty an instant:
I am his proxy.
  Gov.   The Count's word is law!
Again, young scapegrace! How com'st thou admitted?
  De Ber. Oh! a most filial fellow: Huguet's son!
I found him whimpering in the court below.
I pray his leave to say good-bye to father,
Before that very long, unpleasant journey,
Father's about to take. Let him wait here
Till I return.
  Fran. No; take me with you.
  De Ber.   Nay;
After *me*, friend—the Public first!
  Gov.   The Count's
Commands are strict. No one must visit Huguet
Without his passport.
  De Ber. Here it is! Pshaw! nonsense!
I'll be your surety. See, my Cerberus,
He is no Hercules!
  Gov.   Well, you're responsible.
Stand there friend. If, when you come out, my Lord,
The youth slip in, 'tis *your* fault.
  De Ber.   So it is!
      [*Exit through the door of the cell, followed by the* Gaoler.
  Gov. Be calm, my lad. Don't fret so. I had once
A father, too! I'll not be hard upon you,
And so, stand close. I must not *see* you enter:
You understand! Between this innocent youth
And that intriguing monk there is, in truth,
A wide distinction.

      Re-enter Gaoler.

      Come, we'll go our rounds;
I'll give you just one quarter of an hour;
And if my Lord leave first, make my excuse.
Yet stay, the gallery's long and dark: no sentry
Until he reach the grate below. He'd best
Wait till I come. If he should lose the way,
We may not be in call.
  Fran.   I'll tell him, sir. [*Exeunt* Governor *and* Gaoler.
He's a wise son that knoweth his own father.
I've forged a precious one! So far, so well!
Alas! what then? this wretch hath sent to Baradas—
Will sell the scroll to ransom life. Oh, Heaven!
On what a thread hangs hope!   [*Listens at the door.*
     Loud words—a cry! [*Looks through the keyhole.*
They struggle! Ho!—the packet!!! [*Tries to open the door*
      Lost! He has it—
The courtier has it—Huguet, spite his chains,
Grapples!—well done! Now—now!   [*Draws back.*
     The gallery's long—

And this is left us!
> *Drawing his dagger, and standing behind the door. Re-enter* DE BERINGHEN *with the packet.*

            Victory!
                    Yield it, robber—
Yield it—or die—   [*A short struggle.*
    De Ber.   Off! ho!—there!—
    Fran. [*grappling with him*].   Death or honor!   [*Exeunt struggling.*

SCENE II.

The King's closet at the Louvre. A suite of rooms in perspective at one side.

BARADAS *and* ORLEANS.

Bar. All smiles! the Cardinal's swoon of yesterday
Heralds his death to-day. Could he survive,
It would not be as minister—so great
The King's resentment at the priest's defiance!
All smiles!—And yet, should this accursed De Mauprat
Have given our packet to another—'Sdeath!
I dare not think of it!
    Orle.   You've sent to search him?
    Bar. Sent, sir, to search?—that hireling hands may find
Upon him, naked, with its broken seal,
That scroll, whose every word is death! No—No—
These hands alone must clutch that awful secret.
I dare not leave the palace, night nor day,
While Richelieu lives—his minions—creatures—spies—
Not one must reach the King!
    Orle.   What hast thou done?
    Bar. Summon'd De Mauprat hither.
    Orle.   Could this Huguet,
Who pray'd thy presence with so fierce a fervor,
Have thieved the scroll?
    Bar.   Huguet was housed with us,
The very moment we dismiss'd the courier.
It cannot be! a stale trick for reprieve.
But, to make sure, I've sent our trustiest friend
To see and sift him.—Hist!—here comes the King—
How fare you, Sire?

Enter LOUIS.

    Louis.   In the same mind. I have
Decided!—Yes, he would forbid your presence,
My brother—yours, my friend,—then Julie, too!
Thwarts—braves—defies—[*suddenly turning to* BARADAS] We make you minister.
Gaston, for you—the bâton of our armies.
You love me, do you not?

Orle.   Oh, love you, Sire?
[*Aside.*] Never so much as now.
    Bar.   May I deserve
Your trust [*aside*] until you sign your abdication!
My liege, but one way left to daunt De Mauprat,
And Julie to divorce,—We must prepare
The death-writ; what though sign'd and seal'd? we can
Withhold the enforcement.
    Louis.   Ah, you may prepare it;
We need not urge it to effect.
    Bar.   Exactly!
No haste, my liege. [*Looking at his watch and aside.*] He may live one hour longer

                    Enter Courtier.

    Cour. The Lady Julie, Sire, implores an audience.
    Louis. Aha! repentant of her folly!—Well,
Admit her.
    Bar.   Sire, she comes for Mauprat's pardon,
And the conditions——
    Louis.   You are minister—
We leave to you our answer.
      [*As* Julie *enters, the* Captain of the Archers *by another door, and whispers*
      Baradas.
    Capt.   The Chevalier
De Mauprat waits below.
    Bar. [*aside*].   Now the despatch!
                                                                     [*Exit with* Officer.

                    Enter Julie.

    Julie. My liege, you sent for me. I come where Grief
Should come when guiltless, while the name of King
Is holy on the earth! Here at the feet
Of Power, I kneel for mercy.
    Louis.   Mercy, Julie,
Is an affair of state. The Cardinal should
In this be your interpreter.
    Julie.   Alas!
I know not if that mighty spirit now
Stoop to the things of earth. Nay, while I speak,
Perchance he hears the orphan by the throne
Where kings themselves need pardon; O my liege,
Be father to the fatherless; in you
Dwells my last hope!

                    Enter Baradas.

    Bar. [*aside.*]   He has not the despatch;
Smiled, while we search'd, and braves me.—Oh!
    Louis. [*gently*].   What wouldst thou?
    Julie. A single life.—You reign o'er millions.—What
Is *one man's* life to you?—and yet to *me*
'Tis France—'tis earth—'tis everything!—a life—
A human life—my husband's.

Louis [*aside*].   Speak to her,
I am not marble,—give her hope—or——
    Bar.   Madam,
Vex not your King, whose heart, too soft for justice,
Leaves to his ministers that solemn charge.   [LOUIS *walks up the stage.*
    Julie. You *were* his friend.
    Bar.   I *was* before I loved thee.
    Julie. Loved me!
    Bar.   Hush, Julie: couldst thou misinterpret
My acts, thoughts, motives, nay, my very words,
Here—in this palace?
    Julie.   Now I know I'm mad;
Even that memory fail'd me.
    Bar.   I am young,
Well-born and brave as Mauprat!—for thy sake
I peril what he has not—fortune—power;
All to great souls most dazzling. I alone
Can save thee from yon tyrant, now my puppet:
Be mine; annul the mockery of this marriage,
And on the day I clasp thee to my breast
De Mauprat shall be free.
    Julie.   Thou durst not speak.
Thus in *his* ear [*pointing to* LOUIS]. Thou double traitor!—tremble!
I will unmask thee.
    Bar.   I will say thou ravest,
And see this scroll! its letters shall be blood:
Go to the King, count with me word for word;
And while you pray the life—I write the sentence!
    Julie. Stay, stay, [*rushing to the* King]. You have a kind and princely heart,
Tho' sometimes it is silent: you were born
To *power*—it has not flush'd you into madness,
As it doth meaner men. Banish my husband—
Dissolve your marriage—cast me to that grave
Of human ties, where hearts congeal to ice,
In the dark convent's everlasting winter—
(Surely eno' for justice—hate—revenge)—
But spare this life, thus lonely, scath'd, and bloomless;
And when thou stand'st for judgment on thine own,
The deed shall shine beside thee as an angel.
    Louis [*much affected*]. Go, go, to Baradas: annul thy marriage,
And——
    Julie [*anxiously, and watching his countenance*]. Be his bride!
    Louis.   A form, a mere decorum;
Thou know'st I love thee.
    Julie.   O thou sea of shame,
And not one star!
        [*The* King *goes up the stage, and passes through the suite of rooms at the side,
            in evident emotion.*
    Bar   Well, thy election, Julie;
This hand—his grave!
    Julie.   His grave! and I——
    Bar.   Can save him.—
Swear to be mine.

Julie. ' That were a bitterer death !
Avaunt, thou tempter ! I did ask his life
A boon, and not the barter of dishonor.
The heart can break, and scorn you: wreak your malice;
Adrien and I will leave you this sad earth,
And pass together hand in hand to Heaven !

Bar. You have decided. [*Withdraws to the side scene for a moment, and returns*
Listen to me, Lady;
I am no base intriguer. I adored thee
From the first glance of those inspiring eyes;
With thee entwined ambition, hope, the future.
I will not lose thee ! I can place thee nearest—
Ay, to the throne—nay, on the throne, perchance;
My star is at its zenith. Look upon me;
Hast thou decided ?

Julie. No, no; you can see
How weak I am: be human, sir—one moment.

Bar. [*stamping his foot,* DE MAUPRAT *appears at the side of the stage guarded*].
Behold thy husband !—Shall he pass to death,
And know thou couldst have saved him ?

Julie. Adrien, speak !
But say you wish to *live !*—if not, your wife,
Your slave,—do with me as you will.

De Mau. Once more !—
Why this is mercy, Count ! Oh, think, my Julie,
Life, at the best, is short,—but love immortal !

Bar. [*taking* JULIE'S *hand*]. Ah, loveliest—

Julie. Go, that touch has made me iron.
We have decided—death !

Bar. [*to* DE MAUPRAT]. Now say to whom
Thou gavest the packet, and thou yet shalt live.

De Mau. I'll tell thee nothing !

Bar. Hark,—the rack !

De Mau. Thy penance
For ever, wretch !—What rack is like the conscience ?

Julie. I shall be with thee soon.

Bar. [*giving the writ to the* Officer.] Hence to the headsman !

[*The doors are thrown open. The* Huissier *announces* " His Eminence the Cardinal Duke de Richelieu."

[*Enter* RICHELIEU, *attended by* Gentlemen, Pages, &c., *pale, feeble, and leaning on* JOSEPH, *followed by three* Secretaries of State, *attended by* Sub-Secretaries *with papers, &c.*

Julie [*rushing to* RICHELIEU]. You live—you live—and Adrien shall not die !

Rich. Not if an old man's prayers, himself near death,
Can aught avail thee, daughter ! Count, you now
Hold what I held on earth :—one boon, my Lord,
This soldier's life,

Bar. The stake,—my head !—you said it.
I cannot lose one trick.—Remove your prisoner.

Julie. No !—No !—

Enter LOUIS *from the rooms beyond.*

Rich. [*to* Officer]. Stay, Sir, one moment. My good liege,
Your worn-out servant, willing, Sire, to spare you
Some pain of conscience, would forestall your wishes.
I do resign my office.
    De Mau.   You!
    Julie.   All's over!
    Rich. My end draws near. These sad ones, Sire, I love them.
I do not ask his life; but suffer justice
To halt, until I can dismiss his soul,
Charged with an old man's blessing.
    Louis.   Surely!
    Bar.   Sire——
    Louis. Silence—small favor to a dying servant.
    Rich. You would consign your armies to the bâton
Of your most honored brother. Sire, so be it!
Your minister, the Count de Baradas;
A sagacious choice!—Your Secretaries
Of State attend me, Sire, to render up
The ledgers of a realm. I do beseech you,
Suffer these noble gentlemen to learn
The nature of the glorious task that waits them,
Here, in my presence.
    Louis.   You say well, my Lord. [*To* Secretaries, *as he seats himself.*
Approach, Sirs.
    Rich.   I—I—faint!—air—air!
    [JOSEPH *and a* Gentleman *assist him to a sofa, placed beneath a window.*
                        I thank you—
Draw near, my children.
    Bar.   He's too weak to question.
Nay, scarce to speak; all's safe.

SCENE III.

Mannet RICHELIEU, MAUPRAT, *and* JULIE, *the last kneeling beside the* Cardinal; *the* Officer *of the Guard behind* MAUPRAT. JOSEPH *near* RICHELIEU, *watching the* King. LOUIS. BARADAS *at the back of the* King's *chair, anxious and disturbed.* ORLEANS *at a greater distance, careless and triumphant. The* Secretaries. *As each* Secretary *advances in his turn, he takes the portfolios from the* Sub-Secretaries.

    First Sec.   The affairs of Portugal,
Most urgent, Sire: One short month since the Duke
Braganza was a rebel.
    Louis.   And is still!
    First Sec. No, Sire, *he has succeeded!* He is now
Crown'd King of Portugal—craves instant succor
Against the arms of Spain.
    Louis.   We will not grant it
Against his lawful king. Eh, Count?

Bar.   No, Sire.
    First Sec. But Spain's your deadliest foe: whatever
Can weaken Spain must strengthen France. The Cardinal
Would send the succors:—[*solemnly*]—balance, Sire, of Europe !
    Louis. The Cardinal !—balance !—We'll consider.—Eh, Count ?
    Bar. Yes, Sire;—fall back.
    First Sec.   But——
    Bar.   Oh ! fall back, Sir.
    Joseph.   Humph !
    Second Sec. The affairs of England, Sire, most urgent: Charles
The First has lost a battle that decides
One half his realm,—craves moneys, Sire, and succor.
    Louis. He shall have both.—Eh, Baradas ?
    Bar.   Yes, Sire.
(Oh that despatch !—my veins are fire !)
    Rich. [*feebly, but with great distinctness*]. My liege—
Forgive me—Charles's cause is lost ! A man,
Named Cromwell, risen,—a great man !—your succor
Would fail—your loans be squander'd !—Pause—reflect. *
    Louis. Reflect.—Eh, Baradas ?
    Bar.   Reflect, Sire.
    Joseph.   Humph !
    Louis [*aside*]. I half repent !—No successor to Richelieu !
Round me thrones totter !—dynasties dissolve !—
The soil he guards alone escapes the earthquake !
    Joseph. Our star not yet eclipsed !—you mark the King ?
Oh ! had we the despatch !
    Rich.   Ah ! Joseph !—Child—
Would I could help thee !

        Enter Gentleman, *whispers* Joseph, *who exit hastily.*

Bar. [*to* Secretary].   Sir, fall back.
Second Sec.   But——
Bar.   Pshaw, Sir !
Third Sec. [*mysteriously*]. The *secret correspondence*, Sire, most urgent,—
Accounts of Spies—deserters—heretics—
Assassins—poisoners—schemes against yourself !——
    Louis. Myself !—most urgent !—[*looking on the documents*].
      Re-enter Joseph *with* François, *whose pourpoint is streaked with blood.*
        François *passes behind the* Cardinal's Attendants, *and, sheltered by them
from the sight of* Baradas, *etc., falls at* Richelieu's *feet.*
    Fran.   O ! my Lord !
    Rich.   Thou art bleeding !
    Fran. A scratch—I have not fail'd——   [*Gives the packet.*
    Rich.   Hush !—   [*Looking at the contents.*
    Third Sec. [*to* King].   Sire, the Spaniards
Have reinforced their army on the frontiers.
The Duc de Bouillon——
    Rich.   Hold !—In this department—

---

* See in " Cinq Mars," Vol. V., the striking and brilliant chapter from which the interlude of the Secretaries
is borrowed.

A paper—here, Sire,—read yourself—then take
The Count's advice in't.

Enter De Beringhen *hastily, and draws aside* Baradas.

[Richelieu *to* Secretary, *giving an open parchment.*

Bar. [*bursting from* De Beringhen]. What! and reft it from thee!
Ha!—hold!

Joseph. Fall back, son, it is your turn now!

Bar. Death!—the despatch!

Louis [*reading*]. To Bouillon—and sign'd Orleans!—
Baradas, too!—league with our foes of Spain!—
Lead our Italian armies—what! to Paris!—
Capture the King—my health requires repose—
Make me subscribe my proper abdication—
Orleans, my brother, Regent!—Saints of Heaven!
These are the men I loved!

[Baradas *draws,—attempts to rush out,—is arrested.—*Orleans, *endeavoring to escape more quickly, meets* Joseph's *eye and stops short.* Richelieu *falls back.*

Joseph. See to the Cardinal!

Bar. He's dying! and I yet shall dupe the King!

Louis [*rushing to* Richelieu]. Richelieu!—'tis *I* resign!—
Reign thou!

Joseph. Alas! too late!—he faints!

Louis. Reign, Richelieu!

Rich. [*feebly*]. With absolute power?——

Louis. Most absolute!—Oh! live!
If not for me—for France!

Rich. FRANCE!

Louis. Oh! this treason!—
The army—Orleans—Bouillon—Heavens!—the Spaniard!—
Where will they be next week?——

Rich. [*starting up*]. There,—at my feet!

[*To* First *and* Second Secretary.

Ere the clock strike!—the Envoys have their answer!

[*To* Third Secretary, *with a ring.*

This to De Chavigny—he knows the rest—
No need of parchment here—he must not halt
For sleep—for food.—In *my* name,—MINE!—he will
Arrest the Duc de Bouillon at the head
Of his army!—Ho!—there, Count de Baradas,
Thou hast lost the stake!—Away with him!*

[*As the* Guards *open the folding-doors, a view of the ante-room beyond, lined with* Courtiers. Baradas *passes through the line.*

Ha!—ha!—

[*Snatching* De Mauprat's *death-warrant from the* Officer.

See here De Mauprat's death-writ, Julie!—

---

* The passion of the drama requires this catastrophe for Baradas. He however survived his disgrace, though stripped of all his rapidly-acquired fortunes; and the daring that belonged to his character won him distinction in foreign service. He returned to France after Richelieu's death, but never regained the same court influence. He had taken the vows of a Knight of Malta, and Louis made him a Prior.

Parchment for battledores !—Embrace your husband
At last the old man blesses you !
    Julie.   O joy !
You are saved: you live—I hold you in these arms.
    De Mau. Never to part—
    Julie.   No—never, Adrien—never !
    Louis [*peevishly*]. One moment makes a startling cure, Lord Cardinal.*
    Rich. Ay, Sire, for in one moment there did pass
Into this wither'd frame the might of France !—
My own dear France—I have thee yet—I have saved thee !
I clasp thee still !—it was thy voice that call'd me
Back from the tomb !—What mistress like our country ?
    Louis. For Mauprat's pardon—well ! But Julie,—Richelieu,
Leave me one thing to love !—
    Rich.   A subject's luxury !
Yet, if you must love something, Sire,—*love me !*
    Louis [*smiling in spite of himself*]. Fair proxy for a young fresh Demoiselle !
    Rich. Your heart speaks for my clients:—Kneel, my children,
And thank your King,—
    Julie.   Ah, tears like these, my liege,
Are dews that mount to Heaven.
    Louis.   Rise—rise—be happy.
                                        [RICHELIEU *beckons to* DE BERINGHEN.
    De Ber. [*falteringly*]. My lord—you are—most—happily—recover'd.
    Rich. But you are pale, dear Beringhen:—this air
Suits not your delicate frame—I long have thought so:—
Sleep not another night in Paris:—Go,—
Or else your precious life may be in danger.
Leave France, dear Beringhen !
    De Ber.   I shall have time,
More than I ask'd for—to discuss the pâté.   [*Exit* DE BERINGHEN.
    Rich. [*to* ORLEANS]. For you, repentance—absence—and confession !
                                              [*To* FRANÇOIS.
Never say *fail* again.—Brave boy !   [*To* JOSEPH.
                        He'll be—
A Bishop first.
    Joseph.   Ah, Cardinal—
    Rich.   Ah, Joseph !
                      [*To* LOUIS—*as* DE MAUPRAT *and* JULIE *converse apart.*
See, my liege—see thro' plots and counterplots—
Thro' gain and loss—thro' glory and disgrace—
Along the plains, where passionate Discord rears
Eternal Babel—still the holy stream
Of human happiness glides on !
    Louis.   And must we
Thank for *that* also—our prime Minister ?

---

* The sudden resuscitation of Richelieu (not to strain too much on the real passion which supports him in this scene) is in conformance with the more dissimulating part of his character. The extraordinary nobility of his countenance (latterly so deathlike, save when the mind spoke in the features) always lent itself to stage effect of this nature. The queen-mother said of him, that she had seen him one moment so feeble, cast down, and " semi-mort," that he seemed on the point of giving up the ghost—and the next moment he would start up full of animation, energy, and life.

Rich. No—let us own it:—there is ONE above
Sways the harmonious mystery of the world,
Ev'n better than prime ministers;—
                              Alas !
Our glories float between the earth and heaven
Like clouds which seem pavilions of the sun,
And are the playthings of the casual wind;
Still, like the cloud which drops on unseen crags
The dews the wild flower feeds on, our ambition
May from its airy height drop gladness down
On unsuspected virtue;—and the flower
May bless the cloud when it hath pass'd away ! *

* The image and the sentiment in the concluding lines are borrowed from a passage in one of the writings attributed to the Cardinal.

NOT SO BAD AS WE SEEM;

OR,

MANY SIDES TO A CHARACTER.

DEDICATION.

TO

HIS GRACE THE DUKE OF DEVONSHIRE, K.G.

My Lord Duke,

This play is respectfully dedicated to your Grace in token of the earnest gratitude, both of Author and Performers, for the genial and noble sympathy which has befriended their exertions in the cause of their brotherhood.

The debt that we can but feebly acknowledge, may those who come after us seek to repay; and may each loftier Cultivator of Art and Letters, whom the Institution established under your auspices may shelter from care and penury, see on its corner-stone your princely name,—and perpetuate to distant times the affectionate homage it commands from ourselves.

It is this hope that can alone render worthy the tribute which, in my own name as Author, and in the names of my companions the Performers, of the Play first represented at Devonshire House, I now offer to your Grace, with every sentiment that can deepen and endear the respect and admiration

With which I have the honor to be,

My Lord Duke,

Your Grace's most obedient and faithful Servant,

E. BULWER LYTTON.

DRAMATIS PERSONÆ.

Original Cast.

The Duke of Middlesex,	*Peers attached to the son of James II.,*	Mr. Frank Stone.
The Earl of Loftus,	*commonly called the First Pretender.*	Mr. Dudley Costello.

Lord Wilmot, *a young man at the head of the Mode more than a century ago, son to Lord Loftus* . . . Mr. Charles Dickens.

Mr. Shadowly Softhead, *a young gentleman from the city, friend and double to Lord Wilmot* . . . . Mr. Douglas Jerrold.

Hardman, *a rising Member of Parliament, and adherent to Sir Robert Walpole* . . . . Mr. John Forster.

Sir Geoffrey Thornside, *a gentleman of good family and estate* . . . . Mr. Mark Lemon.

Mr. Goodenough Easy, *in business, highly respectable, and a friend of Sir Geoffrey* . . . . . . Mr. E. W. Topham.

Lord Le Trimmer	*Frequenters of Will's Coffee House*	Mr. Peter Cunningham.
Sir Thomas Timid		Mr. Westland Marston.
Colonel Flint, *a Fire-eater*		Mr. R. H. Horne.

Mr. Jacob Tonson, *a Bookseller* . . . . . Mr. Charles Knight.
Smart, *Valet to Lord Wilmot* . . . . . . Mr. Wilkie Collins.
Hodge, *Servant to Sir Geoffrey Thornside* . . . Mr. John Tenniel.
Paddy O'Sullivan, *Mr. Fallen's Landlord* . . . Mr. Robert Bell.
Mr. David Fallen, *Grub Street Author and Pamphleteer* . Mr. Augustus Egg, A.R.A.

Coffee-House Loungers, Drawers, Newsmen, Watchmen, etc. etc.

Lucy, *Daughter to Sir Geoffrey Thornside* . . . Mrs. Compton.
Barbara, *daughter to Mr. Easy* . . . . . Miss Ellen Chaplin.
The Silent Lady of Deadman's Lane (Lady Thornside) . . . .

Date of Play—The reign of George I.   *Scene*—London.

Time supposed to be occupied, from the noon of the first day to the afternoon of the second.

First performed on Friday, the 16th of May, 1851, before the Queen and the Prince Consort, at Devonshire House, Piccadilly.

DRAMATIS PERSONÆ.

THE DUKE OF MIDDLESEX	MR. STUART.
THE EARL OF LOFTUS	MR. BRAID.
LORD WILMOT	MR. LEIGH MURRAY.
MR. SHADOWLY SOFTHEAD	MR. KEELEY.
HARDMAN	MR. BARRY SULLIVAN.
SIR GEOFFREY THORNSIDE	MR. BENJAMIN WEBSTER.
MR. GOODENOUGH EASY	MR. BUCKSTONE.
COLONEL FLINT	MR HASTINGS.
MR. JACOB TONSON	MR. ROGERS.
SMART	MR. CLARK.
HODGE	MR. COE.
PADDY O'SULLIVAN	MR. H. BEDFORD.
MR. DAVID FALLEN	MR. HOWE.
LUCY	MISS ROSA BENNETT.
BARBARA	MISS AMELIA VINING.
THE SILENT LADY OF DEADMAN'S LANE	MRS. LEIGH MURRAY.

First performed on Saturday, the 12th of February, 1853, at the Haymarket Theatre.

NOT SO BAD AS WE SEEM:

OR,

MANY SIDES TO A CHARACTER.

ACT I—SCENE I.

Lord Wilmot's *Apartment in* St. James's.

Smart [*showing in a* Masked Lady]. My Lord is dressing. As you say, madam, it is late. But though he never wants sleep more than once a week, yet when he does sleep, I am proud to say he sleeps better than any man in the three kingdoms.

Lady. I have heard much of Lord Wilmot's eccentricities—but also of his generosity and honor.

Smart. Yes, madam, nobody like him for speaking ill of himself and doing good to another.

Enter Wilmot.

Wil. "And sleepless lovers just at twelve awake." Any duels to-day, Smart? No—I see something more dangerous—a woman. [*To* Smart.] Vanish. [*Placing a chair for* Lady.] Madam, have I the honor to know you? Condescend to remove your vizard. [Lady *lifts her mask.*] Very fine woman, still—decidedly dangerous. Madam, allow me one precautionary observation—My affections are engaged.

Lady. So I conjectured; for I have noticed you from the window of my house, walking in the garden of Sir Geoffrey Thornside with his fair daughter: and she seems worthy to fix the affections of the most fickle.

Wil. My dear madam, do you know Sir Geoffrey? Bind me to you for life, and say a kind word to him in my favor.

Lady. Can you need it?—young, highborn, accomplished——

Wil. Sir Geoffrey's very objections against me. He says I am a fine gentleman, and ha. a vehement aversion to that section of mortals, because he implies that a fine gentleman once did him a mortal injury. But you seem moved—dear lady, what is your interest in Sir Geoffrey or myself?

Lady. You shall know later. Tell me, did Lucy Thornside ever speak to you of her mother?

Wil. Only to regret, with tears in her eyes, that she had never known a mother—that lady died, I believe, while Lucy was but an infant.

Lady. When you next have occasion to speak to her, say that you have seen a friend of her mother, who has something to impart that may contribute to her father's happiness and her own.

Wil. I will do your bidding this day, and——

Soft. [*without.*]. Oh, never mind announcing me, Smart.

Lady. [*starting up*]. I would not be seen here—I must be gone. Call on me at nine o'clock this evening; this is my address.

Enter SOFTHEAD, *as* LORD WILMOT *is protecting* Lady's *retreat, and stares aghast.*

Wil. [*aside*]. Do not fear him—best little fellow in the world, ambitious to be thought good for nothing, and frightened out of his wits at the sight of a petticoat. [*Aloud, as he attends her out.*] Allow me to escort your Ladyship.

Soft. Ladyship!—lucky dog. But then he's such a villain!

Wil. [*returning, and looking at the address*]. Very mysterious visitor—sign of Crown and Portcullis, Deadman's Lane—a very funeral residence. Ha, Softhead! my Pylades—my second self! *Animæ*——

Soft. Enemy!

Wil. Dimidium meæ.

Soft. Dimi! that's the oath last in fashion, I warrant. [*With a swagger and a slap on the back.*] *Dimidum meæ*, how d'ye do? But what is that lady?—masked too? Oh, Fred, Fred, you are a monster!

Wil. Monster! ay, horrible! That lady may well wear a mask. She has poisoned three husbands.

Soft. Dimidum meæ.

Wil. A mere harmless gallantry has no longer a charm for me.

Soft. Nor for me either! [*Aside.*] Never had.

Wil. Nothing could excite us true men of pleasure but some colossal atrocity, to bring our necks within an inch of the gallows!

Soft. He's a perfect demon! Alas, I shall never come up to *his* mark!

Enter SMART.

Smart. Mr. Hardman, my Lord.

Wil. Hush! Must not shock Mr. Hardman, the most friendly, obliging man, and so clever—will be a minister some day. But not one of *our* set.

Enter HARDMAN.

Hard. And how fares my dear Lord?

Wil. Bravely—and you? Ah! you men who live for others have a hard life of it. Let me present you to my friend, Mr. Shadowly Softhead.

Hard. The son of the great clothier who has such weight in the Guild? I have heard of you from Mr. Easy and others, though never so fortunate as to meet you before, Mr. Softhead.

Soft. Shadowly Softhead:—my grandmother was one of the Shadowlys—a genteel family that move about Court. She married a Softhead——

Wil. A race much esteemed in the city.

Hard. A new picture, my lord? I'm no very great judge—but it seems to me quite a master-piece.

Wil. I've a passion for art. Sold off my stud to buy that picture. [*Aside.*] And please my poor father. 'Tis a Murillo.

Hard. A Murillo! you know that Walpole, too, has a passion for pictures.—In despair at this moment that he can't find a Murillo to hang up in his gallery. If ever you want to corrupt the Prime Minister's virtue, you have only to say, "I have got a Murillo."

Wil. Well, if, instead of the pictures, he'll just hang up the *men* he has bought, you may tell him he shall have my Murillo for nothing!

Hard. Bought! now really, my Lord, this is so vulgar a scandal against Sir Robert. Let me assure your Lordship——

Wil. Lordship! Plagues on these titles among friends. Why, if the Duke of Middlesex himself—commonly styled "The Proud Duke"—who said to his Duchess, when she astonished his dignity one day with a kiss, " Madam, my first wife was a Percy, and *she* never took such a liberty;"——*

Hard. Ha! ha! well, " if the Proud Duke"——

Wil. Could deign to come here, we would say, " How d'ye do, my dear Middlesex!"

Soft. So we would, Fred, Middlesex.—Shouldn't you like to know a Duke, Mr. Hardman?

Hard. I have known one or two—in opposition: and had rather too much of 'em.

Soft. Too much of a Duke! La! I could never have eno' of a Duke?

Hard. You may live to think otherwise.

Enter SMART.

Smart. His grace the Duke of Middlesex.

Enter DUKE.

Duke. My Lord Wilmot, your most obedient servant.

Wil. [*Aside.* Now then courage!] How d'ye do, my dear Middlesex?

Duke. " How d'ye do?" " Middlesex!" Gracious Heaven; what will this age come to?

Hard. [*to* SOFTHEAD]. Well, it *may* be the fashion,—yet I can *hardly* advise you to adopt it.

Soft. But if Fred.——

Hard. Oh! certainly Fred is an excellent model——

Soft. Yet there's something very awful in a live Duke!

Hard Tut! a mere mortal like ourselves, after all.

Soft. D'ye really think so!—upon your honor?

Hard. Sir, I'm sure of it,—upon my honor, a mortal!

Duke [*turning stiffly round, and half rising from his chair in majestic condescension*]. Your Lordship's friends? A good day to you, gentlemen!

Soft. And a good day to yourself. My Lord Du——I mean, my dear boy!—Middlesex. how d'ye do?

Duke. " Mid!"—" boy"—" sex!"—" dear!" I must be in a dream.

Wil. [*to* SOFTHEAD]. Apologise to the Duke. [*To* HARDMAN.] Then hurry him off into the next room. Allow me to explain to your Grace.

Soft. But what shall I say?

Hard. Anything most civil and servile.

Soft. I—I—my Lord Duke, I really most humbly entreat your Grace's pardon I,——

Duke. Small man, your pardon is granted, for your existence is effaced. So far as my recognition is necessary to your sense of being, consider yourself henceforth annihilated!

Soft. I humbly thank your Grace! Annihilated! what's that?

Hard. Duke's English for excused. [SOFTHEAD *wants to get back to the* DUKE.] What! have not you had enough of the Duke?

Soft. No, now we've made it up. I never bear malice. I should like to know more of him; one can't get at a Duke every day. If he did call me " small man" he *is* a Duke,—and such a remarkably fine one!

Hard. [*drawing him away*]. You deserve to be haunted by him! No—no! Come into the next room.

[*Exeunt through side door.* SOFTHEAD *very reluctant to leave the* DUKE.

Duke. There's something portentous in that small man's audacity.—Quite an abberration

---

* This well-known anecdote of the Proud Duke of Somerset, and some other recorded traits of the same eminent personage, have been freely applied to the character, intended to illustrate the humor of pride, in the comedy. None of our English memoirs afford, however, instances of that infirmity so extravagant as are to be found in the French. Tallamant has on anecdote of the celebrated *Duchesse de Longueville*, which enlivens the burlesque by a bull that no Irish imagination ever surpassed. A surgeon having probably saved her life by bleeding her too suddenly and without sufficient ceremonial—the *Duchesse* said, on recovering herself, that " he was an insolent fellow to have bled her—*in her presence.*"

of nature! But we are alone now, we two gentlemen. Your father is my friend, and his son must have courage and honor.

Wil. Faith, I had the courage to say I would call your Grace "Middlesex," and the honor to keep to my word. So I've given good proof that I've courage and honor enough for anything!

Duke. [*affectionately*]. You're a wild boy. You have levities and follies. But alas! even rank does not exempt its possessor from the faults of humanity. Very strange! My own dead brother—[*with a look of disgust*].

Wil. Your brother, Lord Henry de Mowbray? My dear Duke, pray forgive me; but I hope there's no truth in what Tonson, the bookseller, told me at Will's,—that your brother had left behind certain Confessions or Memoirs, which are all that might be apprehended from a man of a temper so cynical, and whose success in the gay world was so—terrible. [*Aside.* Determined seducer and implacable cut-throat!]

Duke. Ha! then those Memoirs exist! My brother kept his profligate threat. I shall be ridiculed, lampooned. I, the head of the Mowbrays. Powers above, is nothing on earth, then, left sacred! Can you learn in whose hands is this scandalous record?

Wil. I will try. Leave it to me. I know Lord Henry bore you a grudge for renouncing his connection, on account of his faults—of humanity! I remember an anecdote how he fought with a husband, some poor devil named Morland, for a boast in a tavern, which—Oh, but we'll not speak of that. We *must* get the Memoir. We gentlemen have all common cause here.

Duke [*taking his hand*]. Worthy son of your father. You deserve, indeed, the trust that I come to confide to you. Listen. His Majesty, King James, having been deceived by vague promises in the Expedition of 'Fifteen, has very properly refused to imperil his rights again, unless upon the positive pledge of a sufficient number of persons of influence, to risk life and all in his service. Myself and some others, not wholly unknown to you, propose to join in a pledge which our King with such reason exacts. Your assistance, my lord, would be valuable, for you are the idol of the young. Doubts were entertained of your royalty. I have come to dispel them—a word will suffice. If we succeed, you restore the son of a Stuart; if we fail,—you will go to the scaffold by the side of John Duke of Middlesex! Can you hesitate? or is silence assent?

Wil. My dear Duke, forgive me that I dismiss with a jest a subject so fatal, if gravely entertained. I have so many other engagements at present that, just to recollect them, I must keep my head on my shoulders. Accept my humblest excuses.

Duke. Accept mine for mistaking the son of Lord Loftus. [*Goes up to C. D.*

Wil. Lord Loftus again! Stay. Your Grace spoke of persons not wholly unknown to me. I entreat you to explain.

Duke. My Lord, I have trusted you with my own life; but to compromise by a word the life of another!—permit me to remind your Lordship that I am John Duke of Middlesex.

Wil. Can my father have entangled himself in some Jacobite plot? How shall I find out?—Ha! Hardman, Hardman, I say! Here's a man who finds everything out.

Enter HARDMAN *and* SOFTHEAD.

Softhead, continue annihilated for the next five minutes or so. These books will help to the cessation of your existence, mental and bodily, Mr. Locke, on the Understanding, will show that you have not an innate idea; and the Essay of Bishop Berkely will prove you have not an atom of matter.

Soft. But——

Wil. No buts!—they're the fashion.

Soft. Oh, if they're the fashion——

[*Seats himself at the further end of the room; commences vigorously with Berkely and Locke, first one and then the other, and after convincing himself that they are above his comprehension, gradually subsides from despair into dozing.*

Wil. [*to* HARDMAN]. My dear Hardman, you are the only one of my friends whom, in spite of your politics, my high Tory father condescends to approve of. Every one knows that his family were stout cavaliers attached to the Stuarts.

Hard. [*aside*]. Ah! I guess why the Jacobite Duke has been here. I must look up David Fallen; he is in all the schemes for the Stuarts. Well—and——

Wil. And the Jacobites are daring and numerous; and,—in short, I should just like to know that my father views things with the eyes of our more wise generation.

Hard. Why not ask him yourself?

Wil. Alas! I'm in disgrace; he even begs me not to come to his house. You see he wants me to marry.

Hard. But your father bade me tell you, he would leave your choice to yourself;—would marriage then seem so dreadful a sacrifice?

Wil. Sacrifice! Leave my choice to myself? My dear father. [*Rings the hand-bell.*] Smart! [*Enter* SMART.] Order my coach.

Hard. This impatience looks very like love.

Wil. Pooh! what do you know about love?—you,—who love only ambition? Solemn old jilt, with whom one's never safe from a rival.

Hard. Yes;—always safe from a rival, both in love and ambition, if one will watch to detect, and then scheme to destroy him.

Wil. Destroy—ruthless exterminator! May we never be rivals? Pray keep to ambition.

Hard. [*aside*]. But ambition lures me to love. This fair Lucy Thornside, as rich as she's fair! woe indeed to the man who shall be my rival with her. I will call there to-day.

Wil. Then, you'll see my father, and sound him?

Hard. I will do so.

Wil. You are the best friend I have. If ever I can serve you in return—— [*Exit.*

Hard. Tut! in serving my friends, 'tis myself that I serve.

Wil. [*after a moment's thought*]. Now to Lucy. Ha! Softhead.

Soft. [*waking up*]. Heh!

Wil. [*aside*]. I must put this suspicious Sir Geoffrey on a wrong scent. If Softhead were to make love to the girl—violently—desperately.

Soft. [*yawning*] I would give the world to be tucked up in bed now.

Wil. I've a project—an intrigue—be all life and all fire! Why you tremble——

Soft. With excitement. Proceed!

Wil. There's a certain snarling, suspicious Sir Geoffrey Thornside, with a beautiful daughter, to whom he is a sort of a one-sided bear of a father—all growl and no hug.

Soft. I know him!

Wil. You. How?

Soft. Why, his most intimate friend is Mr. Goodenough Easy.

Wil. Lucy presented me to a Mistress Barbara Easy. Pretty girl.

Soft. You are not courting her?

Wil. Not at present. Are you?

Soft. Why, my father wants me to marry her.

Wil. You refused?

Soft. No. I did not.

Wil. Had *she* that impertinence?

Soft. No; but her father had. He wished for it once; but since I've become *à la mode,* and made a sensation at St. James's, he says that his daughter shall be courted no more by a man of such fashion. Oh! he's low, Mr. Easy: very good-humored and hearty, but respectable, sober, and square-toed;—decidedly low!—City bred! So I can't go much to his house; but I see Barbara sometimes at Sir Geoffrey's.

Wil. Excellent! Listen: I am bent upon adding Lucy Thornside to the list of my conquests. But her churl of a father has already given me to understand that he hates a lord——

Soft. Hates a lord! Can such men be?

Wil. And despises a man *à la mode.*

Soft. I knew he was eccentric, but this is downright insanity.

Wil. Brief. I see very well that he'll soon shut his doors in my face, unless I make him believe that it is not his daughter who attracts me to his house; so I tell you what we will do; ---you shall make love to Lucy—violent love, you rogue.

Soft. But Sir Geoffrey knows I'm in love with the other.

Wil. That's over. Father refused you—transfer of affection; natural pique and human inconstancy. And, in return, to oblige you, I'll make love just as violent to Mistress Barbara Easy.

Soft. Stop, stop; I don't see the necessity of that.

Wil. Pooh! nothing more clear. Having thus duped the two lookers on, we shall have ample opportunity to change partners, and hands across, then down the middle and up again.

Enter SMART.

Smart. Your coach waits, my Lord.

Wil. Come along. Fie! that's not the way to conduct a cane. Has not Mr. Pope, our great poet of fashion, given you the nicest instructions in that art?

"Sir Plume, of amber snuff-box justly vain,
And the nice conduct of a clouded cane."

The cane does not conduct you; you conduct the cane. Thus with a *debonnair* swing. Now, t'other hand on your haunch; easy, *dégagé*—impudently graceful; with the air of a gentleman, and the heart of a—monster! *Allons! Vive la joie.*

Soft. Vive la jaw, indeed. I feel as if I were going to be hanged. *Allons! Vive la jaw!* [*Exeunt.*

ACT II.—SCENE I.

Library in the house of SIR GEOFFREY THORNSIDE—*At the back a large window opening nearly to the ground—Side door to an adjoining room—Style of decoration, that introduced from the Dutch in the reign of William III. (old-fashioned, therefore, at the date assigned to the Play)—rich and heavy; oak panels, partly guilt; high-backed chairs, etc.*

Enter SIR GEOFFREY *and* HODGE.

Sir Geof. But I say the dog did howl last night, and it is a most suspicious circumstance.

Hodge. Fegs, my dear Measter, if you'se think that these Lunnon thieves have found out that your honor's rents were paid last woik, mayhap I'd best sleep here in the loibery.

Sir Geof. [*aside*]. How does he know I keep my moneys here?

Hodge. Zooks! I'se the old blunderbuss, and that will boite better than any dog, I'se warrant!

Sir Geof. [*Aside.* I begin to suspect him. For ten years have I nursed that viper at my hearth, and now he wants to sleep in my library, with a loaded blunderbuss, in case I should come in and detect him. I see murder in his very face. How blind I've been!] Hodge, you are very good—very; come closer. [*Aside.* What a felon step he has!] But I don't keep my rents here, they're all gone to the banker's.

Hodge. Mayhap I'd best go and lock up the plate; or will you send that to the banker's.

Sir Geof. [*Aside.* I wonder if he has got an accomplice at the banker's! It looks uncommonly like it.] No, I'll not send the plate to the bankers, I'll—consider. You've not detected the miscreant who has been flinging flowers into the library the last four days?—or observed any one watching your master when he walks in his garden, from the window of that ugly old house in Deadman's Lane?

Hodge. With the sign of the Crown and Poor Culley! Why, it maun be very leately. 'Tint a week ago 'sint it war empty.

Sir Geof. [*Aside.* How he evades the question!—just as they do at the Old Bailey.] Get along with you and feed the house-dog—*he's* honest!

Hodge. Yes, your honor. [*Exit.*

Sir Geof. I'm a very unhappy man, very. Never did harm to any one—done good to many. And ever since I was a babe in the cradle, all the world have been conspiring and plotting against me. It certainly is an exceedingly wicked world; and what its attraction can be to the other worlds, that they should have kept it spinning through space for six thousand years, I can't possibly conceive—unless they are as bad as itself; I should not wonder. That new theory of attraction is a very suspicious circumstance against the planets—there's a gang of 'em! [*A bunch of flowers is thrown in at the window.*] Heaven defend me! There it is again! This is the fifth bunch of flowers that's been thrown at me through the window— what can it possibly mean?—the most alarming circumstance.

[*Cautiously poking at the flowers with his sword.*

Mr. Goodenough Easy [*without*]. Yes, Barbara, go and find Mistress Lucy. [*Entering.*] How d'ye do, my hearty?

Sir Geof. Ugh! hearty, indeed!

Easy. Why, what's the matter? what are you poking at those flowers for?—is there a snake in them?

Sir Geof. Worse than that, I suspect! Hem! Goodenough Easy, I believe I may trust you——

Easy. You trusted me once with five thousand pounds.

Sir Geof. Dear, dear, I forgot that. But you paid me back, Easy?

Easy. Of course: but the loan saved my credit, and made my fortune: so the favor's the same.

Sir Geof. Ugh! Don't say that; favors and perfidy go together! a truth I learned early in life. What favors I heaped on my foster-brother. And did not he conspire with my cousin to set my own father against me; and trick me out of my heritage?

Easy. But you've heaped favors as great on the son of that scamp of a foster-brother; and he——

Sir Geof. Ay! but he don't know of them. And then there was my——that girl's mother——

Easy. Ah! that was an affliction which might well turn a man, pre-inclined to suspicion, into a thorough self-tormentor for the rest of his life. But she loved you dearly once, old friend; and were she yet alive, and could be proved guiltless after all——

Sir Geof. Guiltless! Sir?

Easy. Well—well! we agreed never to talk upon that subject. Come, come, what of the nosegay?

Sir Geof. Yes, yes, the nosegay! Hark! I suspect some design on my life. The dog howled last night. When I walk in the garden, somebody or something (can't see what it is) seems at the watch in a window in Deadman's Lane—pleasant name for a street at the back of one's premises! And what looks blacker than all, for five days running, has been thrown in at me, yonder, surreptitiously and anonymously, what you call—a nosegay!

Easy. Ha! ha! you lucky dog!—you are still not bad-looking! Depend on it the flowers come from a woman.

Sir Geof. A woman!—my worse fears are confirmed? In the small city of Placentia, in one year, there were no less than seven hundred cases of slow poisoning, and all by women. Flowers were among the instruments they employed, steeped in laurel water and other mephitic preparations. Those flowers are poisoned. Not a doubt of it!—how very awful!

Easy. But why should any one take the trouble to poison you, Geoffrey?

Sir Geof. I don't know. But I don't know why seven hundred people in one year were poisoned in Placentia. Hodge! Hodge!

Enter HODGE.

Sweep away those flowers!—lock 'em up with the rest in the coal-hole. I'll examine them all chemically, by and by, with precaution. [*Exit* HODGE.] Don't smell at 'em; and, above all, don't let the house-dog smell at 'em.

Easy. Ha! ha!

Sir Geof. [*Aside.* Ugh!—that brute's laughing!—no more feeling than a brick-bat!] Goodenough Easy, you are a very happy man.

Easy. Happy, yes. I could be happy on bread and water.

Sir Geof. And would toast your bread at a conflagration, and fill your jug from a deluge! Ugh! I've a trouble you are more likely to feel for, as you've a girl of your own to keep out of mischief. A man named Wilmot, and styled "my Lord," has called here a great many times; he pretends he saved my——ahem!—that is, Lucy, from footpads, when she was coming home from your house in a sedan chair. And I suspect that man means to make love to her!——

Easy. Egad! that's the only likely suspicion you've hit on this many a day. I've heard of Lord Wilmot. Softhead professes to copy him. Softhead, the son of a trader! *he* be a lounger at White's and Will's, and dine with wits and fine gentlemen! *He* lives with lords!—*he* mimic fashion! No! I've respect for even the faults of a man; but I've none for the tricks of a monkey.

Sir Geof. Ugh! you're so savage on Softhead, I suspect 'tis from envy. Man and monkey, indeed! If a ribbon is tied to the tail of a monkey, it is not the man it enrages; it is some other monkey whose tail has no ribbon!

Easy [*angrily*]. I disdain your insinuations. Do you mean to imply that I am a monkey? I will not praise myself; but at least a more steady, respectable, sober——

Sir Geof. Ugh! sober!—I suspect you'd get as drunk as a lord, if a lord passed the bottle.

Easy. Now, now, now. Take care; you'll put me in a passion.

Sir Geof. There—there—beg pardon. But I fear you've a sneaking respect for a lord.

Easy. Sir, I respect the British Constitution and the House of Peers as a part of it; but as for a lord in himself, with a mere handle to his name, a paltry title! *That* can have no effect on a Briton of independence and sense. And that's just the difference between Softhead and me. But as you don't like for a son-in-law the real fine gentleman; perhaps you've a mind to the copy. I am sure you are welcome to Softhead.

Sir Geof. Ugh! I've other designs for the girl.

Easy. Have you? What? Perhaps your favorite, young Hardman?—by the way, I've not met him here lately.

Enter LUCY *and* BARBARA.

Lucy. O, my dear father, forgive me if I disturb you; but I did so long to see you!

Sir Geof. Why?

Lucy. Ah, father is it so strange that your child——

Sir Geof. [*interrupting her*]. Why?

Lucy. Because Hodge told me you'd been alarmed last night,—the dog howled! But it was full moon last night, and he will howl at the moon!

Sir Geof [*aside*]. How did she know it was full moon? I suspect she was looking out of the window——

[*Enter* HODGE, *announcing* LORD WILMOT *and* MR. SHADOWLY SOFTHEAD].—Wilmot! my suspicions are confirmed; she *was* looking out of the window! This comes of Shakspeare having written that infernal incendiary trash about Romeo and Juliet!

Enter WILMOT *and* SOFTHEAD.

Wil. Your servant, ladies;— Sir Geoffry, your servant. I could not refuse Mr. Softhead's request to inquire after your health.

Sir Geof. I thank your lordship; but when my health wants inquiring after I send for the doctor.

Wil. Is it possible you can do anything so dangerous and rash?

Sir Geof. How?—how?

Wil. Send for the very man who has an interest in your being ill!

Sir. Geof. [*aside*]. That's very true. I did not think he had so much sense in him!

[SIR GEOFFREY *and* EASY *retire up the stage.*

Wil. I need not inquire how you are, ladies. When Hebe retired from the world, she divided her bloom between you. Mistress Barbara, vouchsafe me the honor a queen accords to the meanest of her gentlemen.

[*Kisses* BARBARA'S *hand, and leads her aside, conversing in dumb show.*

Soft. Ah, Mistress Lucy, vouchsafe me the honor which—[*Aside.* But she don't hold her hand in the same position].

Easy. Bravo!—bravo! Master Softhead!—*Encore!*

Soft. Bravo!—*Encore!* I don't understand you, Mr. Easy.

Easy. That bow of yours! Perfect. Plain to see you have not forgotten the old Dancing Master in Crooked Lane.

Soft. [*Aside.* I'm not an inconstant man; but I'll show that City fellow, there are other ladies in town besides his daughter.]—*Dimidum meæ,* how pretty you are, Mistress Lucy!

[*Walks aside with her.*

Sir Geof. That popinjay of a lord is more attentive to Barbara than ever he was to the other.

Easy. Hey! hey! D'ye think so?

Sir Geof. I suspect he has heard how rich you are.

WILMOT *and* BARBARA *approaching.*

Bar. Papa, Lord Wilmot begs to be presented to you.

[*Bows interchanged.* WILMOT *offers snuff-box.* EASY *at first declines, then accepts—sneezes violently; unused to snuff.*

Sir Geof. He! he! quite clear!—titled fortune-hunter. Over head and ears in debt, I dare say. [*Takes* WILMOT *aside.*] Pretty girl, Mistress Barbara! Eh?

Wil. Pretty! Say beautiful!

Sir Geof. He! he! Her father will give her fifty thousand pounds down on the wedding-day.

Wil. I venerate the British merchant who can give his daughter fifty thousand pounds! What a smile she has! [*Hooking his arm into* SIR GEOFFREY'S.] I say, Sir Geoffrey, you see I'm very shy—bashful, indeed—and Mr. Easy is watching every word I say to his daughter: so embarrassing! Couldn't you get him out of the room?

Sir Geof. Mighty bashful, indeed! Turn the oldest friend I have out of my room, in order that you may make love to his daughter! [*Turns away.*

Wil. [*to* EASY]. I say, Mr. Easy. My double, there, Softhead, is so shy—bashful, indeed—and that suspicious Sir Geoffrey is watching every word he says to Mistress Lucy: so embarrassing! Do get your friend out of the room, will you!

Easy. Ha! ha! Certainly, my lord. [*Aside.* I see he wants to be alone with my Barbara. What will they say in Lombard-street, when she's my lady? Shouldn't wonder if they returned me M.P. for the city.] Come into the next room, Geoffrey; and tell me your designs for Lucy.

Sir Geof. Oh, very well! You wish to encourage that pampered young—Satrap! How he does love a lord, and how a lord does love fifty thousand pounds! He! he!

[*Exeunt* SIR GEOFFREY *and* SOFTHEAD

Wil. [*running to* LUCY *and pushing aside* SOFTHEAD]. Return to your native allegiance. Truce with the enemy and exchange of prisoners.

[*Leads* LUCY *aside—she rather grave and reluctant.*

Bar. So, you'll not speak to me, Mr. Softhead; words are too rare with you fine gentlemen to throw away upon old friends.

Soft. Ahem'

Bar. You don't remember the winter evenings you used to pass at our fire-side? nor the mistletoe bough at Christmas? nor the pleasant games at Blind-man's Buff and Hunt the Slipper? nor the strong tea I made you when you had the migraine? Nor how I prevented your eating Banbury cake at supper, when you know it always disagrees with you?—But I suppose you are so hardened that you can eat Banbury cake every night now!—I'm sure 'tis nothing to me!

Soft. Those recollections of one's early innocence are very melting! One renounces a great deal of happiness for renown and ambition.—Barbara!

Bar. Shadowly!

Soft. However one may rise in life—however the fashion may compel one to be a monster——

Bar. A monster!

Soft. Yes, Fred and I are both monsters! Still—still—still—'Ecod, I do love you with all my heart, and that's the truth of it.

WILMOT *and* LUCY *advancing.*

Lucy. A friend of my lost mother's. Oh! yes, dear Lord Wilmot, do see her again—learn what she has to say. There are times when I so long to speak of that—my mother; but my father shuns even to mention her name. Ah, he must have loved her well!

Wil. What genuine susceptibilty! I have found what I have sought all my life, the union of womanly feeling and childlike innocence.

[*Attempts to take her hand:* LUCY *withdraws it coyly.*

Nay, nay, if the renunciation of all youthful levities and follies, if the most steadfast adherance to your side—despite all the chances of life, all temptations, all dangers——

[HARDMAN'S *voice without.*

Bar. Hist! some one coming.

Wil. Change partners; hands across. My angel Barbara!

Enter HARDMAN.

Hard. Lord Wilmot here!

Wil. What! does *he* know Sir Geoffrey?

Bar. Oh yes. Sir Geoffrey thinks there's nobody like him.

Wil. Well met, my dear Hardman. So you are intimate here?

Hard. Ay; and you?

Wil. An acquaintance in its cradle. Droll man, Sir Geoffrey; I delight in odd characters. Besides, here are other attractions.   [*Returning to* BARBARA.

Hard. [*aside.*] If he be my rival! Hum! I hear from David Fallen that his father's on the brink of high treason! That secret gives a hold on the son.   [*Joins* LUCY.

Wil. [*to* BARBARA]. You understand; 'tis a compact. You will favor my stratagem?

Bar. Yes; and you'll engage to cure Softhead of his taste for the fashion, and send him back to——the City.

Wil. Since you live in the City, and condescend to regard such a monster!

Bar. Why, we were brought up together. His health is so delicate; I should like to take care of him. Heigho! I am afraid 'tis too late, and papa will never forgive his past follies.

Wil. Yet papa seems very good-natured. Perhaps there's another side to his character?

Bar. Oh yes! He is such a very independent man, my papa! and has *such* a contempt for people who go out of their own rank, and make fools of themselves for the sake of example.

Wil. Never fear; I'll ask him to dine, and open his heart with a cheerful glass.

Bar. Cheerful glass! You don't know papa—the soberest man! If there's anything on which he's severe, 'tis a cheerful glass.

Wil. So, so! does not he *ever*—get a little excited?

Bar. Excited! Don't think of it? Besides, he is so in awe of Sir Geoffrey, who would tease him out of his life, if he could but hear that papa was so inconsistent as to—as to——

Wil. As to get—a little excited? [*Aside.* These hints should suffice me! 'Gad, if I could make him tipsy for once in a way!—I'll try.] Adieu, my sweet Barbara, and rely on the zeal of your faithful ally. Stay; tell Mr. Easy that he must lounge into Will's. I will look out for him there in about a couple of hours. He'll meet many friends from the City, and all the wits and fine gentlemen. *Allons! Vive la joie!* Softhead, we'll have a night of it!

Soft. Ah! those were pleasant nights when one went to bed at half after ten. Heigho!

[*As* HARDMAN *kisses* LUCY'S *hand*, WILMOT *gaily kisses* BARBARA'S—HARDMAN *observes him with a little suspicion*—WILMOT *returns his look lightly and carelessly*—LUCY *and* BARBARA *conscious.*

ACT III.—SCENE I.

Will's Coffee-house; occupying the depth of the stage. Various groups; some seated in boxes, some standing. In a box at the side, DAVID FALLEN *seated writing.*

Enter EASY, *speaking to various acquaintances as he passes to the background.*

How d'ye do?—Have you seen my Lord Wilmot?—Good day.—Yes; I seldom come here; but I've promised to meet an intimate friend of mine—Lord Wilmot.—Servant, sir!—looking for my friend Wilmot:—Oh! not come yet!—hum—ha!—charming young man, Wilmot: head of the mode; generous, but prudent. I know all his affairs.

Enter Newsman.

Great news! great news! Suspected Jacobite Plot! Fears of ministers!—Army to be increased!—Great news!

[*Coffee-house frequenters gather round* Newsman—*take papers—form themselves into fresh groups.*

Enter HARDMAN.

Hard. I have sent off my letter to Sir Robert Walpole. This place, he must give it; the first favor I have asked. Hope smiles; I am at peace with all men. Now to save Wilmot's father. [*Approaches the box at which* DAVID FALLEN *is writing, and stoops down, as if arranging his buckle.*] [*To* FALLEN. Hist! Whatever the secret, remember, not a word save to me.] [*Passes down the stage, and is eagerly greeted by various frequenters of the Coffee-house.*

Enter LORD LOFTUS.

Lord Lof. Drawer, I engage this box; give me the newspaper. So—" Rumored Jacobite plot—"

Enter the DUKE OF MIDDLESEX.

Duke. My dear Lord, I obey your appointment. But is not the place you select rather strange?

Lof. Be seated, I pray you. No place so fit for our purpose. First, because its very publicity prevents all suspicion. We come to a coffee-house, where all ranks and all parties assemble, to hear the news, like the rest. And, secondly, we could scarcely meet our agent anywhere else. He is a Tory pamphleteer: was imprisoned for our sake in the time of William and Mary. If we, so well known to be Tories, are seen to confer with him here, 'twill only be thought that we are suggesting some points in a pamphlet. May I beckon our agent!

Duke. Certainly. He risks his life for us; he shall be duly rewarded. Let him sit by our side——[LORD LOFTUS *motions to* DAVID FALLEN, *who takes up his pamphlet and approaches openly.*]—I have certainly seen somewhere before that very thin man. Be seated, sir. Honorable danger makes all men equal.

Fal. No, my Lord Duke. I know not you. It is the Earl I confer with. [*Aside.* I never stood in *his* hall, with lacqueys and porters.]

Duke. Powers above! That scare-crow rejects my acquaintance! Portentous!
[*Stunned and astonished.*

Lof. Observe, Duke, we speak in a sort of jargon. Pamphlet means messenger. [*To* FALLEN *aloud.*] Well, Mr. Fallen, when will the pamphlet be ready?

Fal. [*aloud*]. To-morrow, my Lord, exactly at one o'clock.

Duke [*still bewildered*]. I don't understand—

Lof. Hush! Walpole laughs at pamphlets, but would hang messengers. [*Aloud.*] To-morrow, not to-day! Well, more time for——

Fal. Subscribers. Thank you, my Lord. [*Whispering*]. Where shall the messenger meet you?]

Lof. At the back of the Duke's new house, there a quiet, lone place——

Fal. [*whispering*]. By the old mill near the Thames? I know it. The messenger shall be there. The signal word, "Marston Moor." No conversation should pass. But who brings the packet? That's the first step of danger.

Duke [*suddenly rousing himself, and with dignity*]. Then 'tis mine, sir, in right of my birth.

Fal. [*aloud*]. I'll attend to all your Lordship's suggestions; they're excellent, and will startle this vile administration. Many thanks to your Lordship.

[*Returns to his table and resume his writing. Groups point and murmur.* JACOB TONSON *advances.*

Easy. That pestilent scribbler, David Fallen! Another libellous pamphlet as bitter as the last, I'll swear.

Ton. Bitter as gall, sir, I am proud to say. Your servant; Jacob Tonson, the bookseller, —at your service. I advanced a pound upon it.

Duke. I will meet you in the Mall to-morrow, a quarter after one precisely. We may go now? Powers above!—his mind's distracted—he walks out before me!

Lof. [*drawing back at the door*]. I follow you, Duke.

Duke. My dear friend—if you really insist on it? [*Exeunt bowing.*

Hard. [*as the* Drawer *places the wine, etc., on the table*]. Let me offer you a glass of wine, Mr. Fallen—[*Aside.* Well?—] [FALLEN, *who has been writing, pushes the paper towards him.*

Hard. [*reading*]. "At one to-morrow—by the old mill near the Thames—Marston Moor —the Duke in person"—So! We must save these men.—I will call on you in the morning, and concert the means.

Fal. Yes, save, not destroy, these enthusiasts. I'm resigned to the name of a hireling— not to that of a butcher!

Hard. You serve both Whig and Jacobite; do you care then for either?

Fal. Sneering politician! what has either cared for me? I entered the world, devoted heart and soul to two causes—the throne of the Stuart, the glory of Letters. I saw them both as a poet. My father left me no heritage, but loyalty and learning. Charles the Second praised my verse, and I starved; James the Second praised my prose, and I starved; the reign of King William—I passed *that* in prison!

Hard. But the ministers of Anne were gracious to writers.

Fal. And offered me a pension to belie my past life, and write Odes on the Queen who had dethroned her own father. I was not then disenchanted—I refused. That's years ago. If I starved, I had fame. Now came my worst foes, my own fellow-writers. What is fame but a fashion? A jest upon Grub Street, a rhyme from young Pope, could jeer a score of gray laborers like me out of their last consolation. Time and hunger tame all. I could still starve myself; I have six children at home—they must live.

Hard. [*Aside.* This man has genius—he might have been a grace to his age.] I'm perplexed; Sir Robert——

Fal. Disdains letters—I've renounced them. He pays services like these. Well—I serve him. Leave me; go.

Hard. [*rising*]. Not so bad as he seems—another side to the character.

Enter Drawer *with a letter to* HARDMAN.

Hard. [*Aside*]. From Walpole! Now then! my fate—my love—my fortunes!

Easy [*peeping over* HARDMAN'S *shoulder*]. He has got a letter from the Prime Minister, marked "private and confidential." [*Great agitation.*] After all, he *is* a very clever fellow.

[*Coffee-house frequenters evince the readiest assent, and the liveliest admiration.*

Hard. [*advancing and reading the letter*]. "My dear Hardman,—Extremely sorry. Place in question absolutely wanted to conciliate some noble family otherwise dangerous.* Another time, more fortunate. Fully sensible of your valuable service.—ROBERT WALPOLE." —Refused! Let him look to himself! I will—I will—Alas! he is needed by my country; and I am powerless against him.   [*Seats himself.*

Enter WILMOT *and* SOFTHEAD.

Wil. Drawer! a private room—covers for six—dinner in an hour!† And—Drawer! Tell Mr. Tonson not to go yet.—Softhead, we'll have an orgy to-night, worthy the days of King Charles the Second.

Softhead, let me present you to our boon companions;—my friend, Lord Strongbow (hardest drinker in England); Sir John Bruin, best boxer in England—threshed Figg; quarrelsome but pleasant: Colonel Flint—finest gentleman in England, and, out and out, the best fencer; mild as a lamb, but can't bear contradiction, and, on the point of honor, inexorable. Now, for the sixth. Ha, Mr. Easy! (I ask him to serve you.) Easy, your hand! So charmed that you've come. You'll dine with us—give up five invitations on purpose. Do— *sans cérémonie.*

Easy. Why, really, my Lord, a plain sober man like me would be out of place——

Wil. If that's all, never fear. Live with us, and we'll make another man of you, Easy?

Easy. What captivating familiarity! Well, I cannot resist your lordship. [*Strutting down the room, and speaking to his acquaintances.*] Yes, my friend Wilmot—Lord Wilmot —will make me dine with him. Pleasant man, my friend Wilmot. We dine together to-day.

[SOFTHEAD *retires to the background with the other invited guests; but trying hard to escape* SIR JOHN BRUIN, *the boxer, and* COL. FLINT, *the fencer, fastens himself on* EASY *with an air of patronage.*

Wil. [*Aside.* Now to serve the dear Duke.] You have not yet brought the memoir of a late Man of Quality.

Ton. Not yet, My Lord; just been trying; hard work. [*Wipes his forehead.*] But the person who has it is luckily very poor! one of my own authors.

---

* As Walpole was little inclined to make it a part of his policy to conciliate those whose opposition might be dangerous, while he was so fond of power as to be jealous of talent not wholly subservient to him, the reluctance to promote Mr. Hardman, implied to the insincerity of his excuse, may be supposed to arise from his knowledge of that gentleman's restless ambition and determined self-will.

† It was not the custom at Will's to serve dinners; and the exception in favor of my Lord Wilmot proves his influence as a man *a la mode.*

Wil. [*Aside.* His eye turns to that forlorn-looking spectre I saw him tormenting.] That must be one of your authors: he looks so lean, Mr. Tonson?

Ton. Hush; that's the man! made a noise in his day; David Fallen.

Wil. David Fallen, whose books, when I was but a schoolboy, made me first take to reading,—not as taskwork, but pleasure. How much I do owe him!

[*Bows very low to* Mr. Fallen.

Ton. My Lord bows very low! Oh, if your Lordship knows Mr. Fallen, pray tell him not to stand in his own light. I would give him a vast sum for the memoir,—two hundred guineas; on my honor I would! [*Whispering.*] Scandal, my Lord; sell like wild-fire.—I say, Mr. Hardman, I observed you speak to poor David. Can't you help me here? [*Whispering*]. Lord Henry de Mowbray's Private Memoirs! Fallen has them, and refuses to sell. Love Adventures; nuts for the public. Only just got a peep myself. But *such* a confession about the beautiful Lady Morland.

Hard. Hang Lady Morland!

Ton. Besides—shows up his own brother! Jacobite family secrets. Such a card for the Whigs!

Hard. Confound the Whigs! What do I care?

Wil. I'll see to it, Tonson. Give me Mr. Fallen's private address.

Ton. But pray be discreet, my Lord. If that knave Curll should get wind of the scent, he'd try to spoil my market with my own author. The villain!

Wil. [*Aside.* Curll? Why, I have mimick'd Curll so exactly that Pope himself was deceived, and, stifling with rage, ordered me out of the room. I have it! Mr. Curll shall call upon Fallen the first thing in the morning and outbid Mr. Tonson. Thank you, sir. [*Taking the address.*] Moody, my Hardman? some problem in political ethics? You turn away,—you have a grief you'll not tell me—why, this morning I asked you a favor; from that moment I had a right to your confidence, for a favor degrades when it does not come from a friend.

Hard. You charm, you subdue me, and I feel for once how necessary to a man is the sympathy of another. Your hand, Wilmot. This is secret—I, too, then presume to love. One above me in fortune; it may be in birth. But a free state lifts those it employs to a par with its nobles. A post in the Treasury of such nature is vacant; I have served the minister, men say, with some credit; and I asked for the gift without shame—'twas my due. Walpole needs the office, not for reward to the zealous, but for bribe to the doubtful. See, [*giving letter*] "Noble family to conciliate." Ah, the drones have the honey!

Wil. [*reading and returning the letter*]. And had you this post, you think you could gain the lady you love?

Hard. At least it would have given me courage to ask. Well, well, well,—a truce with my egotism,—you at least, my fair Wilmot, fair in form, fair in fortune, you need fear no rebuff where you place your affections.

Wil. Why, the lady's father sees only demerits in what you think my advantages.

Hard. You mistake, I know the man much better than you do; and look, even now he is gazing upon you as fondly as if on the coronet that shall blazon the coach of my lady, his daughter.

Wil. Gazing on me?—where?

Hard. Yonder—Ha! is it not Mr. Easy, whose——

Wil. Mr. Easy! you too taken in! Hark, secret for secret—'tis Lucy Thornside I love.

Hard. You—stun me!

Wil. But what a despot love is, allows no thought, not its slave! They told me below that my father had been here; have you seen him?

Hard. Ay.

Wil. And sounded?

Hard. No—better than that—I have taken precautions. I must leave you now; you shall know the result to-morrow afternoon. [*Aside.* Your father's life in these hands—his ransom what I please to demand.—Ah, joy! I am myself once again. Fool to think man

could be my friend! Ah, joy! born but for the strife and the struggle, it is only 'mid foes that my invention is quickened! Half-way to my triumph, now that I know the rival to vanquish!] [*To* FALLEN. Engage the messenger at one, forget not. Nothing else till I see you.] [*To* WILMOT.] Your hand once again. To-day I'm your envoy; [*Aside*: to-morrow your master.]
[FALLEN *folds up papers and exit.*

Wil. The friendliest man that ever lived since the days of Damon and Pythias: I'm a brute if I don't serve him in return. To lose the woman he loves for want of this pitiful place. Saint Cupid forbid! Let me consider! Many sides to a character—I think I could here hit the right one better than the Hardman. Ha! ha! Excellent! My Murillo! I'll not sell myself, but I'll buy the Prime Minister! Excuse me, my friends; urgent business; I shall be back ere the dinner hour; the room is prepared. Drawer, show in these gentlemen: Hardman shall have his place and his wife, and I'll bribe the arch-briber! Ho! my lackies, my coach, there! Ha, ha! bribe the Prime Minister! There never was such a fellow as I am for crime and audacity.
[*Exit* WILMOT

Colonel Flint. Your arm, Mr. Softhead.

Soft. And Fred leaves me in the very paws of this tiger!
[*Exeunt.*

SCENE II.

The Library in SIR GEOFFREY'S *House.*

Enter SIR GEOFFREY.

I'm followed! I'm dogged! I go out for a walk unsuspiciously; and behind creeps a step, pit, pat; feline and stealthy; I turn, not a soul to be seen—I walk on; pit, pat, stealthy and feline! turn again; and lo! a dark form like a phantom, muffled and masked—just seen and just gone. Ouf! The plot thickens around me—I can struggle no more.
[*Sinks into a seat.*

Enter LUCY.

Who is there?

Lucy. But your child, my dear father.

Sir Geof. Child, ugh! what do you want?

Lucy. Ah, speak to me gently. It is your heart that I want!

Sir Geof. Heart—I suspect I'm to be coaxed out of something!—Eh; eh! Why she's weeping. What ails thee, poor darling?

Lucy. So kind. Now I have courage to tell you. I was sitting alone, and I thought to myself—"my father often doubts of me—doubts of all"—

Sir Geof. Ugh—what now?

Lucy. "Yet his true nature is generous—it could not always have been so. Perhaps in old times he has been deceived where he loved. Ah, his Lucy, at least, shall never deceive him." So I rose and listened for your footstep—I heard it—and I am here, on your bosom, my own father!

Sir Geof. You'll never deceive me—right, right—go on, pretty one, go on. [*Aside.* If she should be my child after all?]

Lucy. There is one who has come here lately—one who appears to displease you—one whom you've been led to believe comes not on my account, but my friend's. It is not so, my father; it is for me that he comes. Let him come no more—let me see him no more—for—I feel that his presence might make me too happy—and that would grieve you, O my father!
[Mask *appears at the window watching.*

Sir Geof. [*Aside.* She must be my child! Bless her!] I'll never doubt you again. I'll bite out my tongue if it says a harsh word to you. I'm not so bad as I seem. Grieve me?—yes, it would break my heart. You don't know these gay courtiers—I do!—tut—tut—tut—don't cry. How can I console her?

Lucy. Shall I say?—let me speak to you of my mother.

Sir Geof. [*recoiling*]. Ah!

Lucy. Would it not soothe you to hear that a friend of hers was in London, who——

Sir Geof. [*rising, and a change in his whole deportment*]. I forbid you to speak to me of your mother,—she dishonored me—

Mask [*in a low voice of emotion*]. It is false! [*Mask disappears.*

Sir Geof. [*starting.*] Did you say "false?"

Lucy [*sobbing*]. No—no—but my heart said it!

Sir Geof. Strange; or was it but my own fancy?

Lucy. Oh, father, father!—How I shall pity you if you discover that your suspicions erred. And again I say—I feel—feel in my heart of woman—that the mother of the child who so loves and honors you, was innocent.

Hardman's voice without. Is Sir Geoffrey at home?

[LUCY *starts up, and exit.—Twilight.—During the preceding dialogue in the scene, the stage has gradually darkened.*

Enter HARDMAN.

Hard. Sir Geoffrey, you were deceived; Lord Wilmot has no thought of Mr. Easy's daughter.

Sir Geof. I know that—Lucy has told me all, and begged me not to let him come here again.

Hard. [*joyfully*]. She has! Then she does not love this Lord Wilmot?—But still be on your guard against him. Remember the arts of corruption—the emissary—the letter—the go-between—the spy!

Sir Geof. Arts! Spy! Ha! if Easy was right after all. If those flowers thrown in at the window; the watch from that house in the lane; the masked figure that followed me; all bode designs but on Lucy——

Hard. Flowers have been thrown in at the window? You've been watched? A masked figure has followed you? One question more. All this since Lord Wilmot knew Lucy?

Sir Geof. Yes, to be sure; how blind I have been! [*Masked figure appears.*

Hard. Ha! look yonder! Let me track this mystery [*Figure disappears*]: and if it conceal a scheme of Lord Wilmot's against your daughter's honor, it shall need not your sword to protect her. [*Leaps from the window.*

Sir Geof. What does he mean? Not *my* sword? Zounds! he don't think of his own! If he does, I'd discard him. I'm not a coward, to let other men risk their lives in my quarrel. Served as a volunteer under Marlbro', at Blenheim; and marched on a cannon! Whatever my faults, no one can say I'm not brave. [*Starting.*] Ha! bless my life! What is that? I thought I heard something—I'm all on a tremble! Who the deuce *can* be brave when he's surrounded by poisoners—followed by phantoms; with an ugly black face peering in at his window?—Hodge, come and bar up the shutters—lock the door—let out the house-dog! Hodge! Hodge! Where on earth is that scoundrel? [*Exit.*

SCENE III.

The Streets—in perspective, an Alley inscribed Deadman's Lane—a large, old fashioned, gloomy House in the Corner, with the door on the stage, above which is impanelled a sign of the Crown and Portcullis. Enter a Female Figure, masked—looks round, pauses, and enters the door. —Dark—Lights down.

Enter HARDMAN.

Hard. Ha! enters that house. I have my hand on the clue! some pretext to call on the morrow, and I shall quickly unravel the skein.   [*Exit.*

Goodenough Easy [*singing without*].—

"Old King Cole
Was a jolly old soul,
And a jolly old soul was he——

[*Entering, with* LORD WILMOT *and* SOFTHEAD, EASY, *his dress disordered, a pipe in his mouth, in a state of intoxication, hilarious, musical, and oratorical.—* SOFTHEAD *in a state of intoxication, abject, remorseful, and lachrymose—* WILMOT *sober, but affecting inebriety.*

"He called for his pipe, and he called for his bowl
And he called for his fiddlers three."

Wil. Ha! ha! I imagine myself like Bacchus between Silenus and his—ass!

Easy. Wilmot, you're a jolly old soul, and I'll give you my Barbara.

Soft. [*blubbering*]. Hegh! hegh! hegh! Betrayed in my tenderest affections.

Wil. My dear Mr. Easy, I've told you already that I'm pre-engaged.

Easy. Pre-engaged! that's devilish unhandsome! But now I look at you, you do seem double: and if you're double, you're not single; and if you're not single, why you can't marry Barbara, for that would be bigamy! But I don't care; you're a jolly old soul!

Wil. Not a bit of it. Quite mistaken, Mr. Easy. But if you want, for a son-in-law, a jolly old soul—there he is!

Soft. [*bursting out afresh*]. Hegh! hegh! hegh!

Easy. Hang a lord! What's a lord? I'm a respectable, independent family Briton!—Softhead, give us your fist: you're a jolly old soul, and you shall have Barbara!

Soft. Hegh! hegh! I'm not a jolly old soul. I'm a sinful, wicked miserable monster! Hegh! hegh!

Easy. What's a monster? I like a monster? My girl shan't go a-begging any farther. You're a precious good fellow, and your father's an alderman, and has got a great many votes, and I'll stand for the City: and you shall have my Barbara.

Soft. I don't deserve her, Mr. Easy; I don't deserve such an angel! I'm not precious good. Lords and tigers have corrupted my innocence. Hegh! hegh! I'm going to be hanged.

Watch. [*without*]. Half-past eight o'clock!

Wil. Come along, gentlemen; we shall have the watch on us!

Easy.
"And the bands that guard the City,
Cried—'Rebels, yield or die!'"

Enter Watchman.

Watch. Half-past eight o'clock!—move on! move on!

Easy. Order, order! Mr. Vice and gentlemen, here's a stranger disturbing the harmony of the evening. I knock him down for a song. [*Seizes the* Watchman's *rattle.*] Half-past Eight, Esq., on his legs! Sing, sir; I knock you down for a song.

Watch. Help! help! Watch! watch! [*Cries within* "Watch!"

Soft. Hark! the officers of justice! My wicked career is approaching its close!

Easy [*who has got astride on the* Watchman's *head, and persuades himself that the rest of the* Watchman *is the table*]. Mr. Vice and gentleman, the toast of the evening——what's the matter with the table? 'Tis bobbing up and down. The table's drunk! Order for the chair —you table, you! [*Thumps the* Watchman *with the rattle.*] Fill your glasses—a bumper toast. Prosperity to the City of London—nine times nine—Hip, hip, hurrah! [*Waves the rattle over his head; the rattle springs, and makes all the noise of which rattles are capable.*] [*Amazed.*] Why, the Chairman's hammer is as drunk as the table!

Enter Watchmen *with staves, springing their rattles.*

Wil. [*drawing* SOFTHEAD *off into a corner*]. Hold your tongue—they'll not see us here!

Watch. [*escaping*]. Murder!—murder!—this is the fellow!—most desperate ruffian.

[EASY *is upset by the escape of the* Watchman, *and, after some effort to remove him otherwise, the Guardians of the Night hoist him on their shoulders.*

Easy. I'm being chaired member for the City! Freemen and Electors! For this elevation to the post of member for your metropolis, I return you my heartfelt thanks! Steady there, steady! The proudest day of my life.—'Tis the boast of the British Constitution that a plain, sober man like me may rise to honors the most exalted! Long live the British Constitution. Hip—hip—hurrah!

[*Is carried off waving the rattle.* SOFTHEAD *continues to weep in speechless sorrow.*

Wil. [*coming forth*]. Ha! ha! ha!—My family Briton being chaired for the City! "So severe on a cheerful glass." Well, he has chosen a son-in-law drunk; and, egad! he shall keep to him sober! Stand up; how do you feel?

Soft. Feel! I'm a ruin!

Wil. Faith, I never saw a more mournful one! It must be near Sir Geoffrey's!—Led them here—on my way to this sepulchral appointment, Deadman's Lane. Where the plague can it be? Ha! the very place. Looks like it! How get rid of Softhead.—Ha, ha! I have it. Softhead, awake! the night has begun—the time for monsters and their prey. Now will I lift the dark veil from the mysteries of London. Behold that house, Deadman's Lane!

Soft. Deadman's Lane! I'm in a cold perspiration!

Wil. In that house—under the antique sign of Crown and Portcullis—are such delightful horrors at work as would make the wigs of holy men stand on end! The adventure is dangerous, but deliriously exciting. Into that abode which woman were lost did she enter, which man is oft hanged when he leaves—into that abode will we plunge, and gaze, like Macbeth, "on deeds without a name."

[*Enter Masked Figure from the door in Deadman's Lane, and approaches* WILMOT, *who has, till now, hold of* SOFTHEAD.

Soft. Hegh? hegh! hegh! I won't gaze on deeds without a name! I won't plunge into Deadman's abodes! [*Perceiving the figure.*] Ha! Look there! Dark veil, indeed! Mysteries of London! Horrible apparition, avaunt! [*Breaks from* WILMOT, *who releases him here, and not till now, as he sees the figure.*] Hegh! hegh! I'll go home to my mother.

[*Exit.*

[*Mask motions to* WILMOT, *who follows her into the house.*]

[*Exeunt* Mask *and* WILMOT *within the house.*

ACT IV.—SCENE I.

The Library in Sir Geoffrey's *house*

Hardman *and* Sir Geoffrey.

Sir Geof. Yes! I've seen that you're not indifferent to Lucy. But before I approve or discourage, just tell me more of yourself,—your birth, your fortune, past life. Of course, you are the son of a gentleman? [*Aside.*] Now as he speaks truly or falsely I will discard him as a liar, or reward him with Lucy's hand.—He turns aside. He will lie!

Hard. Sir, at the risk of my hopes, I will speak the hard truth. "The son of a gentleman!" I think not. My infancy passed in the house of a farmer; the children with whom I played told me I was an orphan. I was next dropped, how I know not, in the midst of that rough world called school. "You have talent," said the master, "but you're idle; you have no right to holidays; you must force your way through life; you are sent here by charity!"

Sir Geof. Charity! *There,* the old fool was wrong!

Hard. My idleness vanished—I became the head of the school. Then I resolved no longer to be the pupil of—Charity. At the age of sixteen I escaped, and took for my motto —the words of the master—"You must force your way through life." Hope and pride whispered—"You'll force it!"

Sir Geof. Poor fellow! What then?

Hard. Eight years of wandering, adventure, hardship, and trial. I often wanted bread— never courage. At the end of those years I had risen—to what? A desk at a lawyer's office in Norfolk.——

Sir Geof. [*Aside*]. My own lawyer? where I first caught trace of him again.

Hard. Party spirit ran high in town. Politics began to bewitch me. There was a Speaking Club, and I spoke. My ambition rose higher—took the flight of an author. I came up to London with ten pounds in my pocket, and a work on the "State of the Nation." It sold well; the publisher brought me four hundred pounds. "Vast fortunes," said he, "are made in the South Sea Scheme. Venture your hundreds,—I'll send you a broker."——

Sir Geof. He! he! I hope he was clever, that broker!

Hard. Clever indeed; in a fortnight he said to me, "Your hundreds have swelled into thousands. For this money I can get you an Annuity on land, just enough for a parliamentary qualification." The last hint fired me—I bought the Annuity. You now know my fortune, and how it was made.

Sir Geof. [*Aside*]. He! he! I must tell this to Easy: how he'll enjoy it.

Hard. Not long after, at a political coffee-house, a man took me aside. "Sir," said he, "you are Mr. Hardman who wrote the famous work on 'The State of the Nation.' Will you come into Parliament! We want a man like you for our borough; we'll return you free of expense; not a shilling of bribery."

Sir Geof. He! he! Wonderful! not a shilling of bribery.

Hard. The man kept his word, and I came into Parliament—inexperienced and friendless. I spoke, and was laughed at; spoke again, and was listened to; failed often; succeeded at last. Here, yesterday, in ending my tale I must have said, looking down, "Can you give your child to a man of birth more than doubtful; and of fortunes so humble?" Yet aspiring even then to the hand of your heiress, I wrote to Sir Robert for a place just vacated by a man of high rank, who is raised to the peerage. He refused.

Sir Geof. Of course. [*Aside.*] I suspect he's very rash and presuming.

Hard. To-day the refusal is retracted—the office is mine.

Sir Geof. [*astonished and aside*]. Ha! I had no hand in that!

Hard. I am now one—if not of the highest—yet still *one* of that Government through which the Majesty of England administers her laws. And, with front erect, I say to you—as I would to the first peer of the realm—" I have no charts of broad lands, and no roll of proud fathers. But alone and unfriended, I have fought my way against Fortune. Did your ancestors more? My country has trusted the new man in her councils, and the man whom she honors is the equal of all."

Sir Geof. Brave fellow, your hand. Win Lucy's consent, and you have mine. Hush! no thanks! Now listen; I have told you my dark story—these flowers cannot come from Wilmot. I have examined them again—they are made up in the very form of the posies I had the folly to send, in the days of our courtship, to the wife who afterwards betrayed me——

Hard. Be not so sure that she betrayed. No proof but the boast of a profligate.

Sir Geof. Who had been my intimate friend for years—so that, O torture! I am haunted with the doubt whether my heiress be my own child! and to whom (by the confession of a servant) she sent a letter in secret the very day on which I struck the mocking boast from the villain's lips, in a public tavern. Ah, he was always a wit and a scoffer—perhaps it is from him that these flowers are sent, in token of gibe and insult. He has discovered the man he dishonored, in spite of the change of name——

Hard. You changed your name for an inheritance. You have not told me that which you formerly bore.

Sir Geof. Morland?

Hard. Morland—Ha—and the seducer's——

Sir Geof. Lord Henry de Mowbray——

Hard. The reprobate brother of the Duke of Middlesex! He died a few months since.

Sir Geof. [*sinking down*]. Died too! Both dead!

Hard. [*Aside*]. Tonson spoke of Lord Henry's Memoir—Confession about Lady Morland in Fallen's hands.—I will go to Fallen at once. [*Aloud.*] You have given me a new clue. I will follow it up.—When can I see you again?

Sir Geof. I'm going to Easy's—you'll find me there all the morning. But don't forget Lucy,—we must save her from Wilmot.

Hard. Fear Wilmot no more.—This day he shall abandon his suit. [*Exit* HARDMAN.

Sir Geof. Hodge!—Well—well——

Enter HODGE

—Hodge take your hat and your bludgeon—attend me to the City. [*Aside.*] She'll be happy with Hardman. And if she were my own child after all! [*Exeunt* SIR GEOFFREY *and* HODGE.

SCENE II.

DAVID FALLEN'S *Garret. The scene resembling that of Hogarth's " Distress Poet."*

Fal [*opening the casement*]. So, the morning air breathes fresh! One moment's respite from drudgery. Another line to this poem, my grand bequest to my country! Ah! this description; unfinished; good, good.

" Methinks we walk in dreams on fairy land
Where—golden ore—lies mix'd with——" *

---

* As it would be obviously presumptuous to assign to an author so eminent as Mr. David Fallen, any verses composed by a living writer, the two lines in the text are taken from Mr. Dryden's *Indian Emperor*.

Enter PADDY.

Paddy. Please, sir, the milkwoman's score!

Fal. Stay, stay;—

"Lies mixed with—common sand!"

Eh? Milkwoman? She must be paid, or the children—I—I—[*Fumbling in his pocket, and looking about the table*]. There's another blanket on the bed; pawn it.

Paddy. Agh, now! don't be so ungratful to your ould friend, the blanket. When Mr. Tonson, the great book-shiller, tould me, says he, "Paddy, I'd giv you two hunder gould guineas for the papursh Mr. Fallen has in his disk!"

Fal. Go, go!   *Knock.*

Paddy. Agh, murther! Who can that be distarbin' the door at the top of the mornin'?

[*Exit.*

Fal. Oh! that fatal Memoir! My own labors scarce keep me from starving, and this wretched scrawl of a profligate worth what to me were Golconda! Heaven sustain me! I'm tempted.

Enter PADDY, *and* WILMOT *disguised as* EDMUND CURLL.

Paddy. Stoop your head, sir. 'Tis not a dun, sir; 'tis Mr. Curll; says he's come to out-bid Mr. Tonson, sir.

Fal. Go quick; pawn the blanket. Let me think my children are fed. [*Exit* PADDY.] Now, sir, what do you want?

Wil. [*taking out his handkerchief and whimpering*]. My dear good Mr. Fallen—no offence —I do so feel for the distress of genius. I *am* a bookseller, but I have a heart—and I'm come to buy——

Fal. Have you? this poem? it is nearly finished—twelve books—twenty years' labor— twenty-four thousand lines!—ten pounds, Mr. Curll, ten pounds?

Wil. Price of *Paradise Lost!* Can't expect such prices for poetry now-a-days, my dear Mr. Fallen. Nothing takes that is not sharp and spicy. Hum! I hear you have some most interesting papers; private Memoirs and Confessions of a Man of Quality recently deceased. Nay, nay, Mr. Fallen! don't shrink back; I'm not like that shabby dog, Tonson. Three hundred guineas for the Memoir of Lord Henry de Mowbray.

Fal. Three hundred guineas for that garbage!—not ten for the Poem!—and—the children! Well! [*Takes out the Memoir in a portfolio, splendidly bound, with the arms and supporters of the Mowbrays blazoned on the sides.*] Ah!—but the honor of a woman—the secrets of a family—the——

Wil. [*grasping at the portfolio which* FALLEN *still detains*]. Nothing sells better, my dear, dear Mr. Fallen! But how, how did you come by these treasures, my excellent friend?

Fal. How? Lord Henry gave them to me himself on his death-bed.

Wil. Nay; what could he give them for, but to publish, my sweet Mr. Fallen; no doubt to immortalize all the ladies who loved him.

Fal. No, sir; profligate as he was, and vile as may be much in this Memoir, that was not his dying intention, though it might be his first. There was a lady he had once foully in- jured—the sole woman he had ever loved eno' for remorse. This Memoir contains a confes- sion that might serve to clear the name he himself had aspersed; and in the sudden repent- ance of his last moments, he bade me seek the lady, and place the whole in her hands, to use as best might serve to establish her innocence.

Wil. How could you know the lady, my benevolent friend?

Fal. I did not; but she was supposed to be abroad with her father,—a Jacobite exile,— and I, then a Jacobite agent, had the best chance to trace her.

Wil. And you did?

Fal. But to hear she had died somewhere in France.

Wil. Then, of course you may *now* gratify our intelligent Public for your own personal profit. Clear as day, my magnanimous friend! Three hundred guineas! I have 'em here in a bag!

Fal. Begone! I will not sell man's hearth to the public.

Wil. [*Aside.* Noble fellow!] Gently, gently, my too warm, but high-spirited friend! To say the truth, I don't come on my own account. To whom, my dear sir, since the lady is dead, *should* be given these papers, if unfit for a virtuous, but inquisitive public? Why, surely to Lord Henry's nearest relation. I am employed by the rich Duke of Middlesex. Name your terms.

Fal. Ha! ha! Then at last he comes crawling to me, your proud Duke? Sir, years ago, when a kind word from his Grace, a nod of his head, a touch of his hand, would have turned my foes into flatterers, I had the meanness to name him my patron—inscribed to him a work, took it to his house, and waited in his hall among porters and lackeys—till, sweeping by to his carriage, he said, "Oh! you are the poet? take this."—and entending his alms, as if to a beggar. "You look very thin, sir; stay and dine with my people." People—his servants!

Wil. Calm yourself, my good Mr. Fallen! 'tis his Grace's innocent way with us all.

Fal. Go! let him know what these Memoirs contain! They would make the proud Duke the butt of the town—the jeer of the lackeys, who jeered at my rags; expose his frailties, his follies, his personal secrets. Tell him this; and then say that my poverty shall not be the tool of his brother's revenge: but my pride shall not stoop from its pedestal to take money from him. Now, sir, am I right? Reply, not as tempter to pauper; but if one spark of manhood be in you, as man speaks to man.

Wil. [*resuming his own manner*]. I reply, sir, as man to man, and gentleman to gentleman. I am Frederick, Lord Wilmot. Pardon this imposture. The Duke is my father's friend. I am here to obtain, what is clear that he alone should possess. Mr. Fallen, your works first raised me from the world of the senses, and taught me to believe in such nobleness as I now hope for in you. Give me this record to take to the Duke—no price, sir; for such things are priceless—and let me go hence with the sight of this poverty before my eyes, and on my soul the grand picture of the man who has spurned the bribe to his honor, and can humble by a gift the great prince who insulted him by alms.

Fal. Take it—take it! [*Gives the portfolio.*] I am saved from temptation. God bless you, young man!

Wil. Now you indeed make me twofold your debtor—in your books, the rich thought; in yourself the heroic examaple. Accept from my superfluities, in small part of such debt, a yearly sum equal to that which your poverty refused as a bribe from Mr. Tonson.

Fal. My Lord—my Lord—— [*Bursts into tears.*

Wil. Oh, trust me the day shall come, when men will feel that it is not charity we owe to the ennoblers of life—it is tribute! When your Order shall rise with the civilization it called into being; and shall refer its claim to just rank among freemen, to some Queen whom even Milton might have sung, and even a Hampden have died for.

Fal. O dream of my youth! My heart swells and chokes me!

Enter HARDMAN.

Hard. What's this? Fallen weeping?—Ah! is not that the tyrannical sneak, Edmund Curil?——

Wil. [*changing his tone to* FALLEN *into one of imperiousness*]. Can't hear of the poem, Mr. Fallen. Don't tell me. Ah! Mr. Hardman [*concealing the portfolio*], your most humble! Sir—sir—if you want to publish something smart and spicy—Secret Anecdotes of Cabinets—Sir Robert Walpole's Adventures with the Ladies—I'll come down as handsomely as any man in the Row—smart and spicy——

Hard. Offer to bribe *me*, you insolent rascal!

Wil. Oh, my dear good Mr. Hardman, I've bribed the Premier himself. Ha! ha! Servant, sir; servant. [*Exit.*

Hard. Loathsome vagabond! My dear Mr. Fallen, you have the manuscript Memoir of Lord Henry de Mowbray. I know its great value. Name your own price to permit me just to inspect it.

Fal. It is gone; and to the hands of his brother, the Duke.

Hard. The Duke! This is a thunder-stroke! Say, sir: you have read this Memoir—does it contain aught respecting a certain Lady Morland?

Fal. It does. It confesses that Lord Henry slandered her reputation as woman in order to sustain his own as a seducer. That part of the Memoir was writ on his death-bed.

Hard. His boast, then——

Fal. Was caused by the scorn of her letter rejecting his suit.

Hard. What joy for Sir Geoffrey! And that letter?

Fal. Is one of the documents that make up the Memoir.

Hard. And these documents are now in the hands of the Duke!

Fal. They are. For, since Lady Morland is dead——

Hard. Are you sure she is dead?

Fal. I only go by report—

Hard. Report often lies. [*Aside.* Who *but* Lady Morland can this mask be? I will go at once to the house and clear up that doubt myself. But the the Duke's appointment! Ah! that must not be forgotten; my rival must be removed ere Lucy can be won. And what hold on the Duke himself to produce the Memoir, if I get the Despatch.] Well, Mr. Fallen, there is no more to be said as to the Memoir. Your Messenger will meet his Grace, as we settled. I shall be close at hand; and mark! the messenger must give me the despatch which is meant for the Pretender. [*Exit* HARDMAN.

Enter PADDY.

Paddy. Plase, sur, an' I've paid the milk-score——

Fal. [*interrupting him*]. I'm to be rich—so rich! 'Tis my turn now. I've shared your pittance, you shall share my plenty! [*Scene closes.*

SCENE III.

The Mall.

Enter SOFTHEAD, *his arms folded, and in deep thought. He is forming a virtuous resolution.*

Soft. Little did I foresee, in the days of my innocence, when Mr. Lillo read to me his affecting tragedy of George Barnwell,* how I myself was to be led on, step by step, to the brink of deeds without a name. Deadman's Lane!—the funeral apparition in black!—a warning to startle the most obdurate conscience!

Enter EASY, *recently dismissed from the Watch-house; slovenly, skulking, and crestfallen.*

Easy. Not a coach on the stand! A pretty pickle I'm in if any one sees me! A sober, respectable man like me, to wake in the watch-house, be kept there till noon among thieves and pickpockets, and at last to be fined five shillings for drunkenness and disorderly conduct; all from dining with a lord who had no thoughts of making Barbara my Lady after all!—Deuce take him!

Easy. [*discovering* SOFTHEAD]. Softhead! how shall I escape him?

Soft. [*discovering* EASY]. Easy! WHAT A FALL! I'll appear not to remember. Barbara's father should not feel degraded in the eyes of a wretch like myself! How d'ye do Mr. Easy? You're out early to day.

---

* We have only, I fear, Mr. Softhead's authority for supposing *George Barnwell* to be then written: it was not acted till some years afterwards.

Easy. [*aside.* Ha! He was so drunk himself he has forgotten all about it.] Yes, a headache. You were so pleasant at dinner. I wanted the air of the park.

Soft. Why, you look rather poorly, Mr. Easy!

Easy. Indeed, I feel so. A man in business can't afford to be laid up—so I thought, before I went home to the City, that I'd just look into—Ha, ha, a seasoned toper like you will laugh when I tell you—I thought I'd just look into the 'pothecary's!

Soft. Just been there myself, Mr. Easy. [*Showing a phial.*

Easy. [*regarding it with mournful disgust*]. Not taken physic since I was a boy! It looks very nasty!

Soft. 'Tis worse than it looks! And this is called *Pleasure!* Ah! Mr. Easy, don't give way to Fred's fascination; you don't know how it ends.

Easy. Indeed I do [*Aside.* It ends in the watch-house]. And I'm shocked to think what will become of yourself, if you are thus every night led away by a lord, who———

Soft. Hush! talk of the devil—look! he's coming up the Mall!

Easy. He is? then I'm off; I see a sedan-chair. Chair! chair! stop!—chair! chair!
[*Exit.*

Enter WILMOT *and* DUKE.

Duke. [*looking at portfolio*]. Infamous indeed! His own base lie against that poor lady, whose husband he wounded. Her very letter attached to it. Ha!—what is this?—Such ribaldry on me! Gracious Heaven! My name thus dragged through the dirt, and by a son of my house! Oh, my Lord, how shall I thank you?

Wil. Thank not me; but the poet, whom your Grace left in the hall.

Duke. Name it not—I'll beg his pardon myself! Adieu; I must go home and lock up this scandal till I've leisure to read and destroy it; never again shall it come to the day! And then, sure that no blot shall be seen in my 'scutcheon, I can peril my life without fear in the cause of my king. [*Exit* DUKE.

Wil. [*chanting*].

"Gather you rosebuds while you may,
For time is still a-flying."

Since my visit last night to Deadman's Lane, and my hope to give Lucy such happiness, I feel as if I trod upon air. Ah, Softhead! why, you stand there as languid and lifeless, as if you were capable of—fishing!

Soft. I've been thinking——

Wil. Thinking! you *do* look fatigued! What a horrid exertion it must have been to you!

Soft. Ah! Fred, Fred, don't be so hardened. What atrocity did you perpetrate last night?

Wil. Last night? Oh, at Deadman's Lane: monstrous, indeed. And this morning, too, another! Never had so many atrocities on my hands as within the last twenty-four hours. But they are all nothing to that which I perpetrated yesterday, just before dinner. Hark! I bribed the Prime Minister.

Soft. Saints in Heaven!

Wil. Ha! ha! Hit him plump on the jolly blunt side of his character! I must tell you about it. Drove home from Will's; put my Murillo in the carriage, and off to Sir Robert's —shown into his office,—"Ah! my Lord Wilmot," says he, with that merry roll of his eye; "this *is* an honor, what can I do for you?"—"Sir Robert," says I, "we men of the world soon come to the point; 'tis a maxim of yours that all have their price."—"Not quite that," says Sir Robert, "but let us suppose that it is." Another roll of his eye, as much as to say, "I shall get this rogue a bargain!" "So, Sir Robert," quoth I, with a bow, "I've come to buy the Prime Minister."—Buy me," cried Sir Robert, and he laughed till I thought he'd have choked; "my price is rather high, I'm afraid." Then I go to the door, bid my lackeys bring in the Murillo. "Look at that, if you please; about the mark, is it not?"—Sir Robert runs to the picture, his breast heaves, his eyes sparkle: "A Murillo!" cries he, name your price!"—"I have named it." Then he looks at me *so*, and I look at him *so!*—turn out the lackeys, place pen, ink, and paper before him; "That place in the Treasury just vacant, and the Murillo is yours."—"for yourself?—I am charmed," cried Sir Robert. "No, 'tis for a friend of your own, who's in want of it."—"Oh, that alters the case: I've so many troubled with the same sort of want."—"Yes, but the Murillo is *genuine*,—pray what are the friends?" Out laughed Sir Robert, "There's no resisting you and the Murillo together! There's the appointment. And now, since your Lordship has bought me, I must insist upon buying your Lordship. Fair play is a jewel." Then I take my grand holiday air: "Sir Robert," said I, "you've bought me long ago! you've given us peace where we feared civil war; and a Constitutional King instead of a despot. And if that's not enough to buy the vote of an Englishman, believe me, Sir Robert, he's not worth the buying." Then he stretched out his bluff hearty hand, and I gave it a bluff hearty shake. He got the Murillo—Hardman the place. And here stand I, the only man in all England, who can boast that he bought the Prime Minister! Faith, you may well call me hardened: I don't feel the least bit of remorse.

Soft. Hardman! you got Hardman the place?

Wil. I did not say Hardman——

Soft. You did say Hardman. But as 'tis a secret that might get you into trouble, I'll keep it.—Yet, *Dimidum meæ*, that's not behaving much like a monster?

Wil. Why, it does seem betraying the Good Old Cause;—but if there's honor among thieves, there is among monsters; and Hardman is in the same scrape as ourselves—in love;—this place may secure him the hand of the lady. But mind—he's not to know I've been meddling with his affairs. Hang it! no one likes that. Not a word then——

Soft. Not a word. My dear Fred, I'm so glad you're not so bad as you seem. I'd half a mind to desert you; but I have not the heart; and I'll stick by you as long as I live!

Wil. [*Aside*]. Whew? This will never do! Poor dear little fellow! I'm sorry to lose him; but my word's passed to Barbara; and 'tis all for his good. [*Aloud.*] As long as you live? Alas! that reminds me of your little affair. I'm to be your second, you know.

Soft. Second!—affair!

Wil. With that fierce Colonel Flint. I warned you against him; but you have such a deuce of a spirit. Don't you remember?

Soft. No; why, what was it all about?

Wil. Let me see—oh, Flint said something insolent about Mistress Barbara.

Soft. He did?—Ruffian!

Wil. So—you called him out! But if you'll empower me in your name to retract and apologize——

Soft. Not a bit of it. Insolent to Barbara! *Dimidum meæ.* I'd fight him if he were the first swordsman in England.

Wil. Why, that's just what he is!

Soft. Don't care; I'm his man—though a dead one.

Wil. [*Aside.* Hang it—he's as brave as myself, on that side of his character. I must turn to another.] No, Softhead, that was not the cause of the quarrel—said it to rouse you, as you seemed rather low. The fact is that it was a jest on yourself, that you took up rather warmly.

Soft. Was that all—only myself?

Wil. No larger subject; and Flint is *such* a good fencer!

Soft. My dear Fred; I retract, I apologize; I despise duelling—absurd and unchristianlike.

Wil. Leave all to me. Dismiss the subject. I'll settle it; only, Softhead, you see our set has very stiff rules on such matters. And if you apologize to a bravo like Flint; nay, if you don't actually, cheerfully, rapturously fight him—though sure to be killed—I fear you must resign all ideas of high life!

Soft. Dimidum meæ, but low life is better than no life at all!

Wil. There's no denying that proposition. It will console you to think that Mr. Easy's kind side is Cheapside. And you may get upon one, if you return to the other.

Soft. I was thinking so, when you found me—*thinking* [*hesitatingly*]—But to leave you——

Wil. Oh, not yet! Retire at least with *éclat*. Share with me one grand, crowning, last, daring, and desperate adventure.

Soft. Deadman's Lane again, I suppose? I thank you for nothing. Fred, I have long been your faithful follower. [*With emotion.*] Now, my Lord, I'm your humble servant.* [*Aside.* Barbara will comfort me. She's perhaps at Sir Geoffrey's.] [*Exit.*

Wil. Well! his love will repay him, and the City of London will present me with her freedom, in a gold box for restoring her prodigal son to her Metropolitan bosom. Deadman's Lane—that was an adventure, indeed. Lucy's mother still living—implores me to get her the sight of her child. Will Lucy believe me? Will——

Enter SMART.

—Ha, Smart? Well—Well?—You—baffled Sir Geoffrey?

Smart. He was out.

Wil. And you gave the young lady my letter?

Smart. Hist! my Lord, it so affected her—that—here she comess. [*Exit* SMART.

Enter LUCY.

Lucy. Oh, my Lord, is this true? Can it be? A mother lives! Do you wonder that I forget all else?—that I am here—and with but one prayer, lead me to that mother! She says, too, she has been slandered—blesses me—that my heart defended her,—but—but—this is no snare—you do not deceive me?

Wil. Deceive you! Oh, Lucy—I have a sister myself at the hearth of my father.

Lucy. Forgive me—lead on—quick, quick—oh, mother, mother!

[*Exeunt* LUCY *and* WILMOT.

ACT V.—SCENE I.

Old Mill near the Thames.

Enter HARDMAN.

Hard. The Despatch to the Pretender [*opening it*]. Ho! Wilmot is in my power; here ends his rivalry. The Duke's life, too, in exchange for the Memoir? No! Fear is not his weak point; but how can this haughtiest of men ever yield such memorials? Even admit the base lie of his brother? Still her story has that which may touch him. Since I have seen her, I feel sure of her innocence. The Duke comes; now all depends on my chance to hit the right side of a character.

Enter DUKE OF MIDDLESEX.

Duke. Lord Loftus not here yet! Strange!

Hard. My Lord Duke—forgive this intrusion!

Duke. T'other man I met at Lord Wilmot's. Sir, your servant; I'm somewhat in haste.

Hard. Still I presume to delay your Grace; for it is on a question of honor!

Duke. Honor! that goes before all! Sir, my time is your own.

Hard. Your Grace is the head of a house, whose fame is a part of our history; it is

---

* A play upon words plagiarized from Farquhar. The reader must regret that the author had not the courage to plagiarize more from Farquhar.

therefore that I speak to you boldly, since it may be that wrongs were inflicted by one of its members——

Duke. How, sir !

Hard. Assured that if so (and should it be still in your power), your Grace will frankly repair them, as a duty you took with the ermine and coronet.

Duke. You speak well, sir.—[*Aside.* Very much like a gentleman !]

Hard. Your Grace had a brother, Lord Henry de Mowbray.

Duke. Ah ! Sir, to the point.

Hard. At once, my Lord Duke. Many years ago a duel took place between Lord Henry and Sir Geoffrey Morland—your Grace knows the cause.

Duke. Hem ! yes; a lady—who—who——

Hard. Was banished her husband's home, and her infant's cradle, on account of suspicions based, my Lord Duke, on—what your Grace cannot wonder that the husband believed —the word of a Mowbray !

Duke. [*Aside.* Villain !] But what became of the husband, never since heard of ? He——

Hard. Fled abroad from men's tongues, and dishonor. He did not return to his native land, till he had changed for another the name that a Mowbray had blighted. Unhappy man ! he lives still.

Duke. And the lady—the lady——

Hard. Before the duel, had gone to the house of her father, who was forced that very day to fly the country. His life was in danger.

Duke. How ?

Hard. He was loyal to the Stuarts,—and—a Plot was discovered.

Duke. Brave, noble gentleman ! Go on, sir.

Hard. Her other ties wrenched from her, his daughter went with him into exile—his stay, his hope, his all. His lands were confiscated. She was high-born: she worked for a father's bread. Conceive yourself, my Lord Duke, in the place of that father—loyal and penniless; noble; proscribed; dependent on the toils of a daughter; and that daughter's name sullied by——

Duke. A word ?——

Hard. From the son of that house to which all the chivalry of England looked for example.

Duke. [*Aside.* Oh, Heaven; can my glory thus be turned to my shame ?] But they said she had died, sir.

Hard. When her father had gone to the grave, she herself spread or sanctioned that rumor—for she resolved to die to the world. She entered a convent, prepared to take the noviciate—when she suddenly learned that a person had been inquiring for her at Paris, who stated that Lord Henry de Mowbray had left behind him a Memoir——

Duke. Ah !

Hard. Which acquits her. She learned, too, the clue to her husband—resolved to come hither—arrived six days since. No proof of her innocence save those for which I now appeal to your Grace !

Duke. O pride, be my succour ! [*Haughtily.*] Appeal to me, sir, and wherefore ?

Hard. The sole evidence alleged against this lady are the fact of a letter sent from herself to Lord Henry, and the boast of a man now no more. She asserts that that letter would establish her innocence. She believes that, on his deathbed, your brother retracted his boast: and that the Memoir he left will attest to its falsehood.

Duke. Asserts—believes—go on—go on.

Hard. No, my Lord Duke, I have done. I know that that letter, that Memoir exist; that they are now in your hands. If her assertion be false—if they prove not her innocence—a word, nay, a sign, from the chief of a house so renowned for its honor, suffices. I take my leave, and condemn her. But if her story be true, you have heard the last chance of a wife and a mother to be restored to the husband she loves and forgives, to the child who has grown into womanhood remote from her care; and these blessings I pledged her my faith to obtain, if that letter, that Memoir, should prove that the boast was——

Duke. A lie, sir, a lie, a black lie!—the coward's worst crime—a lie on the fair name of a woman! Sir, this heat, perhaps, is unseemly; thus to brand my own brother! But if we, the peers of England, and the representatives of her gentlemen, can hear, can think, of vile things done, whoever the doer, with calm pulse and cold heart—perish our titles; where would be the use of a Duke?

Hard. [*Aside*]. A very bright side of his character.

Duke. Sir, you are right. The Memoir you speak of is in my hands; and with it, Lady Morland's own letter. Much in that Memoir relates to myself; and so galls all the pride I am said to possess, that not ten minutes since methought I had rather my duchy were forfeit than have exposed its contents to the pity or laugh of a stranger. I think no more of myself? A woman has appealed for her name to mine honor as a man. Now, sir, your commands?

Hard. No passage is needed, save that which acquits Lady Morland. Let the Memoir still rest in your hands. Condescend but to bring it forthwith to my house; and may I hope that my Lord Loftus may accompany you—there is an affair of moment on which I would speak to you both.

Duke. Your address, sir; I will but return home for the documents, and proceed at once to your house. Hurry not; I will wait. Allow me to take your hand, sir. You know how to speak to the heart of a gentleman. [*Exit.*

Hard. [*Aside.*] Yet how ignorant we are of men's hearts till we see them lit up by a passion! This noble has made what is honor so clear to my eyes. Let me pause—let me think —let me choose! I feel as if I stood at the crisis of life.

Enter SOFTHEAD.

Soft. What have I seen!—Where go?—Whom consult? Oh, Mr. Hardman! You're a friend of Lord Wilmot's, of Sir Geoffrey's, of Lucy's?

Hard. Speak—quick—to the purpose.

Soft. On my way to Sir Geoffrey's, I passed by a house of the most villanous character. I dare not say how Wilmot himself has described it. [*Earnestly.*] Oh, sir, you know Wilmot! you know his sentiments on marriage. I saw Wilmot and Lucy Thornside enter that infamous house!—Deadman's Lane!

Hard. [*Aside*]. Deadman's Lane? He takes her to the arms of her mother! forestalls my own plan, will reap my reward. Have I schemed, then, for him! No, by yon heavens!

Soft. I ran on to Sir Geoffrey's—he was out.

Hard. [*who has been writing in his tablets, tears out a page*]. Take this to Justice Kite's, hard by; he will send two special officers, placed at the door, Deadman's Lane, to wait my instructions. They must go instantly—arrive as soon as myself. Then hasten to Mr. Easy's; Sir Geoffrey is there. Break your news with precaution, and bring him straight to that house. Leave the rest to my care. Away with you; quick.

Soft. I know he will kill me! But I'm right. And when I'm right,—*Dimidum meæ!*
[*Exit.*

Hard. Ho! ho! It is war! My choice is made. I am armed at all points, and strike for the victory. [*Exit.*

SCENE II.

Apartment in the house, Deadman's Lane, Crown and Portcullis, very old-fashioned and sombre, faded tapestry on the walls, high mantel-piece, with deep ingles; furniture rude and simple; general air of the room not mean, but forlorn, as of that in some house neglected and little inhabited since the days of Elizabeth; the tapestry, drawn aside at the back, shows a door into an inner room—LUCY *and her mother.*—WILMOT *seated.*

Lady Thorn. And you believe me. Dear child—this indeed is happiness.—Ah! if your cruel father—

Lucy. Hush—he will believe you, too.

Lady Thorn. No; I could not venture into his presence, without the proof that he had wronged me.

Wil. Oh, that I had known before what interest you had in this Memoir!—how can I recover it from the Duke!—

Lucy. You will—you must—dear—dear Lord Wilmot—you have restored me to my mother; restore my mother to her home.

Wil. Ah—and this hand—would you withdraw it then?

Lucy. Never from him who reunites my parents.

Lady Thorn. Ha!—a voice without—steps!

Wil. If it should be Sir Geoffrey—in some rash violence he might—retire—quick—quick.
[*Exeunt* LADY THORNSIDE *and* LUCY *in the inner room.*

Enter HARDMAN.

Hard. Alone! Where is Lucy, my lord?

Wil. In the next room with——

Hard. Her mother?

Wil. What! you know?

Hard. I know that between us two there is a strife, and I am come to decide it; you love Lucy Thornside.

Wil. Well! I told you so.

Hard. You told it, my Lord, to a rival. Ay, smile. You have wealth, rank, fashion, and wit; I have none of these, and I need them not. But I say to you—that ere the hand on this dial moves to that near point in time, your love will be hopeless and your suit be withdrawn.

Wil. The man's mad. Unless, sir, you wish me to believe that my life hangs on your sword, I cannot quite comprehend why my love should go by your watch.

Hard. I command you, Lord Wilmot, to change this tone of levity: I command it in the name of a life which, I think, you prize more than your own; a life that is now in my hands. You told me to sound your father. I have not done so—I have detected——

Wil. Detected! Hold, sir! that word implies crime.

Hard. Ay, the crime of the great. History calls it ZEAL. Law styles it HIGH TREASON.

Wil. What do I hear? Heavens!—my father! Sir, your word is no proof?

Hard. But *this* is! [*Producing the Requisition to the Pretender.*] 'Tis high treason, conspiring to levy arms against the King on the throne—here called the Usurper. High treason to promise to greet with banner and trump a pretender—here called James the Third. Such is the purport of the paper I hold—and here is the name of your father.

Wil. [*Aside*]. Both are armed and alone. [*Locks the outer door by which he is standing.*

Hard. [*Aside*]. So, I guess his intention. [*Opens the window.*] Good, the officers are come.

Wil. What the law calls high treason I know not; what the honest call treason I know. Traitor, thou who hast used the confidence of a son against the life of a father, thou shalt not quit these walls with that life in thy grasp—yield the proof thou hast plundered or forged.

[*Seizes him.*

Hard. 'St! the officers of justice are below; loose thine hold, or the life thou demandest falls from these hands into theirs!

Wil. [*recoiling*]. Foiled! Foiled! How act! what do? And thy son set yon bloodhound on thy track, O my father! Sir, you say you are my rival; I guess the terms you now come to impose!

Hard. I impose no terms. What needs the demand? Have you an option? I think better of you. We both love the same woman; I have loved her a year, you a week; you have her father's dislike, I his consent. One must yield—why should I? Rude son of the people though I be, why must I be thrust from the sunshine because you cross my path as the fair and the high-born? What have I owed to your order or you?

Wil. To me, sir? Well, if to me you owed some slight favor, I should scorn at this moment to speak it.

Hard. I owe favor, the slightest to no man; 'tis my boast. Listen still, I schemed to save your father, not to injure. Had you rather this scroll had fallen into the hands of a spy? And now, if I place it in yours—save your name from attainder, your fortunes from confiscation, your father from the axe of the headsman—why should I ask terms? Would it be possible for you to say, "Sir, I thank you; and in return I would do my best to rob your life of the woman you love, and whom I have just known a week?" Could you, peer's son, and gentleman, thus reply,—when, if I know aught of this grand people of England, not a mechanic who walks thro' yon streets, from the loom to the hovel, but what would cry "Shame!" on such answer?

Wil. Sir, I cannot argue with, I cannot rival the man who has my father's life at his will, whether to offer it as a barter, or to yield it as a boon. Either way, rivalry between us is henceforth impossible. Fear mine no more! Give me the scroll—I depart.

Hard. [*Aside.* His manliness moves me!] Nay let me pray your permission to give it myself to your father, and with such words as will save him, and others whose names are hereto attached, from such perilous hazards in future.

Wil. In this too I fear that you leave me no choice; I must trust as I may to your honor! but heed well if——

Hard. Menace not; you doubt, then, my honor?

Wil. [*with suppressed passion*]. Plainly, I do; our characters differ. I had held myself dishonored for ever if our positions had been reversed,—if I had taken such confidence as was placed in you,—concealed the rivalry,—prepared the scheme,—timed the moment,—forced the condition in the guise of benefit. No, sir, no; that may be talent, it is not honor.

Hard. [*Aside.* This stings! scornful fool that he is, not to see that I was half relenting. And now I feel but the foe! How sting again? I will summon him back to witness himself my triumph.] Stay, my Lord! [*Writing at the table.*] You doubt that I should yield up the document to your father? Bring him hither at once! He is now at my house with the Duke of Middlesex; pray them both to come here, and give this note to the Duke. [*With a smile.*] You will do it, my Lord.

Wil. Ay, indeed,—and when my father is safe, I will try to think that I wronged you. [*Aside.* And not one parting word to—to—S'death—I am unmanned. Show such emotion to him—No, no!—And if I cannot watch over that gentle life, why the angels will!] I—I go, sir,—fulfil the compact; I have paid the price. [*Exit.*

Hard. He loves her more than I thought for. But she? Does she love him? [*Goes to the door.*] Mistress Lucy! [*Leads forth* LUCY.

Lucy. Lord Wilmot gone!

Hard. Nay, speak not of him. If ever he hoped that your father could have overcome a repugnance to his suit, he is now compelled to resign that hope, and for ever. [LUCY *turns aside, and weeps quietly.*] Let us speak of your parents—your mother——

Lucy. Oh, yes—my dear mother—I so love her already.

Hard. You have heard her tale! Would you restore her, no blot on her name, to the hearth of your father?

Lucy. Speak!—speak!—can it be so?

Hard. If it cost you some sacrifice?

Lucy. Life has none for an object thus holy.

Hard. Hear, and decide. It is the wish of your father that I should ask for this hand——

Lucy. No!—no!

Hard. Is the sacrifice so hard? Wait and hear the atonement. You come from the stolen embrace of a mother; I will make that mother the pride of your home. You have yearned for the love of a father; I will break down the wall between yourself and his heart—I will dispel all the clouds that have darkened his life.

Lucy. You will—you will! O blessings upon you!

Hard. Those blessings this hand can confer!

Lucy. But—but—the heart—the heart—*that* does *not* go with the hand.

Hard. Later, it will. I only pray for a trial. I ask but to conquer that heart, not to break it. Your father will soon be here—every moment I expect him. He comes in the full force of suspicion—deeming you lured here by Wilmot—fearing (pardon the vile word) your dishonor. How explain? You cannot speak of your mother till I first prove her guiltless. Could they meet till I do, words would pass that would make even union hereafter too bitter to her pride as a woman. Give me the power at once to destroy suspicion, remove fear, delay other explanations. Let me speak—let me act as your betrothed, your accepted. Hark! voices below—your father comes!—I have no time to plead; excuse what is harsh—seems ungenerous——

Sir Geof. [*without*]. Out of my way!—loose my sword!

Lucy. Oh save my mother!—Let him not see my mother.

Hard. Grant me this trial—pledge this hand now—retract hereafter if you will. Your mother's name—your parents' reunion! Ay or no!—will you pledge it?

Lucy. Can you doubt their child's answer? I pledge it!

Enter SIR GEOFFREY, *struggling from* EASY, SOFTHEAD, BARBARA.

Sir Geof. Where is he? where is this villain? let me get at him! What, what, gone? [*Falling on* HARDMAN'S *breast.*] Oh Hardman! You came, you came! I dare not look at her yet. *Is* she saved.

Hard. Your daughter is innocent in thought as in deed—I speak in the name of the rights she has given me; you permitted me to ask for her hand; and here she has pledged it!

Sir Geof. O my child! my child! I never called you that name before. Did I? Hush! I know now that thou art my child; know it by my anguish; know it by my joy. Who could wring from me tears like these, but a child!

Easy. But how is it all, Mr. Hardman? you know everything! That fool Softhead, with his cock-and-bull story, frightened us out of our wits.

Soft. That's the thanks I get! How is it all, Mr. Hardman?

Sir Geof. Ugh, what so clear? He came here—he saved her! My child was grateful. Approach, Hardman, near, near. Forgive me, if your childhood was lonely; forgive me, if you seemed so unfriended. Your father made me promise that you should not know the temptations that he thought had corrupted himself,—should not know of my favors, to be galled by what he called my suspicions,—should not feel the yoke of dependence;—should believe that you forced your own way through the world—till it was made. Now it is so. Ah, not in vain did I pardon him his wrongs against me; not in vain fulfil that sad promise which gave a smile to his lips in dying; not in vain have I bestowed benefits on you. You have saved—I know it—I feel it; saved from infamy—my child.

Lucy. Hush, sir, hush! [*Throws herself into* BARBARA'S *arms.*

Hard. My father? Benefits? You smile, Mr. Easy. What means he? No man on this earth ever bestowed benefits on me!

Easy. Ha! ha! ha! Nay, excuse me; but when I think that that's said by a clever fellow like you—ha!—ha!—the jest is too good; as if any one ever drove a coach through this world but what some other one built the carriage, or harnessed the horses! Why, who gave you the education that helped to make you what you are? Who slily paid Tonson, the publisher, to bring out the work that first raised you into notice? Who sent you the broker with the tale of the South-Sea Scheme? From whose purse came the sum that bought your annuity? Whose land does the annuity burthen? Who told Fleece'em, the boroughmonger, to offer you a seat in Parliament? Who paid for the election that did not cost you a shilling? —who, but my suspicious, ill-tempered, good-hearted friend there? And you are the son of his foster-brother, the man who first wronged and betrayed him!

Soft. And this is the gentleman who knows everybody and everything? Did not even know his own father! Ha! why he's been quite a taken-in! Ha! ha!

Easy. Ha! ha! ha!

Hard. And all the while I thought I was standing apart from others,—needing none; served by none; mastering men; moulding them,—the men whom my father had wronged went before me with noiseless beneficence, and opened my path through the mountain I fancied this right hand had hewn!

Sir Geof. Tut! I did but level the ground; till you were strong eno' to rise of yourself; *I* did not give you the post that you named with so manly a pride; *I* did not raise you to the councils of your country as the "Equal of All!"

Soft. No! for that you'll thank Fred. He bribed the Prime Minister with his favorite Murillo. He said you wanted the post to win the lady you loved. *Dimidium mei,*—I think you might have told him what lady it was.

Hard. So! Wilmot!—It needed but this!

Easy. Pooh, Mr. Softhead! Sir Geoffrey would never consent to a lord. Quite right. Practical, steady fellow is Mr. Hardman; and as to his father, a disreputable connection— quite right not to know him! All you want, Geoffrey, is to secure Lucy's happiness.

Sir Geof. All! That, now, is his charge.

Hard. I accept it. But first I secure yours, O my benefactor! This house, in which you feared to meet infamy, is the home of sorrow and virtue; the home of a woman unsullied, but slandered,—of her who, loving you still, followed your footsteps; watched you night and day from yon windows; sent you those flowers, the tokens of innocence and youth; in romance, it is true—the romance only known to woman—the romance only known to the pure! Lord Wilmot is guiltless! He led your child to the arms of a mother!

Sir Geof. Silence him!—silence him!—'tis a snare! I retract! He shall not have this girl! *Her* house? Do I breathe the same air as the woman so loved and so faithless?

Lucy. Pity, for my mother!—No, no; justice for her! Pity for yourself and for me!

Sir Geof. Come away, or you shall not be my child, I'll disown you. That man speaks——

Enter WILMOT, DUKE, *and* LORD LOFTUS.

Hard. I speak, and I prove—[*To the* DUKE]—The Memoirs—[*Glancing over them.*] Here is the very letter that the menial informed you your wife sent to Lord Henry. Read it; and judge if such scorn would not goad such a man to revenge. What revenge could he wield? Why, a boast!

Sir Geof. [*reading*]. The date of the very day that he boasted. Ha! brave words! proud heart! I suspect! I suspect!

Hard. Lord Henry's confession! It was writ on his deathbed.

Lord Lof. 'Tis his hand. I attest it.

Duke. I, too, John, Duke of Middlesex.

Sir Geof. [*who has been reading the confession*]. Heaven forgive me! Can *she?* The flowers; the figure; the—— How blind I've been! Where is she? where is she? You said she was here! [LADY THORNSIDE *appears at the door.*] Ellinor! Ellinor! to my arms—to my heart—O my wife! Pardon! Pardon!

Lady Thorn. Nay, all was forgiven when I once more embraced our child.

Hard. [*to* LOFTUS *and* DUKE]. My Lords destroy this Requisition! When you signed it, you doubtless believed that the Prince you would serve was of the Church of your Protestant fathers? You are safe evermore; for your honor is freed. The Prince has retired to Rome, and abjured your faith. I will convince you of this later.

[DUKE *and* SOFTHEAD *continue to shun each other with mutual apprehension.*]

Easy [*to* WILMOT]. Glad to find you are not so bad as you seemed, my Lord; and now that Lucy is engaged to Mr. Hardman——

Wil. Engaged already! [*Aside.* So! he asked me here to insult me with his triumph!] Well!

Hard. Lucy, your parents are united—my promise fulfilled; permit me—[*Takes her hand.*] Sir Geoffrey, the son of him who so wronged you, and whose wrongs you pardoned, now reminds you, that he is entrusted with the charge to ensure the happiness of your child! Behold the man of her choice, and take from his presence your own cure of distrust. With his faults on the surface, and with no fault that is worse than that of concealing his virtues;—Here she loves and is loved! And thus I discharge the trust, and ensure the happiness!

[*Placing her hand in* WILMOT'S.

Sir Geof. How?

Lady Thorn. It is true—do you not read in her blush the secret of her heart?

Wil. How can I accept at the price of——

Hard. Hush! For the third time to-day, you have but one option. You cannot affect to be generous to me at the cost of a heart all your own. Take your right. Come, my Lord, less I tell all the world how you bribed the Prime Minister.

Soft. [*who has taken* EASY *aside*]. But, indeed, Mr. Easy, I reform; I repent. Mr. Hardman will have a bride in the country—let me have a bride in the city. After all, I was not such a very bad monster.

Easy. Pooh! Won't hear of it! Want to marry only just to mimic my Lord.

Bar. Dear Lord Wilmot; *do* say a good word for us.

Easy. No, sir; no! Your head's been turned by a lord.

Wil. Not the first man whose head has been turned by a lord, with the help of the Duke of Burgundy—eh, Mr. Easy? I'll just appeal to Sir Geoffrey.

Easy. No—no—hold your tongue, my Lord.

Wil. And you insisted upon giving your daughter to Mr. Softhead; forced her upon him.

Easy. I never—!—When?

Wil. Last night, when you were chaired member for the City of London. I'll just explain the case to Sir Geoffrey——

Easy. Confound it—hold—hold!—You like this young reprobate, Barbara?

Bar. Dear Papa, his health is so delicate! I should like to take care of him.

Easy. There, go, and take care of each other. Ha! ha! I suppose it is all for the best.

[DUKE *takes forth, and puts on, his spectacles; examines* SOFTHEAD *curiously—is convinced that he is human, approaches, and offers his hand, which* SOFTHEAD, *emboldened by* BARBARA, *though not without misgivings, accepts.*]

A great deal of dry stuff, called philosophy, is written about life. But the grand thing is to take it coolly, and have a good-humored indulgence——

Wil. For the force of example, Mr. Easy!

Soft. Ha! ha! ha!

Wil. For the follies of fashion, and the crimes of monsters like myself, and that terrible Softhead!

Sir Geof. Ha! ha!

Hard. You see, my dear Wilmot, many sides to a character!

Wil. Plague on it, yes! But get at them all, and we're not so bad as we seem——

Soft. No, Fred, not quite so bad!

Wil. Taking us as we stand—ALTOGETHER!

"DAVID FALLEN IS DEAD!"

OR,

A KEY TO THE PLAY.

(AN AFTER-SCENE, BY WAY OF AN EPILOGUE.)

(*Intended to have been spoken by the Original Amateur Performers.*)

SCENE.

WILMOT'S *Apartment.*—WILMOT, SIR GEOFFREY, SOFTHEAD, EASY, *and* HARDMAN, *seated at a Table. Wine, Fruits, etc.*

Wil. Pass the wine—what's the news?
Easy. Funds have risen to-day.
Sir Geof. I suspect it will rain.
Easy. Well, I've got in my hay.
Hard. DAVID FALLEN IS DEAD!
Omnes. DAVID FALLEN!
Wil. Poor fellow!
Sir Geof. I should like to have seen him!
Soft. *I* saw him! *So* yellow!
Hard. Your annuity killed him!
Wil. How—how? to the point.
Hard. By the shock on his nerves—at the sight of a joint.
A very great genius——
Easy. I own—now he's dead,
That a writer more charming——
Wil. Was never worse fed!
Hard. His country was grateful——
Soft. [*surprised*]. He looked very shabby!
Hard. His bones——
Soft. You might count them!——
Hard. Repose in the Abbey!
Soft. [*after a stare of astonishment*]. SO THAT is the way that a country is grateful!
Ere his nerves grew so weak,—if she'd sent him a plateful.
Easy [*hastily producing a long paper*]. MY TAXES!
Your notions are perfectly hateful!
[*Pause.—Evident feeling that there's no getting over* MR. EASY'S *paper*

Wil. Pope's epigram stung him.
Hard.   Yes, Pope has a sting.
Wil. But who writes the epitaph?
Hard.   Pope : a sweet thing !
Wil. 'Gad, if I were an author, I'd rather, instead,
Have the epitaph living—the epigram dead.
If Pope had but just considered that matter,
Poor David——
   Soft.   , Had gone to the Abbey much fatter !
   Easy. He was rather a scamp !
   Wil.   Put yourself in his place.
   Easy [*horror struck*]. Heaven forbid !
   Hard.   Let us deem him the Last of a Race !
   Sir Geof. But the race that succeeds may have little more pelf.
   Hard. Ay ; and trials as sharp. I'm an author myself.
But the remedy ? Wherefore should authors not build——
   Easy. An alms house ?
   Hard.   No, merchant, their own noble Guild !
Some fortress for youth in the battle for fame ;
Some shelter that Age is not humbled to claim ;
Some roof from the storm for the Pilgrim of Knowledge ;—
   Wil. Not unlike what our ancestors meant by—a College ;
Where teacher and student alike the subscriber,
Untaxing the Patron,—
   Easy.   The State——
   Hard.   Or the briber,——
   Wil. The son of proud Learning shall knock at the door
And cry *This* * is rich, and not whine *That* † is poor.
   Hard. Oh right ! For these men govern earth from their graves—
Shall the dead be as kings, and the living as slaves !
   Easy. It is all their own fault—they so slave one another;
Not a son of proud Learning but knocks—down his brother !
   Wil. Yes ! other vocations, from Thames to the Border,
Have some *esprit de corps,* and some pride in their order;
Lawyers, soldiers, and doctors, if quarrels do pass,
Still soften their spite from respect to their class;
Why should authors be spitting and scratching like tabbies,
To leave but dry bones——
   Soft.   For those grateful cold Abbeys !
   Hard. Worst side of their character !
   Wil.   True to the letter.
Are their sides, then, so fat, we can't hit on a better?
   Hard. Why—the sticks in the fable !—our Guild be the tether.
   Wil. Ay: the thorns are rubbed off when the sticks cling together.
   Soft. [*musingly*]. I could *be*—yes—I *could* be a Pilgrim of Knowledge,
If you'd change Deadman's Lane to a snug little College.
   Sir Geof. Ugh ! stuff !—it takes money a College to found.
   Easy. I will head the subscription myself—with a pound.
   Hard. Quite enough from a friend: for we authors should feel
We must put our own shoulders like men to the wheel.
Be thrifty when thriving—take heed of the morrow,——
   Easy. And not get in debt——

     * The head.   † The pocket.

Sir Geof. Where the deuce could they borrow?
Hard. Let us think of a scheme.
Easy. He is always so knowing.
Wil. A scheme! I have got one; the wheel's set are going!
A play from one author.
Hard. With authors for actors.—
Wil. And some benefit nights,——
Both. For the world's benefactors.
Sir Geof. Who'll give you the play? it will not be worth giving,
Authors now are so bad; always are while they're living!
Easy. Ah! if David Fallen, great genius, were here——
Omnes. Great genius!
Hard. A man whom all time shall revere!
Soft. [*impatiently*]. But he's dead.
Omnes. [*lugubriously*]. He is dead!
Easy. The true Classical School, sir!
Ah! could he come back!
Wil. He'll not be such a fool, sir.
    [*Taking* HARDMAN *aside, whispers.*
We know of an author.
Hard. [*doubtfully*]. Ye—s—s, David was brighter.
Omnes. But he's dead.
Hard. This might do—as a live sort of writer.
Easy. Alive! that looks bad.
Soft. Must we take a live man?
Wil. To oblige us he'll be, sir,—as dead as he can!
Soft. Alive; and *will* write, sir?
Hard. With pleasure, sir.
Soft. PLEASURE!
Hard. With less than your wit, he has more than your leisure.
Coquets with the Muse——
Sir Geof. Lucky dog to afford her!
Wil. Can we get his good side?
Hard. Yes, he's proud of his order.
Wil. Then he'll do!
Sir Geof. As for wit—he has books on his shelves.
Hard. Now the actors?
Wil. By Jove, we will act it ourselves.
    [*Omnes, at first surprised into enthusiasm, succeeded by great consternation.*
Sir Geof. Ugh, not I!
Soft. Lord ha' mercy!
Easy. A plain, sober, steady—
Wil. I'll appeal to Sir Geoffrey. There's one caught already!
This suspicious old knight; to his blind side, direct us.
Hard. Your part is to act——
Wil. True; and his to suspect us.
I rely upon you.
Hard. [*looking at his watch*]. Me! I have not a minute!
Wil. If the Play has a plot, he is sure to be in it.
Come, Softhead!
Soft. I won't. I'll go home to my mother.
Wil. Pooh! monsters like us always help one another.

Sir Geof. I suspect you will act.

Soft. Well, I've this consolation—
Still to imitate one——

Hard. Who defies imitation.

Wil. Let the public but favor the plan we have hit on,
And we'll chair through all London,—our Family Briton.

Sir Geof. What?—what? Look at Easy! He's drunk, or I dream——

Easy [*rising*]. The toast of the evening—SUCCESS TO THE SCHEME!

MONEY.

"'Tis a very good world we live in,
　To lend, or to spend, or to give in:
　But to beg, or to borrow, or get a man's own,
　'Tis the very worst world that ever was known."
　　　　　　　　　　　　　　—*Old Truism.*

"*Und, es herrscht der Erde Gott, das Geld.*"—SCHILLER.

DEDICATED TO

JOHN FORSTER, ESQ.,

Author of "The Lives of Statesmen of the Commonwealth."

A SLIGHT MEMORIAL

OF SINCERE RESPECT AND CORDIAL FRIENDSHIP;

ALTHOUGH

(FOR WE ARE ALL HUMAN!)

HE HAS, IN ONE INSTANCE, AND BUT ONE,

SUFFERED HIS JUDGMENT TO BE MISLED BY TOO GREAT A REGARD FOR

"MONEY!"

DRAMATIS PERSONÆ.

LORD GLOSSMORE	MR. F. VINING.
SIR JOHN VESEY, Bart., Knight of the Guelph, F.R.S., F.S.A	MR. STICKLAND.
SIR FREDRICK BLOUNT	MR. WALTER LACY.
STOUT	MR. DAVID REES.
GRAVES	MR. BENJAMIN WEBSTER
EVELYN	MR. MACREADY.
CAPTAIN DUDLEY SMOOTH	MR. WRENCH.
SHARP	MR. WALDRON.
TOKE	MR. OXBERRY.
FRANTZ, *Tailor*	MR. O. SMITH.
TABOURET, *Upholsterer*	MR. HOWE.
MACFINCH, *Jeweller and Silversmith*	MR. GOUGH.
MACSTUCCO, *Architect*	MR. MORGUE.
KITE, *Horse dealer*	MR. SANTER.
CRIMSON, *Portrait-painter*	MR. GALLOT.
GRAB, *Publisher*	MR. CAULFIELD.

*Members of the * * * Club, Servants, etc.*

LADY FRANKLIN, *half-sister to Sir John Vesey* . . .	MRS. GLOVER.
GEORGINA, *daughter to Sir John*	MISS P. HORTON.
CLARA, *companion to Lady Franklin, cousin Evelyn* .	MISS HELEN FAUCIT.

Scene—London, 1840.

First performed on Tuesday, the 8th of December, 1840, at the Haymarket Theatre.

MONEY.

ACT I.—SCENE I.

A drawing-room in Sir John Vesey's *house; folding-doors at the back, which open on another drawing-room. To the right, a table, with newspapers, books etc.; to the left, a sofa writing-table.*

Sir John, Georgina.

Sir John [*reading a letter edged with black*]. Yes, he says at two precisely. "Dear Sir John, as since the death of my sainted Maria,"—Hum!—that's his wife; she made him a martyr, and now he makes her a saint?

Geor. Well, as since her death?—

Sir John [*reading*]. "I have been living in chambers, where I cannot so well invite ladies, you will allow me to bring Mr. Sharp, the lawyer, to read the will of the late Mr. Mordaunt (to which I am appointed executor) at your house—your daughter being the nearest relation. I shall be with you at two precisely.—Henry Graves."

Geor. And you really feel sure that poor Mr. Mordaunt has made me his heiress?

Sir John. Ay, the richest heiress in England. Can you doubt it? Are you not his nearest relation? Niece by your poor mother, his own sister. All the time he was making this enormous fortune in India did we ever miss sending him little reminiscences of our disinterested affection? When he was last in England, and you only so high, was not my house his home? Didn't I get a surfeit out of complaisance to his execrable curries and pillaws? Didn't he smoke his hookah—nasty old—that is, poor dear man—in my best drawing-room? And didn't you make a point of calling him your " handsome uncle " ?—for the excellent creature was as vain as a peacock,—

Geor. And so ugly!—

Sir John. The dear deceased! Alas, he *was,* indeed;—like a kangaroo in a jaundice! And *if* after all these marks of attachment you are *not* his heiress, why then the finest feelings of our nature—the ties of blood—the principles of justice—are implanted in us in vain.

Geor. Beautiful, sir. Was not that in your last speech at the Freemasons' Tavern upon the great Chimney-sweep Question?

Sir John. Clever girl!—what a memory she has! Sit down, Georgy. Upon this most happy—I mean melancholy—occasion, I feel that I may trust you with a secret. You see this fine house—our fine servants—our fine plate—our fine dinners: every one thinks Sir John Vesey a rich man.

Geor. And are you not, papa?

Sir John. Not a bit of it—all humbug, child—all humbug, upon my soul! As you hazard a minnow to hook in a trout, so one guinea thrown out with address is often the best bait for a hundred. There are two rules in life—First, Men are valued not for what they *are,* but what they *seem* to be. Secondly, If you have no merit or money of your own, you must trade on the merits and money of other people. My father got the title by services in the army, and died penniless. On the strength of his services I got a pension of £400 a year; on the strength of £400 a year I took credit for £800; on the strength of £800 a year I married your mother with £10,000; on the strength of £10,000 I took credit for £40,000 and paid Dicky Gossip three guineas a week to go about everywhere calling me "Stingy Jack!"

Geor. Ha! ha! A disagreeable nickname.

Sir John. But a valuable reputation. When a man is called stingy, it is as much as calling him rich; and when a man's called rich, why he's a man universally respected. On the strength of my respectability I wheedled a constituency, changed my politics, resigned my seat to a minister, who, to a man of such stake in the country, could offer nothing less in return than a patent office of £2,000 a year. That's the way to succeed in life. Humbug, my dear!—all humbug, upon my soul.

Geor. I must say that you——

Sir John. Know the world, to be sure. Now, for your fortune,—as I spend more than my income, I can have nothing to leave you; yet, even without counting your uncle, you have always passed for an heiress on the credit of your expectations from the savings of "Stingy Jack." The same with your education. I never grudged anything to make a show —never stuffed your head with histories and homilies; but you draw, you sing, you dance, you walk well into a room; and that's the way young ladies are educated nowadays, in order to become a pride to their parents, and a blessing to their husband—that is, when they have caught him. Apropos of a husband: you know we thought of Sir Frederick Blount.

Geor. Ah, papa, he is charming.

Sir John. He *was so*, my dear, before we knew your poor uncle was dead; but an heiress such as you will be should look out for a duke.—Where the deuce is Evelyn this morning?

Geor. I've not seen him, papa. What a strange character he is!—so sarcastic; and yet he can be agreeable.

Sir John. A humorist—a cynic? one never knows how to take him. My private secretary,—a poor cousin, has not got a shilling, and yet, hang me, if he does not keep us all at a sort of a distance.

Geor. But why do you take him to live with us, papa, since there's no good to be got by it?

Sir John. There you are wrong; he has a great deal of talent: prepares my speeches, writes my pamphlets, looks up my calculations. My Report on the last Commission has got me a great deal of fame, and has put me at the head of the new one. Besides he *is* our cousin —he has no salary: kindness to a poor relation always tells well in the world; and Benevolence is a useful virtue,—particularly when you can have it for nothing! With our other cousin, Clara, it was different: her father thought fit to leave me her guardian, though she had not a penny— mere useless encumbrance: so, you see, I got my half-sister, Lady Franklin, to take her off my hands.

Geor. How much longer is Lady Franklin's visit to be?

Sir John. I don't know, my dear; the longer the better,—for her husband left her a good deal of money at her own disposal. Ah, here she comes!

SCENE II.

Lady Franklin, Clara, Sir John, Georgina.

Sir John. My dear sister, we were just loud in your praises. But how's this?—not in mourning?

Lady Frank. Why should I go into mourning for a man I never saw?

Sir John. Still, there may be a legacy.

Lady Frank. Then there'll be less cause for affliction! Ha! ha! my dear Sir John, I'm one of those who think feelings a kind of property, and never take credit for them upon false pretences.

Sir John. [*aside*]. Very silly woman! But, Clara, I see you are more attentive to the proper decorum: yet you are very, *very*, VERY distantly connected with the deceased—a third cousin, I think?

Clara. Mr. Mordaunt once assisted my father, and these poor robes are all the gratitude I can show him.

Sir John. Gratitude! humph! I am afraid the minx has got expectations.

Lady Frank. So, Mr. Graves is the executor—the will is addressed to him? The same Mr. Graves who is always in black—always lamenting his ill-fortune and his sainted Maria, who led him the life of a dog?

Sir John. The very same. His liveries are black—his carriage is black—he always rides a black galloway—and, faith, if he ever marry again, I think he will show his respect to the sainted Maria by marrying a black woman.

Lady Frank. Ha! ha! we shall see.—[*Aside.*] Poor Graves, I always liked him: he made an excellent husband.

Enter EVELYN [*seats himself, and takes up a book unobserved*].

Sir John. What a crowd of relations this Will brings to light! Mr. Stout, the Political Economist—Lord Glossmore—

Lady Frank. Whose grandfather kept a pawnbroker's shop, and who, accordingly, entertains the profoundest contempt for everything popular, *parvenu*, and plebeian.

Sir John. Sir Frederick Blount—

Lady Frank. Sir Fwedewick Blount, who objects to the letter R as being too *w*ough, and therefore *dw*ops its acquaintance: one of the new class of prudent young gentlemen, who, not having spirits and constitution for the hearty excesses of their predecessors, intrench themselves in the dignity of a lady-like languor. A man of fashion in the last century was riotous and thoughtless—in this he is tranquil and egotistical. He never does anything that is silly, or says anything that is wise. I beg your pardon, my dear; I believe Sir Frederick is an admirer of yours, provided, on reflection, he does not see "what harm it could do him" to fall in love with your beauty and expectations. Then, too, our poor cousin the scholar—Oh, Mr. Evelyn, there you are!

Sir John. Evelyn—the very person I wanted: where have you been all day? Have you seen to those papers?—have you written my epitaph on poor Mordaunt?—Latin, you know?—have you reported my speech at Exeter Hall?—have you looked out the debates on the Customs?—and, oh, have you mended up all the old pens in the study?

Geor. And have you brought me the black floss silk?—have you been to Storr's for my ring?—and, as we cannot go out on this melancholy occasion, did you call at Hookham's for the last H B. and the Comic Annual?

Lady Frank. And did you see what was really the matter with my bay horse?—did you get me the Opera-box?—did you buy my little Charley his peg-top?

Eve. [*always reading*]. Certainly, Paley is right upon that point; for, put the syllogism thus——[*looking up*] Ma'am—Sir—Miss Vesey—you want something of me?——Paley observes, that to assist even the undeserving tends to the better regulation of our charitable feelings—No apologies—I am quite at your service.

Sir John. Now he's in one of his humors!

Lady Frank. You allow him strange liberties, Sir John.

Eve. You will be less surprised at that, madam, when I inform you that Sir John allows me nothing else.—I am now about to draw on his benevolence.

Lady Frank. I beg your pardon, sir, and like your spirit. Sir John. I'm in the way, I see; for I know your benevolence is so delicate that you never allow any one to detect it!

[*Walks aside.*

Eve. I could not do your commissions to-day—I have been to visit a poor woman, who was my nurse and my mother's last friend. She is very poor, *very*—sick—dying—and she owes six months' rent!

Sir John. You know I should be most happy to do anything for yourself. But the nurse—[*Aside.* Some people's nurses are always ill!]—there are so many impostors about?—We'll talk of it to-morrow. This most mournful occasion takes up all my attention. [*Looking at his watch.*] Bless me! so late! I've letters to write, and—none of the pens are mended. [*Exit.*

Geor. [*taking out her purse*]. I think I will give it to him—and yet, if I don't get the fortune, after all!—Papa allows me so little!—then I *must* have those earrings [*puts up the purse*] Mr. Evelyn, what is the address of your nurse?

Eve. [*writes and gives it*]. She has a good heart with all her foibles!—Ah! Miss Vesey, if that poor woman had not closed the eyes of my lost mother, Alfred Evelyn would not have been this beggar to your father. [CLARA *looks over the address.*

Geor. I will certainly attend to it—[*aside*] if I get the fortune.

Sir John [*calling without*]. Georgy, I say!

Geor. Yes, papa. [*Exit.*

[EVELYN *has seated himself again at the table (to the right), and leans his face on his hands.*

Clara. His noble spirit bowed to this!—Ah, at least here I may give him comfort—[*sits down to write*]. But he will recognize my hand.

Lady Frank. What bill are you paying, Clara?—putting up a bank-note?

Clara. Hush!—O Lady Franklin, you are the kindest of human beings. This is for a poor person—I would not have her know whence it came, or she would refuse it. Would you?—No,—he knows *her* handwriting also!

Lady Frank. Will I—what?—give the money myself? with pleasure! Poor Clara Why this covers all your savings—and I am so rich!

Clara. Nay, I would wish to do all myself!—it is a pride—a duty—it is a joy; and I have so few joys! But, hush!—this way.

[*They retire into the inner room and converse in dumb show.*

Eve. And thus must I grind out my life for ever!—I am ambitious, and Poverty drags me down; I have learning, and Poverty makes me the drudge of fools!—I love, and Poverty stands like a sceptre before the altar! But no, no—if, as I believe, I am but loved again, I will—will—what?—turn opium-eater, and dream of the Eden I may never enter.

Lady Frank. [*to* CLARA]. Yes I will get my maid to copy and direct this—she writes well, and *her* hand will never be discovered. I will have it done and sent instantly. [*Exit.*

CLARA *advances to the front of the stage, and seats herself*—EVELYN *reading.*—*Enter* SIR FREDERICK BLOUNT.

SCENE III.

CLARA, EVELYN, SIR FREDERICK BLOUNT.

Blount. No one in the woom!—Oh, Miss Douglas!—Pway don't let me disturb you. Where is Miss Vesey—Georgina? [*Taking* CLARA'S *chair as she rises.*

Eve. [*looking up, gives* CLARA *a chair and re-seats himself*]. [*Aside.*] Insolent puppy!

Clara. Shall I tell her you are here, Sir Frederick?

Blount. Not for the world. Vewy pwetty girl this companion!

Clara. What did you think of the Panorama the other day, Cousin Evelyn?

Eve. [*reading*].—

"I cannot talk with civet in the room,
A fine puss gentleman that's all perfume!"

Rather good lines these.

Blount. Sir !

Eve. [*offering the book*]. Don't you think so?—Cowper.

Blount [*declining the book*]. Cowper !

Eve. Cowper.

Blount [*shrugging his shoulders, to* CLARA]. Strange person, Mr. Evelyn !—quite a chawacter !—Indeed the Panowama gives you no idea of Naples—a delighful place. I make it a wule to go there evewy second year—I am vewy fond of twavelling. You'd like Wome (Rome)—bad inns, but very fine wuins; gives you quite a taste for that sort of thing !

Eve. [*reading*].—

"How much a dunce that has been sent to roam
Excels a dunce that has been kept at home !"

Blount [*aside*]. That fellow Cowper says vewy odd things !—Humph !—it is beneath me to quawwell.—[*Aloud.*] It will not take long to wead the will, I suppose. Poor old Mordaunt !—I am his nearest male welation. He was vewy eccentwic. By the way, Miss Douglas, did you wemark my cuwicle ? It is bwinging cuwicles into fashion. I should be most happy if you will allow me to dwive you out. Nay—nay—I should upon my word.

[*Trying to take her hand.*

Eve. [*starting up*]. A wasp !—a wasp !—just going to settle. Take care of the wasp, Miss Douglas !

Blount. A wasp !—where !—don't bwing it this way,—some people don't mind them ! I've a particular dislike to wasps; they sting damnably !

Eve. I beg pardon—it's only a gadfly.

Enter Servant.

Ser. Sir John will be happy to see you in his study, Sir Frederick. [*Exit* Servant

Blount. Vewy well. Upon my word, there is something vewy nice about this girl. To be sure, I love Georgina—but if this one would take a fancy to me [*thoughtfully*]—Well, I don't see what harm it could do me !—*Au plaisir !* [*Exit.*

SCENE IV.

EVELYN *and* CLARA.

Eve. Clara !

Clara. Cousin !

Eve. And you too are a dependent !

Clara. But on Lady Franklin, who seeks to make me forget it.

Eve. Ay, but can the world forget it ? This insolent condescension—this coxcombry of admiration—more galling than the arrogance of contempt ! Look you now—Robe Beauty in silk and cashmere—hand Virtue into her chariot—lackey their caprices—wrap them from the winds—fence them round with a golden circle—and Virtue and Beauty are as goddesses both to peasant and to prince. Strip them of the adjuncts—see Beauty and Virtue poor—dependent—solitary—walking the world defenceless ! oh, *then* the devotion changes its character—the same crowd gather eagerly around—fools—fops—libertines—not to worship at the shrine, but to sacrifice the victim !

Clara. My cousin, you are cruel !

Eve. Forgive me ! There is a something when a man's heart is better than his fortunes, that makes even affection bitter. Mortification for myself—it has ceased to chafe me. I can mock where I once resented. But *you*—YOU, so delicately framed and nurtured—one slight to you—one careless look—one disdainful tone—makes me feel the true curse of the poor man. His pride gives armor to *his own* breast, but it has no shield to protect another.

Clara. But I, too, have pride of my own—I, too, can smile at the pointless insolence——

Eve. Smile—and he took your hand! Oh, Clara, you know not the tortures that I suffer hourly! When others approch you—young—fair—rich—the sleek darlings of the world—I accuse you of your very beauty—I writhe beneath every smile that you bestow. No—speak not!—my heart has broken its silence, and you shall hear the rest. For you I have endured the weary bondage of this house—the fool's gibe—the hireling's sneer—the bread purchased by toils that should have led me to loftier ends: yes, to see you—hear you—breathe the same air—be ever at hand—that if others slighted, from one at least you might receive the luxury of respect:—for this—for this I have lingered, suffered, and forborne. Oh! Clara, we are orphans both—friendless both: you are all in the world to me: turn not away—my very soul speaks in these words—I LOVE YOU!

Clara. No—Evelyn—Alfred—No! say it not; think it not! it were madness.

Eve. Madness!—nay, hear me yet. I am poor, penniless—a beggar for bread to a dying servant. True!—But I have a heart of iron! I have knowledge—patience—health,—and my love for you gives me at last ambition! I have trifled with my own energies till now, for I despised all things till I loved you. With you to toil for—your step to support—your path to smooth—and I—I poor Alfred Evelyn—promise at last to win for you even fame and fortune! Do not withdraw your hand—*this* hand—shall it not be mine?

Clara. Ah, Evelyn! Never—never!

Eve. Never.

Clara. Forget this folly; our union is impossible, and to talk of love were to deceive both!

Eve. [*bitterly*]. Because I am poor!

Clara. And *I too!* A marriage of privation—of penury—of days that dread the morrow! I have seen such a lot!—Never return to this again.

Eve. Enough—you are obeyed. I deceived myself—ha!—ha!—I fancied that I too was loved. I, whose youth is already half gone with care and toil!—whose mind is soured—whom nobody *can* love—who ought to have loved no one!

Clara [*aside*]. And if it were only *I* to suffer, or perhaps to starve?—Oh, what shall I say? [*Aloud.*] Evelyn—Cousin?

Eve. Madam.

Clara. Alfred—I—I—

Eve. Reject me!

Clara. Yes! It is past! [*Exit.*

Eve. Let me think. It was yesterday her hand trembled when mine touched it. And the rose I gave her—yes, she pressed her lips to it once when she seemed as if she saw me not. But it was a trap—a trick—for I was as poor then as now. This will be a jest for them all! Well, courage! it is but a poor heart that a coquet's contempt can break! And now, that I care for no one, the world is but a great chess-board, and I will sit down in earnest and play with Fortune!

Enter LORD GLOSSMORE, *preceded by* Servant.

Ser. I will tell Sir John, my Lord! [EVELYN *takes up the newspaper.*

Gloss. The secretary—hum! Fine day, sir; any news from the East?

Eve. Yes!—all the wise men have gone back there!

Gloss. Ha, ha!—not all, for here comes Mr. Stout, the great political economist.

SCENE V.

Stout, Glossmore, Evelyn.

Stout. Good morning, Glossmore.
Gloss. Glossmore !—the parvenu !
Stout. Afraid I might be late—been detained at the Vestry—Astonishing how ignorant the English poor are ! Took me an hour and a half to beat it into the head of a stupid old widow, with nine children, that to allow her three shillings a week was against all the rules of public morality.
Eve. Excellent !—admirable !—your hand, sir !
Gloss. What ! you approve such doctrines, Mr. Evelyn ? Are old women only fit to be starved ?
Eve. Starved ! popular delusion ! Observe, my lord—to squander money upon those who starve is only to afford encouragement to starvation.
Stout. A very superior person that !
Gloss. Atrocious principles ! Give me the good old times, when it was the duty of the rich to succor the distressed.
Eve. On second thoughts, *you* are right, my Lord.—I, too, know a poor woman—ill—dying—in want. Shall *she*, too, perish ?
Gloss. Perish ! horrible !—in a Christian country ! Perish ! Heaven forbid !
Eve. [*holding out his hand*]. What, then, will you give her ?
Glos. Ahem ! Sir—the parish ought to give.
Stout. No !—no !—no ! Certainly not ! [*with great vehemence*].
Gloss. No ! no ! But I say, yes ! yes ! And if the parish refuse to maintain the poor, the only way left to a man of firmness and resolution, holding the principles that I do, and adhering to the constitution of our fathers, is to force the poor *on* the parish by never giving them a farthing one's self.

SCENE VI.

Sir John Blount, Lady Franklin, Georgina, Glossmore, Stout, Evelyn.

Sir John. How d'ye do ?—Ah ! How d'ye do, gentlemen ? This is a most melancholy meeting ! The poor deceased ! what a man he was !
Blount. I was chwistened Fwedewick after him ! He was my first cousin.
Sir John. And Georgina his own niece—next of kin !—an excellent man, though odd—a kind heart, but no liver ! I sent him twice a year thirty dozen of the Cheltenham waters. It's a comfort to reflect on these little attentions at such a time.
Stout. And I, too, sent him the Parliamentary debates regularly, bound in calf. He was my second cousin—sensible man—and a follower of Malthus: never married to increase the surplus population, and fritter away his money on his own children. And now——
Eve. He reaps the benefit of celibacy in the prospective gratitude of every cousin he had in the world !
Lady Frank. Ha ! ha ! ha !
Sir John. Hush ! Hush ! decency, Lady Franklin; decency !

Enter Servant.

Ser. Mr. Graves—Mr. Sharp.

Sir John. Oh, here's Mr. Graves; that's Sharp the lawyer, who brought the will from Calcutta.

SCENE VII.

Graves, Sharp, Sir John, etc.

Chorus of Sir John, Glossmore, Blount, Stout.

Ah, Sir,—Ah, Mr. Graves! [Georgina *holds her handkerchief to her eyes.*

Sir John. A sad occasion!

Graves. But everything in life is sad. Be comforted, Miss Vesey. True, you have lost an uncle; but I—I have lost a wife—such a wife!—the first of her sex—and the second cousin of the defunct! Excuse me, Sir John; at the sight of your mourning my wounds bleed afresh. [Servants *hand round wine and sandwiches.*

Sir John. Take some refreshment—a glass of wine.

Graves. Thank you!—(very fine sherry!)—Ah! my poor sainted Maria! Sherry was *her* wine: everything reminds me of Maria! Ah, Lady Franklin! *you* knew her. Nothing in life can charm me now.—[*Aside.*] A monstrous fine woman that!

Sir John. And now to business. Evelyn, you may retire.

Sharp [*looking at his notes*]. Evelyn—Any relation to Alfred Evelyn?

Eve. The same.

Sharp. Cousin to the deceased, seven times removed. Be seated, sir; there may be some legacy, though trifling: all the relations, however distant, should be present.

Lady Frank. Then Clara is related—I will go for her. [*Exit.*

Geor. Ah, Mr. Evelyn; I hope you will come in for something—a few hundreds, or even more.

Sir John. Silence! Hush; Whugh! ugh! Attention!

[*While the Lawyer opens the will, re-enter* Lady Franklin *and* Clara.

Sharp. The will is very short—being all personal property. He was a man that always came to the point.

Sir John. I wish there were more like him!—[*Groans and shakes his head.*]

[*Chorus groan and shake their heads*

Sharp [*reading*]. "I, Frederick James Mordaunt, of Calcutta, being at present date of sound mind, though infirm body, do hereby give, will and bequeath—Inprimis, To my second cousin, Benjamin Stout, Esq., of Pall Mall, London—— [*Chorus exhibit lively emotion.* Being the value of the Parliamentary Debates with which he has been pleased to trouble me for some time past—deducting the carriage thereof, which he always forgot to pay—the sum of £14 2s. 4d. [*Chorus breathe more freely.*

Stout. Eh, what?—£14? Oh, hang the old miser!

Sir John. Decency—decency! Proceed, sir.

Sharp. "Item.—To Sir Frederick Blount, Baronet, my nearest male relative——"

[*Chorus exhibit lively emotion.*

Blount. Poor old boy! [Georgina *puts her arm over* Blount's *chair.*

Sharp. "Being, as I am informed, the best-dressed young gentleman in London, and in testimony to the only merit I ever heard he possessed, the sum of £500 to buy a dressing-case." [*Chorus breathe more freely;* Georgina *catches her father's eye, and removes her arm.*

Eve. Oh, it will come—will it? Georgina, refused the trifler—*she* courts him [*taking up a portrait*]. Why, what is this?—my own——
—*Money*, Act II., Sc. 1.

Blount [*laughing confusedly*]. Ha! ha! ha! Vewy poor wit—low!—vewy—vewy low!

Sir John. Silence, now, will you?

Sharp. "Item.—To Charles Lord Glossmore—who asserts that he is my relation—my collection of dried butterflies, and the pedigree of the Mordaunts from the reign of King John."
[*Chorus as before.*

Gloss. Butterflies!—Pedigree!—I disown the plebeian!

Sir John [*angrily*]. Upon my word, this is too revolting! Decency! Go on.

Sharp. "Item.—To Sir John Vesey, Baronet, Knight of the Guelph, F.R.S., F.S.A. etc."
[*Chorus as before.*

Sir John. Hush! *Now* it is really interesting!

Sharp. "Who married my sister, and who sends me every year the Cheltenham waters, which nearly gave me my death—I bequeath—the empty bottles."

Sir John. Why, the ungrateful, rascally, old ——

Chorus. Decency, Sir John—decency.

Sharp. "Item.—To Henry Graves, Esq., of the Albany——" [*Chorus as before.*

Graves. Pooh! Gentlemen—my usual luck—not even a ring I dare swear!

Sharp. "The sum of £5,000 in the Three Per Cents."

Lady Frank. I wish you joy!

Graves. Joy—pooh! Three per Cents!—Funds sure to go! Had it been *land*, now—though only an acre!—just like my luck.

Sharp. "Item.—To my niece Georgina Vesey——" [*Chorus as before.*

Sir John. Ah, now it comes!

Sharp. "The sum of £10,000 India Stock, being, with her father's reputed savings, as much as a single woman ought to possess."

Sir John. And what the devil, then, does the old fool do with all his money?

Chorus. Really, Sir John, this is too revolting. Decency! Hush!

Sharp. "And, with the aforesaid legacies and exceptions, I do will and bequeath the whole of my fortune, in India Stock, Bonds, Exchequer Bills, Three per Cent Consols, and in the Bank of Calcutta, (constituting him hereby sole residuary legatee and joint executor with the aforesaid Henry Graves, Esq.) to Alfred Evelyn, now, or formerly of Trinity College, Cambridge— [*Universal excitement.*
Being, I am told, an oddity, like myself—the only one of my relations who never fawned on me; and, who having known privation, may the better employ wealth."—And now, Sir, I have only to wish you joy, and give you this letter from the deceased—I belive it is important.

Eve. [*crossing over to* CLARA]. Ah, Clara, if you had but loved me!

Clara [*turning away*]. And his wealth, even more than poverty, separates us for ever!
[*Omnes crowd round to congratulate* EVELYN.

Sir John [*to* GEORGINA]. Go, child—put a good face on it—he's an immense match! My dear fellow, I wish you joy: you are a great man now—a very great man!

Eve. [*aside*]. And *her* voice alone is silent!

Lord Gloss. If I can be of any use to you——

Stout. Or I, sir——

Blount. Or I! Shall I put you up at the clubs?

Sharp. You will want a man of business. I transacted all Mr. Mordaunt's affairs.

Sir John. Tush, tush! Mr. Evelyn is at home *here*—always looked on him as a son! Nothing in the world we would not do for him! Nothing!

Eve. Lend me £10 for my old nurse! [*Chorus put their hands into their pockets*

ACT II.—SCENE I.

An anteroom in EVELYN'S *new house; at one corner, behind a large screen,* MR. SHARP, *writing at a desk, books and parchments before him.*—MR. CRIMSON, *the portrait-painter;* MR. GRAB, *the publisher;* MR. MACSTUCCO, *the architect;* MR. TABOURET, *the upholsterer;* MR. MACFINCH, *the silversmith;* MR. PATENT, *the coachmaker;* MR. KITE, *the horse-dealer; and* MR. FRANTZ, *the tailor.*—(Servants *cross to and fro the stage.*)

Patent [*to* FRANTZ, *showing a drawing*]. Yes, sir; this is the Evelyn vis-à-vis! No one more the fashion than Mr. Evelyn. Money makes the man, sir.

Frantz. But de tailor, de schneider, make de gentleman! It is Mr. Frantz, of St. James's who take his measure and his cloth, and who make de fine handsome noblemen and gentry, where the faders and de mütters make only de ugly little naked boys!

Macstuc. He's a mon o' teeste, Mr. Evelyn. He taulks o' buying a veela (villa), just to pool down and build oop again.—Ah, Mr. Macfinch! a design for a piece of pleete, eh?

Macfinch [*showing the drawing*]. Yees, sir; the shield o' Alexander the Great, to hold ices and lemonade! It will cost two thousand poon'!

Macstuc. And it's dirt cheap—ye're Scotch, arn't ye?

Macfinch. Arberdounshire!—scraitch me, and I'll scraitch you!

[*Door at the back thrown open.—Enter* EVELYN.

Eve. A levee, as usual. Good day. Ah, Tabouret, your designs for the draperies; very well. And what do you want, Mr. Crimson?

Crim. Sir, if you'd let me take your portrait, it would make my fortune. Every one says you're the finest judge of paintings.

Eve. Of paintings! paintings! Are you sure I'm a judge of paintings?

Crim. Oh, sir, didn't you buy the great Correggio for £4,000.

Eve. True—I see. So £4000 makes me an excellent judge of paintings. I'll call on you, Mr. Crimson,—good day. Mr. Grab—oh, you're the publisher who once refused me £5, for a poem? You are right, it was a sad doggerel.

Grab. Doggerel! Mr. Evelyn, it was sublime! But times were bad then.

Eve. Very bad times with me.

Grab. But now, sir, if you will give me the preference, I'll push it, sir—I'll push it! I only publish for poets in high life, sir; and a gentleman of your station ought to be pushed! —£500 for the poem, sir!

Eve. £500 when I don't want it, where £5 once would have seemed a fortune.

"Now I am rich, what value in the lines!
How the wit brightens—how the sense refines!"

[*Turns to the rest who surround him.*

Kite. Thirty young horses from Yorkshire, sir!

Patent [*showing drawing*]. The Evelyn vis-à-vis!

Macfinch [*showing drawing*]. The Evelyn salver!

Frantz. [*opening his bundle, and with dignity*]. Sare, I have brought de coat—de great Evelyn coat.

Eve. Oh, go to——that is, go home! Make me as celebrated for vis-à-vis, salvers, furniture, and coats, as I already am for painting, and shortly shall be for poetry. I resign myself to you—go!

[*Exeunt* MACFINCH, PATENT, &c.

Enter STOUT.

Eve. Stout, you look heated!

Stout. I hear you have just bought the great Groginhole property.

Eve. It is true. Sharp says it's a bargain.

Stout. Well, my dear friend Hopkins, member for Groginhole, can't live another month—but the interests of mankind forbid regret for individuals! The patriot Popkins intends to start for the borough the instant Hopkins is dead!—your interest will secure his election!—now is your time! put yourself forward in the march of enlightenment!——By all that is bigoted, here comes Glossmore!

SCENE II.

STOUT, GLOSSMORE, EVELYN; SHARP *still at his desk.*

Gloss. So lucky to find you at home! Hopkins, of Groginhole, is not long for this world. Popkins, the brewer, is already canvassing underhand (so very ungentlemanlike!). Keep your interest for young Lord Cipher—a most valuable candidate. This is an awful moment—the CONSTITUTION depends on his return! Vote for Cipher.

Stout. Popkins is your man!

Eve. [*musingly*]. Cipher and Popkins—Popkins and Cipher! Enlightenment and Popkins—Cipher and the Constitution! I AM puzzled! Stout, I am not known at Groginhole.

Stout. Your *property's* known there!

Eve. But purity of election—independence of votes——

Stout. To be sure: Cipher bribes *abominably*. Frustrate his schemes—preserve the liberties of the borough—turn every man out of his house who votes against enlightenment and Popkins!

Eve. Right!—down with those who take the liberty to admire any liberty except *our* liberty! That *is* liberty!

Gloss. Cipher has a stake in the country—will have £50,000 a year—Cipher will never give a vote without considering beforehand how people of £50,000 a year will be affected by the motion.

Eve. Right: for as without law there would be no property, so to be the law for property is the only proper property of law!—That *is* law!

Stout. Popkins is all for economy—there's a sad waste of the public money—they give the Speaker £5,000 a year, when I've a brother-in-law who takes the chair at the vestry, and who assures me confidentially he'd consent to be speaker for half the money!

Gloss. Enough, Mr. Stout.—Mr. Evelyn has too much at stake for a leveller.

Stout. And too much sense for a bigot.

Eve. Mr. Evelyn has no politics at all!—Did you ever play at *battledore?*

Both. Battledore?

Eve. Battledore!—that is a contest between two parties: both parties knock about something with singular skill—something is kept up—high—low—here—there—everywhere—nowhere! How grave are the players! how anxious the bystanders! how noisy the battledores! But when this something falls to the ground, only fancy—it's nothing but cork and feather! Go, and play by yourselves—I'm no hand at it!

Stout [*aside*]. Sad ignorance!—Aristocrat!

Gloss. Heartless principles!—Parvenu!

Stout. Then you don't go *against* us?—I'll bring Popkins to-morrow.

Gloss. Keep yourself free till I present Cipher to you.

Stout. I must go to inquire after Hopkins. The return of Popkins will be an era in history. [*Exit.*

Gloss. I must be off to the club—the eyes of the country are upon Groginhole. If Cipher fail, the constitution is gone! [*Exit.*

Eve. Both sides alike! Money *versus* Man!—Sharp, come here—let me look at you! You are my agent, my lawyer, my man of business. I believe you honest;—but what *is* honesty?—where does it exist?—in what part of us?

Sharp. In the heart, I suppose, sir.

Eve. Mr. Sharp, it exists in the breeches-pocket! Observe: I lay this piece of yellow earth on the table—I contemplate you both; the man there—the gold here! Now, there is many a man in those streets honest as you are, who moves, thinks, feels and reasons as well as we do; excellent in form—imperishable in soul; who, if his pockets were three days empty, would sell thought, reason, body, and soul too, for that little coin! Is that the fault of the man?—no! it is the fault of mankind! God made man; behold what mankind have made a god! When I was poor, I hated the world; now I am rich, I despise it! Fools—knaves—hypocrites!——By the bye, Sharp, send £100 to the poor bricklayer whose house was burned down yesterday!——

Enter GRAVES.

Ah, Graves, my dear friend! what a world this is!—a cur of a world, that fawns on its master, and bites the beggar! Ha! ha! it fawns on *me* now, for the beggar has bought the cur.

Graves. It is an atrocious world!—But astronomers say that there is a travelling comet which must set it on fire one day,—and that's some comfort!

Eve. Every hour brings its gloomy lesson—the temper sours—the affections wither—the heart hardens into stone! Zounds, Sharp! what do you stand gaping there for?—have you no bowels?—why don't you go and see to the bricklayer? [*Exit* SHARP.

SCENE III.

GRAVES *and* EVELYN.

Eve. Graves, of all my new friends—and there name is Legion—you are the only one I esteem; there is sympathy between us—we take the same views of life. I am cordially glad to see you!

Graves [*groaning*]. Ah! why should you be glad to see a man so miserable?

Eve. Because I am miserable myself.

Graves. You! Pshaw! you have not been condemned to lose a wife!

Eve. But plague on it, man, I may be condemned to take one?—Sit down, and listen. I want a confidant!—Left fatherless, when yet a boy, my poor mother grudged herself food to give me education. Some one had told her that learning was better than house and land—that's a lie, Graves.

Graves. A scandalous lie, Evelyn!

Eve. On the strength of that lie I was put to school—sent to college, a sizar. Do you know what a sizar is? In pride he is a gentleman—in knowledge he is a scholar—and he crawls about, amidst gentlemen and scholars, with the livery of a pauper on his back! I carried off the great prizes—I became distinguished—I looked to a high degree, leading to a fellowship; that is, an independence for myself—a home for my mother. One day a young lord insulted me—I retorted—he struck me—refused apology—refused redress. I was a sizar! —a Pariah!—a thing to be struck! Sir, I was at least a man, and I horsewhipped him in the hall before the eyes of the whole College! A few days, and the lord's chastisement was forgotten. The next day the sizar was expelled—the career of a life blasted! That in the difference between Rich and Poor: it takes a whirlwind to move the one—a breath may uproot the other! I came to London. As long as my mother lived, I had one to toil for; and I did toil—did hope—did struggle to be something yet. She died, and then, somehow, my spirit broke—I resigned myself to my fate; the Alps above me seemed too to high ascend—I ceased to care what became of me. At last I submitted to be the poor relation—the hanger-on and gentleman-lackey of Sir John Vesey. But I had an object in that—there was one in that house whom I had loved at the first sight.

Graves. And were you loved again?

Eve. I fancied it, and was deceived. Not an hour before I inherited this mighty wealth I confessed my love and was rejected because I was poor. Now, mark: you remember the letter which Sharp gave me when the will was read?

Graves. Perfectly; what were the contents?

Eve. After hints, cautions, and admonitions—half in irony, half in earnest (Ah, poor Mordaunt had known the world!), it proceeded—but I'll read it to you:—" Having selected you as my heir, because I think money a trust be placed where it seems likely to be best employed, I now—not impose a condition, but ask a favor. If you have formed no other and insuperable attachment, I could wish to suggest your choice; my two nearest female relations are my niece Georgina, and my third cousin, Clara Douglas, the daughter of a once dear friend. If you could see in either of these one whom you could make your wife, such would be a marriage that, if I live long enough to return to England, I would seek to bring about before I die." My friend, this is not a legal condition—the fortune does not *rest* on it; yet, need I say that my gratitude considers it a moral obligation? Several months have elapsed since thus called upon—I ought now to decide: you hear the names—Clara Douglas is the woman who rejected me!

Graves. But now she would accept you!

Eve. And do you think I am so base a slave to passion, that I would owe to my gold what was denied to my affection?

Graves. But you must choose one, in common gratitude; you *ought* to do so—yes, there you are right. Besides, you are constantly at the house—the world observed it: you must have raised hopes in one of the girls. Yes; it is time to decide between her whom you love and her whom you do not!

Eve. Of the two, then, I would rather marry where I should exact the least. A marriage, to which each can bring sober esteem and calm regard, may not be happiness, but it may be content. But to marry one whom you could adore, and whose heart is closed to you—to yearn for the treasure, and only to claim the casket—to worship the statue that you never may warm to life—Oh! such a marriage would be a hell, the more terrible because Paradise was in sight!

Graves. Georgina is pretty, but vain and frivolous.—[*Aside.*] But he has no right to be fastidious—he has never known Maria!—[*Aloud.*] Yes, my dear friend, now I think on it, you *will* be as wretched as myself!—When you are married, we will mingle our groans together!

Eve. You may misjudge Georgina; she may have a nobler nature than appears on the surface. On the day, but before the hour, in which the will was read, a letter, in a strange or disguised hand, signed "*From an unknown friend to Alfred Evelyn,*" and enclosing what to a girl would have been a considerable sum, was sent to a poor woman for whom I had implored charity, and whose address I had only given to Georgina.

Graves. Why not assure yourself?

Eve. Because I have not dared. For sometimes, against my reason, I have hoped that it might be Clara! [*taking a letter from his bosom and looking at it*]. No, I can't recognize the hand. Graves, I detest that girl.

Graves. Who? Georgina?

Eve. No; Clara! But I've already, thank Heaven! taken some revenge upon her. Come nearer.—[*Whispers.*] I've bribed Sharp to say that Mordaunt's letter to me contained a codicil leaving Clara Douglas £20,000.

Graves. And didn't it? How odd, then, not to have mentioned her in his will!

Eve. One of his caprices: besides, Sir John wrote him word that Lady Franklin had adopted her. But I'm glad of it—I've paid the money—she's no more a dependent. No one can insult her now—she owes it all to me, and does not guess it, man—does not guess it !—owes it to me,—me, whom she rejected;—me, the poor scholar !—Ha ! ha !—there's some spite in that, eh ?

Graves. You're a fine fellow, Evelyn, and we understand each other. Perhaps Clara may have seen the address, and dictated this letter after all !

Eve. Do you think so ?—I'll go to the house this instant !

Graves. Eh ? Humph ! Then I'll go with you. That Lady Franklin is a fine woman ! If she were not so gay, I think—I could——

Eve. No, no; don't think any such thing; women are even worse than men.

Graves. True; to love is a boy's madness !

Eve. To feel is to suffer.

Graves. To hope is to be deceived.

Eve. I have done with romance !

Graves. Mine is buried with Maria !

Eve. If Clara did but write this——

Graves. Make haste, or Lady Franklin will be out !—A vale of tears !—a vale of tears !

Eve. A vale of tears, indeed ! [*Exeunt.*

Re-enter GRAVES *for his hat.*

Graves. And I left my hat behind me ! Just like my luck ! If I had been bred a hatter, little boys would come into the world without heads. * [*Exit.*

SCENE V.

Drawing-rooms at SIR JOHN VESEY'S, *as in Act I., Scene I.*

LADY FRANKLIN, CLARA, Servant.

Lady Frank. Past two, and I have so many places to go to ! Tell Philipps I want the carriage directly—instantly.

Ser. I beg pardon, my lady; Philipps told me to say the young horse had fallen lame, and and could not be used to-day. [*Exit.*

Lady Frank. Well, on second thoughts, that is lucky; now I have an excuse for not making a great many tedious visits. I must borrow Sir John's horses for the ball to-night. Oh, Clara, you must see my new turban from Carson's—the prettiest thing in the world and so becoming !

Clara. Ah, Lady Franklin, you'll be so sorry—but—but——

Lady Frank. But what ?

Clara. Such a misfortune ! poor Smith is in tears—I promised to break it to you. Your little Charley had been writing his copy, and spilt the ink on the table; and Smith not seeing it—and taking out the turban to put in the pearls as you desired—she—she——

Lady Frank. Ha ! ha ! laid it on the table, and the ink spoilt it. Ha ! ha !—how well I can fancy the face she made ! Seriously, on the whole it is fortunate; for I think I look best, after all, in the black hat and feathers.

Clara. Dear Lady Franklin, you really have the sweetest temper !

Lady Frank. I hope so, for it's the most becoming turban a woman can wear ! Think of that when you marry. Oh, talking of marriage, I've certainly made a conquest of Mr. Graves.

Clara. Mr. Graves ! I thought he was inconsolable.

* For this melancholy jest Mr. Graves is indebted to a poor Italian poet.

Lady Frank. For his sainted Maria! Poor man! not contented with plaguing him while she lived, she must needs haunt him now she is dead.

Clara. But why does he regret her?

Lady Frank. Why? Because he has everything to make him happy—easy fortune—good health, respectable character. And since it is his delight to be miserable, he takes the only excuse the world will allow him. For the rest—it's the way with widowers; that is, whenever they mean to marry again. But, my dear Clara, you seem absent—pale—unhappy—tears, too?

Clara. No—no—not tears. No!

Lady Frank. Ever since Mr. Mordaunt left you £20,000 every one admires you. Sir Frederick is desperately smitten.

Clara. [*with disdain*]. Sir Frederick!

Lady Frank. Ah! Clara, be comforted—I know your secret: I am certain that Elevyn loves you.

Clara. He did—it—it is past now. He misconceived me when he was poor; and now he is rich, it is not for me to explain.

Lady Frank. My dear child, happiness is too rare to be sacrificed to a scruple. Why does he come here so often?

Clara. Perhaps for Georgina!

Enter SIR JOHN, *and turns over the books, etc., on the table, as if to look for the newspaper.*

Lady Frank. Pooh! Georgina is my niece; she is handsome and accomplished—but her father's worldliness has spoilt her nature—she is not worthy of Evelyn! Behind the humor of his irony there is something noble—something that may yet be great. For his sake as well as yours, let me at least——

Clara. Recommend me to his pity? Ah, Lady Franklin! if he addressed me from dictation, I should again refuse him. No; if he cannot read my heart—if he will not seek to read it, let it break unknown.

Lady Frank. You mistake me, my dear child: let me only tell him that you dictated that letter—that you sent that money to his old nurse. Poor Clara! it was your little all. He will then know, at least, if avarice be your sin.

Clara. He would have guessed it had *his* love have been like *mine*.

Lady Frank. Guessed it!—nonsense! The handwriting unknown to him—every reason to think it came from Georgina.

Sir John [*aside*]. Hum! Came from Georgina!

Lady Frank. Come, *let* me tell him *this*. I know the effect it would have upon his choice.

Clara. Choice! oh, that humiliating word! No, Lady Franklin, no! Promise me!

Lady Frank. But——

Clara. No! Promise—faithfully—sacredly.

Lady Frank. Well, I promise.

Clara. You know how fearful is my character—no infant is more timid: if a poor spider cross the floor, you often laugh to see me grow pale and tremble; and yet I would lay this hand upon the block—I would walk bare-foot over the ploughshare of the old ordeal—to save Alfred Evelyn one moment's pain. But I have refused to share his poverty, and I should die with shame if he thought I had now grown enamoured of his wealth. My kind friend, you will keep your promise?

Lady Frank. Yes, since it must be so.

Clara. Thanks. I—I—forgive me—I am not well. [*Exit*

Lady Frank. What fools these girls are!—they take as much pains to lose a husband as a poor widow does to get one!

Sir John. Have you seen "The Times" newspaper? Where the deuce is the newspaper? I can't find "The Times" newspaper.

Lady Frank. I think it is in my room. Shall I fetch it?

Sir John. My dear sister—you're the best creature. Do! [*Exit* LADY FRANKLIN.
Ugh! you unnatural conspirator against your own family! What can this *letter* be? Ah! I recollect something.

Enter GEORGINA.

Geor. Papa, I want——
Sir John. Yes, I know what you want well enough! Tell me—were you aware that Clara had sent money to that old nurse Evelyn bored us about the day of the will?
Geor. No! He gave me the address and I promised, if——
Sir John. Gave you *the address?*—that's lucky! Hush!

Enter Servant.

Mr. Graves—Mr. Evelyn.

SCENE V.

GRAVES, EVELYN, SIR JOHN, GEORGINA, LADY FRANKLIN.

Lady Frank. [*returning*]. Here is the newspaper.
Graves. Ay—read the newspapers!—they'll tell you what this world is made of. Daily calendars of roguery and woe! Here, advertisements from quacks, money-lenders, cheap warehouses, and spotted boys with two heads. So much for dupes and impostors! Turn to the other column—police reports, bankruptcies, swindling, forgery, and a biographical sketch of the snub-nosed man who murdered his own three little cherubs at Pentonville. Do you fancy these but exceptions to the *general* virtue and health of the nation?—Turn to the leading articles; and your hair will stand on end at the horrible wickedness or melancholy idiotism of that half the population who think differently from yourself. In my day I have seen already eighteen crises, six annihilations of Agriculture and Commerce, four overthrows of the Church, and three last, final, awful, and irremediable destructions of the entire Constitution. And that's a newspaper!
Lady Frank. Ha! ha! your usual vein! always so amusing and good-humored!
Graves [*frowning and very angry*]. Ma'am—good humored!——
Lady Frank. Ah! you should always wear that agreeable smile; you look so much younger—so much handsomer—when you smile!
Graves [*softened*]. Ma'am——A charming creature, upon my word!
Lady Frank. You have not seen the last HB.? It is excellent. I think it might make you *laugh*. But, by the bye, I don't think you can laugh.
Graves. Ma'am—I have not laughed since the death of my sainted Ma——
Lady Frank. Ah! and that spiteful Sir Frederick says you never laugh, because——But you'll be angry?
Graves. Angry!—pooh! I despise Sir Frederick too much to let anything he says have the smallest influence over me! He says I don't laugh, because——
Lady Frank. You have lost your front teeth!
Graves. Lost my front teeth! Upon my word! Ha! ha! ha! That's too good—capital! Ha! ha! ha! [*laughing from ear to ear*].
Lady Frank. Ha! ha! ha! [*They retire to the table in the inner drawing-room.*
Eve. [*aside*]. Of course Clara will not appear!—avoids me as usual! But what do I care?—what is she to me? Nothing! I'll swear this is her glove!—no one else has so small a hand. She'll miss it—so—so—! Nobody's looking—I'll keep it, just to vex her.
Sir John [*to* GEORGINA]. Yes—yes—leave me to manage: you took his portrait, as I told you?

Geor. Yes—but I could not catch the expression. I got Clara to touch it up.

Sir John. That girl's always in the way!

Enter CAPTAIN DUDLEY SMOOTH.

Smooth. Good morning, dear John. Ah, Miss Vesey, you have no idea of the conquests you made at Almack's last night!

Eve. [*examining him curiously while* SMOOTH *is talking to* GEORGINA]. And that's the celebrated Dudley Smooth!

Sir John. More commonly called Deadly Smooth!—the finest player at whist, écarté, billiards, chess, and picquet, between this and the Pyramids—the sweetest manners!—always calls you by your Christian name. But take care how you play at cards with him!

Eve. He does not cheat, I suppose?

Sir John. Hist! No!—but he always *wins!* Eats up a brace of lords and a score or two of guardsmen every season, and runs through a man's fortune like a course of the Carlsbad waters. He's an uncommonly clever fellow!

Eve. Clever? yes! When a man steals a loaf we cry down the knavery—when a man diverts his neighbor's mill-stream to grind his own corn, we cry up the cleverness!—And every one courts Captain Dudley Smooth!

Sir John. Why, who could offend him?—the best-bred, civillest creature—and a dead shot! There is not a cleverer man in the three kingdoms.

Eve. A study—a study!—let me examine him! Such men are living satires on the world.

Smooth [*passing his arm caressingly over* SIR JOHN'S *shoulder*]. My dear John, how well you are looking! A new lease of life! Introduce me to Mr. Evelyn.

Eve. Sir, it's an honor I've long ardently desired. [*They bow and shake hands.*

Enter SIR FREDERICK BLOUNT.

Blount. How d'ye do, Sir John? Ah, Evelyn—I wished so much to see you.

Eve. 'Tis my misfortune to be visible!

Blount. A little this way. You know, perhaps, that I once paid my addwesses to Miss Vesey; but since that vewy eccentwic will Sir John has shuffled me off, and hints at a pwior attachment—[*aside*] which I know to be false.

Eve. [*seeing* CLARA]. A prior attachment!—(Ha! Clara!) Well, another time, my dear Blount.

Enter CLARA.

Blount. Stay a moment—I want you to do me a favor with regard to Miss Douglas.

Eve. Miss Douglas!

Blount. Yes;—you see, though Georgina has gweat expectations, and Stingy Jack will leave her all that he has, yet she has only her legacy of £10,000 at the moment—no doubt closely settled on herself too: Clawa has £20,000. And, I think, Clawa always liked me a little.

Eve. You! I dare say she did!

Blount. It is whispered about that you mean to pwopose to Georgina. Nay, Sir John more than hinted that was her pwior attachment!

Eve. Indeed!

Blount. Now, as you are all in all with the family, if you could say a word for me to Miss Douglas, I don't see what harm it could do me!—[*Aside.*] I will punish Georgina for her pwerfidy.

Eve. 'Sdeath, man! speak for yourself! you are just the sort of man for young ladies to like—they understand you—you're of their own level. Pshaw! you're too modest—you want no mediator!

Blount. My dear fellow, you flatter me. I'm well enough in my way. But you, you know, would cawwy evewything before you!—you're so confoundedly wich!

Eve. [*turning to* CLARA]. Miss Douglas, what do you think of Sir Frederick Blount? Observe him. He is well dressed—young—tolerably handsome—(BLOUNT *bowing*) bows with an air—has plenty of small talk—every thing to captivate. Yet he thinks that, if he and I were suitors to the same lady, I should be more successful because I am richer.—What say you! Is love an auction?—and *do* women's hearts go to the highest bidder?

Clara. Their hearts?—No.

Eve. But their hands—yes! You turn away. Ah, you dare not answer that question!

Geor. [*aside.*] Sir Frederick flirting with Clara? I'll punish him for his perfidy. You are the last person to talk so, Mr. Evelyn!—you, whose wealth is your smallest attraction—you, whom every one admires—so witty, such taste, such talent! Ah, I'm very foolish!

Sir John [*clapping him on the shoulder*]. You must not turn my little girl's head. Oh, you're a sad fellow! Apropos, I must show you Georgina's last drawings. She has wonderfully improved since you gave her lessons in prospective.

Geor. No, papa!—No, pray, no! Nay, don't!

Sir John. Nonsense, child!—it's very odd, but she's more afraid of you than of any one!

Smooth [*to* BLOUNT *taking snuff*]. He's an excellent father, our dear John! and supplies the place of a mother to her.   [*Turns away to* LADY FRANKLIN *and* GRAVES.

[EVELYN *and* GEORGINA *seat themselves, and look over the drawings;* SIR JOHN *leans over them;* SIR FREDERICK *converses with* CLARA; EVELYN *watching them.*

Eve. Beautiful!—a view from Tivoli. (Death!—she looks down while he speaks to her!) Is there a little fault in that coloring? (She positively blushes!) But this Jupiter is superb. (What a d——d coxcomb it is!) [*Rising.*] Oh, she certainly loves him—I too can be loved elsewhere—I too can see smiles and blushes on the face of another.

Geor. Are you not well?

Eve. I beg pardon. Yes, you are indeed improved! Ah, who so accomplished as Miss Vesey?   [*Takes up the drawings; pays her marked attention in dumb show.*

Clara. Yes, Sir Frederick, the concert was very crowded. Ah, I see that Georgina consoles him for the past! He has only praises for her, nothing but taunts for me!

Blount. I wish you would take my opewa-box next Saturday—'tis the best in the house. I'm not wich, but I spend what I have on myself! I make a point to have evewything the best in a quiet way. Best opewa-box—best dogs—best horses—best house of its kind. I want nothing to complete my establishment but the best wife!

Clara [*abstractedly*]. That will come in good time, Sir Frederick.

Eve. Oh, it will come—will it? Georgina refused the trifler—*she* courts him [*taking up a portrait*]. Why, what is this?—my own——

Geor. You must not look at that—you must not, indeed. I did not know it was there.

Sir John. Your own portrait, Evelyn! Why, child, I was not aware you took likenesses: that's something new. Upon my word it's a strong resemblance.

Geor. Oh, no—it does not do him justice. Give it to me. I will tear it. [*Aside.*] That odious Sir Frederick!

Eve. Nay, you shall not.

Clara. So—so—he loves her, then! Misery—misery! But he shall not perceive it! No—no—I can be proud too. Ha! ha!—Sir Frederick—excellent—excellent—you are so entertaining—ha! ha! [*laughs hysterically*].

Eve. Oh, the affectation of coquets—they cannot even laugh naturally!

[CLARA *looks at him reproachfully, and walks aside with* SIR FREDERICK.

But where is the new guitar you meant to buy, Miss Vesey—the one inlaid with tortoiseshell? It is nearly a year since you set your heart on it, and I don't see it yet!

Sir John [*taking him aside confidentially*]. The guitar—oh, to tell you a secret—she applied the money I gave her for it to a case of charity several months ago—the very day the will was read. I saw the letter lying on the table, with the money in it. Mind, not a word to her—she'd never forgive me!

Eve. Letter!—money! What was the name of the person she relieved—not Stanton?

Sir John. I don't remember, indeed.

Eve. [*taking out the letter*]. This is not her hand!

Sir John. No! I observed at the time it was not her hand, but I got out from her that she did not wish the thing to *be known*, and had employed some one else to copy it. May I see the letter? Yes, I think this is the wording. But I did not mean to tell you what case of charity it was. I promised Georgy I would not. Still, how did she know Mrs. Stanton's address?—you never gave it to me!

Eve. I gave it to her, Sir John.

Clara [*at the distance*]. Yes, I'll go to the opera, if Lady Franklin will. Do go, dear Lady Franklin!—on Saturday, then, Sir Frederick. [*Exit* BLOUNT.

Eve. Sir John, to a man like me, this simple act of unostentatious generosity is worth all the accomplishments in the world. A good heart—a tender disposition—a charity that shuns the day—a modesty that blushes at its own excellence—an impulse towards something more divine than Mammon;—such are the true accomplishments which preserve beauty for ever young. Such I have sought in the partner I would take for life;—such have I found—alas! not where I had dreamed!—Miss Vesey, I will be honest—I say then, frankly—[*as* CLARA *approaches, raising his voice and looking fixedly at her*]—I have loved another—deeply—truly —bitterly—*vainly!* I cannot offer to you, as I did to her, the fair first love of the human heart—rich with all its blossoms and its verdure. But if esteem—if gratitude—if an earnest resolve to conquer every recollection that would wander from your image;—if these can tempt you to accept my hand and fortune, my life shall be a study to deserve your confidence. [CLARA *stands motionless, clasping her hands, and then slowly seats herself.*

Sir John. The happiest day of my life! [CLARA *falls back in her chair.*

Eve. [*darting forward*]. [*Aside.*] She is pale; she faints! What have I done? Oh heaven!—Clara!

Clara [*rising with a smile*]. Be happy, my cousin—be happy! Yes, with my whole heart I say it—be happy, Alfred Evelyn!

ACT III.—SCENE I.

The drawing-rooms in SIR JOHN VESEY'S *house.*

SIR JOHN, GEORGINA.

Sir John. And he has not pressed you to fix the wedding-day?

Geor. No; and since he proposed he comes here so seldom, and seems so gloomy. Heigho! Poor Sir Frederick was twenty times more amusing.

Sir John. But Evelyn is fifty times as rich!

Geor. Sir Frederick dresses so well!

Sir John. You'll have magnificent diamonds; but a word with you: I saw you yesterday in the square with Sir Frederick; that must not happen again. When a young lady is engaged to one man, nothing is so indecorous as to flirt with another. It might endanger your marriage itself. Oh, it's highly indecorous!

Geor. Don't be afraid, papa,—he takes up with Clara.

Sir John. Who, Evelyn?

Geor. Sir Frederick. Heigho!—I hate artful girls.

Sir John. The settlements will be splendid! if anything happens, nothing can be handsomer than your jointure.

Geor. My own kind papa, you always put things so pleasantly. But do you not fear lest he discover that Clara wrote the letter?

Sir John. No; and I shall get Clara out of the house. But there is something else that makes me very uneasy. You know that no sooner did Evelyn come into possession of his fortune than he launched out in the style of a prince. His house in London is a palace, and he has bought a great estate in the country. Look how he lives!—Balls—banquets—fine arts—fiddlers—charities—and the devil to pay!

Geor. But if he can afford it ——

Sir John. Oh! so long as he stopped *there* I had no apprehension; but since he proposed for you he is more extravagant than ever. They say he has taken to gambling: and he is always with Captain Smooth! No fortune can stand Deadly Smooth! If he gets into a scrape he may fall off from the settlements. We must press the marriage at once.

Geor. Heigho! Poor Frederick! You don't think he is *really* attached to Clara!

Sir John. Upon my word I can't say. Put on your bonnet, and come to Storr and Mortimer's to choose the jewels.

Geor. The jewels; yes—the drive will do me good. So you'll send away Clara?—she's so very deceitful.

Sir John. Never fear—yes—tell her to come to me. [*Exit* GEORGINA.

Yes! I must press on this marriage; Georgina has not wit enough to manage him—at least till he's her husband, and then all women find it smooth sailing. This match will make me a man of prodigious importance! I suspect he'll give me up her ten thousand pounds. I can't think of his taking to gambling, for I love him as a son—and I look on his money as my own.

SCENE II.

CLARA *and* SIR JOHN.

Sir John. Clara, my love!

Clara. Sir——

Sir John. My dear, what I am going to say may appear a little rude and unkind, but you know my character is frankness. To the point then; my poor child, I am aware of your attachment to Mr. Evelyn——

Clara. Sir! *my attachment?*

Sir John. It is generally remarked. Lady Kind says you are falling away. My poor girl, I pity you—I do, indeed! Now, there's that letter you wrote to his old nurse—it has got about somehow—and the world is so ill-natured. I don't know if I did right; but after he had proposed to Georgy—(of course not before!)—I thought it so unpleasant for you as a young lady, to be suspected of anything forward with respect to a man who was not attached to you, that I rather let it be supposed that Georgy *herself* wrote the letter.

Clara. Sir, I don't know what right you had to——

Sir John. That's very true, my dear: and I've been thinking since that I ought perhaps to tell Mr. Evelyn that the letter was yours—shall I?

Clara. No, sir; I beg you will not. I—I—[*weeps*].

Sir John. My dear Clara, don't cry; I would not have said this for the world, if I was not a little anxious about my own girl. Georgina is so unhappy at what everyone says of your attachment——

Clara. Every one?—Oh, torture!

Sir John. That it preys on her spirits—it even irritates her temper! You see, although the marriage will take place almost immediately, Mr. Evelyn does not come so often as he ought. In a word, I fear these little jealousies and suspicions will tend to embitter their future union.—I'm a father—forgive me.

Clara. Embitter their union! Oh, never! What would you have me do, sir?

Sir John. Why, you're now independent. Lady Franklin seems resolved to stay in town. Surely she can't mean to take her money out of the family by some foolish inclination for Mr. Graves? He is always purring and whining about the house, like a black cat in the megrims. What think you, eh?

Clara. Sir, it was of myself—my unhappy self, you were speaking.

Sir John. Sly!——True; true! What I meant to say was this;—Lady Franklin persists in staying *here*: you are your own mistress. Mrs. Carlton, aunt to my late wife, is going abroad for a short time, and would be delighted if you would accompany her.

Clara. It is the very favor I would have asked of you. [*Aside.*] I shall escape at least the struggle and the shame. When does she go?

Sir John. In five days—next Monday.—You forgive me?

Clara. Sir, I thank you.

Sir John [*Drawing the table*]. Suppose, then, you write a line to her yourself, and settle it at once?

Enter Servant.

Servant. The carriage, Sir John; Miss Vesey is quite ready.

Sir John. Wait a moment. Shall I tell Evelyn you wrote the letter?

Clara. No, sir, I implore you.

Sir John. But it would be awkward for Georgy, if discovered.

Clara. It *never* shall be.

Sir John. Well, well, as you please. I know nothing could be so painful to a young lady of pride and delicacy.——James, if Mr. Serious, the clergyman, calls, say I'm gone to the great meeting at Exeter Hall: if Lord Spruce calls, say you believe I'm gone to the rehearsal of Cinderella. Oh! and if MacFinch should come—(MacFinch, who duns me three times a week)—say I've hurried off to Garraway's to bid for the great Bulstrode estate. Just put the Duke of Lofty's card carelessly on the hall table. And I say, James, I expect two gentlemen a little before dinner—Mr. Squab the Radical, and Mr. Qualm of the great Marylebone Conservative Association. Show Squab into the study, and be sure to give him the "Weekly True Sun."—Qualm into the back parlor, with the "Times" and the "Morning Post." One must have a little management in this world. All humbug!—all humbug, upon my soul!

[*Exit.*

Clara [*folding the letter*]. There—it is decided! A few days, and we are parted forever! —a few weeks, and another will bear his name—his wife! Oh, happy fate! She will have the right to say to him—though the whole world should hear her—"I am thine!" And I embitter their lot—I am the cloud upon their joyous sunshine! And yet, O Alfred! if she loves thee—if she knows thee—if she values thee—and, when thou wrong'st her, if she can forgive, as I do—I can bless her when far away, and join her name in my prayer for thee!

Eve. [*without*]. Miss Vesey just gone? Well, I will write a line.

SCENE III.

Evelyn *and* Clara.

Eve. [*aside*]. So—Clara! Do not let me disturb you, Miss Douglas.

Clara [*going*]. Nay, I have done.

Eve. I see that my presence is always odious to you, it is a reason why I come so seldom. But be cheered, madam: I am here but to fix the day of my marriage, and I shall then go into the country—till—till——In short, this is the last time my visit will banish you from the room I enter.

Clara [*aside*]. The last time!—and we shall then meet no more!—and to part thus for ever—in scorn—in anger—I cannot bear it! [*Approaching him.*] Alfred, my cousin, it is true, this may be the last time we shall meet—I have made my arrangements to quit England.

Eve. To quit England?

Clara. But before I go let me thank you for many a past kindness, which it is not for an orphan easily to forget.

Eve. [*mechanically*]. To quit England!

Clara. I have long wished it; but enough of me.——Evelyn, now that you are betrothed to another—now, without recurring to the past—now, without the fear of mutual error and mistake—something of our old friendship may at least return to us.——And if, too, I dared, I have that on my mind which only a friend—a sister—might presume to say to you.

Eve. [*moved*]. Miss Douglas—Clara—if there is ought that I could do—if, while hundreds —strangers—beggars tell me that I have the power, by opening or shutting this worthless hand, to bid sorrow rejoice, or poverty despair—if—if my life—my heart's blood—could render to *you* one such service as my gold can give to others—why, speak!—and the past you allude to —yes, even that bitter past—I will cancel and forget.

Clara [*holding out her hand*]. We are friends, then! you are again my cousin! my brother.

Eve. [*dropping her hand*]. Brother! Ah! say on!

Clara. I speak, then, as a sister—herself weak, inexperienced, ignorant, nothing—*might* speak to a brother, in whose career she felt the ambition of a man. Oh, Evelyn, when you inherited this vast wealth I pleased myself with imagining how you would wield the power delegated to your hands. I knew your benevolence—your intellect—your genius!—the ardent mind coached beneath the cold sarcasm of a long-baffled spirit! I saw before me the noble and bright career open to you at last—and I often thought that, in after-years, when far away —as I soon shall be—I should hear your name identified, not with what fortune can give the base, but with deeds and ends to which, for the *great*, fortune is but the instrument;—I often thought that I should say to my own heart—weeping proud and delicious tears—"And once this man loved me!"

Eve. No more, Clara!—oh, Heavens!—no more!

Clara. But *has* it been so?—have you been true to your own self?——Pomp—parade— luxuries—pleasures—follies!—all these might distinguish others—they do but belie the ambition and the soul of Alfred Evelyn!——Oh! pardon me—I am too bold—I pain—I offend you.——Ah, I should not have dared thus much had I not thought at times, that—that——

Eve. That these follies—these vanities—this dalliance with a loftier fate were your own work! You thought that, and you were right! Perhaps, indeed, after a youth steeped to the lips in the hyssop and gall of penury—perhaps I might have wished royally to know the full value of that dazzling and starry life which, from the last step in the ladder, I had seen indignantly and from afar. But a month—a week would have sufficed for that experience. Experience!—Oh, how soon we learn that hearts are as cold and souls as vile—no matter whether the sun shine on the noble in his palace, or the rain drench the rags of the beggar cowering at the porch. The extremes of life differ but in this:—Above, *Vice* smiles and revels—below, *Crime* frowns and starves. But you—did not you reject me because I was poor? Despise me if you please!—my revenge might be unworthy—I wished to show you the luxuries, the gaud, the splendor I thought you prized,—to surround with the attributes your sex seems most to value the station that, had you loved me, it would have been yours to command. But vain—vain alike my poverty and my wealth! You loved me not in either, and my fate is sealed.

Clara. A happy fate, Evelyn!—you love!

Eve. And at last I am beloved. [*After a pause, and turning to her abruptly.*] Do you doubt it?

Clara. No, I believe it firmly!—[*Aside.*] Were it possible for her not to love him?

Eve. Georgina, perhaps, is vain—and light—and——

Clara. No—think it not! Once removed from the worldly atmosphere of her father's counsels, and you will form and raise her to your own level. She is so young yet—she has beauty, cheerfulness, and temper;—the rest you will give, if you will but yet do justice to your own nature. And, now that there is nothing unkind between us—not even regret—and surely [*with a smile*] not revenge, my cousin, you will rise to your nobler self—and so, farewell!

Eve. No; stay, one moment;—you will feel interest in my fate! Have I been deceived? Oh, why—why did you spurn the heart whose offerings were lavished at your feet? Could you still—still——? Distraction—I know not what I say;—my honor pledged to another—my vows accepted and returned! Go, Clara, it is best so! Yet you will miss some one, perhaps, more than me—some one to whose follies you have been more indulgent—some one to whom you would permit a yet tenderer name than that of brother!

Clara [*aside*]. It will make him, perhaps, happier to think it! Think so, if you will!—but part friends.

Eve. Friends—and that is all! Look you, this is life! The eyes that charmed away every sorrow—the hand whose lightest touch thrilled to the very core—the presence that, like moonlight, shed its own hallowing beauty over the meanest things; a little while—a year—a month—a day, and we smile that we could dream so idly. All—all—the sweet enchantment, known but once, never to return again, vanished from the world! And the one who forgets the soonest—the one who robs your earth for ever of its summer—comes to you with a careless lip, and says—" Let us part friends!"——Go, Clara,—go—and be happy if you can!

Clara [*weeping*]. Cruel—cruel—to the last!——Heaven forgive you, Alfred! [*Exit.*

Eve. Soft! let me recall her words, her tones, her looks.—*Does she love me?* She defends her rival—she did not deny it when I charged her with attachment to another; and yet—and yet—there is a voice at my heart which tells me I have been the rash slave of a jealous anger.——But I have made my choice—I must abide the issue!

Enter GRAVES, *preceded by* Servant.

Ser. Lady Franklin is dressing, sir.

SCENE IV.

GRAVES *and* EVELYN.

Graves. Well, I'll wait. [*Exit* Servant.] She was worthy to have known the lost Maria! So considerate to ask me hither—not to console me, *that* is impossible—but to indulge the luxury of woe. It will be a mournful scene.——[*Seeing* EVELYN.]—Is that you, Evelyn?—I have just heard that the borough of Groginhole is vacant at last. Why not stand yourself?—with your property you might come in without even a personal canvass.

Eve. I, who despise these contests for the color of a straw—this everlasting litigation of Authority *versus* Man—I to be one of the wranglers?—never!

Graves. You are quite right and I beg your pardon.

Eve. [*aside*]. And yet Clara spoke of ambition. She would regret me if I could be distinguished.——[*Aloud.*] To be sure, after all, Graves, corrupt as mankind are, it is our duty to try at least to make them a little better. An Englishman owes something to his country.

Graves. He does, indeed! [*counting on his fingers.*] East winds, Fogs, Rheumatism, Pulmonary Complaints, and Taxas—[EVELYN *walks about in disorder*]. You seem agitated—a quarrel with your intended? Oh! when you've been married a month, you'll not know what to do with one!

Eve. You are a pleasant comforter.

Graves. Do you deserve a comforter? One morning you tell me you love Clara, or at least detest her, which is the same thing (poor Maria often said she detested *me*)—and that very afternoon you propose to Georgina!

Eve. Clara will easily console herself—thanks to Sir Frederick!

Graves. He is young!

Eve. Good looking!

Graves. A coxcomb!

Eve. And therefore irresistible!

Graves. Nevertheless, Clara has had the bad taste to refuse him. I have it from Lady Franklin, to whom he confided his despair in re-arranging his neck-cloth!

Eve. My dear friend—is it possible?

Graves. But what then? You *must* marry Georgina, who, to believe Lady Franklin, is sincerely attached to—your fortune. Go and hang yourself, Evelyn; you have been duped by them.

Eve. By them—bah! If deceived, I have been my own dupe. Is it not a strange thing that in matters of reason—of the arithmetic and logic of life—we are sensible, shrewd, prudent men; but touch our hearts—move our passions—take us for an instant from the hard safety of worldly calculation—and the philosopher is duller than the fool? *Duped*—if I thought it!—

Graves. To be sure!—you tried Clara in your *poverty;* it was a safe experiment to try Gorgina in your *wealth.*

Eve. Ha! that is true—very true. Go on.

Graves. You'll have an excellent father-in-law. Sir John positively weeps when he talks of your income!

Eve. Sir John, possibly—but Georgina?

Graves. Plays affection to you in the afternoon, after practising first with Frederick in the morning.

Eve. On your life, sir, be serious: what do you mean?

Graves. That in passing this way I see her very often walking in the square with Sir Frederick.

Eve. Ha! say you so?

Graves. What then? Man is born to be deceived. You look nervous—your hand trembles; that comes of gaming. They say at the clubs that you play deeply.

Eve. Ha! ha! Do they say that?—a few hundreds lost or won—a cheap opiate—anything that can lay the memory to sleep. The poor man drinks, and the rich man gambles—the same motive to both! But you are right—it is a base resource—I will play no more.

Graves. I am delighted to hear it, for your friend Captain Smooth has ruined half the young heirs in London. To play with him is to advertise yourself a bankrupt.—Even Sir John is alarmed. I met him just now in Pall Mall; he made me stop, and implored me to speak to you. By the by, I forgot—do you bank with Flash, Brisk, Credit, and Co.?

Eve. So, Sir John is alarmed?—[*Aside.*] Gulled by this cogging charlatan?—Ah! I may beat him yet at his own weapons!——Humph! Bank with Flash! Why do you ask me?

Graves. Because Sir John has just heard that they are in a very bad way, and begs you to withdraw anything you have in their hands.

Eve. I'll see to it. So Sir John is *alarmed* at my gambling?

Graves. Terribly! He even told me he should go himself to the club this evening, to watch you.

Eve. To watch me!—good—I will be there.

Graves. But you will promise not to play?

Eve. Yes—to play. I feel it is impossible to give it up!

Graves. No—no! 'Sdeath, man! be as wretched as you please; break your heart, that's nothing! but damme, take care of your pockets.

Eve. I will be there—I will play with Captain Smooth—I will lose as much as I please—thousands—millions—billions; and if he presume to spy on my losses, hang me if I don't lose

Sir John himself in the bargain! [*Going out and returning.*] I am so absent? What was the bank you mentioned? Flash, Brisk, and Credit? Bless me, how unlucky! and it's too late to draw out to-day. Tell Sir John I'm very much obliged to him, and he'll find me at the club any time before day-break, hard at work with my friend Smooth! [*Exit.*

Graves. He's certainly crazy! but I don't wonder at it! What the approach of the dog-days is to the canine species, the approach of the honeymoon is to the human race.

Enter Servant.

Ser. Lady Franklin's compliments—she will see you in the *boudoir*.

Graves. In the *boudoir!*—go, go—I'll come directly. [*Exit* Servant.

My heart beats—it must be for grief. Poor Maria! [*Searching his pockets for his handkerchief.*] Not a white one!—just my luck: I call on a lady to talk of the dear departed, and I've nothing about me but a cursed gaudy, flaunting, red, yellow, and blue abomination from India, which it's even indecent for a disconsolate widower to exhibit. Ah! Fortune never ceases to torment the susceptible. The *boudoir!*—ha! ha! the *boudoir!* [*Exit.*

SCENE V.

A Boudoir in the same house.

Lady Frank. I take so much compassion on this poor man, who is determined to make himself wretched, that I am equally determined to make him happy! Well, if my scheme does but succeed, he shall laugh, he shall sing, he shall——Mum!—here he comes!

Enter GRAVES.

Graves [*sighing*]. Ah, Lady Franklin!

Lady Frank. [*sighing*]. Ah, Mr. Graves! [*They seat themselves.*] Pray excuse me for having kept you so long. Is it not a charming day?

Graves. An east wind, ma'am! but nothing comes amiss to you!—'tis a happy disposition! Poor Maria! *she*, too, was naturally gay.

Lady Frank. Yes, she was gay. So much life, and a great deal of spirit.

Graves. Spirit? Yes!—nothing could master it. She *would* have her own way! Ah! there was nobody like her!

Lady Frank. And then, when her spirit was up, she looked so handsome! Her eyes grew so brilliant!

Graves. Did not they?—Ah! ah! ha! ha! ha! And do you remember her pretty trick of stamping her foot?—the tiniest little foot—I think I see her now. Ah! this conversation is very soothing!

Lady Frank. How well she acted in your private theatricals!

Graves. You remember her Mrs. Oakley, in "The Jealous Wife?" Ha! ha! how good it was!—ha! ha!

Lady Frank. Ha! ha! Yes, in the very first scene, when she came out with [*mimicking*] "Your unkindness and barbarity will be the death of me!"

Graves. No—no! that' not it! more energy. [*Mimicking.*] "Your unkindness and barbarity will be the DEATH of me." Ha! ha! I ought to know how she said it, for she used to practice it on me twice a day. Ah! poor dear lamb! [*Wipes his eyes.*]

Lady Frank. And then she sang so well! was such a composer! What was that little French air she was so fond of?

Graves. Ha! ha! sprightly? was it not? Let me see—let me see.

Lady Frank [*humming*]. Tum ti—ti tum—ti—ti-ti. No, that's not it.

Graves [*humming*]. Tum ti—ti—tum ti—ti—tum—tum—tum.
Both. Tum ti—ti—tum ti—ti—tum—tum—tum. Ha! ha!
Graves [*throwing himself back*]. Ah! what recollections it revives! It is too affecting.
Lady Frank. It *is* affecting; but we are all mortal. [*Sighs.*] And at your Christmas party at Cyprus Lodge, do you remember her dancing the Scotch reel with Captain Macnaughten?
Graves. Ha! ha! ha! To be sure—to be sure.
Lady Frank. Can you think of the step!—somehow thus, was it not? [*Dancing.*]
Graves. No—no—quite wrong!—just stand there. Now then [*humming the tune*].—La—la-la-la.—La la, etc. [*They dance.*
That's it—excellent—admirable!
Lady Frank. [*aside*]. Now 'tis coming.

Enter SIR JOHN, BLOUNT, GEORGINA,—*they stand amazed.*
[LADY FRANKLIN *continues to dance.*

Graves. Bewitching—irresistible! 'Tis Maria herself that I see before me! Thus—thus—let me clasp——Oh, the devil! Just like my luck!—[*Stopping opposite* SIR JOHN].
[LADY FRANKLIN *runs off.*

Sir John. Upon *my* word, Mr Graves!
Geor., Blount. Encore—encore! Bravo—bravo!
Graves. It's all a mistake! I—I—Sir John. Lady Franklin, you see—that is to say—I——Sainted Maria! you are spared, at least, this affliction!
Geor. Pray go on!
Blount. Don't let us interwupt you.
Graves. Interrupt me! I must say that this rudeness—this gross impropriety—to pry into the sorrows of a poor bereaved sufferer, seeking comfort from a sympathizing friend—But such is human nature!
Geor. But, Mr. Graves!—[*following him*].
Graves. Heartless!
Blount. My dear Mr. Graves!—[*following him*].
Graves. Frivolous!
Sir John. Stay and dine!—[*following him*].
Graves. Unfeeling!
Omnes. Ha!——ha!——ha!
Graves. Monsters! Good day to you.* [*Exit, followed by* SIR JOHN, *&c.*

SCENE VI.

*The interior of * * * *'s Club; night; lights, &c. Small sofa-tables, with books, papers, tea, coffee, &c. Several Members grouped by the fireplace; one Member with his legs over the back of his chair; another with his legs over his table; a third with his legs on the chimney-piece. To the left, and in front of the Stage, an old Member reading the newspaper, seated by a small round table; to the right a card-table, before which* CAPTAIN DUDLEY SMOOTH *is seated, and sipping lemonade; at the bottom of the Stage another card-table.*

GLOSSMORE *and* STOUT.

Gloss. You don't come often to the club, Stout?
Stout. No; time is money. An hour spent at a club is unproductive capital.

---

* For the original idea of this scene the author is indebted to a little *proverbe*, never, he believes, acted in public.

Old Mem. [*reading the newspaper*]. Waiter !—the snuff-box. [Waiter *brings it.*
Gloss. So, Evelyn has taken to play ? I see Deadly Smooth, " hushed in grim repose, awaits his evening prey." Deep work to-night, I suspect, for Smooth is drinking lemonade—keeps his head clear—monstrous clever dog !

Enter EVELYN; *salutes and shakes hands with different members in passing up the Stage.*

How d'ye do, Glossmore? How are you, Stout ? *you* don't play, I think ? Political economy never plays at cards, eh ?—never has time for anything more frivolous than Rents and Profits, Wages and Labor, High Prices, and Low—Corn-Laws, Poor-Laws, Tithes, Currency—Dot-and-go-one—Rates, Puzzles, Taxes, Riddles, and Botheration ! Smooth is the man. Aha, Smooth. Piquet, eh ? You owe me my revenge !

[*Members touch each other significantly;* STOUT *walks away with the snuff-box;* Old Member *looks at him savagely.*

Smooth. My dear Alfred, anything to oblige. [*They seat themselves.*
Old Mem. Waiter ! the snuff-box.

[Waiter *takes it from* STOUT, *and brings it back to* Old Member.

Enter BLOUNT.

Blount. So, so ! Evelyn at it again,—eh, Glossmore ?
Gloss. Yes, Smooth sticks to him like a leech. Clever fellow, that Smooth !
Blount. Will you make up a wubber ?
Gloss. Have you got two others ?
Blount. Yes; Flat and Green.
Gloss. Bad players.
Blount. I make it a wule to play with bad players; it is five per cent. in one's favor. I hate gambling. But a quiet wubber, if one is the best player out of four, can't do one any harm.
Gloss. Clever fellow, that Blount !

[BLOUNT *takes up the snuff-box and walks off with it;* Old Member *looks at him savagely.*
[BLOUNT, GLOSSMORE, FLAT, *and* GREEN *make up a table at the bottom of the Stage.*

Smooth. A thousand pardons, my dear Alfred,—ninety repique—ten cards !—game !
Eve. [*passing a note to him.*] Game ! Before we go on, one question. This is Thursday—how much do you calculate to win of me before Tuesday next ?
Smooth. Ce cher Alfred ! He is so droll !
Eve. [*writing in his pocket-book*]. Forty games a-night—four nights, minus Sunday—our usual stakes—that would be right, I think !
Smooth [*glancing over the account*]. Quite—if I win all—which is next to impossible.
Eve. It shall be possible to win twice as much, on one condition. Can you keep a secret ?
Smooth. My dear Alfred, I have kept myself ! I never inherited a farthing—I never spent less than £4,000 a-year—and I never told a soul how I managed it.
Eve. Hark ye, then—a word with you—[*they whisper*].
Old Mem. Waiter !—the snuff-box ! [Waiter *takes it from* BLOUNT, etc.

Enter SIR JOHN.

Eve. You understand ?
Smooth. Perfectly; anything to oblige.
Eve. [*cutting*]. It is for you to deal. [*They go on playing.*
Sir John [*groaning*]. There's my precious son-in-law, that is to be, spending *my* consequence, and making a fool of himself.

[*Takes up the snuff-box;* Old Member *looks at him savagely.*
Blount. I'm out. Flat, a poney on the odd twick. That's wight.—[*Coming up, counting his money.*] Well, Sir John, you don't play !

Sir John. Play? no! Confound him—lost again!

Eve. Hang the cards!—double the stakes!

Smooth. Just as you please—done!

Sir John. Done, indeed!

Old Mem. Waiter!—the snuff-box. [*Waiter takes it from* SIR JOHN.

Blount. I've won eight points and the bets—I never lose—I never play in the Deadly Smooth set! [*Takes up the snuff-box;* Old Member *as before.*

Sir John [*looking over* SMOOTH'S *hand, and fidgeting backwards and forwards*]. Lord, have mercy on us! Smooth has seven for his point! What's the stakes?

Eve. Don't disturb us—I only throw out four. Stakes, Sir John?—immense! Was ever such luck?—not a card for my point. Do stand back, Sir John—I'm getting irritable.

Old Mem. Waiter! the snuff-box. [*Waiter brings it back.*

Blount. One hundred pounds on the next game, Evelyn.

Sir John. Nonsense—nonsense—don't disturb him! All the fishes come to the bait! Sharks and minnows all nibbling away at my son-in-law!

Eve. One hundred pounds, Blount? Ah! the finest gentleman is never too fine a gentleman to pick up a guinea. Done! Treble the stakes, Smooth!

Sir John. I'm on the rack! [*seizing the snuff-box*]. Be cool, Evelyn! take care, my dear boy! Be cool—be cool.

Eve. What—what? You have four queens!—five to the king. Confound the cards! a fresh pack. [*Throws the cards behind him over* SIR JOHN.]

Old Mem. Waiter! the snuff-box. [*Different members gather round.*

First Mem. I never before saw Evelyn out of temper. He must be losing immensely!

Second Mem. Yes, this is interesting!

Sir John. Interesting! There's a wretch!

First Mem. Poor fellow! he'll be ruined in a month.

Sir John. I'm in a cold sweat.

Second Mem. Smooth is the very devil.

Sir John. The devil's a joke to him!

Gloss. [*slapping* SIR JOHN *on the back*]. A clever fellow that Smooth, Sir John, eh? [*Takes up the snuff-box.* Old Member *as before.*] £100 on this game, Evelyn?

Eve. [*half-turning round.*] You! well done the Constitution! yes, £100!

Old Mem. Waiter!—the snuff-box.

Stout. I *think* I'LL venture £200 on this game, Evelyn?

Eve. [*quite turning round*]. Ha! ha! ha!—Enlightenment and the Constitution on the same side of the question at last! Oh Stout, Stout! greatest happiness of the greatest number—greatest number, number one! Done, Stout!—£200! ha! ha! ha!—deal, Smooth. Well done, Political Economy—ha! ha! ha!

Sir John. Quite hysterical—drivelling! Ar'nt you ashamed of yourselves? His own cousins—all in a conspiracy—a perfect gang of them. [*Members indignant.*

Stout [*to Members*]. Hush! he's to marry Sir John's daughter.

First Mem. What, Stingy Jack's? oh!

Chorus of Mems. Oh! oh!

Old Mem. Waiter! the snuff-box.

Eve. [*rising in great agitation.*] No more, no more—I've done!—quite enough. Glossmore, Stout, Blount—I'll pay you to-morrow. I—I—Death!—this is ruinous! [*Seizes the snuff-box;* Old Member *as before.*

Sir John. Ruinous? I dare say it is. What has he lost? what *has* he lost, Smooth? Not much? eh? eh? [*Omnes gather round* SMOOTH.

Smooth. Oh, a trifle, dear John!—excuse me! we never tell our winnings—[*To* BLOUNT.] How d'ye do, Fred?—[*To* GLOSSMORE.] By the by, Charles, don't you want to sell your house in Grosvenor Square?—£12,000, eh?

Gloss. Yes, and the furniture at a valuation. About £3,000 more.

Smooth [*looking over his pocket-book*]. Um!—Well, we'll talk of it.

Sir John. 12 and 3—£15,000. What a cold-blooded rascal it is!—£15,000, Smooth?

Smooth. Oh, the house itself is a trifle; but the establishment—I'm considering whether I have enough to keep it up, my dear John.

Old Mem. Waiter, the snuff-box! [*Scraping it round, and with a wry face*]—And it's all gone!   [*Gives it to the* Waiter *to fill.*

Sir John. [*turning round*]. And it's all gone!

Eve. [*startiug up and laughing hysterically*]. Ha! ha! all gone? not a bit of it. Smooth, this club is so noisy. Sir John, you are always in the way. Come to my house! come! Champagne and a broiled bone. Nothing venture, nothing have! The luck must turn, and by Jupiter we'll make a night of it!

Sir John. A night of it!!! For Heaven's sake, Evelyn! EVELYN!!—think what you are about!—think of Georgina's feelings! think of your poor lost mother!—think of the babes unborn! think of——

Eve. I'll think of nothing! Zounds!—you don't know what I have lost, man; it's all your fault, distracting my attention. Pshaw—pshaw! Out of the way, do! Come, Smooth. Ha! ha! a night of it, my boy—a night of it!   [*Exeunt* SMOOTH *and* EVELYN.

Sir John [*following*]. You must not, you shall not! Evelyn, my dear Evelyn! he's drunk,—he's mad! Will no one send for the police?

Mems. Ha! ha! ha! Poor old stingy Jack!

Old Mem. [*rising for the first time, and in a great rage*]. Waiter!—the snuff-box!

ACT IV.—SCENE I.

The Ante-room in EVELYN'S *house, as in Scene I., Act II.*

TABOURET, MACFINCH, FRANTZ, *and other* Tradesmen.

Tabou. [*half whispers*]. So, I hear that Mr. Evelyn has turned gamester! There are strange reports about to-day—I don't know what to make of it! We must look sharp, Mr. Macfinch, we poor tradesmen, and make hay while the sun shines.

Macfinch. I wuish those geeming-houses were aw at the devil!—It's a cheam and a sin for gentlemen to gang and ruin themselves, when we honest tradesmen could do it for them with sae muckle advantage to the arts and coummerce o' the country! [*Omnes shake their heads approvingly.*]

Enter SMOOTH *from the inner room, with a pocket-book and pencil in his hand.*

Smooth [*looking round*]. Hum! ha! Fine pictures!—[*Feeling the curtains.*] The new-fashioned velvet, hum! good proportioned rooms! Yes, this house is better than Glossmore's! On, Mr. Tabouret, the upholsterer! you furnished these rooms? All of the best, eh?

Tabou. Oh, the VERY best. Mr. Evelyn is not a man to grudge expense, sir.

Smooth. He is not, indeed. You've been paid, I suppose, Tabouret?

Tabou. No, sir, no—I never send in my bills when a customer is rich. [*Aside*]. Bills are like trees, and grow by standing.

Smooth. Humph! Not PAID? humph!   [*Omnes gather round.*

Macfinch. I dinna like that hoomph, there's something vara suspeecious abun' it.

Tabou. [*to the tradesmen*]. It is the great card-player, Captain Smooth—finest player in Europe—cleaned out the Duke of Sillyvale. Uncommonly clever man!

Smooth [*pacing about the room*]. Thirty-six feet by twenty-eight—Um! I think a bow-window *there* would be an *improvement:* could it be done easily, Tabouret?

Macfinch. If Mr. Evelyn wants to pool about his house, there's no mon like my friend Mr. MacStucco.

Smooth. Evelyn! I was speaking of *myself*. Mr. MacStucco?—humph!

Tabou. Yourself? Have you bought the house, sir?

Smooth. Bought it?—hum!—ha!—it depends—So you've not been paid yet?—um! Nor you—nor you—nor you? Hum! ha!

Tabou. No, sir!—what *then?* No fear of Mr. EVELYN? Ha! ha!

Omnes [*anxiously*]. Ha! ha!—what then?

Macfinch. Ah, sir, what then? I'm a puir mon with a family: this way, Captain! You've a leetle account in the buiks; an' we'll e'en wipe it out altogether, gin you'll say what you mean by that Hoom ha!

Smooth. Macfinch, my dear fellow, don't oblige me to cane you; I would not have Mr. Evelyn distressed for the world. Poor fellow! he holds very bad cards. So you've not been paid yet? Don't send in your bills on any account—Mind! Yes; I don't dislike the house with some alteration. Good day to you—Hum! ha!

[*Exit, looking about him, examining the chairs, tables, etc.*

Tabou. Plain as a pike-staff! staked his very house on an odd trick!

SCENE II.

The foregoing.—Enter SHARP *from the inner room, agitated, and in a hurry.*

Sharp. O Lord! O Lord;—who'd have thought it? Cards are the devil's books! John!—Thomas!—Harris!—[*ringing the bell*].

Enter Two Servants.

Tom, take this letter to Sir John Vesey's. If not at home, find him—he will give you a cheque. Go to his banker's, and get it cashed *instantly*. Quick—quick! off with you!

Tabou. [*seizing* Servant]. What's the matter—what's the matter? How's Mr. Evelyn?

Ser. Bad—very bad! Sate up all night with Captain Smooth! [*Runs off.*

Sharp [*to the other* Servant]. Yes, Harris, your poor master! O dear! O dear! You will take this note to the Belgian minister, Portland-place. Passport for Ostend! Have the travelling carriage ready at a moment's notice!

Macfinch [*stopping* Servant]. Passport! Harkye, my mon; is he gaun to pit the saut seas between us and the siller?

Ser. Don't stop me—something wrong in the chest—change of air—late hours—and Captain Smooth! [*Exit.*

Sharp [*walking about*]. And if the bank should break!—if the bank *is* broke, and he can't draw out!—bound to Smooth!

Tabou. Bank!—what bank?

Sharp. Flash's bank! Flash, brother-in-law to Captain Smooth! What have *you* heard?—eh?—eh?

Tabou. That there's an awful run on it!

Sharp. I must be off. Go—go—you can't see Mr. Evelyn to-day!

Tabou. My account, sir!

Macfinch. I've a muckle bairns and a sma' bill!

Frantz. O sare, de great gentlemen always tink first of de tailor!

Sharp. Call again—call again at Christmas. The bank,—the cards,—the bank! O dear! O dear! [*Exit.*

Tabou. The bank!

Macfinch. The passport!

Frantz. And all dat vil be seen of de great Evelyn coat is de back of it. Donner und Hagel!—I vil arrest him—I vil put de salt on de tail of it!

Tabou. [*aside*]. I'll slip down to the city and see how the bank goes!

Macfinch [*aside*]. I'll e'en gang to my coosin the la'yer. Nothing but peetience for us, Mr. Tabouret.

Tabou. Ay, ay—stick by each other—share and share alike—that's my way, sir.

Omnes. Share and share alike. [*Exeunt.*

SCENE III.

Enter Servant, GLOSSMORE, *and* BLOUNT.

Ser. My master is not very well, my lord! but I'll let him know. [*Exit.*

Gloss. I am very curious to learn the result of his gambling tête-à-tête.

Blount. Oh, he's so howwidly wich, he can afford even a tête-à-tête with Deadly Smooth!

Gloss. Poor old Stingy Jack! why Georgina was *your* intended.

Blount. Yes; and I really liked the girl, though out of pique I pwoposed to her cousin. But what can a man do against money?

Enter EVELYN.

If we could start fair, you'd see whom Georgina would pwefer: but she's sacwificed by her father! She as much as told me so!

Eve. So, so, gentleman, we've a little account to settle—one hundred each.

Both. Don't talk of it.

Eve. [*putting up his pocket-book*]. Well, I'll not talk of it!—[*Taking* BLOUNT *aside.*] Ha! ha! you'd hardly believe it—but I'd rather not pay you just at present: my money is locked up, and I must wait, you know, for the Groginhole rents. So, instead, of owing you one hundred pounds, suppose I owe you *five?* You can give me a cheque on the other four. And, harkye! not a word to Glossmore.

Blount. Glossmore! the gweatest gossip in London! I shall be delighted!—[*Aside*]. It never does harm to lend to a rich man; one gets it back somehow. By the way, Evelyn, if you want my gway cab-horse, you may have him for to hundwed pounds, and that will make seven.

Eve. [*Aside*]. That's the fashionable usury: your friend does not take interest—he sells you a horse—[*Aloud*]. Blount, it's a bargain.

Blount [*writing the cheque, and musingly*]. No; I don't see what harm it can do me; that off-leg must end in a spavin.

Eve. [*to* GLOSSMORE]. That hundred pounds I owe you is rather inconvenient at present; I've a large sum to make up for the Groginhole property—perhaps you would lend me five or six hundred more—just to go on with?

Gloss. Certainly! Hopkins is dead: your interest for Cipher would——

Eve. Why, I can't promise *that* at this moment. But as a slight mark of friendship and gratitude, I shall be very much flattered if you'll accept a spendid gray cab-horse I bought to-day—cost two hundred pounds!

Gloss. Bought *to-day!*—then I'm safe. My dear fellow, you're always so princely!

Eve. Nonsense! just write the cheque; and, harkye, not a syllable to Blount!

Gloss. Blount! He's the town crier! [*Goes to write.*

Blount. [*giving* EVELYN *the cheque*]. Wansom's, Pall-mall East.

Eve. Thank you. So you *proposed* to Miss Douglas!

Blount. Hang it! yes; I could have sworn that she fancied me; her manner, for instance, that vewy day you pwoposed for Miss Vesey, otherwise Georgina——

Eve. Has only half what Miss Douglas has.

Blount. You forgot how much Stingy Jack must have saved! But I beg your pardon.

Eve. Never mind; but not a word to Sir John, or he'll fancy I'm ruined.

Gloss. [*giving the cheque.*] Ransom's, Pall-mall East. Tell me, did you win or lose last night?

Eve. Win! lose! oh! No more of that, if you love me. I must send off at once to the banker's [*looking at the two cheques*].

Gloss. [*aside*]. Why! he's borrowed from Blount, too!

Blount. [*aside*]. That's a cheque from Lord Glossmore!

Eve. Excuse me; I must dress; I have not a moment to lose. You remember you dine with me to-day—seven o'clock. You'll meet Smooth. [*With tears in his voice*]. It may be the last time I shall ever welcome you here! My——what am I saying?—Oh, merely a joke?—good bye—*good* bye. [*Shaking them heartily by the hand. Exit by the inner door.*

Blount. Glossmore!

Gloss. Blount!

Blount. I'm afraid all's not wight!

Gloss. I incline to your opinion!

Blount. But I've sold my gway cab-horse.

Gloss. Gray cab horse! you! What is he really worth now?

Blount. Since he is sold, I will tell you—Not a sixpence!

Gloss. Not a sixpence? he gave it to me!

[EVELYN *at the door giving directions to a* Servant *in dumb show.*

Blount. That was devilish unhandsome! Do you know, I feel nervous!

Gloss. Nervous! Let us run and stop payment of our checks.

[EVELYN *shuts the door, and* Servant *runs across the stage.*

Blount. Hollo, John! where so fast?

Ser. [*in great haste*]. Beg pardon, Sir Frederick, to Pall-mall East—Messrs. Ransom. [*Exit.*

Blount [*solemnly*]. Glossmore, we are fwoored?

Gloss. Sir, the whole town shall know of it. [*Exeunt.*

SCENE IV.

Enter TOKE *and other* Servants.

Toke. Come, come, stir yourselves! we've no time to lose. This room is to be got ready for the shawls. Mrs. Crump and the other ladies of the household are to wait here on the women before they go up to the drawing-room. Take away that desk: don't be lazy! and give me the newspaper. [TOKE *seats himself; the* Servants *bustle about.*

Strange reports about my patron! and the walley is gone for the passport!

Enter FRANTZ *with a bundle.*

Frantz. Mr. Toke, my goot Mr. Toke, I've brought you von leetel present.

Toke. John and Charles vanish! [*Exeunt* Servants.

I scorn to corrupt them 'ere working classes!

Frantz [*producing a pair of small-clothes which* TOKE *examines*]. Your master is von beggar! He vants to run avay; ve are all in de same vat-you-call-it—de same leetel nasty boat, Mr. Toke! Just let my friend Mr. Clutch up through the area. I vill put vat you call un execution on de gutes and de cattles dis very tay.

Toke. I accept the abridgements: but you've forgotten to line the pockets!

Frantz. Blesh my soul, so I have! [*giving a note*].

Toke. The area-gate shall be left undefended. Do it quietly, no *claw*, as the French say.

Frantz. Goot Mr. Toke—to morrow I vill line de oter pocket. [*Exit.*

Toke. My patron does not give me satisfaction!

Enter Footman.

Foot. What chandeliers are to be lighted, Mr. Toke?—it's getting late.

Toke. Don't disturb me—I'm rum-mynating! yes, yes, there's no doubt of it! Charles, the area-gate is open.

Foot. And all the plate in the pantry! I'll run and—

Toke. Not a step! leave it open.

Foot. But——

Toke [*with dignity*.] 'Tis for the sake of wentilation! [*Exeunt.*

SCENE V.

A splendid saloon in EVELYN'S *house.*

EVELYN *and* GRAVES.

Graves. You've withdrawn your money from Flash and Brisk?

Eve. No.

Graves. No!—then——

Enter SIR JOHN, LADY FRANKLIN, *and* GEORGINA.

Sir John. You got the cheque for £500 safely?—too happy to——

Eve. [*interrupting him*]. My best thanks!—my warmest gratitude! So kind in you! so seasonable!—that £500—you don't know the value of that £500. I shall never forget your nobleness of conduct.

Sir John. Gratitude!—Nobleness!—[*Aside.*] I can't have been taken in?

Eve. And in a moment of such distress!

Sir John [*aside*]. Such distress! He picks out the ugliest words in the whole dictionary!

Eve. I've done with Smooth. But I'm still a little crippled, and you must do me *another* favor. I've only as yet paid the deposit of ten per cent for the great Groginhole property. I am to pay the rest this week—nay, I fear to-morrow. I've already sold out the Funds! the money lies at the banker's, and of course I can't touch it; for if I don't pay by a certain day, I forfeit the estate and the deposit.

Sir John. What's coming now, I wonder?

Eve. Georgina's fortune is £10,000. I always meant, my dear Sir John, to present you with that little sum.

Sir John. Oh, Evelyn! your generosity is positively touching [*wipes his eyes*].

Eve. But the news of my losses has frightened my tradesmen! I have so many heavy debts at this moment that—that—that——. But I see Georgina is listening, and I'll say what I have to say to her.

Sir John. No, no—no, no. Girls don't understand business!

Eve. The very-reason I speak to her. This is an affair not of business, but of *feeling*. Stout, show Sir John my Correggio.

Sir John [*aside*]. Devil take his Correggio! The man is born to torment me!

Eve. My dear Georgina, whatever you may hear said of me, I flatter myself that you feel confidence in my honor.

Geor. Can you doubt it.

Eve. I confess that I am embarrassed at this moment: I have been weak enough to lose money at play; and there are other demands on me. I promise you never to gamble again as long as I live. My affairs can be retrieved; but for the first few years of our marriage it may be necessary to retrench.

Geor. Retrench !

Eve. To live, perhaps, altogether in the country.

Geor. Altogether in the country !

Eve. To confine ourselves to a modest competence.

Geor. Modest competence ! I knew something horrid was coming !

Eve. And now, Georgina, you may have it in your power at this moment to save me from much anxiety and humiliation. My money is locked up—my debts of honor must be settled —you are of age—your £10,000 in your own hands——

Sir John [STOUT *listening as well as* SIR JOHN]. I'm standing on hot iron !

Eve. If you could lend it to me for a few weeks——You hesitate ! oh ! believe the honor of the man you will call your husband before all the calumnies of the fools whom we call the world ! Can you give me this proof of your confidence ? Remember, without confidence what is wedlock ?

Sir John [*aside to her*]. No ! [*Aloud, pointing his glass at the Correggio.*] Yes, the painting may be fine.

Stout. But you don't like the subject ?

Geor. [*aside*]. He may be only trying me ! Best leave it to papa.

Eve. Well——

Geor. You—you shall hear from me to-morrow.—[*Aside.*] Ah, there's that dear Sir Frederick ! [*Goes to* BLOUNT.

Enter GLOSSMORE *and* SMOOTH; EVELYN *salutes them, paying* SMOOTH *servile respect.*

Lady Frank. [*to* GRAVES]. Ha ! ha ! To be so disturbed yesterday,—was it not droll ?

Graves. Never recur to that humiliating topic.

Gloss. [*to* STOUT]. See how Evelyn fawns upon Smooth !

Stout. How mean in him !—*Smooth*—a professional gambler—a fellow who lives by his wits ! I would not know such a man on any account !

Smooth [*to* GLOSSMORE]. So Hopkins is dead—you want Cipher to come in for Groginhole, eh ?

Gloss. What !—could *you* manage it ?

Smooth. Ce cher Charles !—anything to oblige !

Stout. Groginhole ! What can he have to do with Groginhole ?—Glossmore, present me to Smooth.

Gloss. What ! the gambler—the fellow who lives by his wits ?

Stout. Why, his wits seem to be an uncommonly productive capital ? I'll introduce myself. How d'ye do, Captain Smooth ? We have met at the club, I think—I am charmed to make your acquaintance in private. I say, sir, what do you think of the affairs of the nation ? Bad ! very bad !—no enlightenment !—great fall off in the revenue !—no knowledge of finance ! There's only one man who can save the country——and that's POPKINS !

Smooth. Is he in Parliament, Mr. Stout ? What's your Christian name, by-the-bye ?

Stout. Benjamin.—No; constituencies are so ignorant, they don't understand his value. He's no orator; in fact, he stammers so much—but devilish profound. Could not we ensure him for Groginhole ?

Smooth. My dear Benjamin, it is a thing to be thought on.

Eve. [*advancing*]. My friends, pray be seated;—I wish to consult you. This day twelve months I succeeded to an immense income, and as, by a happy coincidence, on the same day

I secured your esteem, so now I wish to ask you if you think I could have spent that income in a way more worthy your good opinion.

Gloss. Impossible! excellent taste—beautiful house!

Blount. Vewy good horses—[*Aside to* GLOSSMORE] especially the gwey cob!

Lady Frank. Splendid pictures!

Graves. And a magnificent cook, ma'am!

Smooth. [*thrusting his hands into his pockets*]. It is my opinion, Alfred—and I'm a judge—that you could not have spent your money better!

Omnes. [*except* SIR JOHN]. Very true!

Eve. What say *you*, Sir John? You may think me a little extravagant; but you know that in this world the only way to show one's self thorougly respectable is to make a thoroughly repectable show.

Sir John. Certainly—certainly! No, you could not have done better. [*Aside.*] I don't know what to make of it.

Geor. Certainly.—[*Coaxingly.*] Don't retrench, my dear Alfred!

Gloss. Retrench! nothing so plebeian!

Stout. Plebeian, sir!—worse than plebeian!—it is against all the rules of public morality. Every one knows, now-a-days, that extravagance is a benefit to the population—encourages art—employs labor—and multiplies spinning-jennies.

Eve. You reassure me! I own I did think that a man worthy of friends so sincere might have done something better than feast—dress—drink—play——

Gloss. Nonsense!—we like you the better for it. [*Aside.*] I wish I had my £600 back, though.

Eve. And you are as much my friends now as when you offered me £10 for my old nurse?

Sir John. A thousand times more so, my dear boy! [*Omnes approve.*

Enter SHARP.

Smooth. But who's our new friend?

Eve. Who! the very man who first announced to me the wealth which you allow I have spent so well. But what's the matter, Sharp?

SHARP [*whispering* EVELYN].

Eve. [*aloud*]. The bank's *broke!*

Sir John. Broke!—what bank?

Eve. Flash, Brisk, and Co.

Gloss. [*to* SMOOTH]. And Flash was your brother-in-law. I'm very sorry.

Smooth [*taking snuff*]. Not at all, Charles,—I did not bank there.

Sir John. But I warned you—you withdrew?

Eve. Alas! no!

Sir John. Oh! Not much in their hands?

Eve. Why, I told you the purchase-money for Groginhole was at my bankers'——but no, no: don't look so frightened! It was not placed with Flash—it is at Hoare's—it is, indeed. Nay, I assure you it is. A mere trifle at Flash's, upon my word, now! To-morrow, Sharp, we'll talk of this! One day more—one day, at least, for enjoyment.

Sir John. Oh! a pretty enjoyment!

Blount. And he borrowed £700 of me!

Gloss. And £600 of me!

Sir John. And £500 of me!

Stout. Oh! a regular Jeremy Diddler!

Smooth [*to* SIR JOHN]. John, do you know, I think I would take a handsome offer for this house just as it stands—furniture, plate, pictures, books, bronzes, and statues!

Sir John. Powers above!

Stout [*to* SIR JOHN]. I say, you have placed your daughter in a very unsafe investment.

What then?—a daughter's like any other capital—transfer the stock in hand to t'other speculation.

Sir John [going to GEORGINA]. Ha! I'm afraid we've been very rude to Sir Frederick. A monstrous fine young man!

Enter TOKE.

Toke [to EVELYN]. Sir, I beg your pardon, but Mr. Macfinch insists on my giving you this letter instantly.

Eve. [*reading*]. How! Sir John, this fellow, Macfinch, has heard of my misfortunes and insists on being paid;—a lawyer's letter—quite insolent!

Toke. And, sir, Mr. Tabouret is below, and declares he will not stir till he's paid.

Eve. Not stir till he's paid! What's to be done, Sir John?—Smooth, what *is* to be done?

Smooth. If he'll not stir till he's paid, make him up a bed, and I'll take him in the inventory, as one of the fixtures, Alfred!

Eve. It is very well for you to joke, Mr. Smooth. But——

Enter Sheriff's Officer, *giving a paper to* EVELYN, *and whispering.*

Eve. What's this? Frantz, the tailor. Why, the impudent scoundrel! Faith, this is more than I bargained for—Sir John, the bailiffs are in the house!

Stout [*slapping* SIR JOHN *on the back with glee*]. The bailiffs are in the house, old gentleman! But I did'nt lend him a farthing.

Eve. And for a mere song—£150! Sir John, pay this fellow, will you? or see that my people kick out the bailiffs, or do it yourself, or something,—while we go to dinner!

Sir John. Pay—kick—I'll be d——d if I do!—Oh, my £500! my £500! Mr. Alfred Evelyn, I want my £500!

Graves. I'm going to do a very silly thing—I shall lose both my friend and my money;—just like my luck!—Evelyn, go to dinner—I'll settle this for you.

Lady Frank. I love you for that!

Graves. Do you? then I am the happiest—Ah! ma'am, I don't know what I am saying!

[*Exeunt* GRAVES *and* Officer.

Eve [*to* GEORGINA]. Don't go by these appearances! I repeat £10,000 will more than cover all my embarrassments. I shall hear from you to-morrow?

Geor. Yes—yes!

Eve. But you're not going?—You, too, Glossmore?—you, Blount?—you, Stout—you, Smooth?

Smooth. No; I'll stick by you as long as you've a guinea to stake!

Gloss. Oh, this might have been expected from a man of such ambiguous political opinions!

Stout. Don't stop me, sir. No man of common enlightenment would have squandered his substance in this way. Pictures and statues?—baugh!

Eve. Why, you all said I could not spend my money better! Ha! ha! ha!—the absurdest mistake!—you don't fancy I'm going to prison?—Ha! ha!—Why don't you laugh, Sir John?—Ha! ha! ha!

Sir John. Sir, this horrible levity!—Take Sir Frederick's arm, my poor, injured, innocent child!—Mr Evelyn, after this extraordinary scene, you can't be surprised that I—I—Zounds! I'm suffocating!

Smooth. But, my dear John, it is for us at least to put an execution on the dinner.

Stout [*aside*]. The election at Groginhole is to-morrow. This news may not arrive before the poll closes—[*Rushing to* EVELYN.] Sir Popkins never bribes: but Popkins will bet you £1,000 that he don't come in for Groginhole.

Gloss. This is infamous, Mr. Stout! Cipher is a man who scorns every subterfuge!—[*Aside to* EVELYN]. But, for the sake of the Constitution, name your price.

Eve. I know the services of Cipher—I know the profundity of Popkins: but it is too late—the borough's engaged!

Toke. Dinner is served.

Gloss. [*pausing*]. Dinner!

Stout. Dinner! a very good smell!

Eve. [*to* SIR JOHN]. Turtle and venison too. [*They stop irresolute.*]

Eve. That's right—come along. But, I say, Blount—Stout—Glossmore—Sir John—one word first; will you lend me £10 for my old nurse? [*They all fall back.*

Ah! you fall back.—Behold a lesson for all who build friendship upon their fortune, and not their virtues!—You lent me hundreds this morning to squander upon pleasure—you would refuse me £10 now to bestow upon benevolence. Go—we have done with each other—go!

[*Exeunt, indignantly, all but* EVELYN *and* SMOOTH.

Re-enter GRAVES.

Graves. Heyday!—what's all this?

Eve. Ha! ha!—the scheme prospers—the duper *is* duped! Come, my friends—come: when the standard of money goes down, in the great battle between man and fate—why, a bumper to the brave hearts that refuse to desert us. [*Exeunt.*

ACT V.—SCENE I.

* * * * *'s Club;* SMOOTH, GLOSSMORE—*other Members.*

Gloss. Will his horses be sold, think you?

Smooth. Very possibly, Charles!—a fine stud—hum!—ha! Waiter, a glass of sherry!

Gloss. They say he must go abroad!

Smooth. Well; 'tis the best time of year for travelling, Charles!

Gloss. We are all to be paid to-day; and that looks suspicious!

Smooth. Very suspicious, Charles! Hum!—ah!

Gloss. My dear fellow, you must know the rights of the matter: I wish you'd speak out. What have you really won? Is the house itself gone?

Smooth. The house itself is certainly not gone, Charles, for I saw it exactly in the same place this morning at half-past ten—it has not moved an inch.

[Waiter *gives a letter to* GLOSSMORE.

Gloss. [*reading*]. From Groginhole—an express! What's this? I'm amazed!!! [*Reading.*] "They've actually, at the eleventh hour, started Mr. Evelyn; and nobody knows what his politics are! We shall be *beat!*—the Constitution is gone!—CIPHER!" Oh! this is infamous in Evelyn! Gets into Parliament just to keep himself out of the Bench.

Smooth. He's capable of it.

Gloss. Not a doubt of it, sir!—Not a doubt of it!

Enter SIR JOHN *and* BLOUNT, *talking.*

Sir John. My dear boy, I'm not flint! I am but a man! If Georgina really loves you—and I am sure that she *does*—I will never think of sacrificing her happiness to ambition—she is yours: I told her so this very morning.

Blount [*aside*]. The old humbug!

Sir John. She's the best of daughters!—the most obedient, artless creature! Oh! she's been properly brought up! a good daughter makes a good wife. Dine with me at seven, and we'll talk of the settlements.

Blount. Yes; I don't care for fortune;—but——

Sir John. Her £10,000 will be settled on herself—that of course.

Blount. All of it, sir? Weally, I——

Sir John. What *then*, my dear boy? I shall leave you both all I've laid by. Ah! you know I'm a close fellow! "Stingy Jack," eh? After all, worth makes the man!

Smooth. And the more a man's worth, John, the worthier man he must be. [*Exit.*

Blount. [*aside*]. Yes, he has no other child! she *must* have all his savings; I don't see what harm it could do me. Still that £10,000,—I want that £10,000: if she would but wun off now, one could get wid of the settlements.

Enter STOUT [*wiping his forehead*], *and takes* SIR JOHN *aside.*

Stout. Sir John, we've been played upon! My secretary is brother to Flash's head clerk; Evelyn had not £300 in the bank!!

Sir John. Bless us and save us! you take away my breath! But then—Deadly Smooth—the execution—the——oh, he must be done up!

Stout. As to Smooth, he'd "do anything to oblige." All a trick, depend upon it! Smooth has already deceived me, for before the day's over, Evelyn will be member for Groginhole. I've had an express from Popkins; he's in despair! not for *himself*—but for the *country*, Sir John—what's to become of the country?

Sir John. But what could be Evelyn's *object*?

Stout. Object? Do you look for an object in a whimsical creature like that?—a man who has not even any political opinions! Object! Perhaps to break off his match with your daughter! Take care, Sir John, or the borough will be lost to your family!

Sir John. Aha! I begin to smell a rat! But it is not too late yet.

Stout. My interest in Popkins made me run to Lord Spendquick, the late proprietor of Groginhole. I told him that Evelyn could not pay the rest of the money! and *he* told me that——

Sir John. What?

Stout. Mr. Sharp had just paid it him; there's no hope for Popkins! England will rue this day!

Sir John. Georgina shall lend him the money! *I'll* lend him—every man in my house shall lend him—I feel again what it is to be a father-in-law!—[*Aside.*] But stop; I'll be cautious. Stout may be on his side—a trap—not likely; but I'll go first to Spendquick myself. Sir Frederick, excuse me—you can't dine with me to-day. And, on second thoughts, I see that it would be very unhandsome to desert poor Evelyn, now he's down in the world. Can't think of it, my dear boy—can't think of it! Very much honored, and happy to see you as a friend. Waiter, my carriage! Um! What, humbug *Stingy Jack*, will they? Ah! a good joke, indeed!

Blount. Mr. Stout, what have you been saying to Sir John? Something against my chawacter; I know you have; don't deny it. Sir, I shall expect satisfaction.

Stout. Satisfaction, Sir Frederick,? as if a man of enlightenment had any satisfaction in fighting! Did not mention your name; we were talking of Evelyn. Only think?—he's no more ruined than you are.

Blount. Not wuined! Aha, now I understand! So, so! Stay, let me see—she's to meet me in the square! [*pulls out his watch; a very small one.*

Stout [*pulling out his own; a very large one*]. I must be off to the vestry.

Blount Just in time!—ten thousand pounds! 'Gad, my blood's up, and I won't be tweated in *this* way, if he were fifty times Stingy Jack! [*Exit.*

SCENE II.

The drawing-rooms in SIR JOHN VESEY'S *house.*

LADY FRANKLIN, GRAVES.

Graves. Well, well, I am certain that poor Evelyn loves Clara still, but you can't persuade me that she cares for him.

Lady Frank. She been breaking her heart ever since she heard of his distress. Nay, I am sure she would give all she has, could it save him from the consequences of his own folly.

Graves [*half aside*]. She would only give him his own money, if she did. I should just like to sound her.

Lady Frank. [*ringing the bell*]. And you shall. I take so much interest in her, that I forgive your friend everything but his offer to Georgina.

Enter Servant.

Where are the young ladies?

Ser. Miss Vesey is, I believe, still in the square: Miss Douglas is just come in, my lady.

Lady Frank. What! did she go out with Miss Vesey?

Ser. No, my lady; I attended her to Drummond's the banker. [*Exit*

Lady Frank. Drummond's!

Enter CLARA.

Why, child, what on earth could take you to Drummond's at this hour of the day?

Clara [*confused*]. Oh, I——that is—I—Ah, Mr. Graves! How is Mr. Evelyn? How does he bear up against so sudden a reverse?

Graves. With an awful calm. I fear all is not right here. [*Touching his head.*]—The report in the town is, that he must go abroad instantly—perhaps to-day.

Clara. Abroad!—to-day!

Graves. But all his creditors will be paid; and he only seems anxious to know if Miss Vesey remains true in his misfortunes.

Clara. Ah? he loves her so *much*, then!

Graves. Um!—That's more than I can say.

Clara. She told me last night, that he said to the last that £10,000 would free him from all his liabilities—that was the sum, was it not?

Graves. Yes; he persists in the same assertion. Will Miss Vesey lend it?

Lady Frank. [*aside.*] If she does, I shall not think so well of her poor dear mother; for I am sure she'd be no child of Sir John's!

Graves. I should like to convince myself that my poor friend has nothing to hope from a woman's generosity.

Lady Frank. Civil! And are men, then, less covetous?

Graves. I know one man, at least, who, rejected in his poverty by one as poor as himself, no sooner came into a sudden fortune than he made his lawyer invent a codicil which the testator never dreamt of, bequeathing independence to the woman who had scorned him.

Lady Frank. And never told her?

Graves. Never! There's no such document at Doctor's Commons, depend on it! You seem incredulous, Miss Clara! Good day!

Clara [*following him*]. One word, for mercy's sake! Do I understand you right? Ah, how could I be so blind! Generous Evelyn!

Graves. *You* appreciate, and *Georgina* will desert him. Miss Douglas, he loves you still.—if that's not just like me! Meddling with other people's affairs, as if they were worth it—hang them! [*Exit.*

Clara. Georgina will desert him. Do you think so? [*Aside.*] Ah, he will soon discover that she never wrote that letter!

Lady Frank. She told me last night that she would never see him again. To do her justice, she's less interested than her father,—and as much attached as she can be to another. Even while engaged to Evelyn, she has met Sir Frederick every day in the square.

Clara. And he is alone—sad—forsaken—ruined. And I, whom he enriched—I the creature of his bounty—I, once the woman of his love—I stand idly here to content myself with tears and prayers! Oh, Lady Franklin, have pity on me—on him! We are both of kin to him—as relations, we have both a right to comfort! Let us go to him—come!

Lady Frank. No! it would scarcely be right—remember the world—I cannot!

Clara. All abandon him—then I will go alone!

Lady Frank. You!—so proud—so sensitive!

Clara. Pride—when he wants a friend?

Lady Frank. His misfortunes are his own fault—a gambler!

Clara. Can you think of his faults now? *I* have no right to do so. All I have—all—his gift!—and I never to have dreamed it!

Lady Frank. But if Georgina do indeed release him—if she have already done so—what will he think? What but——

Clara. What but—that, if he love me still, I may have enough for both, and I am by his side! But that is too bright a dream. He told me I might call him brother! Where now, should a sister be? But—but—I—I—I—tremble! If, after all—if—if——In one word, am I too bold? The world—my conscience can answer *that*—but do you think that HE could despise me?

Lady Frank. No, Clara, no! Your fair soul is too transparent for even libertines to misconstrue. Something tells me that this meeting may make the happiness of both! You cannot go alone. My presence justifies all. Give me your hand—we will go together!

[*Exeunt.*

SCENE III.

A room in EVELYN's *house.*

Eve. Yes; as yet, all surpasses my expectations. I am sure of Smooth—I have managed even Sharp; my election will seem but an escape from a prison. Ha! ha! True, it cannot last long; but a few hours more are all I require, and for that time at least I shall hope to be thoroughly ruined.

Enter GRAVES.

Well, Graves, and what do people say of me?

Graves. Everything that's bad!

Eve. Three days ago I was universally respected. I awake this morning to find myself singularly infamous. Yet I'm the same man.

Graves. Umph!—why, gambling——

Eve. Cant! it was not criminal to gamble—it was criminal to lose. Tut!—Will you deny that if I had ruined Smooth instead of myself, every hand would have grasped mine yet more cordially, and every lip would have smiled congratulation on my success? Man—Man! I've not been rich and poor for nothing! The Vices and the Virtues are written in a language the world cannot construe; it reads them in a vile translation, and the translators are—FAILURE and SUCCESS! You alone are unchanged.

Graves. There's no merit in that. I am always ready to mingle my tears with any man. —[*Aside.*] I know I'm a fool, but I can't help it. Hark ye, Evelyn! I like you—I'm rich; and anything I can do to get you out of your hobble will give me an excuse to grumble for the rest of my life. There, now 'tis out.

Eve. [*touched*]. There's something good in human nature, after all! My dear friend, I will now confide in you: I am not the spendthrift you think me—my losses have been trifling —not a month's income of my fortune. [GRAVES *shakes him heartily by the hand.*] No!—it has been but a stratagem to prove if the love, on which was to rest the happiness of a whole life, were given to the Money or the Man. Now you guess why I have asked from Georgina this one proof of confidence and affection.—Think you she will give it?

Graves. Would you break your heart if she did not?

Eve. It is in vain to deny that I still love Clara; our last conversation renewed feelings which would task all the energies of my soul to conquer. What then? I am not one of those, the Sybarites of sentiment, who deem it impossible for humanity to conquer love—who call their own weakness the voice of a resistless destiny. Such is the poor excuse of every woman who yields her honor—of every adulterer who betrays his friend. No! the heart was given to the soul as its ally, not as its traitor.

Graves. What do you tend to?

Eve. This:—If Georgina still adhere to my fortunes (and I will not put her to too harsh a trial); if she can face the prospect, not of ruin and poverty, but of a moderate independence; if, in one word, she love me for myself, I will shut Clara for ever from my thoughts. I am pledged to Georgina, and I will carry to the altar a soul resolute to deserve her affection and fulfil its vows.

Graves. And if she reject you?

Eve. [*joyfully*]. If she do, I am free once more! And then—then I will dare to ask, for I can ask without dishonor, if Clara can explain the past and bless the future!

Enter Servant *with a letter.*

Eve. [*after reading it*]. The die is cast—the dream is over! Generous girl! Oh, Georgina! I will deserve you yet.

Graves. Georgina! is it possible?

Eve. And the delicacy, the womanhood, the exquisite grace of this! How we misjudge the depth of the human heart! How, seeing the straws on the surface, we forget that the pearls may lie hid below!* I imagined her incapable of this devotion.

Graves. And *I* too.

Eve. It were base in me to continue this trial a moment longer. I will write at once to undeceive that generous heart [*writing*].

Graves. I would have given £1,000 if that little jade Clara had been beforehand. But just like may luck: if I want a man to marry one woman, he's sure to marry another on purpose to vex me. [EVELYN *rings the bell.*

Enter Servant.

Eve. Take this instantly to Miss Vesey; say I will call in an hour. [*Exit* Servant.] And now Clara is resigned for ever! Why does my heart sink within me? Why, why, looking to the fate to come, do I see only the memory of what has been?

Graves. You are re-engaged then to Georgina?

Eve. Irrevocably.

* "Errors like straws," &c.

SCENE IV.

Enter Servant, *announcing* Lady Franklin *and* Miss Douglas.

Evelyn *and* Graves.

Lady Frank. My dear Evelyn, you may think it strange to receive such visitors at this moment; but, indeed, it is no time for ceremony. We are your relations—it is reported you are about to leave the country—we come to ask frankly what we can do to serve you?

Eve. Madam—I——

Lady Frank. Come, come—do not hesitate to confide in us; Clara is less a stranger to you than I am: your friend here will perhaps let me consult with him.—[*Aside to* Graves.] Let us leave them to themselves.

Graves. You're an angel of a widow; but you come too late, as whatever is good for anything generally does. [*They retire into the inner room, which should be partially open.*

Eve. Miss Douglas, I may well want words to thank you, this goodness—this sympathy——

Clara [*abandoning herself to her emotion*]. Evelyn! Evelyn! Do not talk thus!—Goodness!—sympathy!—I have learned *all—all!* It is for ME to speak of *gratitude!* What! even when I had so wounded you—when you believed me mercenary and cold—when you thought that I was blind and base enough not to know you for what you are; even *at that time* you thought but of my happiness—my fortunes—my fate!—And to you—you—I owe all that has raised the poor orphan from servitude and dependence! While your words were so bitter, your deeds so gentle! Oh, noble Evelyn, this then was your revenge!

Eve. You owe me no thanks—that revenge was sweet! Think you it was nothing to feel that my presence haunted you, though you knew it not?—that in things the pettiest as the greatest, which that gold could buy—the very jewels you wore—the very robe in which, to other eyes, you might seem more fair—in all in which you took the woman's young and innocent delight—*I* had a part—a share? that, even if separated for ever—even if another's—even in distant years—perhaps in a happy home, listening to sweet voices that might call you "mother!"—even then should the uses of that dross bring to your lips one smile—that smile was mine—due to me—due, as a sacred debt, to the hand that you rejected—to the love that you despised!

Clara. Despised! See the proof that I despise you!—see: in this hour, when they say you are again as poor as before, I forget the world—my pride—perhaps too much my sex: I remember but your sorrows—I am here!

Eve. [*aside*]. Oh, Heaven! give me strength to bear it!—[*Aloud.*] And is this the same voice that, when I knelt at your feet—when I asked but *one day* the hope to call you mine—spoke only of poverty, and answered, "*Never*"?

Clara. Because I had been unworthy of your love if I had insured your misery. Evelyn, hear me! My father, like you, was poor—generous; gifted, like you, with genius—ambition: sensitive, like you, to the least breath of insult. He married, as you would have done—married one whose only dower was penury and care! Alfred, I saw that genius the curse to itself!—I saw that ambition wither to despair!—I saw the struggle—the humiliation—the proud man's agony—the bitter life—the early death!—and heard over his breathless clay my mother's groan of self-reproach! Alfred Evelyn, now speak! Was the woman you loved so nobly to repay you with such a doom?

Eve. Clara, we should have shared it!

Clara. Shared? Never let the woman who really loves, comfort her selfishness with such delusion! In marriages like this, the wife cannot share the burden; it is he—the husband—to provide, to scheme, to work, to endure—to grind out his strong heart at the miserable wheel! The wife, alas! cannot share the struggle—she can but witness the despair! And therefore, Alfred, I rejected you.

Eve. Yet you believe me as poor now as I was then.

Clara. But *I* am not poor: *we* are not so poor. Of this fortune, which is all your own—if, as I hear, one half would free you from your debts, why, we have the other half still left. Evelyn! it is humble—but it is not penury.

Eve. Cease, cease—you know not how you torture me. Oh, that when hope was possible;—oh, that you had bid me take it to my breast and wait for a brighter day!

Clara. And so have consumed your life of life upon a hope perhaps delayed till age—shut you from a happier choice, from fairer fortunes—shackled you with vows that, as my youth and its poor attributes decayed, would only have irritated and galled—made your whole existence one long suspense! No, Alfred, even *yet* you do not know me.

Eve. Know you! Fair angel, too excellent for man's harder nature to understand!—at least it is permitted me to revere. Why were such blessed words not vouchsafed to me before?—why, why come they now?—too late! Oh, Heaven—too late!

Clara. Too late! What, then, have I said?

Eve. Wealth! what is it without you? *With* you, I recognize its power; to forestall your every wish—to smooth your every path—to make all that life borrows from Grace and Beauty your ministrant and handmaid; and then, looking to those eyes, to read there the treasures of a heart that excelled all that kings could lavish;—why *that* were to make gold indeed a god! But vain—vain—vain! Bound by every tie of faith, gratitude, loyalty, and honor, to another!

Clara. Another? Is she, then, true to your reverses? I did not know this—indeed I did not! And I have thus betrayed myself? O, shame! he must despise me now!

SCENE V.

The foregoing.—Enter Sir John; *at the same time* Graves *and* Lady Franklin *advance from the inner room.*

Sir John [*with dignity and frankness*]. Evelyn, I was hasty yesterday. You must own it natural that I should be so. But Georgina has been so urgent in your defence, that——[*as* Lady Franklin *comes up to listen*] Sister, just shut the door, will you ——that I cannot resist her. What's money without happiness? So give me your security; for she insists on lending you the £10,000.

Eve. I know, and have already received it.

Sir John. Already received it! Is he joking? Faith, for the last two days I believe I have been living amongst the Mysteries of Udolpho! Sister, have you seen Georgina?

Lady Frank. Not since she went out to walk in the square.

Sir John [*aside*]. She's not in the square nor the house—where the deuce can the girl be?

Eve. I have written to Miss Vesey—I have asked her to fix the day for our wedding.

Sir John [*joyfully*]. Have you? Go, Lady Franklin, find her instantly—she must be back by this time: take my carriage, it is but a step—you will not be two minutes gone.—[*Aside.*] I'd go myself, but I'm afraid of leaving him a moment while he's in such excellent dispositions.

Lady Frank. [*repulsing* Clara]. No, no: stay till I return. [*Exit.*

Sir John. And don't be down-hearted, my dear fellow; if the worst come to the worst, you will have everything I can leave you. Meantime, if I can in any way help you——

Eve. Ha!—you!—*you,* too?—Sir John, you have seen my letter to Miss Vesey?—[*Aside*]—or could she have learned the truth before she ventured to be generous?

Sir John. No! on my honor. I only just called at the door on my way from Lord Spend——that is, from the City. Georgina was out;—was ever anything so unlucky?—[*Without.*] [Hurrah—hurrah! Blue for ever!]—What's that?

Enter SHARP.

Sharp. Sir, a deputation from Groginhole—poll closed in the first hour—you are returned! Holloa, sir—holloa!

Eve. And it was to please Clara!

Sir John. Mr. Sharp—Mr. Sharp—I say, how much has Mr. Evelyn lost by Messrs. Flash and Co.?

Sharp. Oh, a great deal, sir,—a great deal.

Sir John [*alarmed*]. How?—a great deal!

Eve. Speak the truth, Sharp,—concealment is all over.

Sharp. £223 6s. 3d.—a great sum to throw away!

Graves. Ah, I comprehend now! Poor Evelyn caught in his own trap!

Sir John. Eh! what, my dear boy?—what? Ha! ha! all humbug was it?—all humbug, upon my soul! So, Mr. Sharp, isn't he ruined after all?—not the least, wee, rascally, little bit in the world, ruined?

Sharp. Sir, he has never even lived up to his income.

Sir John. Worthy man! I could jump up to the ceiling! I am the happiest father-in-law in the three kingdoms.—And that's my sister's knock, too.

Clara. Since I was mistaken, cousin,—since, now, you do not need me,—forget what has passed; my business here is over. Farewell!

Eve. Could you but see my heart at this moment, with what love, what veneration, what anguish it is filled, you would know how little, in the great calamities of life, fortune is really worth. And must we part now,—*now*, when—when——I never wept before, since my mother died!

Enter LADY FRANKLIN *and* GEORGINA, *followed by* BLOUNT, *who looks shy and embarrassed.*

Graves. Georgina herself—then there's no hope.

Sir John. What the deuce brings that fellow Blount here?—Georgy, my dear Georgy, I want to——

Eve. Stand back, Sir John!

Sir John. But I must speak a word to her—I want to——

Eve. Stand back, I say,—not a whisper—not a sign. If your daughter is to be my wife, to *her* heart only will I look for a reply to *mine*.

Lady Frank. [*to* GEORGINA]. Speak the truth, niece.

Eve. Georgina, it is true, then, that you trust me with your confidence—your fortune? It is also true, that when you did so you believed me ruined? Oh, pardon the doubt! Answer as if your father stood not there—answer me from that truth the world cannot yet have plucked from your soul—answer as if the woe or weal of a life trembled in the balance—answer as the woman's heart, yet virgin and unpolluted, *should* answer to one who has trusted to it his all!

Geor. What can he mean?

Sir John [*making signs*]. She'll not look this way; she will not—hang her—HEM!

Eve. You falter. I implore—I adjure you—answer!

Lady Frank. The truth!

Geor. Mr. Evelyn, your fortune might well dazzle me, as it dazzled others. Believe me, I sincerely pity your reverses.

Sir John. Good girl! you hear her, Evelyn.

Geor. What's money without happiness?

Sir John. Clever creature!—my own sentiments!

Geor. And so, as our engagement is now annulled,—papa told me so this very morning,—I have promised my hand where I have given my heart—to Sir Frederick Blount.

Sir John. I told you,—I? No such thing—no such thing: you frighten her out of her wits—she don't know what she's saying.

Eve. Am I awake? But this letter—this letter, received to-day——

Lady Frank. [*looking over the letter.*] Drummond's—from a banker!

Eve. Read—read.

Lady Frank. "Ten thousand pounds just placed to your account—from the same unknown friend to Evelyn." Oh, Clara, I know now why you went to Drummond's this morning.

Eve. Clara! What!—and the former one with the same signature, on the faith of which I pledged my hand and sacrificed my heart——

Lady Frank. Was written under my eyes, and the secret kept that——

Eve. Look up, look up, Clara—I am free!—I am released! you forgive me?—you love me?—you are mine! We are rich—rich! I can give you fortune, power,—I can devote to you my whole life, thought, heart, soul—I am all yours, Clara—my own—my wife!

Sir John [*to* GEORGINA]. So, you've lost the game by a revoke, in trumping your own father's best of a suit!—Unnatural jade!—Aha, Lady Franklin—I am to thank you for this!

Lady Frank. You've to thank me that she's not now on the road to Scotland with Sir Frederick. I chanced on them by the Park just in time to dissuade and save her. But, to do her justice, a hint of your displeasure was sufficient.

Geor. [*half-sobbing*]. And you know, papa, you said this very morning that poor Frederick had been very ill-used and you would settle it all at the club.

Blount. Come, Sir John, you can only blame yourself and Evelyn's cunning device. After all, I'm no such vewy bad match; and as for the £10,000——

Eve. I'll double it. Ah, Sir John, what's money without happiness?

Sir John. Pshaw—nonsense—stuff! Don't humbug me!

Lady Frank. But if you don't consent, she'll have no husband at all.

Sir John. Hum! there's something in that. [*Aside to* EVELYN.] Double it, will you? Then settle it all *tightly* on her. Well—well—my foible is not avarice. Blount, make her happy. Child, I forgive you.—[*Pinching her arm.*] Ugh, you fool!

Graves [*to* LADY FRANKLIN]. I'm afraid it's catching. What say you? I feel the symptoms of matrimony creeping all over me. Shall we, eh? Frankly, now, frankly——

Lady Frank. Frankly, now, there's my hand, on one condition,—that we finish our reel on the wedding-day.

Graves. Accepted. Is it possible? Sainted Maria! thank Heaven you are spared this affliction!

Enter SMOOTH.

Smooth. How d'ye do, Alfred? I intrude, I fear! Quite a family party.

Blount. Wish us joy, Smooth—Georgina's mine, and—

Smooth. And our four friends there apparently have made up another rubber. John, my dear boy, you look as if you had something at stake on the odd trick.

Sir John. Sir, your very——Confound the fellow!—and he's a dead shot, too!

Enter STOUT *and* GLOSSMORE *hastily, talking with each other.*

Stout. I'm sure he's of our side; we've all the intelligence.

Gloss. I'm sure he's of our's if his fortune is safe, for we've all the property.—My dear Evelyn, you were out of humor yesterday—but I forgive you.

Stout. Certainly!—what would become of public life if man were obliged to be two days running in the same mind?—I rise to explain.—Just heard of your return, Evelyn. Congratulate you. The great motion of the session is fixed for Friday. We count on your vote. Progress with the times!

Gloss. Preserve the Constitution!

Stout. Your money will do wonders for the party!—Advance!

Gloss. The party respects men of your property!—Stick fast!

Eve. I have the greatest respect, I assure you, for the worthy and intelligent flies upon both sides the wheel; but whether we go too fast or too slow, does not, I fancy, depend so much on the flies as on the Stout Gentleman who sits inside and pays the post-boys. Now all my politics as yet is to consider what's best for the Stout Gentleman!

Smooth. Meaning John Bull. *Ce cher* old John!

Stout. I'm as wise as I was before.

Gloss. Sir, he's a trimmer!

Eve. Smooth, we have yet to settle our first piquet account and our last! And I sincerely thank you for the service you have rendered to me, and the lesson you have given these gentlemen.—[*Turning to* CLARA.] Ah, Clara, you—you have succeeded where wealth had failed! You have reconciled me to the world and to mankind. My friends—we must confess it—amidst the humors and the follies, the vanities, deceits, and vices that play their parts in the great Comedy of Life—it is our own fault if we do not find such natures, though rare and few, as redeem the rest, brightening the shadows that are flung from the form and body of the TIME with glimpses of the everlasting holiness of truth and love.

Graves. But for the truth and the love, when found, to make us tolerably happy, we should not be without——

Lady Frank. Good health;

Graves. Good spirits;

Clara. A good heart;

Smooth. An innocent rubber;

Geor. Congenial tempers;

Blount. A pwoper degwee of pwudence;

Stout. Enlightened opinions;

Gloss. Constitutional principles;

Sir John. Knowledge of the world;

Eve. And——plenty of Money!

THE RIGHTFUL HEIR.

TO ALL FRIENDS AND KINSFOLK

IN

THE AMERICAN COMMONWEALTH,

THIS DRAMA IS DEDICATED

WITH AFFECTION AND RESPECT.

LONDON,
Sept. 28, 1868.

PREFACE.

MANY years ago this Drama was re-written from an earlier play by the same Author called "The Sea Captain," the first idea of which was suggested by a striking situation in a novel by M. A. Dumas (*Le Capitaine Paul*). The Author withdrew "The Sea Captain" from the stage (and even from printed publication), while it had not lost such degree of favor as the admirable acting of Mr. Macready chiefly contributed to obtain for it; intending to replace it before the public with some important changes in the histrionic cast, and certain slight alterations in the conduct of the story. But the alterations once commenced, became so extensive in character, diction, and even in revision of plot, that a new play gradually rose from the foundation of the old one. The task thus undertaken, being delayed by other demands upon time and thought, was scarcely completed when Mr. Macready's retirement from his profession suspended the Author's literary connection with the stage, and "The Rightful Heir" has remained in tranquil seclusion till this year, when he submits his appeal to the proper tribunal;—sure, that if he fail of a favorable hearing, it will not be the fault of the friends who take part in his cause and act in his behalf.

LONDON,
Sept. 28, 1868.

NOTE.

"The Spanish Armada was ready in the beginning of May, but the moment it was preparing to sail, the Marquis of Santa Croce, the Admiral, was seized with a fever, of which he soon after died. . . . At last the Spanish fleet, full of hope and alacrity, set sail from Lisbon May 29th, but next day met with a violent tempest, which scattered the ships—sunk some of the smallest, and forced the rest to take shelter in the Groyne, where they waited till they could be re-fitted. When news of this event was carried to England, the Queen concluded that the design of an invasion was disappointed for the summer, and, being always ready to lay hold on every pretence for saving money, she made Walsingham write to the Admiral, directing him to lay up some of the larger ships, and to discharge the seamen. But Lord Effingham, who was not so sanguine in his hopes, used the freedom to disobey these orders, and he begged leave to retain all the ships in service, though it should be at his own expense. . . .

" Meanwhile, all the damages to the Armada were repaired, and the Spaniards, with fresh hopes, set out again to sea."—*Hume*.

DRAMATIS PERSONÆ.

LORD BEAUFORT, *Son to Lady Montreville* . . . . MR. NEVILLE.
SIR GREY DE MALPAS, *the poor cousin, distantly connected to Lady Montreville, but next in succession to the earldom, on failure of the direct line* . . . . } MR. HERMAN VEZIN.
WRECKLYFFE, *a disinherited and ruined gentleman—who, after a vicious and lawless career on land, has turned pirate* . . } MR. LAWLOR.
SIR GODFREY SEYMOUR, *a justice of the peace* . . . . MR. GEORGE PEEL.
VYVYAN, *the captain of the* Dreadnought, *a privateer* . . MR. BANDMANN.
FALKNER, *Vyvyan's first lieutenant and friend* . . . MR. LIN RAYNE.
HARDING, *Vyvyan's second lieutenant* . . . . . . MR. T. ANDERSON.
MARSDEN, *seneschal to Lady Montreville* . . . . MR. DAVID EVANS.
ALTON, *a village priest* . . . . MR. BASIL POTTER.
A SUB-OFFICER *on board the* Dreadnought . . . . MR. EVERARD.

Servants, Sailors, Clerk, and Halberdiers attendant on Sir Godfrey.

LADY MONTREVILLE, *a countess in her own right* . . . MRS. HERMAN VEZIN.
EVELINE, *her ward—distantly related to her, and betrothed to Vyvyan*. . . . . } MISS H. PALMER.

TIME OCCUPIED.—*In the first four acts, one day. Between the 4th and 5th acts the interval of a year. Time supposed to be occupied by the events in the 5th act, little more than that required for representation on the stage.*

DATE OF THE PLAY.—*In the first four acts, July,* 1588—*the year of the Armada. The 5th act, the Summer of* 1589.

*** There are a few omissions and verbal alterations in the stage representation of the Play; but they are too slight to require special notice in the printed text.

First performed on Saturday, the 3d of October, 1868, at the Lyceum Theatre.

THE RIGHTFUL HEIR.

ACT I.—SCENE I.

In the foreground the house of Sir Grey de Malpas, *small and decayed, the casements broken, etc. Ruins around, as if the present house were but the remains of some more stately edifice of great antiquity. In the background, a view of the sea. On a height at some little distance, the castle of Montreville, the sun full upon its turrets and gilded vanes.*

N.B. The scene to be so contrived that the grandeur of the castle and the meanness of the ruin be brought into conspicuous contrast.

Sir Grey *at work on a patch of neglected garden ground, throws down his spade and advances*

    Sir G. I cannot dig ! Fie what a helpless thing
Is the hand of well-born poverty !
And yet between this squalor and that pomp
Stand but two lives, a woman's and a boy's—
But two frail lives. I may outlive them both.

Enter Wrecklyffe.

    Wreck. Ay, that's the house—the same; the master changed,
But less than I am. Winter creeps on him,
Lightning hath stricken me. Good day.
    Sir G.   Pass on.
No spendthrift hospitable food spreads here
The board for strangers. Pass.
    Wreck.   Have years so dimmed
Eyes once so keen, De Malpas ?
    Sir. G. [*after a pause*].   Ha ! Thy hand.
What brings thee hither ?
    Wreck.   'Brings me ?' say 'hurls back.'
First, yellow pestilence, whose ghastly wings
Guard, like the fabled griffin, India's gold;
Unequal battle next; then wolfish famine;
And lastly, storm (rough welcome home to England)
Swept decks from stern to stem; to shore was flung
A lonely pirate on a battered hulk !
One wreck rots stranded;—you behold the other.
    Sir G. Penury hath still its crust and roof-tree—share them
Time has dealt hardly with us both, since first
We two made friendship—thou straight-limbed, well-favored,
Stern-hearted, disinherited dare-devil !
    Wreck. And thou !——

Sir G. A stroke paints me. My lord's poor cousin.
How strong thou wert, yet I could twist and wind thee
Round these slight hands;—that is the use of brains!
　Wreck. Still jokes and stings?
　Sir G. Still a poor cousin's weapons.
　Wreck. Boast brains, yet starve?
　Sir G. Still a poor cousin's fate, sir.
Pardon my brains, since oft thy boasts they pardoned;
(Sad chance since then), when rufflers aped thy swagger,
And village maidens sighed and, wondering, asked
Why heaven made men so wicked—and so comely.
　Wreck. 'Sdeath! Wilt thou cease?
　Sir G. That scar upon thy front
Bespeaks grim service.
　Wreck. In thy cause, de Malpas;
The boy, whom at thine instance I allured
On board my bark, left me this brand of Cain.
　Sir G. That boy——
　Wreck. Is now a man—and on these shores.
This morn I peered from yonder rocks that hid me,
And saw his face. I whetted then this steel:
Need'st thou his death? In me behold Revenge!
　Sir G. He lives!—he lives! There is a third between
The beggar and the earldom!
　Wreck. Steps and voices!
When shall we meet alone? Hush, it is he!
　Sir G. He with the plume?
　Wreck. Ay.
　Sir G. Quick; within.
　Wreck. And thou?
　Sir G. I dig the earth; see the grave-digger's tool.
　　　　　　　　　　　　　[*Exit* WRECKLYFFE *within the house.*

Enter HARDING *and* Sailors.

　Hard. Surely 'twas here the captain bade us meet him
While he went forth for news?
　1st Sailor. He comes.

Enter VYVYAN.

　Hard. Well, captain,
What tidings of the Spaniards' armament?
　Vyv. Bad, for they say the fighting is put off,
And storm in Biscay driven back the Dons.
This is but rumor—we will learn the truth.
Harding, take horse and bear these lines to Drake—
If yet our country needs stout hearts to guard her,
He'll not forget the men on board the Dreadnought,
Thou can'st be back ere sunset with his answer,
And find me in yon towers of Montreville. [*Exit* HARDING.
Meanwhile make merry in the hostel, lads,
And drink me out these ducats in this toast:—
"No foes be tall eno' to wade the moat
Which girds the fort whose only walls are men." [*Sailors* cheer, *and exeunt.*

Vyv. I never hailed reprieve from war till now.
Heaven grant but time to see mine Eveline,
And learn my birth from Alton.

Enter FALKNER.

Falk. Captain.
Vyv. Falkner!
So soon returned? Thy smile seems fresh from home.
All well there?
Falk. Just in time to make all well.
My poor old father!—bailiffs at his door;
He tills another's land, and crops had failed.
I poured mine Indian gold into his lap,
And cried "O father, wilt thou now forgive
The son who went to sea against thy will?"
Vyv. And he forgave.—Now tell me of thy mother;
I never knew one, but I love to mark
The quiver of a strong man's bearded lip
When his voice lingers on the name of mother.
Thy mother bless'd thee——
Falk. Yes, I—— [*Falters and turns aside*]
Pshaw! methought
Her joy was weeping on my breast again!
Vyv. I envy thee those tears.
Falk. Eno' of me!
Now for thyself. What news? Thy fair betrothed—
The maid we rescued from the turbaned corsair
With her brave father in the Indian seas—
Found and still faithful?
Vyv. Faithful, I will swear it;
But not yet found. Her sire is dead—the stranger
Sits at his hearth—and with her next of kin,
Hard by this spot—yea, in yon sunlit towers,
Mine Eveline dwells.
Falk. Thy foster father, Alton.
Hast thou seen him?
Vyv. Not yet. My Falkner, serve me.
His house is scarce a two hours' journey hence,
The nearest hamlet will afford a guide;
Seek him and break the news of my return,
Say I shall see him ere the day be sped.
And, hearken, friend (good men at home are apt
To judge us sailors harshly), tell him this—
On the far seas his foster son recalled
Prayers taught by age to childhood, and implored
Blessing on that grey head. Farewell! Now, Eveline.

[*Exeunt severally*, VYVYAN *and* FALKNER

Sir G. [*advancing*]. Thou seekest those towers—go. I will meet thee there.
He must not see the priest—the hour is come
Absolving Alton's vow to guard the secret;
Since the boy left, two 'scutcheons moulder o'er
The dust of tombs from which his rights ascend;
He must not see the priest—but how forestall him?—

Within ! For there dwells Want, Wit's counsellor,
Harboring grim Force, which is Ambition's tool.   [*Exit* SIR GREY.

SCENE II.

The gardens of the castle of Montreville, laid out in the formal style of the times. Parterres sunk deep in beds of arabesque design. The gardens are enclosed within an embattled wall, which sinks, here and there, into low ornamented parapets, over which the eye catches a glimpse of the sea, which is immediately below. A postern gate in the wall is open, through which descends a flight of steps, hewn out of the cliff.

Enter LADY MONTREVILLE.

Lady M. This were his birthday, were he living still!
But the wide ocean is his winding sheet,
And his grave—here! [*Pressing her hand to her heart.*] I dreamed of him
    last night!
Peace! with the dead, died shame and glozing slander;
In the son left me still, I clasp a world
Of blossoming hopes which flower beneath my love,
And take frank beauty from the flattering day.
And——but my Clarence!——in his princely smile
How the air brightens!

Enter LORD BEAUFORT, *speaking to* MARSDEN.

Lord B.   Yes, my gallant roan,
And, stay—be sure the falcon, which my lord
Of Leicester sent me; we will try its metal.
    Mars. Your eyes do bless him, madam, so do mine:
A gracious spring; Heaven grant we see its summer!
Forgive, dear lady, your old servant's freedom.
    Lady M. Who loves him best with me ranks highest, Marsden. [*Exit* MARSDEN.
Clarence, you see me not.
    Lord B.   Dear mother, welcome.
Why do I miss my soft-eyed cousin here?
    Lady M. It doth not please me, son, that thou should'st haunt
Her steps, and witch with dulcet words her ear.
Eveline is fair, but not the mate for Beaufort.
    Lord B. Mate! Awful word! Can youth not gaze on beauty.
Save by the torch of Hymen? To be gallant,
Melt speech in sighs, or murder sense in sonnets;
Veer with each change in Fancy's April skies,
And o'er each sun-shower fling its fleeting rainbow.
All this——
    Lady M. [*gloomily.*] Alas, is love.
    Lord B.   No! Love's light prologue,
The sportive opening to the serious drama;
The pastime practice of Dan Cupid's bow,
Against that solemn venture at the butts
At which fools make so many random shafts,

And rarely hit the white! Nay, smile, my mother;
How does this plume become me?
 Lady M.   Foolish boy!
It sweeps too loosely.
 Lord B.   Now-a-days man's love
Is worn as loosely as I wear this plume—
A glancing feather swept with every wind
Into new shadows o'er a giddy brain
Such as your son's. Let the plume play, sweet mother!
 Lady M. Would I could chide thee!
 Lord B.   Hark, I hear my steed
Neighing impatience; and my falcon frets
Noon's lazy air with lively silver bells;
Now, madam, look to it—no smile from me
When next we meet,—no kiss of filial duty,
Unless my fair-faced cousin stand beside you,
Blushing 'Peccavi' for all former sins—
Shy looks, cold words, this last unnatural absence,
And taught how cousins should behave to cousins. [*Exit* LORD BEAUFORT.
 Lady M. Trifler! And yet the faults that quicken fear
Make us more fond—we parents love to pardon.

Enter EVELINE, *weaving flowers—not seeing* LADY MONTREVILLE.

 Evel. [*Sings*]—

> Bud from the blossom,
> And leaf from the tree,
> Guess why in weaving
> I sing "Woe is me!"—
>
> 'Tis that I weave you
> To drift on the sea,
> And say, when ye find him,
> Who sang "Woe is me!"—

[*Casts the flowers, woven into a garland, over the parapet, and advances*
 Lady M. A quaint but mournful rhyme.
 Evel.   You, madam!—pardon!
 Lady M. What tells the song?
 Evel.   A simple village tale
Of a lost seaman, and a crazed girl,
His plighted bride—good Marsden knew her well,
And oft-times marked her singing on the beach,
Then launch her flowers, and smile upon the sea.
I know not why—both rhyme and tale do haunt me.
 Lady M. Sad thoughts haunt not young hearts, thou senseless child.
 Evel. Is not the child an orphan?
 Lady M.   In those eyes
Is there no moisture softer than the tears
Which mourn a father? Roves thy glance for Beaufort?
Vain girl, beware! The flattery of the great
Is but the eagle's swoop upon the dove,
And, in descent, destroys.
 Evel.   Can you speak thus,
Yet bid me grieve not that I am an orphan? [*Retires up the garden*

Lady M. [*to herself*]. I have high dreams for Beaufort; bright desires!
Son of a race whose lives shine down on Time
From lofty tombs, like beacon-towers o'er ocean,
He stands amidst the darkness of my thoughts,
Radiant as Hope in some lone captive's cell.
Far from the gloom around, mine eyes, inspired,
Pierce to the future, when these bones are dust,
And see him loftiest of the lordly choirs
Whose swords and coronals blaze around the throne,
The guardian stars of the imperial isle—
Kings shall revere his mother.

Enter Sir Grey, *speaking to* Servant.

Sir G. What say'st thou?
Servant [*insolently*]. Sir Grey—ha! ha!—Lord Beaufort craves your pardon,
He shot your hound—its bark disturbed the deer.
Sir G. The only voice that welcomed me! A dog—
Grudges he that?
Servant. Oh sir, 'twas done in kindness
To you and him; the dog was wondrous lean, sir!
Sir G. I thank my lord. [*Exit* Servant.
So, my poor Tray is killed!
And yet *that* dog but barked—can *this* not bite?
[*Approaches* Lady Montreville *vindictively, and in a whisper*—
He lives!
Lady M. He! who?
Sir G. The heir of Montreville!
Another, and an elder Beaufort, lives!
[*Aside*] So—the fang fixes fast—good—good!
Lady M. Thou saidst
Ten years ago—" Thy first-born is no more—
Died in far seas."
Sir G. So swore my false informant.
But now, the deep that took the harmless boy
Casts from its breast the bold-eyed daring man.
Lady M. Clarence! My poor proud Clarence!
Sir G. Ay, *poor* Clarence!
True; since his father, by his former nuptials
Had other sons, if you, too, own el ler,
Clarence is poor—as poor as his r cousin.
Ugh! but the air is keen, an Pov rty
Is thinly clad; subject to rheums and agues [*shivers*],
Asthma and phthisis [*coughs*], pains in the loins and limbs,
And leans upon a crutch, like your poor cousin.
If Poverty begs, Law sets it in the stocks;
If it is ill, the doctors mangle it;
If it is dying, the priests scold at it;
And when 'tis dead, rich kinsmen cry, "Thank heaven!"
Ah! if the elder prove his rights, dear lady,
Your younger son will know what's poverty!
Lady M. Malignant, peace! why dost thou torture me?
The priest who shares alone with us the secret
Hath sworn to guard it.

Sir G.   Only while thy sire
And second lord survived. Yet, what avails
In law his tale, unbacked by thy confession?
    Lady M. All! He hath proofs, clear proofs. Thrice woe to Clarence!
    Sir G. Proofs—written proofs?
    Lady M.   Of marriage, and the birth!
    Sir G. Wherefore so long was this concealed from me?
    Lady M. Thou wert my father's agent, Grey de Malpas,
Not my familiar.
    Sir G.   Here, then, ends mine errand.
    Lady M. Stay, sir—forgive my rash and eager temper;
Stay, stay, and counsel me. What! sullen still?
Needest thou gold?—befriend, and find me grateful.
    Sir G. Lady of Montreville, I once was young,
And pined for gold, to wed the maid I loved:
Your father said, "Poor cousins should not marry,"
And gave that sage advice in lieu of gold.
A few years later, and I grew ambitious,
And longed for wars and fame, and foolish honors:
Then I lacked gold, to join the knights, mine equals,
As might become a Malpas and your kinsman:
Your father said he had need of his poor cousin
At home to be his huntsman, and his falconer!
    Lady M. Forgetful! After my first fatal nuptials
And their sad fruit, count you as naught——
    Sir G.   My hire!
For service and for silence; not a gift.
    Lady M. And spent in riot, waste, and wild debauch!
    Sir G. True; in the pauper's grand inebriate wish
To know what wealth is,—tho' but for an hour.
    Lady M. But blame you me or mine, if spendthrift wassa
Run to the dregs? Mine halls stand open to you;
My noble Beaufort hath not spurned your converse;
You have been welcomed——
    Sir G.   At your second table,
And as the butt of unchastised lackeys;
While your kind son, in pity of my want,
Hath this day killed the faithful dog that shared it.
'Tis well; you need my aid, as did your father,
And tempt, like him with gold. I take the service;
And, when the task is done, will talk of payment.
Hist! the boughs rustle. Closer space were safer;
Vouchsafe your hand, let us confer within.
    Lady M. Well might I dream last night! A fearful dream.
                           [*Exeunt* LADY MONTREVILLE *and* SIR GREY.

                   Re-enter EVELINE.

    Evel. O, for some fairy talisman to conjure
Up to these longing eyes the form they pine for!
And yet in love, there's no such word as absence;
The loved one glides beside our steps for ever;
Its presence gave such beauty to the world,
That all things beautiful its tokens are,

And aught in sound most sweet, to sight most fair,
Breathes with its voice, and haunts us with its aspect.

Enter VYVYAN *through the postern gate.*

There spoke my fancy, not my heart ! Where art thou,
My unforgotten Vyvyan ?
   Vyv.   At thy feet !
Look up—look up !—these are the arms that sheltered
When the storm howled around ; and the lips
Where, till this hour, the sad and holy kiss
Of parting lingered, as the fragrance left
By angels, when they touch the earth and vanish.
Look up ; night never hungered for the sun
As for thine eyes my soul !
   Evel.   Oh ! joy, joy, joy !
   Vyv. Yet weeping still, tho' leaning on my breast !
My sailor's bride, hast thou no voice but blushes ?
Nay from those drooping roses let me steal
The coy reluctant sweetness !
   Evel.   And, methought
I had treasured words, 'twould take a life to utter
When we should meet again !
   Vyv.   Recall them later.
We shall have time eno', when life with life
Blends into one ;—why dost thou start and tremble ?
   Evel. Methought I heard her slow and solemn footfall !
   Vyv. Her ! Why, thou speak'st of woman · the meek word
Which never chimes with terror.
   Evel.   You know not
The dame of Montreville.
   Vyv.   Is she so stern ?
   Evel. Not stern, but haughty: as if high-born virtue
Swept o'er the earth to scorn the faults it pardoned.
   Vyv. Haughty to thee ?
   Evel.   To all, ev'n when the kindest;
Nay, I do wrong her; never to her son;
And when those proud eyes moisten as they hail him,
Hearts lately stung, yearn to a heart so human !
Alas, that parent love ! how in its loss
All life seems shelterless !
   Vyv.   Like thee, perchance,
Looking round earth for that same parent shelter,
I too may find but tombs. So, turn we both,
Orphans, to that lone parent of the lonely,
That doth like Sorrow ever upward gaze
On calm consoling stars—the mother Sea.
   Evel. Call not the cruel sea by that mild name.
   Vyv. She is not cruel if her breast swell high
Against the winds that thwart her loving aim
To link by every raft whose course she speeds,
Man's common brotherhood from pole to pole;
Grant she hath danger—danger schools the brave,
And bravery leaves all cruel things to cowards.

Grant that she hardens us to fear,—the hearts
Most proof to fear are easiest moved to love,
As on the oak whose roots defy the storm,
All the leaves tremble when the south-wind stirs.
Yet if the sea dismay thee, on the shores
Kissed by her waves, and far, as fairy isles
In poets dreams, from this grey care-worn world,
Blooms many a bower for the Sea Rover's bride.
I know a land where feathering palm-trees shade
To delicate twilight, suns benign as those
Whose dawning gilded Eden;—Nature, there,
Like a gay spendthrift in his flush of youth,
Flings whole treasure on the lap of Time.
There, steeped in roseate hues, the lakelike sea
Heaves to an air whose breathing is ambrosia;
And, all the while, bright-winged and warbling birds,
Like happy souls released, melodious float
Thro' blissful light, and teach the ravished earth
How joy finds voice in Heaven. Come, rest we yonder,
And, side by side, forget that we are orphans!

[VYVYAN *and* EVELINE *retire up the stage.*

Enter LADY MONTERVILLE *and* SIR GREY.

Lady M. Yet still, if Alton sees——
Sir G. Without the proofs,
Why, Alton's story were but idle wind;
The man I send is swift and strong, and ere
This Vyvyan (who would have been here before me
But that I took the shorter path) depart
From your own threshold to the priest's abode,
Our agent gains the solitary dwelling,
And——
Lady M. But no violence!
Sir G. Nay, none but fear—
Fear will suffice to force from trembling age
Your safety, and preserve your Beaufort's birthright.
Lady M. Let me not hear the ignominious means;
Gain thou the end;—quick—quick!
Sir G. And if, meanwhile,
This sailor come, be nerved to meet—a stranger;
And to detain—a guest.
Lady M. My heart is wax,
But my will, iron—go.
Sir G. [*aside*]. To fear add force—
And this hand closes on the proofs, and welds
That iron to a tool. [*Exit* SIR GREY

Re-enter VYVYAN *and* EVELINE.

Evel. Nay, Vyvyan—nay,
Your guess can fathom not how proud her temper.
Vyv. Tut for her pride! a king upon the deck

Is every subject's equal in the hall.
I will advance. [*He uncovers.*]

Lady M. Avenging angels spare me!

Vyv. Pardon the seeming boldness of my presence.

Evel. Our gallant countryman, of whom my father
So often spake—who from the Algerine
Rescued our lives and freedom.

Lady M. Ah! Your name sir?

Vyv. The name I bear is Vyvyan, noble lady.

Lady M. Sir, you are welcome. Walk within, and hold
Our home your hostel, while it lists you.

Vyv. Madam,
I shall be prouder in all after time
For having been your guest.

Lady M. How love and dread
Make tempest here! I pray you follow me. [*Exit* LADY MONTREVILLE.

Vyv. A most majestic lady—her fair face
Made my heart tremble, and called back old dreams:
Thou saidst she had a son?

Evel. Ah, yes.

Vyv. In truth
A happy man.

Evel. Yet he might envy thee:

Vyv. Most arch reprover, yes. As kings themselves
Might envy one whose arm entwines his all. [*Exeunt* EVELINE *and* VYVYAN.

ACT II—SCENE I.

A Gothic chamber. On one side a huge hearth, over which an armorial scutcheon and an earl's coronet, boldly carved. The walls covered with old portraits—tall beaufets in recesses filled with goblets and other vessels of silver. An open door admits a view of a cloister, and the alleys in the courtyard without.

A table spread with fruits and wines, at which are seated LADY MONTREVILLE, VYVYAN *and* EVELINE.

Vyv. Ha! ha! In truth we made a scurvy figure
After our shipwreck.

Lady M. You jest merrily
On your misfortunes.

Vyv. 'Tis the way with sailors:
Still in extremes. I can be sad sometimes.

Lady M. That sigh, in truth, speaks sadness. Sir, if I
In aught could serve you, trust me.

Evel. Trust her, Vyvyan.
Methinks the mournful tale of thy young years
Would raise thee up a friend, wherever pity
Lives in the heart of woman.

Vyv. Gentle lady,
The key of some charmed music in your voice

Unlocks a haunted chamber in my soul;
And—would you listen to an outcast's tale,—
'Tis briefly told. Until my fifteenth year,
Beneath the roof of a poor village priest,
Not far from hence, my childhood wore away;
Then stirred within me restless thoughts and deep;—
Throughout the liberal and harmonious nature
Something seemed absent,—what, I scarcely knew,
Till one calm night, when over slumbering seas
Watched the still heaven, and down on every wave
Looked some soft lulling star—the instinctive want
Learned what it pined for; and I asked the priest
With a quick sigh—" Why I was motherless ?"

  Lady M. And he ?—

  Vyv.   Replied that—I was nobly born,
And that the cloud which dimmed a dawning sun,
Oft but foretold its splendor at the noon.
As thus he spoke, faint memories struggling came—
Faint as the things some former life hath known.

  Lady M. Of what ?

  Vyv.   A face sweet with a stately sorrow,
And lips which breathed the words that mothers murmur.

  Lady M. [*aside*]. Back, tell-tale tears !

  Vyv.   About that time, a stranger
Came to our hamlet; rough, yet, some said, well-born;
Roysterer, and comrade, such as youth delights in.
Sailor he called himself, and naught belied
The sailor's metal ringing in his talk
Of El Dorados, and Enchanted Isles,
Of hardy Raleigh, and of fearless Drake,
And great Columbus with prophetic eyes
Fixed on a dawning world. His legends fired me—
And, from the deep whose billows washed our walls,
The alluring wave called with a siren's music.
And thus I left my home with that wild seaman.

  Lady M. The priest, consenting, still divulged not more ?

  Vyv. No; nor rebuked mine ardor. "Go," he said,
" The noblest of all nobles are the men
In whom their country feels herself ennobled."

  Lady M. [*aside*]. I breathe again. Well, thus you left these shores—

  Vyv. Scarce had the brisker sea-wind filled our sails,
When the false traitor who had lured my trust
Cast me to chains and darkness. Days went by,
At length—one belt of desolate waters round,
And on the decks one scrowl of swarthy brows,
(A hideous crew, the refuse of all shores)—
Under the flapping of his raven flag
The pirate stood revealed, and called his captive.
Grimly he heard my boyish loud upbraidings,
And grimly smiled in answering: " I, like thee,
Cast off, and disinherited, and desperate,
Had but one choice, death or the pirate's flag—
Choose *thou*—I am more gracious than thy kindred;

I proffer life; the gold *they* gave me paid
Thy grave in ocean !
  Lady M.   Hold ! The demon lied !
  Vyv. Swift, as I answered so, his blade flashed forth;
But self-defence is swifter still than slaughter;
I plucked a sword from one who stood beside me,
And smote the slanderer to my feet. Then all
That human hell broke loose; oaths rang, steel lightened
When in the death-swoon of the caitiff chief,
The private next in rank forced back the swarm,
And—in that superstition of the sea
Which makes the sole religion of its outlaws—
Forbade my doom by bloodshed—griped and bound me
To a slight plank; spread to the winds the sail,
And left me on the waves alone with God.
  Evel. Pause. Let my hand take thine—feel its warm life,
And, shuddering less, thank Him whose eye was o'er thee.
  Vyv. That day, and all that night, upon the seas
Tossed the frail barrier between life and death;
Heaven lulled the gales; and when the stars came forth,
All looked so bland and gentle that I wept,
Recalled that wretch's words, and murmured, " All,
Ev'n wave and wind, are kinder than my kindred ! "
But—nay, sweet lady——
  Lady M.   Heed me not. Night passed——
  Vyv. Day dawned; and, glittering in the sun, behold
A sail—a flag !
  Evel. Well—well ?
  Vyv.   Like hope, it vanished !
Noon glaring came—with noon came thirst and famine,
And with parched lips I called on death, and sought
To wrench my limbs from the stiff cords that gnawed
Into the flesh, and drop into the deep:
And then—the clear wave trembled, and below
I saw a dark, swift-moving, shapeless thing,
With watchful, glassy eyes;—the ghastly shark
Swam hungering round its prey—then life once more
Grew sweet, and with a strained and horrent gaze
And lifted hair I floated on, till sense
Grew dim, and dimmer; and a terrible sleep
(In which still—still—those livid eyes met mine)
Fell on me—and——
  Evel.   Quick—quick !
  Vyv.   I woke, and heard
My native tongue ! Kind looks were bent upon me.
I lay on deck—escaped the ravening death—
For God had watched the sleeper.
  Evel.   Oh, such memories
Make earth, for ever after, nearer heaven;
And each new hour an altar for thanksgiving.
  Lady M. Break not the tale my ear yet strains to listen.
  Vyv. True lion of the ocean was the chief
Of that good ship. Beneath his fostering eyes,

Nor all ungraced by Drake's illustrious praise,
And the frank clasp of Raleigh's kingly hand,
I fought my way to manhood. At his death
The veteran left me a more absolute throne
Than Cæsar filled—his war-ship; for my realm
And to the ocean, hope,—and measure it!
Nameless, I took his name. My tale is done—
And each past sorrow, like a wave on shore,
Dies on this golden hour. [*Turns to* EVELINE.

Lady M. [*observing them.*] He loves my ward,
Whom Clarence, too—that though piles fear on fear;
Yet, hold—that very rivalship gives safety—
Affords pretext to urge the secret nuptials,
And the prompt parting, ere he meet with Alton.
I—but till Nature sobs itself to peace,
Here's that which chokes all reason. Will ye not
Taste summer air cooled through yon shadowy alleys?
Anon I'll join you. [*Exit* LADY MONTREVILLE.

Vyv. We will wait your leisure.
A most compassionate and courteous lady—
How couldst thou call her proud?

Evel. Nay, ever henceforth,
For the soft pity she hath shown to thee,
I'll love her as a mother.

Vyv. Thus I thank thee [*kissing her hand*].
[*Exeunt through the cloisters.*

SCENE II.

Exterior of the castle. On one side, a terrace, with a low embattled parapet, hangs over the rock on which the castle is built, and admits a glimpse of the scene below. On another side, the ground stretches away into avenues and alleys. The castle thus seen, takes the character of a strong fortified hold.

N. B. The scene should present the space within a vast, but irregular embattled wall, large enough to enclose trees and undulating ground. The cloister, with the door leading to LADY MONTREVILLE'S *apartment, will form part of the building, and a gate of great strength, with portcullis, etc., should form a side scene. Through this gate, as the principal portal, will enter* LORD BEAUFORT, *and, towards the end of the act,* FALKNER.

Enter SIR GREY DE MALPAS *from the terrace.*

Lord B. [*speaking without*]. A noble falcon! Marsden, hood him gently.

Enter LORD BEAUFORT.

Good day, old knight, thou hast a lowering look,
As if still ruffled by some dire affray
With lawless mice, at riot in thy larder.

Sir G. Mice in my house! magnificent dreamer, **mice**!
The last was found three years ago last Christmas,
Stretched out beside a bone; so lean and worn

With pious fast—'twas piteous to behold it;
I canonized its corpse in spirits of wine,
And set it in the porch—a solemn warning
To its—poor cousins! [*Aside*] Shall I be avenged?
He killed my dog too.

Enter VYVYAN *and* EVELINE, *lingering in an alley in the background.*

  Lord B.   Knight, look there!—A stranger,
And whispering with my cousin.
  Sir G. [*aside*].   Jealous? Ha!
Something should come of this: Hail, green-eyed fiend;
[*Aloud*] Let us withdraw—tho' old I have been young;
The whispered talk of lovers should be sacred.
  Lord B. Lovers!
  Sir G.   Ah! true! You know not, in your absence
Your mother hath received a welcome guest
In your fair cousin's wooer. Note him well,
A stalwart comely gallant.
  Lord B.   Art thou serious?
A wooer to my cousin—quick, his name!
  Sir G. His name?—my memory doth begin to fail me—
Your mother will recall it. Seek—ask *her*——
  Lord B. [*advancing*]. Whom have we here? Familiar sir, excuse me,
I do not see the golden spurs of knighthood.
  Vyv. Alack, we sailors have not so much gold
That we should waste it on our heels! The steeds
We ride to battle need no spurs, Sir Landsman;
  Lord B. And overleap all laws; methinks thou art
One of those wild Sea Rovers who——
  Vyv.   Refuse
To yield to Spain's proud tyranny, her claim
To treat as thieves and pirates all who cross
The line Spain's finger draws across God's ocean.
We, the Sea Rovers, on our wandering decks
Carry our land, its language, laws and freedom;
We wrest from Spain the Sceptre of the seas,
And in the New World build up a new England.
For this high task, if we fulfil it duly,
The Old and New World both shall bless the names
Of Walter Raleigh and his bold Sea Rovers.
  Lord B. Of those names thine is——
  Vyv.   Vyvyan.
  Lord B.   Master Vyvyan
Our rank scarce fits us for a fair encounter
With the loud talk of blustering mariners.
We bar you not our hospitality;
Our converse, yes. Go, ask the Seneschal
To lodge you with your equals!
  Vyv.   Equals, stripling!
Mine equals truly should be bearded men,
Noble with titles carpet lords should bow to—
Memories of dangers dared, and service done,
And scars on bosoms that have bled for England!

Sir G. Nay, coz, he has thee there. [*withholding* LORD BEAUFORT.]
Thou shalt not, Clarence.
Strike *me*. I'm weak and safe—but *he* is dangerous.

Enter LADY MONTREVILLE *from the cloister as* LORD BEAUFORT *breaks from* SIR GREY *and draws his sword.*

Evel. Protect your guest from your rash son.
Lady M. Thy sword
Draw on thy——Back, boy! I command thee, back!
To you, sir guest, have I in aught so failed,
That in the son you would rebuke the mother?
Vyv. Madam, believe, my sole offence was this,
That rated as a serf, I spoke as man.
Lady M. Wherefore, Lord Beaufort, such unseemly humors?
Lord B. [*drawing her aside*]. Wherefore?—and while we speak, his touch profanes her!
Who is this man? Dost thou approve his suit?
Beware!
Lady M. You would not threaten——Oh, my Clarence,
Hear me, you——
Lord B. Learned in childhood from my mother
To brook no rival—and to curb no passion.
Aid'st thou yon scatterling against thy son,
Where most his heart is set?
Lady M. Thy heart, perverse one?
Thou saidst it was not love.
Lord B. That was before
A rival made it love—nay, fear not, mother,
If you dismiss this insolent;—but, mark me,
Dismiss him straight, or, by mine honor, madam,
Blood will be shed.
Lady M. Thrice miserable boy!
Let the heavens hear thee not!
Lord B. [*whispering as he passes* VYVYAN]. Again, and soon, sir!
[*Exit* LORD BEAUFORT.
Lady M. [*seeing* SIR GREY]. Villain!—but no, I dare not yet upbraid——
[*Aloud*] After him, quick! Appease, soothe, humor him.
Sir G. Ay, madam, trust to your poor cousin. [*Exit* SIR GREY.
Lady M. Eveline,
Thou lov'st this Vyvyan?
Evel. Lady—I—he saved
My life and honor.
Lady M. Leave us, gentle child,
I would confer with him. May both be happy!
Evel. [*to* VYVYAN]. Hush! she consents; well mayst thou bid me love her.
[*Exit* EVELINE.
Lady M. Sir, if I gather rightly from your speech,
You do not mean long sojourn on these shores?
Vyv. Lady, in sooth, mine errand here was two-fold.
First, to behold, and, if I dare assume
That you will ratify her father's promise,
To claim my long affianced; next, to learn
If Heaven vouchsafe me yet a parent's heart.

I gained these shores to hear of war and danger—
The long-suspended thunderbolt of Spain
Threatened the air. I have despatched an envoy
To mine old leader, Drake, to crave sure tidings;
I wait reply: If England be in peril,
Hers my first service; if, as rumor runs,
The cloud already melts without a storm,
Then, my bride gained, and my birth tracked, I sail
Back to the Indian seas, where wild adventure
Fulfils in life what boyhood dreamed in song.

    Lady M. 'Tis frankly spoken—frankly I reply.
First—England's danger: Now, for five slow years
Have Spain's dull trumpets blared their braggart war,
And Rome's grey monk-craft muttered new crusades;
Well, we live still—and all this deluge dies
In harmless spray on England's scornful cliffs.
And, trust me, sir, if war beleaguer England,
Small need of one man's valor: lacked she soldiers,
Methinks a Mars would strike in childhood's arm,
And woman be Bellona.

    Vyv.   Stately matron,
So would our mother country speak and look,
Could she take visible image !

    Lady M.   Claim thy bride
With my assent, and joyous gratulation.
She shall not go undowried to your arms.
Nor deem me wanting to herself and you
If I adjure prompt nuptials and departure.
Beaufort—thou see'st how fiery is his mood—
In my ward's lover would avenge a rival:
Indulge the impatient terrors of a mother,
And quit these shores. Why not this night?

    Vyv.   This night?
With her—my bride?

    Lady M.   So from the nuptial altar.
Pledge thou thy faith to part—to spread the sail
And put wide seas between my son and thee.

    Vyv. This night, with Eveline!—dream of rapture! yet—
My birth untracked——

    Lady M.   Delay not for a doubt
Bliss when assured. And, heed me, I have wealth
To sharpen law, and power to strengthen justice;
I will explore the mazes of this mystery;
I—I will track your parents.

    Vyv.   Blessed lady;
My parents—find me one with eyes like thine,
And were she lowliest of the hamlet born,
I would not change with monarchs.

    Lady M. [*aside*].   Can I bear this?
Your Eveline well nigh is my daughter; you
Her plighted spouse; pray you this kiss—O, sweet!

            [*He sinks on his knee as she kisses his forehead.*

    Vyv. Ah, as I kneel, and as thou bendest o'er me,

Methinks an angel's hand lifts up the veil
Of Time, the great magician, and I see
Above mine infant couch, a face like thine.
  Lady M. Mine, stranger!
  Vyv.   Pardon me; a vain wild thought
I know it is; but on my faith, I think
My mother was like thee.
  Lady M.   Peace, peace: We talk
And fool grave hours away. Inform thy bride;
Then to thy bark, and bid thy crew prepare;
Meanwhile, I give due orders to my chaplain.
Beside the altar we shall meet once more:—
And then—and then—Heaven's blessing and farewell! [*Exit* LADY MONTREVILLE.
  Vyv. Most feeling heart! its softness hath contagion,
And melts mine own. Her aspect wears a charm
That half divides my soul with Eveline's love!
Strange! while I muse a chill and ominous awe
Creeps thro' my veins! Away, ye vague forebodings!
Eveline. At thy dear name the phantoms vanish,
And the glad future breaks like land on sea,
When rain-mists melt beneath the golden morn.

      Enter FALKNER.

  Falk. Ha! Vyvyan!
  Vyv.   Thou!
  Falk.   Breathless with speed to reach thee.
I guessed thee lingering here. Thy foster sire
Hath proofs that clear the shadow from thy birth.
Go—he awaits thee where yon cloud-capt rock
Jags air with barbed peaks —St. Kinian's Cliff.
  Vyv. My birth! My parents live?
  Falk.   I know no more.

      Enter HARDING.

  Hard. Captain, the rumor lied. I bring such news
As drums and clarions and resounding anvils
Fashioning the scythes of reapers into swords,
Shall ring from Thames to Tweed.
  Vyv.   The foeman comes!
  Hard. [*giving letter*]. These lines will tell thee; Drake's own hand.
  Vyv. [*reading*].   "The Armada
Has left the Groyne, and we are ranging battle.
Come! in the van I leave one gap for thee."
Poor Eveline! Shame on such unworthy weakness!
  Falk. [*Taking him aside*]. Time to see her and keep thy tryst with Alton.
Leave me to call the crew and arm the decks.
Not till the moon rise in the second hour
After the sunset, will the deepening tide
Float us from harbor—ere that hour be past
Our ship shall wait thee by St. Kinian's Cliff.
Small need to pray thee not to miss the moment
Whose loss would lose thee honor.
  Vyv.   If I come not

Ere the waves reel to thy third signal gun
Deem Death alone could so delay from duty,
And step into my post as o'er my corpse.

   Falk. Justly, my captain, thou rebuk'st my warning,
And couldst thou fail us, I would hold the signal
As if thy funeral knell—crowd every sail,
And know thy soul——

   Vyv.   Was with my country still.   [*Shouts without.*

   Enter Sub-officer, Sailors, Retainers, *and* Villagers, *confusedly.*

   Sub-officer. [*with broadsheet*]. Captain, look here. Just come!
   Vyv.   The Queen's Address
From her own lips to the armed lines at Tilbury.
   Voices. Read it, sir, read it.
   Vyv.   Hush then [*reading*]. "Loving people,
Let tyrants fear! I, under Heaven, have placed
In loyal hearts my chiefest strength and safeguard,
Being resolved in the midst and heat of the battle
To live and die amongst you all; content
To lay down for my God and my people
Honor and life-blood in the dust: I know
I have the body of a feeble woman,
But a King's heart, a King of England's too;
And think foul scorn that Parma, Spain, or Europe,
Dare to invade the borders of my realm!
Where England fights—with concord in the camp,
Trust in the chief, and valor in the field,
Swift be her victory over every foe
Threatening her crown, her altars and her people."

The noble Woman King! These words of fire
Will send warm blood through all the veins of Freedom
Till England is a dream! Uncover, lads!
God and St. George! Hurrah for England's Queen!

ACT III.—SCENE I.

St. Kinian's Cliff, a wild and precipitous headland. In front the ground is broken with crags, here and there interspersed with stunted brushwood. The scene to be so contrived as to give some notion of the height of the cliff. Time, a little before sunset.

ALTON *and* VYVYAN *seated.*

Alton. And I believed them when they said "He died
In the far seas." Ten years of desolate sorrow
Passed as one night—Now thy warm hand awakes me.
   Vyv. Dear friend, the sun sets fast.
   Alton.   Alas! then listen.
There was a page, fair, gentle, brave, but low-born—
And in those years when, to young eyes, the world,
With all the rough disparities of fortune,
Floats level thro' the morning haze of fancy,
He loved the heiress of a lordly house:
She, scarce from childhood, listening, loved again,
And secret nuptials hallowed stolen meetings—
'Till one—I know not whom (perchance a kinsman,
Heir to that house—if childless died its daughter)
Spied—tracked the bridegroom to the bridal bower,
Aroused the sire, and said, "Thy child's dishonored!"
Snatching his sword, the father sought the chamber:
Burst the closed portal—but his lifted hand
Escaped the crime. Cold as a fallen statue,
Cast from its blessed pedestal for ever,
The bride lay senseless on the lonely floor
By the oped casement, from whose terrible height
The generous boy, to save her life or honor,
Had plunged into his own sure death below.
   Vyv. A happy death, if it saved her he loved!
   Alton. A midnight grave concealed the mangled clay,
And buried the bride's secret. Few nights after,
Darkly as life from him had passed away,
Life dawned on thee—and, from the unconscious mother,
Stern hands conveyed the pledge of fatal nuptials
To the poor priest, who to thy loftier kindred
Owed the mean roof that sheltered thee.
   Vyv.   Oh say
I have a mother still!
   Alton.   Yes, she survived—
Her vows, thy birth, by the blind world unguessed;
And, after years of woe and vain resistance,
Forced to a lordlier husband's arms.
   Vyv.   My soul

Ofttimes recalls a shadowy Mournfulness,
With woman's patient brow, and saddest tears
Dropped fast from woman's eyes;—they were my mother's.

 Alton. In stealth a wife—in stealth a mother! yes,
Then did she love thee, *then* aspired to own
In coming times, and bade me hoard these proofs
For that blest day. But, ah! with the new ties
Came new affections—to the second nuptials
A second son was born; she loved him better,
Better than thee—than her own soul!

 Vyv.   Poor mother!

 Alton. And haughtier thoughts on riper life arose,
And worldly greatness feared the world's dread shame,
And she forsook her visits to thy pillow,
And the sire threatened and the kinsman prayed,
Till, over-urged by terror for thy safety,
I took reluctant vows to mask the truth,
And hush thy rights while lived thy mother's sire,
And he, her second unsuspecting lord.
Thus thy youth, nameless, left my lonely roof.
The sire and husband died while thou wert absent.
Thou liv'st—thou hast returned; mine oath is freed;
These scrolls attest my tale and prove thy birthright—
Hail, Lord of Beaufort—Heir of Montreville!

 Vyv. 'Tis she—'tis she! At the first glance I loved her!
And when I told my woes, she wept—she wept!
This is her writing. Look—look where she calls me
"Edmond and child." Old man, how thou hast wronged her!
Joy—joy! I fly to claim and find a Mother!   [*Exit* VYVYAN.

 Alton. Just Power, propitiate Nature to that cry.
And from the hardened rock, let living streams
Gush as in Horeb! Ah, how faintly flags,
Strained by unwonted action, weary age!
I'll seek the neighboring hamlet—rest and pray.   [*Exit* ALTON.

SCENE II.

The exterior of the castle, as in Scene II., Act II. *Sunset. The twilight creeps on during the scene.*

Enter SIR GREY *and* WRECKLYFFE.

 Sir G. The priest had left his home?
 Wreck.   The hour I reached it.
 Sir G. With but one man? Didst thou not hound the foot-track?
 Wreck. I did.
 Sir G.   Thou didst—and yet the prey escaped!
I have done: I gave thee thy soul's wish, revenge,
Revenge on Vyvyan—and thou leav'st his way

Clear to a height as high from thy revenge
As is yon watch-tower from a pirate's gibbet.

   Wreck. Silence ! thou——

   Sir G. [*haughtily*].   Sir !

   Wreck. [*subdued and cowed*]. Along the moors I track'd them,
But only came in sight and reach of spring
Just as they gained the broad and thronging road,
Aloud with eager strides, and clamorous voices—
A surge of tumult, wave to wave rebooming
How all the might of Parma and of Spain
Hurried its thunders on.

   Sir G.   Dolt, what to us
Parma and Spain? The beggar has no country !

   Wreck. But deeds like that which thou dost urge me to
Are not risked madly in the populous day.
I come to thy sharp wit for safer orders.

   Sir G. My wit is dulled by time, and must be ground
Into an edge by thought. Hist !—the door jars,
She comes. Skulk yonder—hide thee—but in call !
A moment sometimes makes or marreth fortune,
Just as the fiend Occasion springs to hand—
Be *thou* that fiend !   [WRECKLYFFE *passes among the trees, and exit.*

Enter LADY MONTREVILLE *from the cloister.*

   Lady M.   Look on me! What, nor tremble?
Couldst thou have deemed my father's gold a bribe
For my son's murder? Sold to pirates ! Cast
On the wild seas !

   Sir G.   How ! I knew nought of this.
If such the truth, peace to thy father's sins,
For of those sins is this. Let the past sleep,
Meet present ills—the priest hath left his home
With Vyvyan's comrade, and our scheme is foiled.

   Lady M. I will, myself, see Alton on the morrow—
Edmond can scarce forestall me ; for this night
Fear sails with him to the far Indian main.

   Sir G. Let me do homage to thy genius. Sorceress,
What was thy magic?

   Lady M.   Terror for my Clarence,
And Edmond's love for Eveline.

   Sir G. [*aside*].   I see !
Bribed by the price of which she robs his rival !—
This night—so soon?—this night——

   Lady M.   I save my Clarence !
Till then, keep close, close to his side. Thou hast soothed him?

   Sir G. Fear not—these sudden tidings of the foe
With larger fires have paled receding love—
But where is Vyvyan?

   Lady M.   Doubtless with his crew,
Preparing for departure.

   Lord B. [*without*]. This way, Marsden.

Enter Lord Beaufort, *with* Marsden *and armed* Attendants.

    Lord B. Repair yon broken parapets at dawn ;
Yonder the culverins !—delve down more sharply
That bank ;—clear out the moat. Those trees—eh, Marsden,—
Should fall ? They'd serve to screen the foe ! Ah mother,
Make a scarf to wear above the armor
In which thy father, 'mid the shouts of kings,
Shivered French lances at the Cloth of Gold.
    Mars. Nay, my young lord, too vast for you that armor.
    Lord B. No; you forget that the breast swells in danger,
And honor adds a cubit to the stature.
    Lady M. Embrace me, Clarence, I myself will arm thee.
Look at him, Marsden—yet they say I spoil him !
    Sir G. [*who has been leaning over the low parapet, advances, draws aside* Lady
        Montreville *and whispers.*
I mark i' the distance, swift disordered strides,
And the light bound of an impatient spirit;
Vyvyan speeds hither, and the speed seems joy.
He sought his crew—Alton might there await him.
    Lady M. His speed is to a bride.
    Sir G.   Ay, true—old age
Forgets that Love's as eager as Ambition;
Yet hold thyself prepared.
    Lady M. [*to herself.*]   And if it were so !
Come, I will sound the depths of Beaufort's heart;
And, as that answers, hush or yield to conscience.
Lead off these men.   [*Exeunt* Sir Grey *and* Attendants.
[*To* Marsden.]   Go, meet my this day's guest,
And see he enter through the garden postern.   [*Exit* Marsden.
Clarence, come back.
    Lord B. [*peevishly.*]. What now ?
    Lady M.   Speak kindly, **Clarence.**
Alas, thou'lt know not till the grave close o'er me,
How I did need thy kindness !
    Lord B.   Pardon, mother,
My blunt speech now, and froward heat this morning.
    Lady M. Be all such follies of the past, as leaves
Shed from the petals of the bursting flower.
Think thy soul slept, till honor's sudden dawn
Flashed, and the soil bloomed with one more hero !
Ah, Clarence, had I, too, an elder-born,
As had thy father by his former nuptials !—
Could thy sword carve out fortune ?
    Lord B.   Ay, my mother !
    Lady M. Well the bold answer rushes from thy lips !
Yet, tell me frankly, dost thou not, in truth,
Prize over much the outward show of things;
And couldst thou—rich with valor, health and beauty,
And hope—the priceless treasure of the young—
Couldst thou endure descent from that vain height
Where pride builds towers the heart inhabits not;
To live less gorgeously, and curb thy wants

Within the state, not of the heir to earls,
But of a simple gentleman?
    Lord B.   If reared to it,
Perchance contented so; but *now*—no, never!
Such as I am, thy lofty self hath made me;
Ambitious, haughty, prodigal; and pomp
A part of my very life. If I could fall
From my high state, it were as Romans fell,
On their swords' point! Why is your check so hueless?
Why daunt yourself with airiest fantasies?
Who can deprive me of mine heritage—
The titles borne at Palestine and Crecy,
The seignory, ancient as the throne it guards,
That will be mine in trust for sons unborn,
When time—from this day may the date be far!
Transfers the circlet on thy stately brows
(Forgive the boast!) to no unworthy heir?
    Lady M. [*aside*]. My proud soul speaks in his, and still remorse;
I'll know no other son! Now go, Lord Beaufort.
    Lord B. So formal—fie!—has Clarence then offended?
    Lady M. Offended?—thou! Resume thy noble duties,
Sole heir of Montreville!   [*Exit* LORD BEAUFORT.
                        My choice is made.
As one who holds a fortress for his king,
I guard this heart for Clarence, and I close
Its gates against the stranger. Let him come.   [*Exit*

Enter VYVYAN *and* EVELINE. *Twilight, but still clear; a few stars come out gradually.*

    Evel. I would not bid thee stay, thy country calls thee—
But thou hast stunned my heart i' the midst of joy
With this dread sudden word—part—part!
    Vyv.   Live not
In the brief present. Go forth to the future!
Wouldst thou not see me worthier of thy love?
    Evel. Thou canst not be so.
    Vyv.   Sweet one, I am now.
Obscure and nameless. What, if at thy feet
I could lay rank and fortune?
    Evel.   These could give
To me no bliss save as they blest thyself.
Into the life of him she loves, the life
Of woman flows, and nevermore reflects
Sunshine or shadow on a separate wave.
Be his lot great, for his sake she loves greatness;
Humble—a cot with *him* is Arcady!
Thou art ambitious; thou wouldst arm for fame,
Fame then fires me too, and without a tear,
I bid thee go where fame is won—as now;
Win it and I rejoice; but fail to win,
Were it not joy to think I could console?
    Vyv. O that I could give vent to this full heart!
Time rushes on, each glimmering star rebukes me—
Is that the Countess yonder? This way—come.   [*Retire up the stage.*

Enter LORD BEAUFORT *and* SIR GREY.

Lord B. Leave England, say'st thou—and with her?
Sir G. Thou hast wrung
The secret from me. Mark—I have thy promise
Not to betray me to thy mother.
Lord B. Ah!
Thought she to dupe me with that pomp of words,
And blind ambition while she beggared life?
No, by yon heavens, she shall not so befool me!
Sir G. Be patient. Had I guessed how this had galled,
I had been dumb.
Lord B. Stand from the light! Distraction!
She hangs upon his breast!

[*Hurries to* VYVYAN, *and then, uncovering with an attempt at courtesy, draws him to the front of the stage.*

[WRECKLYFFE, *who at the first entrance of* VYVYAN, *has looked forth and glided after him, as if not to lose sight of his revenge, now creeps through the foilage, within hearing.*

Lord B. Sir, one word with you.
This day such looks and converse passed between us
As men who wear these vouchers for esteem,
Cancel with deeds.
Vyv. [*aside*]. The brave boy! How I love him!
Lord B. What saidst thou, sir?
Evel. [*approaching*]. Oh, Clarence.
Lord B. Fear not, cousin.
I do but make excuses for my rudeness
At noon, to this fair cavalier.
Sir G. If so,
Let us not mar such courteous purpose, lady,
Evel. But—
Sir G. Nay, you are too timid! [*Draws* EVELINE *away.*
Lord B. Be we brief, sir,
You quit these parts to-night. This place beseems not
The only conference we should hold. I pray you
Name spot and hour in which to meet again,
Unwitnessed save by the broad early moon.
Vyv. Meet thee again—oh yes!
Lord B. There speaks a soldier,
And now I own an equal. Hour and place?
Vyv. Wait here till I have—
Lord B. No, sir, on thy road.
Here we are spied.
Vyv. So be it, on my road.
[*Aside.* There where I learned that heaven had given a brother,
There the embrace.] Within the hour I pass
St. Kinian's Cliff.
Lord B. Alone?
Vyv. Alone.
Lord B. Farewell!
Sir G. [*catching at* LORD BEAUFORT *as he goes out*]. I heard St. Kinian's Cliff.
I'll warn the Countess.
Lord B. Do it, and famish!

Sir G.   Well, thy fence is skilful.
Lord B. And my hand firm.
Sir G.   But when?
Lord B.   Within the hour!
                                                                  [*Exit* LORD BEAUFORT.

Evel. I do conjure thee on thine honor, Vyvyan,
Hath he not——
    Vyv.   What?
    Evel.   Forced quarrel on thee?
    Vyv.   Quarrel!
That were beyond his power. Upon mine honor,
No, and thrice no!
    Evel.   I scarce dare yet believe thee.
    Vyv. Why then, I thus defy thee still to tremble.
Away this weapon! [*throwing down his sword*]. If I meet thy cousin,
Both must be safe, for one will be unarmed.
    Evel. Mine own frank hero-lover, pardon me;
Yet need'st thou not——
    Vyv.   Oh, as against the Spaniard,
There will be swords enow in Vyvyan's war-ship—
But art thou sure his heart is touched so lightly?
    Evel. Jealous, and now!
    Vyv.   No, the fair boy, 'tis pity!

                        Enter MARSDEN.

    Mars. My lady, Sir, invites you to her presence;
Pray you, this way.
    Evel.   Remember—O, remember
One word again, before we part; but one!
    Vyv. One word. Heaven make it joyous.
    Evel.   Joyous!
    Vyv. Soft, let me take that echo from thy lips
As a good omen. How my loud heart beats! [*aside*].
Friend, to your lady.   [*Exeunt* VYVYAN *and* MARSDEN *within the castle.*
    Evel.   Gone! The twilight world
Hath its stars still—but mine! Ah, woe is me!   [*Exit* EVELINE.
    Sir G. Why take the challenge, yet cast off the weapon?
Perchance, if, gentle he forbears the boy;
Perchance, if wordly wise, he fears the noble;
Or hath he, in his absence, chanced with Alton?
It matters not. Like some dark necromancer,
I raise the storm, then rule it thro' the fiend!
Where waits this man without a hope?
    Wreck. [*advancing*].   Save vengeance!
    Sir G. Wert thou not as near when Beaufort spoke with Vyvyan?
    Wreck. Shall I repeat what Vyvyan said to Beaufort?
    Sir G. Thou know'st——
    Wreck.   I know, that to St. Kinian's Cliff
Will come the man whose hand wrote "felon" here.
    Sir G. Mark, what I ask is harder than to strike;
'Tis to forbear—but 'tis revenge with safety.
Let Vyvyan first meet Beaufort; watch what pass,
And if the boy, whose hand obeys all passion,

Should slay thy foeman, and forestall thy vengeance,
Upon thy life (thou know'st, of old, Grey Malpas)
Prevent not, nor assist.
    Wreck.   That boy slay Vyvyan!
    Sir G. For Vyvyan is unarmed.
    Wreck.   Law calls that—murder!
    Sir G. Which by thy witness, not unbacked by proof,
Would give the murderer to the headsman's axe,
And leave Grey Malpas heir of Montreville,
And thee the richest squire in all his train.
    Wreck. I do conceive the scheme. But if the youth
Fail or relent——
    Sir G.   I balk not thy revenge.
And, if the corpse of Beaufort's rival be
Found on the spot where armed Beaufort met him,
To whom would justice track the death blow?—Beaufort!
    Wreck. No further words. Or his, or mine the hand,
Count one life less on earth; and weave thy schemes—
As doth the worm its coils—around the dead.   [*Exit* WRECKLYFFE.
    Sir G. One death avails as three, since for the mother
Conscience and shame were sharper than the steel.
So, I o'erleap the gulf, nor gaze below.
On this side, desolate ruin; bread begrudged;
And ribald scorn on impotent gray hairs;
The base poor cousin Boyhood threats with famine—
Whose very dog is butchered if it bark:—
On that side bended knees and fawning smiles,
Ho! ho! there—Room for my Lord's knights and pages!
Room at the Court—room there, beside the throne!
Ah, the new Earl of Montreville! His lands
Cover two shires. Such men should rule the state—
A gracious lord—the envious call him old;
Not so—the coronet conceals gray hairs.
He limp'd, they say, when he wore hose of serge.
Tut, the slow march becomes the robes of ermine.
Back, Conscience, back! Go scowl on boors and beggars—
Room, smiling flatterers, room for the new Earl!   [*Exit* SIR GREY.

ACT IV.—SCENE I.

Lady Montreville's *apartment as in* Sc. I., Act II. *Lights. During the scene the moon rises, seen through the casement.* Lady Montreville *seated.*

Enter Vyvyan.

Lady M. Thou com'st already to demand thy bride?
Vyv. Alas! such nuptials are deferred. This night
The invader summons me—my sole bride, Honor,
And my sole altar—England! [*Aside.*] How to break it?
Lady M. My Clarence on the land, and thou on sea,
Both for their country armed! Heaven shield ye both!
Vyv. Say thou that?—*Both?*—You, who so love your son?
Lady M. Better than life, I love him!
Vyv. [*aside*]. I must rush
Into the thick. Time goads me! [*Aloud.*] Had you not
Another son? A first-born?
Lady M. Sir!
Vyv. A son,
On whom those eyes dwelt first—whose infant cry
Broke first on that divine and holiest chord
In the deep heart of woman, which awakes
All Nature's tenderest music? Turn not from me!
I know the mystery of thy mournful life.
Will it displease thee—will it—to believe
That son is living still?
Lady M. Sir—sir—such license
Expels your listener [*rises*].
Vyv. No, thou wilt not leave me?
I say, thou wilt not leave me—on my knees
I say, thou *shalt* not leave me!
Lady M. Loose thine hold!
Vyv. I am thy son—thine Edmond—thine own child!
Saved from the steel, the deep, the storm, the battle;
Rising from death to thee—the source of life!
Flung by kind heaven once more upon thy breast,
Kissing thy robe, and clinging to thy knees.
Dost thou reject thy son?
Lady M. I have no son,
Save Clarence Beaufort.
Vyv. Do not—do not hear her,
Thou who, enthroned amid the pomp of stars,
Dost take no holier name than that of Father!
Thou hast no other son? O, cruel one!
Look—look—these letters to the priest who reared him—
See where thou call'st him "Edmond"—"child"—"life's all!"

Can the words be so fresh on this frail record,
Yet fade, obliterate from the undying soul?
By these—by these—by all the solemn past,
By thy youth's lover—by his secret grave—
By every kiss upon thine infant's cheek—
By every tear that wept his fancied death—
Grieve not that still a first-born calls thee "Mother!"

   Lady M. Rise. If these prove that such a son once lived,
Where are your proofs that still he lives in you?

   Vyv. There! in thine heart!—thine eyes that dare not face me!
Thy trembling limbs, each power, each pulse of being,
That vibrates at my voice! Let pride encase thee
With nine-fold adamant, it rends asunder
At the great spell of Nature—Nature calls;
Parent, come forth!

   Lady M. [*aside*]. Resolve gives way! Lost Clarence!
What! "Fall as Romans fell, on their swords' point?"
No, Clarence, no! [*turning fiercely*]. Impostor! If thy craft
Hath, by suborning most unworthy spies,
Sought in the ruins of a mourner's life
Some base whereon to pile this labored falsehood,
Let law laugh down the fable—Quit my presence.

   Vyv. No. I will not.

   Lady M.   Will not! Ho!

   Vyv.   Call your hirelings,
And let them hear me [*striding to the hearth*]. Lo, beneath thy roof,
And on the sacred hearth of sires to both,
Under their 'scutcheon, and before their forms
Which from the ghostly canvas I invoke
To hail their son—I take my dauntless stand,
Armed with my rights; now bid your menials thrust
From his own hearth the heir of Montreville!

               Enter Servants.

   Lady M. Seize on——[*Clasping her hands before her face.*] Out—out! His
        father stands before me
In the son's image. No, I dare not!

   Servant.   Madam,
Did you not summon us?

   Vyv.   They wait your mandate,
Lady of Montreville.

   Lady M.   I called not, Go!   [*Exeunt* Servants.
Art thou my son? If so, have mercy, Edmond!
Let Heaven attest with what remorseful soul
I yielded to my ruthless father's will,
And with cold lips profaned a second vow.
I *had* a child—I was a parent, true;
But exiled from the parent's paradise,
Not mine the frank joy in the face of day,
The pride, the boast, the triumph, and the rapture;
Thy couch was sought as with a felon's step,
And whispering nature shuddered at detection.
Oh, could'st thou guess what hell to the loftier minds

It is to live in one eternal lie !
Yet, spite of all, how dear thou *wert !*
  Vyv.   I was ?
Is the time past for ever ? What my sin ?
  Lady M. I loved thee till another son was born,
A blossom 'mid the snows. Thou wert afar,
Seen rarely—alien—on a stranger's breast
Leaning for life. But this thrice-blessed one
Smiled in mine eyes, took being from my breast,
Slept in mine arms; here love asked no concealment—
Here the tear shamed not—here the kiss was glory—
Here I put on my royalty of woman—
The guardian, the protector: food, health, life—
It clung to me for all. Mother and child,
Each was the all to each.
  Vyv.   O, prodigal,
Such wealth to him, yet nought to spare to me !
  Lady M. My boy grew up, my Clarence. Looking on him
Men prized his mother more—so fair and gracious,
And the world deemed to such high state the heir !
Years went; they told me that by Nature's death
Thou hadst in boyhood passed away to heaven,
I wept thy fate; and long ere tears were dried,
The thought that danger, too, expired for Clarence,
Did make thy memory gentle.
  Vyv.   Do you wish
That I were still what once you wept to deem me ?
  Lady M. I did rejoice when my lip kissed thy brow;
I did rejoice to give thy heart its bride;
I would have drained my coffers for her dowry;
But wouldst thou ask me if I can rejoice
That a life rises from the grave abrupt
To doom the life I cradled, reared, and wrapt
From every breeze, to desolation ?—No !
  Vyv. What would you have me do ?
  Lady M.   Accept the dowry,
And, blest with Eveline's love, renounce thy mother.
  Vyv. Renounce thee ! No—*these* lips belie not Nature !
Never !
  Lady M. Eno'—I can be mean no more,
Ev'n in the prayer that asked his life. Go, slay it.
  Vyv. Why must my life slay his ?
  Lady M.   Since his was shaped
To soar to power—not grovel to dependence—
And I do seal his death-writ when I say,
" Down to the dust, Usurper; bow the knee
And sue for alms to the true Lord of Beaufort."
Those words shall not be said—I'll find some nobler.
Thy rights are clear. The law might long defer them—
I do forestall the law. These lands be thine.
Wait not my death to lord it in my hall:
Thus I say not to Clarence, " Be dependent "—
But I *can* say, " Share poverty with me."

I go to seek him; at his side depart;
He spurns thine alms:—I wronged thee—take thy vengeance!

Vyv. Merciless—hold, and hear me—I—alms!—vengeance!—
True—true, this heart a mother never cradled,
Or she had known it better.

    Lady M.   Edmond!

    Vyv.   Hush!
Call me that name no more—it dies for ever!
Nay, I renounce thee not, for that were treason
On the child's lip. Parent, renounce thy child!
As for these nothings [*giving the papers*], take them; if you dread
To find words, once too fond, they're blurr'd already—
You'll see but tears: tears of such sweetness, madam.
I did not think of lands and halls, pale Countess,
I did but think—these arms shall clasp a mother.
Now they are worthless—take them. Never guess
How covetous I was—how hearts cast off,
Pine for their rights—rights not a parchment, lady.
Part we, then, thus? No, put thine arms around me;
Let me remember in the years to come,
That I have lived to say, a mother blessed me!

    Lady M. Oh, Edmond, Edmond, thou hast conquered, Edmond!
Thy father's voice!—his eyes! Look down from heaven,
Bridegroom, and pardon me; I bless thy child!

    Vyv. Hark! she has blessed her son! It mounts to heaven,
The blessing of the mother on her child!
Mother, and mother;—how the word thrills thro' me!
Mother, again dear mother! Place thy hand
Here—on my heart. Now thou hast felt it beat,
Wilt thou misjudge it more? Recoil'st thou still?

    Lady M. [*breaking from him*]. What have I done?—betrayed, condemned my Clarence!

    Vyv. Condemned thy Clarence! By thy blessing, No!
That blessing was my birthright. I have won
That which I claimed. Give Clarence all the rest.
Silent, as sacred, be the memory
Of this atoning hour. Look, evermore [*kissing her*]
Thus—thus I seal the secret of thy first born!
Now, only Clarence lives! Heaven guard thy Clarence!
Now deem me dead to thee. Farewell, farewell!   [*Exit* VYVYAN.

    Lady M. [*rushing after him*]. Hold, hold—too generous, hold! Come back, my son!   [*Exit* LADY MONTREVILLE.

SCENE II.

St. Kinian's Cliff. The ship on the sea. WRECKLYFFE *standing in the shadow of a broken rock.*

    Enter LORD BEAUFORT.

    Lord B. And still not here! The hour has long since passed.
I'll climb yon tallest peak, and strain mine eyes
Down the sole path between the cliff and ocean.   [*Exit* LORD BEAUFORT.

Wreck. [*advancing*]. The boors first grinned, then paled, and crept away;
The tavern-keeper slunk, and muttered "Hangdog!"
And the she-drudge whose rough hand served the drink,
Stifled her shriek, and let the tankard fall!
It was not so in the old merry days:
Then the scarred hangdog was "fair gentleman."
And—but the reckoning waits. Why tarries he? [*Signal gun from the ship.*
A signal! Ha!

Vyv. [*without*]. I come! I come!

Wreck. [*grasping his knife but receding as he sees* BEAUFORT, *who appears above*].
                                    Hot lordling!
I had well nigh forestalled thee. Patience!
    [*Creeps under the shadow of the rock, and thence steals out of sight in the background.*

                Enter LORD BEAUFORT.

Lord B.   Good!
From crag to crag he bounds—my doubts belied him;
His haste is eager as my own.

                Enter VYVYAN.

                Sir, welcome.

Vyv. Stay me not, stay me not! Thou hast all else
But honor—rob me not of that! Unhand me!

Lord B. Unhand thee? yes—to take thy ground and draw.

Vyv. Thou know'st not what thou sayest. Let me go!

Lord B. Thyself didst name the place and hour!

Vyv.   For here
I thought to clasp—[*aside*] I have no brother now!

Lord B. He thought to clasp his Eveline. Death and madness!

Vyv. Eveline! Thou lov'st not Eveline. Be consoled.
Thou hast not known affliction—hast not stood
Without the porch of the sweet home of men;
Thou hast leaned upon no reed that pierced the heart;
Thou hast not known what it is, when in the desert
The hopeless find the fountain: happy boy,
Thou hast not loved. Leave love to man and sorrow!

Lord B. Dost thou presume upon my years? Dull scoffer!
The brave is man betimes—the coward never.
Boy if I be, my playmates have been veterans;
My toy a sword, and my first lesson valor.
And, had I taken challenge as thou hast,
And on the ground replied to bold defiance
With random words implying dastard taunts,
With folded arms, pale lip, and haggard brow,
I'd never live to call myself a man.
Thus says the boy, since manhood is so sluggard,
Soldier and captain. Do not let me strike thee!

Vyv. Do it,—and tell thy mother, when thy hand
Outraged my cheek, I pardoned thee, and pitied.

Lord B. Measureless insult! Pitied! [*Second gun.*

Vyv.   There, again!
And still so far! Out of my path, insane one!

Were there nought else, thy youth, thy mother's love
Should make thee sacred to a warrior's arm—
Out of my path.   Thus, then   [*suddenly lifts, and puts him aside*].
              Oh, England—England !
Do not reject me too !—I come ! I come !   [*Exit up the cliff.*
   Lord B. Thrust from his pathway—every vein runs fire !
Thou shalt not thus escape me—Stand or die !   [*Rushes after him.*]
   [VYVYAN *retreats to the edge of the cliff, and grasps for support at the bough
      of a tree.*
   Vyv. Forbear, forbear !
   Lord B.   Thy blood on thine own head !   [*Third gun.*
   [*As* BEAUFORT *lifts his sword and strikes,* VYVYAN *retreats—the bough breaks,
      and* VYVYAN *falls down the precipice.*
   Wreck. [*who has followed part of the way, peering down the precipice*].—Is the
      deed done ?   If not this steel completes it.   [*Descends the cliff, and disappears.*
   [LORD BEAUFORT *sinks on his knee in horror.   The ship sails on as the scene
      closes slowly.*

ACT V.—SCENE I.

St. Kinian's Cliff.   A year is supposed to have passed since the date of Act IV.

Enter SIR GREY DE MALPAS.

   Sir G. A year—and Wreckliffe still is mute and absent.
Even as Vyvyan is !   Most clear !   He saw,
And haply shared, the murderous deed of Beaufort;
And Beaufort's wealth hath bribed him to desert
Penury and me.   That Clarence slew his brother
I cannot doubt.   He shuts me from his presence;
But I have watched him, wandering, lone, yet haunted—
Marked the white lip and glassy eyes of one
For whom the grave has ghosts, and silence, horror.
His mother, on vague pretext of mistrust
That I did sell her first-born to the pirate,
Excludes me from her sight, but sends me alms
Lest the world cry, "See, her poor cousin starves !"
Can she guess Beaufort's guilt ?   Nay !   For she lives !
I know that deed, which, told unto the world,
Would make me heir of Montreville.   O, mockery !
For how proceed ?—no proof !   How charge ?—no witness !
How cry, "Lo ! murder !" yet produce no corpse !

Enter ALTON.

   Alton. Sir Grey de Malpas !   I was on my way
To your own house.
   Sir G.   Good Alton—can I serve you ?
   Alton. The boy I took from thee, returned a man
Twelve months ago: mine oath absolved.
   Sir G.   'Tis true.

Alton. Here did I hail the rightful lord of Montreville,
And from these arms he rushed to claim his birthright.

Sir G. [*aside*]. She never told me this.

Alton. That night, his war-ship
Sailed to our fleet. I deemed him with the battle.
Time went; Heaven's breath had scattered the Armada.
I sate at my porch to welcome him—he came not.
I said, "his mother had abjured her offspring,
And law detains him while he arms for justice."
Hope sustained patience till to-day.

Sir G. To-day?

Alton. The very friend who had led me to his breast
Returns, and——

Sir G. [*soothingly*]. Well?

Alton. He fought not with his country.

Sir G. And this cold friend lets question sleep a year?

Alton. His bark too rashly chased the flying foe;
Was wrecked on hostile shores; and he a prisoner.

Sir G. Lean on my arm, thou'rt faint.

Alton. Oh, Grey de Malpas,
Can men so vanish—save in murderous graves?
You turn away.

Sir G. What murder without motive?
And who had motive here?

Alton. Unnatural kindred.

Sir G. Kindred! Ensnare me not! Mine, too, that kindred.
Old man, beware how thou asperse Lord Beaufort!

Alton. Beaufort! Oh, horror! How the instinctive truth
Starts from thy lips.

Sir G. From mine—priest!

Alton. Not of man
Ask pardon, if accomplice——

Sir G. I accomplice!
Nay, since 'tis my good name thou sulliest now—
This is mine answer: Probe; examine; search;
And call on justice to belie thy slander.
Go, seek the aid of stout Sir Godfrey Seymour;
A dauntless magistrate; strict, upright, honest:
[*Aside.*] At heart a Puritan, and hates a Lord,
With other slides that fit into my grooves.

Alton. He bears with all the righteous name thou giv'st him.
Thy zeal acquits thyself.

Sir G. And charges none.

Alton. Heaven reads the heart. Man can but track the deed.
My task is stern. [*Exit* ALTON.

Sir G. Scent lies—suspicious dogs—
And with hot breath pants on the flight of conscience.
Ah! who comes here? Sharp wit, round all occasion!

Enter FALKNER *with* Sailors.

Falk. Learn all you can—when latest seen, and where—Meanwhile I seek yon towers. [*Exeunt* Sailors.

Sir G. Doubtless, fair sir.

I speak to Vyvyan's friend. My name is Malpas—
Can it be true, as Alton doth inform me,
That you suspect your comrade died by murder?
    Falk. Murder!
    Sir G.   And by a rival's hand? Amazed!
Yet surely so I did conceive the priest.
    Falk. Murder!—a rival!—true, he loved a maiden!
    Sir G. In yonder halls!
    Falk.   Despair! Am I too late
For all but vengeance! Speak, sir,—who this rival?
    Sir G. Vengeance!—fie!—seek those towers, and learn compassion,
Sad change, indeed, since here, at silent night,
Your Vyvyan met the challenge of Lord Beaufort.
    Falk. A challenge?—here?—at night?
    Sir. G.   Yes, this the place.
How sheer the edge! crag, cave, and chasm below!
If the foot slipped,—nay, let us think slipped heedless,—
Or some weak wounded man were headlong plunged,
What burial place more secret?
    Falk.   Hither, look!
Look where, far down the horrible descent,
Through some fresh cleft rush subterranean waves,
How wheel and circle ghastly swooping wings!
    Sir G. The sea-gulls ere a storm.
    Falk.   No! Heaven is clear!
The storm they tell, speeds lightning towards the guilty.
So have I seen the foul birds in lone creeks.
Sporting around the shipwrecked seamen's bones.
Guide me, ye spectral harbingers!   [*Descends the cliff.*
    Sir G.   From bough
To bough he swings—from peak to slippery peak
I see him dwindling down;—the loose stones rattle;
He falls—he falls—but 'lights on yonder ledge,
And from the glaring sun turns stedfast eyes
Where still the sea-gulls wheel; now crawls, now leaps;
Crags close around him—not a glimpse nor sound!
O, diver for the dead,—bring up but bones,
And round the scull I'll wreathe my coronet.   [*Scene closes on* SIR GREY *seated*

SCENE II.

A room in the castle of Montreville—with casement opening on a balcony that overhangs the sea.

    Enter LADY MONTREVILLE *and* MARSDEN.

    Lady M. Will he not hunt nor hawk? This constant gloom!
Canst thou not guess the cause? He *was* so joyous!
    Mars. Young plants need air and sun; man's youth the world.
Young men should pine for action. Comfort, madam.
The cause is clear, if you recall the date.
    Lady M. Thou hast marked the date.

Mars.   Since that bold seaman's visit.
    Lady M. Thy tongue runs riot, man. How should that stranger,—
I say a stranger, strike dismay in Beaufort?
    Mars. Dismay! Not that, but emulation!
    Lady M.   Ay!
You speak my thoughts, and I have prayed our Queen
To rank your young lord with her chivalry;
This day mine envoy should return.
    Mars.   This day?
Let me ride forth and meet him!
    Lady M.   Go!   [*Exit* MARSDEN.
                            'Tis true!
Such was the date. Hath Clarence guessed the secret—
Guessed that a first-born lives? I dread to question!
Yet sure the wronged was faithful, and the wrong
Is my heart's canker-worm and gnaws unseen.
Where wanderest thou, sad Edmond? Not one word
To say thou liv'st—thy very bride forsaken,
As if love, frozen at the parent well-spring,
Left every channel dry! What hollow tread,
Heavy and weary falls? Is that the step
Which touched the mean earth with a lightsome scorn,
As if the air its element?

Enter BEAUFORT—*his dress neglected—wrapped in a loose mantle of fur.*

    Lord B.   Cold! cold!
And I saw the beggar doff his frieze,
Warm in his rags. I shiver under ermine.
For me 'tis never summer—never—never!
    Lady M. How fares my precious one?
    Lord B.   Well;—but so cold.
Ho! there! without!

Enter Servant.

                        Wine—wine!   [*Exit* Servant.
    Lady M.   Alas! alas!
Why, this is fever—thy hand burns
    Lord B.   That hand!
Ay, *that* hand always burns

Re-enter Servant, *with wine, and a goblet of rich workmanship, set in jewels.*

                            Look you—the cup
The wondrous Tuscan jeweller, Cellini,
Made for a king! A king's gift to thy father!
What? Serve such gauds to me!
    Lady M.   Thyself so ordered
In the proud whims thy light heart made so graceful.
    Lord B. Was I proud once? Ha! ha! What's this?—not wine?
    Servant. The Malvoisie your lordship's friends, last year,
Esteemed your rarest.
    Lord B.   How one little year
Hath soured it in to nausea! Faugh—'tis rank.

Lady M. [*to* Servant]. Send for the leech—quick—go.   [*Exit* Servant.
Oh, Clarence! Clarence!
Is this the body's sickness, or the soul's?
Is it life's youngest sorrow, love misplaced?
Thou dost not still love Eveline?
    Lord B.   Did I love her?
    Lady M. Or one whose birth might more offend my pride?
Well, I *am* proud. But I would hail as daughter
The meanest maiden from whose smile thy lip
Caught smiles again. Thy smile is day to me.
    Lord B. Poor mother, fear not. Never hermit-monk,
Gazing on skulls in lone sepulchral cells,
Had heart as proof to woman's smile as mine.
    Lady M. The court—the camp—ambition—

Enter MARSDEN *with a letter.*

    Mars.   From the Queen!
       [*While the* COUNTESS *reads,* MARSDEN, *turning to* LORD BEAUFORT.
My dear young lord, be gay! The noblest knight
In all the land, Lord Essex, on his road
From conquered Cadiz, with the armed suite
That won his laurels, sends before to greet you,
And prays you will receive him in your halls.
    Lord B. The flower of England's gentry, spotless Essex!
Sully him not, old man, bid him pass on.
    Lady M. Joy, Beaufort, joy! August Elizabeth
Owns thee her knight, and bids thee wear her colors,
And break thy maiden lance for England's lady.
    Lord B. I will not go. Barbed steeds and knightly banners—
Baubles and gewgaws!
    Mars.   Glorious to the young.
    Lord B. Ay—to the young! Oh, when did poet-dreams
Ever shape forth such fairy land as youth!
Gossamer hopes, pearled with the dews of morn,
Gay valor, bounding light on welcome peril,—
Errors themselves, the sparkling overflow,
Of life as headlong, but as pure as streams
That rush from sunniest hill-tops kissing heaven,—
Lo! *that* is youth. Look on my soul, old man,
Well—is it not more gray than those blanched hairs?
    Lady M. He raves—heed not his words. Go, speed the leech!
                                                               [*Exit* MARSDEN.
    Lady M. [*aside*]. I know these signs—by mine own soul I know them;
This is nor love, nor honor's sigh for action,
Nor Nature's milder suffering. This is guilt!
Clarence—now, side by side, I sit with thee!
Put thine arms round me, lean upon my breast—
It is a mother's breast. So, that is well;
Now—whisper low—what is thy crime?
    Lord B. [*bursting into tears*].   O, mother!
Would thou hadst never born me!
    Lady M.   Ah, ungrateful!
    Lord B. No—for thy sake I speak. Thou—justly proud,

For thou art pure; thou, on whose whitest name
Detraction spies no soil—dost thou say " crime "
Unto thy son; and is his answer tears?

Enter EVELINE, *weaving flowers as in first act.*

Evel.—
    Blossoms, I weave ye
     To drift on the sea,
    Say when ye find him
    Who sang " Woe is me!"—

[*Approaching* BEAUFORT.] Have you no news?
Lord B.   Of whom?
Evel.   Of Vyvyan?
Lord B. That name! Her reason wanders; and O, mother,
When that name's uttered—so doth mine—hush, hush it.
     [EVELINE *goes to the balcony and throws the garland into the sea.*
Lady M. Kill me at once—or when I ask again,
What is thy crime?—reply, 'No harm to Vyvyan!'
  Lord B. [*breaking away*]. Unhand me! Let me go! [*Exit* LORD BEAUFORT.
  Lady M.   This pulse beats still!
Nature rejects me!
  Evel. [*from the balcony*]. Come, come—see the garland,
It dances on the waves so merrily.

Enter MARSDEN.

  Mars. [*drawing aside* LADY M.] Forgive this haste. Amid St. Kinian's cliffs,
Where, once an age, on glassy peaks may glide
The shadow of a man, a stranger venturing
Hath found bleached human bones, and to your hall,
Nearest at hand, and ever famed for justice,
Leads on the crowd, and saith the dead was Vyvyan.
  Evel. Ha! who named Vyvyan? Has he then come back?
  Mars. Fair mistress, no.
  Lady M.   If on this terrible earth
Pity lives still—lead her away. Be tender.
  Evel. [*approaching* LADY M.] I promised him to love you as a mother.
Kiss me, and trust in Heaven! He will return! [*Exeunt* EVELINE *and* MARSDEN
  Lady M. These horrors are unreal.

Enter a Servant.

  Servant.   Noble mistress,
Sir Godfrey Seymour, summoned here in haste,
Craves your high presence in the Justice Hall.
  Lady M. Mine—Mine? Where goest thou?
  Servant.   Sir Godfrey bade me
Seek my young lord.
  Lady M.   Stir not. My son is ill.
Thyself canst witness how the fever [*hurrying to the side scene*] Marsden!

Enter MARSDEN.

My stricken Clarence!—In his state, a rumor
Of—of what passes here, might blast life—reason:
Go, lure him hence—if he resist, use force

As to a maniac. Good old man, thou lov'st him;
His innocent childhood played around thy knees—
I know I can trust *thee*. Quick—speak not:—Save ! [*Exit* MARSDEN.
[*to* Servant.] Announce my coming. [*Exit* Servant.
        This day, life to shield
The living son:—Death, with the dead, to-morrow ! [*Exit* LADY MONTREVILLE.

SCENE III.

A vast feudal hall in the castle. At the extreme end, the carved screen work of later date, supporting the minstrels' gallery (similar to that in Hampton Court). The opening in the screen is made the principal entry on the scene. In another part of the hall a high Gothic casement forms a recess, over which a curtain is drawn aside. In the recess a tressel, serving as bier for the remains of the dead, which are covered with a cloth. At each side of the screen entry, a halberdier in the service of SIR GODFREY SEYMOUR, *officiating as constable.* ALTON *kneeling before the tressel in the the recess.*

In front of the stage, a table, before which SIR GODFREY SEYMOUR *seated. A* Clerk *employed in writing.* SIR GREY DE MALPAS *standing near* SIR GODFREY. FALKNER *a little apart.*

 Sir Godf. [*to* FALKNER]. Be patient, sir, and give us ample proof
To deem yon undistinguishable bones
The relics of your friend.
 Falk.   That gentleman
Can back my oath, that these, the plume, the gem
Which Vyvyan wore—I found them on the cliff.
 Sir Godf. Verily, is it so?
 Sir Grey. [*with assumed reluctance*]. Sith law compel me—
Yes, I must vouch it.

Enter Servant.

 Servant. [*placing a chair of state.*] Sir, my lady comes.
 Sir Godf Let not that sight appal her——
 Sir Grey.   And her son.
  [*Servant draws the curtain round the recess, leaving* ALTON *still kneeling
   within, and exit.*

Enter LADY MONTREVILLE, *and seats herself.*

 Sir Godf. You pardon, madam, mine imperious duties,
And know my dismal task——
 Lady M.   Pray you be brief, sir.
 Sir Godf. Was, this time year, the captain of a war-ship,
Vyvyan his name, your guest?
 Lady M.   But one short day—
To see my ward, whom he had saved from pirates.
 Sir Godf. I pray you, madam, in his converse with you
Spoke he of any foe, concealed or open,
Whom he had cause to fear?
 Lady M.   Of none !
 Sir Godf.   Nor know you
Of any such?

Lady M. [*after a pause*]. I do not.
Sir Godf. [*aside to* FALKNER]. Would you farther
Question this lady, sir?
Falk. No, she is woman,
And mother; let her go. I wait Lord Beaufort.
Sir Godf. Madam, no longer will we task your presence.

Enter LORD BEAUFORT, *breaking from* MARSDEN, *and other* Attendants.

Lord B. Off, dotard, off! Guests in our hall!
Lady M. He is ill.
Sore ill—fierce fever—I will lead him forth.
Come, Clarence; darling, come!
Lord B. Who is this man?
Falk. The friend of Vyvyan, whose pale bones plead yonder.
Lord B. I—I will go. Let's steal away, my mother.
[SIR GREY *intercepts the retreat of* BRAUFORT, *and, with by-play intimating
remonstrance and encouragement, urges him forward.*
Falk. Lost friend, in war, how oft thy word was 'spare.'—
Methinks I hear thee now. [*drawing aside* LORD BEAUFORT.]
Young lord, I came
In these halls, demanding blood for blood—
But thy remorse [this *is* remorse] disarms me.
Speak; do but say—(look, I am young myself,
And know how hot is youth;) speak—do but say,
After warm words, struck out from jealous frenzy,
Quick swords were drawn: Man's open strife with man—
Passion, not murder: Say this, and may law
Pardon thee, as a soldier does!
Sir Grey [*to* MARSDEN]. Call Eveline,
She can attest our young lord's innocence. [*Exit* MARSDEN.
Falk. He will not speak, sir, let my charge proceed.
Lady M. [*aside*] Whate'er the truth—of that—of that hereafter,
Now but remember, child, thy birth, thy name;
Thy mother's heart, it beats beside thee—take
Strength from its pulses.
Lord B. Keep close, and for thy sake
I will not cry—''Twas passion, yet still, murder!'
Sir Godf. [*who has been conversing aside with* SIR GREY]. Then jealous love the
motive? Likelier that
Than Alton's wilder story.

Enter EVELINE *and* MARSDEN.

Sweet young madam,
If I be blunt, forgive me; we are met
On solemn matters which relate to one
Who, it is said, was your betrothed:
Evel. To Vyvyan!
Sir Godf. 'Tis also said, Lord Beaufort crossed his suit,
And your betrothed resented.
Evel. No! forgave.
Sir Grey. Yes, when you feared some challenge from Lord Beaufort,
Did Vyvyan not cast down his sword and say,

'Both will be safe, for one will be unarmed?'

[*Great sensation through the hall.* FALKNER *and* SIR GODFREY *both.*] Unarmed!

Evel. His very words!

Falk. Oh, vile assassin!

Sir Godf. Accuser, peace! This is most grave. Lord Beaufort,
Upon such tokens, with your own strange bearing,
As ask appeal to more august tribunal,
You stand accused of purposed felon murder
On one named Vyvyan, Captain of the *Dreadnought*—
Wouldst thou say aught against this solemn charge?

Evel. Murdered!—he—Vyvyan! Thou his murderer, Clarence,
In whose rash heat my hero loved frank valor?
Lo! I, to whom his life is as the sun
Is to the world—with my calm trust in heaven
Mantle thee thus.

Lady M. [*aside*]. Be firm—deny, and live.

Lord B. [*with a vacillating attempt at his former haughtiness.*] You call my bearing "strange"—what marvel, sir?
Stunned by such charges, of a crime so dread.
What proof against me?

Lady M. [*whilst* LADY M. *speaks,* SIR GREY *steals behind the curtain.*] Words deposed by whom?
A man unknown;—a girl's vague fear of quarrel—
His motive what? A jealous anger! Phantom!
Is not mine son mine all?—And yet this maid
I plighted to another. Had I done so
If loved by him, and at the risk of life?
Again, I ask all present what the motive?

Alton. [*advancing from the recess with* SIR GREY]. Rank, fortune, birthright. Miserable woman!

Lady M. Whence com'st thou, pale accuser?

Alton. From the dead!
Which of ye two will take the post I leave?
Which of ye two will draw aside that veil,
Look on the bones behind, and cry, "I'm guiltless?"
Hast thou conspired with him to slay thy first-born,
Or knows he not that Vyvyan was his brother?

[LADY MONTREVILLE *swoons. Till now* EVELINE *has held to* BEAUFORT— *now she rushes to* LADY MONTREVILLE.

Lord B. My brother! No! no! no! [*clutching hold of* SIR GREY]. Kinsman, he lies!

Sir Grey. Alas!

Lord B. Wake, mother, wake. I ask not speech.
Lift but thy brow—one flash of thy proud eye
Would strike these liars dumb!

Alton. Read but those looks
To learn that thou art——

Lord B. Cain! [*grasping* FALKNER.] Out with thy sword—
Hew off this hand. Thou calledst me "Assassin!"
Too mild—say "Fratricide!" Cain, Cain, thy brother! [*Falls*

Evel. It cannot be so! No. Thou wondrous Mercy,
That from the pirate's knife, the funeral seas

And all their shapes of death, didst save the lone one,
To prove to earth how vainly man despairs
While God is in the heavens—I cling to thee,
As faith unto its anchor ! [*to* SIR GREY] Back, false kinsman !
I tell thee Vyvyan lives—the boy is guiltless !

Falk. Poor, noble maid ! How my heart bleeds for her !

Lady M. [*starting up*]. Sentence us both ! or stay,—would law condemn,
A child so young, if I had urged him to it ?

Sir Godf. Unnatural mother, hush ! Sir Grey, to you,
Perchance ere long, by lives too justly forfeit,
Raised to this earldom, I entrust these—prisoners.

   [*Motions to the halberdiers, who advance to arrest* BEAUFORT *and* LADY MONTREVILLE.

Mars. O, day of woe !

Sir Grey.   Woe—yes ! Make way for us.   [*Trumpet*

     Enter Servant.

Servant. My lord of Essex just hath passed the gates;
But an armed knight who rode beside the Earl,
After brief question to the crowd without,
Sprang from his steed, and forces here his way !

Enter KNIGHT *in half armor—wrapped in his horseman's cloak, his visor three parts down.*

Knight. Forgiveness of all present !

Sir Godf.   Who art thou ?

Knight. A soldier, knighted by the hand of Essex
Upon the breach of Cadiz.

Sir Godf.   What thy business ?

Knight. To speak the truth. Who is the man accused
Of Vyvyan's murder.

Sir Grey.   You behold him yonder.

Knight. 'Tis false.

Sir Grey.   His own lips have confessed his crime.

Knight. [*throwing down his gauntlet*]. This to the man whose crushing lie bows
  down
Upon the mother's bosom that young head !
Say you " confess'd ! " O tender, tender conscience !
Vyvyan, rough sailor, galled him and provoked;
He raised his hand. To the sharp verge of the cliff,
Vyvyan recoiled, backed by an outstretched bough.
The bough gave way—he fell, but not to perish;
Saved by a bush-grown ledge that broke his fall;
Long stunned he lay; when opening dizzy eyes,
On a gray crag between him and the abyss
He saw the face of an old pirate foe;
Saw the steel lifted, saw it flash and vanish,
As a dark mass rushed thro' the moonlit air
Dumb into deeps below—the indignant soil
Had slid like glass beneath the murderer's feet,
And his own death-spring whirled him to his doom.
Then Vyvyan rose, and, crawling down the rock,
Stood by the foe, who, stung to late remorse
By hastening death, gasped forth a dread confession.

The bones ye find are those of Murder's agent—
Murder's arch-schemer—Who?—Ho! Grey de Malpas,
Stand forth! Thou art the man!

  Sir Grey.   Hemm'd round with toils,
Soul, crouch no more! Base hireling, doff thy mask,
And my sword writes the lie upon thy front.
By Beaufort's hand died Vyvyan—

  Knight.   As the spell
Shatters the sorcerer when his fiends desert him,
Let thine own words bring doom upon thyself!
Now face the front on which to write the lie.   [*Casts off his helmet.*

    [SIR GREY *drops his sword and staggers back into the arms of the retainers.*

  Evel. Thou liv'st, thou liv'st—

  Vyv. [*kneeling to her*].   Is life worth something still?

  Sir Grey. Air, air—my staff—some chord seems broken here. [*Pressing his heart.*
Marsden, your lord shot his poor cousin's dog;
In the dog's grave—mark!—bury the poor cousin. [*Sinks exhausted, and is borne out.*

  Vyv. Mine all on earth, if I may call thee mine.

  Evel. Thine, thine, thro' life, thro' death—one heart, one grave!
I knew thou wouldst return, for I have lived
In thee so utterly, thou couldst not die
And I live still—the dial needs the sun;
But love reflects the image of the loved,
Tho' every beam be absent!—Thine, all thine!

  Lady M. My place is forfeited on thy breast, not his. [*Pointing to* BEAUFORT
Clarence, embrace thy brother, and my first-born.
His rights are clear—my love for thee suppressed them—
He may forgive me yet—wilt *thou?*

  Beau.   Forgive thee!
Oh mother, what is rank to him who hath stood
Banished from out the social pale of men,
Bowed like a slave, and trembling as a felon?
Heaven gives me back mine ermine, innocence;
And my lost dignity of manhood, honor.
I miss nought else.—Room there for me, my brother

  Vyv. Mother, come first!—love is as large as heaven!

  Falk. But why so long——

  Vyv.   What! could I face thee, friend,
Or claim my bride, till I had won back honor?
The fleet had sailed—the foeman was defeated—
And on the earth I laid me down to die.
The prince of England's youth, frank-hearted Essex,
Passed by——But later I will tell you how
Pity woke question; soldier felt for soldier.
Essex then, nobly envying Drake's renown,
Conceived a scheme, kept secret till our clarions,
Startling the towers of Spain, told earth and time
How England answers the invader. Clarence,
Look—I have won the golden spurs of knighthood!

For worldly gifts, we'll share them—hush, my brother;
Love me, and thy gift is as large as mine.
Fortune stints gold to some; impartial Nature

Shames her in proffering more than gold to all—
Joy in the sunshine, beauty on the earth,
And love reflected in the glass of conscience ;
Are these so mean ? Place grief and guilt beside them,
Decked in a sultan's splendor, and compare !
The world's most royal heritage is his
Who most enjoys, most loves, and most forgives.

WALPOLE;

OR,

EVERY MAN HAS HIS PRICE.

DRAMATIS PERSONÆ.

THE RIGHT HON. ROBERT WALPOLE, M.P., *Chancellor of the Exchequer, and First Lord of the Treasury.*
JOHN VEASEY, M.P., *his Confidant.*
SELDEN BLOUNT, M.P.
SIR SIDNEY BELLAIR, BART., M.P.
LORD NITHSDALE.
1ST JACOBITE LORD.
2D JACOBITE LORD.

Frequenters of Tom's Coffee-House, Servants, etc.

WOMEN.

LUCY WILMOT.   MRS. VIZARD.

Scene—London, 1716.

Time occupied by the Events of the Play—*One Day.*

WALPOLE.

ACT I.—SCENE I.

Tom's Coffee-house. In the background, gentlemen seated in different compartments, or "boxes."

Enter WALPOLE *and* VEASEY *from opposite sides.*

Vea. Ha! good day, my dear patron.
Wal.   Good day, my dear friend,
You can spare me five minutes?
Vea.   Five thousand.
Wal.   Attend;
I am just from the king, and I failed not to press him
To secure to his service John Veasey.
Vea.   God bless him!
Wal. George's resign, just begun, your tried worth will distinguish.
Vea. Oh, a true English king!
Wal.   Tho' he cannot speak English.
Vea. You must find that defect a misfortue, I fear.
Wal. The reverse; for no rivals can get at his ear.
It is something to be the one public man pat in
The new language that now governs England, dog Latin.
Vea. Happy thing for these kingdoms that you have that gift,
Or, alas! thro' what shoals all our counsels would drift.
Wal. Yes, the change from Queen Anne to King George we must own,
Renders me and the Whigs the sole props of the throne.
For the Tories their Jacobite leanings disgrace,
And a Whig is the only safe man for a place.
Vea. And the Walpoles of Houghton, in all their relations,
Have been Whigs to the backbone for three generations.
Wal. Ay, my father and mother contrived to produce
Their eighteen sucking Whigs for the family use,
Of which number one only, without due reflection,
Braved the wrath of her house by a Tory connection.
But, by Jove, if her Jacobite husband be living,
I will make him a Whig.
Vea.   How?
Wal.   By something worth giving:
For I loved her in boyhood, that pale pretty sister;
And in counting the Walpoles still left, I have mist her.
                  [*Pauses in emotion, but quickly recovers himself.*
What *was* it I said?—Oh,—the State and the Guelph,

For their safety, must henceforth depend on myself.
The revolt, scarcely quenched, has live sparks in its ashes;
Nay, fresh seeds for combustion were sown by its flashes.
Each example we make dangerous pity bequeathes;
For no Briton likes blood in the air that he breathes.

Vea. Yes: at least there's one rebel whose doom to the block
Tho' deserved, gives this soft-hearted people a shock.

Wal. Lord Nithsdale, you mean; handsome, young, and just wedded,—
A poor head, that would do us much harm if beheaded.

Vea. Yet they say you rejected all prayers for his life.

Wal. It is true; but in private I've talked to his wife:
She had orders to see him last night in the Tower.
And——

Vea. Well?

Wal. [*looking at his watch*]. Wait for the news—tis not yet quite the hour.
Ah! poor England, I fear, at the General Election,
Will vote strong in a mad anti-Whiggish direction.
From a Jacobite Parliament we must defend her,
Or the King will be Stuart, and Guelph the Pretender.
And I know but one measure to rescue our land
From the worst of all ills—Civil War.

Vea. True; we stand
At that dread turning-point in the life of a State
When its free choice would favor what freedom should hate;
When the popular cause, could we poll population——

Wal. Would be found the least popular thing in the nation.

Vea. Scarce a fourth of this people are sound in their reason——

Wal. But we can't hang the other three-fourths for high treason.

Vea. Tell me, what is the measure your wisdom proposes?

Wal. In its third year, by law, this Whig Parliament closes.
But the law! What's the law in a moment so critical?
Church and State must be saved from a House Jacobitical.
Let this Parliament then, under favor of heaven,
Lengthen out its existence from three years to seven.

Vea. Brilliant thought! could the State keep its present directors
Undisturbed for a time by those rowdy electors,
While this new German tree, just transplanted, takes root,
Dropping down on the lap of each friend golden fruit,
Britain then would be saved from all chance of reaction
To the craft and corruption of Jacobite faction.
But ah! think you the Commons would swallow the question?

Wal. That depends on what pills may assist their digestion,
I could make—see this list—our majority sure,
If by buying two men I could sixty secure;
For as each of these two is the chief of a section
That will vote black or white at its leader's direction,
Let the pipe of the shepherd but lure the bell-wether,
And he folds the whole flock, wool and cry, altogether.
Well, the first of these two worthy members you guess.

Vea. Sure, you cannot mean Blount, virtuous Selden Blount?

Wal. Yes.

Vea. What! your sternest opponent, half Cato, half Brutus,
He, whose vote incorruptible——

Wal.   Just now would suit us ;
For a patriot so stanch could with dauntless effrontery——
    Vea. Sell himself ?
    Wal.   Why, of course, for the good of his country.
True, his price will be high—he is worth forty votes,
And his salary must pay for the change in their coats.
Prithee, has not his zeal for his fatherland—rather
Overburthened the lands he received from his father ?
    Vea. Well, 'tis whispered in the clubs that his debts somewhat tease him.
    Wal. I must see him in private, and study to ease him.
Will you kindly arrange that he call upon me
At my home, not my office, to-day—just at three ?
Not a word that can hint at the object in view—
Say some bill in the House that concerns him and you ;
And on which, as distinct from all party disputes,
Members meet without tearing each other like brutes.
    Vea. Lucky thought—Blount and I both agree in Committee
On a bill for amending the dues of the City——
    Wal. And the Government wants to enlighten its soul
On the price which the public should pay for its coal.
We shall have him, this Puritan chief of my foes.
Now the next one to catch is the chief of the Beaux;
All our young members mimic his nod or his laugh;
And if Blount be worth forty votes, he is worth half.
    Vea. Eh ! Bellair, whose defence of the Jacobite peers——
    Wal. Thrilled the House; Mister Speaker himself was in tears.
Faith, I thought he'd have beat us.   [*Taking snuff.*
    Vea.   The fierce peroration——
    Wal. Which compared me to Nero—superb [*brushing the snuff from his lace lappet*] declamation !
    Vea. Yes; a very fine speaker.
    Wal.   Of that there's no doubt.
For he speaks about things he knows nothing about,
But I still to our party intend to unite him—
Secret Service Department—Bellair—a small item.
    Vea. Nay, you jest—for this gay maiden knight in debate,
To a promise so brilliant adds fortune so great——
    Wal. That he is not a man to be bought by hard cash;
But he's vain and conceited, light-hearted and rash.
Every favorite of fortune hopes still to be greater,
And a beau must want something to turn a debater.
Hem ! I know a Duke's daughter, young, sprightly, and fair;
She will wed as I wish her; hint that to Bellair;
Ay, and if he will put himself under my steerage,
Say that with the Duke's daughter I throw in the peerage.
    Vea. Those are baits that a vain man of wit may seduce.
    Wal. Or, if not, his political creed must be loose;
To some Jacobite plot he will not be a stranger,
And to win him securely——
    Vea.   We'll get him in danger.
Hist !   [*Enter* BELLAIR *humming a tune.*

SCENE II.

WALPOLE, VEASEY, BELLAIR.

Wal. Good morning, Sir Sidney; your speech did you credit;
And whatever your party, in time you will head it.
Your attack on myself was exceedingly striking,
Tho' the subject you chose was not quite to my liking.
Tut! I never bear malice.   You hunt?
    Bel.   Yes, of late.
    Wal. And you ride as you speak?
    Bel.   Well, in both a light weight
    Wal. But light weights have the odds in their favor, I fear.
Come and hunt with my harriers at Houghton this year;
I can show you some sport.
    Bel.   Sir, there's no doubt of that.
    Wal. We will turn out a fox.
    Bel. [*aside*].   As a bait for a rat!
    Wal. I expect you, next autumn!   Agreed then: good day.   [*Exit* WALPOLE

SCENE III.

VEASEY, BELLAIR.

    Bel. Well, I don't know a pleasanter man in his way;
'Tis no wonder his friends are so fond of their chief.
    Vea. That you are not among them is matter for grief.
Ah, a man of such stake in the land as yourself,
Could command any post in the Court of the Guelph.
    Bel. No, no; I'm appalled.
    Vea.   By the king?   Can you doubt him?
    Bel. I'm appalled by these Gorgons, the ladies about him.
    Vea. Good! ha, ha! yes, in beauty his taste may be wrong,
But he has what we want, sir, a government strong.
    Bel. Meaning petticoat government?   Mine too is such,
But my rulers don't frighten their subjects so much.
    Vea. Nay, your rulers?   Why plural!   Legitimate sway
Can admit but one ruler to love——
    Bel.   And obey.
What a wife!   Constitutional monarchy?   Well,
If I choose my own sovereign I might not rebel.
    Vea. You may choose at your will!   With your parts, wealth, condition,
You, in marriage, could link all the ends of ambition.
There *is* a young beauty—the highest in birth,
And her father, the Duke——
    Bel.   Oh, a duke!
    Vea.   Knows your worth.
Listen; Walpole, desiring to strengthen the Lords

With the very best men whom the country affords,
Has implied to his Grace, that his choice should be clear. [*Carelessly.*
If you wed the Duke's daughter, of course you're a peer.
    Bel. With the Lords and the lady would Walpole ally me?
    Vea. Yes; and if I were *you*——
    Bel.   He would certainly buy me;
But I,—being a man—— [*Draws himself up haughtily.*
    Vea.   No offence. Why that frown?
    Bel. [*relapsing into his habitual ease*]. Nay, forgive me. Tho' man, I'm
        a man about town;
And so graceful a compliment could not offend
Any man about town, from a Minister's friend.
Still, if not from the frailty of mortals exempt,
Can a mortal be tempted where sins do not tempt?
Of my rank and my fortune I *am* so conceited,
That I don't, with a wife, want those blessings repeated.
And tho' flattered to learn I should strengthen the Peers—
Give me still our rough House with its laughter and cheers.
Let the Lords have their chamber—I grudge not its powers;
But for badgering a Minister nothing like ours!
Whisper that to the Minister;—sir, your obedient. [*Turns away.*
    Vea. [*aside*]. Humph! I see we must hazard the ruder expedient.
If some Jacobite pit for his feet we can dig,
He shall hang as a Tory, or vote as a Whig. [VEASEY *retires into the background.*
    Bel. [*seating himself*]. Oh, how little these formalist middle-aged schemers
Know of *us* the bold youngsters, half sages, half dreamers!
Sages half? Yes, because of the time rushing on,
Part and parcel are *we: they* belong to time gone.
Dreamers half? Yes, because in a woman's fair face
We imagine the heaven they find in a place.
At this moment I, courted by Whig and by Tory,
For the spangles and tinsel which clothe me with glory,
Am a monster so callous, I should not feel sorrow
If an earthquake engulfed Whig and Tory to-morrow,
" What an heartless assertion!" the aged would say:
True, the young have no heart, for they give it away.
Ah, I love! and here—joy!—comes the man who may aid me. [*Enter* BLOUNT.

SCENE IV.

BELLAIR, BLOUNT, VEASEY, ETC.

Blount [*to Coffee-house loungers, who gather round him as he comes down the
    stage*]. Yes, sir, just from Guildhall, where the City has paid me
The great honor I never can merit enough,
Of this box, dedicated to Virtue—— [*Coffee-house loungers gather round.*
    Vea.   And snuff.
    Blount. Yes, sir, Higgins the Patriot, who deals in rappee,
Stored that box with pulvillio, superfluous to me:
For a public man gives his whole life to the nation,
And his nose has no time for a vain titillation.

Vea. On the dues upon coal—apropos of the City—
We agreed——
    Blount. And were beat; Walpole bribed the Committee.
    Vea. You mistake; he leans tow'rds us, and begs you to call
At his house—three o'clock.
    Blount [*declaiming as if in Parliament*]. But I say, once for all,
That the dues——
    Vea.   Put the case as you only can do,
And we carry the question.
    Blount.   I'll call, sir, at two.
    Vea. He said three.
    Blount.   I say *two*, sir; my honor's at stake,
To amend every motion that Ministers make. [VEASEY *retires into the background.*
    Blount [*advancing to* BELLAIR]. Young debater, your hand. One might tear into shreds
All your plea for not cutting off Jacobite heads;
But that burst against Walpole redeemed your whole speech,
Be but honest, and high is the fame you will reach.
    Bel. Blount, your praise would delight, but your caution offends.
    Blount. 'Tis my way—I'm plain spoken to foes and to friends.
What are talents but snares to mislead and pervert you,
Unless they converge in one end—Public Virtue!
Fine debaters abound: we applaud and despise them;
For when the House cheers them the Minister buys them.
Come, be honest, I say, sir—away with all doubt;
Public Virtue commands! Vote the Minister out!
    Bel. Public Virtue when construed means private ambition.
    Blount. This to me—to a Patriot——
    Bel.   In fierce opposition;
But you ask for my vote.
    Blount.   England wants every man.
    Bel. Well, tho' Walpole can't buy me, I think that you can.
Blount, I saw you last evening cloaked up to your chin;
But I had not a guess who lay, *perdu*, within
All those bales of broad cloth—when a gust of wind rose,
And uplifting your beaver it let out your nose.
    Blount [*somewhat confusedly*]. Yes, I always am cloaked—half disguised, when I go
Certain rounds—real charity hides itself so;
For one good deed concealed is worth fifty paraded.
    Bel. Finely said. Quitting, doubtless, the poor you had aided,
You shot by me, before I had time to accost you,
Down a court which contains but one house;—there I lost you.
    Blount. One house!
    Bel.   Where a widow named Vizard——
    Blount [*aside*].   I tremble.
Yes——
    Bel. Resides with an angel——
    Blount [*aside*].   'Twere best to dissemble.
With an angel! bah! say with a girl—what's her name?
    Bel. On this earth, Lucy Wilmot.
    Blount.   Eh!—Wilmot?
    Bel.   The same.

Blount [*after a short pause*].   And how knew you these ladies?
Bel.   Will you be my friend?
Blount. I? of course.   Tell me all from beginning to end.
Bel. Oh, my story is short.   Just a fortnight ago,
Coming home tow'rds the night from my club——
Blount.   Drunk?
Bel.   So, so.
"Help me, help!" cries a voice—'tis a woman's—I run—
Which may prove I'd drunk less than I often have done.
And I find—but, dear Blount, you have heard the renown
Of a set called the Mohawks?
Blount.   The scourge of the town.
A lewd band of night savages, scouring the street,
Sword in hand,—and the terror of all whom they meet
Not as bad as themselves;—*you* were safe, sir; proceed.
  Bel. In the midst of the Mohawks I saw her and freed——
  Blount. You saw *her*—Lucy Wilmot—at night, and alone?
  Bel. No, she had a protector—the face of that crone.
  Blount. Mistress Vizard?
  Bel.   The same, yet, tho' strange it appear,
When the rogues saw her face they did *not* fly in fear.
Brief—I came, saw, and conquered—but own, on the whole,
That my conquest was helped by the City Patrol.
I escorted them home—at their threshold we part—
And I mourn since that night for the loss of my heart.
  Blount. Did you call the next day to demand back that treasure?
  Bel. Yes.
  Blount.   And saw the young lady?
  Bel.   I had not that pleasure;
I saw the old widow, who told me politely
That her house was too quiet for visits so sprightly;
That young females brought up in the school of propriety
Must regard all young males as the pests of society.
I will spare you her lectures, she showed me the door,
And closed it.
  Blount.   You've seen Lucy Wilmot no more?
  Bel. Pardon, yes—very often; that is, once a-day.
Every house has its windows——
  Blount.   Ah! what did you say?
  Bel. Well, by words very little, but much by the eyes.
Now instruct me in turn,—from what part of the skies
Did my angel descend?   What her parents and race?
She is well-born, no doubt—one sees *that* in her face.
What to her is Dame Vizard—that awful duenna,
With the look of a griffiness fed upon senna?
Tell me all.   Ho there!—drawer, a pottle of clary!
  Blount. Leave in peace the poor girl whom you never could marry.
  Bel. Why?
  Blount.   Her station's too mean.   In a small country town,
Her poor mother taught music.
  Bel.   Her father?
                [DRAWER *places wine and glasses on the table*
  Blount.   Unknown.

From the mother's deathbed, from the evil and danger
That might threaten her youth, she was brought by a Stranger
To the house of a lady who——
  Bel.   Showed me the door?
  Blount. Till instructed to live, like her mother before,
As a teacher of music. My noble young friend,
To a match so unmeet you could never descend.
You assure me, I trust, that all thought is dismist
Of a love so misplaced.
  Bel.   No [*filling* BLOUNT's *glass*]—her health!
  Blount.   You persist?
Dare you, sir, to a man of my tenets austere,
Ev'n to hint your designs if your suit persevere?
What!—you still would besiege her?
  Bel.   Of course, if I love.
  Blount. I am Virtue's defender, sir—there is my glove.
     [*Flings down his glove, and rises in angry excitement.*
  Bel. Noble heart! I esteem you still more for this heat.
In the list of my sins there's no room for deceit;
And to plot against innocence helpless and weak—
I'd as soon pick a pocket!
  Blount.   What mean you then? Speak.
  Bel. Blount, I mean you to grant me the favor I ask.
  Blount. What is that?
  Bel. To yourself an agreeable task.
Since you know this Dame Vizard, you call there to-day,
And to her and to Lucy say all I would say.
You attest what I am—fortune, quality, birth,
Adding all that your friendship allows me of worth.
Blount, I have not a father; I claim you as one;
You will plead for my bride as you'd speak for a son.
All arranged—to the altar we go in your carriage,
And I'll vote as you wish the month after my marriage.
  Blount [*aside*]. Can I stifle my fury?

       Enter Newsman *with papers.*

  Newsman.   Great news!
  Bel.   Silence, ape!
   [*Coffee-house loungers rise and crowd round the* Newsman—VEASEY
     snatching the paper.
  Omnes. Read.
  Vea. [*reading*]. Lord Nithsdale, the rebel, has made his escape.
His wife, by permission of Walpole last night,
Saw her lord in the Tower——"   [*Great sensation.*
  Bel. [*to* BLOUNT.]   You will make it all right.
  Vea. [*continuing*]. "And the traitor escaped in her mantle and dress."
  Bel. [*to* BLOUNT]. Now my fate's in your hands—I may count on you.
  Blount.   Yes.

ACT II.—SCENE I.

A room in WALPOLE'S *house. Pictures on the wall. A large table with books, papers, etc.*

WALPOLE *and* VEASEY *seated*.

Wal. And so Nithsdale's escaped ! His wife's mantle and gown;
Well—ha, ha ! let us hope he's now out of this town,
And in safer disguise than my lady's attire,
Gliding fast down the Thames—which he'll not set on fire.
  Vea. All your colleagues are furious.
  Wal. Ah, yes; if they catch him,
Not a hand from the crown of the martyr could snatch him !
Of a martyr so pitied the troublesome ghost
Would do more for his cause than the arms of a host.
These reports from our agents, in boro' and shire,
Show how slowly the sparks of red embers expire.
Ah ! what thousands will hail in a general election
The wild turbulent signal for——
  Vea. Fresh insurrection.
  Wal. [*gravely.*] Worse than that;—Civil War !—at all risk, at all cost,
We must carry this bill, or the nation is lost.
  Vea. Will not Tory and Roundhead against it unite ?
  Wal. Every man has his price; I must bribe left and right.
So you've failed with Bellair—a fresh bait we must try.
As for Blount——

Enter Servant.

  Serv. Mr. Blount.
  Wal. Pray admit him. Good-bye. [*Exit* VEASEY.

SCENE II.

WALPOLE, BLOUNT.

Blount. Mr. Walpole, you ask my advice on the dues
Which the City imposes on coal.
  Wal. Sir, excuse
That pretence for some talk on more weighty a theme,
With a man who commands——
  Blount [*aside*]. Forty votes.
  Wal. My esteem.
You're a patriot, and therefore I courted this visit.
Hark ! your country's in danger—great danger, sir.

Blount [*drily*]. Is it?

Wal. And I ask you to save it from certain perdition.

Blount. Me!—I am——

Wal. Yes, at present in hot opposition.
But what's party? Mere cricket—some out and some in:
I have been out myself. At that time I was thin,
Atrabilious, sir—jaundiced; now, rosy and stout,
Nothing pulls down a statesman like long fagging out.
And to come to the point, now there's nobody by
Be as stout and as rosy, dear Selden, as I.
What! when bad men conspire, shall not good men combine!
There's a place—the Paymastership—just in your line;
I may say that the fees are ten thousand a year,
Besides extras—not mentioned. [*Aside.*] The rogue will cost dear

Blount. What has that, sir to do with the national danger
To which——

Wal. You're too wise to be wholly a stranger.
Need I name to a man of your Protestant true heart
All the risks we yet run from the Pope and the Stuart?
And the indolent public is so unenlightened
That 'tis not to be trusted, and scarce to be frightened.
When the term of this Parliament draws to its close,
Should King George call another, 'tis filled with his foes.

Blount. You pay soldiers eno' if the Jacobites rise——

Wal. But a Jacobite house would soon stop their supplies.
There's a General, on whom you must own, on reflection,
The Pretender relies.

Blount. Who?

Wal. The General election.

Blount. That election must come; you have no other choice.
Would you juggle the People and stifle its voice?

Wal. That is just what young men fresh from college would say,
And the People's a very good thing in its way.
But what is the People?—the mere population?
No, the sound-thinking part of this practical nation,
Who support peace and order, and steadily all poll
For the weal of the land!

Blount [*aside*]. In plain words, for Bob Walpole.

Wal. Of a people like this I've no doubts nor mistrustings,
But I have of the fools who vote wrong at the hustings.
Sir, in short, I am always frank-spoken and hearty,
England needs all the patriots that go with your party.
We must make the three years of this Parliament seven.
And stave off Civil War. You agree?

Blount. Gracious heaven!
Thus to silence the nation, to baffle its laws,
And expect Selden Blount to defend such a cause!
What could ever atone for so foul a disgrace?

Wal. Everlasting renown—[*aside*] and the Paymaster's place.

Blount. Sir, your servant—good day; I am not what you thought;
I am honest——

Wal. Who doubts it?

Blount. And not to be bought.

Wal. You are not to be bought, sir—astonishing man!
Let us argue that point. If creation you scan,
You will find that the children of Adam prevail
O'er the beasts of the field but by barter and sale.
Talk of coals—if it were not for buying and selling,
Could you coax from Newcastle a coal to your dwelling?
You would be to your own fellow-men good for nought,
Were it true, as you say, that you're not to be bought.
If you find men worth nothing—say, don't you despise them?
And what proves them worth nothing?—why, nobody buys them.
But a man of such worth as yourself! nonsense—come,
Sir, to business ; I want you—I buy you ; the sum?
 Blount. Is corruption so brazen? are manners so base?
 Wal. [*aside*]. That means he don't much like the Paymaster's place.
[*With earnestness and dignity.*
Pardon, Blount, I spoke lightly ; but do not mistake,—
On mine honor, the peace of the land is at stake.
Yes, the peace and the freedom! Were Hampden himself
Living still, would he side with Stuart or Guelph?
When the Cæsars the freedom of Rome overthrew,
All its forms they maintained—'twas its spirit they slew!
Shall the freedom of England go down to the grave?
No! the forms let us scorn, so the spirit we save.
 Blount. England's peace and her freedom depend on your bill?
 Wal. [*seriously*]. Thou know'st it—and therefore—
 Blount. My aid you ask still?
 Wal. Nay, no longer *I* ask, 'tis thy country petitions.
 Blount. You talked about terms.
 Wal. [*pushing pen and paper to him*]. There, then, write your conditions.
 [BLOUNT *writes, folds the paper, gives it to* WALPOLE, *bows, and exit.*
 Wal. [*reading*]. "'Mongst the men who are bought to save England
  inscribe me,
And my bribe is the head of the man who would bribe me."
Eh! my head! That ambition is much too high-reaching;
I suspect that the crocodile hints at impeaching.
And he calls himself honest! What highwayman's worse?—
Thus to threaten my life when I offer my purse.
Hem! he can't be in debt, as the common talk runs,
For the man who scorns money has never known duns.
And yet *have* him I must! Shall I force or entice?
Let me think—let me think; every man has his price. [*Exit* WALPOLE.

SCENE III.

A room in Mrs. Vizard's *house. At the back a large window opening on a balcony. In one angle of the room a small door, concealed in the wainscoting. In another angle folding-doors, through which the visitors enter. At each of the side scenes in front, another door.*

Enter Mrs. Vizard.

Mrs. V. 'Tis the day when the Jacobite nobles bespeak
This safe room for a chat on affairs once a-week.   [*Knock without.*
Ah, they come.

Enter two Jacobite Lords, *and* Nithsdale *disguised as a woman.*

1st. J. L.   Ma'am, well knowing your zeal for our king,
To your house we have ventured this lady to bring.
She will quit you at sunset—nay, haply, much sooner—
For a voyage to France in some trusty Dutch schooner.
Hist!—her husband in exile she goes to rejoin,
And our homes are so watched——
   Mrs. V.   That she's safer in mine.
Come with me, my dear lady, I have in my care
A young ward——
   1st J. L. [*hastily*]. Who must see her not! Till we prepare
Her departure, conceal her from all prying eyes;
She is timid, and looks on new faces as spies.
Send your servant on business that keeps her away
Until nightfall;—her trouble permit me to pay.   *Giving a purse.*
   Mrs. V. Nay, my lord, I don't need——
   1st J. L.   Quick, your servant release.
   Mrs. V. I will send her to Kent with a note to my niece.
                                              [*Exit* Mrs. Vizard.
   1st J. L. [*to* Nith.] Here you're safe; still, I tremble until you are freed;
Keep sharp watch at the window—the signal's agreed.
When a pebble's thrown up at the pane, you will know
'Tis my envoy;—a carriage will wait you below.
   Nith. And if, ere you can send him, some peril befall?
   1st J. L. Risk your flight to the inn near the steps at Blackwall.

Re-enter Mrs. Vizard.

   Mrs. V. She is gone.
   1st J. L.   Lead the lady at once to her room.
   Mrs. V. [*opening door to right of side scene*]. No man dares enter here.
   Niths. [*aside.*]   Where she sleeps, I presume.
                                  [*Exeunt* Mrs. Vizard *and* Nithsdale.
   2d J. L. You still firmly believe, tho' revolt is put down,
That King James is as sure to recover his crown.
   1st J. L. Yes; but wait till this Parliament's close is decreed,
And then up with our banner from Thames to the Tweed.
                                              [*Knock at the street-door*
Who knocks? Some new friend?

Enter Mrs. Vizard.

Mrs. V. [*looking out of the window*]. Oh! quick—quick—do not stay! It is Blount.

Both L.   What!—the Roundhead?

Mrs. V. [*opening concealed door in the angle*]. Here—here—the back way.   [*Exit* Mrs. Vizard.

1st J. L. [*as they get to the door*]. Hush! and wait till he's safe within doors.

2d J. L.   But our foes She admits?

1st J. L.   By my sanction,—their plans to disclose.

[*Exeunt* Jacobite Lords *just as enter* Blount *and* Mrs. Vizard

---

SCENE IV.

Mrs. Vizard, Blount.

Mrs. V. I had sent out my servant; this is not your hour.

Blount. Mistress Vizard.

Mrs. V. Sweet sir! [*Aside.*] He looks horridly sour.

Blount. I enjoined you, when trusting my ward to your care——

Mrs. V. To conceal from herself the true name that you bear.

Blount. And she still has no guess——

Mrs. V.   That is Jones, christened John. 'Tis the great Selden Blount whom she gazes upon.

Blount. And my second injunction——

Mrs. V.   What was duly to teach her To respect all you say, as if said by a preacher.

Blount. A preacher!—not so; as a man she should rather Confide in, look up to, and love as——

Mrs. V.   A father.

Blount. Hold! I did not say "Father." You might, for you can, Call me——

Mrs. V. What?

Blount.   Hang it, madam, a fine-looking man. But at once to the truth which your cunning secretes, How came Lucy and you, ma'am, at night in the streets?

Mrs. V. I remember. Poor Lucy so begged and so cried—On that day, a year since——

Blount.   Well!

Mrs. V.   Her poor mother died; And all her wounds opened, recalling that day: She insisted—I had not the heart to say nay—On the solace religion alone can bestow; So I led her to church,—does that anger you?

Blount.   No! But at nightfall——

Mrs. V.   I knew that the church would be dark; And thus nobody saw us, not even the clerk.

Blount. And returning——

Mrs. V. We fell into terrible danger.
Sir, the Mohawks——

Blount. I know; you were saved by a stranger.
He escorted you home; called the next day, I hear.

Mrs. V. But I soon sent him off with a flea in his ear.

Blount. Since that day the young villain has seen her.

Mrs. V. Oh no!

Blount. Yes.

Mrs. V. And where?

Blount. At the window.

Mrs. V. You do not say so!
What deceivers girls are? how all watch they befool!
One should marry them off, ere one sends them to school!

Blount. Ay, I think you are right. All our plans have miscarried.
Go; send Lucy to me—it is time she were married.

[*Exit* Mrs. Vizard *by door to left of side scene.*

Blount. When I first took this orphan, forlorn and alone,
From the poor village inn where I sojourned unknown,
My compassion no feeling more sensitive masked.
She was grateful—that pleased me; was more than I asked.
'Twas in kindness I screened myself under false names,
For she told me her father had fought for King James;
And, embued in the Jacobite's pestilent error,
In a Roundhead she sees but a bugbear of terror.
And from me, Selden Blount, who invoked our free **laws**
To behead or to hang all who side with that cause.
She would start with a shudder! O fool! how above
Human weakness I thought myself! This, then, is love!
Heavens! to lose her—resign to another those charms?
No, no! never! Why yield to such idle alarms?
What's that fop she has seen scarcely once in a way
To a man like myself, whom she sees every day?
Mine she must be! but how!—the world's laughter I dread.
Tut! the world will not know, if in secret we wed.

[*Enter* Lucy *by door to left of side scene.*

SCENE V.

Blount, Lucy.

Lucy. Dear sir, you look pale. Are you ill?

Blount. Ay, what then?
What am I in your thoughts?

Lucy. The most generous of men.
Can you doubt of the orphan's respectful affection,
When she owes ev'n a home to your sainted protection?

Blount. In that home I had hoped for your youth to secure
Safe escape from the perils that threaten the pure;
But, alas! where a daughter of Eve is, I fear
That the serpent will still be found close at her ear.

Lucy. You alarm me !
Blount. I ought. Ah, what danger you ran !
You have seen—have conversed with——
Lucy. Well, well.
Blount. A young man.
Lucy. Nay, he is not so frightful, dear sir, as you deem;
If you only but knew him, I'm sure you'd esteem.
He's so civil—so pleasant—the sole thing I fear
Is—heigh-ho ! are fine gentleman always sincere?
Blount. You are lost if you heed not the words that I say.
Ah ! young men are not now what they were in my day.
Then their fashion was manhood, their language was truth,
And their love was as fresh as a world in its youth;
Now they fawn like a courtier, and fib like his flunkeys,
And their hearts are as old as the faces of monkeys.
Lucy. Ah ! you know not Sir Sidney——
Blount. His nature I do,
For he owned to my friend his designs upon you.
Lucy. What designs ?
Blount. Of a nature too dreadful to name.
Lucy. How ! His words full of honor——
Blount. Veiled thoughts full of shame.
Heard you never of wolves in sheep's clothing ? Why weep ?
Lucy. Indeed, sir, he don't look the least like a sheep.
Blount. No, the sheepskin for clothing much finer he trucks ;
Wolves are nowaday clad not as sheep—but as bucks.
'Tis a false heart you find where a fine dress you see,
And a lover sincere in a plain man like me.
Dismiss then, dear child, this young beau from your mind—
A young beau should be loathed by good young womankind.
At the best he's a creature accustomed to roam ;
'Tis at sixty man learns how to value a home.
Idle fancies throng quick at your credulous age,
And their cure is companionship, cheerful but sage ;
So, in future, I'll give you much more of my own.
Weeping still !—I've a heart, and it is not of stone.
Lucy. Pardon, sir, these vain tears; nor believe that I mourn
For a false-hearted——
Blount. Coxcomb, who merits but scorn.
We must give you some change—purer air, livelier scene—
And your mind will soon win back its temper serene.
You must quit this dull-court with its shocking look-out.
Yes, a cot is the home of contentment, no doubt
A sweet cot with a garden—walled round—shall be ours,
Where our hearts shall unite in the passion—for flowers,
Ah ! I know a retreat, from all turmoil remote,
In the suburb of Lambeth—soon reached by a boat.
So that every spare moment to business not due
I can give, my sweet Lucy, to rapture and you. .
Lucy. What means he ? His words and his looks are alarming;
Mr. Jones, you're too good !
Blount. What !—to find you so charming
Yes; tho' Fortune has placed my condition above you,

Yet Love levels all ranks. Be not startled—I love you.
From all dreams less exalted your fancies arouse;
The poor orphan I raise to the rank of my spouse.
    Lucy. What! His spouse! Do I dream?
    Blount.   Till that moment arrives,
Train your mind to reflect on the duty of wives.
I must see Mistress Vizard, and all things prepare;
To secure our retreat shall this day be my care.
And—despising the wretch who has caused us such sorrow—
Our two lives shall unite in the cottage to-morrow.
    Lucy. Pray excuse me—this talk is so strangely——
    Blount.   Delightful!
    Lucy [*aside*]. I am faint; I am all of a tremble: how frightful!
                                                                         [*Exit through side door to left.*
    Blount. Good; my mind overawes her! From fear love will grow,
And by this time to-morrow a fig for the beau.   [*Calling out.*
Mistress Vizard!   [*Enter* MRS. VIZARD.

SCENE VI.

BLOUNT, MRS. VIZARD.

    Blount.   Guard well my dear Lucy to-day,
For to-morrow I free you, and bear her away.
I agree with yourself—it is time she were married,
And I only regret that so long I have tarried.
Eno'!—I've proposed.
    Mrs. V.   She consented?
    Blount.   Of course;
Must a man like myself get a wife, ma'am, by force?
    Newsman [*without, ringing a bell*]. Great News.
    Mrs. V. [*running to the window, listening and repeating*]. What! " Lord
        Nithsdale escaped from the tower."
                                [NITHSDALE *peeps through the door of his room.*
" In his wife's clothes disguised!—the gown gray, with red flower,
Mantle black, trimmed with ermine." My hearing is hard.
Mr. Blount, Mr. Blount! Do you hear the reward?
    Blount. Yes; a thousand——
    Mrs. V. What!—guineas?
    Blount.   Of course; come away.
I go now for the parson—do heed what I say.
              [NITHSDALE *shakes his fist at* MRS. VIZARD, *and retreats.*
We shall marry to-morrow—no witness but you;
For the marriage is private. I'm Jones still. Adieu!   [*Exit* BLOUNT.
                                                                   [LUCY *peeps out.*
    Mrs. V. Ha! a thousand gold guineas!   [*Locks* NITHSDALE'S *door.*

Re-enter BLOUNT.

    Blount.   Guard closely my treasure.
That's her door; for precaution, just lock it.

Mrs. V. With pleasure.
                          [*As she shows out* BLOUNT, LUCY *slips forth.*
Lucy. Eh! locked up! No, I yet may escape if I hide.
                                 [*Gets behind the window-curtains.*

                    Re-enter MRS. VIZARD.

Mrs. V. Shall I act on this news? I must quickly decide.
Surely Nithsdale it is! Gray gown, sprigged with red;
Did not walk like a woman—a stride, not a tread.   [*Locks* LUCY'S *door.*
Both my lambs are in fold; I'll steal out and inquire.
Robert Walpole might make the reward somewhat higher.
                                       [*Exit* MRS. VIZARD.
Lucy [*looking out from the window*]. She has locked the street-door.
    She has gone with the key,
And the servant is out. No escape; woe is me!
How I love him! And yet I must see him with loathing.
Why should wolves be disguised in such beautiful clothing?
    Niths. [*knocking violently*]. Let me out. I'll not perish entrapped.
        From your snare
Thus I break——   [*Bursts the door, and comes out brandishing a poker.*
    Treacherous hag!

SCENE VII.

LUCY, NITHSDALE.

Lucy.   'Tis the wolf. Spare me; spare!
                          [*Kneeling, and hiding her face.*
Niths. She's a witch, and has changed herself!
Lucy.   Do not come near me.
Niths. Nay, young lady, look up!
Lucy.   'Tis a woman!
Niths.   Why fear me?
Perchance, like myself, you're a prisoner?
Lucy.   Ah yes!
Niths. And your kinsfolk are true to the Stuart, I guess.
Lucy. My poor father took arms for King James.
Niths.   So did I.
Lucy. You!—a woman! How brave!
Niths.   For that crime I must die
If you will not assist me.
Lucy.   Assist you—how? Say.
Niths. That she-Judas will sell me, and goes to betray.
Lucy. Fly! Alas! she has locked the street-door!
Niths.   Lady fair,
Does not Love laugh at locksmiths? Well, so does Despair!
                                 [*Glancing at the window.*
Flight is here. But this dress my detection ensures.
If I could but exchange hood and mantle for yours!
Dare I ask you to save me?

Lucy.   Nay, doubt not my will;
But my door is locked.
    Niths. [*raising the poker.*] And the key is *here* still.
                            [*Bursts the door of* Lucy's *room and enters.*
    Lucy. I have read of the Amazons; this must be one.
    Niths. [*coming from the door with hood, gown, and mantle on his arm*].
       I have found all I need for the risk I must run.
    Lucy. Can I help you?
    Niths.   Heaven bless thee, sweet Innocence, no.
Haste, and look if no back way is open below.
Stay; your father has served the king over the water;
And this locket may please your brave father's true daughter—
The gray hair of poor Charles, intertwined with the pearl.
Go; vouchsafe me this kiss.   [*Kissing her hand, and exit within the door.*
    Lucy.   What a wonderful girl!

SCENE VIII.

The exterior of Mrs. Vizard's *house. Large window. Balcony, area rails below. A court. Dead walls for side scenes, with blue posts at each end, through which the actors enter.*

Enter Blount.

    Blount. For the curse of celebrity nothing atones.
The sharp parson I call on, as simple John Jones,
Has no sooner set eyes on my popular front,
Than he cries, "Ha'! the Patriot, the great Selden Blount!"
Mistress Vizard must hunt up some priest just from Cam,
Who may gaze on these features, nor guess who I am.   [*Knocks.*
Not at home. Servant out too! Ah! gone forth, I guess,
To enchant the young bride with a new wedding-dress.
I must search for a parson myself.   [*Enter* Bellair *from the opposite side.*

SCENE IX.

Blount, Bellair.

    Bel. [*slapping him on the shoulder*]. Blount your news?
    Blount. You! and here, sir! What means——
    Bel.   My impatience excuse.
You have seen her?
    Blonnt.   I have.
    Bel.   And have pleaded my cause:
And of course she consents, for she loves me? You pause.
    Blount. Nay, alas! my dear friend——
    Bel.   Speak and tell me my fate.
    Blount. Quick and rash though your wooing be, it is too late;
She has promised her hand to another. Bear up!

Bel. There is many a slip 'twixt the lip and the cup.
Ah! my rival I'll fight. Say his name if you can.
    Blount. Mr. Jones. I am told he's a fine-looking man.
    Bel. His address?
    Blount.   Wherefore ask? You kill *her* in this duel—
Slay the choice of her heart!
    Bel.   Of her heart; you are cruel.
But if so, why, heaven bless her!
    Blount.   My arm—come away!
    Bel. No, my carriage waits yonder. I thank you. Good day. [*Exit.*
    Blount. He is gone; I am safe—[*shaking his left hand with his right*]
    wish you joy, my dear Jones! [*Exit.*
    [NITHSDALE, *disguised in* LUCY's *dress and mantle, opens the window.*
    Niths. All is still. How to jump without breaking my bones?
    [*Trying to flatten his petticoats, and with one leg over the balcony.*
Curse these petticoats! Heaven, out of all my lost riches,
Why couldst thou not save me one thin pair of breeches!
Steps!   [*Gets back—shuts the window.*

Re-enter BELLAIR.

    Bel. But Blount may be wrong. From her own lips alone
Will I learn.   [*Looking up at the window.*
    I see some one; I'll venture this stone. [*Picks up, and throws,
    a pebble at the window.*
    Niths. [*opening the window*]. Joy!—the signal!

SCENE X.

BELLAIR, NITHSDALE.

    Bel. 'Tis you; say my friend was deceived.
           [NITHSDALE *makes an affirmative sign.*
You were snared into——
    Niths.   Hush!
    Bel.   Could you guess how I grieved!
But oh! fly from this jail; I'm still full of alarms.
I've a carriage at hand: trust yourself to these arms.
    [NITHSDALE *tucks up his petticoats, gets down the balcony backwards,
    setting his foot on the area rail.*
    Bel. Powers above!—what a leg!
    [LORD NITHSDALE *turns round on the rail, rejects* BELLAIR's *hand,
    and jumps down.*
    Bel.   O my charmer! one kiss.
    Niths. Are you out of your senses?
    Bel. [*trying to pull up her hood*]. With rapture!
    Niths. [*striking him*].   Take this
    Bel. What a fist! If it hits one so hard before marriage.
What *would* it do after?
    Niths.   Quick—where is the carriage?
Now, sir, give me your hand.
    Bel.   I'll be hanged if I do

Till I snatch my first kiss! [*Lifts the hood and recoils astounded.*
Who the devil are you?
[NITHSDALE *tries to get from him. A struggle.* BELLAIR *prevails.*
   Bel. I will give you in charge, or this moment confess
How you pass as my Lucy, and wear her own dress?
   Niths. [*aside*]. What! His Lucy? I'm saved.
To her pity I owe
This last chance for my life; would you sell it, sir?
   Bel. No.
But your life! What's your name? Mine is Sidney Bellair.
   Niths. Who in Parliament pleaded so nobly to spare
From the axe——
   Bel. The chiefs doomed in the Jacobite rise?
   Niths. [*with dignity*]. I am Nithsdale. Quick—sell me or free me—time flies.
   Bel. Come this way. There's my coach: I will take you myself
Where you will;—ship you off.
   Niths. Do you side with the Guelph?
   Bel. Yes. What then?
   Niths. You would risk your own life by his laws,
Did you ship me to France. They who fight in a cause
Should alone share its perils. Farewell, generous stranger!
   Bel. Pooh! no gentleman leaves a young lady in danger;
You'd be mobbed ere you got half a yard through the town;
Why, that stride and that calf—let me settle your gown.
[*Clinging to him, and half spoken without.*
No, no; I will see you at least to my carriage. [*Behind scene.*
To what place shall it drive?
   Niths. To Blackwall.

Enter LUCY *from the window.*

   Lucy. Hateful marriage!
But where's that poor lady? What!—gone? She is free!
Could she leap from the window? I wish I were she. [*Retreats.*

SCENE XI.

BELLAIR, LUCY.

   Bel. Now she's safe in my coach, on condition, I own,
Not flattering, sweet creature, to have her alone.
   Lucy. [*peeping*]. It is he.
   Bel. Ah! if Lucy would only appear!
[*Stoops to pick up a stone, and in the act to fling as* LUCY *comes out.*
O my Lucy!—mine angel!
   Lucy. Why is he so dear?
   Bel. Is it true? From that face am I evermore banished?
In your love was the dream of my life? Is it vanished?
Have you pledged to another your hand and your heart?

Lucy. Not my heart. Oh, not that.
 Bel. But your hand? By what art,
By what force, are you won heart and hand to dissever,
And consent to loathed nuptials that part us for ever?
 Lucy. Would that pain you so much?
 Bel. Can you ask? Oh, believe me.
You're my all in the world!
 Lucy. I am told you deceive me;
That you harbor designs which my lips dare not name,
And your words full of honor veil thoughts full of shame.
Ah, sir! I'm so young and so friendless—so weak!
Do not ask for my heart if you take it to break.
 Bel. Who can slander me thus? Not my friend, I am sure.
 Lucy. His friend!
 Bel. Can my love know one feeling impure
When I lay at your feet all I have in this life—
Wealth and rank, name and honor—and woo you as wife?
 Lucy. As your wife! All about you seems so much above
My mean lot——
 Bel. And so worthless compared to your love.
You reject, then, this suitor?—my hand you accept?
 Lucy. Ah! but do you not see in what prison I'm kept?
And this suitor——
 Bel. You hate him!
 Lucy. Till this day, say rather——
 Bel. What?
 Lucy. I loved him.
 Bel. You loved!
 Lucy. As I might a grandfather.
He has shielded the orphan;—I had not a notion
That he claimed from me more than a grandchild's devotion?
And my heart ceased to beat between terror and sorrow
When he said he would make me his wife, and to-morrow.
 Bel. Fly with me and at once!
 Lucy. She has locked the street door.
 Bel. And my angel's not made to jump down from that floor.
Listen—quick; I hear voices:—I save you; this night
I arrange all we need both for wedlock and flight.
At what time after dark does your she-dragon close
Her sweet eyes, and her household consign to repose?
 Lucy. About nine in this season of winter. What then?
 Bel. By the window keep watch. When the clock has struck ten
A slight stone smites the casement;—below I attend.
You will see a safe ladder; at once you descend.
We then reach your new home, priest and friends shall be there,
Proud to bless the young bride of Sir Sidney Bellair.
Hush! the steps come this way; do not fail! She is won. [*Exit* BELLAIR.
 Lucy. Stay;—I tremble as guilty. Heavens! what have I done?

ACT III.—SCENE I.

St. James's Park.   Seats, etc.   Time—Sunset.

Enter BLOUNT.

 Blount. So the parson is found and the cottage is hired—
Every fear was dispelled when my rival retired.
Ev'n my stern mother country must spare from my life
A brief moon of that honey one tastes with a wife!
And then strong as a giant, recruited by sleep,
On corruption and Walpole my fury shall sweep.
'Mid the cheers of the House I will state in my place
How the bribes that he proffered were flung in his face.
Men shall class me amid those examples of worth
Which, alas! become daily more rare on this earth;
And Posterity, setting its brand on the front
Of a Walpole, select for its homage a Blount.   [*Enter* BELLAIR, *singing gaily.*

SCENE II.

BLOUNT, BELLAIR.

 Bel. "The dove builds where the leaves are still green on the tree———"
 Blount [*rising*]. Ha!
 Bel.   "For May and December can never agree."
 Blount. I am glad you've so quickly got over that blow.
 Bel. Fallala!
 Blount. [*aside*]. What this levity means I must know.
The friend I best loved was your father, Bellair—
Let me hope your strange mirth is no laugh of despair.
 Bel. On the wit of the wisest man it is no stigma
If the heart of a girl is to him an enigma;
That my Lucy was lost to my arms you believed—
Wish me joy, my dear Blount, you were grossly deceived.
She is mine!—What on earth are you thinking about?
Do you hear?
 Blount.   I am racked!
 Bel.   What?
 Blount.   A twinge of the gout.
            [*Reseating himself.*
Pray excuse me.
 Bel.   Nay, rather myself I reproach
For not heeding your pain.   Let me call me you a coach.

  Blount. Nay, nay, it is gone. I am eager to hear
How I've been thus deceived—make my blunder more clear.
You have seen her?
  Bel.   Of course. From her own lips I gather
That your good Mr. Jones might be Lucy's grandfather.
Childish fear or of Vizard—who seems a virago—
Or the old man himself——
  Blount.   Oh!
  Bel.   You groan?
  Blount.   The lumbago!
  Bel. Ah! they say gout is shifty—now here and now there.
  Blount.—Pooh; continue. The girl then——
  Bel.   I found in despair.
But no matter—all's happily settled at last.
  Blount. Ah! eloped from the house?
  Bel.   No, the door was made fast.
But to-night I would ask you a favor.
  Blount   What? Say.
  Bel. If your pain should have left you, to give her away.
For myself it is meet that I take every care
That my kinsfolk shall hail the new Lady Bellair.
I've induced my two aunts (who are prudish) to grace
With their presence my house, where the nuptials take place.
And to act as her father there's no man so fit
As yourself, dear old Blount, if the gout will permit.
  Blount. 'Tis an honor——
  Bel.   Say pleasure.
  Blount.   Great pleasure! Proceed.
How is *she*, if the door be still fast, to be freed?
Is the house to be stormed?
  Bel.   Nay; I told you before
That a house has its windows as well as its door.
And a stone at the pane for a signal suffices,
While a ladder——
  Blount.   I see. [*Aside.*] What infernal devices!
Has she no maiden fear——
  Bel.   From the ladder to fall?
Ask her that—when we meet at my house in Whitehall.
         [*Enter 1st* Jacobite Lord.

SCENE III.

Blount, Bellair, 1*st* Jacobite, *afterwards* Veasey.

  J. L. [*giving note to* Bellair]. If I err not, I speak to Sir Sidney Bellair?
Pray vouchsafe me one moment in private.   [*Draws him aside.*
  Blount.   Despair!
How prevent?—how forestall? Could I win but delay,
I might yet brush this stinging fly out of my way.
      [*While he speaks, enter* Veasey *in the background.*

Vea. Bellair whispering close with that Jacobite lord——
Are they hatching some plot? [*Hides behind the trees—listening.*
    Bel. [*reading*]. So he's safely on board——
    J. L. And should Fortune shake out other lots from her urn,
We, poor friends of the Stuart, might serve you in turn.
You were talking with Blount—Selden Blount—is he one
Of your friends?
    Bel.   Ay, the truest.
    J. L.   Then warn him to shun
That vile Jezabel's man-trap—I know he goes there.
Whom she welcomes she sells.
    Bel.   I will bid him beware.
        [*Shakes hands. Exit* JACOBITE LORD.
    Bel. [*to* BLOUNT]. I have just learned a secret, 'tis fit I should tell you.
Go no more to old Vizard's, or know she will sell you.
Nithsdale hid in her house when the scaffold he fled.
She received him, and went for the price on his head;
But—the drollest mistake—of that tale by and-by——
He was freed; is safe now!
    Blount.   Who delivered him?
    Bel.   I.
    Blount. Ha!—you did!
    Bel.   See, he sends me this letter of thanks.
    Blount [*reading*]. Which invites you to join with the Jacobite ranks.
And when James has his kingdom——
    Bel.   That chance is remote;
    Blount. Hints an earldom for you.
    Bel.   Bah!
    Blount.   Take care of this note.
    [*Appears to trust it into* BELLAIR'S *coat-pocket—lets it fall, and puts his foot on it.*
    Bel. Had I guessed that the hag was so greedy of gold,
Long ago I had bought Lucy out of her hold;
But to-night the dear child will be free from her power.
Adieu! I expect you then.
    Blount.   Hold! at what hour?
    Bel. By the window at ten, self and ladder await her;
The wedding—eleven; you will not be later.   [*Exit.*
    Blount. [*picking up the letter*]. Nithsdale's letter. Bright thought!—
and what luck! I see Veasey.

Re-enter BELLAIR.

    Bel. Blount, I say, will old Jones be to-morrow uneasy?
Can't you fancy his face?
    Blount.   Yes; ha! ha!
    Bel.   I am off.   [*Exit*

SCENE IV.

BLOUNT, VEASEY.

Blount. What? shall I, Selden Blount, be a popinjay's scoff?
Mr. Veasey, your servant.
    Vea.   I trust, on the whole,
That you've settled with Walpole the prices of coal.
    Blount. Coals be—lighted below? Sir, the country's in danger.
    Vea. To that fact Walpole says that no patriot's a stranger.
    Blount. With the safety of England myself I will task,
If you hold yourself licensed to grant what I ask.
    Vea. Whatsoever the terms of a patriot so stanch,
Walpole gives you—I speak as his proxy—*carte blanche.*
    Blount. If I break private ties where the Public's at stake,
Still my friend is my friend: the condition I make
Is to keep him shut up from all share in rash strife,
And secure him from danger to fortune and life.
    Vea. Blount—agreed. And this friend? Scarce a moment ago
I marked Sidney Bellair in close talk with——
    Blount.   I know.
There's a plot to be checked ere it start into shape.
Hark! Bellair had a hand in Lord Nithsdale's escape!
    Vea. That's abetment of treason.
    Blount.   Read this, and attend.
            [*Gives* NITHSDALE's *note to* BELLAIR, *which* VEASEY *reads.*
Snares atrocious are set to entrap my poor friend
In an outbreak to follow that Jacobite's flight——
    Vea. In an outbreak. Where?—when?
    Blount.   Hush! in London to-night.
He is thoughtless and young. Act on this information,
Quick—arrest him at once; and watch over the nation.
    Vea. No precaution too great against men disaffected.
    Blount. And the law gives you leave to confine the suspected.
    Vea. Ay, this note will suffice for a warrant. Be sure,
Ere the clock strike the quarter, your friend is secure. [*Exit* VEASEY.
    Blount. Good; my rival to-night will be swept from my way,
And John Jones shall wake easy eno' the next day.
Do I still love this girl? No, my hate is so strong,
That to me, whom she mocks, she alone shall belong.
I need trust to that saleable Vizard no more.
Ha! I stand as Bellair the bride's window before.
Oh, when love comes so late now it maddens the brain,
Between shame for our folly, and rage at our pain! [*Exit.*

SCENE V.

Room in WALPOLE'S *house.* [*Lights.*]

Enter WALPOLE.

Wal. So Lord Nithsdale's shipped off. There's an end of one trouble;
When his head's at Boulogne the reward shall be double.
    [*Seating himself, takes up a book—glances at it, and throws it down.*
Stuff! I wonder what lies the Historians will tell
When they babble of one Robert Walpole! Well, well,
Let them sneer at his blunders, declaim on his vices,
Cite the rogues whom he purchased, and rail at the prices,
They shall own that all lust for revenge he withstood;
And, if lavish of gold, he was sparing of blood;
That when England was threatened by France and by Rome,
He forced Peace from abroad and encamped her at home,
And the Freedom he left, rooted firm in mild laws.
May o'ershadow the faults of deeds done in her cause! [*Enter* VEASEY.

SCENE VI.

WALPOLE, VEASEY.

Vea. [*giving note*]. Famous news! See, Bellair has delivered himself
To your hands. He must go heart and soul with the Guelph,
And vote straight, or he's ruined.
    Wal. [*reading*].   This note makes it clear
That he's guilty of Nithsdale's escape.
    Vea.   And I hear
That to-night he will lead some tumultuous revolt,
Unless chained to his stall like a mischievous colt.
    Wal. Your informant?
    Vea.   Guess! Blount; but on promise to save
His young friend's life and fortune!
    Wal.   What Blount says is grave.
He would never thus speak if not sure of his fact. [*Signing warrant.*
Here, then, take my State warrant; but cautiously act.
Bid Bellair keep his house—forbid exits and entries;—
To make sure, at his door place a couple of sentries.
Say I mean him no ill; but these times will excuse
Much less gentle precautions than those which I use.
Stay, Dame Vizard is waiting without: to her den
Nithsdale fled. She came here to betray him.
    Vea.   What then?
    Wal. Why, I kept her, perforce, till I sent, on the sly,
To prevent her from hearing Lord Nithsdale's good bye.

When my agent arrived, I'm delighted to say
That the cage-wires were broken,—the bird flown away;
But he found one poor captive imprisoned and weeping;
I must learn how that captive came into such keeping.
Now, then, off—nay, a moment; you would not be loth
Just to stay with Bellair?—I may send for you both.

 Vea. With a host more delightful no mortal could sup,
But a guest so unlooked for——

 Wal.   Will cheer the boy up! [*Exit* VEASEY.

 Wal. [*ringing hand-bell*].   [*Enter* Servant.
Usher in Mistress Vizard.

SCENE VII.

WALPOLE, MRS. VIZARD.

 Wal.   Quite shocked to detain you,
But I knew a mistake, if there were one, would pain you.

 Mrs. V. Sir, mistake there is not; that vile creature is no man.

 Wal. But you locked the door?

 Mrs. V.   Fast.

 Wal.   Then, no doubt, 'tis a woman,
For she slipped thro' the window.

 Mrs. V.   No woman durst!

 Wal.   Nay.
When did woman want courage to go her own way?

 Mrs. V. You jest, sir. To me 'tis no subject of laughter.

 Wal. Do not weep. The reward?—we'll discuss that hereafter.

 Mrs. V. You'd not wrong a poor widow who brought you such news?

 Wal. Wrong a widow!—there's oil to put in her cruise.
             [*Giving a pocket-book.*
Meanwhile, the tried agent despatched to your house,
In that trap found a poor little terrified mouse,
Which did call itself "Wilmot"—a name known to me.
Pray you, how in your trap did that mouse come to be?

 Mrs. V. [*hesitatingly*]. Sir, believe me——

 Wal.   Speak truth—for your own sake you ought.

 Mrs. V. By a gentleman, sir, to my house she was brought.

 Wal. Oh! some Jacobite kinsman perhaps?

 Mrs. V.   Bless you, no;
A respectable Roundhead. You frighten me so!

 Wal. A respectable Roundhead intrust to your care
A young girl, whom you guard as in prison!—Beware!
'Gainst decoy for vile purpose the law is severe.

 Mrs. V. Fie! you libel a saint, sir, of morals austere.

 Wal. Do you mean Judith Vizard?

 Mrs. V.   I mean Selden Blount.

 Wal. I'm bewildered! But why does this saint (no affront)
To your pious retreat a fair damsel confide?

 Mrs. V. To protect her as ward till he claims her as bride.

Wal. Faith, his saintship does well until that day arrive
To imprison the maid he proposes to wive.
But these Roundheads are wont but with Roundheads to wed,
And the name of this lady is Wilmot she said.
Every Wilmot I know of is to the backbone
A rank Jacobite; say, can that name be her own?

Mrs. V. Not a doubt; more than once I have heard the girl say
That her father had fought for King James on the day
When the ranks of the Stuart were crushed at the Boyne.
He escaped from the slaughter, and fled to rejoin
At the Court of St. Germain's his new-wedded bride.
Long their hearth without prattlers; a year ere he died,
Lucy came to console her who mourned him bereft
Of all else in this world.

Wal. [*eagerly*].   But the widow he left;
She lives still?

Mrs. V.   No; her child is now motherless.

Wal. [*aside*].   •Fled!
Fled again from us, sister! How stern are the dead!
Their dumb lips have no pardon! Tut! shall I build grief
On a guess that perchance only fools my belief?
This may *not* be her child.   [*Rings.*

Enter Servant.

My coach waits?

Servant.   At the door.

Wal. Come; your house teems with secrets I long to explore.
                    [*Exeunt* WALPOLE *and* MRS. VIZARD.

SCENE VIII.

MRS. VIZARD'S *house. A lamp on the table.*

Enter LUCY *from her room.*

Lucy. Mistress Vizard still out!   [*Looking at the clock.*
                    What! so late? O my heart!
How it beats! Have I promised in stealth to depart?
Trust him—yes! But will *he*, ah! long after this night,
Trust the wife wooed so briefly, and won but by flight?
My lost mother!   [*Takes a miniature from her breast.*
        Oh couldst thou yet counsel thy child!
No, this lip does not smile as it yesterday smiled.
From thine heaven can no warning voice come to mine ear;
Save thy child from herself;—'tis myself that I fear.

Enter WALPOLE *and* MRS. VIZARD *through the concealed door.*

Mrs. V. Lucy, love, in this gentleman (curtsy, my dear)
See a friend.

Wal.   Peace, and leave us.   [*Exit* MRS. VIZARD.

SCENE IX.

WALPOLE, LUCY.

Wal. Fair girl I would hear
From yourself, if your parents——
Lucy. My parents; oh say
Did you know them?—my mother?
Wal. The years roll away.
I behold a gray hall, backed by woodlands of pine;
I behold a fair face—eyes and tresses like thine—
By her side a rude boy full of turbulent life,
All impatient of rest, and all burning for strife—
They are brother and sister. Unconscious they stand—
On the spot where their paths shall divide—hand in hand.
Hush! a moment, and lo! as if lost amid night,
She is gone from his side, she is snatched from his sight.
Time has flowed on its course—that wild boy lives in me;
But the sister I lost! Does she bloom back in thee?
Speak—the name of thy mother, ere changing her own
For her lord's?—who her parents?
Lucy. I never have known.
When she married my father, they spurned her, she said,
Bade her hold herself henceforth to them as the dead;
Slandered him in whose honor she gloried as wife,
Urged attaint on his name, plotted snares for his life;
And one day when I asked what her lineage, she sighed
" From the heart they so tortured their memory has died."
Wal. Civil war slays all kindred—all mercy, all ruth.
Lucy. Did you know her?—if so, was this like her in youth?
[*Giving miniature*
Wal. It is she; the lips speak! Oh, I knew it!—thou art
My lost sister restored!—to mine arms, to mine heart.
That wild brother the wrongs of his race shall atone;
He has stormed his way up to the foot of the throne.
Yes! thy mate thou shalt choose 'mid the chiefs of the land.
Dost thou shrink?—heard I right?—is it promised this hand,
And to one, too, of years so unsuited to thine?
Lucy. Dare I tell you?
Wal. Speak, sure that thy choice shall be mine.
Lucy. When my mother lay stricken in mind and in frame,
All our scant savings gone, to our succor there came
A rich stranger, who lodged at the inn whence they sought
To expel us as vagrants. Their mercy he bought;
Ever since I was left in the wide world alone,
I have owed to his pity this roof——
Wal. Will you own
What you gave in return?
Lucy. Grateful reverence.
Wal. And so
He asked more!

Lucy. Ah! that more was not mine to bestow.

Wal. What! your heart some one younger already had won.
Is he handsome?

Lucy. Oh yes!

Wal. And a gentleman's son.

Lucy. Sir, he looks it.

Wal. His name is——

Lucy. Sir Sidney Bellair.

Wal. Eh! that brilliant Lothario? Dear Lucy, beware;
Men of temper so light may make love in mere sport.
Where on earth did you meet?—in what terms did he court?
Why so troubled? Why turn on the timepiece your eye?
Orphan trust me.

Lucy. I will. I half promised to fly——

Wal. With Bellair. [*Aside.*] He shall answer for this with his life.
Fly to-night as his—what!

Lucy. Turn your face—as his wife.
[Lucy *sinks down, burying her face in her hands.*

Wal. [*going to the door*]. Jasper—ho!

Enter Servant *as he writes on his tablets.*

Take my coach to Sir Sidney's, Whitehall
Mr. Veasey is there; give him this—that is all.
[*Tearing out the leaf from the tablet and folding it up.*
Go out the back way; it is nearest my carriage.*
[*Opens the concealed door, through which Exit* Servant.
I shall very soon know if the puppy means marriage.

Lucy. Listen; ah! that's his signal!

Wal. A stone at the pane!
But it can't be Bellair—*he* is safe.

Lucy. There, again!

Wal. [*peeps from the window*]. Ho!—a ladder! Niece, do as I bid
you; confide
In my word, and I promise Sir Sidney his bride!
Ope the window and whisper, "I'm chained to the floor;
Pray, come up and release me!"

Lucy. [*out of the window*]. "I'm chained to the floor;
Pray, come up and release me."

Wal. I watch by this door.
[*Enters* Lucy's *room and peeping out.*
[Blount *enters through the window.*

---

* In obeying this instruction, the servant would not see the ladder, which (as the reader will learn by what immediately follows) is placed against the balcony in the *front* of the house.

SCENE X.

BLOUNT, LUCY, WALPOLE *at watch unobserved.*

Lucy. Saints in heaven, Mr. Jones!
Wal. [*aside*]. Selden Blount, by Old Nick!
Blount. What! you are not then chained! Must each word be a trick?
Ah! you look for a gallant more dainty and trim;
He deputes me to say he abandons his whim;
By his special request I am here in his place—
Saving him from a crime and yourself from disgrace.
Still, ungrateful, excuse for your folly I make—
Still, the prize he disdains to my heart I can take.
Fly with me, as with him you would rashly have fled;—
He but sought to degrade you, I seek but to wed.
Take revenge on the false heart, give bliss to the true!
Lucy. If he's false to myself, I were falser to you,
Could I say I forget him;
Blunt. You will, when my wife.
Lucy. That can never be——
Blount. Never!
Lucy. One love lasts thro' life!
Blount. Traitress! think not this insult can tamely be borne—
Hearts like mine are too proud for submission to scorn.
You are here at my mercy—that mercy has died;
You remain as my victim or part as my bride. [*Locks the door.*
See, escape is in vain, and all others desert you;
Let these arms be your refuge.
Wal. [*tapping him on the shoulder*]. Well said, Public Virtue!

[BLOUNT, *stupefied, drops the key, which* WALPOLE *takes up, stepping out into the balcony, to return as* BLOUNT, *recovering himself, makes a rush at the window.*

Wal. [*stopping him*]. As you justly observed, "See, escape is in vain"—
I have pushed down the ladder,
Blount. [*laying his hand on his sword*]. 'Sdeath! draw, sir!—
Wal. Abstain
From that worst of all blunders, a profitless crime.
Cut my innocent throat? Fie! one sin at a time.
Blount. Sir, mock on, I deserve it; expose me to shame,
I've o'erthrown my life's labor,—an honest man's name.
Lucy. [*stealing up to* BLOUNT.] No; a moment of madness can not sweep away
All I owed, and—forgive me—have failed to repay: [*To* WALPOLE.
Be that moment a secret.
Wal. If woman can keep one,
Then a secret's a secret. Gad, Blount, you're a deep one!

[*Knock at the door;* WALPOLE *opens it.*
Enter BELLAIR *and* VEASEY, *followed by* MRS. VIZARD.

SCENE XI.

WALPOLE, LUCY, BLOUNT, VEASEY, BELLAIR, MRS. VIZARD *in the background*.

  Bel. [*not seeing* WALPOLE, *who is concealed behind the door which he opens and hurrying to* BLOUNT]. Faithless man, canst thou look on my face undismayed?
Nithsdale's letter disclosed, and my friendship betrayed!
What! and *here* too! Why *here?*
  Blount [*aside*].   I shall be the town's scoff.
  Wal. [*to* BELLAIR *and* VEASEY]. Sirs, methinks that you see not that lady—hats off.
I requested your presence, Sir Sidney Bellair,
To make known what you owe to the friend who stands there.
For that letter disclosed, your harsh language recant——
It's condition your pardon;—full pardon I grant.
He is here—you ask why; 'tis to save you to-night
From degrading your bride by the scandal of flight. [*Drawing him aside.*
Or—hist!—*did* you intend (whisper close in my ear)
Honest wedlock with one so beneath you I fear?
You of lineage so ancient——
  Bel.   Must mean what I say.
Do their ancestors teach the Well-born to betray?
  Wal. Wed her friendless and penniless?
  Bel.   Ay.
  Wal.   Strange caprice
Deign to ask, then, from Walpole the hand of his niece.
Should he give his consent, thank the friend you abuse.
  Bel. [*embracing* BLOUNT]. Best and noblest of men, my blind fury excuse!
  Wal. Hark! her father's lost lands may yet serve for her dower.
  Bel. All the earth has no lands worth the bloom of this flower.
  Lucy. Ah! too soon fades the flower.
  Bel.   True, I alter the name.
Be my perfect pure chrysolite—ever the same.
  Wal. Hold! I know not a chrysolite from a carbuncle,
     [*With insinuating blandishment of voice and look*
But my nephew-in-law should not vote out his uncle.
  Bel. Robert Walpole, at last you have bought me, I fear.
  Wal. Every man has his price. My majority's clear.
If,——   [*Crossing quickly to* BLOUNT.
    Dear Blount, did your goodness not rank with the best,
What you feel as reproach, you would treat as a jest.
Raise your head—and with me keep a laugh for the ass
Who has never gone out of his wits for a lass:
Live again for your country—reflect on my bill.
  Blount. [*with emotion, grasping* WALPOLE'S *hand*]. You are generous;
   I thank you. Vote *with* you?—I will!
  Vea. How dispersed are the clouds seeming lately so sinister!
  Wal. Yes, I think that the glass stands at Fair—for the Minister.
  Vea. Ah! what more could you do for the People and Throne?
  Wal. Now I'm safe in my office, I'd leave well alone.

DARNLEY.

PREFACE TO "DARNLEY."

My father left to my unfettered discretion the task of dealing with his numerous unpublished manuscripts. Amongst them was one which, under the title of "Darnley," is here added to the collection of his dramatic works. Its author had given to it no name and no conclusion. It consisted of four acts of a five-act play, finished only it the rough, and some few notes. The four acts had not received those important final touches which, in the case of acting plays, are best reserved for consultation with the principal actors concerned in their performance. Of the fifth act no trace existed; except in the few notes to which reference will be found at the conclusion of the fourth act as printed in this Edition. Such was the condition of the manuscript I had to deal with under a twofold sense of obligation to the living and the dead. The literary remains of celebrated authors constitute a kind of property not easily classified. It is not altogether private: for the public has a legitimate interest in the result of all literary labor undertaken by a great author for its enjoyment or instruction. And of this interest the author's literary executors are to some extent trustees. But, on the other hand, they are also the guardians of a reputation not their own. Death has placed in their hands the key of a workshop, only interesting to the public on account of the worthy and famous works which have issued from it. In its secret chambers are materials collected, and instruments arranged, which may serve to illustrate the master's method, though they cannot reveal his incommunicable secret; and, with them, fragments of work reserved either for destruction or completion by the hand that has left it incomplete. Shall all these be consigned for ever to that "wallet," wherein "Time puts alms for Oblivion?" If not, how many of them will it be right to save for the satisfaction of a not irreverent curiosity?

Such questions present themselves in a form comparatively simple to the literary executors of the philosopher or the man of science; whose roughest notes possess an interest and importance which owe nothing to art. But the literary value of work done by the poet, the novelist, or the dramatist, is largely dependent on the artistic finish of it. And those who display the unpublished work of a great artist, must recall in fear and trembling the curse invoked by Shakespeare on the disturber of his bones.

I was not uninfluenced by these reflections when considering what I should do with the present dramatic fragment. I cannot precisely fix the date at which it was written; but the allusions it contains to an attempt on the life of Louis Philippe, and the military action of Sir Harry Pottinger, leave no doubt that it must have lain for many years undisturbed in the portfolio of its author. Why did he leave it so long unfinished? Why, in the course of those many years, had he made no effort to place it on the stage? Was it because he deemed the work undeserving of completion and performance? If so, the posthumous publication of it would have been wholly unwarrantable. But I had many and strong reasons for attributing to other causes my father's apparent neglect of a work which, even in its present rough-hewn and unfinished condition, is powerfully constructed and full of vigorous handiwork.

In the first place; although, during my father's lifetime, I was not aware of the existence of this unfinished play, yet in conversations with me on the subject of dramatic structure he had frequently illustrated his views of that most difficult art by describing scenes and situations which occur in "Darnley;" and he often expressed to me his conviction that a most powerful domestic drama might be constructed out of the conception he has here embodied. In the next place; this unfinished play belongs to an important series of carefully completed dramas which, though he reckoned them among the best of his dramatic works, my father never published. They were all written for the stage. They were never published because they had never been performed; and they were never performed because no theatre in this country united all the requisite conditions of their efficient performance. With Mr. Macready's retirement from the stage, my father had lost his chief incentive to write for it. Here and there, it still furnished an excellent actor, but nowhere an acting company, or a school of acting, able to give adequate expression to the ideas embodied in a form possessing any pretension to literary value. But the bent of my father's genius was so emphatically dramatic, that the form first assumed by many of his most important fictions was that of the drama. Of these dramatic sketches, some were eventually developed into novels and romances; which probably owe much of their structural symmetry and emotional strength to the concise dramatic form wherein the conception of them was first cast. Others he retained in this form; hopeful, no doubt, of an occasion that never came during his lifetime, when they might be placed upon the stage with a reasonable prospect of that perfect co-operation of intelligence between the author, the actors, and the public, which is indispensable to the satisfactory effect of an acting play.

Notwithstanding the unfinished condition of it, the manuscript of Darnley appeared to me too vigorous and valuable a specimen of it's authors dramatic workmanship to be permanently withheld from the public. In this impression I was confirmed by the unqualified opinion of the late Mr. John Forster, and the late Mr. George Henry Lewes, to whom I showed it. Those competent judges of dramatic writing also shared my conviction that for the publication of this work the stage was the only adequate vehicle. The late Mr. Rogers, when told by one of his guests that the author of Philip van Arteveldt had written a new play, asked "Is it an acting play, or a reading play?" And on hearing that it was a reading play, he drily replied, "Then I shan't read it." Few people do read with complete satisfaction that hybrid kind of composition which is commonly called a reading play. But poems are poems; and not to be talked of, or thought of, as plays, merely because they happen to be written in dialogue, and divided into acts and scenes. Such dramatic poems as those of Sir Henry Taylor are literary treasures, of which the value has no relation to their acting capabilities. To be rightly appreciated, they must be read. It is just the reverse with a genuine play. To be rightly appreciated it must be acted. In the case of this play, however, the unfinished condition of it was an insuperable obstacle to placing it upon the stage in a thoroughly satisfactory form. In Germany the play-going public is interested by the performance of such a mere dramatic fragment as the "Demetrius" of Schiller, when it is from the pen of a famous national author. But from an English audience it would be idle to expect a similar interest in the performance of an unfinished play, however illustrious its authorship. And, even in Germany, an unfinished play by Goethe, Schiller, Lessing or Grillparzer, though sure of a permament place in the *répretoire* of the national stage, would probably fail to fill the theatre for many consecutive nights. In order to place this play upon the stage, therefore, it was necessary to add to it a fifth act, by a hand not that of its author. For such a task it was not easy to find in any one writer all the requisite qualifications. In some who were not unwilling to undertake it I could reckon upon knowledge of the stage, in others upon literary capacity. In none upon a combination of both, commensurate with the difficulty of the undertaking. Wholly unqualified to undertake it myself, I asked Monsieur Alexandre Dumas whether he would be willing to write the fifth act of this play with a view to its performance, as thus completed, at the Théâtre Français, in Paris. That eminent dramatist declared himself much pleased and flattered by the proposal. After reading the four acts written by my father, however, he found that their adaptation to the taste of a French audience would require alterations of the original text more or less inconsistent with fidelity to the main idea of it; and to Monsieur Dumas no less than to myself this consideration appeared conclusive against the project of bringing out the play in France. Shortly afterwards, I received from Mr. Hare proposals for the production of it at the Court Theatre in London. In accepting Mr. Hare's proposals I felt assured, both from the finished excellence of his own acting and the general intelligence with which it was supported by the company then associated with him, that the play could not be performed in England under conditions more favorable to its success, if only the dramatic interest of it were adequately sustained in the fifth act still to be written for it. The composition of this act was intrusted to Mr. Coghlan; and I hoped to assist him in it by various suggestions which are submitted to the reader in the explanatory remarks I have appended to the fourth act. The fulfilment of that hope, however, was prevented by circumstances which involved my lengthened absence from England before I had any communication with Mr. Coghlan on the subject of his work. He completed it without reference to me, during my absence; and I was busily occupied in India when the play, as finished by him, was brought out at the Court Theatre in London.

No effort to ensure success was neglected. It was placed upon the stage with great intelligence and expense: and I am assured by all who witnessed it that Mr. Hare's impersonation of the character of Mainwaring was one of his most finished and admirable performances. Nevertheless the play was not successful; and after a short run it was withdrawn. Translated into German, it had been simultaneously produced in Vienna, at the Burg Theatre, by some of the best actors in Europe. The announcement of its performance on that celebrated stage had been received with lively interest by a population to whom the name of its author was a household word. The performance was honored by the presence of the Emperor and the whole Imperial Court, as well as by all the representatives of the literary world in Austria. The actors had undertaken their parts with enthusiasm; and the Darnley of Herr Sonenthal was, I am told by those who saw it, most effective and affecting. The audience followed the progress of the play with animated and increasing interest to the close of the fourth act. But its permanent interest as a drama could not survive the anti-climax of the fifth act. Thus at Vienna, as in London, the play was withdrawn after a short run. I should leave both the author and the actors of "Darnley," under a reproach which they do not deserve if I recorded this failure without stating what I believe to be the cause of it.

I have no doubt whatever that, had my father himself prepared this play for the stage, he would have made in the four acts, here printed just as they were left by him, various alterations sugested by the experience of rehersal. That was his practice in the composition of those dramas which have taken so permanent a hold upon the English stage.

However strong or accurate may be the dramatic instinct of an author's genius, if he is not professionally connected with the stage, he cannot possibly possess that intimate knowledge of it which best qualifies the experienced actor or manager to suggest, though it does not equally qualify them to carry out, alterations in the acting copy of a play. Molière's plays were probably much improved by attention to the criticism of his housekeeper.* But the housekeeper would not have improved them, had she herself undertaken the alterations which her remarks suggested to their author. Mr. Coghlan's alterations of my father's manuscript were sparing and judicious. For acting purposes I believe every one of them to have been necessary in the peculiar circumstances of the case. They were mostly in the way of omision, and rightly so. If it were in his power, it was not in his function, to strengthen and develop any part of the author's original work. Yet there are parts of it which would certainly have been strengthened and developed by its author had they received his final touches. For, like a skilful painter, he never worked up his minor tones till he had put in his strongest light. In completing this play he would certainly have been careful to make the first four acts of it conducive and subservient to the effect of the fifth. But the fifth act added to it by Mr.

---

* An erroneous tradition, however. The housekeeper was Montaigne's.

Coghlan was not only ineffective itself; it was also destructive, I think, to the effect of the four preceding ones. This was perhaps inevitable under the very difficult conditions of a somewhat invidious task. Nor is it in any spirit of reproach that I attribute the failure of "Darnley" as an acting play, mainly, though not entirely, to the incongruity of the fifth act added by Mr. Coghlan to the acting copy of it. But in justice to my father's work, I think it right to place before the readers of it a statement of the principles on which I believe the fifth act of this play would have been constructed had my father written it himself; and to indicate the *dénouement* intended by the author. This I have done in a note appended to the fourth act.

LYTTON.

KNEBWORTH, *May 16th,* 1882.

DRAMATIS PERSONÆ.

DARNLEY	MR. CHARLES KELLY.
PARSONS, *his Clerk*	MR. R. CATHCART.
MAINWARING, *his Friend*	MR. HARE.
SIR FRANCIS MARSDEN. . . ⎫ *His Acquaintances.* ⎧	MR. TITHERADGE.
SELFBY FYSHE . . . . ⎭ ⎩	MR. A. BISHOP.
LORD FITZHOLLOW, *his Father-in-Law* . . .	MR DENISON.
SERVANT	MR. CARNE.
LADY JULIET DARNLEY	MISS ELLEN TERRY.
FANNY DARNLEY	MISS BROWN.
MISS PLACID	MISS AMY ROSELLE.
THE LADY OF THE VILLA	MISS B. HENRI.

First performed on Saturday, the 6th of October, 1877, at the Court Theatre.

DARNLEY.

ACT I.—SCENE I.

SIR FRANCIS MARSDEN'S *lodgings*.

[NOTE FOR THE SCENE-PAINTER.—*Pictures of race-horses, and prints of opera-dancers on the wall; Turkish pipes and weapons arranged in a recess; foils and boxing-gloves on one of the tables. A toilet table. And the general character of the apartment that of a young single man of fortune and fashion.*]

Marsden [*seated, and reading the newspaper.*] "Private French Theatricals at the Duchess of Dashmore's. The brilliant Sir Francis Marsden (much obliged for the epithet!) performed the Maréchal de Richelieu, and in the gaiety of the part seemed perfectly at home." At home? Ignoramus! as if gaiety and "at home" were not a contradiction in terms! [*yawns*] It takes a vast deal of pains to be a Man of Pleasure! What's this? "The beautiful Lady Juliet Darnley"—a long paragraph on her charms and her diamonds. Yes; she's very attractive, and her conquest would make me the envy of London! [*yawns again*] One must be always falling in love just to keep oneself awake.

Enter SELFBY FYSHE.

Mars. How d'ye do? You find me getting up the news of the day for the small talk of the evening.

Fyshe. News? I don't care for news. What's news to me? News means other people's concerns; I don't care for other people.

Mars. [*reading.*] What a horrible fire last night in St. Giles's!

Fyshe. Ah! I've no property in that direction.

Mars. So, Louis Philippe has been shot at again! What would become of France if she lost that sagacious king?

Fyshe. It's all one to me. I've nothing in the French funds.

Mars. Heavens! What is this? Your poor friend Dick Squander—blew out his brains at a quarter before six yesterday evening!

Fyshe. Did he? Thank Heaven I never lent him anything—except my umbrella! I must send for it.

Mars. Unparalleled philosopher, unmoved by the conflagration of a parish, the murder of a king, the danger of a realm, and the suicide of a friend!

Fyshe. Why, certainly, we ought all to be thankful when the calamities of others do not injure ourselves. [*offers snuff.*] My mixture—the Selfby Fyshe mixture.

Mars. No, man! I abhor your puny excitements of Rappee and Havannah. Give me those which stir the blood, and rock the heart—Fighting, Politics, Gaming, Drinking, Wine, Love!

Fyshe. Marsden, don't bore!

Mars. Ha! ha! Why even you are not insensible to love. Own that you are prodigiously stricken with the fair Amelia Placid—

Fyshe. More propriety in your expression—"stricken" is violent, and "prodigiously" hyperbolical. Amelia Placid's uncle was my father's intimate friend. This uncle left Amelia £30,000 of which she forfeits the half if she does not marry me—unless, indeed, *I* refuse to ensure her happiness by making her Mrs. Fyshe. But I'm not marble. I shall marry her. I'm very fastidious. My wife must be subdued and ladylike. Miss Placid seems tolerably quiet: understands draughts and double dummy. I could conceive a sort of a kind of conjugal tranquillity in retiring to Fyshe Hall with a sort of a kind of tranquil companion who would not give me much trouble. [*thoughtfully*] She don't look as if she'd have noisy children!

Mars. Well, I wish you tranquillity with your Amelia. Wish me rapture with my Juliet.

Fyshe. Your Juliet's married already, and they put a very high price upon rapture at Doctors' Commons.

Mars. Pshaw! I would give my whole fortune for a smile.

Fyshe [*aside.*] He'd have the smile at a bargain. His fortune's all gone to the Jews. [*aloud.*] Really, though it's no business of mine, I must say I think it's very immoral to destroy the happiness of an excellent man—who gives excellent dinners.

Mars. Happiness? No, I'm a sad dog where love is concerned, but not so bad as you think me. There can be no happiness in my cousin Juliet's marriage with Darnley.

Fyshe. Why? He's a very gentlemanlike man—for a merchant, or rather a speculator, for he's more the last than the first.

Mars. Oh! his father was a cabinet minister, his boyhood was spent in a court. When he came of age his father offered him a sinecure, and a relation of his mother's offered him a share in a mercantile establishment. He chose the latter; spent his youth at the desk; at the age of thirty-three saw my cousin Juliet, then only seventeen; fell in love with her, and was accepted. For two or three years I dare say they lived like most married people. But twelve months ago this Darnley, whose genius for speculation is wonderful, by a series of lucky hits became, from a man of easy fortune, one of the richest subjects in Europe. From that time he has only lived for speculation, and Juliet has only lived for the world. They scarcely ever see each other. Juliet is without a guide, and Darnley without a companion.

Fyshe. Darnley must be occupied indeed if he does not observe your more than cousinly attentions. Does he never seem to suspect you.

Mars. You know his singular calm and thorough high breeding. An enthusiast at the counter, but a stoic in the world. If he suspect me, he shows it only by an ironical politeness that looks confoundedly like contempt. [*Looks at his watch.*] I did not know it was so late. I am going to Lady Juliet's, shall I take you in my cab?

Fyshe. No? Cabs are liable to accidents. I have patent safety close little carriage.

Mars. Then you shall take me.

Fyshe. No! the Selfby Fyshe Patent Safety only holds one. Built on purpose not to be crowded by self-invited companions. [*Opens the window and puts out his hand.*] It's going to rain. I left my carriage at the corner, that damned fellow before he blew out his brains should have sent me back my umbrella.

Mars. Pshaw! the country wants rain—the crops are perishing.

Fyshe. Very likely. I don't grow oats and barley on the nap of my new hat. [*Exit.*

Mars. Ha! ha! Go thy way, thou incarnation of the languid egotism of the nineteenth century. Like Major Longbow, if the lightning struck thy bride in the honey-moon, thou would'st ring the bell for thy valet to bring clean glasses, and sweep away Mrs. Fyshe. [*Rings the bell.*] John, is my cab come?

John. Yes, sir.

Mars. [*dressing.*] My coat. Certainly, I adore this Juliet. The eau-de-cologne. Never loved anyone so much—except Jane, and Kate, and Caroline; ah! and poor Susan [*in an altered voice.*] Poor Susan, if she had not left me I had been perhaps another man. Into how many wild excesses have I plunged, to silence my remorse! But she deserted me and I am free. Plague on these late hours, how they shake the nerves. John, the laudanum drops. [*drinks.*] Pshaw! Again I am a true Epicurean. The past is irrevocable, the future not at our command. He who would enjoy life must seize every joy of the moment!

John. Mr. Plunder's bill, sir, and Mr. Rackett's, and Squabb the horsedealer's.

Mar. These are "messengers that feeling persuade us what we are." John—John—John—one word for all. It hurts the feelings of a man of honor not to pay what he fairly owes. Spare my feelings and burn the bill.

[*Singing.*]

"C' est l' armour, l' armour
Qui fait le monde a la ronde,
Et chaque jour, a son tour
L' amour, fait passer le monde."

[*Exit.*

SCENE II.

A library in DARNLEY'S *house.*

DARNLEY *and* PARSONS (DARNLEY'S Head Clerk).

Darn. An imprudent speculation, do you say, sir? A company to light the towns of Germany with gas!—Buy up all the shares you can—*all*. As the loadstone attracts the needle, civilization attracts capital. In the nineteenth century every investment in Human Improvement is a safe speculation. Buy up the shares.

Par. Well, sir—as you please. But these Spanish Funds, they are falling sadly. Better sell out.

Darn. Sell out? pooh! I shall throw in another ten thousand, and redress the market. Ha, ha! the glorious thing called *capital!* I, a plain English Merchant, can have an effect on the very destinies of Spain.

Par. But, sir——

Darn. I tell you I know to day when these Funds will rise ten per cent. Here [*gives a paper*]—see to these instructions. [*Exit* Clerk *and enter* MAINWARNING.

Main. Ah, money-making, money-making—always making!

Darn. Well, and what benefactor to the world like the money-maker? Charity feeds one man, but Capital a million. It reaches Genius, and up springs Art. It converts the desert to a garden, the hamlet to a city. Without competition no excellence, but without capital no competition. Without energy no virtue, but no energy without gold. Your money-maker is the great civilizer.

Main. Hem! You are fortunate in having a wife who puts so much energy and virtue into constant circulation.

Darn. Always some sneer at my poor Juliet. For shame!

Main. For shame yourself, Harry Darnley! This extravagant wife of yours is——

Darn. Beware!

Main. Beware? Dammee, sir, don't take that tone with me! 'Tis not generous. Don't I owe everything to you? and does not that give me the right to say whatsoever I please? When years ago, I, born a gentleman and reared in luxury, was left by my father's improvidence to poverty and despair—when but for my young sister (then an infant looking to me for bread) I might have sunk to the cowardice of the suicide—who alone remembered the old schoolfellow in the ruined pauper? Who, not then rich himself, came to the sordid and wretched garret? Who gave a home to my sister, a future to my hope? Who was that man? you, Harry Darnley, you! Blame yourself if I am a troublesome, honest, disagreeable friend—and zounds, sir, I don't care how uncomfortable I may make you, so long as I save you from a single sorrow.

Darn. My dear Mainwaring!

Main. Don't "dear" me, sir! I won't be wheedled out of my right to reprove you. You procured me an appointment abroad. I, too, became a money-maker. I saw my sister grow up to womanhood—fair and innocent the joy of my life. Suddenly my affairs summoned me to England. A fortune is left me by a relation whose name I now bear. I was absent but three months. I returned—my sister had left my roof. Gone with some villain—gone, and not a word! Oh, then I knew the nothingness of the money-making you boast of! Darnley, Darnley, I tell you, gold may civilize a nation; it does not consecrate a home.

Darn. Calm yourself. Your sister may yet return.

Main. Return? I would rather stand by her grave than look upon her face. Fortunately the estate bequeathed me obliged me to change the name she stains and bears. And to you alone I have confided the history of her shame. You said "Live with me, and find the home that you have lost." I came—and you have no home of your own. Man has no home when the wife is absent from the hearth.

Darn. Ah, that you had seen the first happy years of our marriage!

Main. They can return—if you but exercise your rights. Take warning from me. You indulge your wife as I indulged my sister. My reward was desertion and disgrace. All women are alike. Would you be safe? Be stern.

Darn. What would you have me do? Have I not myself encouraged what you ask me now to reprove? In the blaze of my sudden wealth my eyes saw but Juliet shine. Too busy, perhaps too simple in my own person, to enjoy what my millions placed at my command, I enjoyed it, as it were, through her. She was the incarnation of my wealth. The splendor of my fortune became visible in the delight that it gave to her. Recall the difference of our years. Shall I bid her renounce her youth, because the pleasures of youth are but dull to me?

Main. Among the pleasures of youth, do you include a handsome, good-for-nothing cousin?

Darn. Hold, hold! [*checking himself*]. Nay, man, indulge your spleen—I have no cause for fear.

Main. A man who counts on the faith of a woman has everything to fear.

Darn. And the moment a husband shows such fear, dignity and trust are gone for ever. His happiness is in his wife's love, his honor in her virtue. I will not forfeit the one by harshness, nor shake the other by distrust. Juliet may have faults, but her heart is generous. For the faults of the generous what cure so effectual as confidence and indulgence? [*Seats himself.*] Enough. What are these? "Designs for Elgrove Lodge, the villa of Henry Darnley, Esq., after the Alhambra."

Main. Oh, yes. Lady Juliet's last proof of generosity. I never knew a woman more generous with her husband's fortune.

[*Folding doors open. Enter* LADY JULIET, FYSHE, MISS PLACID (*tatting*), *and* SIR FRANCIS MARSDEN.

Lady J. Yes, I must show you the drawings for our villa. A thousand pardons, dear Henry, for so abrupt an invasion. Look, Sir Francis, are they not charming?

Mars. Superb! after the Alhambra. Ah, the style's so effective; then, too, the associations. I always found the highest interest in the accounts of the Moors——

Darn. Really! I had fancied you had found a still higher interest in the accounts of the Jews.

Mars. [*aside.*] Hang his impertinence!

Lady J. You *must* like the idea. Next week we'll begin. You can't guess my impatience.

Darn Still, it takes some time to move an Alhambra all the way from Granada. Give me leave to consider.

Lady J. Consider? I hate consideration. Next month, you know, I may care nothing about it.

[Scene III.]

Main. Very true. This month 'tis an Alhambra on the banks of the Thames. Next month it will be a Pagoda at the top of St. Paul's!

Lady J. Ha! ha! I dare say it will. But, meanwhile, why not all go to Elgrove to-day, and examine its Moorish capabilities?

Darn. To-day? ah! to-day I am so busy.

Mars. Fyshe, here's an opportunity for urging your suit to Miss Placid. Press Lady Juliet to go. The loveliest villa!

Fyshe. I hate villas, they're full of earwigs and thorough draughts.

Miss P. Come, Mr. Mainwaring! Since Mr. Fyshe does not go, you must be my cavalier.

Fyshe. She's piqued, poor thing! I suppose I must go. (*to Mainwaring*) Always tatting—the quietest creature! We can put up all the windows, and sit down to rest, the moment we arrive.

Lady J. [*who has been conversing with* DARNLEY]. Well, then, it's arranged. Adieu, Henry. Mr. Fyshe, will you take the designs? And, oh, this book,—Robert's Views of the Alhambra! I shall be back early.

Darn. Will you? a thousand thanks!

Lady J. Oh, yes. For the opera. Well, Mr. Mainwaring, how do you like me in this bonnet of Herboult's?

Main. Not at all.

Lady J. I admire your sincerity, and compassionate your taste. Mr. Fyshe, will you charge yourself with my parasol?

Miss P. And mine.

Lady J. Oh! and where is poor little Shock? he will break his heart if I leave him!

Mars. Run for Shock, Fyshe, he's in his basket.

Fyshe. Run yourself. Shock bites. Miss Placid, under my right arm a small cavity is still left.

Miss P. Won't you come, Mr. Mainwaring?

Main. No.

Miss P. Heigh ho! Mr. Fyshe, I shall tat all the way.

Fyshe. It's a charming accomplishment, and refreshingly noiseless.

Mars. Good bye, Darnley. We shall miss you dreadfully.

Darn. To be missed by Sir Francis is an honor that can even console for the loss of his company.

Main. Ha! ha!

Mars. [*disconcerted, and offering his arm*] Come, Lady Juliet—*allons!*

Darn. [*stopping him.*] You forget—this arm is destined to Shock. You must go for him. Take care. He is snappish, but if you handle him properly you will find him as harmless a puppy as—the rest of his species.

Mars. [*enraged.*] Sir, I—— [*aside.*] Damn it, the master bites worse than the dog. [*Exit.*

Darn. [*as* MARS. *goes out.*] Adieu, Lady Juliet. This poor Marsden! what a good creature it is.

[*Exeunt* LADY JULIET, FYSHE, *and* MISS P.

SCENE III.

MAINWARING *and* DARNLEY.

Darn. My heart stands still. Yes, I fear that man!

Main. Most complaisant of husbands!

Darn. I've a great mind to call her back.

Main. A cousin is so proper a companion!

Darn. She shall not go.

Main. Ha! ha!

Darn. She shall not—[*going to the door*]. [*Enter* LADY J.

Lady J. My heart chides me—dear Henry! Perhaps after all you wish me to stay at home?

Main. To be sure he does.

Darn. No, my dear Juliet, I'm not so selfish. And yet—[*aside*]—out on my jealous heart!

Lady J. Yet what?

Darn. If you had another female companion!

Lady J. True. I will take old Lady Babbleton.

Darn. [*aside*]. I will give her a safer companion for a young wife. [*aloud.*] Why not take your child?

Lady J. Ah, yes—dear Fanny! that will be charming; now, indeed, I shall scarcely miss you.

Darn. The weight's gone. She does not fear the eyes of her child

Lady J. Grave still?

Darn. No, happy in your happiness. Go, my Juliet, and be gay. Gaiety with you is but the natural language of innocence and youth. [*Opens the door for her.*]

Main. What! going after all?

Lady J. With your leave. Ha, ha! see how awful he looks. Poor bachelor! what can he know of us strange married folks? Poor Mainwaring!

Darn. Ha! ha! poor Mainwaring! [*kissing her hand.*] [*Exit Lady J.*

Main. I've done with you!

Darn. Nay, forgive me. After all, what a temper she has!

Main. Oh, charming! The true female mixture for curing refractory husbands. Three drachms of the steel of obstinacy to an ounce of the oil of coaxing.

Darn. Obstinacy? Never contradicts!

Main. And always has her own way.

Darn. Ever ready to yield her inclination to mine!

Main. And ever doing every mischief she's inclined to.

Darn. Hum!

Main. Hum!

Darn. This Alhambra will cost thousands—Well, I can the less afford to be idle. Come with me to the city. I want to consult you. Such a vast speculation! If it succeeds, I shall clear half a million.

Main. And would be just as happy without it.

Darn. True! The money is nothing—but, oh, the excitement of the pursuit! For the happy, sweet must be repose. For the disappointed, no solace but in action! In the fever of our schemes we forget the goad of our cares. I seem to rise from the earth when I return to my desk.

Enter Servant.

Servant. Sir, a lady wishes to see you in the library.

Darn. A——what?

Servant. A lady, sir. She will not give her name.

Darn. Pshaw! I'm busy.

Servant. She seems in distress, sir. [*aside*] I knew that would touch him.

Darn. In distress? I won't keep her a moment. You see, while there's distress on the earth there's something godlike in making money.

Main. Some pinched old beggar, eh? [*taking out his purse.*

Servant. No, so young, and so handsome, sir!

Main. [*putting up his purse.*] Then, I'll keep my mite for the old and the ugly. [*Exit Servant.*] If Darnley were a man to be seduced, that sort of beggar would find this a lucky time for her purpose. 'Tis an ominous conjunction for a poor dog of a husband, when the wife goes a-gadding, and young girls come a-begging. Oh, these women, these women, what torments they are! There's that malignant Amelia, asking me to go to the villa that I might see her angling for Fyshe. Oh, but he has money! and I verily think that, for the sake of a handsome settlement, a woman would marry a gudgeon, and live in a pond.

Enter DARNLEY.

Darn. My poor Mainwaring—I mean my dear friend—How can I get him out of the house? Oh, will you kindly take these papers to Parsons, my clerk? I will meet you in an hour—at my office—pray go instantly!

Main. What the deuce is the matter? This young lady's distress seems to move you very much.

Darn. It does, indeed—that is—I—but be off, I beseech you! Parsons must have these papers before the markets are closed.

Main. But——

Darn. [*pushing him out.*] There's your hat—and your stick. Take a cab, or you won't be in time.

Main. Oh, these women, these women! old and young, giddy and sober, sinner and saint, it's all alike to them.

Darn. 'Sdeath man, if my character—

Main. Character? Lord help you, they're no more respect for a man's character than a wolf has for a lamb's. Well, I go, I go. Take care of yourself. Don't let her cry. Hold your character well over your head. But, when a woman once taken to crying, you'll find it a very sorry umbrella. [*Exit* MAINWARING.

Darn. Thank heaven, he's gone! [*Rings.*] [*Enter* Servant.] Not at home to a soul—send for the chariot. [*Exit* Servant.

Where can I find her lodging? Where I may visit her unknown? So young, so charming! In my whole life I've never been more touched and affected. [*Exit.*

ACT II.—SCENE I.

Drawing-room in DARNLEY'S *house.*

Enter Servant *preceding* MARSDEN *and* FYSHE.

Fyshe. It is Miss Placid I wish to see.

Servant. Yes, sir. [*Exit.*

Mars. What! are you about to propose?

Fyshe. Not exactly. There are many things to consider before one admits another to the right of sharing one's existence, and crowding one's carriage. The girl's certainly quiet and silent. But has she all the other qualifications for a conjugal partner? There's the question! Take off all trouble, claim no authority, recollect what one likes when she orders the dinner, and never presume to appropriate to herself the liver-wing of the chicken?

Mars. A most original epitome of a bridegroom's expectations and a bride's perfections! I think Miss Placid will suit you exactly. A picture of still life, framed in white muslin.

Fyshe. Yes, but I'm very comfortable as a bachelor; and though, as you say, the picture is one of very still life, I would not hang it up in my drawing-room if it were worth less than £30,000. [*Looking out, aside.*] This fellow's in my way. [*Aloud.*] When Miss Placid comes you'll be good enough to go?

Mars. Oh, certainly. Lady Juliet will receive me in her boudoir.

Fyshe. Ever since that excursion to the villa, you've made way in her ladyship's heart.

Mars. I've not come yet to the heart, but I'm on the high-road,—through the fancy. Still, shall I own it? my conscience is a perpetual check on my hopes. Ah, what would I give to detect some frailty in Darnley, to justify the diversion of Juliet's affections!

Fyshe. [*aside.*] What would he give? What has he got that would be useful to me? Hum—ha. Frailty—ha—hum.

Mars. But that is impossible!

Fyshe. Impossible? That's very good—hum—ha.

Mars. What do you know of——

Fyshe. I—it's not my business to know anything. Nothing to be got by meddling with other people's affairs—hum—ha.

Mars. This fellow has certainly wormed out a secret. But he'll never give even a secret for nothing. You affect to be mighty wise, Master Fyshe; but I bet you my brown cob (the one I refused to sell you last week) to the old umbrella you got back from poor Squander's executors, that you can't say a word against Darnley's moral reputation.

Fyshe. Will you? The brown cob? Done

Mars. Done.

Fyshe. It never stumbles?

Mars. No.

Fyshe. Darnley does. I've a villa in St. John's Wood—my aunt's legacy. I told my agent to let it. He has done so—to a female—young and exceedingly pretty. By-the-bye, you will throw in the bridle and saddle?

Mars. Yes, yes! For Heaven's sake go on.

Fyshe. Darnley pays the rent—the establishment, the bills—keeps the lady a carriage, and visits her almost daily.

Mars. The formal hypocrite! Are you sure?

Fyshe. Sure? Have not I bet my umbrella? There's the address. Saw the girl with my own eyes, when I called about moving some things of mine. Darnley don't know I'm the owner—settles all with the agent. Don't mention me as your authority.

Mars. My last scruple is vanished!

Enter Servant.

Servant. My lady will see you, Sir Francis.

Mars. I come. Aha, saintly sinner!

Fyshe. You are sure it's quite safe?

Mars. Safe?

Fyshe. The cob.

Mars. Oh, certainly, and if ever it grows restive, you can lend it to the future Mrs. Fyshe.

[*Exit.*

Enter Miss Placid, *tatting.*

Fyshe. Heaven forbid Mrs. Fyshe should do anything so boisterous as ride. Ah, Miss Placid, always occupied? A nice employment! Better than singing—not so noisy.

Miss P. You don't like noisy people?

Fyshe. No, indeed. You agree with me? [Miss Placid *nods assent.*

Fyshe. Man's first care should be his health. Noise shatters the nerves, and disturbs the digestion. [Miss Placid *nods.*

Fyshe. What a dumb little thing she is! She was born to be a Fyshe! A-hem! You know, my dear young lady, the wishes of my poor friend, your late uncle?

Miss P. Yes—he wished me to marry you. I cannot guess why.

Fyshe. Charming simplicity! Your uncle consulted your happiness in choosing a man of good fortune and moral character. I never gamble—it's expensive. I never drink—it's unhealthy. I never flirt—for it's troublesome. In short, I may say without vanity that, thinking that vice always injures oneself—I have not a vice in the world. That's why your uncle chose me.

Miss P. But my uncle said you were very sensible, and you know I'm rather silly than not.

Fyshe. So much the better. What they call a superior woman is always fidgetty, and generally cracked.

Miss P. But, they say Mr. Fyshe, married people ought to love each other. I am afraid I sha'n't love you.

Fyshe. Love? Human Nature was not made for such violent emotions. Love—the Enemy of Repose and the Prompter of Dyspepsia!

Miss P. Heigho! I don't think I can marry you—I don't indeed. And as for the forfeit of £15,000 if I refuse you—you are too generous to take it.

Fyshe. You render justice to my disposition. But I must do my duty, however painful—and in money matters a conscientious man owes a duty to himself.

Miss P. [*aside.*] Odious creature! [*aloud.*] But is my uncle's will so decisive?

Fyshe. It is indeed. Shall I bring you my copy?

Miss. P. Yes—to-morrow at twelve.—One can't give up so much money.

Fyshe. A very sensible remark. Ah, Miss Amelia, believe me, we shall be exceedingly happy. Fyshe Hall is the quietest place—game in abundance and the poultry suberb. By the way, what part of the chicken do you prefer?

Miss. P. I've no preference.

Fyshe. Thank Heaven! the liver wing is save! No preference? Excellent creature—a perfect treasure! [*passionately.*] Oh, my Amelia, my Amelia!

Miss. P. La! you frighten me. Go away, now, and at twelve to-morrow.

Fyshe. I will call with the will. [*Admiringly.*] How serenely she tats! Nothing disturbs her. Made on purpose for me—quite an automation! Might as well not be married at all. Ah, I'm a lucky dog! Adieu, my Amelia. [*Exit.*

Miss. P. The monster! I could hardly help boxing his ears. They said he was so sensible. I thought to revolt him by playing the fool. O woman's wit, quicken my invention! Ah, he hates noisy people, does he? If I could but save the forfeit, and bring my whole fortune to that dear rude disagreeable Mainwaring—that is provided that dear rude disagreeable Mainwaring will condescend to accept me.

Enter MAINWARING.

Main. I wish I was a book—or a chair—or a table—or a pair of tongs—or a hearthrug—or a philosopher—anything that don't feel.

Miss P. Always in a passion! Why don't you take to tatting? Come, I'll teach you.

Main. Don't be pert, child!

Miss P. Don't be saucy, man! Sit down. Just wind this on the shuttle.

Main. Pshaw!

Miss P. What, unkind? When I wish to consult you! I'm very unhappy!

Main. Unhappy! You—how—what!

Miss P. Sit down.

Main. [*sitting*] Yes: but unhappy——

Miss P. Wind this—carefully.

Main. [*winding the skein rapidly, and into most horrible confusion.*] Certainly: but unhappy?

Miss P. [*aside but affected.*] Dear Mainwaring! [*aloud.*] You know that I forfeit half my fortune if I refuse to marry Mr. Fyshe.

Main. Oh, you'll marry him. Anything rather than lose money!

Miss P. Very true!

Main. Very true? There's a mercenary baggage!

Miss P. But if I've no affection for him?

Main. So much the better. What's affection, but the power we give another to torment us?

Miss P. Well, I suppose you're right; and if you advise me to marry, I've that confidence in your judgment—that desire for your approbation [*offering to take his hand.*]

Main. Don't touch me!

Miss P. [*aside.*] He loves me! [*aloud.*] Well, but if Mr. Fyshe does as you do—refuse my hand—I preserve my fortune.

Main. Ah, that's the great consideration!

Miss P. Why, one's never thought half so good-looking when one has lost half one's fortune. Who'd marry poor me except for my money?

Main. Who? I know a fool who, if it were *not* for your money, would—but, no—you're too pretty for him.

Miss P. What, would he marry me if I lost——

Main. Every farthing! I dare say he would—but, then, he is a fool.

Miss P. Tell me more of him! Is he very agreeable, and good-tempered, and handsome?

Main. No, a quarrelsome, violent, testy, ill-looking brute. Pshaw! take your skein!

Miss P. Well, I know one thing. I never will marry Mr. Fyshe, or any one else, till I see Mr. Darnley and Lady Juliet as happy as they derserve.

Main. Ah, that reminds me—Poor Darnley! poor fellow!

Miss P. What has happened?

Main. What, have you not heard? This last speculation of Darnley's—a very vast one—has failed. His credit is shaken. There is a run on his house. And, foremost among those who press on the husband, are the creditors whose claims have been created by his wife.

Miss P. Is it possible? The rich Mr. Darnley! the millionnaire!

Main. Yes, the man never satisfied with one million, if he could grasp at two! But, why do I blame him? It contents a man to count the smiles upon the faces of wife and children; but it never contents him to count his gold. If Darnley, driven by regret and disappointment to seek the excitement of the speculator, is a bankrupt—to-morrow let his fine-lady wife blame herself, and be hanged to her!

Miss P. Hush!

Darn. [*without*] Very well. Let him wait in my study. He shall be paid.

[*Enter* DARNLEY *followed by* Servant.

Servant. And, please, sir—Madame Cramousin has been very troublesome—called twice this morning——

Darn. Madame Cramousin? Who's she?

Servant. My lady's dressmaker.

Darn. True. Let her send her receipt to my office to-morrow. Well, Amelia, where is Lady Juliet?

Miss P. In her boudoir.

Darn. Alone?

Miss P. Little Fanny, is with her.

Darn. Anyone else?

Miss P. I—I'm not sure.

Darn. She falters! Torture, she too suspects—[*calmly*] Well, and—and her cousin—my—my friend, Marsden——

Main. Oh, that's of course!

Darn. [*after a pause.*] But, you say that—*her child is with her?*

Miss P. Yes, and Sir Francis only called to bring Fanny a puzzle of the History of England, which he's helping her to put together. [*To* MAINWARING.] Mischief-maker! My shuttle, sir. A pretty confusion you make of things when you take them in hand. *You tat*, indeed! [*Exit.*

Main. That girl bewitches me. I wish I was gay, and handsome, and rich. No! I wish

I was a poker, a hearthrug, a philosopher. What a beast I am! thinking of myself, and Darnley sad! [*Goes up to* DARNLEY, *puts his hand on his shoulder, and with feeling.*] My friend!

Darn. Those bills of Marsden's that you bought up at my request, some time since—they are due this week?

Main. Yes, the improvident rascal! Bills for £10,000, and the brokers sold them for two—the worst speculation you ever made!

Darn. [*to himself.*] The time is past when Knowledge was Power! Money is power, and I will yield it!

Main. [*overhearing.*] Money, power? No! can money ensure you a wife's love? Can money buy me back a sister's virtue?

Darn. A sister! Ah, Mainwarning, be not so hard. If your sister were less guilty than you deem her, if——

Main. Cease!

Darn. Can no suffering atone? no penitence win your pardon?

Main. [*fiercely.*] Yes! when she has told me the name of her betrayer. Yes! when his heart's blood has washed away my shame. Not till then!

Darn. [*aside*]. I must wait some happier moment.

Main. Let's talk the news—the weather—the markets. How go affairs to-day!

Darn. New losses. The next few days my house will be sorely tried. Let the waves beat—we are on a rock.

Main. Lady Juliet's extravagance could give a shock to Gibraltar.

Darn. Well, it must be checked when this crisis is once past.

Main. What time so fit as the present? Why not take this very hour to rouse her conscience by the sight of her folly?

Darn. Why? Simply because I love her! Because this extravagance it pleased me to indulge. Because this wealth, which has been to me but a burden, a drudgery and a toil, became bright and glorious when it invested her with the splendor of a queen. And, now, even now, grasper and speculator as men deem me,—it is not the fear of poverty that makes my heart sick, and my brain dizzy. Fortune once lost can be repaired. But, Home—Honor—Happiness—these lost, what philosoyhy can console, what energy restore? Mainwaring you are right. Money is *not* Power!

Main. Pardon me that I have so pained you! But, now that you are roused from your seeming indifference, all will be well. Assert your authority. Reprove Lady Juliet for her levity. Thrust this gay Lothario from your house.

Darn. And so, perhaps, root him in her heart. Shall I, who have sworn to honor and cherish the young creature that came to my hearth without one stain upon her soul—shall I, perhaps for a groundless fear, a visionary doubt, proclaim the jealousy that brings disgrace? When did the world ever acquit the wife whom the husband sullies my suspicion? Shall I suffer this man, whose vanity would exult even in the obstacle to his crime, to tell to every gossip how he made the proud Darnley tremble for his honor? And, what should I gain? If as yet she is indifferent to him, my harshness, that would insult her, might invest him with attractions not his own. If she loves him—if—if—O Heaven! her *virtue*—I fear not *that*! But, her *heart?* There I am a coward! [*Pauses, in great disorder.*] No, no! As I have begun so will I proceed. I will not combat mine enemy with his own weapons, but I will debase him with my contempt, and, if need be, I will crush him with my gold! And for Juliet—for her whose affection I have cherished with a miser's care—for her, there shall be no meaner guardians than the wife's purity, and the husband's trust.

Enter FANNY.

Fan. Papa, dear papa!
Darn. My pretty one!
Fan. Mamma has just heard you are come in. Pray go to her!

Darn. Does she wish it?

Fan. To be sure. You'll see how nicely I've done the puzzle Sir Francis brought me.

Darn. [*putting her aside.*] Ah, Sir Francis. You love him?

Fan. No I don't.

Darn. [*smiling*]. Why, my Fanny?

Fan. Because he's a naughty man, and tells stories.

Darn. Eh?

Fan. Yes, only think! He tells mamma he's so fond of [*mimicking*] "sweet little Fanny,"—and I heard him tell Mr. Fyshe, I was a troublesome little thing, always in the way. Not like dear good scolding Mr. Mainwaring, who don't say one thing and mean another. Where's my doll, sir?

Main. My darling, I've got it for you. Such a beauty! Come into the nursery, come!

Darn. And I shall see Marsden with her. Courage! [*Exeunt severally.*

SCENE II.

Lady Juliet's *Boudoir.*

Lady Juliet *and* Marsden *seated.*

Mars. Nay, I cannot agree with you my fair cousin. I cannot believe that persons can be permanently happy with dissimilar dispositions; that the grave can harmonize with the gay, or methodical reason with joyous fancy.

Lady J. Have you never seen the grandsire playing with the grandchild? What so dissimilar? The old man to whom the world itself is worn and hacknied; the infant who finds a plaything even in the gray locks of age! Yet the old man's brow smooths from its furrows at the merry laugh of the infant; and the infant will steal from his noisy playmates to clamber up the old man's knee. Can you not conceive that light lends a joy to shadow, and shadow gives repose to light?

Mars. Grandsire and grandchild! an innocent illustration. I spoke of two persons linked in nearer union. Lovers, or—married.

Lady J. Well, take even the married. Henry and myself. I so frivolous, he so wise. I the creature of every impulse, he so serene and calm. Were he like me, I fear I should despise him. Were I like him, I should tease him less—but should I please him more!

Mars. Ah, my fair cousin, you take ground I may not venture to dispute. Still, do you not deny the charm that you have not known?—the perfect harmony of character, the interchange of two hearts that beat with a common pulse; thoughts, feelings the echo of each other—if you are sad, all cloud for the one that loves you; if gay, all sunshine.

Lady J. [*half-touched.*] Ah, that is poetry. Is it life?

Mars. Life, real life—if we but dare to seize it. [*Enter* Darnley.] If, when we find the one congenial spirit, never found but once, we can free oneself from the cold thraldom of the world—if we can see, through all things, but the one dear, ever-gracious, ever-welcome image of—Damn it! the husband!

Darn. Go on, pray! Charming! "Congenial spirit"—"cold thraldom"—"ever welcome image"—Some scene out of the Sorrows of Werter, eh?

Mars. I—I was saying—that is, I was remarking to Lady Juliet that, as a general proposition—that in short merely as a philosophical observation—you understand—

Darn. Perfectly. As a philosophical observation—a congenial disposition——

Mars. Exactly so—is a very agreeable sort of thing.

Darn. The peroration is less brilliant than the exordium,—eh, Juliet? This poor Marsden! As they say in the House of Commons, his delivery is not equal to his matter.

Mars. [*aside.*] Confusion!

Lady J. My cousin is abashed by your irony. We were discussing a foolish question and disagreed. How did it begin? Oh, apropos of Mr. Fyshe and Amelia. My dear Henry, you will never consent to such a sacrifice?

Darn. Amelia is now of age, and can decide for herself. Mr. Fyshe has one recommendation. He is Sir Francis Marsden friend.

Lady J. Friend? He cares for nobody but himself.

Darn. He has the character of being exceedingly sensible.

Lady J. Because he never neglects his own interest.

Darn. And of being scrupulously moral, and prudently economical.

Lady J. Because he is too covetous to spend, and too passionless to feel.

Darn. You show great discernment in character. You are right. There is one class of men too egotistical for error. There is another class whose egotism is less amusing, and yet more contemptible. What say you, Sir Francis?

Mars. I have not studied the species.

Lady J. Perhaps you'll define it.

Darn. I will—by a specimen. Conceive a man who denies himself no pleasure, and is restrained by no duty. Without honesty, frank: without generosity, profuse; a lover of beauty; but as the worm loves the rose, not to delight in the fragrance, but to prey upon the flower. Viewing his fortune as the food of his vices; cultivating his talents as the servants of deceit; careless what misery he occasions so that his vanity is pleased; and undoing the happiness of a life, for the diversion of an hour. Such a man, though the world may call him warm-hearted and lavish, though he seem to the shallow too wild and extravagant to be selfish—such a man is the deadliest and most loathsome egotist; and amidst the ties, the charities, the affections of this breathing world, his only god is himself. Is not that true, Sir Francis?

Lady J. Hush, Cynic! there is no such monster.

Darn. Pardon me, I know an illustration in point. Once on a time, Sir Francis, I had a friend—who did not repent to have married a wife younger than himself. In that wife was centered the charm of his austere existence, the honor of his spotless name. That wife had a cousin—a fair faced and brilliant gentleman, who pressed the husband's hand, feasted at his board, was familiar at his house, and under the guise of the relative aimed at the distinction of the betrayer. You see there is such a monster. Sir Francis recognizes the description!

Lady J. What can this mean?

Darn. I call this man an egotist. For, had he loved, he had respected the honor and the happiness of the woman in whose ruin he sought but the gratification of his own vanity. One day my friend entered the room where the wife and the cousin were alone. He overheard the tawdry sentiment in which the egotist wrapped the insidious poison——

Lady J. Henry!—Henry!——

Mars. [*haughtily.*] Fear not, madam. The egotist perhaps could reply to a calumny, unmask a hypocrite, and avenge an insult. Well, sir, what did your friend do?

Darn. My friend, sir, made himself merry with the confusion he excited. But then, seeing that the hour was come at last to open the eyes of Innocence to the designs of Guilt, he told some such story as I tell now. And having told it, such was his unconquerable trust in his wife's purity and love, such his belief that, the treason once revealed, the traitor was for ever baffled, that he bowed triumphantly to the one whom he did not fear, smiled confidingly on the one whom he could not doubt, took up his hat, and left them. [*Exit.*

[LADY JULIET *sinks down, and covers her face with her hands.*

Mars. [*aside.*] What! He exasperates the foe and then abandons the field? Fool as well as hypocrite! [*aloud.*] Lady Juliet, forgive me if action or word of mine has exposed you to suspicions so insulting and unjust.

Lady J. Suspicion! of me?

Mars. To accuse *me* is to suspect *you*.

Lady J. And has my thoughtless levity stung that generous heart?

Mars. Generous? True! indifference is always generous.

Lady J. Indifference!

Mars. It is easy for a man to be generous to the faults—if such there be—of his wife, when his own affections are given to another.

Lady J. Calumniator!

Mars. Pardon me—I have said too much. Yet pity, even more than indignation. But no! Till you learn the truth—not from me. . . . Ah, Juliet, think what you will of the accuser and the unaccusing! Farewell!

Lady J. Yes, go! I never knew your true character till now. Shame on one who can insinuate the slander which——

Mars. Hold! Taunt me not to your own misery.

Lady J. Speak! that Darnley's life may belie you!

Mars. Alas!

Lady J. Ah, you falter! it is false.

Mars. By heaven, I have not uttered a syllable which I do not believe to be true; and true the more, because experience bids me doubt of the mortal who affects to be the saint. What in the frank is but error, in the hypocrite is sin. If another man, gay and young, hires a house in the superb, and makes a fair lady its inhabitant; if he maintains the establishment, defrays the expenses, and visits the lady daily—why, it is but a venial gallantry as the world goes. But, if this be done by a formal moralist who preaches to others, and gives his life, as you say, for an example, why,—let us hope that it is only charity!

Lady J. And you dare to charge Mr. Darnley with——

Mars. With what I have said and no more. You have wrung it from me.

Lady J. Prove your accusation.

Mars. I have not the right. But this address may enable those who have it, to convict the egotist, or unmask the dissembler. [*Exit.*

Lady. J. [*after a pause.*] where am I? Alone?—alone! O heaven, I never knew till now how I loved him! *

ACT III.—SCENE I.†

A room in a Villa in St. John's Wood.

The Lady of the Villa. How wearily creep the hours! How desolate seems the present, and yet, what happier moments can I hope for in the future? [*sees a guitar lying on the table*] And in these strings sleeps the voice of the past! The past, when all nature seemed to have no sound but music, and I heard his whisper in every murmur of the air [*strikes a few chords*] My only solace. For, when I sing the words he loved, I feel as though my voice could reach him from afar.

SONG.

O, wouldst thou from the blighting wind
  Protect life's early flowers,
And, like the dial, only count
  The time by sunny hours?
        Love not! love not!

And wouldst thou keep from youth to age
  Some trace of childhood's bloom,
Thro' cheerful days and careless nights,
  That sigh not for the tomb?
        Love not! love not!

---

* The conclusion of this scene is altered in the acting version.
† Omitted in the acting version.

When this sad heart shall rest at last
Beneath the funeral shade,
Upon the nameless headstone write,
To warn some happier maid,
"Love not! love not!"

Enter Maid Servant.

Servant. These books, and this letter, from Mr. Darnley. [*Exit.*

The Lady [*in a tone of disappointment*]. He will not come to-day! [*reads the letter*]—" I regret extremely that urgent business may prevent my seeing you for a few days. Meanwhile, take comfort and hope for the best. As soon as the affairs that now engross me will permit, be assured that I will devote every energy to secure your happiness, and repair your wrongs." —Generous Darnley! In you rests, indeed, all that can take the name of hope! Books— they have lost their charm! My own sad thoughts start up from every page. [*Knock at the door.*] A visitor to me!—is it possible? Who can have discovered——

Enter LADY JULIET, *veiled.*

Lady J. [*aside.*] So young! and with that look of innocence! [*aloud.*] Madam, forgive this intrusion.

The Lady. I fear there is some mistake.

Lady J. And I hope it. [*aside.*] What can I say? I have come here by an irresistible impulse, and now I am more confused than herself. [*aloud.*] Madam, a friend of mine—a—I cannot proceed!

The Lady. Her voice falters. Tears! What new misery does she come to announce to me?

Lady J. Away with weakness! At once, madam—are you acquainted with Mr. Darnley?

The Lady. [*starting.*] Mr. Darnley? You terrify me! What has happened to Mr. Darnley? Speak!

Lady J. [*ironically.*] Compose yourself. He is well.

The Lady. Strange! This tone—these looks—this disorder—Whom have I the honor to receive?

Lady J. One who has forgotten herself to come hither. One who knows the secret of your shame.

The Lady. Oh, spare me! spare me!

Lady J. Poor child! not yet reconciled to dishonor.

The Lady. If you know my secret, you know also how I was misled—how deceived. But no! I will not accuse him. I deserved it all. What right had I to confide? I who betrayed the confidence of another, I who may yet have on my soul the weight of a brother's curse, the stain of a brother's blood? O Madam, I know not who you are, nor what brings you hither. But by your womanhood itself I adjure you to remember that this secret is not mine alone. If my brother learn my wrongs and discover the betrayer, he will avenge them with his life—or the life of one still too dear.

Lady J. Life? Oh, fear not. Your secret is my own, and it shall not even rise up in reproach to him who has wronged me, not less than you.

The Lady. Wronged you? You know him? You——

Lady J. [*haughtily.*] Enough, madam. My wrongs are not as yours, for mine have no remorse.

The Lady. [*covering her face with her hands.*] Ah!

Lady J. [*walking to and fro.*] No, I will not parade my injuries. I will not bring the world's obloquy on my child's father. And his life? Oh heaven! should I risk his life because, like Man, he has looked on Woman as his toy? Ah! she hides her face—the face that has allured from me a heart—O torture! torture! [*coming to the table and seeing the letter*] His hand! [*reads*]—" Be assured that I will devote every energy to secure your happiness, and repair your wrongs." Woman, whom on earth hast thou left to me? The sinner has her comforter, the abandoned one has none!

The Lady. You? How have I injured you? How provoked the reproaches of a stranger?

Lady J. How? Know that I am—No, I may not lower my name by breathing it in these walls.

The Lady. Speak to me! speak! I am more sinned against that sinning. Go not till you have lifted from my heart the terror that your words have left there. Oh, turn not from me in such disdain!

Lady J. I turn that I may not see your face: I turn that I may not insult the fallen: I turn that I may leave to one who has robbed me of my all—compassion and forgiveness!
[*Exit.*

The Lady. Forgiveness? A light breaks on me. How my shame blinded me before! Another of his victims—another whom perhaps he owns as wife. Stay! stay!

As she goes to the door, enter Servant.

Servant. What has happened, ma'am? This strange lady——

The Lady. Stay me not! I must see her again.——

Servant. Alas, ma'am, she is gone; you are ill—you faint!

The Lady. Give me your arm. Jane, you remember me in my merry childhood?

Servant. I placed you in your cradle.

The Lady. And saw my mother watch beside me?

Servant. Dear heart, yes——

The Lady. I have no mother now—and yet I am more defenceless. Well, well, Innocence sleeps not so soundly in the cradle, as Sorrow in the Grave! [*Exeunt.*

SCENE II.

The Library in DARNLEY'S *House.*

Enter MAINWARING *fanning himself with his hat.*

Main. Phew! phew! The run on Darnley's house is at fever heat. Well, I've secretly taken all I have in the world to the head clerk. If Darnley's ruined, I'm ruined, and that's a great comfort. So I ought to be! I owe all to him—all that I scraped and saved for my little sister—who I hope is now starving! If she were, I would not give her a farthing, not a loaf, not a crumb. [*Pauses and seats himself.*] Poor thing! I'd give this right hand to hear her gay voice singing on the stairs. She never sang when she'd done anything to vex me. Confound these fine chairs! There's no sitting in comfort in this house. And that villainous Lady Juliet, out gadding as usual, while her husband struggles against ruin and despair. [*Takes out a cigar case and lights a cigar.*] Oho! by the way, this would horrify her dainty ladyship. She swallows the incense of a lover, and swoons at the perfume of a cigar.

Enter MISS PLACID, *speaking to a* Servant.

Miss P. If Mr. Fyshe calls, show him in here. That is, don't announce him—say I expect him in the library. Aha! I will see now in good earnest if I cannot shock him into resigning my alliance, and so sparing me the forfeit. I failed as a fool, perhaps I may succeed as a vixen. Somebody smoking! O dear me, Mr. Mainwaring!

Main. Beg pardon. Darnley allows it in the library. A good cigar is as great a comfort to a man as a good cry to a woman.

Miss P. To be sure. Never mind me. I like it. [*Aside.*] How astonished he looks!

I'll just practise on Mainwaring the part intended for Fyshe. [*Aloud.*] Bless you, when I lived with my poor uncle in Leicestershire, I've smoked a cigar myself, while riding to cover.

Main. Riding to cover!

Miss P. Don't you know my celebrity at Melton? Did you never hear of my great day at Langley Broom?

Main. My poor dear young friend, let me feel your pulse, will you?

Miss P. No, it always gallops a little when I think of that great day at Langley Broom. [*Knock at the door. Aside.*] There he is! Now for it. [*Aloud.*] That *was* a day!

> " A southerly wind and a cloudy sky
> Proclaim it a hunting morning!"—

Fifteen miles to cover. Uncle rather gouty; so we went in a chaise and four, and sent on the horses. Mounted at Crutch Hollow. The field quite on fire with expectation and scarlet. Here the Duke—his brows knit—hounds don't find. There—just where you stand—Count Scamper [*enter* FYSHE]—and there Handsome Tom [*pointing towards* FYSHE *without seeming to see him*]—Suddenly, yap, yap, yap! Hounds find. Horses snort. Freshmen look nervous. Out slips the fox—there, just by the fireplace—Yeo, yeo, yoicks! Tallyho! over the stone-wall, up the hill, on through the wood, Handsome Tom leads the way—stops at the fence and goes plump into the ditch on the other side. "Lie still for your life!" and over I go upon Brown Bess—fence, ditch, Tom, and all! Fox takes to the mill—Hounds at fault—all at a standstill. "Stole away!" cries the Duke. "Yoicks! yoicks!" cries the Huntsman, "there he sneaks the other side of the mill-stream." Harkaway! Harkaway!"—Into the stream—dash, dash, splash, splash! Safe on the bank—halt a moment to breathe—drip, drip, pant, pant! To it again! Count Scamper and I, neck and neck. Yap, yap, helter skelter—hurry scurry! Here we are, in at the death! "Mettlesome girl!" cries the Duke. Oh, what a day! Let me light a cigar.

[*Lights a cigar, and throws herself on the sofa upon which* MR. FYSHE *has sunk in speechless consternation.*

Fyshe. Mad as Bedlam! Lady Juliet's nasty little dog has certainly bit her.

Miss P. Oh, Mr. Fyshe, Mr. Fyshe, I'm perfectly shocked.

Fyshe. So am I. [*To* MAINWARING.] What's all this?

Main. How should I know? Do you take me for a key to the Family Riddle Book?

Miss P. Ah, Mr. Fyshe, I hope I've not lost your good opinion.

Main. Oh, she wants his good opinion, does she?—Hark ye, sir. Marry her and be miserable. You were born to be henpecked. [*Exit.*

Fyshe. Really, Miss Placid, I never knew that your spirits were so remarkably the reverse of low.

Miss P. Why, it's useless to continue the disguise. You see, my guardian has so often lectured me for being a little too vehement, and said "Mr. Fyshe is a very polite, sensible man, and likes young ladies to behave pretty and proper," that—ha! ha! so I took you in, did I?

Fyshe. Took me in!

Miss P. Oh, come now, I dare say you've more fun in you than one would suppose by your looks? Own that you are a little wild now and then. I sha'n't like you the less. And since we must pull together, we'll see which can go fastest.

Fyshe. Pull together? go fastest?

Miss P. By the by, there's no fun like a tandem. Do you handle the ribbons?

Fyshe. Great heavens! all the slang of a groom!

Miss P. Oh, you've got the will [*snatching it*]. Ah, I see. Here is the clause. Quite true. I forfeit half unless you refuse me. When shall it be? Next week? The sooner the better. I want to be my own mistress, and have it all my own way.

Fyshe. Really, Miss Placid, you must permit me to observe that hunting and driving and smoking cigars—[*aside*] I dare say she drinks too [*aloud*] are qualifications. I was scarcely prepared to expect in the female companion of an elegant retirement.

Miss P. Oh, I dare say I shall surprise you a great deal more when we're married.

Fyshe. [*aside.*] I feel uncommonly nervous. I wish she'd refuse me. As to that ma'am, the authority of a husband——

Miss P. Is what I never shall suffer.

Fyshe. [*aside.*] What a virago! Let me look at the will. Ah! £30,000 in the three per cent's—I shall be wretched for life!—but, £30,000! I shall hang myself at my bed-post—but £30,000!—If it were a farthing less—Well, Miss Placid, I suppose we must name the day.

Miss P. [*aside.*] I have failed then! Poor Mainwaring! To lose half the fortune I would bring him! It must be [*aloud*]—No, Mr. Fyshe, I fear I must be content to sacrifice——

Fyshe. Go on! go on!—[*aside.*] She refuses me, and pays the forfeit! £15,000 and no wife! Go on, sweet Amelia!

Enter LADY JULIET *in great agitation.*

Lady J. [*falls on Amelia's neck.*] Oh! my friend—I—I [*weeps.*]

Miss P. Heavens! what has happened? Compose yourself! Sir, you see Lady Juliet is ill. I wish you good morning.

Fyshe. Yes, she seems very ill. Still, as you were saying——

[LADY JULIET *goes to the table and writes.*

Miss P. [*calling to the servant.*] Mr. Fyshe's carriage. Sir, if you don't go this moment, I'll——

Fyshe. Yes, you'll——

Miss P. Accept you!

Fyshe. Miss Amelia, your most obedient. [*Exit.*

[LADY JULIET *seals her letter and rings the bell.*

Enter Servant.

Lady J. Mr. Darnley is not returned?

Servant. No, my lady. He is still in the city, and——

Lady J. Let him have this when he returns. No! send it instantly. Instantly!

Servant. Yes, my lady, I will take it myself.

Lady J. Do so. [*Exit* Servant.

Miss P. You alarm me. What letter is this? What have you written?

Lady J. What have I written? My intention to part from Mr. Darnley at once and for ever! [*Exit through the folding doors.*

Miss P. Part! Do I hear aright? Alas! that this brilliant creature should be the slave of every impulse. Hark! Sobs? I must go—and——

Servant *announces* MARSDEN, *who enters.*

Mars. Pardon me, Miss Placid. Where is Lady Juliet? I must see her—I—Surely that is her voice! [*Goes to the door.*

Miss P. [*arresting him.*] No! no! you cannot see Lady Juliet now!

Mars. And why?

Miss P. Some vile treachery has been at work to distract her mind and destroy her happiness! In such an hour——

Mars. In such an hour, friendship claims the privilege to console. [*Bows and exit.*

Miss P. Console! Ah, with him to console is to betray! I will not leave her disordered reason to his arts. The grief of woman, woman alone should soothe.

[*Exit after* SIR FRANCIS.*

---

* The conclusion of this scene altered in the Acting Version.

SCENE III.

DARNLEY'S *Counting House.*

Enter DARNLEY *followed by* PARSONS.

Darn. And the run strengthens, eh?

Par. Sir, the panic swells every moment, the vast sum in our hands last Monday is nearly drained.

Darn. [*holding up his watch.*] Is my watch right?

Par. Sir, yes—certainly.

Darn. Then all is safe. In less than an hour the day's demand will be over—[*Enter* MAINWARING.]—And to-morrow arrive my supplies from Hamburg.

Par. And the day after——

Darn. And the day after—those shares on which we perilled so much shall take such a rise in the market that we could pave Lombard-street with gold; and the next day, if the wind hold, "The Adventurer" will be at the mouth of the Thames; and the next day, return my agents from Rotterdam and Frankfort; and the next day, the crowd around my column at the Exchange shall know that the House of Darnley, recovered from every shock, complete the mightiest loan merchant ever lent to monarch. Go back. We are safe! [*Exit* PARSONS.

Main. But if these resources fail you? If the Hamburg supplies are delayed? If the shares continue to fall instead of rising? If——

Darn. Well the Science of Life is the calculation of Ifs. While you speak, I am counting what else to depend on. Humph! my shares in the Australian Bank can be sold—next week come my remittances from Guiana and Barbadoes—[*looking over his books.*]

Main. Your coolness fevers me. Your gigantic speculations have scattered all your resources; and, should the succor that depends upon a thousand accidents not come to the very hour, you are undone!

Darn. Undone? we are never undone while the mind is firm and the name is spotless. The spider reweaves her web: the brave man rebuilds his fortunes.

Main. Stoic, be human!

Darn. I am human. Where Humanity is weakest—in the affections! If I am calm in the midst of the storm, it is because I see at last the sunshine breaking upon my home. Yesterday I found the courage to warn Juliet, and in Marsden's presence. I watched her while I warned, and there was innocence on her cheeks. Henceforth the danger is banished from my house, the jealous agony from my heart. I have saved the wealth that brings the sweetest return, and all meaner treasure seems to have lost the value it had before. Stoic? It is only fortune that menaces me, and I am a Stoic now.

Enter Servant.

Servant [*giving letter.*] From my lady, Sir.

Darn. From Juliet! Ah, I was detained so late last night, and have not seen her since I left her with the man I no longer fear. Uneasy at my absence or alarmed at these reports—Wait without. [*Exit* Servant.] [*Reads.*]—" Sir "—Sir!—" I have long been convinced of the utter dissimilarity in our habits and our tastes. The affront you passed on me yesterday, in implying a doubt which, however disguised, could only reflect upon myself—" upon her!—" has decided me to adopt a resolution "—I will read no more. I am not in my senses! I have not slept for many nights, my eyes deceive me. Did the man say this was from Lady Juliet Darnley?

Main. From Lady Juliet—Yes.

Darn. I will read on—" a resolution which "—The air is close—heavy—[MAINWARING *opens the window*]—Thank you! It revives me—" to ask your consent to an immediate separation. The details I will leave to you and to my father."—It is not her writing. Ha, ha! a forgery! Read—read!

Main. [*reads.*] O, Darnley, be a Stoic now!

Darn. I tell you it is a forgery. Three months since, a poor wretch forged my signature for a handful of dross—and I would not prosecute. But oh what punishment stern enough for one who has thus lyingly—lyingly, look you!—counterfeited the hand of her, who—A forgery! a vile forgery!

Main. Not a forgery; but still, perhaps, a delusion. Some one has maddened her to this —Ha! [*calls the* Servant.] Did your lady go out this morning?

Servant. Yes, sir.

Main. Where?

Servant. I don't know, sir.

Main. Was no one with her when you left?

Servant. Sir Francis Marsden just called as I came away. Any answer, sir?

Darn. [*calmly.*] Say I shall be detained from home till to-morrow afternoon, when I will see Lady Juliet. [*Exit* Servant.] Marsden—Marsden—with her! An immediate separation!—it is well—well——

Enter PARSONS.

Par. Oh, sir! Such tidings! The house at Hamburg, Meyer and Vandervelt, on which you relied for to-morrow, has failed.

Darn. Failed? No matter. It will not affect me.

Par. [*aside.*] What a man! Nothing daunts him. [*Exit.*

Main. For your child's sake, take courage! Tear this woman from your heart!

Darn. I do—I do. I am not base enough to mourn a wanton——

Main. Those bills of Marsden's, that you bade me buy up long since,—shall I not sell them? They may bring something: you will want all.

Darn. Sell them? not for millions! I will smite him with my wand—my sceptre—my gold—ere it leaves my grasp. Hush! Meyer and Vandervelt fail me. How much did I count on? Reach me that book. I see. And in her love I was so rich! Yes, as you say, heavy bills will be due to-morrow. Where is the list? Pshaw! we can meet these. I must raise money on Elgrove. You know the old willows by the riverside—our favorite walk in the first happy summers. She loved me then, and yet I was not then so rich. Foolish thoughts these, and at such a time. True, true!

Main. Rouse yourself. But just now you defied fortune.

Darn. And do still—[*rings. Enter* PARSONS.] Send for Mr. Simmonds the Bill-broker, privately.

Par. Yes, sir. I beg pardon but here is a draft for £3,000 signed by Lady Juliet—to Mr. Fringe for decorations for Elgrove. Really, we need not pay this. It is not your signature. We cannot spare this sum.

Darn. [*taking the cheque.*] This is her hand [*comparing it with the letter.*] Here, Mainwaring, here. These characters differ, eh?

Main. For heaven's sake——

Darn. No! no! no! it is not a forgery. You know Lady Juliet had my leave to draw upon the house. Pay the cheque.

Par. But, indeed, sir——

Darn. Begone? [*Exit* PARSONS.] You see I denied her nothing.

Main. Hark you, Darnley. To-day you owe a duty to your clients, your name, your child, and your country's commerce. Think of these alone. Any day will suffice to expel the faithless wife from the home to which she brings but ruin and disgrace. Go over these accounts. Prepare for the morrow. If you lose your self-possession you will be a bankrupt, your child a beggar.

Darn. [*writing.*] You are right. You shall not blush for your friend. I have all the evening left—I will gather up all my resources. [*Rings. Enter* PARSONS.] This letter to Messrs. Richmore. This to Sir John Gould. The messenger will wait for answers. Fetch me the iron box with the title deeds of Elgrove. [*Exit* PARSONS.] That paper yonder— [MAINWARING *gives it to him.*] These sums are complicated. There, see my head is clear— I can still compute in a glance what would be a puzzle for Algebra. Why, to-morrow shall find me ready for all. Next week wealth shall roll back like an ocean. Next week—and home—Juliet—that smile—that voice! O God!—my heart is broken!

ACT IV.—SCENE I.*

A Drawing-room in DARNLEY'S *House.*

Lady J. No, I will not deign to proclaim the cause of my resolution. I will not be that pitiable object, a jealous and abandoned wife. I will part as becomes my dignity, my innocence, and my wrongs, without the weakness of reproach. His footstep! I will be firm.

Enter DARNLEY.

Darn. She cannot conceal her emotion. Even yet it may not be too late. Juliet!
Lady J. Mr. Darnley.
Darn. "Mr. Darnley?"—It *is* too late. Lady Juliet Darnley, is this your writing?
Lady J. Certainly.
Darn. And you persist in the same desire? You would forsake your husband's roof?
Lady J. Phrase it as you will. I desire your consent to part.
Darn. Madam, you have it.
Lady J. How calmly he consents! I am glad my reasons have convinced you.
Darn. Reasons? They are not found in this letter. They are written, where I have no longer power to search, in the heart which has abjured its vows. "Uncongenial habits"— Ah, that was not the phrase upon your lips when,—but no matter! "The affront of a doubt," when another man might have . . . But let it pass! I seek no explanation: and I suffer without a murmur—the penalty of a blind trust and a weak indulgence.
Lady J. [*ironically.*] May the consciousness of your defects console you for mine. Indulgence, ha! ha!
Darn. By heaven, this levity! But no, you shall not make me forget—all that is left me in misfortune—my indignation and my pride. Indulgence—what! was the word misapplied? I might have expected to find, even in so high-born and fair a partner, a companion, a friend, the helpmate and guardian of a home. Can you deny that I have found them not? But, when did I repine while you were happy? If, wearied and exhausted, I returned from the cares and anxieties of the day to a solitary hearth, still it soothed me to think that these, my "uncongenial habits," had saddened not your joyous youth. You were shining elsewhere— delighting others. In your gaiety I was gay; in your youth I was young again.
Lady J. Darnley! Henry! [*Aside.*] Ah, shall I tell him all!
Darn. Oh! let man beware of marriage until he thoroughly know the mind of her on whom his future must depend. Woe to him, agony and woe when the wife feels no sympathy with the toil, when she soothes not in the struggle, when her heart is far from that world within, to which her breath gives the life, and her presence is the sun! How many men in humbler life have fled, from a cheerless hearth, to the haunts of guilt! How many in the convict's exile, in the felon's cell, might have shunned the fall—if woman (whom Heaven meant for our better angel) had allured their step from the first paths to hell by making a paradise of home! But by the poor the holy household ties are at least not scorned and trifled with, as by those among whom you were reared. *They* at least do not deem it a mean ambition that contents itself with the duties of wife and mother. Look round the gay world you live in, and when you see the faithless husband wasting health, fortune, honor, in un-

---

* In the acting version this scene is, with obvious propriety, transferred to the house of Lord Fitzhollow.

seemly vices—behold too often the cause of all in the cold eyes and barren heart of the fashionable wife.

Lady J. [*aside*]. He seeks to excuse himself! [*aloud*]. And the fashionable wife is alone to blame if the husband transfer his affections to some tenderer object?

Darn. At least she must share the blame.

Lady J. Enough, Mr. Darnley. You will now be released from one whom you judge so severely—who—who—[*bursts into tears.*]

Darn. Her heart softens—she weeps! Juliet, Juliet, retract those fatal words.

Lady J. Retract? Never! It was a moment's weakness, and is past. [*Rings the bell. Enter* Servant.] Go to my lord and beg him to come here instantly. Now, sir, we shall both be happy.

Darn. Happy! May you be so, not in revel and in pomp, in stately equipage, in applauded beauty—least of all in hallow flattery from the lips of guilt. But happy in a good name, in a calm conscience, in prayers that leave no repentance. Oh! ere warning be all in vain, beware, Juliet, beware! You forsake me, but I leave your daughter in my place: and if ever your heart trembles before temptation, go to your child—look into its pure eyes—listen to its innocent voice—and let the mother save the wife! [*Exit.*

Lady J. Beware! save! Vain dissimulation! He knows himself faithless, and counterfeits distrust of me. Oh, Heaven pity me! I am desolate and wretched!

Enter MARSDEN [*putting aside a* Servant *who announces him*].

Mars. At last I see you, and alone. I had no opportunity yesterday, while your friend was by, to tell you how truly I share your sorrows, how deeply I feel your wrongs. My cousin, my dear cousin [*attempts to take her hand*].

Lady J. Leave me! leave me!

Mars. Leave you?—no! Ah, that I had the privilege which Darnley has despised, in joy or in grief to be for ever by your side!

Lady J. For ever! There is no for ever in man's thoughts when he speaks to woman! Betrayed—forsaken—even reproach denied me—O why are women so powerlesss to avenge?

Mars. Powerless? no! what vengeance like the fransfer of your love? Ah, need you learn now that I but live for you? How truly, how patiently, how hopelessly, till this hour—I have sighed for the affection which the ingrate has cast away!

[*As he kneels, and* JULIET *weeps on, unheeding him,* DARNLEY *with* FANNY *in his arms, opens the door—darts forward, then halts, and retires.*

Lady J. Rise! rise! This is but cruelty, insult——

Mars. Nay, in my love behold, at least, the means of your revenge. Listen to me!

Lady J. Speak not to me now! These walls reel before my eyes. I know not what I say, or think, or feel. Am I listening to guilt or shame? [*Enter* MAINWARING. LADY JULIET *hastening to him.*] Sit down—here—here—sit down! Remain! Thank Heaven there is something present, now, to interpose between crime and madness!

Mars. [*aside.*] Mainwaring! 'Sdeath in the very moment of success!

Main. [*looking at them steadily.*] Thank you. Yes, I am very glad to sit down—and feel as if I should not get up for a twelvemonth.

Mars. Indeed, Mr. Mainwaring, I appeal to your delicacy. I have something very important to say to my relation, Lady Juliet. Leave us but for a few minutes, I entreat you.

Main. Lady Juliet, is it your wish that I should leave you with Sir Francis Marsden?

Lady J. No, stay, stay!

Main. Then, with your permission, Sir Francis, I'll read the newspaper. Hum! What do you think of affairs in China?

Mars. Sir, this trifling——

Main. Trifling! Nay, really, Sir Henry Pottinger seems pretty well in earnest.

Mars. [*To* LADY JULIET] Grant me one moment? Can I not speak to you elsewhere?

Main. Ah, if I disturb you, you'll find Darnley in the next room. Pray, Sir Francis, do you know the precise latitude of the Island of Hong Kong?

Mars. Zounds! is it always to be my fate to be made ridiculous? [*Whispering.*] Juliet, remember! When we meet again, I will take your answer.

[LADY JULIET *remains as if insensible, her eyes fixed on space.*

Main. [*watching them and then turning to the paper.*] Bless me! a Divorce case. God help the false wife's abandoned children!

Lady J. [*starting*]. Ah!

Mars. [*muttering*]. Confound him! [*Exit.*

Main. From this daily oracle comes a voice for every conscience. [*dropping the paper and seizing* LADY JULIET'S *hand*] Your hand is cold. So be it ever to the clasp of every man, save your noble husband's. Wake yourself, Juliet Darnley! Why are you here? Why listening to that soft-tongued knave, when your post should be by Darnley's side in his hour of reverse and woe. Do you not know that he is on the verge of ruin?

Lady J. Ruin!

Main. Ruin—and you the cause. Had you been contented to bless the wealth he had acquired, Darnley had not been driven to seek the distraction of absorbing schemes and feverish speculations. To supply your extravagance no enterprise seemed too rash. Sudden reverse—endangered credit—the very splendor that surrounds you but feeding the fears of every claimant—this is the state in which you would desert your husband! And in the hour when he most needs support and solace, his wife forsakes her husband, and listens to her lover!

Lady J. Hold, Sir! you presume. But no! your warmth shall not offend me. I knew not, so help me Heaven, I knew not Henry's misfortunes. I thought—I think still, that I have wrongs, deep wrongs. Let them pass. We were to part—I will not leave my husband now—no, not in his care and sorrow—no—not unless he drive me from his hearth.

Main. He drive you! he who so loves——

Lady J. Loves? We will not speak of love. Tell me more of his affairs.

Main. The supplies counted on for to-day have failed; the run continues. Could we but get through the next twelve hours, we may be safe. To-morrow new resources will pour in. But to-day! And Darnley, whose energy alone could sustain and avert the danger, for the first time flies from the storm—sinks beneath his fate, crushed by the grief that you have heaped upon his heart. But I waste time. This is the hour to seek friends. As if friends were not like mammoths and iguanodons—a species of monsters that never survive a deluge. A month ago a quarter of a million would so have served the great House of Darnley as twenty, nay ten, thousand pounds would to-day.

Lady J. How! Are you serious? Twenty thousand pounds——

Main. Ay, or ten.

Lady J. Joy, joy, oh, joy! Wait here, one instant! Wait—— [*Exit.*

Main. Certainly, the more I consider, the more I'm convinced that a woman is a kind of quicksilver. She is here and there, come and gone, lost and found, vaporizes at a common temperature, and only becomes solid when she's below zero. But, properly confined, and nailed up in the parlor, she's a capital weather-glass; for she falls with every cloud, and rises with every sunbeam.

Re-enter LADY JULIET.

Lady J. Here Mr. Mainwaring. These diamonds were my mother's. They are mine to give, for they made my only dowry. These, too, were Henry's wedding gift. Ah, happy days! These too—these—these, take them all. They will raise more than you say he requires. Haste! quick! quick! But mind, one condition—one promise—not a word to Henry! Pledge me your honor.

Main. Pshaw? Why?

Lady J. Why? because you know his pride. Because, in our present relation towards each other, he would refuse them, and it would be mean in me to seem as if I would buy back his love.

Main. Well, for the present you may be right. I don't scruple to accept the relief. It may save him yet.

Lady J. Save him? Fly!

Main. But are you sure you will not repent? Jewels that belonged to your ancestors; can even money replace them?

Lady J. Money, no! If you would replace them, bring me back my husband's heart. [*Exit.*

Main. This would be a very happy marriage if Darnley could be ruined every day of his life. I'm half afraid I'm beginning to fall in love with her myself. Hang her! [*Exit.*

SCENE II.

The Library.

DARNLEY *and* FANNY.

DARNLEY *seated; his hands before his eyes.* FANNY *attempts to withdraw them.*

Fan. Papa! speak to me, papa!

Darn. Child! child!

Fan. Don't call me child, Nurse calls me 'child' when she's angry. Call me Fanny, your own Fanny. You are sad. Stay, I will bring mamma.

Darn. [*starting up and putting aside the child*]. O, the happy hour when I first taught these lips to lisp the mother's name! [*Pauses, and opens his arms.*] Do you love me? do you love me? Say you love me, O my child!

Fan. Fanny loves you with her whole heart, papa.

Enter Servant *announcing* LORD FITZHOLLOW.

Lord F. My dear Darnley; do you know you alarm me terribly? Juliet sends for me: I come: and now she is in her room, too ill to see even me. You are disturbed. Can these dreadful reports be true?

Darn. I have much to say to you [*puts down the child who goes into a corner of the room and amuses herself with building a house of cards*].

Lord F. I listen.

Darn. Why did you choose me for your daughter's husband?

Lord F. Why? My dear Darnley, that's a strange question! Though a merchant, you were of noble family: you were rising, already rich, and an irreproachable public character— of my own politics. I knew you would do credit to me as a connection.

Darn. But did you consider whether I should make your daughter happy as a husband?

Lord F. Why not? Your house is admirably appointed. She has the best box at the opera; no one is more thoroughly the mode. I don't think there's a woman in London more to be envied than Lady Juliet Darnley

Darn. It was to my wealth, then, that you looked, when you thought of your daughter's happiness?

Lord F. My dear Darnley, we don't live in Arcadia; and of course, as a man of some birth and station, I could not have consented to Juliet's marriage with any man who could not give her an establishment suitable to the daughter of Lord Fitzhollow.

Darn. I understand you. My wealth is gone. With it, my power of conferring happiness. Take back your daughter.

Lord F. Sir!

Darn. By her settlements an ample income is secured to Lady Juliet. Whatever may chance so me, that income I surrender. I took her poor. I return her rich. Are you contented?

Lord F. Mr Darnley, you speak bluntly. But still, if your affairs are, as you seem to fear, it would be unpleasant for me to think my daughter involved in misfortunes that might lower her dignity,—and my own. In short, till your affairs are retrieved, a separation would be a very proper proceeding—if Juliet can be induced to consent.

Darn. It is her own wish.

Lord F. Indeed? Ah, she was brought up with a proper sense of her station.

Darn. To-morrow (if you will do me the honor to attend), my Lawyer shall be prepared with the deed of separation.

Lord F. It is a very sad business, and we must make the best of it to the world. You have no fault to find with Lady Juliet?

Darn. No one is more thoroughly the mode.

Lord F. Um! Sarcastic! Of course you leave her daughter to her care?

Darn. No. An hour ago I had intended that cruel sacrifice. I have changed my mind. One victim is enough.

Lord F. But——

Darn. On this head, I am immoveable.

Lord F. Well, I cannot dictate to you; the law is on your side. But for my grandchild's future prospects, her entrance into society, her ensurance of a suitable alliance in point of fortune,—my house, and the experience of Lady Fitzhollow, present unequalled advantages.

Darn. What education did you give your daughters?

Lord F. The very best. Bochsa for the harp, and Hertz for the piano. My daughters speak seven languages; and are universally admitted to be most highly accomplished.

Darn. And these are the walls of tinsel which are to fortify the human conscience in the hour of trial! Unguided the temper that should bless a home, unstrengthened the principles that should subdue the world. O, yes, you taught your daughters all that could feed the vanity, and starve the heart; all that could make them turn from the holy tranquillity of the household altar, to crave the applause that contaminates, and the excitement that consumes!

Lord F. Opinions on education differ. Still, I have the consolation of thinking that everyone says my daughters reflect great credit on myself.

Darn. "Credit on yourself!" How this egotism pervades the world, and poisons the fountains of the holiest affections! Our children are educated, that their accomplishments may pander to our vanity; and married, that their alliance may gratify our pride. And we only regard their destiny as an investment that is to yield an usurer's interest to our prudent selves.

Lord F. [*aside.*] I have always observed that when a man becomes poor he loses a great deal of his good breeding. [*Aloud.*] Well, Mr. Darnley, you'll excuse me if I don't reply to your homilies. Nothing, in my opinion, is more *mauvais ton* than family recriminations. At two to-morrow, eh? *Au plaisir!* Oh, by the way, there should be another trustee to this deed of separation. Whom would you suggest? Some quiet, moral, sensible, worthy man —not over-curious about the affairs of other people.

Darn. Why not Mr. Fyshe? He is, openly, what you all are in disguise.

Lord F. How d'ye mean?

Darn. A quiet, sensible, moral, worthy man—not over-curious about other people's affairs.

Lord F. Mr. Fyshe? I never heard anything against Mr. Fyshe. Mr. Fyshe let it be.

[*Exit.*

Fan. Papa, come and see what a nice house I have built [*claps her hands*]. Ah, it is down now!

Darn. Grieve not. Thy father's house is as frail as thine.

Enter MAINWARING.

Main. Give me your hand, Darnley! Huzza! a timely aid has enabled us to pay off the last demands of the day. The panic is subsiding. The shares in the great Gas Company (on which you so wisely counted to repair all losses) are rising. What dumb? I say you are saved.

Darn. [*helping the child with the card-house.*] It is too late. Pretty one, see! we cannot build up the house again.

Main. [*whispering.*] Juliet retracts—repents. She loves you!

Darn. Hush! hush!—[*opens the door and puts out the child.*] Play there, my Fanny! [*coming back.*] Breathe not the mother's name before the sinless child.

Main. Pshaw! Lady Juliet has her faults—her errors. But, remember her youth, her training, the corruption of this damnable great world. She shall ask your pardon.

Darn. Heaven can pardon all sins. There are wrongs which man cannot forgive.

Main. Darnley, I have never pleaded for your wife before. I plead for her now. She loves you. Be patient! This Marsden——

Darn. [*fiercely.*] I saw him at her feet! saw it, and *was* patient—[*After a pause*] Yes, but a few minutes before, we parted, my heart relented; I said to myself, "*My* words failed to move her, she shall hear her better angel speak from her child's lips." I came to place her child in her arms and say, "Blind one, behold thy guide, and let it lead thee from the abyss!" I came, and saw—her lover at her feet. I sprang forward in man's natural instinct of just revenge—and my eyes fell upon my child. The mother vanished from my soul: the child alone remained upon the earth. Should the world hiss in my daughter's ear, "Thy mother was an adulteress, and the blood of her paramour is on thy father's hands!" And so,—darkness fell on me, and I knew no more, till small rosy fingers plucked my hands from my face, and before me smiled innocent, unconscious eyes, and—I thanked Heaven that I *had* been patient!

Main. Darnley, take comfort! What you have seen is no proof of guilt. Nay, ra· can I prove to you that at this very hour your wife's heart is with you; your wife's——

Darn. Cease. All confidence is gone—all excuse too late. Wedded faith is too sole to be blown to and fro by every wind.

Enter JULIET *who stands by the door timidly.*

Lady J. Henry! he hears me not. My voice fails me!

Main. Listen to me—one word——

Darn. Not one! I am weary of this woman! My sole happiness is in the thought that seas and lands shall divide us evermore. Let her face, as she will, the storms of the noisy world. I fly for refuge from mankind to the shelter of the only heart that is left me to cherish. [*going towards the room where he has left* FANNY.]

Lady. J. What do I hear? Henry!—Mercy, mercy!

Main. Now look at her——

[DARNLEY, *turns round as* LADY JULIET *clasps her hands, and looks for a moment.*

Main. And relent! [DARNLEY *turns, and Exit.*

Lady J. "Weary of this woman?"—the only heart left to him to cherish?" Tell him I obey. Tell him I am content to part—tell him—O lost! lost to me for evermore!

[*Falls as* MAINWARING *supports her.*

NOTE TO DARNLEY.

NOTE TO DARNLEY.

The next of the four preceding acts is printed from the second of two rough drafts of them found amongst my father's manuscripts. The drafts do not materially differ from each other. In both, the *dramatis personæ* have the same names and characters, with the exception of Selfby Fyshe; who, in the first draft, is sometimes named Fyshe, but more frequently Languid. The author, when writing the first draft, was apparently undecided which of the two names he should finally adopt for this character. Of the fifth act I have been able to find amongst my father's papers no trace beyond some fragments of scenes apparently belonging to it, and such slight indication of its main incidents as may be gathered from the following synopsis of the whole play.

ACT I.

Scene   I.—Stand as now,—with alteration of Marsden's character.
"   II.—Mainwaring and Darnley.
"   III.—Lady Juliet and Sir Francis. Sentimental.
"   IV.—Mainwaring and Darnley. To aid Darnley in his plot.

ACT II.

Lady Juliet and Marsden. Sentimental and dangerous. Enter Darnley. Strong situation. Enter Mainwaring. Excites her jealousy. She goes out. Darnley re-enters. To him Languid; who has taken a villa from Marsden, and let it again to Darnley. Act to end with comedy between Mainwaring and Miss Placid.

ACT III.

Scene   I.—Miss Placid and Languid. Asks him to let her off. He won't.
"   II.—Lady Juliet and Miss Placid. Lady Juliet's jealousy. Writes to her husband that she will separate.
"   III.—Darnley. First his equanimity, then his despair.

ACT IV.

Languid and Miss Placid. He is led to suppose her fortune gone. Not as now. Altered.

ACT V.

Marsden and Languid. The joy of the former at separation. Has been invited as a relative to sign final arrangements. Room in D.'s house. Darnley and Marsden. Final scene. Discovery and reconciliation.

It will be seen at once that the second draft, which has been selected for the text of this Edition, differs in some important particulars from the above synopsis as regards the sequence and arrangement of incidents. Both the draft and synopsis also contain internal evidence of the author's intention to make further alterations in the structure of the plot, and especially in the situations which serve to explain and develop the character of Marsden. This character, as at present sketched, is the most artificial and least intelligible feature of the play. Yet all of its *dramatis personæ* Marsden is dramatically the most important, since the main plot of the play grows directly out of his action. It is essential to the effect of the whole play that the action of this character should be dramatically justified. And the method of its dramatic justification (which Mr. Coghlan seems to have thought unnecessary or impossible) appears to me sufficiently indicated by the author of the play even in his unaltered sketch of Marsden's character. Neither dramatically nor morally is Marsden a villain. His character should be so presented as to enable us to perceive that, although without principle, he is not altogether without heart. From the moment he appears upon the stage, the audience is meant, and should be made, to understand that, in the life of frivolity and excitement he is leading, he has no other interest or object than distraction from some painful memory. "Poor Susan!" he says, if she had not left me, I had been perhaps another man." He adds, "But she deserted me, and I am free;" and then, with a curse on late hours and shaken nerves, he calls for the laudanum drops. He is selfish, not like Fyshe, upon principle, but from recklessness. And he is reckless, because the wreck of something serious in his life has left him without any serious interest or purpose.

There is nothing serious in his pursuit of Lady Juliet. The *dénouement* contemplated by the author of the play would be impossible if Marsden were seriously in love with Juliet; and, were the audience led to suppose him seriously in love with her, the artificiality of his sentiments and language would have been a grave defect in the treatment of those scenes wherein he makes love to her. As it is, the artistic truth of the whole play would be grievously injured by any attempt to render the part of Marsden, in these scenes, more natural. The author has taken care to let us know that Marsden is not in love with Juliet. Rightly therefore, he has made him woo her as an actor, not as a lover. In retouching this character the author, I doubt not, would have slightly strengthened the sympathetic side of it, and softened some of its more repulsive features. But, of course, he would have reserved for the fifth act the solution of the problem which requires that, till then, the dramatic motive of the character should remain somewhat enigmatical.

I shall here venture to suggest what I believe to be the explanation of Marsden's character, and the right *dénouement* of the plot so far as it depends upon this character.

Marsden may be supposed to have begun life with expensive tastes, small means, and good expectations dependent on the will of some relation (father or uncle), who would be deeply offended by a *mésalliance*, or even an imprudent marriage, on his part. Abroad, he has become acquainted with Susan, the sister of Mainwaring. She is younger than he; of humble station though gently born; penniless and entirely dependent on the exertions of her only brother, whose name is not then Mainwaring. That brother has been summoned to England by the illness of the kinsman whose name and fortune he afterwards inherits. The girl is alone, and motherless. Marsden's acquaintance with her may have been brought about by some act of generosity or compassion on his part; an act which has protected her from insult, or extricated her from some distressing difficulty; and which, from the nature and conditions of it, draws them closely together. On his part compassion, warmed by admiration of her beauty, on hers gratitude idealised, in a girl's imagination, by the fascinations of an apparition from some world more brilliant than her own, ripen into a passionate attachment. That attachment is on both sides innocent and pure. In Marsden's love for Susan, there is no thought of seduction or betrayal; but his union with her, if known, would be fatal to his prospects. He persuades her to a secret marriage; and, in order to ensure its secrecy, he contracts it under an assumed name. I apprehend that the assumed name would not *per se* invalidate the contract, if it were valid in all other respects, and its validity undisputed by either party to it. But at any rate it is to be assumed that Marsden had strong and reasonable ground for believing that the circumstances which induced him to conceal his marriage would be of the briefest possible duration, and that he would be in a position to repair an irregularity not committed with any fraudulent intention before it could jeopardise the legitimacy of his offspring. But the occasion he had reckoned on calls him suddenly away from Susan; and in his absence some accident reveals to her the unexplained deception, from which she draws the worst conclusions. Reared in veneration of the proud and stern honesty embodied in the character of her brother, and overwhelmed by the horror and humiliation of this discovery, she flies from the house of her supposed seducer.

Thenceforth her predominant instinct is to hide herself from all who have known her. Marsden, now free to declare his marriage, returns from England. The life before him is a vision of virtuous joys, and beneficent activities. He is elated by the prospect of sharing wealth, station, and, perhaps, future eminence, with a woman in whose affection he has concentrated all the romance of a boy's first love, all the incentives to youth's vague ambition, and all the felicities of an honest home. That home he finds deserted. The wife he was impatient to rejoin has left there only a farewell letter filled with reproaches. His search for her proves fruitless. And then, what his position in life? what his relations to the world around him? Those of a man in the freshest prime of youth and health, with passions unappeased, warm affections unsatisfied, hope blighted, memory embittered. Married, yet wifeless, childless, homeless. Single, yet not free. Bound by a broken tie; and forbidden to replace it by any new one that is not illicit. Equally out of unison with himself and the world around him, he cannot rest in the unrevealed affliction which is all that remains to him of the past; yet in the present he has no peace, and in the future no escape from it. The apparent artificiality of his character springs from the profound unreality of his position. This position is made up of false appearances from which it is not in his power to escape. It imposes on him a character which, though fictitious, is fixed to him by circumstance as firmly as was the iron mask to its unwilling wearer. The fathers and mothers of society see in him a man who, from every point of view independent of his character or conduct, is an eligible husband for their marriageable daughters. Yet his relations with women must necessarily be confined to the already married. With an ardent temperament capable of keen enjoyment and vigorous activity, he stands upon the threshold of life prematurely purposeless: or, at least, with no other purpose than to escape from recollections in the pursuit of excitement. To such temperaments life offers only two strong excitements: pleasure and politics. The acquisition of influence either over women or over men. But a political career is exciting only to ambition or enthusiasm; and the majority of men are neither ambitious nor enthusiastic. Possessing, at the outset of life, a fortune which tempts to pleasure and exempts from toil, Marsden is under no compulsion to work for bread. Wifeless and childless, in the future as well as the present, he has no motive to work for fame. It is not power, or public influence, that he misses and craves to recover: for these he has never known. It is affection: and what the loss of this leaves vacant in his life he seeks to fill by those emotions which are, at least, the imitations of it. It is the heart, not the head, that, in his case, craves occupation. Thus, his need of excitement has made him a man of pleasure; and his disdain of excitements that fail to fill the void in his affections has made him a heartless man of pleasure. In this secret of his life lies the explanation of his character and conduct. And it is an explanation which, if given, with passion and dignity, by himself, at the close of the drama, to the woman he has never ceased to love, and never voluntarily injured, would assuredly contain all the conditions of a powerful and affecting situation.

But, by the dramatic Calvinism of Mr. Coghlan's merciless fifth Act, Marsden is made to seduce Susan Mainwaring in a manner peculiarly infamous. Accused by her, in the presence of Lady Juliet, not only of having betrayed and abandoned his victim, but also of having deliberately left her to starve, or do worse, he carelessly, almost cheerfully, admits the truth of this accusation; making his final exit with the inane remark, that it is hard upon a man to be scolded by two women at once. Could anything be more revolting? And, notwithstanding Susan's plain avowel that she is 'an abandoned woman' in every sense of the word, Mainwaring, inconsistently with his whole character throughout the four previous acts, is, in this act, persuaded by Miss Placid to 'go and embrace his sister.'

In one of the wittiest scenes ever written by Congreve, when Sir Harry Wildare places his guineas on the mantlepiece of the young lady whose character and situation are misconceived by him, she exclaims in astonishment, "What, Sir Harry, is that all your wit and manners?' To which he replies, ''Pon my soul, my dear, 'tis all the wit and manners I have about me at present.' I am persuaded that this barbarous *dénouement* can be no fair specimen of Mr. Coghlan's dramatic wit and manners. But all the wit and manners he had about him when he wrote it imply a strange misconception of the situation and characters with which he was dealing.

Indications of the right *dénouement* are not wanting in the four acts to which this note is appended. But they are conclusive in what remains to be added here from the author's rough drafts and notes. Thus in a fragment of my father's manuscript which would seem to be part of some cancelled sketch of the first act, Mainwaring says of his sister, " I loved her more than a father loves his first-born. She fell ill. I gave up all other undertakings, broke off the engagements on which my chance of easier fortune was then depending, to accompany and attend her abroad. Was suddenly summoned home. Left her at Tours for a few weeks. And in the meanwhile she was gone. Eloped with some villain. Gone! and and from that day not one word. Ah, she did well to be silent." So again, in the same draft of the first scene of the play, Marsden, shaking off the recollection of Susan, exclaims, what is life? a barren future, an irrevocable past. Let us clutch the present moment ere it fleets, and enjoy it,—if we can!" But the strongest confirmation of the view here taken of the character assigned by the author to the relations between Marsden and Susan, is to be found in some cancelled passages of the original manuscript of the scene at the villa with which my father has opened his third act. From his acting version of the play, Mr. Coghlan has omitted this scene altogether. And not injudiciously. For acting purposes, it obviously requires considerable development and alteration.

Such a task could scarcely be accomplished with success by any writer not in the secret of the author's intentions: and there is evidence that by the author himself it was felt to be a task of considerable delicacy, which he reserved for careful consideration after the completion of the fifth act, or in connection with it. In real life it would be almost impossible, and certainly incredible, that this scene should take place between Lady Juliet and her supposed rival without putting an end to the misunderstanding, which, in the play, it is designed to argument. This, I think, would be strongly felt by the spectators of the scene, if it were acted just as it now stands: and such a feeling would be seriously prejudical to the dramatic effect of the whole play. To the prolongation of misunderstanding between Lady Juliet and her husband, the audience, after witnessing an unterrupted interview between the wife and the supposed mistress on the subject of these misunderstandings, would scarcely be reconciled by the incidents of the scene as it is sketched in the unfinished manuscript. And, indeed this scene is more blotted, crossed, and underlined than any other part of the manuscript: a fact which suggests and justifies the conclusion that the author was not satisfied with it in its present form. The passages cancelled by his own pen are omitted from the text of this edition. But in one of them the Lady of the Villa exclaims—" If you know my secret, you know also how I was deceived: how I listened only to vows which had all the eloquence of sincerity; how I was misled, not to the conscious commission of a false act, but into innocent reliance on the truth of a false name; how I yielded only to a union invested with every evidence of virtue, and sealed by every sanction of honor; how I believed myself a wife, till I found myself an outcast." And when Lady Juliet observes that, whatever his errors, ' he ' (meaning Darnley) is incapable of the villainy implied by this story of the false name and the sham marriage, the Lady of the Villa (in this cancelled passage) replies, " I meant not to accuse him. Alas, what right have I to accuse my betrayer, when I myself have betrayed an affection truer than his? I who, beguiled by a blind passion, have irreparably wronged the tenderest, the noblest of human hearts! I who, if my secret were revealed, might have upon my soul the burden of a brother's curse, the stain perhaps of a brother's blood!'

It is evident from all this that Susan Mainwaring has consented to a secret, but not to a false, marriage. It is evident that she did not leave her brother to become the mistress of Marsden, that she never was the mistress of Marsden, and that the wrong done by her to Mainwaring was limited to her unexplained flight, and the temporary concealment of a marriage which she believed to be valid and honorable. It is equally evident that Marsden has not seduced Susan Mainwaring, and that he never desired, intended, or attempted to seduce her. He has deceived her by marrying her under a false name, but in the full, and not erroneous, belief that their marriage is still a valid one, and with every intention of "setting matters right" as soon as he can do so without forfeiting the fortune he expects. He is not a good character, and still less is he a fine one. Unscrupulous he certainly is, inconsiderate, self-indulgent, somewhat selfish, lax in his morals, but neither a villain nor a blackguard. In another cancelled passage of this scene the Lady of the Villa explains to her servant that Darnley has advised her to frequent the park and all places of public amusement, with a view to the recognition of her supposed betrayer. And, since Darnley is known to pay for her carriage and establishment, her fulfilment of this injunction would, of course, tend to strengthen the impression made on Fyshe and others that she is Darnley's mistress—a mistress moreover of the most ordinary type. Evidently Darnley is not cognizant of the real facts of the case, and supposes it to be worse than it is. In yet another part of the scene as originally sketched, which has, also been struck out by the author, the following incident occurs. Immediately after the departure of Lady Juliet, the servant hurriedly enters, conjuring the Lady of the Villa, to hasten with her to the window of the next room, and look through it, at the gentleman who is talking to her late visitor in the street. 'What do you mean?' exclaims the Lady of the Villa: and the scene ends thus:—

[*Servant*. I think it is Mr. Swynford. I'm sure it is he. On horseback. By the carriage of the lady who has just gone.
Lady. Swynford? Ah, heaven! one look, one glance, and then— (*Exit with Servant.*)]

From this it is obvious that Swynford is the name under which Marsden has married Susan. I do not pretend even to suggest how my father, had he completed this play, or prepared it for the stage, would have worked out the *dénouement* of it on the lines thus indicated. I know not how Susan Mainwaring's discovery that she had been married under a false name would have been reconciled by him with her obvious ignorance of Marsden's real name. And there are many other details in which the construction of the plot must for ever remain incomplete. The wand of Prospero is buried in the deep; and with it all the secrets of his art. But, in order to justify both her brother's forgiveness, and the sympathy her situation is intended to elicit, it is essential that Mainwaring's sister should not have deliberately left her brother's house for the purpose of living with Marsden as his mistress; and to her ultimate reconciliation with Marsden himself, the validity of the marriage she contracted without any doubt of its honesty, is no less indispensable. Of the dramatic importance of this condition in its relation to the character of Mainwaring, further illustration will be found in the following fragment of a scene found amongst the author's notes for his fifth act.

[ACT V.—SCENE I.

DARNLEY's Library. DARNLEY and MAINWARING seated.

Darn. I tell you, Mainwaring, I have not been to the firm to-day. I care not what befall. Henceforth, wealth and poverty are the same to me. Enough of this, and of myself. Before I leave England, there is one matter in which I still feel an interest. I must turn from my sorrows to your own. What if I had tidings of your sister?

Main. (*at first eagerly*) My sister! Is she safe? is she well? (*in altered voice*) Has she still the right to call me brother?

Darn. Can that right ever be forfeited? My friend, give your kind heart its natural vent.

Main. Only say that she bears a husband's name! Only say that she is—she is—the word strangles me—Darnley, is she honest?

Darn. Recall her youth, her innocence, her beauty. What if she had been deceived, betrayed? her virtue ensnared, her——

Main. Hold! Enough! I renounce her. Let her reap in sorrow what she has sowed in shame.

Darn. But——

Main. Name her not! name her not!

Darn. Well, then, when I quit these shores, let your sister . . . . who shall protect her if . . . Ah, Mainwaring, see her. Listen to her once. Hear her own tale.

Main. I will not see her, for I will not spurn my——]

Here the scene breaks off unfinished.

And now, as to the *dénouement* of the whold play. Two plots are involved in it—a sentimental and a comic plot. It appears to me suggested by sound principles of dramatic construction, *firstly*, that the action of the lighter plot should be directly conducive to the development and *dénouement* of the more serious plot; *secondly*, that the House of Darnley should be saved in that *dénouement*—not (as in Mr. Coghlan's acting version) by Darnley's ward, Miss Placid, who has no direct connection with the cause of its impending ruin—but by his wife Lady Juliet, whose relation to the plot is the meeting point of those forces and influences which affect her husband's fortunes through his feelings; connecting the house, with the home, and giving to the whole drama its moral significance. That all this was intended by the author of the drama, may be confidently assumed, both from the structure of its four first acts, and from the two remaining fragments of scenes written by him for the fifth act of it, which I now subjoin.

[ACT V.—SCENE V.

MISS PLACID and FYSHE.

Fyshe. What do I hear? you deceive me!

Miss P. Upon my honor it is true. But with £15,000 and your own patrimony, we can still drive a tandem, and hunt twice a week.

Fyshe. S'death! This is a blow. Deranges all my calculations. Hunting, driving, smoking, on *one* side, and £30,000 on the *other*, was a very near balance of items. Substract £15,000 from the one account, and add Kissing Dick Mainwaring to the other, and, faith! it's a devilish bad book. I should like to hedge.

Miss P. You are silent? I can't bear silent people. Talk! laugh! rattle! Hang money, and drown care! (*She sings.*)

Fyshe. (*aside.*) The creature exhausts me. Takes away all my oxygen. I feel like a mouse in an air-pump!

Enter Servant.

Servant. Lady Juliet wishes to see you, ma'am.

Miss P. Mr. Fyshe, excuse me. If you wait for Lord Fitzhollow in the little parlor next to the library, you will see a portfolio. My last caricatures.

Fyshe. So, she draws caricatures. too!

Miss P. A little likeness of yourself. Will divert you. You've no idea how all your friends have enjoyed it. Ah, you don't know half my accomplishments.

Fyshe. Not yet, thank heaven! (*Aside.*) I see the accomplishments increase in an inverse rate to the money. Not a farthing less than £30,000 could compensate for the misery of a life, and only half her accomplishments. Shooting, hunting, driving, smoking, kissing caricaturing. . . . It is too much! That is, the *quid pro quo* is too little. (*Aloud.*) I release you. I see that we shall not be happy. I will write——

Miss P. Release me! What, you won't marry me?

Fyshe. I'd sooner marry the chimpanzee. I'll write the release—while I look at my caricature. (*Aside.*) Good heavens, what frisky obstreperous children she would have had! (*Exit.*)

Miss P. Ha! ha! I have won the victory for myself. Now then, I must bring up my forces to aid my friend.]

It was probably intended that the half of Miss Placid's fortune should appear to have been lost in the bankruptcy which is averted by the sale of Lady Juliet's jewels. On the eve of Darnley's departure from England, Mainwaring, who not being in Miss Placid's plot, believes in reality of her alleged loss, urges her to accept from him the home which Darnley can no longer give her. And hence a scene between them, concluded by an embrace in which Fyshe has surprised them. The manuscript of Darnley includes another version of this scene, through which the author has drawn his pen. But the cancelled scene contains a situation which throws some light on the *dénouement* of the play. It is thus sketched.

[*Enter* Servant (*followed by a lady, veiled.*)

Servant. A lady wishes to see you, ma'am.

Miss P. Me? Be seated, madam. Mr. Fyshe, excuse me.

Fyshe. Good heavens! what is this? Darnley's mistress, Miss Placid's friend? In her own house? Lord have mercy on us! "Birds of a feather" indeed! What an escape I have had! What an escape! What frisky obstreperous children she would have had! (*Exit*.)]

This last fragment completes the number of indications left in my father's handwriting, of his general intentions respecting the act he had left unwritten. I have thought it expedient to collect them all, with some explanatory observations, in this edition of "Darnley"; and although they are few in number, and faint in outline, they will, I think, suffice to enable the readers of the play, as here printed, to form a fairly correct notion of its intended *dénouement*.

LYTTON.

KNEBWORTH, *May 16th*, 1882.

END OF BULWER'S DRAMAS.